History of
Scott County, Missouri

HISTORY & FAMILIES

SCOTT COUNTY, MISSOURI

ESTABLISHED 1822

TURNER PUBLISHING COMPANY

Turner
PUBLISHING COMPANY

TURNER PUBLISHING COMPANY
Publishers of America's History

Book Commitee Chairman: Margaret Cline Harmon
Publishing Consultant: Douglas W. Sikes
Book Designer: Emily Sikes
Scott County Logo Design: Elizabeth Sikes

Library of Congress Control Number: 2003111474
ISBN: 978-1-68162-450-1

Limited Edition. First Printing 2003 A.D.
Additional copies may be purchased from Turner Publishing Company
and the Scott County Historical and Genealogy Society.

Table of Contents

History Book Committee

The Scott County Historical Society was organized November 15, 1980 in Morley, MO. Charter members were Janice Thomeston, Morley; Mason Emerson, Sikeston; Sylvester and Ramona Glastetter, Kelso; Louis Hirschowitz, Oran; Fred and Mildred Laster, Sikeston; and Mary McArthur, Morley.

Margaret Cline Harmon was Chairman of the Scott County History Book Committee and wrote the general county history and individual personal vignettes. She is currently a senior at Southeast Missouri State University in Historic Preservation and is married to Tom Harmon. Margaret is past president of the Scott County Historical and Genealogy Society and also wrote the society newsletter for over five years. She is now serving as Historical Director on the Board of Directors of the Missouri State Genealogy Society. Margaret enjoys writing about local and state history and is a published newspaper author and winner of several essay contests.

Lois Dirnberger Spalding has been the treasurer of the Scott County Historical and Genealogy Society for five years. Her contribution to the publishing of this History book consisted of contacting families and asking them to write their family histories, collecting family histories and logging them, collecting and logging all orders for the book and accounting for all funds collected toward purchases of the book.

Lois is a member of St. Denis church in Benton, MO. She worked for twenty years for the Missouri State Division of Family Services and helped her late husband, Joe Spalding, with his trucking business. She is also a member of the Daughters of the American Revolution, Nancy Hunter Chapter, Cape Girardeau, MO.

Tom Lett has been president of the Scott County Historical and Genealogy Society since January 2000. He is a native of Scott County and now lives in Cape Girardeau County, MO. He is retired from the U.S. Department of Agriculture and owned and operated Lett's Nursery for some twenty years before retiring again. He now volunteers for organizations he believes in. He served as church and business sales representative for the Scott County History and Family History book.

Carolyn Graham Frey is vice-president of the Scott County Historical and Genealogy Society. Throughout the duration of the book she collected family stories and edited for grammar. She logged the families and pictures, submitted them as to be mailed or picked up, and forwarded finished stories to the publisher. She wishes to thank all those that contributed family histories and pictures, as well as a special thanks to Peggy for her help.

Supportive Committee Members:

Donna Cannon, Ramona Glastetter, Caryl Hairston, Conrad Hudson, Carolyn Johnson, Betty Mirly, and Carolyn Pendergass.

Introduction

The pioneers that built Southeast Missouri with wagons, oxen, and traveled on horses, steamboats and stage coaches are no more. In their place is modern civilization with automobiles, comfortable combines to harvest the cotton, and people enjoying life in an easier life style. Let us not forget the connection between the past and present. This book shows that one's genealogy and history are inseparable.

Missouri's willingness to stand back while others rush ahead prompts some observers to dismiss her as a state which somehow faltered after a promising beginning as the gateway to the west. Evidence can be selected to show that the ancient ways and cautious spirit of southeast Missouri, the Ozark Hills, the farms and hamlets along the river valleys, and the rolling countryside have made Missouri an artifact in these United States. One can see relics in Scott Countians to show a willingness to pause while others rush ahead. Scott County is only one of a few counties where cotton plants are found growing in the city limits of its largest town, Sikeston. Agriculture is still of primary importance to its citizens and gives them roots.

Although Scott County's citizens are still divided in culture, all of her people are well grounded in the traditions of family values, a respect for the environment and a determined spirit to meet each day with hope and perseverance. Scott County has many generational families tracing back to the early 1800s. It appears the younger generations realize, in farming some of the same family land, the appeal agriculture carried a century or more before. The county's people's realism and frankness may show other counties, states, and the Nation the realization that thoughtful restraints are needed, if democracy is to survive a third century.

The Scott County Historical and Genealogy Society will continue to preserve and make available to citizens of Scott County and other researchers the records that document and preserve our rich heritage. By doing so, we will help to preserve the collective memory of the men and women who make up Scott County today and yesterday. The Book Committee wishes to thank everyone who has contributed in any way to the successful publication of this history book.

Blodgett, MO, circa 1892. Wagons of watermelons waiting for the train. (Photo courtesy of Mike Marshall)

History of Scott County, Missouri

Scott County Early Development

The first known human occupants of the region of Southeast Missouri were the Mound Builders. They were not numerous, though Southeast Missouri has over 18,000 identifiable mounds. Undoubtedly these ancient people hunted, fished, and farmed a bit in this area as they did in most of the Mississippi and Ohio valleys.[1]

The close of the American Revolutionary War brought American immigrants to the bounties of Spanish territory. The Spanish authorities agreed to a tentative plan for a buffer colony. Settlers were to be offered liberal grants of land, religious freedom, local self-government, and the creation of a port of entry that would eliminate the necessity of carrying goods to New Orleans. Spain was to donate 15 million acres for this project, which had been suggested by, and was under the control of, Colonel George Morgan, an American Revolutionary War veteran from Virginia.

Early in 1789, Morgan selected the site of New Madrid as his "capital," and the town was laid out on a rectangular plan extending four miles along the river. Sites for schools, churches, and market places were provided, and in the center of town a generous driveway was platted around a lake. No trees were to be cut along the streets or in the parks of the new town without official permission; laws protected the game in the surrounding country. That was Morgan's plan anyway.

The project generated great interest among American colonists, who considered Morgan's plan a better method of attracting settlers to the West than any suggested by Congress. There were many followers from Vincennes and Kaskaska who believed in Morgan's plan. Unfortunately, Morgan had political problems with Governor Miro of Louisiana. As often happens, what one politician promised, another took away and the once invisioned grand city of New Madrid failed to materialize. Many of Morgan's group returned to their homes east of the Mississippi River, but a few stayed in New Madrid along with Francis and Joseph LeSieur.[2]

Probably the first settler in present day Scott County was William Smith who came up the Mississippi River and settled in Tywappity bottoms in 1797. He built an establishment, sort of a tavern, for the convenience of travelers. It was opposite Cat Island at the future site of Commerce.[3] The census of the area taken in 1803 showed that William Smith's family included three males, six females and no slaves. His farm production that year was 1,000 bushels of corn and 2,000 pounds of cotton. Livestock on hand included 30 head of cattle and six horses.[4]

The years of the Napoleonic Wars (1789-1815) were very difficult for the average person in Europe. Both political and religious rights were greatly diminished and everyday life presented hardships we can only imagine. These reasons made exile-compelling motives for migration. Beyond these push factors of declining everyday life; immigration to America presented a strong pull factor to Europeans too. They were pulled toward the possibility of becoming landowners and of experiencing a better life for themselves and family in America.[5]

In the early days, eastern Missouri was divided into five original districts: New Madrid, Cape Girardeau, Ste. Genevieve, St. Louis, and St. Charles. The districts continued after the Louisiana Purchase was completed, until the Territory of Missouri was organized by Congress. Most of the settlers immigrated just after the Louisiana Purchase in 1803. They were from Virginia, Kentucky, North Carolina and Tennessee. Congress organized the Territory of Missouri on June 4, 1812 and immigration accelerated.[6]

Among the families from Kentucky were Hartwell Baldwin, Joseph Hunter, Edward N. Matthews, Isaac Ogden, Samuel Phillips, Stephen Ross, John Shields Sr., Moses Shelby and other lesser known families but equally important to the development of the area.[7]

In 1789, a road known as King's Highway was marked out from Ste. Genevieve to New Madrid and it was along this road that the settlements were most numerous in New Madrid District and what is now Scott County. Other early settlers west of the Mississippi River were Edward Robertson, who with this son-in-law, Moses Hurley, located near where Sikeston is now. Hurley was an extensive land speculator, and also kept a store and trading post. He was uneducated and could not write his name but he was a shrewd business man and succeeded in keeping most of the other settlers in his debt.

In 1796 or 1797 Capt. Charles Friend, with his family, came from Monongahela County, Virginia and secured a concession of land near the present site of Oran. He had been a captain in the Revolutionary War, and was at this time about 75 years of age. He had a family of nine sons, three of whom, Jonas, John and Jacob, each received the customary concession of 800 arpents of land, an inducement to settlers at that time.

In the early 1800s, William Meyers moved with his parents to what is now the Benton area.

During the Spanish domination, the territory now comprised in Scott County was attached to the post of Cape Girardeau. Governor Harrison defined the boundaries of the districts of Upper Louisiana, in 1804, and the line between New Madrid and Cape Girardeau did not change until June 7, 1805. Governor Wilkinson, by proclamation, fixed the line as follows: "Beginning at an outlet of the river Mississippi, called the Great Swamp, below the Cape Girardeau, and extending through the center of the same to the River St. Francois, and thence until it strikes the present northern boundary of the district of New Madrid, and with the same westward as far as the same extends." This change proved inconvenient to the people living in Tywappity Bottoms, who had transacted all their business at Cape Girardeau in the past. They developed a petition and presented it to the Governor and on August 15, 1806, the boundary was changed as follows: "The southern boundary of the district of Cape Girardeau shall form and, after the date hereof, be fixed and determined by a due west line, to be commenced on the right bank of the Mississippi adjoining to and below the plantation of Abraham Bird, opposite to the mouth of the Ohio." This remained the boundary between the districts of New Madrid and Cape Girardeau until the organization of the counties in 1813.[8]

The first settlement recorded in Scott County was in **COMMERCE**, alongside the Mississippi River. The first actual documentation of settlements in Commerce is provided in the Spanish land grants dating from 1791 to 1804. The land upon which the town built was originally granted to Thomas W. Waters, and was owned by his heirs when the survey was made. Early residences of the town were John Brown (hotel keeper), J. W. Echols, Samuel & William Gray (manufacturers of stoneware), Archibald Price and James Weaver.

Thomas Willoughby Waters arrived at Commerce in March of 1804. Shortly after arriving here he formed a trading partnership with Robert Hall under the firm name Waters & Hall. He also formed a partnership with James Brady and their firm was known as Thomas Waters & Company.

On August 23, 1804 Waters wrote President Thomas Jefferson, applying for the position of commandant of the district, pointing out that, as a Major in the Revolutionary War, "he had filled a higher military office than any one here, except for one man upwards of sixty years old."[9] No record of a response was found. Waters also operated a stage coach out of Commerce and the Tywappity Bottoms, as one was listed on a February 15, 1809 personal property appraisal. It was valued at $21.75.[10]

Under the statutes in effect in the period

immediately after Missouri became a state, the circuit courts were given control over executors, administrators, guardians and minors. As Thomas and his wife Fannie Waters had died, there were much litigated and long overdue settlements of their estates. In an effort to speed and facilitate this process, the court, in 1823, ordered a board of commissioners to be appointed to lay out lots at the present site of Commerce and "to expose and sell them at public venue." Many of the out lots and town lots were bought by absentee speculators or bid on by individual members of the Waters family. Among the better known in the first category were Nathaniel W. Watkins, William Myers and Nathaniel Wickliffe. Myers was then a resident of Benton, Watkins lived in Jackson at the time, and Wickliffe was then residing in Kentucky.[11]

During the War Between the States, the County Seat was moved from Benton to Commerce as Commerce was under Union Control. Plans were drawn, copying the first brick Courthouse in Benton, and was completed by mid-1865. It remained the County Seat until 1879 when voters, by more than two-thirds of the votes, expressed their desire that the "Seat of Justice" be returned to Benton.

Commerce was a thriving town in the 1800's with steamboats arriving and departing on schedule, and the 1875 edition of Campbell's Gazetteer listed the town with a population of 600, besides a considerable suburban population. The town had 8 stores, 4 shops, 4 hotels, 2 stave mills, 1 pottery (Koch's) factory, 1 steam flour mill, 2 churches, a Methodist and Baptist. The first newspaper published in Commerce was the *Dispatch*, established in 1867 by William Ballentine and H. P. Lynch. It was published under the management of various editors until the removal of the county seat back to Benton.

Robert S. Douglas's *History of Southeast Missouri,* written in 1912, featured a brief biography of Benjamin F. Anderson as follows: Benjamin F. Anderson was born in 1852. In his early youth he attended local subscription schools, but otherwise was self-educated. At the age of 15 he went to work in a store at Commerce that his brother, Joseph Anderson, owned. He continued this job until 1874, when he went into the mercantile business for himself, and continued to run his store until 1882. At that juncture he became a partner with another brother, William B. Anderson, in a commission grain and milling business.

At the time Douglas's book was published (1912), Ben Anderson owned two elevators that had a combined capacity of 100,000 bushels and shipped grain in carload lots to various markets. He also owned a 200 acre farm which he rented out and was a co-owner with his son, Norwell Anderson, of a store in Commerce. Other Anderson family members living in Commerce were merchants too. Benjamin's wife, Mary Ellen, who was born on April 22, 1852 and died seven years after her husband on June 30, 1935. Joseph T. Anderson, born April 27, 1840 and died September 14, 1895, at White Springs, Mo. of typhoid fever. His two wives are buried near him. His first wife was Fannie Ross Gaither Anderson and second wife Clara W. Ranney Anderson. Also, in the cemetery are: Henry

Gaither Anderson, Nowell F. Anderson, Tillman Wylie Anderson, Jessie Gail Anderson, Wade Gray Anderson, Pauline Maupin Anderson and the last to be buried was Virginia A. Anderson, born March 23, 1881 and died August 13, 1971.

The Anderson family lived in Commerce in its prosperous and exciting years. The William

B. Anderson home is now a Bed and Breakfast and it continues to give a hint of the affluent lifestyle the Anderson family enjoyed.

Another prosperous and important family buried in the Commerce/Anderson cemetery is the Moore's. Joseph H. Moore was born June 12, 1836 and died December 21, 1915. He at-

Water Street, Commerce, Missouri, circa 1900. (Photo courtesy of Bob White)

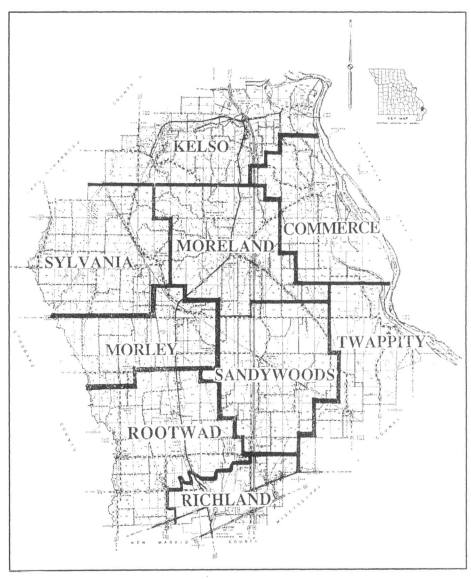

Political township map of Scott County.

First Scott County courthouse in Benton, 1822.

tended Arcadia College in Arcadia, Missouri. He studied law and graduated from Cumberland University in Lebanon, Tennessee. He opened his law office in Benton, Missouri in 1857. He had the first Scott County Abstracts of Land Titles Company in the county. The office was later known as Moore-Harris Abstract Company. In his long career, with many acres in timberland, he cleared land and put it in cultivation and was an extensive stock farmer. He had extensive land holdings in the area immediately south and southwest of Commerce. Reportedly, he once owned 5,000 acres of land.

When the County Courthouse moved from Benton to Commerce during the Civil War, he moved to Commerce and remained there though the Courthouse was moved back to Benton in 1879.

About 1811 John Ramsey moved from Cape Girardeau and located on what was later the Scott County Poor Farm. He remained there until his death in 1837. The Ramsey family played a major roll in the development of Cape Girardeau County too.

The Bird, Byrd, Moore, and Hunter families are several of the oldest and most prominent families of Southeastern Missouri. Migrating from Virginia, Maryland, and Tennessee, they settled in the Missouri Bootheel around the time of the Louisiana Purchase. By virtue of making the initial land entries, and then through a series of marriages and resulting multiple inheritances, the families became among the largest landholders in southeastern Missouri, owning several thousand acres of rich Mississippi delta farmlands. Primarily farmers and stockmen, the families were leading citizens in their communities and furnished representatives to Missouri territorial councils and state legislatures.[12]

Joseph Hunter, one of the most distinguished pioneers of Southeast Missouri, located near the present site of Sikeston about 1806. He was a son of a Scotch Irish Presbyterian who immigrated to America from the North of Ireland prior to the Revolutionary War. During the early settlement of Kentucky the family moved to Louisville. A brother of Joseph, who had been an officer in the Continental army, received a grant of land on the river above Sikeston in what is still known as "Hunter's Bottom." Upon the organization of the Missouri Territory, Joseph Hunter was appointed by President Madison a member of the territorial council.[13] He had a large family and his descendants are very numerous and many are still living in Scott County.

After the disastrous New Madrid earthquakes, the seat of justice for the New Madrid District was moved to Winchester in 1812, the first town in the neighborhood of Sikeston. It was located south of where I-57 is now, south of Sikeston.[14] Today you will only find a corn field and a clump of trees where Winchester once stood and business was conducted.

In November of 1814, County Surveyor Joseph Story laid out the town of **WINCHESTER** on the present day Scott County and New Madrid County border. They named the town in honor of Col. Henderson Winchester who lived in the vicinity. Stephen Ross and Moses Hurley donated fifty acres of land for the town of Winchester. The money obtained from the sale of lots was used to build a jail. Winchester was one of three post offices in the New Madrid area before 1820. Mail was delivered about once a week, by horse, from Cape Girardeau.

Pioneers Daniel Sparks, Edward N. Mathews, Samuel Phillips, Stephen Ross, Thomas Phillips, John Shields, Sr. and Moses Shelby bought early lots in Winchester. Thomas Bartlett opened a general merchandise store and Hartwell Baldwin opened a tavern in the young town. David Hunter, Mark H. Stallcup and Christopher Houts were also engaged in business at Winchester until 1822. Then, Scott County was created and Winchester ceased to be the seat of justice for New Madrid County. The town failed to survive after the county seat was moved to New Madrid.[15]

On December 28, 1821, by act of the Missouri Legislature, New Madrid County was divided into two counties – present day New Madrid and Scott County. By the same act, Enoch Evans, Abraham Hunter, Thomas Roberts, Joseph Smith and Newman Beckwith were appointed to locate the seat of justice for Scott County. The committee selected Benton as its County Seat. Scott County, Missouri was officially founded on December 28, 1821.

The county court was organized at the house of Thomas Houts in February or March, 1822 at which time the judges were Andrew Ramsey, Richard Mathew and Thomas Houts. In 1822 the county contained but two townships, Moreland and Tywappity. Scott County was named after Missouri's first Congressman, John Scott and Benton was named after Missouri's first Senator, Thomas Hart Benton.[16]

Upon entering the Union in 1821, Missouri closed an amazing pioneer period in the western empires of France, Spain, and the United States. Scott County was part of the original five Districts of the Louisiana Purchase along the western banks of the Mississippi River. President Thomas Jefferson dreamed of a slow, deliberate movement of America's frontier through the valleys of the Ohio and Tennessee rivers. Meanwhile, out of conflict's reach, Jefferson had hoped the Osage, Missouri, Iowa, Sacs, Fox, Kickapoo, Shawnee and Delaware Indians in Missouri would undergo a transformation. It was a sublime concept, worthy of Jefferson's best moments of philosophic repose on his Virginia mountaintop.[17] As we know, this was not to be the case.

In 1822, William and Nancy Myers donated 40 acres of land for the new county seat and the town of **BENTON**. Although no legal record of this transaction appears to have survived, there are several historical books that reference the transaction. The town of Benton was surveyed in the fall of 1822 and lots were sold at public auction on October 22, 1822. Edison Shrum makes mention in his *History of Scott County* that Commerce and Benton street names are almost identical. They both include Saint Mary's, New Madrid, Cape Girardeau, North, South, Missouri, and Tywappity Streets. Two distinct streets in Benton are Meyer and Winchester. One certainly was named for its founder, although spelled differently, and the other for the town of Winchester. William and Nancy Myers are buried in the old Benton Cemetery south of town.

The first frame house in Benton was built by Joseph Hunter and used as a storehouse between 1830 and 1840. Other merchants during that time were Dr. E. B. LaValle and John Harbison who occupied the McLaughlin house from 1831 to 1833; George Netherton and Abraham Winchester had a store on the Heiserrer corner and George and Thomas Williams were the leading merchants of the eighteen-forties. The first newspaper in Benton was established by George M. Moore in July 1879, with Louis Dehls as editor. It was named the *Benton Record*.[18]

Scott County has always been primarily

agricultural. Missouri's first senator, Thomas Hart Benton, in the 1820s and 1830s fought to defend a Jeffersonian America by selling public land at low prices and defeating efforts to entice farmers into debt through the availability of paper money. As defender of hard cash, Benton soon earned his nickname, "old Bullion," and a reputation as guarantor of an old order. Generally, Benton's massive influence in Missouri and the nation came to be used to preserve an old-fashioned pastoral society. Through them, he encouraged within Missourians their natural suspicions of big government, glamorous economic legislation, and urban viewpoints.

A great depression occurred after 1837 and it was Benton's Missouri, firm on the rock of fiscal conservatism, which appeared to be the only state faithful to the simple, rural commonwealth that Jefferson had urged and Jackson had echoed. As banks in other states were failing, the Bank of the State of Missouri thrived. Senator Benton's greatest moments in politics occurred in the decade following 1837. These years may also have been Missouri's most significant period in American public affairs.[19]

America received a procession of Catholic pioneers from Alsace-Lorraine between the years 1837 and 1839. The immigrants first settled in an area near Canton, Ohio. The Ohio frontier served as the political, economic and social foundation for the settlement of the Old Northwest. By 1830, the American boundary moved ever westward. By 1837 land costs in Ohio had risen to as high as $40.00 to $50.00 an acre and many Germans found the land too costly to purchase in any quantity. One group of these German-speaking immigrants was from the village of Schirrhein, a border province touching the Rhine River. This group of Catholic pioneers decided to move into Southeast Missouri where land was reported as affordable.[20]

In the early 1800s, the United States depended heavily on immigrants to fuel expansion of the land west of the Mississippi River. The government officials understood that what immigrants wanted most was affordable land. They advertised land in Southeast Missouri for $1.25 per acre. The inducement of affordable land worked. Immigrants flooded westward during the early to mid 1800s. Missouri's eastern bank was the first stop for immigrants. Many German immigrants, including the Catholic pioneers from Alsace-Lorraine, established themselves in Missouri and descendants of these pioneers remain today in the northwestern section of Scott County.

The early Scott County Catholics came by boat down the Ohio River by way of Cairo, Illinois and then up the Mississippi River headed to Commerce. They experienced trouble with their boat and had to land in Tywappity Bottoms, or Horse Shoe or Texas Bend, south of Commerce. It was here the Alsace-Lorraine pioneers built a log cabin church, which they dedicated to God, under the sanctification of St. Francis DeSales, on September 15, 1839.

The Tywappity Bottoms were unhealthy. Many people became victims of malaria, then known as "Swamp Fever," and died. There are no marked graves for these early pioneers. The survivors sought a warmer, healthier climate. In 1841, Xavier Stuppe, Joseph Stuppe, Wendolin Bucher and David Kappler moved to land near Benton.

In 1843, William Myers donated the land on which they built a log church. The first Catholic Church in Scott County was founded in Benton on Hunter Hill on the south side of the town limits. They built near present U. S. Highway 61 and named it St. Mary's Church. Little is known of this pioneer church, its promoters or its organization.

In 1851, a newly found parish of St. Lawrence was dedicated at New Hamburg, Missouri. Scott County's population began to increase with the arrival of new settlers. The trend was for the German Catholics to settle toward the hills around New Hamburg and Kelso. Benton's congregation then went to St. Lawrence in New Hamburg where they had built a small frame church. They abandoned the church at Benton and Union soldiers burned it to the ground in 1864.[21]

The distance of ten or more miles every Sunday was tiresome for old settlers around Benton. A new parish was started in Benton and Denis Diebold, father of Frank L. Diebold, provided $1,000.00 and five acres of land in his will to the Catholic Congregation of Benton. His will stipulated that the church be built within five years. Mrs. Diebold made the same bequest in her will. This enabled the church to be completed. Frank L. Diebold donated six more acres of land to the church to continue the mission begun by his parents. Today, the St. Denis church and cemetery are found on the north side of Benton on the western side of U. S. Highway 61.[22]

Mark Hardin Stallcup, who had served in the War of 1812, moved to Winchester from near Springfield, Kentucky soon after the war and engaged in business. In 1817 he married Hannah Hunter, daughter of Joseph Hunter, and it is interesting to note that he was the man who once owned the whole site of the present town of Sikeston, having bought the land from Michael F. and Luceal Taylor, wife, on December 11, 1844. At his death on December 11, 1848, the property went to his three children: Catherine, Lydia, and James. Catherine married first Andrew Myers, January 9, 1840. He lived about one year and she then married John Sikes on January 14, 1844. Mr. Sikes died in 1867 and much later in life she married Judge Noah Handy of Charleston, Missouri. James Stallcup and Lydia Stallcup Brown, the other heirs to this property, which contained the original town of

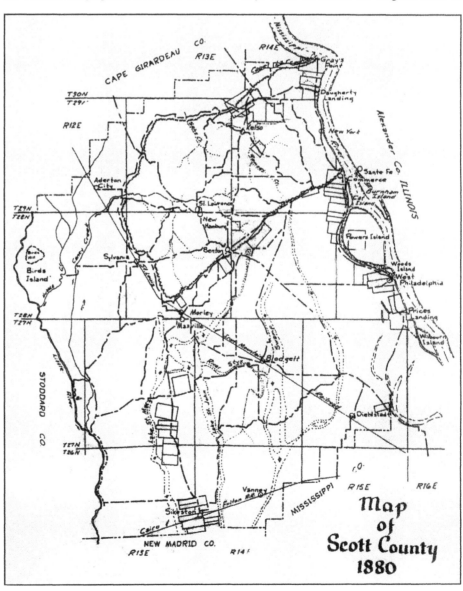

Map of Scott County 1880

11

The first wheat thrashing machine in Southeast Missouri, before 1900, belonged to Carter Foster. (Photo courtesy of Paul Foster)

Four railroad flatcars of Allis-Chalmers #60 combines delivered to and sold by W.R. "Rich" Lewis. The old Sikeston water and ice plant is in the background. (Photo courtesy of Bill Lewis)

Sikeston, sold their interest to John and Catherine Sikes on December 14, 1859.[23]

On June 9, 1853. a meeting of the citizens of Charleston was held at the courthouse to take action to secure a railroad. Judge Noah Handy was chosen chairman, and John C. Thomas secretary. After many trials and tribulations a survey in 1856 was run from Bird's Point. In 1857 construction was began. During the summer contracts were accepted for the grading of the road from Bird's Point to Charleston and on October 1, 1857, the contractor, Colonel H. J. Deal threw the first shovel of dirt. The work was pushed forward as rapidly as circumstances would permit and on April 1, 1859, the first train drawn by the locomotive "Sol G. Kitchen" entered Charleston. The formal opening of the road did not take place until July fourth, when a grand celebration was held. As Abraham Hunter had sold stock in the railroad, he rode into town on the train and made the main speech of the day. The railroad had another locomotive, the "Abraham Hunter," named after him. Construction continued and the road reached Sikeston in 1860.[24]

This railroad was called the Cairo and Fulton (Arkansas). The War Between the States interrupted construction soon after. It was not extended on to Poplar Bluff until about 1872.[25] The nature of American housing changed dramatically as railroads mushroomed across the continent in the decades from 1850 to 1890. Louis Houck, a Cape Girardeau lawyer and businessman, developed railroads in Southeast Missouri. His first venture, the Cape Girardeau Railway Company opened in 1880. In his lifetime, Houck created three railway lines, creating an extensive network that reached into Arkansas and Illinois, and spanned much of Southeast Missouri.[26]

John Sikes had a store where the First Baptist Church was on Kingshighway in Sikeston. He stated in a land title: "I, John Sikes, am going to start me a town and I am going to call it the **TOWN OF SIKESTON**." The original plat of the town is a matter of record in the county courthouse at Benton.

John Sikes was the son of Needham and Mary Shields Sikes who lived south of Sikeston. John and Catherine Stallcup Sikes had one son, Needham Sikes II. They lived on their farm which extended to the railroad in a house directly across the road from the store. It stood back from the road quite a bit.

Many history books allude to the two different cultures of Scott County but do not spell out the difference. Having grown up in Scott County it is clear that north of the Benton Hill, the German Catholics, who fought for the Union in the Civil War, settled and stayed in northern Scott County. Below the Benton Hill, settlers immigrated from Virginia, Kentucky, North Carolina and Tennessee with their customs of agriculture and slaves. They were supportive

of the Confederacy in the War Between the States.

During the War Between the States there were turbulent times throughout Southeast Missouri. There was a band of outlaws, called guerillas, which roamed the countryside and made life miserable for the settlers. During 1864 they came to the Sikes' store and tried to make Mr. Sikes tell them where the family money and jewelry were buried. He refused their request so they hanged him to a big oak tree in the front of the store. Mrs. Sikes, who saw the whole thing, took one hundred dollars hidden in a sack of cotton on the porch and sent it over to them by a Negro girl. Mr. Sikes had turned quite black in the face but they cut him down and he recovered. The Confederate and Federal soldiers both were after the guerillas, but somehow they never were able to catch them.[27]

About a week later the Sikes' house was burned in the night, the family being unaware of it until the structure was falling in. Mr. Frank Boyce, a nephew of Mr. Sikes, ran in and picked

Blodgett Elevator and Grain Co. (Photo courtesy of Harlan Smothers)

up a big featherbed. When he laid it down on the ground, two little girls rolled out of it. One of them was Mary Catherine "Kate" Brown (later Chaney), and the other was Ella May Brown, her sister. Their mother, Lydia Stallcup Brown, Mrs. Catherine Sikes' sister, died in 1863. Mr. and Mrs. Sikes took the two little girls to raise after their mother's death. Conditions continued so unsettled throughout Southeast Missouri that Mr. and Mrs. Sikes and their family went to St. Louis and stayed until the war was over.[28]

After the war they returned to Sikeston. John Sikes went into business with William Hughes. In 1867, a man named William Maulsby came from the country to their business, got drunk, and created a disturbance. Mr. Sikes, knowing him well, took him out to his horse which was tied to a hitch rack at what is now Legion Park, handed him his shotgun and advised him to go home. As Mr. Sikes turned to go back into the store William Maulsby shot him in the back. John Sikes lived about three days after being shot. Mr. Maulsby was arrested and put in jail

at Benton. The next morning he was gone. The jailer said that Maulsby had climbed out the flue hole. He was never seen around there again. It was once reported that he had been seen in Texas.[29]

On August 17, 1874, Sikeston was incorporated. Sikeston merchants in 1875 and 1876, when the population was two hundred fifty, were: W. A. Coffey, proprietor of the Star Saloon; J. O. Davis, fancy groceries; Charles Ebert, bakery, grocery and restaurant; H. C. Edwards, an attorney, Justice of the Peace and collector; A. Griedenberg, general merchandise; O. E. Kendall, druggist; H. Plotz, boot and shoe maker; W. C. Puckett, hotel proprietor; Henry A. Smith and J. R. Tucker, hotel proprietor (from L. A. Wilson), and Dr. J. L. Shumate, general merchandise (and one of the earliest physicians in the area). Another prominent physician was Dr. O. W. Kendall who was born near Martin, Tennessee, and served under General Nathan Bedford Forrest during the War Between the States.[30]

The Americans that immigrated into Scott County early in the 1800s from Virginia were many. One was the Archibald A. Price family. They purchased original Spanish Grant Survey Number 2848 from Robert Lane for $1,075 on March 31, 1834. This land became known as **PRICE'S LANDING**.[31] The 1875 edition of "Campbell's Gazette of Missouri" listed a store and warehouse there at that time and in "Wilson's Gazetteer & Director of Southeast Missouri"; the landing was estimated to have had a population of 25. There was also a post office that opened February 1, 1859, with Archibald Price as postmaster.

Page 191 of the 1850 US Census of Scott County, Missouri listed the family as follows: Price, Archibald A. - 44 year old male farmer, with 13 slaves, born in Virginia and owner of land valued at $5,000.00; Sarah Catherine Price, 13 year old daughter born in Missouri; William M. Price, 10 year old son, born in Missouri; Mary Elizabeth Price, 8 year old daughter, born in Missouri; Louisa Price, 4 year old daughter born in Missouri; Robert A. Price, 2 years old son, born in Missouri and a white male laborer, Thomas H. Hublz, age 40 years old born in Tennessee.

Price's Landing saw a lot of action during the War Between the States as Archibald Price helped his (reported) cousin Gen. Sterling Price warehouse goods for the Southern cause. *"The War of the Rebellion: Official Records of the Union and Confederate Armies," Series I, Vol. III, pages 449 & 450* (1881) relates that Col. C. C. Marsh, Headquartered in Cape Girardeau, took son, William M. Price and his brother-in-law, B. S. Curd, prisoners on or about August 10, 1861, and had William write the following note to his uncle Capt. Charles Price, Missouri State Guard: "The colonel says that if you attack Commerce tonight he will hang

13

us." This brought a letter, dated August 15, 1861, by Thomas C. Reynolds, Acting Governor of Missouri, to be written to Maj. Gen. John C. Fremont:

The gentlemen held by Colonel Marsh are, as I am credibly informed, citizens of this State, and unconnected in any way with military operations. Even were they so connected in a manner justifying their being made prisoners of war, the Articles of War and Army Regulations of the United States require humane treatment of prisoners.

I also learn that the detachment of Colonel Marsh's troops, which captured Mr. William M. Price, wantonly, burned his father's warehouse and took away a large quantity of corn and 60 mules. Similar outrages are believed to have been very lately committed at the farm of General N. W. Watkins, near Cape Girardeau, and by Colonel Marsh's troops. I therefore, in the interest of humanity, lay these matters before you, and request a frank answer to these inquiries:

Does this conduct of Colonel Marsh and his troops meet your approval? If not, what steps do you propose to take in respect to the guilty parties and in order to prevent the repetition of such conduct?

It is the desire of the Missouri State authorities to conduct the present war according to civilized usages, and any departure from them by Missouri forces will be properly punished by their officers if aware of it. I deem it proper to add that on seeing Colonel Marsh's letter I immediately instructed the general commanding the Missouri State Guard in this district (M. Jeff. Thompson) to hold in close custody a number of prisoners recently taken by him and belonging to your forces. Should Colonel Marsh's future treatment of Messrs. Curd and Price necessitate the hanging of any of those prisoners in retaliation, I am content that impartial men shall judge who is morally responsible for their melancholy fate.

I am sir, very respectfully, your obedient servant,

Thos. C. Reynolds,
Acting Governor of Missouri

Col. Marsh responded, "I plead guilty to the charges of having written the note mentioned, and would have done as I promised had Captain Price committed the threatened outrages on the peaceable citizens of Commerce. My threats had the desired effect, and prevented his doing any act of violence there. I tried hard to get hold of Captain Price and his troop of marauders, but they always run, even when but half their number of foot soldiers are opposed to them. The young man Price (William M.) and his brother-in-law, who were taken prisoners, have been notoriously active in aiding the enemy. Their father (Archibald), the brother of Captain Price, was the agent for procuring supplies for the New Madrid forces, and his mules, servants, and families were all engaged in transporting them."

Archibald himself was taken prisoner from Price's Landing by the Union soldiers in late December, 1862, to the Union prison at Cape Girardeau, MO. Bail was set for ten or twenty thousand dollars and he was released, for his good behavior in the future. He then went to his Cousin Charlie Riley's farm near Tiptonville, Tennessee. There he took sick with heart trouble and rheumatism. When he found he was going to die, he sent for his daughters back in Price's Landing, Missouri. He died in about half an hour after their arrival. That was on February 18, 1863. Postal service was discontinued on April 14, 1875, and most of Price's Landing was slowing washed away by the Mississippi River.

Immigration into Scott County continued and new towns started to develop. **NEW HAMBURG** was organized in 1866 by Francis Heuring.[32] The village is located about two miles west of Highway 61, between Benton and Kelso. The St. Lawrence Church is the center of the small town of New Hamburg and is central to the cultural and spiritual lives of its parishioners.

St. Lawrence and St. Denis church in Benton

Confirmation class at St. Denis Catholic Church, Benton. Front row: Zeta Essner and Loretta Bertrand. Second row: Leo LeGrand, Joe Diebold, and Leon Heisserer. Third row: Alponse Robert, Joe Miederhof, Otto Essner, and Phillip Weber. Fourth row: Clemens Miederhof and Leon Essner. Back row: Flora Wilhelm, Clara Diebold Essner, Lena Essner Halter, Emma Essner (Sr. Angeline), and Bertha Bertrand. (Photo courtesy of the family of Alfred Halter)

1924 Benton Tigers. Bottom row, L to R: Avell Williams (sub), Howard Brothers (sub), Tom Haw (sub), Howard Spaulding (sub), and Mr. Rau (coach). Middle row, L to R: Ursal Thompson (right end), Lester Thompson (right tackle), Loomis Lincoln (right guard), Leslie Harris (center), Donald Warner (left guard, captain), Thomas Moody, (left tackle), and Sydney Williams (left end). Back row, L to R: Joe Bucher (half back), Myron Frobase (half back), John Goodin (full back), and Elbert Morrow (quarter back).

and their cemeteries are historically entwined with the early settlement of Scott County. A group of German-speaking immigrants from Alsace-Lorraine, near the Rhine River, established both original churches.

St. Lawrence Church is the mother parish of Benton, Oran, Chaffee, Kelso and Scott City. Prior to the building of the first church, they heard confessions in a chicken house and they said Mass in parishioner's houses, according to the *History of St. Lawrence Church*.

The parish priest told the parishioners in New Hamburg that the church need not be expensive, nor need it be exactly square in the corners. He just wanted a place to worship together. The original St. Lawrence Church stands today in New Hamburg behind the impressive rock church built in 1857.

The first person buried in the cemetery was Sophia Stuppy, wife of Donatus Scherer. She was born Sept. 10, 1823, in Schirrhein, Alsace, France, and died October 5, 1847, in Scott County, Missouri. Her grave was the first dug in St. Lawrence Cemetery and the funeral was the first service held at the church. Denis Diebold hauled her remains and had the brush cut out to let the wagon through. Her monument is 6 feet high and oxen hauled the stone from the quarry at Cape Girardeau to New Hamburg. They carved the inscription in German, rather than English.

German Catholics universally were believers in education. It was not long before the church served as both a church and a school. After completion of the new stone church building, the old church was used to house the parochial grade school. It is the oldest church and schoolhouse still in existence in Scott County.[33]

About this time the railroads played a big part in the building of Southeast Missouri. The two major railroads were Houck's Missouri and Arkansas, and Iron Mountain Railroads and Gould's Frisco Railroad.

ORAN was initially settled by James and John Friend in 1796 when he came by river with his parents, Charles and Nancy (Gouch) Friend to Southeast Missouri. They settled on 640 acres near Oran obtained from the Spanish Government. Later it was settled by a large number of German Catholics, and the many big, square German type houses in the town still easily distinguish this town first called St. Cloud and then Sylvania. These early settlers were hard working, industrious people who were directly responsible for making Oran the center of a busy prosperous agricultural community. The old Iron Mountain Railroad depot still stands near the tracks today.

Oran was laid out in 1869 and was still known as Sylvania for several years. The town had three weekly newspapers over the years. The first was the *Scott County Citizen* from January 1 through December 31, 1904; *The Oran Leader* from April 15 to July 29, 1910 and April 4 through May 10, 1912; and lastly the *Oran News* January 11 through December 26, 1957; January 4, 1963 through April 28, 1967.

In 1912 Oran had five general stores, several minor business establishments and the Bank of Oran. Some of the first merchants were the Brice & Basset store, Ross & Howell. Mr. J.

First Communion of Leo and Blanche Hamm, May 27, 1917, St. Lawrence church, New Hamburg. John I. Hamm and Emma Theresa Hamm were candle carriers. (Photo courtesy of Ramona Glastetter)

St. Lawrence church and school, New Hamburg, 1904. (Photo courtesy of Ramona Glastetter)

W. Clemson began as station agent at Oran about 1892 and continued until the late 1920s when he retired on a pension.

Oran had a population of 940 citizens in 1930. It had a first-class consolidated high school and was modern in every way. It had concrete sidewalks, electricity, a modern fire department and good gravel streets. In 1935 the city voted a bond issue for the purpose of constructing a modern water system.

Oran had two practicing physicians – Dr. Cline and Dr. Loest. The late Dr. H. S. Winters served Oran for many years as a physician and president of the Board of Education, and as Mayor. Dr. E. D. Kimes, dentist of Chaffee, maintained an office three days per week in Oran.

In 1939, the business establishments located at Oran were: The Scott County Milling Company, T. S. Heisserer & Company, large department store; Womack Drug Store, Sturgeon's Garage, Kroger Grocery, Metz Café, Harper's Grocery and Meat Market, Oran State Bank (this bank moved to Oran from Blodgett in 1937), Vogel's Garage, Maddox Grocery, Majestic Theater, Oran Ice and Cold Storage Col, Oran Lumber Company, Scott County Oil Company, Black Bros. Gin Col., and several oil stations, barber shops, and beauty parlors.

Oran is located three miles west of Highway 61, and a mile west of Highway 77.

GRAYSBORO had one of the first mills in Scott County and surrounding area about the year 1844. A small settlement had been started there some time before as grain was brought to the point for miles around to be milled. Capt.

St. Denis Church, Benton, MO, date and event unknown. (Photo courtesy of the family of Alfred Halter)

St. Denis grade school graduation, Benton, MO, June 9, 1929. Boys: Alfred Halter and Sylvester Felter. Girls unknown. (Photos courtesy of the family of Alfred Halter)

Heisserer's Store, Benton, MO. (Photo courtesy of the family of Alfred Halter)

Overview of Oran, Missouri, ca. 1930s. (Photo courtesy of Harlan Smothers)

Blodgett, MO, "Watermelon Capitol of the World," circa 1892, loading melons on freight cars. (Photo courtesy of Mike Marshall)

"Extraordinary Honor Certificate" awarded to Myrtle Flynn in 1920 from the Methodist Sunday School in Deihlstadt. It was awarded for attendance for five Sundays in February and notes, "It is possible for a certificate of this character to be issued only three times in one hundred years" because very rarely does the leap day fall on Sunday, thus being the fifth Sunday of February.

Morley Public School, 1919. (Photo courtesy of Harlan Smothers)

Gray was an early settler in the settlement. He owned steamboats and operated them on the Mississippi River. Capt. Gray built a beautiful mansion near the Mississippi River. It was known as one of the most beautiful mansions in the state at the time. Capt. Gray made acquaintances of men who traveled up and down the river. Members of the Gray family, including Mr. Charles Gray, lived on the old Gray plantation.

During the year 1897, the Cotton Belt on St. Louis Southern Pacific Railroad extended its tract from Delta (at first known as Deray, Missouri) to Grays Point and made Grays Point the northern terminus of the line. This marked the beginning of a town to be known as Graysboro, Missouri. The building of this terminal at Graysboro brought several hundred people to Graysboro and the population increased rapidly. All the work of building the terminus and track was done by men and teams. The business of the railroad increased steadily and so did the population of the little town until it attained a population of around one thousand people.

After the construction of the Thebes Bridge (completed in 1904) it was found that the grade approach to the bridge was too much for the heavy trains to get a start for the grade. So it was decided to move the terminal back about two miles to where Illmo-Fornfelt became located. A great part of the population of Graysboro moved to Illmo-Fornfelt, which marked the decline of Graysboro and the beginning of the above mentioned towns. Most of the business houses in Graysboro also moved their wares to Illmo-Fornfelt. A special train (which was finally taken off) carried workers to and from Graysboro daily.

Some of the houses once located in Graysboro were J. D. Vanneton General Merchandise, Pate Grocery, Bollinger's Meat Market, four saloons, and a rock quarry. Most of the dwellings in Graysboro were razed and moved to Illmo when the city of Illmo was started. Doctors once practicing in Graysboro were Dr. G. S. Cannon, later practicing in Fornfelt and Dr. D. S. Mayfield. Other business houses once located in Graysboro were Gray Bros. General Merchandise, D. I. Bloom Dry Goods, Pate Hotel, Curtus Hotel, O'Donnel Hotel, McDoom Second Hand Furniture, George Hawkins Grocery, and Jasper Belk Dry Goods. The town of Graysboro was a busy town about 1900 and there was plenty of money in circulation in the booming days. Graysboro had board sidewalks. Thebes Bridge was constructed, on large transport boats to Thebes, Illinois.

As history has shown many times, the removal of industry from one town to another often caused the decline of the first town to benefit the new town where industry moves. This was the case for Graysboro. Today it is a ghost town with only memories living there.

DIEHLSTADT is on the tract of land granted by the United States Government to Mr. Henry Kirkpatrick. In 1854 Henry Kirkpatrick and his wife, Jane, deeded the land to John Kirkpatrick and his wife Nancy. They established the first store in the town in 1868. John Kirkpatrick borrowed $500.00 from Henry Diehl to aid him in his venture of platting a town. He thereby named the town Diehlstadt in honor of his friend and keeper. The original deed for the town of Diehlstadt comprised forty acres of land. Mr. Max Ostner built a large mercantile store in which one could purchase anything needed from farm machinery, clothing, groceries and all farm needs. Rev. John T. Ford operated a restaurant in town at 1875. Diehlstadt was incorporated in 1894 and its first mayor was John Rushing.

In 1912, Diehlstadt had five general stores, barber shops, a drug store, besides minor establishments of various kinds. Although Diehlstadt is primarily a farming community, it has supported several successful industries. The Moulten Irrigation Company once provided manufacturing jobs. It once was on the Iron Mountain Railroad line. Today, it is a village located ten miles east of Morley, on State Highway 77.

MORLEY was laid out in 1869. It was a station on the Iron Mountain Railroad and the shipping point for Benton as well as Morley. The town was named in honor of James H. Morley, Chief Engineer, for the planning and building of the Pilot Knob-Belmont line. Streets, except for four that were given women's first names, and one named in honor of Gen. N. W. Watkins, were all named for men connected in one way or another with the railroad.

On October 6, 1868, A. C. Ketchum and 16 other Morley residents petitioned the county court for authority to incorporate the

Kelso, MO, 1903. Left to right: Joe Compas, Frank Seyer, Joe Weidefeld, and Joe Glueck; on porch: Leo Dohogne and Mike Welter; on step: Joe Diebold; far right: Mike Diebold and Amos Drury. The buildings shown are Dr. William's office (built 1892), the old Farmers and Merchant's Bank, and Mike Diebold's Drug Store (each occupied a part of the building with porch), the residence of Charles Logel, and a blacksmith's shop operated by Casmier Martin in 1889. Blattel Street runs East and West between the bank building and Charles Logel home. (Photo courtesy of Romona Glastetter)

St. Augustine School, Kelso, MO, Room 1, May 7, 1912. Front row: Raymond Enderle, Adolph Kirn, Louis Robert, Joe Blattel, Ed Heisserer, Hilda Ressel, Bertha Lauch, Anna Ressel, Josephine Ziegler, Leona Schaefer, Matilda Kirn, Leona Diebold. Second row: Fred Burger, Paul Lieble, Eugene Dumer, Joe Welter, Ervin Messmer, Ann Felter, Alphine Dumey, Dina Blattel, Estella Burger, Sylvia Heisserer, Ada Compas, Bertha Pfefferkorn, Francis Wiedefeld. Third row: Werner Ressel, Frank Compas, Theon Blattel, Leon Ziegler, Father Muhlsiepen, Mary Diebold, Agnes Weissmueller, Mary Enderle, Mary Glastetter, Mary Spalding, Mary Heuring, Leona Staebel. Back row: Hugo Robert, Joe Glastetter, Herman Blattel, Sister Delphine, Emma Dumey, Leona Hess, Anna Seyer, Mary Redman, Irene Glastetter, and Bertha Scherer. (Photo courtesy of Ramona Glastetter)

St. Augustine School, Kelso, Missouri, Room III grade 5 and 6, May 3, 1939. Left to right, front row: Joseph Schwartz, Delores Hopkins Mier, Valeria Ressel Mirgeaux, Leoma Leible Tucker, Mary Lou Enderle Heisserer, Margaret Rogers Bles, Lorena Weissmueller, Elveria Enderle Metheny, Alvina Georger Lett, Ramona Blattel Glastetter, Lena Compas Bucher, Marie Westrich LeGrand, Paul Felter, and Louis Heisserer. Second row: Lloyd Corvick, Ervin Glueck, Frank Bles, Louis Glastetter, Marvin Miller, Benjamin Enderle, Charles Drury, Leroy Blattel, Joseph Glueck, Ruby Peetz, Herbert Blattel, and Leon Blattel. Third row: Paul Diebold, Claude Whaley, Cletus Essner, Norvel Messmer, Florence Welter Diebold, Aurelia Scherer, Melva Jane Heisserer, Edvieria Messmer Rhodes, Emma Compas Scherer, James Crites, Paul Enderle, Leander Drury, William Martin, and William Essner. (Photo courtesy of Ramona Glastetter)

Business district of Blodgett after June 5, 1916 tornado. Ruins of B.F. Marshall Mercantile Co., Hardware and Implement Store. (Photo courtesy of Harlan Smothers)

Blodgett post office and W.H. Stubbs' Café. (Photo courtesy of Harlan Smothers)

Downtown Blodgett, 1905. (Photo courtesy of Mike Marshall)

town. The court approved their petition and appointed A. C. Ketchum, W .J. Welsh, John Riggs, Alexander Courtway and James D. White as trustees. For some reason the actions of the trustees seem not to have met the approval of the townspeople, for on Mar. 23, 1870, Gen. N. W. Watkins, representing James D. White, persuaded the county court to rescind its order of incorporation, and then presented the court another petition of incorporation, signed by White and 40 other residents of the town. This second petition was granted and James Boutwell, Henry Wadsworth, George R. Wilson, B. V. Yandell and L. O'Brien were appointed trustees.

Among the first merchants were B. B. Gaither, W. A. Cade, Hughes and Watkins, Harris & Rosenbaum and J. T. Anderson and Brothers. A grist and corn mill was built soon after the town was established by L. C. Martin and Brothers. The town was incorporated in 1870, with James Boutwell, Henry Wadsworth, George R. Wilson, B. V. Yandell and L. O'Brien as trustees.

According to information in the 1875 edition of "Campbell's Gazetteer of Missouri," Morley, at that time had one public school, two churches, Baptist and Methodist Episcopal South; two hotels, one livery stable, one cotton gin, one mill, ten stores, and several shops.

L.A. Wilson's "Gazetteer and Directory of Southeastern Missouri and Southern Illinois," also published in 1875, estimated the population of Morley in that year was 350 citizens. The town continued to grow, though slowly until, in 1910, it reached 494, where it more or less became stable, and remained so until the decade of the 1960's when its population went from 472 in 1960 to 528 in 1970.

Morley had a school until the Morley and Vanduser Schools consolidated and created the Scott Central School System. The last Morley graduating class was the Class of 1959.

Morley had two weekly newspapers for a brief time. *The Scott County Citizen* was published January 1 through December 31, 1909 and the *Scott County Banner* was published January 1, 1914 through August 4, 1921.[34]

Today, Morley is a bedroom community. The Post Office still operates and there is a bank and a volunteer fire department. However, there is one grocery store, a restaurant, a garage, a beauty shop, a second-hand store, a laundromat, four churches and a Masonic Lodge. A filling station is located on the spur coming into Morley.[35]

BLODGETT was organized in 1870 on the line of the Iron Mountain Railroad about five miles southeast of Morley. By 1900, Blodgett was known as the "Watermelon Capitol" of the world. Ben F. Marshall, Sr., received an award at the World's Fair of 1904 testifying to the fact that Blodgett was known as the biggest watermelon shipping center in the world. At the turn of the twentieth century, Blodgett was a very active city with progressive schools and churches. It also had two large general stores, a drugstore, two saloons, two hotels, and restaurants, barber shop, large livery stable, warehouses and a blacksmith shop.

With the passing of the years and changes in farming conditions, improved transportation and better roads, Blodgett lost its position as capitol of the watermelon production. When all the banks were ordered closed in 1933, until it could be determined which banks were financially sound, the Bank of Blodgett was the first closed bank in Scott County allowed to re-open for business. The bank continued to serve the Blodgett area until 1937. The bank then moved to Oran and became the Oran State Bank.

Two disastrous fires struck Blodgett and a tornado in 1916. The first fire in 1927 destroyed two general stores and the hotel. In 1942, fire completely destroyed the Blodgett business district and it was never rebuilt to its former size.[36]

CROWDER was settled in 1897 by T. A. Cooksey, J. M. Denbow, Dr. C. C. Harris, James & S. P. Marshall, T. A. McCutchen, and Major McKinley, W. H. & W. J. Page, William Utley, E. Virgin and Lee and W. C. Wellman. The first settlement in the town was made in 1897, and the town of Crowder was incorporated in 1902. The first mayor of the town was Sterling P. Marshall. In 1912, there were three general stores, a saw mill, a hoop mill and a stave factory. When the Houck Railway Company of Cape Girardeau built the railroad to Caruthersville in 1896, and came to the point where Crowder is now located, it was suggested that the place be named Crowder after John Crowder, the first engineer to use the new railroad. The town is located on State Highway Z and County Road 480 in the midst of a farming community. In 1910 the population was 288 and in 1930 it was only 130.

Towns After 1900

ANCELL – It had the distinction of being known by three other names before the town officially became known as Ancell. The Cotton Belt Railroad in 1905 located a small depot for public accommodations for neighboring communities. The station was first known as Glenn and then Kelso Station, as it served the town of Kelso as shipping and receiving point for the flour mill located near by. Then a move was made to have the town called Arnold but

Hawkins Street, Blodgett, MO.

Main Street in Illmo, MO, circa 1905. (Photo courtesy of Harlan Smothers)

that too failed as a town by that name near St. Louis was already in existence. Since the Ancell family owned considerable land upon which the town was located and gave a substantial amount for the right of way to the railroad, they were honored by having the town named for them.

Ancell was laid out about 1906 and incorporated in 1911. The town was laid out on land originally owned by the Ancell family who moved from Cobb County, Kentucky to Missouri in the early 1830s. Ancell was located in the northwest corner of Commerce Township. The business interests over time consisted of Arnold's Store, Arnold's Grain and Feed, Ancell Sales, Missouri Propane Gas, the Flamingo Club, Hamil's Barber Shop, Blattel's Filling Station, Tiny's Place, and the Saveway Oil Company with a restaurant and motel courts and Hilleman Garage. The George Blattel family also operated a skating rink in connection with the filling station. The post office was located in the building adjoining Moll's Grocery and Frozen Food Lockers.[37]

In 1957 the Ancell School District was consolidated with Illmo and Fornfelt and the community lost its identity. The only thing left today with the Ancell name is the Cemetery. [38]

BLISSETT SETTLEMENT is located along Highway 61 just south of Morley on the western side of the highway. Mr. E. L. Blissett, a carpet installer in the area, bought up several acres of land in 1946. His children started moving in around the parent's house soon after then. They built the Blissett Temple Church of God and it remained that name until about 2001. In the past few years other Black families have purchased land in the settlement and they voted to change the name of the church to Divine Temple Church of God to attract more members. This settlement has never been incorporated nor had a post office. The Blissett Cemetery is in the rear of the church.[39]

CHAFFEE - the original site of Chaffee was purchased from the government in the early 1800s by a Mr. Cox and was known as "The Old Cox Farm." On June 20, 1905, Mr. Witt sold 1800 acres to the Chaffee Real Estate Company of St. Louis. This company later purchased additional acreage paying as much as $500.00 per acre for cleared land, but considerably less for the remaining hill and swamp lands.

Chaffee was laid out in August of 1905. The checkerboard pattern was platted and sidewalks layed before buildings were erected. The Post Office was established September 23, 1905 and the first postmaster was Carl J. Norseen. The real estate company gave the Frisco Railroad 150 acres for its terminal and a news item in "The Review" of October 1905 stated that the new Frisco passenger station ($35,000.00) and the General Office Building of the railroad ($40,000.00) were nearing completion.

The village was incorporated into a fourth class city on August 6, 1906, and Bob Wright was appointed by the County Court as Chaffee's first mayor. The first weekly newspaper in Chaffee was *The Chaffee Review* established in late 1905. In 1910, C. E. Mattocks came from Oran where he was publishing *The Oran Leader* and began publication of *The Chaffee Signal*. The newspaper is still published today.

Chaffee continued its steady growth with businesses of every description: livery stables, funeral homes, and stores of every description — including one that featured the advertisement "From the cradle to the Grave." It sold infants wear and coffins.

The Bank of Chaffee opened its doors for business in 1937 having been preceded by several unsuccessful banks. It began with a capital stock of $25,000 and in 1955, its total assets were $1,400,000. There is still a bank in Chaffee today.

Many of Chaffee's needs, from its earliest days to modern time, have been met by organizations interested in the betterment of the community. This is true of the public library started in a storeroom in the City Hall in 1930 and housed today in its own modern building. The Public Library has a wide variety of books in its facilities that are used by many organizations of Chaffee. The library is supported by a city tax.[40]

Chaffee is located at the junction of Hwy. 77 and A, eight miles west of Scott City.

FORNFELT owes its beginning to the building of the Thebes bridge across the Mississippi River which was completed in 1905. In 1901 the Missouri Pacific Railroad started the building of the railroad from St. Louis to Thebes, Illinois. The Cotton Belt on the Missouri side was increasing its traffic which led

up to Graysboro. The bridge was very necessary and surveyors selected the site of Fornfelt as the perfect site for the bridge and town to support it. It was located in the northeast part of the county on the Mississippi river.

It was first named Edna after the deceased daughter of Henry Schuette. There being another town with the name Edina in the state so similar in name and causing much confusion, the post office department refused to accept the name and it was officially changed in 1912 to Fornfelt. This was in honor of the family of Mrs. Wilhelmina Fornfelt, who was the mother-in-law of Mrs. Schuette and who owned considerable land south of the railroad tracks which became a part of the town. The name Fornfelt is the English version of the German name Vordemfeld.

Many of the houses were brought over from Graysboro after the removal of the railroad yards from there. The first mayor of Fornfelt was Charley Hamm, who had earlier been a farmer. At the turn of the century Christopher Menz operated a blacksmith shop in the east side of the town. This was not too far from a section known as the "New York Settlement" where the first Lutheran Church of the community was located about 1848. Later the church was moved to its present site in Illmo, now Scott City.

Among the earlier settlers was Dr. G. S. Cannon who served the town as a physician for more than 30 years and equally as long on the Board of Education. He was also postmaster for a time. Ed and Dana Schriefer had a hardware supplies store, J. H. Bollinger Sr., operated a meat market for years and later his son operated it under the name of Dode's Meat Market. The First State Bank of Fornfelt (at the time known as First State Bank of Edna) was organized in the spring of 1905 and erected in 1908. The first president was Henry Schuette, with Emil Steck as the first cashier who remained as such until 1920 when he became the collector of Scott County. He was succeeded by W. L. Tomlinson who had been the assistant cashier from 1913-1920. W. A. Georger succeeded him. Tommy Uelsman has been the cashier for several years, the youngest in the state.[41]

FROEMSDORF was another settlement near Illmo. It was settled a few years before Illmo, but completely abandoned by mid-1900s. The town was named after a woman named Froemsdorf. Here the Frisco depot was once located and a planning mill was operated by A. D. and D. B. Perkins, and a box factory known as the J. P. Mesler Co. This factory was moved to Froemsdorf from Cobden, Illinois in 1907. The factory was then moved to Fornfelt, Missouri.[42]

HAYWOOD CITY is a small town made of blacks about one mile east of Highway 61 off route U, just south of Morley. It has a population of 239 with the New Morning Star Missionary Baptist Church in the city limits. The first court records indicate that the town was founded in December 1947 with P. M. Martin, G. W. Harris and Willie Lockett trustees of the Fellowship Baptist Church of Morley establishing the Fellowship subdivision.[43] Then shortly after the completion of that subdivision the G.

View of Chaffee in 1908, taken East of town.

Local WWI soldiers and period automobile near Lambertville, Missouri (now called Lambert). (Photo courtesy of Mildred F. Sneed)

Judge Warren C. Lambert, Founder of Lambertville, Missouri.

W. Harris lots were sold.[44] The town was officially incorporated in 1960. The citizens use the Morning Star Cemetery to bury their dead and it is off County Road 427.

ILLMO had its beginning, as a result of the removal of the railroad yards, roundhouse and offices of the Cotton Belt Railroad from Graysboro, in 1904. It was incorporated as a fourth class city on May 23, 1905. Illmo was first known as "Whipperwill's Hollow." The name "Illmo" was derived from the abbreviations of Illinois and Missouri. The town of Illmo today is located in the north end of Scott County.

Three major railroads operated in Illmo: Missouri-Pacific, Cotton Belt and Illinois-Central. About this time a few men saw the possibility of the beginning of a new town at what now is Illmo. A company was formed composed of J. S. Norman, J. P. Lightner, R. A. Pellet, H. O. Murphy, and Mr. Wall, and with a few others purchased the land from Casper Roth on which the city of Illmo is now located.

Among the first buildings erected in Illmo were the old Ark building (since razed), a stucco building owned by Joe Pelly and other buildings, known as company buildings, built as an investment. One of the first stores in Illmo was the Illmo Mercantile Co., operated by J. W. Jacobs and a mercantile operated by a Mr. Thomas. The First State Bank of Illmo was organized in 1905. This bank was liquidated some years later and the present Bank was organized. The first factory in Illmo was the building occupied by the Menzie Shoe Company, afterward occupied by the Ely-Walker Dry Goods Company. An addition was added to this factory in 1933 which practically doubled the floor space of the factory and the addition was the pants factory. At one time it employed hundreds but has since closed.

Other active business interests once located at Illmo were Horns Department Store, Carver's Dry Goods, Harris Cleaners, Kjer's Grocery and Meat Market, Model Grocery, Sauer's Meat Market, Peck's Cafe, Domino Café, RJ. R.

Feriell Electric Company, Reliable Shoe Store and Repair Shop, Bishop's Jewelry Store, Bisplinghoff and Hubbard Undertaking, Kroger Grocery, Scott County Building and Loan Association, Hartner's Drug Store, Holliday Insurance Agency, Martin's Bakery, Plaza Theater, McSwains Garage, Cruse Barber Shop, Shipley Bros. Barber Shop, Standard Service Station, Southeast Missouri Lumber Co., a tin shop, two beauty shops, two pool rooms, Wadley Tailor Shop and J. A. Gearing operated a grocery store in Illmo for a number of years. Illmo had four churches, namely, Baptist, Methodist, Christian and Lutheran.

The first school in Illmo was a subscription school and was conducted in the Hubble building by Prof. E. T. Joyce. Previous to this time pupils from Illmo attended the old Washburn School across the railroad tracts. The Illmo school district was organized out of a part of the Washburn district and a part of the head district in 1905. The first part of the present grade school building in Illmo was constructed in 1905 at the cost of $5,000.00.

The first newspaper in Illmo was the "Illmo Headlight." After it suspended operations, Illmo was without a newspaper until 1913 when the "Jimplicate" was organized by E. L. Purcell and was later edited by his daughter, Miss Helen Purcell. It was a progressive newspaper until 1981.

Illmo had such organizations as the Chamber of Commerce, Rotary Club, Brotherhood of Railway Trainmen, Eastern Star, Masonic Lodge, P.T.A., American Legion and a Boy Scout Troop.[45]

In 1957 the Illmo School District was consolidated with Ancell and Fornfelt School Districts and the community lost its identity except for those original residences that remember it well. Illmo is now part of Scott City today.

LAMBERTVILLE, now known as Lambert, was settled by a Warren C. Lambert about 1905. The town set just below the Benton hill east of Benton on Highway 77 East. Judge Lam-

bert had hopes of making Lambert a thriving town. At one time there was a warehouse, a saw mill and two stores or more in Lambertville. Mr. Lambert owned several hundred acres of land in the vicinity. The Depot was located, perhaps before the town was organized, on the Gulf branch of the Frisco, but passed out of existence by 1933. As time passed, the town declined and the railroad tracks were torn up in 1933. The depot served as a shipping point for the town of Benton and for transport of soldiers during World War I. The town has a population of only 32 today, not counting W. C. Lambert and his family members buried in the Lambert Cemetery on the back road of this small village.[46]

LUSK was located at the corner of County roads N & NN. Rev. William M. Lust, an ordained deacon in the Methodist Episcopal Church South for over thirty years, was credited with establishing Lusk Chapel and the small community of Lusk. No other information is known of this small community and all that is there today is one house and the ruins of a service station.[47]

ROCKVIEW is located on the Frisco and Cotton Belt railroads about two miles north of Chaffee. Formerly there were two stores located at Rockview, one operated by a Mrs. Batts and one operated by the late W. F. Foshme, who was killed in his place of business in an attempted robbery in December, 1933. Also at one time Essner Brothers, who later operated a store in Chaffee, and also ran a store in Rockview. At one time Rockview had a post office but does not at the present time. It is now mostly a bedroom community with its citizens working in other towns.[48]

SALCEDO is located at the junction of Highways Y and Z approximately three miles west of Sikeston. The Cantrell family has been prominent in this settlement for many years. Mr. Clarence E. Cantrell moved to Salcedo in 1932 when all that was there was there was an old blacksmith shop and the Baker School. He pur-

Frank Felden's strawberry picking crew May 31, 1917 in Rockview, Missouri. (Photo courtesy of Steve Dumey)

West Ward School, near Scott City. Left to right, front row: Annie Tyler, Mary Alston?, unknown, Mary ? (last name unknown), unknown, Ruth Bruns, Berti Meadows?, Pearl ?, unknown, unknown, unknown. Second row: Betty ?, Edna ?, Ralph Miller, Lorn Tyler, Moses Ulnoy, Howard Morton, Charles Taylor, Frank ?, Theodore Porter, Ernest Taylor, Raymond Jorof, and Dorothy Hocuser?. Third row: Ethel ?, Irma ?, Elizabeth ?, unknown, unknown, unknown, unknown, Lola ?, unknown, unknown, unknown, unknown, unknown. Back row: Elia Lee, Bert Hill, Clifford Payne, Leslie Utnage, Miss Hamel, Ethel Keesee, Roy Utley, Eunice Dodd, Eugene Hudson, Ella Johnson, and Bud Harden. (Photo submitted by Ruth Bardot)

chased 26 acres and started a store on the corner in the blacksmith's shop. He married Mary B. Allard in 1936 and together they improved on the store and expanded Salcedo. They sold the store in the mid 1950s and he went into real estate. He built and sold most of the approximately 125 residences in Salcedo today. Clarence Cantrell is very proud of his community.

When asked how the village got its name,

Mr. Cantrell said there was an old tram train that used to go the area on the ridge above the Little River. A French couple had a cook shack up the road near some large Indian mounds to serve the timber workers. One day while they were on the train there was a doe (deer) standing on top of one of the mounds and the man turned to his wife and said, "Look Sal, see the doe." From that point on, the conductor of the train used to haul logs and passengers referred

to the area as "Sal See Doe," which became Salcedo.[49]

SCOTT CITY was organized after an election on February 29, 1960 in Fornfelt and Ancell for the purpose of consolidation. Representatives of the two old towns (as well as Graysboro and Edna) suggested the name "Scott City" and it was accepted by the County Court. The Fornfelt-Ancell Boosters Club with a membership of 115 was organized in October 1959 to promote the welfare of the two cities and to stimulate a desire for improvements. The name was later changed to Scott City Boosters and it was this group that spearheaded the movement for consolidation. The new town had a population of 1,913 with many business establishments, churches and a consolidated school system with Illmo (R-1).

TANNER was settled by Sikeston business men after the turn of the twentieth century and a store was located there. The community is located of U. S. Highway 61 about five or six miles northwest of Sikeston. It is a center of a great farming community. At one time it had a store but has never had a post office.

VANDUSER is situated about a mile east of Little River, partly on a sandy knoll and partly on gumbo. The Mississippi River is about 20 miles east of Vanduser. The town was once located on the St. Louis & Gulf branch of the Frisco Railroad and until the late 1930's served as the terminus of the Bloomfield branch. The town was laid out about 1895 on land cleared and donated by John S. VanDuser, landowner and merchant, for whom they named the town. The Bank of Vanduser was organized in 1907 with a capital of $10,000.00.

Listed among Vanduser's early business interests were the Layton Company General Store, E. L. Cruse General Merchandise, City Café, Wallance's Café, L. O. Williams General Store, Black & Son General Store, Southeast Missouri Lumber Company and four oil stations. Vanduser also had a cotton gin at one time and The Price & Garet Elevator Company operated in Vanduser for a number of years, but moved away several years ago. The completion of the Frisco Railroad around 1903 eased transportation for the commodities of the growing town. The town was incorporated with H. G. Schatz as mayor and Thomas J. Chaney, Clerk.

When Mr. & Mrs. L. O. Williams were married in Vanduser in 1908, there was only two ways to get around town – on the elevated boardwalk or by boat. The Williams operated the L. O. Williams General Store for 42 years. They remember when water was all the way to Bell City during high water. The St. Louis-Gulf branch of the Frisco ran through Vanduser and probably accounted for the beginnings of the settlement. In the early days, another railroad intersected the Frisco line there.

Vanduser Public School originated from the Batts District in 1904. The first school building was completed in 1907. A four year high school was built in 1922 with the construction of a combined grade and high school. Vanduser later had a consolidated school system and provides transportation. The Vanduser high school building was destroyed by fire in 1931 and replaced by a modern building at a cost of $18,000.00 in 1932. A tornado destroyed much of the town in the 1960s.

Miller's Store, 1955, Benton MO. (Photo couriesy of the family of Alfred Halter)

Today the bank is closed and the education needs is served by a local grade school with the high school students attending the R-5 Scott County Central High School of Highway 61 and about five miles south of Morley. Agriculture is still the life-blood of the community, but frequently people live in Vanduser, and work elsewhere, preferring the small town atmosphere.

OTHER SETTLEMENTS IN SCOTT COUNTY have been: Caney Creek, New York, Philadelphia and San Biding. These communities contributed in the making of Scott County but are no longer in existence.

Bibliography
1 Chaney, Audrey, 1960, *A History of Sikeston, Ramfre Press*, Cape Girardeau, MO
2 Louis Houck, 1908, *A History of Missouri*, R. R. Donnelley & Sons Co., Chicago
3 Ibid.
4 Anon., 1888, *Goodspeed's History of Southeast Missouri*, reprinted by Ramfre Press, Cape Girardeau, MO
5 Davies, Norman, 1996, *EUROPE A History*, Oxford University Press, New York.
6 Chaney, Audrey, 1960, *A History of Sikeston, Ramfre Press*, Cape Girardeau, MO
7 Anon., 1888, *Goodspeed's History of Southeast Missouri*, reprinted by Ramfre Press, Cape Girardeau, MO
8 Ibid.
9 Shrum, Edison, 1996, *COMMERCE, MO. 2—Years of History*, self-published, Cape Girardeau, MO.
10 Ibid.
11 Ibid.
12 Anon., 1888, *Goodspeed's History of Southeast Missouri*, reprinted by Ramfre Press,

Cape Girardeau, MO
13 Ibid.
14 Louis Houck, 1908, *A History of Missouri*, R. R. Donnelley & Sons Co., Chicago (Vol. III)
15 Chaney, Audrey, 1960, *A History of Sikeston, Ramfre Press*, Cape Girardeau, MO
16 Anon., 1888, *Goodspeed's History of Southeast Missouri*, reprinted by Ramfre Press, Cape Girardeau, MO
17 Nagel, Paul C., 1977, *Missouri – A Bicentennial History*, W. W. Norton & Company, New York
18 Scott County Merchant and tax records, found in the Scott County Court House, Benton, MO.
19 Nagel, Paul C., 1977, *Missouri – A Bicentennial History*, W. W. Norton & Company, New York
20 Hurt, Douglas R., 1996, *The Ohio Frontier – Crucible of the Old Northwest, 1720-1830*, Indiana University Press, Bloomington & Indianapolis
21 Anon., *The History of St. Denis Church*, self published, unknown.
22 Ibid.
23 Chaney, Audrey, 1960, *A History of Sikeston, Ramfre Press*, Cape Girardeau, MO
24 Ibid.
25 Ibid.
26 *Houck Papers*, Special Collections Archives, Kent Library, Southeast Missouri State University, Cape Girardeau.
27 Ibid.
28 Ibid.
29 Anon., 1875-76, *History and Directory for Southeast Missouri and Southern Illinois*, Cape Girardeau, MO

30 *Goodspeed's History of Southeast Missouri*, pp 302, 462, and family letters published in *Benton Newsboy*.
31 Ibid.
32 Father Hubert J. Eggermann, 1948. *History of St. Lawrence Catholic Church, New Hamburg, Missouri*
33 Missouri Newspapers on Microfilm at the State Historical Society of Missouri, Columbia, MO
34 Interview with Conrad Hudson, former residence of Morley, MO
35 Blodgett Centennial Booklet, 1870-1970. Betty Marshall-Chairman
36 Mrs. Martin Krieger, *Southeast Missourian*, Cape Girardeau, MO, October 1954
37 Ford, Royal E., 1939 *History of Scott County, Missouri*, self-published, Oak Ridge, MO.
38 *Chaffee Golden Jubilee Souvenir Booklet*, 1955, self published.
39 Interview with Michael T. Blissett on July 21, 2003 by Margaret Cline Harmon.
40 Shrum, Edison, *The History of Scott County, Missouri*, self published for the Scott County Historical Society.
41 Ford, Royal E., 1939 *History of Scott County, Missouri*, self-published, Oak Ridge, MO.
42 Ibid.
43 Plat Book 8, Page 1
44 Plat Book 10, Page 29
45 Ford, Royal E., 1939 *History of Scott County, Missouri*, self-published, Oak Ridge, MO.
46 Ibid.
47 Ibid.
48 Ibid.
49 Interview with Clarence E. Cantrell in May 1999 by Margaret C. Harmon.

Benton High School graduation, May 25, 1933. Front row: Virginia Smith, Clara I. Thompson, Charles Harrison, Georgia Miller, and Cleta Geneva Kirby. Back: Alfred Halter, Clara Mary Vetter, Clarence Ervin, Anna Virginia Eachus, and Norval Turner. (Photo courtesy of the family of Alfred Halter)

One hundred and five Missouri Mules! R.D. Clayton (in foreground, with whip) sold this load of mules to E.P. Coleman in 1933. Others pictured, in foreground, from left: "Toots" Ragland, Sheriff Tom Scott and Paul Scott (on horseback). In background: Brock boys and their father, Coley Brock. Picture taken on the Scott farm on the southern edge of Benton.

Left: Heinrich Christian Lewis Bruns and unknown man on a St. Louis, San Fransisco Railroad (Frisco) train. (Photo Courtesy of ? Bruns)

Left: Iron Mountain Depot, Sikeston, MO. April 14, 1918.

Below: Freddie Joe Graham in front of the root beer stand owned by Fred and Ruth Burns, Benton, MO. (Photo courtesy of Georgia Graham)

Editor's Note: These communities wished to include a more extensive, detailed account of their history, therefore they are separate from the previous histories written by Margaret Cline Harmon.

Chaffee

Founded in 1905

Compiled by: Betty Burnett Dooley Mirly
"God Bless America"

This history has been taken from the *Golden Jubilee Book* written in 1955, our local newspapers, the *Chaffee Signal, Leader, Review* articles, all written by other people. The people of Chaffee are very thankful that someone took the time to write down what they remembered about the early days of our town.

The Chaffee Leader
June 30, 1905

Frisco Yards to Locate near Rockview, Missouri.

The knotty problem as to what the Frisco is intending toward locating railroad yards in this territory seems to be settled beyond a doubt by the action that company has just taken in buying 1800 acres of land near Rockview. All the newspapers of this section have had sites picked for these yards at various places and the Cape Girardeau papers insisted that the yards and shops remain there. But it's all off now. The best informed railroad men who have heretofore been very reticent on this question, now freely admit that Cape will lose all Frisco interests at that point and that all will go to Rockview. Without outside information, this is the only reasonable conclusion that anyone would form in the face of the present developments, as it is certain that this system is not to maintain two separate yards, roundhouses, shops, etc., only 15 miles apart. This road is compelled to have a terminal to handle its bridge business. The Cape is not located good for this, and if it was there is no land there for this purpose which could be gotten at a reasonable price.

Already the work of grading for fourteen switch tracks one and one-quarter miles long has commenced at Rockview. One hundred teams and several hundred laborers and mechanics are being asked for. Two steam shovels and a rock crusher are on the ground.

It is understood that the Frisco will lay out a town there and that a clause prohibiting the dispensation of intoxicating liquors will be attached to each deed of transfer of town lots.

The *Benton Record* says in this connection: "There is no longer any doubt as to the new town to be located with the Frisco car shops in the county on the Witt-Heeb-Owens-Hunt lands near Rockview The cash was paid over by the Chaffee Real Estate Company of St. Louis Tuesday night in Benton, MO, something over $140,000 changing hands.

FRISCO RAILROAD

It was a very exciting time for the nation as a whole; the United States was coming into its own as a world power after the Spanish-American War, and here at home the last great burst of railroad construction was filling out the network of trackage. Here in southeast Missouri, a great deal of railroad track was already in place thanks to Louis Houck of Cape Girardeau; The Houck Lines spread throughout southeast Missouri and northeast Arkansas during the 1880s and 1890s. By the turn of the century, however, the flamboyant style of Houck and the other early-day railroad builders was giving way to that of railroad magnates who were seeking not just to lay track but to build railroad systems that would meet the needs of the future. Among these men was Benjamin Franklin Yoakum, who became Vice-President and General Manager of the Frisco in the mid-1890s and was elected President of the company early in 1900. Yoakum dreamed of nothing less than a railroad empire in the Midwest, and he wasted no time in making his dream come true.

First, the Frisco acquired the Kansas City, Fort Scott and Memphis Railroad, a long-time competitor whose line from Kansas City through Memphis to Birmingham still remained a part of the railroad in 1980. Before the first decade of the twentieth century was half over, Yoakum had succeeded in combining the Frisco, Rock Island, Chicago and Eastern Illinois Railroads into a single system covering the entire midwest from Minnesota and Chicago to Texas.

But the system was incomplete without an outlet to the Gulf Coast, and Yoakum envisioned a water-lever railroad route down the West Bank of the Mississippi River all the way from St. Louis to New Orleans. By 1905, Yoakum had consolidated the operations of his existing system sufficiently to begin construction of his line to the Gulf of Mexico, and it was the construction of that line that brought Chaffee into being.

At that time, the wheat field that occupied the site of Chaffee was surrounded by the lines built by Houck and acquired by the Frisco in 1902. The St. Louis, Memphis and Southeastern Railway had been organized as a subsidiary of the Frisco to rebuild the Houck Lines as necessary and to construct such additional links as were needed to make a through line from St. Louis to Memphis, the first step of the west-bank railroad from St. Louis to New Orleans.

One of the additional links, in fact the one that closed the final gap between St. Louis and Memphis, connected Nash and Lilbourn, MO, passing through the site of Chaffee. Not only would the new line tap traffic from St. Louis, it also would handle traffic moving between Chicago and Memphis by way of the Chicago and Eastern Illinois Railroad and that line's bridge over the Mississippi River to Thebes, IL.

Cape Girardeau, which had traditionally been Frisco's Southeast Missouri headquarters, was north of the junction between the St. Louis and Chicago lines, so land was purchased for a "townsite" just south of the junction and the Frisco system began moving men, machines and offices to the new town of Chaffee, which began growing rapidly. According to a brochure issued by the Chaffee Real Estate Company in 1906, "When southeast Missouri is fully developed there will be no richer nor more prosperous section on this continent, and Chaffee will be its commercial metropolis."

A crew of railroad construction men had moved

Frisco railroad depot, Chaffee

into Chaffee in July of 1905, and by the end of that year railroad facilities here included an office building for Frisco and Chicago and Eastern Illinois Division officials, a substantial passenger station and a roundhouse that could accommodate 30 locomotives, in addition, a freight yard, water works system, car repair shop, powerhouse and a large machine shop building were in place at Chaffee within little more than a year of the time tracks were first laid.

Chaffee was not without its growing pains; some of them caused by the fact that so many railroad installations were built so quickly. It was January of 1908 before the Chaffee correspondent for the *Frisco Man*, a predecessor of today's Frisco employee magazine, *All-Aboard*, could announce, "The labor train operating between Chaffee and Cape for the accommodations of shop employees who live in Cape and work in Chaffee has been pulled off, because of the scarcity of the homes and boarding houses at Chaffee. In fact, Chaffee was quite a booming little town. The *Frisco Man* corespondent boasted that the Hotel Astoria was "one of the most modern hotels in Southeast Missouri." The building boom continued unabated through 1908 and 1909, as a ball park, a planing mill, five store buildings, a restaurant, an elevator, an "electric theater" and numerous cottages and boarding home spread westward from the rails that created Chaffee.

For the first three years of its life, Chaffee faced a major threat from malaria and for that reason acquired somewhat a bad reputation on the Frisco. It developed that in blasting the freight yards in 1907, a few low spots remained to form collecting places for water and thus breeding grounds for the mosquitoes that carried malaria. Dr. R. H. Lucas, Frisco's local physician, soon determined the cause of the malaria epidemic and in cooperation with the Frisco officials saw to it that the smaller pools were filled with gravel and the larger ones drained, and it took care of the problem.

By late 1910, Chaffee had come into its own as a railroad town, and as such was of such vast important that there was talk of moving the county seat here. Few of us now can recognize the complete dependence on railroads in that day. Roads were inadequate for the most part, water transportation was slow and limited in the

territory it could cover, and that left railroads as the only practical means of transportation for people and freight. Six passenger trains a day left Chaffee for such places as St. Louis, Memphis and Chicago, and the seasonal cantaloupe and watermelon harvest in addition to the normal flow of freight traffic kept the rails through Chaffee highly polished.

Those shining rails were more than Chaffee's sustenance: They were its link to what was going on in the world. During the spring and summer, special trains left Chaffee every weekend and sometimes on weekdays to carry baseball fans to St. Louis. One of the largest crowds was drawn by the Chapel Car "Messenger of Peace," which paused at Chaffee for religious services as it made its way around the country in 1910. But change was coming as early as 1912, when a "Good Roads" exhibit car, sponsored by Frisco, stopped at Chaffee to promote the paving of roads to make travel by automobiles easier. Little did anyone know the automobile would surpass and finally eliminate the passenger train as a means of transportation for the people.

More unwelcome changes were on the way that year, however, as the Mississippi River burst its levees and kept low-lying Frisco track in this region under water for almost two months. Traffic through Chaffee was reduced to a trickle, and the Frisco as whole barely stayed out of the red in 1912. In fact, the whole United States economy was sliding into a recession, and the Frisco entered bankruptcy one year later.

Yoakum's dream was shattered. The Frisco, Rock Island and Chicago and Eastern Illinois Railroads went their separate ways, and the line down the West Bank of the Mississippi River would extend only from St. Louis to Memphis. The bankruptcy, and with it the loss of the rail link to Chicago, marked the end of the first chapter in Chaffee's life.

Signal-August 16, 1980

Frisco Day Celebration August 16, 1980 at Chaffee.

Within a few short months of this speech the Frisco merged with the Burlington Northern Railroad and the Frisco nameplate was no more.

EARLY HISTORY OF CHAFFEE

The site of Chaffee was originally purchased

from the government in the early part of the 19th century by a Mr. Cox and was known as the "Old Cox Farm," remaining largely uncultivated until 1890 when it was bought by Mr. John Witt, a farmer from Sikeston, who moved his family there and transformed it into a prosperous farm.

On June 20, 1905, 1800 acres were sold by Mr. Witt to the Chaffee Real Estate Company of St. Louis, who later purchased additional acreage from John Heeb, Otto Heeb, Gus Heeb, Mrs. Emily Hunt and Ottie Owens; paying $100.00 per acre for the 500 acres of cleared land, but considerably less for the remaining hill and swamp portion of it. On the Witt acreage were four houses; a small cabin, a granary a portion which was at 320 Gray Avenue, house on the corner of Black Avenue and Fifth Street, known for years as the "Allen Property" and the original John Witt home, a log house, directly east of the Frisco pump house and facing the old hill road to Rockview. Later the Witt family moved to a two-story home on the site where Carl Smith resident at 317 Elliott Avenue. This house was destroyed by fire.

At the time of the purchase the real estate company was promised possession by July 15, but incessant rains delayed the harvesting of the wheat crop, so it was not until August that engineers were sent to the plat the town. The checker board pattern was platted and sidewalks laid before buildings were erected. The avenues running east and west were named for prominent citizens or railroad officials. The streets running north and south were numbered from Main Street. Circle Park was laid on in the center of Third Street and Yoakum. On the north side the street names were Wright, Black, Cook and Helen, these streets were named after prominent real estate men and Helen was for Helen Gould, daughter of a railroad magnet.

In 1928 East Parker and East Davidson Avenues in the Eastern "A" Addition were added. The streets there were improved and concrete sidewalks were laid.

EARLY BUSINESSES

The first public building was a frame construction; housed the Post Office and the real estate company's office, and was located on the site where the Frisco General Office Building once stood on West Yoakum. The second public building, also of frame construction, was at the corner of West Davidson Avenue and Main Street and housed a grocery and saloon operated by Charles Kagel and Leo Schott and Levi Bechel as bartenders.

Boarding Houses

The first boarding house and third public building was on North Main and was known as the Blue Front Hotel.

The first actual hotel was known as Hotel Astoria, a three-story brick building having 56 rooms, a fine parlor, 8 baths and a cheerful dining room, housing the first local light plant, a saloon, the post office, a drug store. It was advertised as being equipped with steam heat, electric lights, and electric bells. It was built by Mr. L. F. Price and early carpenter for Mr. and Mrs. Jake Astor and was on the corner of Main Street and West Yoakum Avenue. It burned in 1913. And another hotel was not built until 1925, when the Byrd Hotel was erected by C. H. McCarthy.

Frisco railroad depot, Chaffee

Frisco Office building

Hotel Astoria, destroyed by fire.

An advertisement of the Chaffee Supply Company in a paper called *The Review*, dated October 1905 and signed by John J. Brennan, Superintendent, stated, "We have just finished making streets and sidewalks in Chaffee. The new Frisco passenger station and general office are nearing completion and in a few weeks we will start work on the Chaffee State Bank building.

Another article form the same paper stated, "John J. Brennan Jr., Attorney for Chaffee Real Estate Company, is now preparing papers for the telephone system. Under the proposed arrangement Chaffee will be included in a circuit comprising the various important centers of southeast Missouri and will also have connections with the outside world in general." By 1907 there were approximately 75 residential telephones in addition to those in the business establishments and the telephone office was located in the 100 block of Wright Avenue. The crank system of ringing was replaced on Jan. 1, 1952 by the automatic dial system. In 1955 there were 807 telephones in the city.

In 1918 a corporation was formed, known as the Chaffee Iron and Metal Company, that bought and sold scrap iron. Shareholders were: Wm. Pfefferkorn; E. A. Reissaus; George

Sample; G. M. Cohoon; Sam Frissell; Elmer McCutchen and John Krause.

On Aug. 6, 1906, the village was incorporated into a fourth class city with the following officers appointed by the County Court: Bob Wright, mayor; Frank Wilkinson, marshal and collector; W. M. Lee, city attorney; John J. Brennan Jr., justice of peace; and August Heeb, C. D. Rice, J. D. Foucht, Otto Stiehl, and L. E. Lenz, aldermen. During this period lawlessness became such a problem, especially gambling, that a secret civic organization employed a private detective from St. Louis to investigate and make recommendations as to ways of curbing it and means of securing better law enforcement.

Signal-2001

Chief of Police Don Cobb tells of old laws still on the Books

1. The mayor does not have to take bids on city work if an enemy attack is possible.

2. You are guilty of Malicious Mischief if you clip or shave the tail of a horse, or if you remove the nut from a buggy axle.

3. It is illegal to keep a dog that chases horses.

4. It is illegal to tether a mule within 10 feet of an ornamental tree.

Dr. A. W. Frost was Chaffee's first dentist, suc-

ceeded by Drs. Elwood Alley and W. A. Walling, and Dr. H. L. Cordrey was the first physician, succeeded by Drs. R. C. McCabe and H. R. Lucas.

The Post Office was established Sept. 23, 1905 and Carl J. Norseen was the first postmaster. Mr. Norseen was born in Stockholm, Sweden and came to the United States in 1881. He came to Chaffee with the real estate company, where he served as bookkeeper.

The first newspaper was *The Chaffee Review*, established in 1905 and published weekly by J. M. Davey and Company. It is not known when it went out of business. In August 1910 C. E. Mattocks came from Oran and started the publication of *The Chaffee Signal*.

The most prominent merchants of Chaffee's early period were J. W. Graham, Mr. Clifton and J. W. Collier, who owned the first grocery stores; Dr. Elwood Alley and Robert Wright, who opened the first hardware store, handling also hay, corn, coal and later farm machinery. August Heebs Meat Market opened for business in July 1905 and on March 1, 1906, William Guethle and Sons Meat Market was opened. Other grocerymen were H. A. Osman, who later had a variety store, George W. McDonald, John Haley, George Grace, and a firm known as Russler and Hastings Grocery and Market, which advertised "18 pounds of sugar for $1.00 and meat (all kinds) 10 cents per lb. and up," in the Jan. 17, 1908 issue of the *Review*.

The first general merchandise store, known as the Chaffee Mercantile Company, was owned by Frank and Arthur Brockmeyer, who after a few years sold it to E. F. Eggiman and G. F. Thomas. Julius Winer, in the Lankford Drug Store building, and Isaac Kugman, in the 100 block of W. Yoakum, were also early general merchandisers.

A. H. Slagle was a clothier, handling high priced men's wear and ladies' shoes. Mrs. Loretta Mears was Chaffee's first and only milliner. H. F. Stubbs was another early merchant; he owned a hardware store and also the first licensed funeral director and Mr. L. C. (Mayme) Bisplinghoff, the first licensed embalmer. The only funeral chapel in Chaffee is now Amick-Burnett Funeral Chapel, which Jack T. Burnett and Ollie Amick purchased form Lon Bisplinghoff. Today they own funeral homes in Scott City, Oran, Benton and these are run by their sons.

In 1909 T. A. and William Essner came from Rockview and opened the Essner Brothers and Company, a general mercantile store that operated under the slogan "From the cradle to the grave," as they handled everything from cradles to coffins. In 1931 the firm moved from 201 North Main to 110 West Yoakum. In 1947 the grocery and hardware department were separated, Russell Essner assuming management of t he grocery department and Norbert of the hardware. Upon Norbert's death in April 1950, Charles Kielhofner acquired the business which Harlan Whitaker of Portageville purchased April 1952 and operated Whitaker's Hardware, which is still in existence today and is owned and operated by Ronnie and Jean Whitaker.

William Pfefferkorn started a lumber company near the edge of town in 1907, it was called the Chaffee Lumber Company and was in existence until just recently.

An early livery stable on the corner of Main and West Davidson was owned and operated by Mrs. Emily Hunt and son, Cassie. This was sold to Henry Clay and later John Barber operated a second one.

Harry Auchenbaugh opened the first candy shop, making his own candy, Mrs. Ed Preston had the first confectionery, known as the Bon-Ton, where in April 1910 the first soda fountain was installed. This was a favorite afternoon meeting place for the young matrons of the town. Later Eugene Burgess, with his brother Walter, acquired the business from Mrs. Preston and called it the "Arcade." Still later, Bill and Ed Dunn opened the "swank" Green Parrot, eyed longingly from the outside by the adolescents who knew they would have reached the pinnacle of maturity when they could enter those doors and feel themselves welcome beyond the soda fountain. However, prior to this, "necessity being the mother of invention," and mother love removing mountains, Mrs. R. E. West came to the rescue of the "young fry" fully as much as they appreciated her satisfying their "sweet teeth," because it afforded her a means of supporting her family. She told that in a period of adversity, when her cupboards resembled Mother Hubbard's, one evening she had popped corn for the children's supper when the bright idea flashed through her mind of having the youngsters sell the corn and buy more nourishing food for their table. This she did, they had supper that evening and every evening thereafter. This later became the Fisher Candy Store, owned by Mr. and Mrs. E. A. Fisher, which was destroyed by fire. Chaffee's next confectionery was known as Slaughters.

Early after the establishment of the town, Abram Isaac's hung his shingle as a tailor and soon proved himself capable to meeting the demands of his most exacting clientele.

After the death of her husband, Charles Kagle, groceryman and salonkeeper, Mrs. Kitty Kagle started the town's first bakery on the corner of Main and Wright Avenue. The second bakery was owned and operated by C. A. Goddard, which developed into a sizable wholesale, as well as retail firm, having routes throughout the county and supplying baked goods to the stores in the surrounding towns. Raymond Coakley was one of the route men. E. F. Eggiman was later associated with Mr. Goddard in the business, which closed in 1939. Mr. and Mrs. Lloyd Taylor bought the building at 121 West Yoakum on May 1, 1947 and ran a bakery for many years. Chaffee is at the present time without a bakery.

The Standard Oil Filling Station was the first service station, located at Main and Yoakum.

The first manufacturing concerns were the Gill, Cook, Foucht Saw Miller and Lumber Company, the General Lumber Manufacturing Company, and the R. S. Ruch Hoop Mill, later purchased by U. R. Elrod and J. P. Lankford. An early paper stated the Gill, Cook, Foucht Company was a complete saw and planing mill and sawed oak, gum, hickory and cypress for which there was a foreign demand. At one time the Ruch Mill produced an average of 6,000 hoops per day.

On Nov. 5, 1915 the Enterprise Mill and Grain Company came to Chaffee. It was owned by Peter A. Rigdon and sons, Dennis, Herbert and Edwin, and was operated as a flour and grain mill until 1936.

In March 1911 a meeting of citizens was called for the purpose of creating a corporation for the manufacturing of ice and to handle the storage needs of the town. J. S. Wahl was elected president and the board of directors was comprised of H. C. Shults, D. C. Shoptaugh, W. H. Brooks, and William Pfefferkorn.

During the next few years the development of the town was rapid. In a short time three factories were brought here by public subscription; the Bumper Factory, under the management of J. B. Payne of St. Louis; the Premier Manufacturing Company, with Lawrence J. Heyman as manager, made children's play clothes; and the National Garment Factory with Leo J. Rothbarth as president manufactured ladies underwear, converting later to men's and boy's polo shirts and being known as the Patton Garment Company, whose manager was Carl J. Rosenquist.

The old Premier Manufacturing Company building was taken over June 13, 1935 by Oscar Bukstein and began operations as the Chaffee Manufacturing Company with 29 employees and 16 machines. In 1939 an expansion program was launched, bonds sold and the plant enlarged. In 1955 following the death of Oscar Bukstein, a second expansion program was launched, under the presidency of Max Bukstein, and when the new addition was completed the company employed 375. Paul Bukstein was secretary-treasurer of the company.

In 1937 the Bumper Factory building was used as a basis for Collins-Morris Shoe Company, which was in existence for only a few months. On Nov. 6, 1939 a new company, the Sports Specialty Shoemakers, Inc., took its place with Harry Ostermeier of St. Louis as president and L. R. Ward, vice-president. Homer A. Turner was made superintendent.

Mrs. L. R. Ward started a baby shoe factory in collaboration with several out-of-town businessmen. It soon outgrew its quarters in the basement of her home and it was moved to a building in the 100 block of East Yoakum. Soon a larger building was necessary and Chaffee lost this business when it moved to Advance, MO.

In 1928 this article appeared in the *Signal*, "Chaffee made another good record in 1928."

Chaffee, in 1928, enjoyed another good year of steady growth and substantial improvements.

The development of East Parker and East Davidson Avenue in the Eastern "A" Addition was especially noticeable. The streets there were improved and concrete sidewalks were laid, as well as substantial repairs made to a number of dwellings.

The major additions to the city were the securing of a new garment factory, the new water well and erection of three new business rooms on South Main Street.

Both First National Bank and the Chaffee Building and Loan Association enjoyed successful years, the total resources of each nearing the half million-dollar marker.

The local log and timber yard, under the principal management of Harry Hindman, was one of the busiest spots in Chaffee during 1928. A veritable sea of logs, ties, mine props, etc. was constantly on hand, as well as a large number of teams, teamsters and loading equipment. In point in raw material shipment, the Chaffee log yard was one of the largest on the Frisco railroad at the time. Mr. Hindman also ran a sawmill. The timber industry has been one of the largest sources of ready money to many people during 1928.

The Frisco car shops at one time during 1928 had the largest number of men employed here that had ever been employed at one time. The railroad installed its new passenger and freight service to the Gulf of Mexico by way of St. Louis, Chaffee, Memphis and Pensacola, FL. It introduced its "hot shot" freight train called "The Lindberg" which operated on the old running time of fast passenger trains.

Banks

The first bank of Chaffee was opened on May 31, 1906 as the Chaffee State Bank. F. W. Loy was the first president and John Rotherheber, its first cashier. On Oct. 26, 1910 the stockholders voted to increase the capital stock and in November made application to become the First National Bank. Officers were F. W. Loy, president; J. Claude Wylie, vice-president; E. A. Reissaus, cashier; W. D. Loy and L. W. Daniels, assistant cashiers; and directors, William Pfefferkorn, F. W. Loy, Claude Wylie, Dr. G. A. Sample, F. H. Dierssen, W. D. Loy and E. A. Reissaus. This bank closed its doors in November 1931.

The German-American State Bank was organized and opened for business in January 1911. In 1914 it changed to Chaffee Trust Company and on 1917 became Security Savings Bank. It was closed on Nov. 15, 1925.

Following the closing of the First National Bank, Chaffee was without a bank for a few years. On Aug. 21, 1937 the Bank of Chaffee opened its doors for business with Dr. E. D. Kimes as president and O. J. O'Bryant, cashier. In 1955 Fred Thornton was president; John K. Hale, cashier; J. R. Stephens, vice-president; and directors were these men along with Fred Lewallen and Mrs. Fred Thornton.

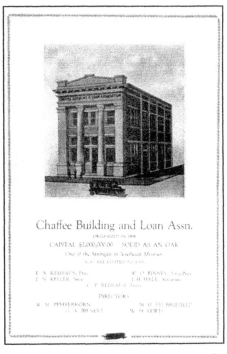

Chaffee Building and Loan Assn.

The Chaffee Building and Loan was organized Nov. 21, 1908. Directors were Frank Brockmeyer, Dr. H. R. Lucas, John Rothenheber, F. W. Loy, R. W. Finley, C. H. McCarthy, William Pfefferkorn, George Bird, John W. Heeb and Dr. Elwood Alley. Officers in 1955 were Dr. W. O. Finney, president; John A. Groseclose, first vice-president; Russell Essner, second vice-president; P. N. Keller, secretary and treasurer; Miss Ann Whitfield, assistant secretary; and directors were M. E. Gisi, Dr. Alvin E. Riehl, Leo J. Trapp, L. R. Ward, Dr. W. O. Finney, John A. Groseclose and Russell Essner.

Today in 2001 Chaffee still supports two banks, the First National Bank and First Commercial Bank.

Utilities

On Nov. 8, 1910 a special election was called for the purpose of accepting or rejecting a proposition to bond the city for $26,000 to construct a waterwork system and city hall. Armor George was named first water superintendent, in which capacity he served until 1947 when he retired and Charles Allen was appointed to fill his vacancy.

Under Mayor Massengill the first electric street lights were installed in an issue of the *Signal* in 1911 was found the account of lights being placed at the intersections of Second and Yoakum and Third and Gray.

First Homes Built in Chaffee

The first residence was built by Mr. Price on the corner of Main Street and Elliott Avenue. It belonged to Mr. and Mrs. George Bienert. Mr. Price was the father of the first child, a daughter, born in Chaffee. She was named "Chaffee."

The house which stands at 103 S. Third, commonly known as the Walling Home, is said by all who remember it, to be quite a showplace.

According to records found at Scott County Recorders Office at Benton, MO says the land on which the house stands was purchased by Chaffee Real Estate Company from John Witt in 1905.

The house was designed by a real estate agent, Frederick Loy and his wife, Fannie, bought the home on Nov. 7, 1908. It is said that Loy designed this house to show visitors to town how prosperous the young town was.

On Jan. 24, 1920 the Loy's sold the property and home to Dr. W. A. Walling and his wife, Lozzetta. The purchase price was $7,000. Dr. Walling set up his dental office in the home.

Mrs. Walling was a very prim and proper lady, as recorded in local newspapers; she gave lavish dinner parties in the large dining room of the home. She had fishponds around the large yard, and inside the hedge that once surrounded the house were beautiful flowers planted throughout.

After Mrs. Walling's death, Dr. Walling married a local lady doctor, Dr. Delezene, who along with her son Edward had a prosperous practice here. The house was bought by Paul and Bernice Horstman Montgomery and served as their home for 10 years.

Later it was turned into an apartment house. Many people lived there over the years.

The house has been sold to Andy Pfefferkorn

The first Chaffee public school building.

and he has remodeled it and has turned into an apartment house.

1923 Fire

Fire which had its origin in the rear of the Grace's Grocery Company located at 205 W. Yoakum, last Friday afternoon at 2 o'clock, starting from a pile of rubbish being burned there, resulted in the most disastrous fire in the history of Chaffee, a total of ten business buildings being totally destroyed resulting in a damage of approximately $50,000.

The fire is believed to have ignited a large tank of kerosene in a shed in the rear of the grocery store.

The fire spread from the grocery on both sides, setting on fire the two-story brick building on the northwest corner of Second and Yoakum, and the two-story frame structure, which housed the Guethle Meat Market. Fire then spread to the building next door to the two-story building belonging to Mrs. Mear and then on to frame building next door occupied by William Evans who had a short order lunch room.

In the meantime the fire had spread to the opposite side of the street, first enveloping the Fischer Confectionery, a one-story frame building, and spreading from this building to buildings on each side of it; the one-story frame building of Santhoff's Shoe Store and Mrs. Stanthoff's Ladies Ready to Wear Store, and the two-story frame building occupied by Huffman's Grocery. It spread from this building to the one and one-half-story building occupied by Henson's Restaurant. However, this building was not burned to the ground.

An extremely high wind from the northwest served to drive flames in a southeasterly direction, which for a time threatened the entire residential section in the southern part of the city. At this point it was evident that fire fighters' apparatus of the city was not sufficient to cope with the situation. In the meantime, several of our citizens, fearing more serious damages, sent in relief calls to Cape Girardeau, Illmo and Fornfelt, MO. At this stage of the fire, Mr. H. E. Hubbard, general foreman at the Frisco

roundhouse, hurried to the shops, and summoned all but three of his men together with the Frisco fire fighting facilities. Five minutes after their arrival the fire was under control. No doubt to the experience these had gained in their weekly fire drills at the shops.

Other buildings and businesses damaged by the fire were L. S. Morrow building; Mr. J. A. Poindexter's second hand furniture store and an apartment above, which was occupied by Mr. and Mrs. Andy Bellis, sustained a loss.

Library

Many of Chaffee's needs have been met by organizations interested in the betterment of the town. This is true of the public library. In the winter of 1929 members of the Chaffee Woman's Club conceived the idea of a city library, whereupon Mrs. R. H. Ballard, president, appointed Mrs. A. W. Aubuchon, Mrs. W. A. Walling, and Mrs. W. H. Richardson to determine the proper procedure for such a project. They conferred with city attorney E. M. Munger, and ascertained that a mill tax for the support of a library could be submitted to the voters after a petition had been presented to the city council. In July 1930 the Club opened the first library in a storeroom of the city hall. Members of the club acted as librarians, without pay, until it became necessary to hire someone. Mrs. L. D. Lankford was employed to serve in this capacity. When first opened it contained approximately 150 books. In 1954 Lon C. Bisplinghoff deeded the corner lot at Second and Wright to the city as the site for the new library. The LeBonehur Junior Federated Club assumed responsibility of raising the necessary funds, which they did by public solicitation and a sizable donation from the city. On March 10, 1955 the contract was let for the $8,822.40 building and that day ground was broken for construction. It was finished in mid-summer.

Swimming Pool Constructed

In the winter of 1938 work was begun on the municipal swimming pool, a long cherished desire of the citizens, who had realized the danger of the "ole" swimming holes in the drainage ditches, but at the same time recognized the

The old Chaffee City Hall housed the city jail and public library.

impossibility and the undesirability of separating boys from swimming holes. Mayor Oscar T. Honey spearheaded the move for the pool, built with government assistance at Harmon Field. It was an elevated one, modeled after one at Grundy Center, IA; the pool was opened in the summer of 1940 and still remains in 2003.

FIRST CHURCH

Realizing that "man does not live by bread alone" the Frisco in the early months of the town's existence furnished a chapel car known as the "Messenger of Peace," which made regular visits to the little town and in which was held interdenominational services. However the residents had no more than procured roofs over their heads to protect them from the elements than they felt the need and desire for a protective shelter for the spiritual side of their lives—a church. Thus in November 1905, Mrs. R. F. Hollinghead circulated a subscription paper and raised enough money to purchase a small tent, 16x24 feet. Here Chaffee's first Sunday School was organized with Dr. Elwood Alley, superintendent and Mrs. Cyrus Stephens, secretary. It was a Union School; the superintendent being a Methodist and the secretary a Baptist. It was quite small at first, there being only two classes; W. H. Kirkendall was first teacher of the adult class and Mrs. Elwood Alley of the primary class.

SCHOOLS

With the demand for churches came also the demand for schools and there was an attempt made in 1906 to have a school, but it was such a discouraging undertaking that the teacher resigned in a few weeks and thus the term ended almost before it had started. However, in September 1907 the second attempt was made and proved successful; classes meeting in a converted granary on Gray Avenue. Miss Ara Finley (Mrs. W. B. Thomson) taught the primary and Miss Blanch Hicks (Mrs. S. J. Crosnoe), the upper elementary grades. There was an enrollment of 134 in the first grade that year, which increased to 157 the following year. This necessitated a division of the group, one-half attending the morning session and the other half the afternoon session. It was this year that the Chaffee Real Estate Company built a small one-room house across the street from the granary and an additional teacher was employed to assist in the upper grades. A further responsibility of these early teachers in bad weather was assisting the children across a plank footbridge, which spanned the ditch at the edge of the walk. There were no library books, references, charts, or blackboards, so portions of the walls were painted to serve as blackboards. The second year Misses Finley and Hicks secured public subscriptions to begin the first school library.

In 1909 a brick building with four rooms and an office was erected on the corner of Fourth and Elliott. In 1910 a one-room frame school was built and used for the primary grades for three years. Then in 1912, four-room addition was made to the brick building, which was known as the Southside Grade School, the cost was $14,900. In 1916 a three-story brick high school was constructed on the corner of Yoakum Avenue and Fifth Street, the bond issue for which was $13,000. A gymnasium was added to the high school campus in 1921.

By this time nearly forty percent of the population was enrolled in the public schools and more room had to be provided. In May 1922, the Board of Education passed a resolution creating the Junior and Senior High School. Bids were opened the first week of services for several more teachers and additional room, so the Board authorized an addition to be built to the high school, when completed, made it a twelve-room building for which the two bond issues had totaled $29,000. The cornerstone was laid June 24, 1922. Prior to this, in 1920, a two-room frame building was erected north of the high school at a cost of $3,000 to relieve congested classrooms of the lower grades and there the first and second grade pupils from the north half of the town was taught.

Having been approved as a first-class high school in 1918, a Commercial Department was added in 1922, a Vocational Home Economics Department in 1931, and a few years later a Manual Arts Department.

Austin C. Walling was the first graduate of the high school in May 1916, completing the last two years study alone. There were no commencement exercises.

St. Ambrose Catholic School

The Rev. Michael J. Clooney followed as shepherd of the parish. His pastorate, though short, was noted for the establishment of St. Ambrose School. Ground was broken for the school building on Aug. 29, 1917 by Father Clooney and members of the parish organization.

The school opened September 3 and included grades 1 through 8 with the Sisters of Mercy from St. Louis staffing it.

Shortly after the school opened, Chaffee was hard hit by an outbreak of Spanish influenza. The Board of Health recommended to the city officials that all public buildings be closed in an attempt to control the spread of the disease.

When school reopened in the fall of 1919, Father Michael O'Leary, who replaced Father Clooney, decided to add a third story to the building to provide a high school department for those students who wished to further their education.

Because of the failure of the school to gain state accreditation (due to lack of physical facilities) and the difficulty of students to gain admission to institutions of higher learning, Father Lonergan chose to discontinue the high school department in 1931. Since that time St. Ambrose parochial school graduates receive their secondary education at the Notre Dame High School in Cape or at the local public school.

In 1931 the economic depression reduced the enrollment of St. Ambrose from 109 to 85. As a result, the seven Sisters teaching in 1930 were reduced to four in 1932. With a continued drop, only three sisters were assigned to Chaffee in 1933.

Six years after the Rev. Walter Craig came to Chaffee; a fire destroyed St. Ambrose Church on April 12, 1942. Because of the war, building materials could not be obtained so Father Craig converted the school basement into a temporary church. Later the basement was enlarged and remodeled.

In 1972 the Sisters of Mercy, who had staffed the school from its beginning, left St. Ambrose, and there was serious consideration of discontinuing the school entirely. But through strong opposition of parishioners and the school board, the school remained open. At this time the school was staffed entirely by lay teachers for the first time since its beginning in 1918.

The Rev. Raymond Kunkel was assigned to St. Ambrose on Sept. 20, 1975. The 1976-77 school year marked the beginning of the first kindergarten class with an enrollment of 15 pupils. The program was initiated through the efforts of the school board and interested parents who wanted to see the continuation and growth of St. Ambrose School.

St. Ambrose School Teacher 1943 – 1948
by Mrs. Dorothy Dees

Sister Mary Constance, R.S.M., taught at St. Ambrose Catholic School, Chaffee, MO, 1943 – 1948. She was principal and teacher of seventh and eighth grades. After leaving Chaffee, she taught in the St. Louis area many years. She still tutors and visits the sick and the infirm at St. John's Convent and St. John's Hospital. The convent, where she and other religious live, is adjacent to the hospital at 611 South New Ballas Road, St. Louis.

Sister Mary Constance was born on Sept. 21, 1913 and enjoys weekly visits with her family, as well as occasional visits with former students and friends from Chaffee.

At age 88, Sister still looks much like this photo, although she doesn't wear the "habit." Her order is now known as the Sisters of Mercy of the Americas.

She tells the story of when one of the sisters ordered a chicken from the grocery store. The clerk said, "Do you want it dressed?" She said, "No" – so when the boy from her class brought the chicken, it was alive, to her dismay.

BANDS

The first band was organized on May 4, 1915 under the leadership of E. O. Brown, foreman of the Frisco car department, and was called locally the Third District Mechanics Band, but outside of Chaffee was known as the Frisco Band. The citizens ready acceptance of this musical organization is attested by the fact that in May 26, 1916 issue of the *Signal* appeared this item: "The Women's Improvement Club will give a dance at the skating rink on next Thursday night beginning at 9:30 for the bandstand benefit." (Circle Park Bandstand).

Many times the Third Mechanics Band barely existed as an organization, but through the persistent efforts of directors, E. O. Brown, Charles Armgardt, and Henry Engleman, the band survived. Mr. Brown was finally instrumental in bringing Oscar T. Hone of Marston, MO to Chaffee to assume the directorship and under him the band progressed in the following years until in July 1921 Col. Warren Mabrey requested it be organized as a National Guard Band to play a the State Fair in Sedalia. It was first known as the Sixth Regimental State Band. It later became the famous 140th Infantry Band of the 35th Division of the National Guard. There were 48 members from Chaffee and the surrounding territory to insure sufficient personnel for its maintenance. In April 1922 the band contracted for equipment to set up a radio station in Chaffee, issuing one hundred membership cards to the Radio Club of Chaffee, which cards would admit members to the Armory for any radio concert during the year. Later Glenn Packwood, a member and assistant cashier of the Security Savings Bank, located a station on the rear of his lot at the corner of Davidson and Second and news received was typed and placed on the window of the bank.

One of the highest honors paid the 140th Infantry Band was the composition, "140th March" written by K. L. Kind and dedicated to Lieut. Honey and the band.

WAR YEARS

Chaffee carried its full responsibility in both World Wars, and WWII had perhaps a near record percentage of the population in service; there being more than one-sixth of the city's total population in the various branches of the Armed Forces. The Women's Defense Club, Red Cross volunteer workers, civil defense workers and others served creditably on the home front. The city's service flag bears 29 Gold Stars.

Chaffee Signal Dec. 17, 1942, "Chaffee Observed Blackout Test"

Chaffee people jointed whole-heartedly in the observance of the test Blackout Monday night from 10 to 10:20 p.m. At the sound of the city fire siren, lights all over the city were immediately turned off.

The Control Center, located at the City Hall, was fully staffed: L. D. Lankford and L. R. Ward, co-commanders, were in charge. Other personnel included C. A. Goddard, chief of the auxiliary police; Charley Allen, chief of fire; Arthur Free, chief air raid warden; Wallace Reynolds, chief of utilities; Dr. W. O. Finney, chief of medical service; Fred Lewallen, chief of communications; Jack Thorne, controller; Allen Brinkman, chief of telephone service. Thirty Boy Scouts from the three local troops served as messengers during the test. Mrs. Robert Capshaw and Miss Jose Finely served as clerks at the Control Center.

Circle Park Bandstand

The Women's Improvement Club of Chaffee certainly deserves a lot of credit and a handsome vote of "Thanks" in their ultimate success in the erection of an elegant and very substantial bandstand in the center of Circle Park. Fred Dobbs, being the contractor and the man who built the structure. This first structure was built in 1916.

This first bandstand was the scene of many an enjoyable concert, and was replaced in 1941 by the present steel and concrete one.

History of Harmon Field

The land where Harmon Field is situated was obtained by the City of Chaffee as a gift from a philanthropist, Wm. E. and Katherine Harmon of New York City. They established the Harmon Foundation because they wanted to leave their money and their properties where it would benefit children.

To comply with the requirements of accepting this grant land, the City of Chaffee had to agree to the following stipulations:

1. That the property be used in perpetuity for playground and recreational purposes.

2. That no building be erected upon the property, except for the furtherance of desirable play and recreation.

3. That the premises shall always be known as Harmon Field.

4. That the land shall be open to all persons.

5. That the premises shall always be kept in such condition as to be attractive as a place of recreation and shall not be permitted to become a nuisance in appearance or unattractive as a place for recreation.

Sister Mary Constance, St. Ambrose School, Chaffee.

Ambrose School, Chaffee 8th grade graduating class, May 14, 1947. Left to right: Father Caig, Don Isaac, Dottie Scheeter, John Biler, Dorothy Halter, Jauad Mier, Florence Kluesner, Barbara Finley, Frank Ludwig, Buster Kluesner, and Jim Westrich. Teacher was Sister Mary Constance, R.S.M. (Photo courtesy of Dorothy Dees)

Chaffee Signal June 12, 1924 "Harmon Foundation offering Free Playground Sites"

The Harmon Foundation, Inc. of New York offers a free playground site for children to be established in fifty small cities in the United States having 3,000 or more population, the sum of $100,000 having been set aside for this purpose. The *Signal* believes that Chaffee is eligible for this favor, and we believe our people should interest themselves and inquire into the matter. The Foundation offers to purchase two acres of ground, but does not furnish the equipment. No less than 500 towns have applied for playgrounds now, applications must be sent in by July 1.

Chaffee Signal July 10, 1924 "Prospects Look for Harmon Foundation Park"

The prospects for a Harmon Foundation Park are looking good. Dr. Geo Huff, a chiropractic doctor, wrote the particulars and the application blank, and has received them.

It is planned to purchase a six-acre tract of land from J. A. Clayton, situated west of Fifth Street, somewhere between Elliott and Davidson Avenue. The Harmon Foundation agrees to donate $2,000 toward the purchase of the land, and they require that it be guaranteed the land will be equipped with playground equipment. It is planned to have a baseball diamond, swimming pool, and tennis courts, besides the playground equipment.

Chaffee Signal Aug. 21, 1924 "Assured of the Harmon Foundation Park"

The Harmon Foundation Park for Chaffee is practically a reality. Monday of this week Dr. Geo Huff received a lengthy letter from the foundation headquarters, stating that Chaffee had been put in Class "A." More than 750 inquiries were received in response to the offer of the Harmon Foundation to give 50 playgrounds this year to growing cities and towns in the United States.

Before the gifts are actually made, there are certain additional important requirements that must be met as stated below.

1. An option must be secured sufficiently long to insure Harmon Foundation getting a free and clear title. Under this revised plan they assume that a sixty-day option will be sufficient and if not already acquired, it need not be secured until actual section of the towns has been made.

2. An abstract of the title and survey must be furnished them, free of cost, prepared by a competent attorney, together with an opinion as to the character of the title, both with respect to its legal soundness and marketability. This need not be ordered until requested.

3. An agreement for maintenance, signed by the governing body of the town, Board of Education, or group responsible must be given providing for the following maintenance program:

A. That the property shall be placed in first class condition.

B. That it shall be maintained, policed and controlled for at least five years.

C. That on properties costing $2,000 or less, $300 will be required the first year, and $200 per annum thereafter for four years. On properties costing more than $2,000 individual arrangements will be made. The $300 install-

ment for the first year's improvement and maintenance program must be deposited with the local bank handling the gift of the Harmon Foundation in advance of conveyance of title.

4. There must be agreement to place in a suitable stone-preferably a rough boulder-a bronze table measuring "10x18" which will be furnished without charge by the Harmon Foundation. This tablet will be inscribed as follows;

"Harmon Field"

This playfield was made ours through the assistance of the Harmon Foundation, 1924. Dedicated forever to the plays of children, the development of youth and the recreation of all.

"The Gift of Land is the Gift Eternal."

Chaffee Signal Oct. 16, 1924 "Chaffee Selected One of Fifty Communities to get Playground-Selection made Subject to Approval of a director who is soon to arrive here to make final investigation"

Dr. Huff has been very actively interested in securing this donation for Chaffee and it is through his untiring efforts that Chaffee has been selected as one of the fifty communities in the United States to receive this award. From all information available Chaffee is the only community in Missouri that is considered for this award.

Chaffee Signal Feb. 12, 1925 "Chaffee Awarded Harmon Field"

The long looked for report from the Harmon Foundation, Inc. of New York, advising that Chaffee is to receive a playground gift was received by Dr. Geo Huff, Chaffee's pioneer chiropractor, last Friday morning in the form of a telegram.

There were 74 applications in Missouri and Chaffee was the only one awarded this grant.

Found in Cornerstone of Bank of Chaffee, 1997

Chaffee, MO, Dec. 9, 1905

The laying of the cornerstone of this building finds the town of Chaffee well under way toward becoming the future "City" of southeast Missouri. At present there are erected, or under course of construction, about forty dwellings and business buildings, most of the business houses being on either side of Yoakum Avenue, west of Second Street. Mettz Brothers have a large two-story building, covering two lots on Main Street, north of Cook, James Alexander store and restaurant on Main Street between Wright and Black Avenues, while August Heeb has a meat market on Main Street facing Parker Avenue. Kagel's large two-story building is not quite completed. Among the merchants of the place may be mentioned J. W. Mears; Alley, Wright and Company; Eli Osman; James Alexander and August Heeb. The Frisco railroad station is ready to turn over to the railroad company, while the office building is nearly completed, the tile roof just being put on. Freight station and roundhouse are well under way, the latter having foundation laid.

The town site of Chaffee is at present owned by the Chaffee Real Estate Company of which Mr. James W. Black is president; Isaac T. Cook, secretary; James F. Cook Jr., assistant secretary; F. W. Loy, manager.

The work of development has been carried on by the Chaffee Development Company of which James W. Black is president, James F.

Cook, secretary-treasurer and John J. Brennan, manager.

Sept. 23, 1965

Last Passenger Train Through Chaffee

Over 60 years of passenger service was ended last Friday, Sept. 17, 1965 when the last Frisco Railroad ran its last passenger train between St. Louis and Memphis. For this run the 807 out of St. Louis, the diesel 2020 known as "Big Red" was used. Three of these six were coaches with other mail and baggage cars.

Ordinarily, one coach would have been enough for the southbound Frisco which has been having three or four passengers to an occasional 50, but for this last memorial trip the Frisco happily put on the extra two coaches for people who wanted to make history by riding this last passenger train.

It was a Chaffee crew that took the 807 on its last run. The southbound crew was Conductor John Montgomery, Fireman Clifford A. Pobst and James A. Barnes.

The northbound Chaffee crew for the last run was Conductor Lon A. Tohill, Fireman S. R. Duncan and Engineer Otis Snyder.

The sadness of all this is that our children born after this date would never know the excitement of riding a passenger train.

Chaffee 2001

From 1905 until 2001 people have come and gone in this small city of a little over 3,000 people, but those who leave seem to come back home. Either to live out their lives and some just to visit.

The railroad is no longer our mainstay, but it still provides opportunity for employment.

The Burlington Northern lines still run four trains south and four or five trains north each day through our depot. We also have two trains north and one south that tie up in Chaffee daily. We have long since had to give up some of our industries that provided employment for our town, Sports Specialties and Thorngate Limited, but fortunately we have other smaller businesses, churches, schools, banks, local city government, police force and people stay as a steady force.

We are second to none as a place to raise our families or to spend out quiet years.

In this year 2001, with the tragedy we have had in our country, most citizens of Chaffee will say I am thankful to live in Chaffee.

We thank the Scott County Historical Society for providing a place for us to let you know about our home place—past, present and a desire for the future.

Commerce Landing

Early Gateway To The West

Scott County was one of the first gateways to the west. In the 1700s, St. Louis was only a fur trading post. The later invention of the steamboat and roads carved through Pennsylvania, Ohio, Indiana and Illinois made St. Louis, at the Missouri and Mississippi River Junction, the gateway to the west.

The Ohio River was the main artery from the original 13 states to the west. When the very early western bound settlers reached the Mississippi River, swamps faced them in every direction except behind them in Kentucky. Down-

Commerce, MO circa 1900. Washington St. looking West between Twappity and Water Streets. (Photo courtesy of Bob White)

Post Brothers drain tile plant in Commerce, MO. (Photo courtesy of the Scott County Signal)

stream the western side of the Mississippi was swampland all the way to the Gulf of Mexico. In order to reach high ground, the settlers had to paddle, pole or pull their rafts and boats 30 miles up the Mississippi to Commerce Landing on Crowleys Ridge in Scott county. This made Commerce a very important landing on the Mississippi. Settlers could take Crowleys Ridge a few miles west, near present day Benton, and find a sand ridge running to present day Morley, Blodgett, Vanduser and Sikeston. This sand ridge became known as the Sikeston Ridge. Another choice was to stay on Crowleys Ridge that ran southwest through Arkansas and into Texas. They could also connect to the Ozarks from Crowleys Ridge and travel west or northwest.

This is why Commerce, for the very early

settlers, wasone of the first Gateways To The West. *By Don May*

Lusk Community

Reaching the junction of State Highways N and NN, approximately nine miles north of Charleston, one has arrived in the Lusk Community. Just across the nearby Mississippi River levee, is the approximate location of Price's Landing, important in the early days, and where this writer's ancestors came ashore April 1, 1846, settling in the adjoining community of Texas Bend, sometimes in early records referred to as "New Texas." All of this flatland area was included in "Tywappity Bottom."

Nearby down river is Buffalo Island, where the two large Cargill elevators are located, both

handling enormous amounts of grain from several counties, which is loaded onto barges destined for the Gulf of Mexico and overseas.

Longtime residents whose homes are located near this highway junction on N, are those of the Doug Glastetters, Oliver Kirkpatricks, Glen Colliers, Randy Keene, and a little farther east is the Larry Brazel home, and just off the road is that of Jim Lovett.

At the southwest corner of the junction of N and NN, stood the landmark "Lusk Chapel" store, for many years the community gathering place. The name "Chapel" derived from the small Methodist church located just south of the store. Legend states that it was built in the early days by a Rev. Lusk, as evidenced by a story relating to an incident which occurred as the Rev. Lusk was logging with his yoke of oxen. Research by Betty R. Darnell found that the marriage of Bernard M. Hagan and Margaret A. Holman was performed at the home of the bride's mother at Price's Landing on Aug. 9, 1869 by Rev. Wm. M. Lusk. Services were held sporadically until about 1950. The modern Leslie Collier home now stands here.

South on NN, about a half-mile, is the stately old white two-story home built by Eliphalet Brown, who had accumulated considerable acreage on both sides of the road. The original home was a log house of two rooms. These two rooms are encased in this two-story house. It has been lovingly maintained by members of the Raymond Gage family, who for over 60 years have farmed the land for the Brown descendants. A unique item, a small cannonball, still lies embedded in a small flower planting in the front lawn, of which it was recently learned, through a daughter in Florida, had been placed there by her mother who resided there during WWI.

Next is the home of Don Gage. Still south on this farm, about one-fourth mile, stood the first small schoolhouse. Broken cemetery stones, several with decorative carvings, found in this field is evidence of a long ago graveyard. The names of Lusk and Rice remain distinct. These are preserved at the Gage farm shop.

The John Harness farm is adjacent, and a deed dated May 28, 1898 shows that his widow Annetta Meisenheimer Harness sold two acres at the edge of their farm to the school district for one hundred forty dollars, for a new school. This was just across the road from the old school. Their daughter, Hannah Harness Stricker, taught at the school during WWI. She had attended the Normal School at Cape Girardeau.

The new Lusk school was well-built and was used until about 1956. A substantial outbuilding was renovated, and hot lunches were served for several years prior to its closing. For a few years following, this building was enlivened each Friday evening by the "Country Cousins" Square Dance Club, which drew dancers from many surrounding towns, including regulars from Wickliffe and Mayfield, KY.

A little farther south is the "blue hole," formed after the devastating floods of 1912-1913. Several tales remembered by some, concerning the depth and dire happenings at this pond, were evidently told by parents to their children, to deter them from entering the water while walking by on their way home from school.

This blue hole is on the Harness farm, now owned by the widow of his grandson, John Joseph Stricker, and their children. Mrs. Stricker and also son, Carl Stricker, have homes just past the pond, direct descendants having resided here since the purchase by John Harness in 1887.

Next down the road is the large two-story house built by Colonel Brown. The farm is owned by the Lochhead family who resides in Arizona. Residents for many years have been the Pemberton families, now by Alen Pemberton.

Other longtime farm owner residents, just off the main road are the Roy Birks, Greg Birks, Alfred Martins, Don Martins, Mrs. Paul Harness Stricker, Marion Strickers and the Randy Brazels.

A mile father south on NN, coming into view, is another well-known landmark, the "Indian Mound, one of the tallest in the county. The Lusk Community seemingly ceases near this area. This road also leads directly to Charleston. *By Margaret Rolwing Stricker*

Miner, Missouri

The land in the 1600s to 1800s that was to become the Miner region, varied from low ridges to overflowed lands, swamps and wilderness.

The bottom lands had forest of giant trees such as cypress, oak, hickory, gum, cottonwood and sycamore. Buffalo, deer, turkey, waterfowl and fish were plentiful. This region was east of the Sikeston ridge.

Indians traveled this region trapping, hunting and fishing. The Mississippian Indians, Capahas and Osage camped nearby farming the crops they needed. French traders traveling down the Mississippi River traded with the Indians. Indian mounds were located in the vicinity of Miner with artifacts of pottery, tools and arrowheads.

There was a crossroad located where Highway 62 and the Blodgett Road now intersect. The road that continued south from Blodgett Road the intersection was known as the "Big Opening Road." This road eventually became the AA Road.

In the early 1860s, the Cairo Fulton Railroad ran from Cairo to Fulton, AR and returning to Tennessee linking the east and west. After the war, the railroad was known as the "CAT" line and was eventually transferred to the Iron Mountain Railroad Company. Later it was acquired by the Missouri Pacific Railroad Company.

Beginning in the 20th century, plans were made to turn the swamp bottom lands into habitable land. Legislation resulted in the formation of the "Little River Drainage District." This involved draining the great Whitewater River swamp and ultimately the St. John's Bayou Basin. These projects began in 1914, diverting these waters into the Mississippi River. This undertaking became the nation's largest drainage project and was completed in 1928. It reclaimed and created some of the richest soil in the region, enabling farmers to grow bountiful crops of wheat, corn, soybeans and vegetables.

This is a school picture of grade seven with teacher, Mrs. Veasman. Students are: first row: Michael Lewis, Sybil Kaiser, Orville Krauss, Hester McGill, Billy Inman, Berva Dean Jones, Harvey Bailey, Glenn McGill. Second row is Billy Peoplemyer, Edsel Lindsay, Mattie Johns, Mable Chadd, Patsy Turner, Wilma Harbinson, Esthel Lee Johns, John A. Matthews, Sonny Isaccs. Top row includes Kenneth Rudisill, Dorsey Dord, Jimmy Peoplemyer, Donald Wyman,

In 1997, a watermelon weighing 213 pounds became a world's record.

The railroad and Drainage system contributed much to the development of Miner's growth. The railroad hauled lumber, crops and goods. Early pioneers were lumbermen, farmers and businessmen.

In 1902, Mr. Minner owned and operated a sawmill until most of the timber cutting had ceased. A small village developed and was named in honor of Mr. Minner. "Minner Switch" was a railroad switching area. It was about three miles east of Sikeston. In 1951, when the railroad company was putting up the "Minner Switch" sign, they left out an "n," so it became "Miner Switch" and later Miner, Missouri.

John A. Matthews came to Sikeston in the early 1900s. He was a farmer and business man, so he bought land around the Miner area. His son, Ben O. Matthews, built Miner's Feed Mill around 1940. It was destroyed by fire and was rebuilt in 1949 on the north side of the railroad tracks where the Ramada Inn is now located. Howard McGill became the manager and later the owner of the M & M Feed Mill.

Minner grew slowly in the early years. There was a post office from 1893 – 1895. The first subdivision was Salmon, founded in 1924 with Smoot's subdivision in 1927. James' subdivision was founded in 1932. Clayton's East Acres was recorded in 1941.

The Harold Lewis family moved to Minner Switch in 1936. There were two stores, a church, and a one-room red brick school. Mr. Lewis bought property and operated the Lewis Salvage Company. He and his wife, Anna, along with other families volunteered and guided the development of Miner.

The first store was owned by C. W. Smoot. Roland Malcolm also owned a store. Mr. Woods owned a dairy. An early gas station was SAVEWAY, located on Hwy. 62 with a sign, "Discount Diesel 5 cents."

Saveway Service Station, Highway 62, Miner, MO, circa 1965. M & M Feedmill in background.

In 1927, the Miner Baptist Missionary Church bought property with a one-room wooden building – on the site now known as the old Miner Cemetery on Matthews Lane. The church voted to build a new church near the center of Miner in the latter part of the 1930s. It was located on the northwest side of the intersection of Highway 62 and Route H. In 1976, a larger facility was needed so they built a new church building located on the east side of Route H, one-half mile north of Highway 62.

The original one-room red brick school was in Miner School District No. 50. It was built around 1925. T. E. Hyatt and Construction crew were the builders. It was located on the west side of miner's intersection, north of the railroad tracks. Grades one though four were taught each year, with grades five and seven, and grades six and eight, taught in alternate years.

A new four-room building was erected in 1941. There were grades one through eight with an enrollment of nearly 80 students. Early teachers were Jewell Allen, Madge Davis, Mrs. Reaves and Mrs. Veasman. After the eighth grade, students went to the Sikeston High School. This building was destroyed by fire in 1947.

Miner was incorporated in 1951 with Howard McGill as the first Chairman of the Board of Trustees (1951-1953). Other chairmen serving were: Joe Bacher, L. F. Wheeler, Harold Lewis, Milton Sadler and L. H. Moore. Mrs. Anna Lewis served as city clerk for 25 years.

A 10-cent tax was set by the board to bring in a little money to operate on. Clayton East Acres Subdivision auctioned off all the lots. As the population grew, needs and problems increased. The board established agreements with MO Utilities Company and other public utilities, receiving franchise taxes from them. The Interstate Highway came through in 1955 and population continued to grow slowly.

Miner became a 4th class city in 1982 with a mayor/council form of government. Billy James Sr. was elected as the first mayor from 1982-1994. The following elected mayors were L. F Wheeler, Don Holman and Betty Barnes.

In order to get a loan from the Federal Government, it was required to have 150 potential water uses signed up. This required getting about 90% of the population to sign. It was approved, and the first water system was installed in 1968, then improved in 1988. An additional 500,000 gallon water tower was installed in 1996. The sewer system was installed in 1977. The aerated sewer lagoon system was installed in 1990. A water treatment plant was built in 1998.

The first fire truck, a used Mack Pumper, was bought in 1967 from Joplin, MO Fire Department and a volunteer fire department was established. A second, later model Mack Pumper, was purchased in 1972. The Miner Fire Department now consists of one full-time fireman and a large volunteer force.

Miner's Police Department was organized with a police commissioner. Joe James was appointed the first City Marshall. The police force now has nine full-time policemen.

City offices were expanded from a very small building in 1993 to the present one. Three jail holding cells and a court room area were added in this expansion.

New subdivisions include Country Estates (1979) and Dockins South Acres (2001). Miner has eight motels, an Outlet Shopping Mall and Lambert's Café, "Home of Throwed Rolls." The 2000 Census records Miner's population as 1056.

It is a member of the Bootheel Regional Planning Commission and partners with the Sikeston/Miner Convention and Visitors Bureau in cooperation with the MO Division of Tourism.

Miner is located a the exits of two interstate highways, I-55 and I-57 into US 62, and is midway between St. Louis and Memphis. *Submitted by Charlotte Johnson*

Dunaver School. Front row, let to right: Archie Lee Mathis, Wallace Wicker, Richard Byrd, Nadine Ferrell Shuppert, Aileen Byrd Laseter, Geneva Aldredge, Anna Mae Terry, Norma Davis, Geraldine Davis, Roberta Aldredge, Clara Terry. Second row, left to right: Warren Holt, Jimmy Ferrell, Carmen Davis Cervantes, Benny Terry, Elmer Wicker, Malcolm Holt, Frank Ferrell, J. V. Ferrell Back row, left to right: Elsie New Holt (teacher), Bonnie Inman, Daveen Davis Alexander, Minnie Lee Byrd Boone, Dan Byrd, Harry Holt.

DUNAVER SCHOOL

Dunaver, District #49, Scott County, MO was the rightful name of the school located east of Miner, MO on Hwy. 62. The one room school was situated on the S. W. corner turning south on County Road 541. It was better known as "Slapout."

Submitted by Minnie Lee Boone

Sikeston

Building on the Past, Preparing for the Future

In 1860 John Sikes recorded a plat with the Scott County Recorder. On it Sikes wrote, "I am going to start me a town, and I am going to call it the Town of Sikeston." From that dream grew a town of over 18,000 – one of the largest and most progressive communities in the Bootheel.

Realizing transportation was a key to development, the railroad was extended to Sikeston in 1860, providing transportation and mail service. By 1868, residents of Sikeston had established a tax-based public school. In 1875 the Town of Sikeston, with a population of 250,, was incorporated by the State of Missouri.

During the next 25 years, Sikeston's first newspaper was published, and commercial telegraph and telephone services were started. The early 1900s saw the establishment of passenger rail service between St. Louis and Memphis, development of City water works and sewer system, and the establishment of the Sikeston Ice, Light and Power Company. Sikeston's first electric generating plant was constructed in 1906.

By 1918, Sikeston's population had almost tripled. Local swamps were being drained, trees harvested for lumber, and cotton became "King." The 1920s were a period of prosperity and economic growth. All of this would grind to a halt during the Great Depression, when two of Sikeston's three banks failed.

1940 marked the opening of the Missouri Delta Medial Center. As the nation entered WWII, Parks Air College opened a campus in Sikeston to train Army Air Corps pilots and mechanics.

In 1952 the Sikeston Jaycees' held their first Sikeston JC Bootheel Rodeo – an event that continues today, 50 years later.

Transportation, once again, became a major aspect of Sikeston's development as Highway 55 was upgraded to an interstate. Within the next 20 years, Sikeston adopted the council/manager form of government.

In 1978 the Sikeston Power Plant was constructed. The Sikeston Business, Education and Technology Park was developed in 1996. Recognizing the need for community-based higher education, a partnership between Southeast Missouri State University, Three Rivers Community College and the City of Sikeston was created. From this grew the Sikeston Area Higher Education Center.

In 2002, Sikeston's voters went to the polls to adopt a home rule charter form of government. The Home Rule Charter will go into effect in April 2003.

CITY OF SIKESTON MAYORS – APRIL 1891 TO APRIL 2003

2002-2003	Phil Boyer
2001-2002	Jerry Pullen
2000-2001	Josh Bill
1999-2000	Bill Mitchell
1998-1999	Bill Mitchell
1997-1998	Alan Keenan
1996-1997	Alan Keenan
1995-1996	Terry Bryant
1994-1995	Mike Moll
1993-1994	Chuck Leible
1992-1993	Terry Bryant
1987-1992	Bill Burch
1985-1986	Bob Stearnes
1984-1985	Bill Burch

1983-1984	Kenny Bridger	
1982-1983	Marion Thompson	
	(12/82 – 4/83)	
	Roger Tolliver (4/82 – 12/82)	
1981-1982	Steve Sikes	
1980-1981	Mary Doggett	
1979-1980	Roger Tolliver	
1978-1979	Lewis H. Conley	
1977-1978	Eric Piel	
1975-1977	Donald Fulton	
1971-1975	Frank Ferrell	
1971-1972	Lee Shell	
1970-1971	Taylor Noles	
1969-1970	Arthur B. Ziegenhorn	
1965-1969	Kendall Sikes	
1960-1965	Harry F. Dudley	
1958-1960	C. E. Felker	
1953-1958	Charles H. Butler	
1950-1953	Joe M. Cravens	
1946-1950	Marvin L. Carroll	
1938-1946	Dr. G. W. Presnell	
1936-1938	N. E. Fuchs	
1934-1936	Dr. G. W. Presnell	
1926-1934	N. E. Fuchs	
1922-1926	C. E. Felker	
1919-1922	C. C. White	
1916-1919	Dr. E. J. Malone	
1914-1916	William S. Smith	
1910-1914	Dr. E. J. Malone	
1908-1910	P. M. Malcolm	
1906-1908	Dr. E. J. Malone	
1902-1906	John L. Tanner	
1898-1902	Calvin Greer	
1896-1898	James H. Shelby	
1985-1896	Calvin Greer	
1894-1895	Elam B. Mills	
1891-1894	C. H. Harris	

CITY OF SIKESTON COUNCILMEN –
1958 TO 2003

2002-2003
  Phil Boyer
  Mike Marshall
  Jerry Pullen
  Michael Harris
  Sue Rogers
2001-2002
  Jerry Pullen
  Phil Boyer
  Bill Mitchell
  Mike Marshall
  Michael Harris
2000-2001
  Josh Bill
  Jerry Pullen
  Bill Mitchell
  Phil Boyer
  Mike Marshall
1999-2000
  Bill Mitchell
  Josh Bill
  Alan Keenan
  Jerry Pullen
  Phil Boyer
1998-1999
  Bill Mitchell
  Josh Bill
  Alan Keenan
  Terry Bryant
  Jerry Pullen
1997-1998

Alan Keenan
Bill Mitchell
Mike Moll
Terry Bryant
Josh Bill
1996-1997
  Alan Keenan
  Mike Moll
  Terry Bryant
  Josh Bill
  Bill Mitchell
1995-1996
  Terry Bryant
  Alan Keenan
  Chuck Lieble
  Mike Moll
  Josh Bill
1994-1995
  Mike Moll
  Alan Keenan
  Terry Bryant
  Chuck Leible
  Josh Bill
1993-1994
  Chuck Leible
  Mike Moll
  Terry Bryant
  Josh Bill
  Marion Thompson (4/1992-3/1993)
  Alan Keenan (3/1993-4/1994)
1992-1993
  Mike Moll
  Josh Bill
  Marion Thompson
  Terry Bryant
  Chuck Leible
1991-1992
  Bill Burch
  Terry Bryant
  Robert Stearnes
  Marion Thompson
  Chuck Leible
1990-1991
  Bill Burch
  Robert Stearnes
  Terry Bryant
  Marion Thompson
  Chuck Leible
1989-1990
  Bill Burch
  Robert Stearnes
  Ira Merideth
  John Houchin
  Marion Thompson
1988-1989
  Bill Burch
  Robert Stearnes
  Ira Merideth
  John Houchin
  Marion Thompson
1987-1988
  Bill Burch
  Robert Stearnes
  Ira Merideth
  John Houchin
  Marion Thompson
1986-1987
  Bill Burch
  Robert Stearnes
  Marion Thompson
  Jean Collins
  Allen Blanton

1985-1986
  Bill Burch
  Robert Stearnes
  Marion Thompson
  Jean Collins
  Allen Blanton
1984-1985
  Kenny Bridger
  Bill Burch
  Robert Stearnes
  Marion Thompson
  Lewis Conley
1983-1984
  Kenny Bridger
  Bill Burch
  Robert Stearnes
  Marion Thompson
  Lewis Conley
1982-1983
  Kenny Bridger
  Bill Burch
  Robert Stearnes
  Marion Thompson
  Lewis Conley
1981-1982
  Steve Sikes
  Mary Doggett
  Lewis Conley
  Roger Tolliver
  Kenny Bridger
1980-1981
  Lewis Conley
  Mary Doggett
  Eric Piel
  Steve Sikes
  Roger Tolliver
1979-1980
  Lewis Conley
  Mary Doggett
  Eric Piel
  Steve Sikes
  Roger Tolliver
1978-1979
  Lewis Conley
  Mary Doggett
  Eric Piel
  Steve Sikes
  Roger Tolliver
1977-1978
  Roger Tolliver
  Mary Doggett
  Lewis Conley
  Steve Sikes
  Eric Piel
1976-1977
  Don Fulton
  Arthur Ziegenhorn
  John Houchin
  Bill Ryan
  Eric Piel
1975-1976
  Frank Ferrell
  Bill Ryan
  Arthur Ziegenhorn
  Don Fulton
  John Houchin
1974-1975
  Chuck Grant
  Frank Ferrell
  Arthur Ziegenhorn
  Bill Ryan
  Don Fulton

1973-1974
    Chuck Grant
    Frank Ferrell
    Arthur Ziegenhorn
    Bill Ryan
    Don Fulton
1972-1973
    Chuck Grant
    Frank Ferrell
    Arthur Ziegenhorn
    Bill Ryan
    Don Fulton
1971-1972
    Lee Shell
    Arthur Ziegenhorn
    Chuck Grant
    Don Fulton
    Kenny Bridger
1970-1971
    Taylor Noles
    Less Shell
    Arthur Ziegenhorn
    Sam Harbin
    Chuck Grant
1969-1970
    Kendall Sikes
    Taylor Noles
    Sam Harbin
    Chuck Grant
    Lee Shell
1968-1969
    Kendall Sikes
    Taylor Noles
    Lee Shell
    Arthur Ziegenhorn

Paul Jobe
1967-1968
    Harry E. Dudley
    Lee Shell
    Arthur Ziegenhorn
    Kendall Sikes
    Taylor Noles
1966-1967
    Harry E. Dudley
    Less Shell
    Arthur Ziegenhorn
    Kendall Sikes
    Taylor Noles
1965-1966
    Kendall Sikes
    Harry E. Dudley
    Taylor Noles
    Arthur Ziegenhorn
    Dr. W. C. Critchlow
1964-1965
    Harry E. Dudley
    Taylor Noles
    Dr. W. C. Critchlow
    Kendall Sikes
    Arthur Ziegenhorn
1963-1964
    Harry E. Dudley
    Kendall Sikes
    Terry Noles
    Dr. W. C. Critchlow
    Don Pasaka
1962-1963
    Harry E. Dudley
    Kendall Sikes
    Terry Noles

Dr. W. C. Critchlow
Don Pasaka
1961-1962
    Harry E. Dudley
    Kendall Sikes
    Terry Noles
    Dr. W. C. Critchlow
    Don Pasaka
1960-1961
    Thomas F. Rafferty
    A. P. Veasman
    Jim Denbow
    Theon Grojean
    Taylor Noles
    Ira Keller
    Vodrel Kirby
    Don Pasaka
1959-1960
    Thomas F. Rafferty
    A. P. Veasman
    Theon Grojean
    Ira Keller
    Taylor Noles
    Vodrel Kirby
    Cecil Boyer
    Shad Old
1958-1959
    Thomas F. Rafferty
    A. P. Veasman
    Fred Smith
    Ira Keller
    Charles Barnett
    Taylor Noles
    Shad Old
    Harry Hambrick

Men's Bible Class, Methodist Church, Sikeston, MO, March 18, 1928. (Photo courtesy of the family of Alfred Halter)

40

Historic Sikeston in Photographs

Left: Unidentified man with set of mules pulling him in a wagon on a dirt road in the early years of Sikeston.

Left: Sikeston Hotel. (Photo courtesty of John Wilson)
Below Left: The Bank of Sikeston. (Photo courtesty of John Wilson)
Below Right: Farmer's Supply Company, Sikeston. (Photo courtesty of John Wilson)

Left: Saturday in Sikeston, MO.

Right: A Common scene in Sikeston, MO.

Left: East Front Street, Sikeston.

Left: Sikeston Sophomore class of 1908. (Photo courtesy of Mildred F. Sneed)

Below: The Drummer's Convention in Sikeston, Missouri, 1910.

Del Ray Hotel, corner of Kingshighway and Center, Sikeston. (Photo courtesy of Judy Bowman)

Malone Park in Sikeston, 1912.

Right: Sikeston, Missouri, 1915.

Right: New Madrid Avenue, looking North, Sikeston, MO.

Right: Holley Matthews Mfg. Col, Sikeston, MO. (Photo courtesy of Harlan Smothers)

Left: Beautiful residential section, Sikeston, MO.

Left: Gladis Avenue, looking East, Sikeston.

Left: Employees of the Sikeston Mercantile Co., Sikeston, Missouri.

More About Scott County

By Margaret Cline Harmon

Missourian Nathaniel W. Watkins

A SOLDER, STATESMAN AND CITIZEN

General Watkins Conservation Area is in Scott County, 15 miles south of Cape Girardeau off Highway 61. The Missouri Conservation Department purchased the 1,108 acres between 1978 and 1997. They named the area for Missouri's statesman and Civil War general, Nathaniel Watkins, who lived here in grand style and is buried in a family cemetery inside the Conservation Area. General Watkins' original Beechland Estate consisted of 1,208.11 acres in the proximity of the Conservation area.

Before visiting the Conservation Area and family cemetery, it will help your experience to understand a little about the man Nathaniel Wilson Watkins. He was the son of Capt. Henry "Hal" Watkins, grandson of James R. Watkins, great grandson of James Randolph Watkins, and great-great grandson of Richard Jerome Watkins. Nathaniel was born January 28, 1796 in Woodford County, Kentucky.

To get a more complete picture of General Watkins, here are some facts about his mother. Elizabeth Hudson first married John Clay in 1765 when she was 15 years old. They were the parents of Henry Clay, the statesman. After the death of John Clay in 1783 she married Capt. Henry Watkins in 1784. This made N. W. Watkins and Henry Clay half-brothers by their mother. Henry Clay, the Senator from Kentucky, is well known in American history. General Nathaniel W. Watkins, Sr. may not be as well known nationally as his half-brother, but was well known in Missouri while he lived. His mother was a woman of great determination and she passed that passion on to at least two of her sons.

Elizabeth nurtured Henry and Nathaniel during their early years and obviously affected her sons' development into leaders. Her grandson, Thomas Bodley Watkins, described her demeanor in his letter of 19 September 1894, according to *Henry Watkins of Henrico County His Descendants and Their Allied Families* compiled by Jane McMurtry Allen. He wrote:

"I can only tell you a part of what my mother, Caroline Milton Watkins, wife of Elizabeth's son John, has many times told me. She was very intimate with my grandmother (Elizabeth Hudson Watkins). From the best information I have, she was rather below the medium in stature and of well-rounded form, dark hair and eyes, and a ruddy complexion. She was a woman of great determination, industrious, and economical."

Jane McMurtry Allen also suggests in her book *Henry Watkins of Henrico County His Descendants and Their Allied Families* that Elizabeth lived with each of her husbands on her father's plantation. It states that there was some litigation regarding George Hudson's plantation after he and his wife's deaths, and she writes the following:

"The homestead Hudson plantation was to be disposed of by terms of the will of George Hudson after the death of his widow. But before such events, Reverend John Clay purchased the undivided half interest of the other heirs, John Watkins and his wife (and Elizabeth's sister) Polly Hudson Watkins. The problem is, he died before the same was fully paid. A friendly suit was brought to legally settle the questions whether this plantation should be sold or disposed of under the provisions of the will of George Hudson or under the contract of sale to Reverend John Clay. The Court decided in favor of the latter, and, by its decree, the plantation was finally sold and purchased by Henry Watkins, who had then married the widow of John Clay (Elizabeth Hudson Clay)."

A letter written by Henry Clay, dated "Ashland, 10th August, 1844" states that he was born on the Hudson Plantation in a house built for his mother. Clay goes on to write, "in 1792 Henry and Elizabeth (Hudson) Watkins moved to Versailles, Kentucky, and kept an inn in Woodford County on the west side of Main Street. The two-story building, built by Henry Watkins, was called Watkins Tavern. The Watkins's quit their tavern between 1815 and 1820 and settled on a farm they owned three miles south of Versailles on the turnpike leading to Mortonsville. Nathaniel, born in 1796, was likely born in the tavern." (I obtained a copy of the letter from the Hudson Family Association.)

Nathaniel Watkins grew up in Kentucky and studied law at Transylvania College. On completion of his studies in 1819, he moved to Jackson, Missouri to practice law. The Cape Girardeau Circuit Court Roll Book of Attorneys and Counselors dated December 9, 1828, shows N. W. Watkins signed on the eleventh line of page one.

He began purchasing property as early as 1823 in Cape Girardeau County. In 1837 he began purchasing land in Scott County. He also owned property in Mississippi County, Dunklin County and New Madrid County, Missouri. It was in New Madrid County that he met his wife, Eliza B. Watson. They were married in New Madrid on May 05, 1828. Eliza was the daughter of Robert G."Goah" and Jane Myers Watson. Her father was a leading merchant in New Madrid for fifty years. He also represented New Madrid County in the Constitutional Convention of 1820, and he was a Judge of the County Court in 1821-1822, 1824-1834 and 1842-1850.

The Jackson newspaper announced their 1828 marriage. Nathaniel W. and Eliza Watson Watkins moved to Jackson after their marriage. They enjoyed a family of seven children born to them in Jackson.

JOHN C. WATKINS, born August 4, 1833, in Cape Girardeau Co., MO; died October 01, 1897, Scott County, Missouri. He married NANCY C. COOPER, December 30, 1860, Cape Girardeau Co., MO. In the 1875 Missouri Business Directory he was listed as a lawyer in Morley, Missouri.

WILLIAM B. WATKINS, born May 28,

General Nathaniel W. Watkins

1839, in Cape Girardeau Co., MO; died July 23, 1926, Crowder, Scott County, Missouri. He married Sarah "Sallie" Madison Grisham. They had two sons and three daughters.

WASHINGTON LEWIS WATKINS, born Abt. 1840, in Cape Girardeau Co., MO. He remained with his parents and never married. He died around 1879, because he was named Administrator of the will but did not live long enough to settle the estate. Court records show that William Ballintine finalized the estate of N. W. Watkins in November 1881.

RICHARD "DICK" JAMES WATKINS, born June 19, 1843, in Cape Girardeau, MO; died November 04, 1913, Morley Hills, Scott, Missouri. He married Eliza J. Harrison around 1867 in Scott County. They had two sons and two daughters.

NATHANIEL "NAT" W. WATKINS, born January 05, 1850, in Cape Girardeau Co., MO; died November 10, 1879, Scott County, Missouri. The 1860 Federal Census of Cape Girardeau County, Missouri shows Nat W. Watkins as 12 years of age (date of birth 1848) but his headstone shows 1850. My research does not show that he ever married.

ELIZA A. WATKINS, born 1850, in Cape Girardeau Co., MO; she married a Mr. Williams. No additional information is known on Eliza and my interviews revealed no knowledge of her. She and her family may have remained in Cape.

AMANDA J. WATKINS, born 1854, Cape Girardeau County, Missouri; died 1916 in Scott County, Missouri. She married George R. Wilson Abt. 1875 in Scott County, Missouri. They had two daughters who both died before the age of five, and one son, Walter F. Wilson who lived to adulthood.

Nathaniel and Eliza named their youngest daughter after Eliza's sister, Amanda Jane, who married William Washington Hunter of New

Madrid. Their home is now a Missouri Historical Site in New Madrid known as the Hunter-Dawson Home. We are sure the two families spent time visiting each other as Jackson and New Madrid were both important cultural towns.

The Watkins Cemetery had to be fenced, because of the isolated area it was necessary to protect the monuments. One should feel free to spend some reflective time and look at the headstones. You will note that over the years, moss has formed on the General's marble monument but you should be able to read all four sides as follows:

"In Memory of Nath'l W. Watkins, born Jan. 28, 1796, Died Mar. 10, 1876 at 80 yrs. 1 Mo. 22 Days. Soldier of the War of 1812, Member of the Mo. State Senate, Speaker of the House, Member State Convention of 1875, A lawyer of 60 years active practice, A solder, statesman, citizen - Sans Peur et sans Reproche"

His Beechland home was quite beautiful with a slate roof, five large windows across the front of the second floor and four large windows across the main floor. After you climbed the impressive stairs, you entered through a ten-foot cypress raised panel front door, with side-lights on each side of the door and a fan light above the door. This provided light for the impressive twenty-four foot tall foyer. The spiral staircase was five feet wide to allow for the ladies large skirts when they entertained. The house had a formal parlor, with a piano, a large formal dining room, butler's pantry, library and study on the first floor. There were six bedrooms and a center hall with setting area on the second floor. The kitchen would have been to the rear of the main house.

The house had a grand circular pathway leading up to the front of the house entrance. In the spring it was bordered by yellow daffodils and centered by a beautiful fountain. It was described in Edison Shrum's "History of Scott County" as a large two story structure, surrounded by grounds featuring a handsome flower garden and large magnolia trees. He obtained this information from unnamed and undated newspaper articles. I was in the Conservation Area where the house once sat in the spring of 2001 with Gene Diebold of Scott City and the daffodils and old varieties of roses are still in the area of the house. The house sat several hundred yards in front of the Watkins Family Cemetery.

The house was built around 1837 or 1838, only a few miles from the Missouri River and south of Benton, and it was used as a retreat from Jackson until the Union troops burned down the General's house, Moss House, in Jackson. However, they did entertain here from the day it was completed. As a legislator and respected attorney many important guests enjoyed parties and being entertained here. Senator Thomas Hart Benton was related by marriage to Henry Clay and I am researching newspapers at this time to locate articles where they would have been guests here from time to time. Sterling Price was a friend of N. W. Watkins and conducted state business together in Jefferson City. He was also a friend of Louis Houck.

We know from census and tax records that the Watkins' had four slaves at their Jackson property, Moss House, and 42 slaves in Scott County. Although none of us today would condone or tolerate slavery, for the period the

General Watkins' Scott County home, Beechland.

Watkins' lived in they were good to their slaves. At a 1939 ceremony in the Scott County Court house honoring Gen. Watkins, a former slave, Lomax, was there and asked to speak. He recalled in a voice made soft by his years of being born to slave parents owned by General Watkins, "The owner and his wife were both very kind. They were very religious. Once they acquired a slave they never sold him." Lomax was a slave for the Watkins for 16 years. This newspaper article highlights the Scott County Court House ceremony.

Nathaniel W. Watkins was a successful lawyer and he held many elective offices, including the Missouri House of Representatives for three terms in 1834, 1846 and 1850. He was proud of being chosen Speaker of the Missouri House in 1850. He went on to be elected to the Missouri State Senate in 1856 and as he neared the end of his life, in 1875 he served as Vice President of the Missouri Constitutional Convention.

He was 65 years old when Missouri voted to support the Confederate Southern states in the Civil War. Missouri Gov. Jackson appointed him Brigadier-General in the Missouri State Guards in 1861. He engaged in raising troops for Missouri's Confederate First District.

Late in 1861, the Union Troops caused great damage to General Watkins' property at Jackson during the Civil War. He sent a communication of protest to President Abraham Lincoln about the destruction of his property. Below is

President Lincoln's reply. It instructs the Union officers at St. Louis to restore, as much as possible, the property damaged and seized.

Since we know that General Watkins did not return to live at Jackson, Missouri, this may be a positive interpretation of what President Lincoln actually wrote about restoring the General's property.

The actual letter was written from the Executive Mansion.

Washington, December 16, 1862

To Major-General Curtis, Saint Louis, Mo.:

N. W. Watkins, of Jackson, Mo. (who is half-brother to Henry Clay), writes me that a colonel of ours has driven him from his home at Jackson. Will you please look into the case and restore the old man to his home, if the public interest will admit?

A. Lincoln

Listed below are just two of the Newspaper Articles referencing Nathaniel W. Watkins.
Western Eagle, Cape Girardeau
Vol. II, Page 1, Col. 2
Friday, April 14, 1848
Resolved, that we have the highest confidence in the ability and integrity of Gen. Nathaniel W. Watkins of Cape Girardeau County and recommend him to the Convention as our candidate for Governor, and James S. Rawlins for Lieutenant Governor.

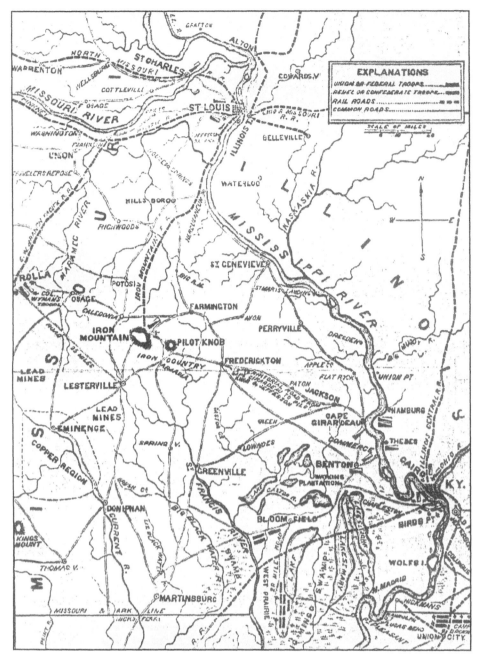

From the New York Harold *War Maps and Diagrams. The Seat of War in the West. Map of the scene of Operations in Southeastern Missouri, Illinois and Tennessee, with the positions of the Rebel Troops and Portions of the Federal Forces, and the defences at Cairo and Bird's Point. Notice the reference to "Watkin's Plantation" South of Benton, Missouri.*

Western Eagle, Cape Girardeau
Vol. II, Page 1, Col. 5
May 19, 1848

On motion of Judge C. A. Davis, of Cape Girardeau, a committee of five, consisting of the following persons to wit: Richard Philip of New Madrid, Charles A. Davis and Nathaniel W. Watkins of Cape Girardeau, and J. Sidney Smith and John F. Darby of St. Louis...

Louis Houck wrote in his Volume III, Pages 32 and 33 of *History of Missouri*, the following quote:

It was my privilege to know two distinguished legal gentlemen of the territorial days of Missouri, General Nathaniel W. Watkins and Greer W. Davis, who survived all their contemporaries, standing alone as it was in the new world, almost amid a new race, after the tempest of the Civil War. When I first met them, they were both still

in active practice, Greer W. Davis giving his attention to legal business in his county, but General Watkins full of energy, aggressive and apparently yet possessed of the unquenchable fire of youth, attended the circuit courts of some of the lower southeastern counties for several years afterward. In 1875 he was elected a member of the constitutional convention, and elected its Vice-President, a fit tribute to his long and useful life. He died in the following year, 1876, on his estate "Beechland" in Scott County. Greer W. Davis, the last of the territorial lawyers, died at Jackson, February 25, 1878, active and industrious almost until his last day. For fifty-four years before his death he was a consistent member of the Methodist church at Jackson.

In summary, N. W. Watkins resigned from his Confederate Commission in 1862. He and his family moved to his plantation and mansion

in Scott County after their Moss House in Cape Girardeau County, Missouri was burned. I was able to obtain a drawing of the mansion from the General's great-grandson, Nat C. Watkins of Farmington (August 1998) and it was a beautiful home. An impressive site for Southeast Missourians in those times, I am sure.

Regrettably, the personal correspondence, private papers and inventory were destroyed by the fire that consumed the home in 1880; however, because he was an elected official and highly successful lawyer we find written records in the state archives and court house minutes, legal filings and briefs throughout southeast Missouri. His life was also recorded in newspapers. One on the articles tells that, at the time of his death, he was the oldest practicing attorney in the United States

I feel fortunate to have this opportunity to help preserve Missouri's pioneer history. My purpose in writing this article is to promote Scott County's pioneer heritage and help people connect with the past visually and spiritually. Some visitors, after walking through the Watkins Conservation Area, perceive and understand that history and genealogy are inseparable, just as nature is renewing and continuing. Many people return often and I hope you will too.

Bibliography:

Henry Watkins of Henrico County His Descendants and Their Allied Families compiled by Jane McMurtry Allen

Encyclopedia of the History of Missouri (Kent Library)

War of the Rebellion Records, Series I, Vol. III, Washington, 1893 (several pages)

Goodspeed's *History of Southeast Missouri*

Missouri Day by Day, by Floyd C. Shoemaker, Vol. I, page 76

History of Scott County, Missouri by Edison Shrum

Scott County Democrat, Sikeston, MO, November 9, 1939

Undated and unidentified newspaper clipping (abt. 1931) from Dorris Minner

Fayette newspaper, June 20, 1828, Column 4 - Wedding Announcement

Various documentation from The State Historical Society of Missouri, Columbia, MO.

Hudson Family Association, Bulletin 13, p. 24 - supplied by Conrad Hudson, May 1998.

1860 US Census, Cape Girardeau County, MO., Jackson Township, Family #1239

1870 US Census, Scott County, MO, Moreland Township, Family #285

Probate records, Box 102, at Scott County Court House, Benton, Missouri

Cape Girardeau County Court Records, Jackson, MO

Watkins Cemetery viewed and transcribed headstones. Located between Morley and Benton, MO on west side of Hwy. 61, and 15 miles south of Cape Girardeau, Missouri.

Southeast Missourian, Cape Girardeau, MO, November 18, 1972, "Ginning Time."

Interviews:

Dorris Maurine Minner, July 3, 1998. She provided me with copies of various Watkins related newspaper clippings and obituaries. Her mother was Eula Emily Page, daughter of Effie Margaret Watkins, who was the daughter of William B. Watkins, son of N. W. Watkins.

Nat C. Watkins in his home at Farmington, MO on August 22, 1998. Photographed a large portrait of Nathaniel W. Watkins, a drawing of Beechwood Plantation home, and a black ebony walking cane. The cane was probably presented to N. W. Watkins on his appointment of Vice President to the Constitutional Convention of Missouri in 1875.

Telephone conversation with Louis Watkins, 3rd great grandson of N. W. Watkins in April 1999 and his sister, Margaret Watkins Ford, in June of 2000.

St. Mark's Masonic Lodge Chartered 100 Years Ago

Wilson Brown died Aug. 27, 1855, in a brick house which he had built in Cape Girardeau. He was serving as lieutenant-governor of Missouri. Born 1804, educated as a physician, but gave much time to public service. His wife was a cousin of Mrs. Louis Houck. He rests in the little grave yard of the Giboney family, south of Girardeau, just over the line in Scott County, where stands the only monument erected by an act of the Missouri legislature to honor a state official in early years. The sinking of the ground under the base has given the marble shaft a slant. It has been suggested that the remains be removed to Cape Girardeau. He was a charter member of the Masonic Lodge. Oct. 14, 1947, *The Southeast Missourian*, page 3.

This headstone has been cleaned and moved to the Scott City Park since this article was written. It stands proudly for everyone visiting the park to appreciate.

The Civil War in the Area of Scott County, Missouri

August 7, 1861

"Upon arrival at (Archibald) Price's Landing, which is located on the Mississippi about 25 miles from Cape Girardeau, Major John McDonald march through cornfields, through deep, dense woods and arrived at the Landing about 2:00 in the morning. He promptly surrounded the premises, and at daylight he entered the house. Price had not returned from his camp, which was located about 14 miles south of his residence. A force of about 1,100 Confederates is reported as being stationed at the camp. McDonald then took as prisoner Price's son, William Price, who is said to hold a captaincy under his father, and his son-in-law. Also found in the warehouse at the Landing was a quantity of stores marked, "General Price, Charleston, Missouri." The loot consisted of 20 barrels containing, in the center, firkins of butter on top of which were potatoes and oats. After setting the torch to the bounty, Major McDonald proceeded on to commerce. He halted at the house of one of Price's officers, but at his home he was told the officer was in camp. Upon arriving at Commerce, he apprehended two notorious rascals known as "the Rebel Post Office." From there he proceeded to Benton, about eight miles west of Commerce. There, supposedly encamped, was Colonel Jeff Thompson with his large Confederate M.S.G. (Missouri State Guard) command. At the approach of the Major's forces, Thompson moved out and up the river to Gen-

eral Pillow's camp, about 48 miles from Benton. Major McDonald, not quite finished, was detailed to Hamburg, about five miles northwest of Benton. There he found the town deserted of male inhabitants. In his report of the affairs of the past few days, Major McDonald makes official complain against Captain T. Q. Hilderbrant for permitting his men to loot and break into a locked house and stray beyond the sentinel lines without permission."[1]

August 30, 1861

"General Jeff Thompson received word today that 4,000 men have landed at Commerce, marching from Cape Girardeau with 150 wagons. A large force under General Prentiss (Union) left Ironton today with the sole purpose of capturing General Hardee. General Thompson also received reports of at least 1,000 Yankees at Dallas, and he reports that he has only 1,200 men at Lakeville and no ammunition."[2]

September 26, 1861

"Belmont, Hunter's farm and Lucas' Bend were the sites of skirmishes. General U. S. Grant took several prisoners in retaliation for those taken for their loyalty throughout the neighborhood."[3]

September 27, 1861

"There was a skirmish near Norfolk and fighting at Beckwith's farm about five miles below Norfolk. The Federals rode into an ambush. Upon the first firing, the Federals under Captain McAdams succeeded in a full rout of the rebels. Although the Confederate steamer *Jeff Davis* is lying at the bank of the river, being anchored only about two miles downstream, it did not molest the raiders. The Federals are scouting in the vicinity of Hunter's farm near the same area."[4]

October 2, 1861

"Expedition from Bird's Point to Charleston. One division of Artillery and 1150 cavalry, under Colonel R. J. Ogelsby moved in force upon Charleston to intercept Confederate Colonel Jeff Thompson. Belmont was evacuated. The "Swamp Fox" slipped by again, supposedly this time toward New Madrid. Thompson really has no choice, he has very little ammunition, so a running feint here and there is necessary, should the opposition find out this crucial fact."[5]

October 7, 1861

"Reconnaissance to Lucus' Bend. (US) Gen. U.S. Grant complains that his men are not armed well enough. He has deployed 1200 men, all armed to Charleston and, MO. Jeff Thompson and Lowe (CSA) are no doubt occupying positions at Sikeston and Benton. Naval commander (US) H. Walke, fired several shots into Camp Belmont, and the rebels immediately answered in kind. Commander Walke was successful in bringing away as a prize, two flat-boats."[6]

December 13, 1861

"Skirmishing at Charleston, Missouri."

December 29, 1861

"Brigadier General Jeff Thompson and his main body was readying for descent upon Commerce to join others of his force who were operating there. Also today there was an unsuccessful attempt to take the Steamer *City of Alton*. All the men of the town of Commerce were made prisoners and taken into the forest. The Confederates hid behind the long rows of woodpiles on the docks awaiting the

Wilson Brown's St. Mark's Masonic Lodge grave. (Photo courtesy of Ramona Glastetter)

arrival of the *City of Alton* with her precious stores and mails. The steamer usually put into the dock at Commerce and took on fuel. To prevent any warning, the women and children were gathered into little groups and were forbidden to give any warning of the ambush upon the threat of death. As the *City of Alton* swung into the landing, the Confederates smiled, clutching their weapons and held their breath for the signal. Suddenly Mrs. Sarah L. Everson sprang out of the midst of the other women and ran to the edge of the river screaming at the top of her voice and waving her arms. There was a clanging of bells. The steamboat's paddlewheel reversed with all power to the engines. The Confederates rose to their feet and sent a volley after the escaping prize, and with many curses, departed. After the war Congress voted to pay Mrs. Everson $15,000 in recognition of her bravery."[7]

January 7, 1862

"From Bird's Point Colonel Nicholas Perczel placed his command on the cars and upon arrival, joined the cavalry and proceeded to the house of one Swank, where supposedly there was a body of about 1,000 Tennessee cavalry encamped. The night being cloudy and rainy the guide lost his way several times. Finally by morning the command had passed the supposed place of encampment in the foggy darkness. From the faint sound of a bugle abut 4:00 in the morning, they knew they were close to camp. Finally locating a house, directions were obtained. About 5:00 in the morning they finally reached the back track into Charleston."[8]

January 8, 1862

"There was skirmishing again at Charleston,

and Colonel Poindexter with 1,000 Confederates took up a strong position on Roan's Tanyard on Silver Creek located seven miles south of Huntsville in Randolph County. Here they were attacked by about 500 men under Confederate Majors Torrence and Hubbard. After about a half-hour of fierce fighting, the troops under Poindexter were routed. The victors promptly set about burning the camp. Federal losses were four killed. Confederates left seven dead on the field and carried many off. A federal encampment is not on the LaMine near Otterville."[9]

[1] Bartell, Carolyn M. 1992. *The Civil War In Missouri Day By Day 1861-1865*, Two Trails Publishing, Independence, MO

[2] Ibid.
[3] Ibid.
[4] Ibid.
[5] Ibid.
[6] Ibid.
[7] Ibid.
[8] Ibid.
[9] Ibid.

The Last Days of Major James Parrott

8th Missouri Cavalry Regiment, C.S.A.

When the 8th Missouri Cavalry Regiment was organized in Southeast Missouri for service to the Confederacy in the fall of 1862, James Parrott, a prominent citizen of Scott County, was elected major. He served for the balance of the war with the regiment, seeing hard fighting during two of Major General John S. Marmaduke's raids into Missouri and Helena, Arkansas, the defense of Little Rock, resisting the advance of a Union army into southern Arkansas during the Camden Expedition, and through all the battles and skirmishes of General Sterling Price's last raid into Missouri in the fall of 1864. At Mine Creek, Kansas on October 25, 1864, the Confederate army was routed in a large cavalry fight. Major Parrott was severely wounded. Taken prisoner in northern Arkansas, he was imprisoned at Fort Smith and then transferred to the military prison at Little Rock. While a prisoner there he contracted small pox, and the effects of the dreaded disease finally cost him his life. The following letters from Parrott, and others, to his wife, provide a poignant account of his last days. The letters are taken from the booklet *At Home in Confederate Arkansas: Letters to and from Pulaski Countians, 1861-1865*, edited by Ted R. Worley in 1955.

Our thanks for some final letters received from James E. McGhee, Jefferson City, Missouri - 1999

Military Prison, Little Rock, Ark.
March 23, 1865
Mrs. M. Maria Parrott
Commerce, Mo.
My ever dear and devoted wife.

Your very kind letter of the 23rd ult. was received upon the 21st inst. It found me slightly indisposed from a very mild attack of Very Alloid (yellow fever). I had some acking of head and Bones for 3 days, with

Document recording the volunteer enlistment of James Muller in the Union Army for one year on September 1, 1864. (Document courtesy of John Maurath)

sore throat also, which are the certain forerunners of small pocks. Where I have been in prison for something over 3 months, some pretty severe cases, but generally rather mild with but five deaths. Be it said to the credit of Surgeon Mills that he understands the disease thoroughly, is kind and attentive to his duty, and a Gentleman by birth and education. I think I will not be marked at all, and am very happy to have it, for it is a loathsome disease, have yourself and children vaccinated if it will save you of danger of more than very alloid.

I am very glad you did not go to Fort Smith, at the time you wished. But could you have gotten there a little earlier I would have been more than happy to have embraced my Dear Love once more in my nice little parlor at Fayetteville. What authority was it prevented your going. Do not, oh my sweet wife, be so disponding. Your dear husband will see you again to live with, love and bless you, and the dear little ones too. Oh, how are they and you, are you all well, I hope Joe's health has improved. God knows you are ever present in my mind, as a rule and guide to my conduct. I know he will again some day smile upon us in the plentitude of his mercies. Do you ever hear

from dear little Bertay in Tenn. with your Ma. How much pleasure it would afford me to meet you there again in the summer, under your Ma's roof. I am very sorry to learn of the severe illness of Bro. Beverly. Hope he has recovered. Tell him I am the same as formerly.

I am informed that the point of exchange for Trans Mississippi troops is the mouth of Red River. My Dear Wife, I wish you to get permission from the proper authorities, for yourself and children to go there, where if I do not meet you, you can get into our lines, leaving a letter or something, so that I can find you. I will go by Memphis, TN. Perhaps you had better go there. If you need money make out a pay Act. in my name, for any amount you need. My last payment was to Dec 30th 1863, all since then is due. That was paid by J. H. Hunter, A.Q.M., leaving due me the last of this month $2,430.00. Gen. Smith will no doubt see to your comfort. Be not uneasy upon that score if you get there. Make yourself and necessities known to the authorities and they will be attended to. If you get to the Regt. you can get what you want. If you want Cage, and he is in reach, send for him. He will make you a decent support. I will not be fit for service soon & wish you to be with me, as I anticipate an early exchange. Please come as soon as you can. My love to all.

Your loving husband until Death
James Parrott, Maj. CSA

Military Prison Little Rock Ark
March 30th,1865
Mrs. M. Maria Parrott
Commerce Scott Co. Mo.
My Dear Love

It is with great pleasure that I can communicate to you, of my recovery from an attack of Vari aloid (yellow fever), that most loathsome of diseases I wrote to you about two weeks since.

Major People and I drew lots a few days since for which should be exchanged for a Federal Major. He beat me and will go out in a few days, or as soon as he recovers, he like myself being sick at the time. My Dear wife, have yourself and children vaccinated, and go south as soon as you hear of my exchange, or before. If you wish, go to the mouth of Red River. Take the children. I want to school them, my last letter contained full instruction. How is your health, are you all well. Farewell my dear love for a while.

James Parrott, Maj. CSA

Cape Girardeau Mo [Undated]
Mrs. Parrott

Madam I have the honor to report I left your husband on the 10th inst. at Little Rock. He is amnestied and will soon be in the Bosom of his Family. He was ill when I left. He is out of prison and I saw him safe at a friend's house where he has all comforts of life and even the Luxuries. I did not know I was going to stop here when I left him or I would have brought you a letter from him For I _____ and admire him and am ready to do you Honor and Service in my humble way.

He may be home by the 10th of June he informed me; he is fast convalescing thoug very weak, in good spirits and surrounded by every comfort. I have been his companion in Prison for four months during which time we have suffered much from disease. He has had the small-pox. He is thoroughly well of them; they left no marks on him.

My kindest wishes attend you Madam your husband's Friend
J. S. Hamilton

Little Rock, Ark.
May 12, 1865
Mrs. Parrott
Dear Madam your husband is sick at my house and not able to write, and he requested me to write to you. He has taken the oath with about fifty other prisoners, and came here not able to go home, but is very anxious to

go to you. He has been sick so long he is very weak. We are trying to do all we can for him, he has a very kind man staying with him. He is also a prisoner, or has been, they are all loyal citizens now. I will do all I can for your husband, and as soon as he gets better he will hasten to his beloved family. He talks a great deal about you and feels very anxious about you but he is very weak. You must try and bear your sorrows with Christian Fortitude and think you are not alone. You have your children to live for, and no one is like a mother to them. I trust in God your husband will recover and return to the loved ones at home.

I have just read what I have written to your husband he says tell you to come and see him leave the baby at home and bring your oldest son with you come by Memphis and Devall's Bluff. You can come as soon as you can.

Yours respectly,
E. L. Cates
P.S. Major says stop in Memphis and see Tom Lacy and see if you can get any funds.
E. L. C.

Little Rock, Ark.
May 14 1865
Mrs. Parrott
Commerce, Scott County, MO
Dear Madam

It is with solemn feelings we pen these lines [to] you to let you know that your Husband departed this life on the night of the 13th inst. He died at 11 o'clock after some thirty days illness, he suffered very much indeed a portion of this time, altho he was conscious of his misery and rational all the time during his illness, he seemed to express a great desire to see home once more. Madam we pen you these lines with Bleeding hearts to think you are separated from one so kind as he. Mrs. Parrott we tried to have his remains sent to you but there has been an order issued not to send any more dead bodies north owing to the warm weather but as it is we have obtained a metallic coffin and will Bury him in Masonic order and at any future day you can get his remains and have them taken home he has been out of Prison one week today he has been staying with a very kind lady. Her name is Mrs. Elen L. Cates, a [next] door neighbor with to Mrs. Susan James they both sympathize with you in your bereaved condition.

The Major has had the best of attention both by physicians and friends. We now make minut [mention] of his affects we will send you his clothing. He has seven shirts, one pare Ladies cessars [scissors], one silver pen, one pare socks, hairbrush, one gold lace Belt. He gave the Belt and cessars

to his Little Daughter the pen to his son.

We the under signed testify that the above statement is a true one.
J. L. Evans
J. L. Tucker
A. W. Barker

Major James Parrott's body was brought by boat from Little Rock to Commerce, Missouri by one of the Parrott's slaves. At that time, Yankees occupied the town of Commerce so the body was smuggled off the boat at night by the family slave and his brother-in-law, Joseph Moore, and carried to the Woodson Parrott plantation. He was buried on the plantation, four and one-half miles north of Benton, MO. It is feasible that his parents, Woodson and Elizabeth Parrott, are also buried there; however, their headstone was not located. In 1999, his grandson, Tom Arnold of Benton, had the tombstone of Maj. James Parrott moved to rest next to his wife in the Benton City Cemetery.

Missourians Who Served in the Union in the Civil War

Name	Company	Unit
Acres, Joseph	H	10 CAV
Albrecht, Julius		Home Guard
Albrecht, Louis	L	10 MO CAV
Allsman, Andrew		Home Guard
Anderson, James C	F	129 INF
Anderson, Washington	F	129 INF
Arngara, Henry	F	2 ART
Arnold, Anthony	F	2 ART
Baldwin, John	F	2 ART
Barnard, William T	F	14 INF CON
Bartlett, Prescott	C	7 CAV
Bates, James S	F	129 INF
Beadles, James H	I	101 INF
Bean, William	F	33 INF
Beasley, James	D	129 INF
Beck, Francis	F	2 ART
Bess, William	F	2 ART
Blumberg, Louis	F	2 ART
Bock, August	F	2 ART
Bock, Charles	F	2 ART
Bock, Frederick	F	2 ART
Bonds, William W	F	129 INF
Bonhardt, Charles	F	2 ART
Bostwick, James L	F	2 ART
Brewer, Eli	D	18 INF
Brewer, William	D	18 INF
Bruno, Henry	F	2 ART
Buchanan, James	F	129 INF
Buchanan, William	F	2 ART
Burch, William	D	129 INF
Calloway, John S	D	129 INF
Campbell, James	A	15 CAV
Campbell, Jefferson	D	129 INF
Campbell, John	F	2 ART
Campbell, Robert	D	129 INF
Carey, Michael	F	2 ART
Carlton, George	D	129 INF
Chapman, Christopher C	F	129 INF
Chapman, John W	F	129 INF
Christison, Jacob	D	129 INF
Chuning, Andrew	F	2 ART
Chuning, James	F	2 ART
Clark, Aaron	F	129 INF
Clark, James R	F	129 INF
Clark, Richard	F	2 ART
Clauton, Jesse	D	129 INF

Major James Parrott

Cleveland, Benjamin F .... F .... 129 INF
Cluley, John M .... F .... 2 ART
Coats, James K .... F .... 2 ART
Cole, Joseph R .... I .... 152 INF
Collins, Thomas .... F .... 129 INF
Counsilor, Solomon .... F .... 2 ART
Cox, John T .... F .... 129 INF
Cox, William G .... F .... 129 INF
Cox, William G .... HQ .... 129 INF
Crabtree, Josiah .... I .... 70 INF
Daily, Joseph .... F .... 33 INF
Dawdy, George W .... D .... 129 INF
Dawdy, James J .... D .... 129 INF
Dawdy, William J .... D .... 129 INF
Diller, Henry .... D .... 129 INF
Dittlenger, Michael .... F .... 2 ART
Dormeier, Henry .... F .... 2 ART
Dorr, Henry .... D .... 129 INF
Eifert, Daniel .... K .... 24 INF
Eifert, Henry .... I .... 155 INF
Eifert, Philip .... B .... 16 INF
Ellis, William .... F .... 2 ART
Eversall, Cyrus M .... A .... 15 CAV
Fisher, Henry .... D .... 129 INF
Flatt, Robert S .... F .... 129 INF
Foster, Scott .... C .... 63 INF
Frame, Peter .... D .... 129 INF
Fuikelder, H .... F .... 24 INF
Funk, Lewis .... F .... 129 INF
Gainson, Jesse .... D .... 129 INF
Gilham, Erastus L .... F .... 129 INF
Gilham, William A .... F .... 129 INF
Glasteller, Fridolin .... F .... 2 ART
Greer, Jackson .... F .... 129 INF
Grunert, William .... D .... 129 INF
Haggard, James R .... D .... 129 INF
Hannant, John .... C .... 27 INF
Harman, Theopholis R .... F .... 129 INF
Harrison, John A .... F .... 2 ART
Hart, Daniel .... F .... 129 INF
Hawkins, Asa .... F .... 2 ART
Hawkins, William .... F .... 2 ART
Held, Carl Frederick "Fritz" .... Home Guard
Held, George .... B .... 52 INF
Held, Jacob .... D .... 43 INF
Held, Nicholas .... A .... 2 INF
Henry, Robert T .... D .... 129 INF
Herold, Valentine .... F .... 2 ART
Hill, James .... D .... 129 INF
Hilleman, August .... Home Guard
Hilleman, Henry .... Home Guard
Hilleman, Charles .... State Militia
Hoover, Joseph .... D .... 129 INF
Horn, Joseph .... D .... 2 ART
Hornbeck, Joseph .... F .... 129 INF
Hosack, Thomas .... D .... 129 INF
Howard, Coleman .... D .... 129 INF
Hucht, William .... F .... 129 INF
Jewitt, Liberty .... D .... 129 INF
Kirkland, John H .... F .... 2 ART
Koch, Frederick .... K .... 5th MO CAV
Kruger, Gottlieb .... F .... 2 ART
Lackey, Nathan W .... F .... 2 ART
Lankford, James M .... D .... 129 INF
Leach, Harvey .... F .... 129 INF
Leadbetter, William F .... F .... 129 INF
Leonard, R F H .... K .... 17 INF
Lopeman, John .... D .... 129 INF
Lutes, Jacob .... F .... 129 INF
Lutes, John F .... F .... 129 INF
Maddox, David .... F .... 129 INF
Maddox, Louis .... F .... 129 INF

Meinz, Christopher .... 50 MO INF
Meinz, Henry L .... B .... 50 MO INF
Mesmer, Charles B .... F .... 2 ART
Mifflin, John .... F .... 2 ART
Mikel, David H .... D .... 129 INF
Mikel, John C .... D .... 129 INF
Miller, Henry C .... F .... 2 ART
Miller, Henry C .... F .... 2 INF
Miller, Joseph .... MO Home Guard
Miller, Philip J .... F .... 2 Art
Miller, Samuel W .... Confederate
Moore, Robert .... D .... 129 INF
Murphy, William .... D .... 129 INF
McAsey, Edward .... D .... 129 INF
McCart, Patrick .... F .... 129 INF
McGlasson, Alfred .... D .... 129 INF
McKinney, McCager .... F .... 129 INF
Newman, Samuel S .... F .... 129 INF
Noles, Francis M .... F .... 129 INF
Northcut, Archibald .... F .... 33 INF
Olothlin, Patrick .... F .... 129 INF
Overstreet, Greenbury .... F .... 129 INF
Peak, George C .... F .... 129 INF
Peetz, Henry .... Home Guard
Penton, Mathias P .... D .... 129 INF
Peters, Henry .... F .... 129 INF
Peters, Joseph .... F .... 129 INF
Priest, John .... D .... 129 INF
Priester, Jacob .... K .... 2 ART
Pruitt, Arthur S .... 13 US INF
Ragland, Benjamin A .... D .... 129 INF
Rankins, Isaiah .... F .... 129 INF
Rasberry, Augustus .... C .... 50 INF
Rasberry, Chuck .... 2 ART
Raspberry, John .... F .... 2 INF
Ray, Scott .... K .... 71 INF
Rea, Scott .... F .... 15 CAV
Robinson, Chesterfield .... D .... 129 INF
Ruble, John .... F .... 2 ART
Sanders, Allen .... 50 INF
Sanders, John .... Home Guard
Sanders, Martin .... 50 INF
Savage, Bailey .... K .... 16 INF
Savage, Hazel .... D .... 129 INF
Scarth, George .... D .... 192 INF
Schaefer, John .... L .... 2 INF
Schaefer, Michael .... 10 CAV
Schaffer, John .... 2 ART
Scheible, Jacob .... F .... 2 ART
Scoby, George R .... F .... 129 INF
Scoby, James A .... F .... 129 INF
Scott, Abel H .... F .... 129 INF
Scott, Thomas .... D .... 129 INF
See, David W .... D .... 129 INF
Sharp, Harrison T .... F .... 129 INF
Shelton, Jesse V .... D .... 129 INF
Shelton, Joseph M .... D .... 129 INF
Simms, J M .... G .... 91 INF
Six, James W .... D .... 129 INF
Smith, John .... I .... 101 INF
Smith, John H .... F .... 2 ART
Smith Rudolf .... F .... 2 ART
Smith, William T .... F .... 129 INF
Sprading, Jesse .... F .... 2 ART
Spradlin, David .... D .... 50 INF
Spradlin, Davis .... D .... 20 LA Vol.
Spradling, Jesse .... F .... 2 INF
Springer, Henry .... Home Guard
Stainsby, John .... D .... 129 INF
Stewart, James W .... F .... 2 ART
Stewart, John W .... F .... 2 ART
Stewart, Samuel M .... F .... 2 ART

Stewart, Virgil .... D .... 129 INF
Stewart, Wash M .... F .... 2 ART
Stewart, William A .... F .... 2 ART
Sunders, John .... Home Guard
Taylor, David H .... F .... 129 INF
Taylor, William M .... F .... 129 INF
Teft, Willis .... I .... 33 INF
Uelsmann, Andrew .... Home Guard
Uhlman, Anton .... F .... 2 ART
Vickers, Charles .... D .... 129 INF
Violett, Leroy .... D .... 129 INF
Vogt, George .... 24 INF
Vogt, John ....
Voss, Henry .... 29 INF
Wagoner, Ely W .... F .... 129 INF
Wagoner, Wesley .... F .... 129 INF
Welch, Nicholas .... F .... 129 INF
Welsh, James .... D .... 129 INF
Welsh, William .... D .... 129 INF
West, Thomas W .... D .... 129 INF
Whewell, John .... I .... 101 INF
White, Thomas W .... F .... 129 INF
Whitehurst, Jordan B .... D .... 129 INF
Whiteside, Augustus R .... K .... 16 INF
Whitworth, Filmer W .... F .... 129 INF
Whitworth, John .... D .... 14 INF
Williams, Alfred .... F .... 129 INF
Williams, Wesley .... F .... 129 INF
Wilson, James W .... D .... 129 INF
Woodey, Lynn B .... D .... 129 INF
Young, Irwin .... D .... 129 INF

The Little River Drainage District

While southeast Missouri had a lot of good farm land, it also contained a lot of swampland. It was joking called "Swampeast Missouri." If the

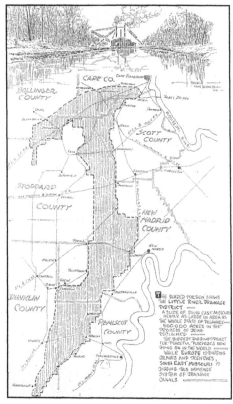

This map, thought to have been drawn during World War I, shows the Little River Drainage District of Southeast Missouri.

swamps could be drained, the acres of farm land would increase dramatically. Draining the swamps was a tangible dream but was recognized as a large engineering problem. Could it be done? The swamps lay where the Ozark foothills gave way to vast flat lands that stretch more than ninety miles over eleven counties into Arkansas. Bordered by where two great rivers, the Mississippi and the Ohio converge and several Ozark streams, most notably the Castor and Ste. Francis rivers, flow into this region – known as the Bootheel of Missouri. The area was made of forests, dirt trails, and full of wildlife. There were bear, deer, otter, beaver and other fur bearing animals. There were fowl of the air, and spring flooding. The swamp's dense forests contained millions of timber trees. The forests were full of pecan, hickory, walnut and butternut trees which yielded a great harvest annually. There were also sassafras, elm and beach, hackberry, ash, the paw-paw, the plum and mulberry trees. Some of the oak trees' circumferences reached 27 feet and some of the Cyprus trees' circumferences reached 10 to 12 feet.

The drainage would be dramatic by any standard but dozens of landowners put their money where their dreams rested. The result was the formation of the Little River Drainage District. The drainage of the swamps of southeast Missouri was long and tedious and required the expertise of some of the best engineering minds in the nation. The drainage was accomplished from 1914 to 1928.

This is what most of southeast Missouri looked like in 1910.

Beginning was in 1893 when the State of Missouri made an appropriation of state funds for a topographical survey of the lowlands of Southeast Missouri. This survey was directed by W. C. Friossell of Cape Girardeau, and showed an average fall of one foot per mile, ample for gravity drainage, provided outlets were constructed.

In January 1905 a group of interested men met at Cape Girardeau and in this meeting they crystallized the idea of constructing a great reclamation district in Southeast Missouri. "There was then no adequate statutory law that would permit the organization of such a district and Senator R. B. Oliver of Cape Girardeau was employed to prepare a bill for presentation to the legislature, then in session, that would enable the constructive idea of the interested group to be put into effect. Such a bill was prepared and introduced into the legislature, approved by the Governor, and became effective on April 8, 1905. A petition was then prepared by the firm of Oliver and Oliver asking for the organization and incorporation of the Little River Drainage District and filed in the Circuit Court of New Madrid County on September 20, 1905."

When the Little River Drainage District had completed its initial task, through construction of 957.8 miles of ditches and 304.43 miles of levees, more than one million cubic yards of earth was displaced; this was a greater mass of soil than in the construction of the Panama Canal.

The Diversion Channel with a levee on its south side drains water from the Ozark foothills into the Mississippi south of Cape Girardeau and the series of ditches drains the water below the channel to the bottom of the Bootheel into wildlife areas in Missouri and Arkansas. At one point in southern New Madrid County five of the ditches converge and flow side-by-side southward into Pemiscot County. A sixth ditch converges with the five in Pemiscot County and they flow side-by-side into Dunklin County. Two of the ditches end in wildlife areas in Dunklin County while three continues into Arkansas. A traveler who does not know the history of southeast Missouri must surely

be surprised when he or she drives over five ditches in a row near Kennett in Dunklin County.

Although setbacks were encountered, in the end, The Little River Drainage Facility proved to be a sound, public corporation which stood the test of time. Since 1931, the Little River Drainage District has been operated and maintained with the assistance from the U.S. Army Corps of Engineers.

The Little River drainage project in Southeast Missouri was the largest ever attempted in the United State and literally lifted the region out of six feet of water. The area benefited is approximately ninety miles long and varies in with from ten to twenty-seven miles. It drains 1,800 square miles of former swamp land in eleven different counties – Bollinger; Butler; Cape Girardeau; Dunklin; Mississippi; New Madrid; Pemiscot; Ripley; Scott; Stoddard and Wayne. Over six hundred ditches were dug in reclaiming land within these counties.

The Little River District was not without controversy. Louis Houck was one of its most ardent opponents. The objectors appealed to the Supreme Court of Missouri on its constitutionality. The court sustained the action of the lower court and the constitutionality of the law under which the district was organized.

Source:

Schultz, Earl L. (1973) *The Little River Drainage District*, publisher unknown

LaCross, Louisa. *St. Louis Post-Dispatch*, St. Louis. October 9, 1924 Issue.

Scott County Poor Farm

The Scott County Poor Farm was located about three miles east of Benton. The homes were built on the cottage plan. The farm was situated just east and south of a long line of hills which protected the buildings from the north and west winds and gave them the benefit of the east and south exposure of the sun most of the day. No exact date of establishment has been determined but an inspection record by Miss Elizabeth Moore dated November 18, 1914 stated that the interior paint had not been changed for approximately five years. Based on this, we can estimate that the County Poor Farm was developed approximately in 1909.

John Spalding or some members of his family supervised the County Poor Farm from the early 1920s through the late 1940s. According to Superintendent Spalding, the Farm consisted of 352 acres of land owned by Scott County, of which 220 acres were cultivated. There was an orchard, and some hilly land, more or less wooded. The superintendent paid a rental of $725 per year for the use of the farm. The county furnished fuel, clothes, bedding, and equipment and paid the superintendent $2.50 per patient per week for board and care. This unusually low rate was to be compensated for by the low rate of rental charged for the farm land.

The County Poor Farm was located on a side road which was impassable in wet weather. The site was selected in an out-of-way and somewhat inaccessible location which had the result, according to reports received, of putting the institution out of the mind of the general public and thereby depriving the inmates (as they were referenced) of many friendly services com-

One of the huge steam-powered, floating dredges whose workers and their families followed close behind living in floating house barges.

Left to right: Joe, Ada Bell, Papa John, Lil and Doc Spalding. A tax payer wrote about this family: "Mr. and Mrs. Spalding, the superintendent and his wife, are patient, kind and considerate of their charges. I have never heard Mrs. Spalding refuse to do anything for these people when they actually need it. Many surgical operations have been done there and Mr. and Mrs. Spalding have practically done all the nursing. I know of several instances when legs and arms have been cut off, and in nearly every instance the patients have recovered, due almost entirely to the close attention these people have given them." (Photo courtesy of Lois Spalding)

The Scott County Poor Farm was located about three miles east of Benton. The homes were built on the cottage plan. Aside from the usual farm buildings, there were three houses on the Scott County Poor Farm for the superintendent and on each side of this were separate inmate's buildings, one for the men and one for the women. Scott County owned 352 acres of land, of which 220 acres, according to Superintendent Spalding, were cultivated. (Photo courtesy of Lois Spalding)

monly rendered by charitable people in places where the County Poor Farm would have been more accessible. Additionally, the location in 1914 was three miles from the nearest electric power line. The grounds upon which the buildings were located were high and dry. They had excellent drainage and the yards were covered with a good growth of blue grass. The yards were amply large to accommodate many more people than were registered at any one time.

Aside from the usual farm buildings, there were three houses on the Scott County Poor Farm, one for the superintendent and on each side of this were separate inmate's buildings, one for the men and one for the women. The buildings were situated on a southern slope. The two wooden framed inmate buildings were exactly alike. They were raised from the ground on brick pillars. At some point sheeting was placed around under the buildings so as to prevent the floors from cold winds.

Each inmate building consisted of a central hallway with five small rooms on each side. Each room had one or two windows that were well lighted and provided an opportunity for ventilation in the summer. There were no shades at windows but shades were on hand to be put up at times of visits. In each building, one room was used for a dining room, the others were bedrooms. The furniture constituted of single iron beds and usually one straight chair per room. Bedding consisted of straw cotton-type mattress, pillow with cotton slip, unbleached sheets or cotton blankets and cotton quilts. The hall served as the inmates' sitting room and was lighted by a half glass door at each end. The illumination was poor when the room doors were closed. Later on a stove with plenty of fuel for fires was placed at each end of the hall. Each room also was issued two good double blankets, two comforts, sheets, pillows, drinking cups and other utensils. In the halls there were cane bottom and several other rocking chairs, a mirror and a long dining table where the meals were served. Meals were served three times a day, winter and summer, and consisted of good, substantial, wholesome food; flour bread served twice a day, hominy, meat, sorghum molasses, peas, beans and potatoes and in the summer seasons garden vegetables. There was only one brand of coffee brought on the county farm and that was made and drunk by inmates and the superintendent's family alike, serving it twice a day to the inmates with sugar and cream.

In the men's building, three kerosene lamps were fastened to the walls of the hall. Inmates who were considered capable were said to be allowed lamps in their rooms, but few were ever seen. In the men's building, there was one small bath tub with drainage through the floor under the building. The tub was provided with an arrangement of buckets hung on the wall, tube and nozzle, which produced a "shower bath." Tobacco was furnished to those who wished it and as much as they desired.

In the women's building, because most inmates were "mentally defective," no lamps and no artificial lighting were allowed. There was no running water on the premises; subsequently, the only toilet facilities were outdoor privies. There was no mention of a tub for bathing in the women's building. The inmates were all furnished with good heavy underwear in the winter seasons, woolen socks for those who desired them, comfortable clothing for men and women alike.

In Miss Moore's inspection report of 1914, she stated that the buildings appeared to be structurally in good repair, inside and out. The interior paint, which had not been removed within five years, was considerably fly-specked and otherwise soiled and worn. The floors were reasonably clean, both in rooms and halls. There were two inmates who had no control over their bodily functions. One was a paralytic insane man and the other was an idiotic girl. The man's bed, both mattress and covers, were filthy; which is probably unavoidable without hospital care. The girl's bedding all soiled was spread outdoors to dry. The girl herself gave rise to a foul odor, which was the only feature of that kind. With these exceptions, the beds on the whole seem reasonably clean. One mattress examined, showed signs of bed bugs, the others did not. One bed-ridden man, who had previously complained of bed bugs, was recently furnished with a new felt mattress.

The inmates' dishes and tableware were washed in the dining rooms by the inmates, using water heated in a kettle on the heating stove. The result varied with the competence of the inmates assigned to the job. The stack of dishes, supposedly washed, in the men's dining room was far from clean. Those on the table, for current use, were in better condition. A box containing the reserve supply of knives, forks, and spoons also contained pieces of chewing tobacco. Both the men's and women's buildings were infested with flies, in spite of its being the last half of November.

At the time of the 1914 inspection, there were 9 inmates at the time of the inspection and two bed-ridden invalids had recently died. There were six men and three women. Of the men, five were white and one colored. The colored man was given his meals at a small table in his own room; otherwise all associated together. Two of the white men were bed-ridden. One was paralytic and the other one was insane, a third was so badly diseased with syphilis he was confined to a wheel chair. None of the other three men were able to more than "get about." The women inmates number three. Two women are white and one is colored. All three are mentally defective to a marked degree. All three women seem to have lived most of their lives at the farm. The idiot girl, who is about 20 years old, can neither walk, talk, nor see and she is badly deformed. The other white woman, about 45 years old, is not physically helpless but she is said to have given birth to five or six children, all fathered by inmates during her institutional career. (It is said that only one of these disasters occurred during the term of the present superintendent.) Four of these children are supposed to be living. The colored woman was old and feeble.

The patients and/or inmates who were not helpless were supposed to wait upon those who were, including bringing the food from the superintendent's kitchen, serving the meals, washing dishes, assisting with washing the clothes and bedding. With the 1914 population it was almost impossible for the superintendent and his wife to secure much assistance in the required way. The County Court authorized the employment of an attendant, but none was secured."

Over time, more was learned about the County Poor Farm from undated newspaper sources. There were several classes of people who usually went to the County Farm. The law stated in order to have the privileges of the County Farm one must have been living in the county one year before application was made.

First – There was the class who had, by unfortunate circumstances, been unable to accumulate enough ahead in way of finances to support themselves in their old age and went there for a home. These people as a rule were very appreciative and never complained.

Second – There was the feeble minded, who hadn't sound mind enough or relatives or friends interested enough in them to care for them.

Third – A class who became diseased from tuberculosis, cancer, dropsy and many other incurable diseases who come to the County Farm to die because no one else was willing to take care of them or give them a home. Of these, many of them died in a few weeks, or months at most, and some in just a few days.

Then there is the professional home seeker. Quite a number had been in many of the different homes of the different counties, never content long in any place, traveling about from county to county trying to find something to suit. This class was never satisfied, always grum-

bling, always complaining. These were the real trouble makers, and in the course of ten or twelve years you would be surprised at the number of this class of visitors.

There was still another class, many more than one would think, who were given the privileges of the county farm when according to the law they were not entitled to it. This class of cases were usually non-resident people, including hoboes, who were seriously injured and without funds, friends or money. They were in every instance sent to the County Farm to be taken care of until they either died or recovered. These would come there injured in railway accidents, burned or crippled or picked up on the highway sick, some filthy, dirty and lousy. Always these people were deloused, bathed and fitted up in new clothes, and shoes. As soon as they were able, they went on their way.

Based on interviews with Spalding relatives it is estimated that the Scott County Poor Farm was closed around 1950. The land is now in private ownership.

Source:
Abstracted from various sources, including Miss Elizabeth Moore's report dated Nov. 18, 1914 and written by Margaret Cline Harmon

Polio Defeated in the 20th Century

The photo below was taken of childhood friends at Warm Springs, Georgia. One of these children was from Chaffee, Missouri and was a famous poster child for the dreaded early 20th century disease Polio. Polio was an acute infectious disease of motor nerves of the spinal cord and brain stem, caused by poliovirus and sometimes resulting in muscular atrophy and skeletal deformity. James M. Stubbs is the child on the right with a puppy friend.

Jim and his friends John Steinhauser of Hendersonville, TN and George Moore of Davis, CA were typical of the children with polio who were sent to the Warm Springs Foundation for treatment between 1927 and the mid 1960's. To-

day the Roosevelt Warm Springs Institute for Rehabilitation is an internationally known comprehensive rehabilitation center providing a wide-range of medical and vocational rehabilitation programs and services for many types of disabilities.

Harvey Parks Airport
Missouri Institute of Aeronautics
309th AAFFTD

When Hilter invaded Poland in 1939, he had 7,000 war-ready airplanes and the personnel to maintain and fly them. The United States Army had 400 less-than-war-ready aircraft and only 1,500 army pilots with limited experience.

In 1939 over the objections of many of his contemporaries and without congressional approval, General Hap Arnold convinced civilian flight school operators to train flying cadets. Hap's suggestion to those operators was risky and unorthodox: "You can borrow the money, can't you, until I get a congressional appropriation?" The AAFFTD stood for Army Air Force Fighter Training Division.

Oliver Parks established five of the civilian primary flight schools requested by General Arnold and graduated 20% of the WWII Aviation Cadets. At the end of WWII there were 63 civilian bases in the United States.

General "Hap" Arnold called a second meeting in Washington, D.C. on May 26, 1940. Oliver L. Parks was in attendance when Arnold told civilian operators to increase aviation cadet training by 100 percent. Out of that order, came the decision to establish a training school in Sikeston, Missouri. At the time of the meeting in Washington, D.C., Parks was already operating civil primary schools at East St. Louis, Illinois and at Tuscaloosa, Alabama. After the meeting, Oliver Parks gave an order to start construction of the Missouri Institute of Aeronautics (MIA) at Sikeston, Missouri on June 11, 1940. The site for Sikeston's base had only been selected the previous day. Sikeston's Missouri Institute of Aeronautics was built in the middle of a cotton field a year and three months before

Children with polio in Warm Springs, Georgia. The boy on the right was from Chaffee, MO. (Photo courtesy of James M. Stubbs)

Harvey Parks Airport, Sikeston, Missouri

Leonard McMullin and his airplane. (Photo courtesy of Charles McMullin)

World War II. The construction began in June 1940 and it was completed August 22, 1940. During this same period Oliver Parks established a school at Jackson, Mississippi, and later Cape Girardeau, Missouri.

The conference in General Arnold's office with Oliver Parks had set a beginning date of September 15, 1940 for activation of MIA. This date coincided with the increased pilot training program from 30,000 to 70,000 pilots per year.

Thirty-two Aviation Cadets, reported to Sikeston on September 10, 1940 – a year and three months before the bombing of Pearl Harbor and the United States declaration of war.

The Missouri Institute of Aeronautics reached a peak of 520 cadets and 170 planes on October 24, 1944. A total of 7,500 men entered the school with 5,100 completing the training. The first plane at Sikeston was the Stearman PT 17 which was replaced by the Fairchild PT 19. The PT 19 was a good plane that had only five instruments on the cockpit panel.

Some very prominent pilots were trained at the Harvey Parks Air Field in Sikeston. The most famous was Robert Johnson, America's leading Ace in Europe during WWII. Director of the X1 Project, Pete Everest, also trained in Sikeston. The X1 was the plane in which Chuck Yeager first broke the speed of sound. The class of 1942 contained 13 U.S. Military Academy Cadets coming directly from West Point to receive their flight training.

Bert Stiles, who had been fiction editor for the *Saturday Evening Post*, did his primary training in Sikeston, went to Europe as a B-17 pilot, and wrote the best selling book, *Serenade to the Big Bird*. The book gave an excellent account of the air war over Europe. Bert Stiles was shot down over Germany and killed before the book was published.

The small town of Sikeston opened its arms to the men. Harvey Woods, one of the cadets, said that Sikeston was one of the highlights of his life. Jim Glass, the first flight instructor hired by Parks Air College, noted that the friendly townsfolk willingly opened their homes. Jim owned a brand new 1941 Chevrolet convertible. The family in whose home he was staying tore down their single car garage and built a two-car garage to share with him, who also met his wife Doris in Sikeston. *Vintage Airplane* surmised, "That's true Midwestern hospitality!"

To establish the air school, a bond issue was passed to provide a City Hospital in Sikeston. A large residence built in 1910 was purchased to make "a modern 20 bed hospital." City Hospital was located on the corner of Gladys and New Madrid Streets.

All work and no play is not health for young men, so the Cadet Hostess arranged dates for dances. The Women's Leagues of Charleston, New Madrid, Dexter, and Cairo were contracted to help. Using a card file, girls were categorized by height and hair color. Sometimes as many as 400 properly chaperoned girls were bused to Sikeston. Additionally, fiancés came from distant states to marry the aviation cadets. Again, Sikeston cadet host helped locate ministers, flowers, witnesses, and places for them to live.

On October 12, 1944, an achievement award was presented to the Missouri Institute of Aeronautics "this award and other ratings which have been given to this base were the result of an organization which functioned smoothly and efficiently during its four years of operation. The success of this operation was the result of the whole-hearted cooperation and effort of both the military and civilian personnel." The base was closed October 16, 1944.

The United States and its allies defeated Hilter with the U. S. Army Air Force playing a major role. Sikeston's contribution to Wings Over America is, indeed, highly commendable. A benefit to Sikeston from General Arnold's civilian flight school was after it was closed for military use Sikeston used it for an elementary school for several years.

Source:
Sikeston Cultural Center Archives at the old Depot. They also have many pictures for viewing at the Depot.

Leonard McMullin, First Licensed Pilot in Missouri

John Leonard McMullin was born October 5, 1890 near Sikeston. He married Warde Matthews in 1914 and they led a very interesting life together with their two sons, Charles and John McMullin.

While attending Sikeston High School in 1908, he served as the first football captain for the team coached by R.E. Bailey. It was Mr. McMullin who named the Sikeston school colors red and black. He spent his entire life in the Skeston community, but he traveled widely in his beloved airplanes.

Leoard McMullin was the first licensed pilot in Missouri and an aviation pioneer. He was the first commercial pilot in the state. He was billed widely over the Midwest as the "Flying Farmer." He and "Spider" Burns gave exhibitions at numerous state fairs. An old clipping from a St. Louis paper told of 50,000 people gathered in Forrest Park in St. Louis for a flying exhibition by Mr. McMullin and a parachute jump by Mr. Burns.

Leonard McMullin's son Charles is also a pilot and is still an active attorney throughout Missouri.

Naturalized Citzens in Scott County

In 1936, the District Director of Naturalization of Washington, D. C., requested Circuit Clerk Leo J. Pfefferkorn to compile a list of the people who had made application for naturalized and those who had completed the procedure prior to 1906. Mr. Pfefferkorn had to use several books to obtain the information but completed the job as requested. Margaret Harmon compiled the information in alphabetical order.

Citizen	Country of Origin	Naturalized
Amrhein, Francis	Bavaria	1855

B

Citizen	Country of Origin	Naturalized
Ballentine, William	Great Britain	1856
Bassler, Theodore	Baden	1873
Bechel, George	France	1854
Behen, Casper	Hanover	1857
Bihan, John	France	1846
Blaes, George	France	1854
Bles, John	France	1853
Boechman, Herman	Prussia	1849
Boeckman, John H.	Prussia	1848
Bohert, Lorentz	France	1856
Bohnhardt, John D.	Switzerland	1848
Bollinger, Peter	Bavaria	1852
Boos, Andreas	Brunswick	1856
Bore, John	Belgium	1857
Brandt, Louis	Hungary	1871
Bronkharst, Peter	Prussia	1870

C

Citizen	Country of Origin	Naturalized
Compass, Morand	France	1860

D

Citizen	Country of Origin	Naturalized
Dannenmueller, Louis	France	1852
Deheck, Stephen	Holland	1857
Dirnberger, Adam	Bavaria	1857
Dirnberger, John	Bavaria	1857
Dirnberger, Michael	Bavaria	1858
Dirnberger, Wolfgang	Bavaria	1858
Dohogne, Joseph	Belgium	1854
Dumay, John	Belgium	1857
Dunican, Frank	England	1870

E

Citizen	Country of Origin	Naturalized
Eichorn, Andrew	Bavaria	1856
Eifert, Rudolph	Germany	1905
Eisele, Casper	Baden (Germany)	1848
Eisert, Henry	Germany	1860
Felthaus, John	Prussia	1852

F

Citizen	Country of Origin	Naturalized
Fisher, Hy.	Kurhassen	1874
Fornfald, William	Prussia	1853
Frish, John	Bavaria	1857

G

Citizen	Country of Origin	Naturalized
Gaengel, George	France	1854
Gangle, Charles	France	1857
Gangle, John	France	1858
Gangle, Joseph	France	1857
, Jacob	Bavaria	1857
George, Joseph	France	1852
Getz, John	France	1860
Glanke, John	Bavaria	1858
Glasser, Stephen	Baden	1853
Glastetter, Fridolin	Baden	1852
Glastetter, John	Baden	1854
Glastetter, Joseph	Baden	1853
Glaus, John	France	1851
Glitz, John	Holland	1856
Granthier, Francis	France	1857
Granthier, John Baptist	France	1857
Grossman, Herman	Russia	1903
Grove, William J.	England	1869

H

Citizen	Country of Origin	Naturalized
Hafler, Lawrence	France	1855
Hahn, John	France	1852
Halter, Ludwig	France	1852
Harris, Benjamin	Prussia	1878
Harris, Renard	Germany	1882
Hartman, John G.	Germany	1842
Heisserer, Andrew	France	1858
Heisserer, Antony	France	1853
Heisserer, Joseph	France	1853
Heisserer, Michael	France	1853
Herman, Frederick Theo.	Germany	1855
Hilleman, Augustus	Germany	1852
Hoffman, Alois	Baden	1858
Holder, Philip	France	1859

J

Citizen	Country of Origin	Naturalized
Jochim, Burhhard	Germany	1892
Job, John	Bier	1858

K

Citizen	Country of Origin	Naturalized
Kabler, David	Bavaria	1850
Kach, Charles	Germany	1867
Kaffenberber, Lenhard	Germany	1865
Kallhofner, Anthony	France	1868
Kamp, Francis	Belgium	1858
Kast, Peter	Bavaria	1856
Kempel, John	Germany	1874
Kenkel, Bernard	Prussia	1871
Kern, Adam	Bavaria	1850
Kern, Lucas	Bavaria	1849
Koelzer, Joacob	Prussia	1859
Kuhn, John	Bavaria	1843
Kurn, Peter	Germany	1870
Kuter, Henry	France	1853

L

Citizen	Country of Origin	Naturalized
Lab, John	France	1857
Lauber, Andrew	France	1851
Lauber, Joseph	France	1858
Lagrand, Joseph	Belgium	1857
LeGrand, Hubert J.	Belgium	1858
LeGrand, Michael	Prussia	1870
Leibel, George	Bavaria	1851
Leibel, Michael	Bavaria	1851
Linck, Michael	France	1851

M

Citizen	Country of Origin	Naturalized
Mames, Michael	Bavaria	1857
Manz, George	Bavaria	1857
Martin, John	France	1857
McLaughlin, Michael	Great Britain	190?
Mier, John	Prussia	1859
Miller, Harry	Russia	1900
Miller, Louis	Baden (Germany)	1852
Miller, Valentine	Hesse (Germany)	1854
Morper, John	Bavaria	1852
Myer, Ferdinand	Germany	1844

N

Citizen	Country of Origin	Naturalized
Naumann, Ianil	Prussia	1871
Nethey, William	England	1858
Nillot, Mathias	France	1857
Nillot, Nicholas	France	1857

O

Citizen	Country of Origin	Naturalized
Oarter, Balthasar	Germany	1848
Oberlin, Alvis	Switzerland	1852
Oberlin, Geroge	Switzerland	1858
Ohlman, Anthony	France	1860
Oupmon, Henry	unknown	1871
Ourth, John	Holland	1866
Ourth, Nicholas	Belgium	1852

P

Citizen	Country of Origin	Naturalized
Pattie, Annie	France	1881
Peppercorn, Andrew	France	1853
Peppercorn, Louis	France	1851

R

Citizen	Country of Origin	Naturalized
Rambo, Mathias	Bavaria	1858
Rapart, Samuel	Prussia	1848

Reinagel, George	France	1880
Reiter, Martin	France	1871
Rembo, Peter	Prussia	1857
Roth, David	Germany	1860
Rubel, Jacob	Bavaria	1852
Rubert, Jacob	Belgium	1858

S

Schaffer, Andrew	Bavaria	1857
Schane, Andrew	unknown	1866
Scherer, Benedict	Baden (Germany)	1855
Scherer, John	Baden (Germany)	1855
Scherer, Valentine	Baden (Germany)	1852
Schetter, Charles	France	1858
Schoat, Michael	France	1856
Schott, Louis	France	1852
Schuber, John	Bavaria	1858
Seigelman, Joseph B.	Hungary	1873
Seufert, Mark	Bavaria	1857
Smith, Ehart	Germany	1842
Sneiman, Henry	Holland	????
Stamfus, Frederick	Hannover (Germany)	1857
Staebler, Louis	France	1856
Steffs, Nicholas	Germany	1880
Stubenrauch, George	Bavaria	1857
Stupey, Joseph	Bavaria	1843
Suppy, Francis A.	France	1846

T

Thole, Henry	Prussia	1857
Treele, Joseph	Baden (Germany)	1843

U

Upman, Frederick	Prussia	1852

V

Vetter, Charles	France	1843

Vetter, Nicholas	Germany	1860
Vogt, Peter	Germany	1858

W

Weaver, John	Bavaria	1857
Weber, Fredrick	Switzerland	1892
Wehling, John	Germany	1876
Weismiller, Jacob	Bavaria	1857
Weismiller, Martin	Bavaria	1858
Winer, Juliua	Russia	1901
Worsley, Jhob	England	1859
Wuhsung, Frederick	Germany	1842

Z

Zeigler, George	Bavaria	1857
Zeingling, Burnhard	Baden (Germany)	1892
Zervis, John	Prussia	1858
Zundel, Frank	Germany	1881

Source: *Scott County Democrat,* Neighbor Day Edition, Section Two, Thursday, October 1, 1936.

Much of northern Scott County was settled by a group of German-speaking immigrants from Alsace-Lorraine, near the Rhine River. Both France and Germany have claimed the citizens of Alsace-Lorraine over the centuries. Today, it is part of France. The immigrants established St. Lawrence Church in New Hamburg, the mother parish of Benton, Oran, Chaffee, Kelso and Illmo (now Scott City).

Factoring in the immigrants from Alsace-Lorrane, Bavaria, Germany, and Prussia, fifty-nine percent (59%) of early Scott County residents who received naturalization papers prior to 1906 were German speaking. Many citizens of Switzerland were also German speaking. During the Civil War northern Scott County fought on the Union side. Citizens of southern Scott County tended to be from Virginia, Kentucky, and Tennessee. They were naturalized citizens before immigrating west of the Mississippi River. Southern Scott County citizens supported the Confederate Southern States in the Civil War.

Scott County Officials

State Legislators Serving Scott County

1826 was the first assembly in which Scott County was entitled to a seat by reason of the county's organization prior to that year.
Source: Missouri Official Manuals

State Representatives

Kelso, William	1826
Allen, Felix G.	1828-1834
Hunter, Abraham	1836, 1846, 1850-52
Brown, Wilson	1838
White, Robert	1840-1842
Sayers, William	1842-1844
Hough, Harrison	1844, 1846-1848
Darnes, William P.	1848 - 1860
Powell, J. A.	1860-1862
Johnson, N. C.	1862-1864
Sillman, B. F.	1866-1868
Winchester, Henderson	1868-1870
Gray, Edward	1870-1872
Wade, R. B.	1872-1878
Arnold, Marshall	1876-1880
Gaither, Benjamin B.	1880-1882
Hunter, Isaac	1882-1886
Frazer, Theodore	1886-1888
Hunter, Benjamin F.	1888-1890
Coffman, John R.	1890-1894
DeReign, Albert	1894-1896
Williams, Lon B.	1896-1904
Hinkle, Thomas F.	1905-1906
Wade, S. J.	1907-1910
Thomas, Matt	1911-1912

Bowman, Joseph D.	1913-1918
Anderson, Tillman W.	1919-1920
Malone, E. J.	1921-1922
Ogilvie, Fred L.	1923-1924
Lindsay, A. Francis	1925-1926
Washburn, H. H.	1927-1928
White, Cornelius C.	1929-1932 & 1935-1938
Munger, Eugene M.	1933-1934
Wallace, J. S.	1939-1948 & 1951-1960
Felker, C. E.	1949-1950
Wallace, J. S.	1950-1960
Germain, George J.	1961-1962
Lankford, Les D.	1963-1964
Heckemeyer, Tony	1964-1972
Cline, C. F.	1972-1978
LaPlant, Clifford	1978-1980
Zeigenhorn, Keith	1980-1988
Amick, Ollie	1988-1994
Heckemeyer, Joe	1994-1998
Myers, Sr. - Peter C.	1998-Present

State Senators

Byrd, Abraham	1822-1824
Dawson, Robert D.	1824-1830
Hunter, Abraham	1830-1834
Lucas, W.	1834-1836
Hunter, Abraham	1838-1842
Snell, Willis W.	1842-1846
White, Edwin	1846-1850
Polk, John	1850-1852
Lindsay, James	1852-1856
Nathaniel W. Watkins	1856-1858

Raines, James S.	1858-1862	Randol, Elijah	1838-1840
Gravelly, J. J.	1862-1866	Randol, C. V.	1840-1842
Deal, H. J.	1867-1869	Harbison, John	1842-1844
Morrison, Thomas J. O.	1869-1884	Shaw, Thomas M.	1844-1846
Hunter, William	1885-1888	Spear, Henry D.	1846-1850
Carleton, George W.	1889-1892	Winchester, W. Henderson	1850-1854
Walker, Benjamin T.	1893-1897	Brock, Hartwell	1854-1858
Marshall, John E.	1898-1904	Winchester, Henderson	1858-1860
Farris, Joseph W.	1904-1909	Howell, William H.	1860-1862
Oliver, Arthur L.	1909-1913	Sillman, B. F.	1862-1866
Cain, Henry	1913-1917	Rhodes, Thomas S.	1866-1870
Mayes, Von	1917-1921	Anderson, Thomas T.	1870-1874
Anderson, Tillman W.	1921-1925	Wright, Alexander	1874-1878
Wammack, Ralph	1925-1933	Trotter, Jasper	1878-1880
McDowell, James C.	1933-1941	Arnold, George W.	1880-1882
Joslyn, Lewis Danforth	1941-1948	Trotter, Jasper	1882-1884
Gilmore, D. W.	1949-1952	Winchester, G. O.	1884-1886
Spradling, Al	1952-1976	Daugherty, H. H.	1886-1888
Dennis, John	1976-1988	Greer, Jasper B.	1888-1890
Kinder, Peter D.	1992-Present	Wade, M. P.	1890-1892
		Miller, B. F.	1892-1894
		Batts, R.	1894-1898
		Henderson, Edward	1898-1901
		Watkins, Joe F.	1901-1906
		Gober, Louis P.	1907-1910
		Ellis, William	1911-1916
		Sneed, Fred K.	1917-1920
		Kirkendall, William E.	1921-1924
		Dye, Everett	1925-1928
		Scott, Tom	1929-1932
		Anderson, Joe	1933-1936
		Anderson, Wade	1936-1938
		Hobb, John	1939-1944
		Malcolm, Early	1945-1952
		Dennis, John	1952-1976
		Ferrell, William "Bill"	1976-Present

Scott County Sheriffs

As we reflect on the life and contributions of former State Senator and Scott County Sheriff John Dennis, let us honor the contributions of all citizens serving in the capacity of Scott County Sheriffs listed below.

The office of Sheriff also had responsibility for the office of collector until 1882, then a separate office of Collector was formed. separate office was legislated for all counties.

Source: Missouri Official State Manual

Hopkins, Joseph A.	1822-1824
Allen, Felix G.	1824-1828
Moore, John	1828-1830
Hutson, Strong N.	1830-1832
Clark, H.	1832-1834
Moore, John	1834-1836
Harbison, John	1836-1838

SEMO Shrine Patrol in 1954. (Photo courtesy of Bill Lewis)

Donald Brad Bedell

Brad Bedell of Sikeston, Missouri was appointed by Governor Holden in April 2001 to serve a six-year term on the Southeast Missouri State University Board of Regents expiring January 1, 2007. He is president of Health Facilities Management Corp., a company established in 1984 by his father Don C. Bedell. The company has 31 nursing facilities throughout Southeast Missouri, Arkansas and Arizona.

In his role as president, Bedell is responsible for providing management and organizational direction to all HFMC personnel as well as comprehensive involvement in general company operations for 40 corporations and 3,000 employees.

Previously Bedell served as executive vice president of HFMC. Prior to that, he was vice president of legal services at HFMC. He holds a bachelor's degree with an emphasis in management and a juris doctorate degree, both from the University of Mississippi. He served as vice magistrate of the Phi Delta Phi legal fraternity at the University of Mississippi and as a member of the Lamar Order with the University of Mississippi School of Law.

He has been a member of the Southeast Missouri University Foundation Board of directors and, in 1998, established the Don C. Bedell Excellence Award through the Foundation to assist business majors at SEMO. Bedell established the scholarship to honor his father.

Bedell has served as a member on the YMCA of Southeast Missouri Board of Directors. Additionally, Bedell currently serves as Missouri Health Care Association president and board member to the American Health Care Association.

Lynn Matthews Dempster

Mrs. Lynn Dempster, a retired Sikeston businesswoman, was appointed to the Southeast Missouri State University Board of Regents in March 1991, for a six-year term. Mrs. Dempster was a legal secretary and office manager for the law firm of Dempster, Barkett & McClellan in Sikeston. She has been active in numerous civic and professional organizations, serving as a member of the Board of Directors for the Southeast Missouri University Foundation, and currently serving as an Emeritus Member of the Foundation Board. She also served as the Chairperson of the "Leadership Gifts Committee" for the Southeast Missouri University Foundation's Vision of Excellence Campaign, and is a member of the President's Council of the Southeast Missouri University Foundation.

Mrs. Dempster, along with her late husband, Robert A. Dempster, who was a prominent Sikeston attorney, has been active in the life of Southeast Missouri State University for many years. They donated $100,000 to the University in 1982 for the renovation of the original Robert A. Dempster Hall of Business, $100,000 to the University's nursing program in 1988 for the construction of the Lynn Dempster Auditorium, and $1,000,000 in 1990 for the construction of the new Robert A. Dempster Hall. In addition, Mrs. Dempster maintains several scholarships at Southeast Missouri State University for students having financial difficulties.

Mrs. Dempster also served as President of the Missouri Delta Medical Center Foundation of Sikeston and Secretary of the Senior Citizens Bootheel Services, Inc. She is a member of the Scott County American Cancer Society, the Administrative Board of the First United Methodist Church, the Menninger's President Club, and the Sikeston Little Theater. Lynn and her husband furnished the Lobby and Family Room of the Wendell Apartments prior to the opening of the complex, and Lynn was one of the original founders of the YMCA in Sikeston.

Mrs. Dempster was born in Johnson County, Clarksville, Arkansas. She was the eldest daughter of Herbert S. Matthews, Sr. and Flora Ann Lee Matthews. Lynn now resides in the Dempster home at 226 North Kingshighway, Sikeston, MO.

Robert A. Dempster

Robert A. Dempster was born April 8, 1912 in Ava, Illinois. He was the only child born to George A. and Emma Dempster. The family moved to Sikeston, Scott County, Missouri in 1915. Robert's father built the house at 226 North Kingshighway in Sikeston where he grew up and continued to live until his death. He first married Beatrice Dobbins of Longmont, Colorado in 1943. She died in June 1973. He married Lynn Matthews on May 23, 1978 in Sikeston, Missouri. Lynn was born in Johnson County, Arkansas, the eldest daughter of Herbert S. Matthews, Sr. and Flora Anne Lee Matthews. She brought three daughters to the marriage: Pam, Paulette and Vicki.

Robert attended the Sikeston Public School System and upon graduation he enrolled in Central Methodist College in Fayette, Missouri. After two years he transferred to the University of Missouri Law School, where he graduated in 1934. During his senior year in law school, he was elected City Attorney for Sikeston. In 1942, he became an officer in the Navy and spent 30 months on the island of Okinawa during World War II. He rose to the rank of Lieutenant Commander before leaving the Navy. He resumed the practice of law in 1945 and served six years as Scott County's Prosecuting Attorney. He practiced law for more than 60 years.

In 1960, he founded the Security National Bank of Sikeston. Mercantile Bank bought it in 1982, and he served as board chairman for the bank from 1960 to 1986. Robert was a devoted friend of Southeast Missouri State University. He helped establish the Southeast Missouri University Foundation in 1983 and served as its first president. In 1984, Robert Dempster was the recipient of the "Friend of the University" award presented by the SEMO University Foundation. The first recipient, in 1983, was Cape Girardeau attorney Rush H. Limbaugh Sr.

In announcing the 1984 selection, Dr. Bill W. Stacy, president of SEMO, said "Not only has Bob Dempster actively guided the foundation through its birth process and growing pains, but he has made significant personal financial contributions. He and Lynn Dempster are 'Heritage Club' members of the Copper Dome Society, a level reached by gifts of over $100,000 to the foundation." Dempster donated $1 million to the construction of a new College of Business building. The new facility—Robert A. Dempster Hall—bears his name.

Southeast was not the only school Dempster aided. He made numerous financial gifts to his alma mater, the University of Missouri, and particularly its law school. He served as a trustee for the law school. He was appointed to the University of Missouri Board of Curators in 1978 by then-Governor Joseph Teasdale and served a six year term. He was chairman of the finance committee during his tenure of the board. He was a Charter member of the Jefferson Club, which was the principal fund raising arm of the University of Missouri. He was also a member of the Board of Trustees of Scarritt College, a Methodist school in Nashville, Tennessee.

Robert Dempster died March 24, 1995 at his home in Sikeston after an extended illness. His wife, Lynn, and died April 11, 2003. The Dempster's were active members of the United Methodist Church of Sikeston.

Gerald Howard

Few persons have demonstrated the dedication to youth development in Sikeston as has Gerald Howard. It begins early in sports and reaches to the high school level in scholarship, sports, and drug awareness training. For over 40 years he has taken a personal interest in our youth. With other services in veterans' groups, church leadership, and emergency police activities, along with his 44 years of work with the Jaycee Rodeo, Gerald Howard is a person worthy of admiration.

He served for four years as a Tech Sergeant assigned to training infantrymen during World War II. He was awarded a Purple Heart after the war, and was very active for several years as a member of the Veterans of Foreign Wars.

Mr. Howard is a member of the First Hunter Memorial church. He has served as Deacon, Elder and Sunday School Superintendent.

He served in the Auxiliary police in the Sikeston Police Department, and also as the City Director of Civil Defense. In 1985, he was appointed as the Missouri State President of Civil Defense.

His services among the city's youth are numerous. He is president of the Just Say No Club in Drug Awareness sponsored by the Elks Club. He is also a chairman for the Sikeston Elks Club Drug Awareness program. He is a chairman for the Elks Club Scholarship program at the Sikeston High School. He is a trustee chairman for the Elks Family, which consists of five children. He is a volunteer at both the Food Bank and the C.P. Center. Gerald Howard coached Little League baseball for ten years and was the president of Senior Babe Ruth baseball for ten years as well.

In his local community volunteer work, Mr. Howard has worked with the Jaycee Rodeo for 44 years. He is chairman of ten Elks Lodges for Drug Awareness. He helped the Just Say No Club collect $20,000.00 for the C.P. Center, as well as helping collect toys and 10,000 cans of food for the needy in the community. He was very active during past floods in the area after the 1986 tornado in Sikeston. He has volunteered at the Sikeston area Food Bank and the Sikeston Depot Art Center.

Sue Marble

Sue Marble is a native of Sikeston. Her family moved to East Chicago, Indiana, where she graduated from St. Riley elementary school. Upon her return to Sikeston she attended Lincoln school until she completed the 10th grade. In order to graduate from the 12th grade, students from the west side of town had to attend another school. Sue graduated from Washington High in East Chicago, Indiana. She attended Sadge Ridley Beauty College for two years in Chicago. She attended the National Institute of Cosmetology in Washington D.C. and received her Bachelor of Arts degree in Cosmetology.

Interested in putting her knowledge of cosmetology to good use, Sue returned to Sikeston and in 1959 she built the first "registered" beauty shop. Concerned about other beauticians' professionalism and the business opportunities offered in the field of cosmetology, she joined Bi-State Cosmetology Association. The association, consisting of beauticians from Missouri and Illinois, elected her Secretary-Treasurer. She was Assistant Secretary of Associated Hairdressers and Cosmetologists of Missouri. Because of her involvement with this group she traveled extensively to such places as Boston, Philadelphia, and New Orleans. In

her business she taught the trade of cosmetology to several apprentices who were able to pass the state board exam. She was an instructor in the Sikeston Public School's cosmetology department. Her motto to the students was "Yes, You Can."

In 1980, she became a widow and had to retire from the beauty shop in order to take over the family business, Aaron's Food Store on Luther Street in Sikeston. As owner/manager, Sue was a quick learner of the retail grocery business and earned the trust and respect of all. She was able to contribute to the community by training individuals in the retail merchandizing business, offering employment to many. She says, "Big business forced me to retire after 15 years."

After working for over 35 years she is now a retired businesswoman. She is a member of St. Francis Xavier Church. She is currently active in her community serving on the board of Directors of the Missouri Delta Medical Center Board member of Sikeston Missouri Arts, and member of the Socialite Club, Progressive Extension Club, and Starlight Club. She is active with the Weed and Seed Program and is a member of the Sikeston Chamber of Commerce. She is a member of the American Legion Women's Auxiliary once serving as 1st Vice-President. In 1984, she and Jessie Lane organized the Daughters of Sunset, an organization to instill pride and beautification in the Sunset community and to give aid and motivation to our young people.

Sue's past involvement in the Sikeston community consists of being past president of the Women's Division of the Sikeston Chamber of Commerce. She holds two certificates of recognition from the City's Public Safety Board, one in 1979 when she was vice-president and the other in 1984. She was awarded a certificate of appreciation from the Sikeston Public School Advisory Board. She is a retired member of the Theta-Nu-Sigma sorority, former vice-president of the Sikeston branch of the NAACP, former member of Sikeston Community 2000, and a former volunteer for the Missouri Delta Medical Center "Pink Ladies."

From 1966 to 1975 Sue served as an active board member of the Sikeston Child Development Center occupying the former Lincoln School building. This licensed, free, child-development program, chaired by Judge Marshall Craig, pioneered daycare for forty pre-school children of the working poor in both black and white communities. She was very active in this operation.

Sue gradually earned the role in the larger community as a peacemaker in racially charged situations. She gained admiration by both black and white people as a fair, forthright thinker whose opinions and leadership carried weight. Politicians, city council members, and church members all sought her help with informing her neighborhood about public issues. She sought the good for all townspeople. It is a role that has continued for her even now.

In the late 1980s she was so fearful about the fast spread of drugs among neighborhood youth that she requested help from the city government. Within hours, the Sikeston mayor had called a meeting of city officials, black and

white parents, and anyone else concerned. The west side church was filled with citizens interested in finding help in stemming the spread of drugs. The resulting solutions were not very effective, but this public meeting instigated by Sue increased a common understanding and awareness of the need to work together. It is a role Sue continues to share.

As presidents of the Daughters of Sunset, she promoted inter-racial dinners celebrating success stories of former African-American natives of Sikeston. This Daughters of Sunset Club of about 12 committed young black women won the Civic Club-of-the-Year Award. They had political candidates come to speak on current election issues in order to better inform Sunset residents.

She was elected to the Board of Directors at Missouri Delta Medical Center where she served on the Public Relations Committee. In January 2002, she was appointed to the Executive Committee.

In 2001, Sue and her Daughters of Sunset friends helped the Sikeston Depot host an exhibit of African-American artists of national fame. These ladies promoted, planned, and prepared the gala reception for the public.

Sue enjoys her daughter Teresa Shumpert and her two grandsons. She spends time each day caring for her disabled 92-year-old mother.

Robert Mitchell

Bob Mitchell has been and is a tremendous asset to the City of Sikeston. He has served the community through various religious, civic and business organizations. In addition to his tireless efforts to promote this city for more than 50 years, he also managed to find time to build a successful business.

Bob Mitchell was born December 8, 1926 in Oklahoma City, OK to Clay and Lucille Mitchell. The family returned to Southeast Missouri when Bob was a young boy. As a lifelong resident of the community, Bob attended Sikeston High School and graduated in 1944. Upon graduation he enlisted in the Army Air Corps and was stations in Biloxi, MS. One year later, on June 23, 1945, he married Sikeston native Betty Jo Heath. After leaving the service, Bob attended the University of Missouri-Columbia and Southeast Missouri State University. While at SEMO, he was a member of the 1946 undefeated SEMO football team.

In October 1948, Bob Mitchell purchased the Malone Insurance Agency, which became what is known today as Mitchell Insurance. Mitchell Insurance was first located a 111 S. Malone (what is now Crader & Crader). In 1963, the company constructed a new office located at 801 N. Main. The agency continued to grow and another office was built. In February 1976, Mitchell Insurance moved to its present location at 901 N. Main. What began as a agency of one producer and one customer service representative is now an agency of seven producers, thirteen customer service representatives and a second location in East Prairie, MO. The agency began as a property and casualty agency but is now a full service, multi-line insurance agency, serving clients in several states. Three generations of family are represented in Mitchell

Insurance. Son, Robert L. Mitchell, Jr. is the President of Mitchell Insurance and grand-daughter Beth Johnson and grandson Deke Lape are producers with the agency.

One of Bob's greatest accomplishments has been the success of Mitchell Insurance. But, he would measure success in a different way than many. While he is proud of the financial success and growth of his business, he is most proud of the kind of place it is to work. He is so proud of the employees of Mitchell Insurance and the job that they do. He wants Mitchell Insurance to be a "good" place to work. He has worked hard over the years to instill that goal in those that lead his company now. It is evident that has created those "good" jobs. Almost half of the 20 employees at Mitchell Insurance have worked for the company for over 10 years.

Kimberly Vance Mothershead

Governor Mel Carnahan appointed Kimberly Vance Mothershead to the Southeast Missouri State University Board of Regents in August of 1997. She is a 1982 graduate of Southeast Missouri State University, where she has been a representative to the National Alumni Council. At Southeast, Mothershead also has been a member of the Copper Dome Society, the Booster Club, the University Presidential Search Committee in 1995-1996 and the search committee for a new basketball coach. During her years at Southeast, she was a majorette with the Golden Eagles Marching Band.

Mothershead has been a teacher of high school educable mentally handicapped students at Thomas W. Kelly High School in Benton, Missouri. She has worked with students with itinerant elementary learning disabilities in Lee Hunter Elementary and Morehouse Elementary schools in the Sikeston Public School District. She has also been a high school teacher of students with learning disabilities and behavior

disorders at North Stoddard County Educational Coop in Bloomfield and Bell City, Missouri.

She is corporate secretary and stockholder of Midwest Agri-Chemico, Inc. and First Missouri Terminals Corp. in Cape Girardeau, as well as corporate treasurer and director of the board of Don Vance Sales, Inc., in Versailles and Marshall, MO. Mothershead has served as presiding officer of the Senate Bill 40 Board of Directors, which distributes funds to those with mental and developmental disabilities as set out in that legislation.

Daniel S. Norton

"Dan" Norton has devoted much of his professional and personal life to the betterment of this community. His "love of the city" and regard for its residents are reflected in his tireless support and personal commitment throughout the years. There is no measure of the contributions he has made, publicly, privately, and often anonymously, to enhance our quality of life. Whether touched personally by his generous spirit, or collectively by his selfless sense of community, citizens of Sikeston can truly say this is a better place because Daniel S. Norton has lived, loved and served here.

Mary Johanna Enderle Spalding

Mary Johanna Enderle Spalding is an example of a citizen who experienced the twentieth century. Mary was born November 22, 1903 at Kelso, Missouri. She attended a rural one room school near Kelso and married Joseph

Lucias Spalding on February 25, 1925 in St. Vincent Catholic Church in Cape Girardeau. They lived within a block of the Benton Court House all their lives. They had four daughters and one son who produced fifteen grandchildren and many great grandchildren. She was the first female school bus driver in Scott County and drove until she was sixty-five years old and retired. She saw one of the first airplanes, talked on an early operator assisted box telephones, witnessed the passing of Amendment XIX, giving women the right to vote in 1920, she rode in horse and buggy and then automobiles. She broke her arm one time when she was cranking an early automobile to get it started. She and her husband sold coal and blocks of ice from the back of their home to citizens of Benton and surrounding areas.

Mary and Joe Spalding started the Spalding Trucking Company in 1925 and she helped him load watermelons, and livestock to sell at the stockyards in St. Louis. It was a long trip in those days without air conditioning and unpaved roads in the beginning.

After she lost her husband Joe in 1952, she worked for Ford Funeral Home in Benton collecting burial insurance, answering the telephones and assisting in the visitation arrangements. She was also known as the town chauffeur for all the widow women and taking them where ever they needed to go. She was active until 1999 when she moved to the Lutheran Home in Cape Girardeau where she now lives. She is still alert, loves to talk about the good ole days and entertain guests. Mary Johanna Enderle Spalding experienced the twenty century as few living today have witnessed.

Frobase Theater in Benton, Missouri, 1944. (Photo courtesy of Tom and Gloria Frobase)

W.R. "Rich" Lewis, Russ Sebastion, and Dale Alcorn at the oil well drilling site in Scott County in 1954. (Photo courtesy Bill Lewis)

Edith Finley, Mabel Finley and Lorena Penny in front of Benton Democrat office on February 15, 1949. (Photo courtesy of Mildred F. Sneed)

Members of the Future Farmers of America chapter at the Kelly High School, near Benton working on a community project on the Chamber of Commerce property at Benton, planting a multiflora rose and loblolly pine. The abandoned grade school is in the background, then equipped as a furniture manufacturing plant. In the foreground is the vocational agriculture instructor, Tom Lett, and the boys, from the left are Larry Lawkes, Corles Hopper, Donald Robert, Jeff Steger, Joe Michael, Dayton King, Larry Hamm, Maurice LeGrand, Kenny Lambert, Jimmy Withrow, Robert LeGrand and Ronnie Glastetter. (Photo from the Cape Girardeau Missourian, *March 18, 1959; courtesy of Tom Lett)*

First Methodist Church, North New Madrid
St., Sikeston, Missouri

Churches & Businesses

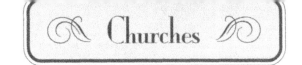

EISLEBEN LUTHERAN CHURCH

A Brief History ... The Lutheran Church In Southeast Missouri by Rev. George D. Hilpert, *The Jimplicate,* Illmo, MO

The following is a history and facts about Eisleben Lutheran Church, Illmo, MO and the settling of Saxon emigrants in southeast Missouri, as published in *The Jimplicate* the first of the year, 1938, as researched and written by a former pastor of the church, Rev. Geo. D. Hilpert. These articles are being re-printed in conjunction with the 125th anniversary of the Lutheran Church, Missouri Synod this year.

VOYAGE AND SETTLEMENT OF SAXON EMIGRANTS A CENTURY AGO

The Saxon Lutheran emigrants who came to Missouri 100 year ago, had chartered 5 ships for their sea voyage from Bremen to New Orleans and were on the ocean about 2 months. The smallest of the ship, the *Amalia* never reached port, was never seen again and all on board perished, making a loss of 56 persons to the emigrant party. During the sea voyage, 8 died and one was born. A total of 602 emigrants arrived in New Orleans. From there the journey proceeded up the Mississippi River on 5 steamboats. In the immigration party were 6 pastors, 10 candidates of the ministry, 5 teachers, 3 lawyers, 2 doctors of medicine, but the majority were farmers, mechanics and common laborers.

St. Louis, then a city of about 16,000 inhabitants, was not to be the final terminus of the emigrants, but for most of them only a temporary stay from where they might cast about for a suitable location which was to become their home in this new land of religious liberty. Quarters were rented in St. Louis, while a committee was entrusted with the selection of a tract of land where they might settle. The members of this "land commission" were one pastor, one lawyer, 3 farmers, Johann Gottlieb Palish, because he was the grandfather or our Mr. Horn, and Mrs. Broeggelmeyer.

The land commission selected a tract of land in Perry County, a few miles from the Mississippi River, about 100 miles south of St. Louis, and about 40 miles north of Illmo. A number of professional men, artisans, merchants and laborers, about 120 in all, remained in St. Louis where they found employment, but the majority soon moved to Perry County. The contract for the tract of land was signed on April 8, 1839. A few days later the surveyor, a few carpenters and laborers arrived. They began the surveying of the purchased land and the erection of temporary shelters for the colonists. The carpenters received $1 and the laborers 50 cents a day, plus food and lodging, and the wife of one of the carpenters, who did the cooking for the men, was paid 40 cents a day. The colonists came to Perry County in groups, the last leaving St. Louis on May 29, 1839.

A Brighter Future For The Saxon Immigrants In Perry County

The period of trial, unrest and confusion which beset the colonists extended over nearly two years. It speaks well for these sturdy pioneers that in spite of all hardships they carried on and determined to make the undertaking a success. During all this time they were not idle. New leadership developed and everyone performed hi study and obligation. The land was parceled out to individuals and families. The people built their homes, churches and schools and tilled the soil. They laid out several little villages; three of them are still in existence and became thriving towns, Altenburg, Frohna and Wittenberg. They became acquainted with their American neighbors and began to adjust themselves to primitive American conditions. If it had not been for the generous help extended by the Americans in Perry County, the Saxon immigrants would have fared much worse than they did.

The wife of one of the immigrants has this to say: "I remember very well how we did our washing at the creek, how we cooked our meals in large kettles, and how we used to sing. Little by little we made our sheds comfortable and even began to visit one another. When the weather was good, the children had their school out of doors,, using logs for benches. Services on Sundays were conducted in the open whenever the weather permitted."

Another wife of the immigrants wrote: "It is remarkable how God always helps us, Besides the fine weather the Americans have a better crop this year than they had had in quite a while. This prompts the people who are most excellent to be helpful to us, providing us with victuals and helping us in other ways. They donate loads of applies and sacks of flour to our people, and you may stay with them as long as you choose to gather apples for the winter. I myself did this twice so far, but in return to the favor shown me I knitted and sewed for them. They appreciate this and repay one generously. They also like to employ the men and young people of the Germans."

The following story is related: "An immigrant widow with seven children was without food and thought of roasting grains of Indian corn, which helped to still the hunger for a while. Then they prayed for bread. The same day an American came along with a sack of flour and offered it to the widow. When she said that she had no money for pay for the flour, he told her that could wait." We are not told whether she ever paid for the flour.

Thus those good American neighbors contributed to the material welfare of the Saxon immigrants, which was much appreciated by them. The colonists themselves came to America with the intention never to return to their native land. They came to stay, and from the very beginning they looked upon America as their homeland, to which they owed allegiance.

THE LUTHERAN CHURCH OF ILLMO AND FORNFELT

When in 1908 I received a call to the Eisleben Church of Scott County, MO, I wondered where "Eisleben" was. T he letter containing the call was mailed from Commerce, Scott County, Missouri, Rural Route No. 1. But Eisleben could not be traced on any map. I soon found that Eisleben was only the name of the congregation and not the name of a city or town. By the way, it is remarkable how "Uncle Sam" through the mail finds his men. Many years ago a letter from Germany addressed to the Pastor of the Lutheran Church, Eisleben, Scott County, MO, U.S.A. was correctly delivered into my hands after it had been sent to Benton. There in the county seat the congregation is incorporated and there they knew about Eisleben and sent the letter to Illmo.

I have often wondered by the local Lutheran Church is called the "Eisleben" Congregation. Eisleben is the name of a city in Germany, where Dr. Martin Luther was born in 1483 and where he died in 1546. Did the first Lutherans who settled in Scott County come from Eisleben or any place in Saxony? This is not the case, for they emigrated from other parts of Germany. The only explanation I can give is that the first Lutheran members named their congregation Eisleben in memory of the birthplace of Dr. Luther the great reformer of the church. There is no connection between the Saxon Lutheran emigrants who came to Perry County a century ago and those early Lutheran settlers of Scott County, who organized the local congregation some years later. Until about 25 years ago Eisleben was the only Lutheran Church in Scott County and the pastor of that church was known among his brethren as the pastor from Scott County.

It is not an easy task to trace the beginning of the local Lutheran church, since there is no chronological record or any minutes of proceedings prior to the year 1867. There still exists an old record book with notations of names of members, of baptisms, marriages, and burials, and other data, dating back to the year 1848. There are also a few written loose leaves from which some information may be obtained. Most of my information of the early history of this congregation I gathered from older members who are no longer with us, especially from the late "Uncle" Henry Hillemann. After much study and research I am able to give what is in my estimation an accurate history of the founding and the early years of the Eisleben Lutheran

Church, one of the first religious institutions of this locality.

As the records of the church go back to the year 1848, we take it for granted that at that time church work began in this neighborhood among Lutheran settlers. Just when the congregation was organized by adopting a constitution is uncertain, as we have no records on this point. But as the beginning was made in 1848 and 40 years ago the congregation celebrated its 50th anniversary we can look upon 90 years of local church history. The first Lutherans of Scott County apparently settled here some years after the Saxons had established their settlements in Perry County. Our Lutheran members soon came in contact with Lutherans in Cape Girardeau County, who in turn, had affiliated with the Saxon Lutherans in Perry County, and thus there is after all some connection between the Centennial Lutheran congregations in Perry County and the Eisleben Lutheran Church in Scott County.

LUTHERANS IN SCOTT COUNTY

The first Lutheran settlers of Scott County did not come to this part of Missouri in large groups, but single or several families came at different times. Neither did they all come from the same county in Germany. Nor did they form a more compact settlement, but were spread over this neighborhood. The first names on record are the following: Blank, Bohnhardt, Buns, Brockmeier, Huelsmann, Hillemann, Kettler, Musbach, Meinz, Vordemfeld. (This is the original later changed to Fornfelt.) Some of their descendants are still members of the church while other names are now unknown and forgotten. Some time later came the Albrechts, Roths, Eiferts, Sprengers, Uelsmanns, and others, of whom there is now a long line.

A few notions taken from the early records may be of interest. The first child baptized was Carl Thoele, born Dec. 28, 1848. The first confirmation class consisted of 10 members, their age being from 13-20 years, confirmed in 1868. Before that year and even after that some were confirmed in Cape Girardeau. Among the first Communion was celebrated the Sunday after Easter 1848, 19 communicants partaking. The first funeral was that of the infant daughter of Wm. Vordemfeld, and the second was that of Erhard Schmidt, age 38 years, both in 1848.

But what can we report of primitive conditions, the way of living, and the poverty of the early settlers? That is an unwritten book and the congregation's records say nothing about it. It is self-evident that they went through and endured all the well known hardships, difficulties, and trials of pioneer life. At that time no one yet dreamed for Fornfelt and Illmo.

All around was primeval forest. They constructed and lived in rude shacks and log houses. There were hardly any roads and no convenience for travel. At first they had no wagons of any kind, but used sleds, dragging them over the ground. True, our members lived in the hills, but they were surrounded by what was known as the Southeast Missouri swamp, a country full of malaria and chills. There was even a cypress swamp that we now find the railroad and depot yards.

The nearest towns were Cape Girardeau, Commerce, and later Kelso. But how to get there? That was often difficult. The swamp was filled with water and mud and was at times impassable. Old settlers told me that when they went to Cape Girardeau in a wagon they often had to stop and poke the mud out from the spokes of the wagon wheels. Or they went on horse back, or even walked, especially in winter time when the mud wand water was frozen over. Then they would carry a small sack of flour home on their shoulders, besides carrying other necessities of life. Talk about lifting Missouri out of the mud! Or t hey went for a doctor in Cape Girardeau or Commerce. It took them hours to get there. Perhaps the doctor was out on a professional trip and they had to wait for him some more hours. Yes, it happened that the doctor finally reached his new patient some time the next day. What would we say today of such conditions? In case of death the body was laid into a home-made coffin, this was placed on a mud sled and thus conveyed to the burial place, while the mourners followed on foot. Compare this with our steel vaults, beautiful caskets, floral wreaths, and funeral processions of costly automobiles.

More could be said, but let this suffice. These old settlers were content with their lot.

THE FIRST LUTHERAN CHURCH AND CONGREGATION MATTERS

There were seven or eight charter members when the Eisleben Lutheran Congregation of Scott County was organized 90 years ago. It was incorporated on April 8, 1870, the Scott County Circuit Court granting the petition for incorporation, and the paper was issued and signed by George W. Arnold, Clerk. The petition for incorporation was presented by J. W. John, Daniel Ruebel, Charles Ebert, Henry Musbach and others.

The first pastor of this congregation was the Rev. A. Lehmann, then Lutheran missionary for this part of Missouri and living in the Bertling congregation (now Hanover Church) four miles from Cape Girardeau on Perryville Road. It is self evident that he could serve this congregation only occasionally and far between. Services were conducted in the homes of members. Rev. Lehmann served this congregation until the year 1855. He had an assistant in the person of Rev. H. T. Jungk, and this man became the first resident pastor of Eisleben. He was installed there on June 10, 1855. He remained with the church until some time in 1860. Pastor Jungk lived not far from the present church in what is now known to us as "Doomstown," a section of Illmo.

During the pastorate of Rev. Jungk the congregation built its first house of worship. It was located in the present city of Fornfelt (formerly Edina) north of the round house. There the congregation had bought 1-1/2 acres of ground, on which a church was built and a cemetery laid out. The small cemetery is still property of our church, but the rest of the land was sold to Mr. Vornfeld for $18.10. Needless to say, that first church was built of logs and not larger than an ordinary room. The members did practically all the work and cash outlay was very little, perhaps not more than the news doors in our present church. Too bad that we have no pictures of that first church. The building served as house of worship until the year 1868, when the famous "Rock Church" was built. The old log church was sold to Mr. Vornfeld for $21.75.

Eisleben Lutheran Church

In recording the early history of Eisleben we must not pass by a very sad visitation which came over the little flock during these years, namely a cholera epidemic. It seems that these epidemics were common in these years, but I have only the record of the one in the year 1852. From July 24 until August 18, seven members died being stricken with this dreadful disease. These were: Wilhelmine Charlotte Vornfeld, age 43; Carl Frederick Huelsmann, 63; Elsie Henriette Thoele, two; August Hilleman, 38 years and Dorthea Louise Thoele, 9 years. In memory of these members a special service was held in August, their obituaries read, and appropriate remarks made by a pastor.

Then came the terrible Civil War between the North and the South. Our congregation being in Missouri, a slave state, and close to the division line, suffered much, both from the Northern and Southern armies, especially the "Bush-wackers" but only in the beginning of the war. There was no local pastor. Church work was nearly at a standstill. The congregation was served occasionally by Pastor Riedel of Cape Girardeau. I was told that when the congregation wanted the service of the pastor it was mostly accomplished in this way: One of the members would ride horseback to Cape Girardeau and the pastor would use this horse for his trip from Cape Girardeau to Eisleben and back, the member staying in Cape during this time. When the pastor had returned he would take the horse and ride home. All this perhaps took three days. And most likely that horse was a mule at times. I have given you a brief history of the first Lutheran settlement and congregation in this part of Scott County and I hope that it interested at least some of the readers. Many thanks to *The Jimplicate* for publishing it.

EISLEBEN LUTHERAN CHURCH

Eisleben's Beginning: Our Frontier, Our Home, Our God, 150 Years
By Gladys Smith, Church Secretary

"I have hallowed this house, which Thou hast built, to put My name there forever, and Mine eyes and Mine heart shall be there always." 1 Kings 9:30

This narrative is only a brief outline of the early history of Eisleben Lutheran Church, Scott City (formerly Illmo), MO and pronounced (Ice-Lay-Ben).

The Missouri Synod began to preach the Word of God in the area south of Cape Girardeau Community in 1848. The territory was then called the "Wooded Hills." Later became the north end of Scott County, Kelso Township.

There were large swamps that were impassable many months of the year. The Big Swamp between the Scott County hills and Cape Girardeau was not drained and the floodwaters of the Mississippi sometimes flowed inland over this vast swamp to near Bell City and Oran, cutting off all road access to Cape Girardeau for weeks at a time. The community around the Old Rock Church was known as "Whippoorwill Hollow" and was near the old "New York Settlement."

On April 2, 1848 Daniel Bohnhardt and Henry Thoele purchased two aces of land from Krammer and Mary Kettler. On April 30, 1848, nineteen Lutherans gathered in a home to celebrate the Lord's Supper. Old records show that beginning with the year 1848, the Word of God was preached in homes. The Lord's Supper was celebrated, children were baptized, and those who died were given Christian funerals. The first Christian marriage was in 1850, uniting Kaspar Roth, a carpenter, and Mrs. Marie Kettler, a widow.

Eisleben was organized and joined what today is the Lutheran Church-Missouri Synod around 1851. Although no one is certain, there are two probable reasons for choosing the unique name of our church as "Eisleben." First, it is possible that it is in honor of the Great Reformer, Dr. Martin Luther. The city of Eisleben in Germany is where Dr. Martin Luther was born and baptized. At the end of his life, Dr. Luther returned to Eisleben to settle a disagreement between the nobility. During his stay, he fell ill and on Feb. 18, 1546, he died in that city of his birth and is buried in Wittenburg. The second possible reason suggested is that Reverend Christian August Lehman, pastor of Hanover Lutheran Church in Cape Girardeau, MO, also served the early settlers. He was born in the city of Kothen, in the Duchy of Anhalt-Kothen. His birthplace is only 30 miles from the city of Eisleben, and he might have suggested or influenced the choice of our name.

There are no records of the effects of the great cholera epidemics of 1832-1833 and 1849-1852 on the citizens of the surrounding area. However, the records of Eisleben Lutheran Church of Scott City, which date back to the 1852 epidemic, have been translated out of the

Members of 50 years ago

German language into English by Mr. Louis Bauer, show that the congregation of Eisleben was hit pretty hard.

The first called pastor of Eisleben was Reverend Fredrich Jacob Theodor Jungk in 1855. Before that, he was an assistant (curate) to Rev. August Lehman at Hanover and Trinity Lutheran in Cape Girardeau and remained as pastor of Eisleben until 1860. During that time, a log building was erected as the first house of worship, which is located near the Old Lutheran Cemetery at the end of Lula Street in (Fornfelt) now Scott City. Being the only cemetery around, the Lutherans were buried on one end and the town people on the other. There was no town at this time. It was just called Kelso Township of Scott County, MO.

The Civil War saw the church without a resident pastor. Pastor Riedel of Trinity Lutheran Church in Cape Girardeau served the congregation occasionally. When the congregation wanted the services of a pastor, one of the members would ride a horse to Cape Girardeau, and the pastor would use this horse for the trip to Eisleben while the member stayed in Cape Girardeau until the pastor returned with the horse.

After the Civil War, Rev. Henry Klockmeyer, the second resident pastor began work here in 1866 and remained for little more than a year. In 1867, the Rev. F. W. John was installed as pastor.

No record of the charter members was kept, but some of the earliest communion and baptismal records are of Albrecht, Blank, Bohnhardt, Buhs, Huelsmann, Hillemann, Kettler, Krieger, Musbach, Meinz, Reppert, Thoele, and Vordemfield families.

During the pastorate of the Rev. F. W. John in 1868, the congregation decided to build a church that was more suitable for the Divine Service and the preaching of God's Word. Property was purchased from David Roth on which was located a house, a cooper shop, and a few other buildings in Illmo, MO. The church was built on this land just a little east of the present church. It was made of pure brown sandstone blocks taken from the bluffs near the Mississippi River. It was called the "Rock Church," and was a widely known landmark until 1913. The rocks from the walls were used for the foundation of the present house of worship.

In 1871, the Rev. Heinrich Grupe began a pastorate that lasted 19 years until 1890. The Rev. C. Schreder became pastor of the congregation and served until 1899.

Two church bells were bought in 1891 and were hung in a bell tower. The large bell, tuned to a "F," weighed 1,600 pounds and the smaller bell, tuned to "A," weighed 850 pounds. In 1963, a devastating fire that burned the church steeple destroyed these bells.

A school building was constructed in 1893, which was used later as a parish hall. It was located in about the same area where the new Parish Hall is now. The school served the church until 1932, when it was closed.

In 1902, the congregation began having English services once a month. In 1905, the Railroad Bridge over the Mississippi River was completed and in the same year, the town of Illmo (abbreviation from Illinois and Missouri) was established on land purchased from George H. Roth. Fornfelt, which was then called Edna, was established about the same time.

The Rock Church being too small for the congregation and in need of repairs led to the building of the present church started in 1913 and completed in 1914. A new Kilgen tracker pipe organ brought over from Germany was purchased from the St. Louis Organ Company and was installed soon after the church was built. It is still being used today after a complete renovation in January 2002.

In 1959 a renovation program was designed to glorify God by bringing new beauty to His house. The work began with remodeling of the chancel, which included the removal of two windows behind the altar and replacing the metal ceiling with plaster. The purpose is to give prominence and beauty to the altar. The tall pulpit was lowered.

On the ceiling above the altar, the symbols of the Father, the son, and the Holy Ghost stand out prominently. The hand of blessing reminds us of the Father, who provides for us bountifully. The Lamb reminds us that Jesus is the sacrifice for all of our sins. He is the One who is worthy to open the seven seals of the Book. He is victorious over sin, death and hell. The dove symbolizes the Holy Ghost, who at the baptism of Jesus, descended upon Him like a dove, lighting on Him.

Two symbols long known and loved by our congregation are the "Alpha" and "Omega," which are placed on the front walls to the right and to the left of the chancel. Formerly these symbols were painted on the altar. "Alpha" is the first letter of the Greek alphabet and "Omega" is the last. In Rev. 1:8, we read: "I am Alpha and Omega, the beginning and the ending, saith the Lord, which is, and which was, and which is to come, the Almighty."

On April 30, 1963 it was a sad day for our church. During the night, there was an electrical storm and lightning struck the wooden steeple housing the bells. The bells were melted and the entire steeple was destroyed. New bells were brought over from Germany and a new belfry and church steeple was built and dedicated in 1964.

Other additions to the current Eisleben property include a parsonage built in 1968 and the

Sophia Kettler and David Eifert, married in the Eisleben Lutheran Church.

new Parish Hall built in 1997. On April 2,1994 the steeple was lit with special lights to illumine the belfry. In 1995 a baby grand piano was given to the church. In 1999 chimes were given and added to the organ and new heavy oak doors were also donated. In 2001 an open-air picnic pavilion for outdoor activities was added to the church grounds.

In 2001 we celebrated our 150th Anniversary of the Church. Special activities were held throughout the year. We are very proud of our heritage and that the Word of God is still being preached here today. We give all praise and honor to our heavenly Father, who has sustained His Church throughout the years.

Pastors who served Eisleben Lutheran Church are:

Rev. August Lehmann – 1848-1855. He was pastor at Hanover Lutheran Church (1846) and helped Eisleben to get organized in 1851.

Rev. H. T. Jungk – 1855-1860.

1860 – 1866, Civil War period. The congregation was without a resident pastor. Pastor Riedel of Cape Girardeau, MO (Trinity) served our congregation occasionally.

Rev. Henry Kockmeyer	1866 – 1867
Rev. F. W. John	1867 – 1870
Rev. Heinrich Grupe	1871 – 1890
Rev. C. Schrader	1890 – 1899
Rev. Alfred Fuehler	1899 – 1908
Rev. George D. Hilpert	1908 – 1940
Rev. Walter Keisker	1940 – 1940
(Vacancy Pastor)	
Rev. R. Borth	1940 – 1946
Rev. Wilbur Maring	1946 – 1961
Rev. George Seboldt	1961 – 1963
(Vacancy Pastor)	
Rev. William Rempfer	1963 – 1968
Rev. Robert Olson	1968 – 1969
(Vacancy Pastor)	
Rev. Ardle Page	1969 – 1973
Rev. Walter Keisker	1973 – 1974
(Vacancy Pastor)	
Rev. Herman Baumann	1974 – 1978
Rev. Julius Strelow	1978 – 1979
(Vacancy Pastor)	
Rev. H. P. Edward Zacharias	1979 – 1986
Rev. Kim Schaerff	1987 – 1987
(Vacancy Pastor)	
Rev. Daniel Wagner	1987 – 1991
Rev. Barry Pfanstiel	1991 – 1992
(Vacancy Pastor)	
Rev. Joel Sarralt	1992 – 1999
Rev. Barry Pfanstiel	1999 – 2000
(Vacancy Pastor)	
Rev. Robert Zinger	2000 – being installed on August 27

Balcony before renovation of organ.

First Christian Church (Disciples of Christ)

The Church had its beginning in the faith and courage of a few consecrated people. To Mrs. Ella Osborn goes the major portion of credit.

The first date on record is February 1906.. The meetings were first held in the Baptist Church, which was one of three existing churches in town.

When families of R. E. Bailey and E. A. Lawrence came to town, the membership increased. The meetings were moved to City Hall and Kendall Opera House. About this time Sunday School was started with Ralph E. Bailey as superintendent. There were times when the Church was without a minister but never without Sunday School and Communion.

In 1910 a one-room wooden building called "The Tabernacle" was erected on a lot at Trotter and New Madrid Streets. Later a brick building was erected. The basement for a permanent church began 1911. The superstructure was begun in 1914 while Rev. T. B. Lockhart was pastor. Membership was 77. The cornerstone was laid in March of that year. The new building, which cost $11,000.00, was dedicated, free of debt on June 20, 1915. In 1939 the membership had grown to 225.

On Nov. 14, 1954 it was voted to buy 3-1/2 acres of land adjacent to Missouri Delta Medical Center.

Groundbreaking ceremonies for the new building were held Oct. 1, 1955. The education unit was built first. The building was dedicated Sept. 16, 1956, free of debt.

Groundbreaking for the sanctuary was April 20, 1958. The formal dedication of the sanctuary was held Dec. 14, 1958 with a cost of $260,000.00 and with a membership of 350.

The church sponsors a Boy Scout Troop which meets at the church.

Communion is served to shut-ins on the first Sunday of each month.

On April 17, 1998, church members voted to raise $250,000 by June 7, 1998 for remodeling and addition of Family Life Center.

A Groundbreaking Ceremony was held on June 7, 1998. The cost of the project was $670,000.

The Family Life Center includes fellowship space, a large kitchen, basketball court and class rooms. Additional parking space will accommodate the church and Missouri Delta Medical Center.

The Family Life Center was dedicated June 13, 1999. Rev. Edmond Pangburn was minister during this project.

Each minister of the church gave their particular ability to church growth. The ministers from 1906 – Rev. John S Zeran, Rev. Field, Rev. J. B. Lockhart, Rev. S. H. Fuller, Rev. John Wells, Rev. J. C. Hoke, Rev. R. M. Houston, Rev. Cyrus Mitchell, Rev. Morton, Rev. E. B. Hensley, Rev. O. P. Bellenger, Rev. McFarland, Rev. W. W. Walker, Rev. R. M. Talbert, Rev. R. S. Rains, Rev. J. P. Read, Rev. G. H. Adkins, Rev. Wayne Davis, Rev. Myron Neal, Rev. Durward Penry, Rev. Paul Walker, Rev. Clark Hargus (interim), Rev. Thomas J. Plumbley, Rev. Jack Barron (interim), Rev. Dr. Lee Brummel, Rev. Gene Akeman (interim), Rev. Edmond Pangburn, Rev. David A. Vernon (interim), Rev. Dr. Allen Shriver (present minister).

This church building was started in 1911.

Present church building.

First United Methodist Church

The first building of First United Methodist Church of Sikeston was erected in 1879 at the corner of Front and Stoddard Streets.

The second building for First United Methodist Church was building 1891, when the church outgrew the first facility.

The third building, called the Dome Church, was completed in 1912 on a triangular lot where Harris Street and New Madrid Street intersect. That building burned in 1968.

The fourth and current building, which is located at 1307 North Main Street, was built and occupied in 1971.

In 1867 the village of Sikeston was approached on horseback by an itinerant preacher, the Rev. Lucilius F. Aspley. He made his way to the home of Mrs. Catherine Stallcup Sikes, who with a few other people, was anxious to organize a Methodist Church and Sunday School. An abandoned freight car became the meeting place.

In 1873 Reece Applegate organized a Methodist Sunday School. It met in a two-story frame building on the site of the old South Grade Schools.

Mrs. Catherine Sikes, the widow of John Sikes and later the wife of Judge Handy, was aware that the church needed a new home. On June 20, 1879 she gave a lot on the corner of Front and Stoddard Streets for construction of a church building. However, by 1890, the congregation saw the need for a larger building The first church was sold to the Roman Catholics for $800 in 1891.

The second church was built in 1891 at the corner of Center and North New Madrid Streets. It was dedicated in 1897 when it was debt free. The church grew so rapidly that the minister and board decided that a larger church must be built again. In October 1910, a committee was elected to erect a new church.

The site of the third church, which came to be called the Dome Church, was a triangular area formed by New Madrid Street and Harris Street going off on an angle to the northwest. The first service in that church was May 5, 1912. Added space for an educational wing became a necessity and in 1951, an annex was added onto the north of the church. The church burned

March 23, 1968, although the education annex survived and remains today. Today the site is marked by huge columns still left standing.

Following the fire, seven and a half acres were purchased at the North Y for the construction of a new church, this triangle location is formed by North Kingshighway and Main Street. It faced the entrance to the north edge of the city. The congregation moved into the new building in 1971, almost three years to the day of the fire.

Since that time, additional building projects have been completed. Construction began in 1989 for a bell gazebo and a new chapel. No provision had been made in the new church for her bell which had been a part of the church since 1987. A gazebo type structure with a bell tower at the top was built and dedicated on Nov. 13, 1990.

In June 1918 a gift was given by Mr. and Mrs. Robert Dempster for the purpose of building a chapel. The Dempster Memorial Chapel, in memory of Mr. Dempster's parents, was consecrated Nov. 11, 1990.

Since 1988, with the exception of a couple of years, the church has hosted Living Christmas Scenes in early December. The scenes now portray major events in the life of Christ from birth through resurrection.

Through the years, the church has grown from having only one service and one Sunday school hour, to today when there are four weekend services and two Sunday School hours..

The church is located at 1307 North Main Street. The mailing address is: First United Methodist Church, P. O. Box 682, Sikeston, MO 63801. The web site is: www.gbgm-umc.org/SikestonFirst. The e-mail address is 1stumc@sbmu.net.

The present building.

The first church building, 1879.

The second building, 1891.

The third building, the "Dome Church," 1912.

St. Augustine Catholic Church

The beginning of our church can actually be traced back to the beginning of our Catholic School. Devout and faithful settlers of the early village of Kelso were finding it increasingly difficult to attend church at the surrounding parishes. To solve this problem, they hoped to establish a church of their own. It was suggested by Father Sosthenes Kleiser, the pastor of St. Mary's Church, Cape Girardeau, that they first open a Catholic School and the church would follow next. He recommended a teacher, Miss Elizabeth Linderman and the school was opened in the fall of 1877. There were thirty students in attendance.

In the spring of 1878, thirty-one families met with Father Kleiser at the home of Carl Messmer to discuss the possibility of building a church. John Blattel, who owned a farm in the area, gave three acres of ground to hold the proposed 60' X 35' church building. Six months later, the building was completed and Father Kleiser was transferred from St. Mary's Parish to the new parish in Kelso. He officiated at the first Catholic service in the church on Nov. 3, 1878.

Father Kleiser dedicated four successful, prosperous years of his life to God through his service to the eager parishioners of this small community. In August 1882, Reverend A. J. Kleinschnittger, or Father Klein, as he came to be known, was assigned as the new pastor of the Kelso congregation after Father Kleiser was transferred. Under the direction of Father Klein, the congregation outgrew the small wood frame church and was in need of something larger. On April 23, 1889, an enthusiastic congregation began work to build a new church that was designed by Brother Adrian, O.S.F., a renowned architect of St. Louis. In August, the splendid structure was completed. The church was a brick, Gothic style church of 120' X 45' with an aspiring steeple of 135'. It had a seating capacity of 500.

On Aug. 28, 1890 the feast of St. Augustine, parishioners came in wagons for the dedication of the new church. Reverend Vicar General Brady dedicated the new church and named St. Augustine as the Patron Saint. The church remained in its original condition until September 1948 when it was remodeled. On June 27, 1979 work began to restore the church to its original condition with a few modern changes. On Feb. 1, 1980, just seven months after the renovation had begun, the parish family of St. Augustine gathered in the church for the two-hour rededication ceremony.

In 1998 it was noted that the 135' steeple was in need of repair. The slate that was so beautifully arranged on the steeple was falling and posed a risk of injury to pedestrians. The slate was replaced with copper. In 2002 a new carillon was donated in memory of Mr. Martin Jansen. The carillon provides elegant music and bell combinations that can be heard for miles.

A rector exists to house the parish priest. The following priests have served St. Augustine Parish since its founding in 1878: Rev. Sosthenes Kleiser, Rev. A. J. Klein, Rev. J. P. Fitzkam, Vicar General Henry Muhlsiepen, Rev. Martin Weissmueller, Right Reverend Monsignor Joseph Keusenkothen, Rev. Robert Landewee, Rev. Phillip Bucher, Rev. James Sullivan, Rev. Justin Brauner, Rev. Michael McDevitt, Rev. Normand Varone, Rev. Raymond V. Orf, Monsignor John H. Westheur and Rev. M. Oliver Clavin.

Today the parish is home to more than 440 families. The Catholic school is still in operation. It is a one-story, brick, eight classroom building with an adjoining gymnasium. There are 115 students enrolled for the 2001-2002 school year. Also on the parish grounds is a building that formerly served as the convent used by the Sisters of the Most Precious Blood from Ruma, IL. The Sisters no longer serve the parish and in 1996 it was named the Ruma Center in their honor for 103 years of dedicated service. Currently it houses the Parish Office, and is used by the school for Art and Science classes, by the Parish Quilters, and by the Parish Council, School Board, and etc. for meetings. The church is what it is today because of the enthusiasm, dedication and faithfulness of those early settlers to Kelso, MO.

St. Denis Catholic Church

The heritage of St. Denis Parish Church consists of settlers who came from Alsace-Lorraine due to religious turmoil and persecution. They came down the Ohio by steamboat to Cairo and then came up the Mississippi River where they settled at Texas Bend; about six miles northeast of Charleston. There were four families, Glaus, Pfefferkorn, Martin and Bisher. There were some Catholic families living in this settlement known as the "Americans" – Kentuckians from Bardstown: Hunters, Spaldings, Deslisles and some Germans. A small church was built there, the land there at that time being in Scott County. These immigrants later moved on to the lowlands of Benton and in 1843 erected a small log cabin and dedicated it to the Mother of God as St. Marys Church. The parish entirely disappeared in 1850. The records of the Vincentian Fathers of Cape Girardeau show baptisms, marriages, confirmations during this period being held in peoples' homes in and around Benton. Later when the church of St. Lawrence was started at New Hamburg, they were members there.

St. Denis Parish was established in 1904 through the generosity of Mr. and Mrs. Denis Diebold and their son, Frank. Denis passed away in 1899 and in his will expressed a wish that $1,000 of his estate be used to construct a Catholic Church in Benton, to be built within a five year period. In early 1904, his son, Frank, decided to donate six acres of land for the church. The construction of a combined church and school was completed in late 1904 through the dedication, hard work and many generous donations of the people of this new parish.

Father Bernard Schathoelter was the priest assigned to the new parish. The first mass was on Christmas Day 1904, at which time the church was dedicated to God under the patronage of St. Dionysius (Denis) in memory of Denis Diebold. In 1904 the school was started with an enrollment of 15 pupils, with Barbara Schumacher as the first teacher and choir director. Shortly after this, the priest's rectory was built. In 1909 the Sisters of St. Francis of Mary Immaculate of Joliet, IL began teaching in the school and a convent was constructed for them. The parish was fast growing and in 1909 the Church was cut in half and a new section was built between the two old sections to enlarge the church. On Jan. 30, 1911 a student at St. Denis, Emma Essner, was the first candidate for the Sisterhood. The first eighth grade class graduated from St. Denis in May 1917. With an ever increasing enrollment, it was necessary to add an addition to the school in 1922. In 1923 electricity was installed in the parish buildings. June 7, 1931 was another proud day for the parish, as the first young man from the parish Father Joseph LeGrand was ordained to the priesthood. He celebrated his first solemn Mass at St. Denis Church followed by a parish celebration in his honor.

As St. Denis continued to grow, the need for a new church was soon being discussed. On Jan. 2, 1940 this need became a necessity as the school and the church were destroyed by fire. On Oct. 9, 1940 a beautiful new red brick school building with four classrooms was completed. The basement of the school was to serve as the church until a new one could be built. Once again, due to the dedication and hard work of the parishioners, enough funds were raised to construct a new church, which was dedicated on Nov. 21, 1954.

In 1985, due to the crowded school conditions a Parish Center was planned. Construction began in 1988, it consisted of a gymnasium, a kitchen, additional classrooms, a teacher's lounge and an office. On Feb. 26, 1989 the proud family of St. Denis parishioners attended the dedication. By 1991 the church was in need of a facelift and again with the help of many parishioners, the inside of the church was redone.

Father Normand Varone is the present pastor of the parish. Through a strong faith and lots of determination, St. Denis Parish has grown from a small group of 31 families to the present 300 families, and the school from an enrollment of 15 pupils to the present 89 pupils.

All under the watchful eyes of God.

St. Denis Catholic Church, Benton, Missouri.

St. Denis School.

St. Francis Xavier Parish

St. Francis Xavier Parish was officially established in 1892 but its beginnings date back to 1885 when Father Joseph Connelly of New Madrid gathered about ten Catholics together in the home of Frank Heisler and celebrated the first Mass in Sikeston. The small group met about once a month there or in other private homes for Mass. In 1887, plans were drawn for the first Catholic Church and Mr. Heisler was commissioned to erect it. Exactly one year later, when only some interior work remained, a cyclone ripped through Sikeston and the new church was demolished.

From 1888 through 1891, the parish was served by a priest from Charleston or Poplar Bluff. Then the old Methodist Church, which stood on the corner of Front and Stoddard Streets, was purchased for $800. Frank Heisler remodeled the old church and it was dedicated to St. Francis Xavier in 1892. Still, pastors from neighboring parishes came only about once a month to celebrate Mass. In July 1905 the fledgling congregation took on new status with the appointment of Father Conrad Brockmeier as first resident pastor.

In the years since then, succeeding priests conducted expansion and building programs.

Father George Ryan opened the parochial school in 1921 with 50 pupils. Three Sisters of Mercy served as teacher. A home located behind the church building was purchased and remodeled for the first school. In 1930, under the direction of Father Thomas Woods, the large Smith House on the corner of Center and Stoddard streets, was purchased for $10,000. It was made into a school with the Sisters' Convent upstairs. This building sufficed until construction of a new three-story brick building was begun in 1950 under the leadership of Monsignor John O'Neill. It was a modern structure and the first eighth grade class graduated from it on May 27, 1951. Cost of the new school in 1951 was $180,000. The school was closed in June 1970 because of a shortage of Sisters to teach. When it closed there were only 68 pupils with a staff of two.

Students began requesting that the school be reopened as early as 1985. On Aug. 25, 1987 the BIG DAY arrived! St. Francis Xavier Catholic School reopened with 42 students in K-2. Sister Agnes Therese Aydt, S.S.N.D. served as principal. The faculty were all lay teachers. One grade was added each year and as more space was needed, the Sisters' Convent was made into classrooms. At present, the school contains K-8 and it also has a pre-school program. At this time, the enrollment is 186 students. Mrs. Susan Long is the principal at the present time. There is a faculty of 15 lay teachers and one religious Sister.

Father John O'Neill (later to be named Monsignor) had a new church built and opening services were held July 31, 1938. The church was solid brick with asphalt tile covering the floor. The ceiling interior was criss-crossed in Old English woodwork. The seating capacity was 350 where as the old church seated but 110. Cost of construction was $24,500.

Father Amel Shibley saw to the construction of a Parish Center and it was dedicated on March 1, 1992. The building consists of a gymnasium, a large meeting room, a state of the art kitchen, three offices and several storage areas.

The Parish is blessed with a number of active organizations. All the ladies of the parish belong to the Altar Society. An organization for men, the Knights of Columbus Council No. 3151, is most active and does charitable works for both the church and the community. Likewise, the ladies' Daughters of Isabella Circle #768 helps the school, church and community in various ways. The Legion of Mary is devoted to spiritual works within the church. There are prayer groups and Bible study groups which meet at different times.

From humble origins, the church family has grown to about 1,500 members. Currently, under the direction of Father Stephen Schneider, adjoining property has been purchased for possible expansion. The Church celebrated its Centennial Year in 1992-93. Under the protection of St. Francis Xavier, the patron of the missions, to whom the church was dedicated in 1892, the congregation hopes to continue to grow in the years to come.

St. Lawrence Church

What an impressive and inspirational sight to see as you come into the small town of New Hamburg, MO – the monumental stone church of St. Lawrence Parish. It is truly a magnificent testimony to the hard work and dedication of parishioners past and present.

St. Lawrence Church was started in 1838 when four families left the Alsace/Lorraine area of Europe because of religious persecution. These included the Louis Pfefferkorn, John Glaus, John Martin, and Martin Bisher (Bessour, Bessier) families. Coming over by boat, a trip that lasted forty-one days, they traveled to Ohio. Land was selling for a steep $50 per acre. They continued down the Ohio River and up the Mississippi River to Texas Bend near Charleston, MO. They finally settled in the hills around the area now called New Hamburg, MO where land sold for $1.25 per acre.

The original log church was started in 1847 when Wendolin Bucher donated three acres for a church to be built. The church was named after his son, Lawrence.

The new stone church was started in 1859 and built without an architect. The designer was a school teacher named Rummeli who remembered the dimensions of the mother church in Schirrhein, Germany. Every family was required to donate $5.00, deliver eight wagon loads of stone, or take off every tenth day and work on building the church.

The community was attacked during the Civil War by Confederate General Jeff Thompson "The Swamp Fox" and Sam Hilderbrand with his group of bushwhackers. The church was burned by Captain Nathan Bolin on May 10, 1864. Many of the records of the parish were lost at this time. Mass was still being said in the old log church when the new church was burned. The church was rebuilt and dedicated in 1869. The total cost of construction, up to this time, was $13,250. The bell tower and the front of the church were added in 1907. A major renovation of the inside of the church was done in 1994 at a cost of over $200,000.

In 1868 construction began on a two-story house for the priest. It was finished and ready for occupation in 1869. An addition of three rooms and an attic were added to the building. All the priests lived in the house until the present rectory was built in 1964/65. When the Catholic School closed in 1968, an auction was held to sell the contents of the house. The house was rented until it was torn down in 1987. It is now the site of the parish center and parking lot.

A large, two-story, brick Parish Center was built and dedicated in 1988. It consists of four meeting/class rooms, restrooms, large kitchen, hall/gym, and storage area.

The first recorded burial in the St. Lawrence Cemetery is that of Sophia Scherer who died on the fifty day of October 1847 at the age of twenty-four. Four priests of the parish are also buried in the St. Lawrence Cemetery. These include Rev. Balthasar Rachor (1891), Rev.

The present church.

Martin Scherer (1898), Rev. Walter Craig (1971), and Rev. Alois Stevens (1994).

St. Lawrence Church has been blessed with twenty-five dedicated priests who, beginning with Rev. Cajetan Zapotti who came in 1847, to our present priest, Rev. Normand G. Varone, have inspired men and women of the parish to serve God, the Father, and his Son, Jesus Christ.

These pastors along with dedicated people of the parish and God's help have made St. Lawrence Church what it is today.

The original church.

St. Paul United Methodist Church

Like all other United Methodist Churches, our roots are in the experience of the English Clergyman, John Wesley, who lived in the 1700s. Wesley was "methodical" in his search to live a proper Christian life, but he lacked the inner feeling of being assured of God's love until at an evangelical meeting, he felt his heart "strangely warmed" and was on fire with the commitment to Christ.

The movement spread rapidly onto the new American continent. Methodist circuit riders, on horseback, preached the "Good News" to the new American settlers in the West. Throughout the nineteenth century, the Methodist Church continued to grow by leaps and bounds.

It was in the 1790s that a few settlers began to drift into the vicinity and in 1802, when it was considered likely that the United States would purchase the Louisiana territory, a trading post was established by Thomas W. Waters and Robert Hall, known as Tywappity. In July 1834 the town of Commerce was incorporated, having been laid out as a town in 1823 on the land which was originally granted by Thomas W. Waters.

The Methodist Church was established in Commerce in 1854 with the services being held in a brick structure. The present structure was built in the year 1889.

St. Paul United Methodist Church is located just two blocks from and facing the Mississippi River in the oldest town of Scott County and one of the oldest towns in the state. On any given day one can stand in the front door of the church and watch the tugs plying their trade on the mighty river.

St. Paul United Methodist Church, Washington and Cape Girardeau Streets, Commerce, Missouri

Tanner Street Church of God

In May 1941, the cornerstone for the Tanner Street Church of God was laid. The original building, consisting primarily of an auditorium, was erected on a lot facing Tanner Street at Taylor and opposite the old Sikeston High School. This was completed under the leadership of Rev. O. C. Lewis. He was the pastor for two years with a Sunday School enrollment of 30 to 65 persons.

Rev. H. McDonough was called as the first full time pastor in 1943. The Sunday School attendance increased to an average of 100.

In 1946, Rev. Vernon and Mrs. Guttenfelder began the first of two 12-year tenures as pastor of the church with an increase in Sunday School attendance above 200. The Sunday School annex and recreational fellowship building was added during this time. The Sanctuary was enlarged by an addition of a side chapel.

Rev. E. D. Johnson served the church as pastor from 1957 to 1961.

In June of 1961, Rev. Oral Withrow and family assumed the pastorate through 1966. During these years, the church completed a construction program which doubled the size of its facilities. The pulpit was moved to the north end of the sanctuary and the entrance moved to the southeast corner of the narthex.

Rev. and Mrs. Guttenfelder returned to Sikeston in 1966 and stayed until 1978. The Children's sanctuary was constructed and continues to provide a strong ministry for the elementary ages.

Rev. Forrest Robinson and his wife, Peggy, accepted the ministerial leadership of the church in 1979. Under his leadership the sanctuary was again remodeled and expanded. The Christian Educational Building was expanded and renovated. Sunday School enrollment increased to 600.

Rev. Robinson initiated the Little League Basketball program in 1979. He also started the Junior High Church Basketball League in Sikeston.

During his eleven years of ministry at Tanner Street, the church grew to become one of the largest and most active churches in the area, a position it continues to enjoy today.

Rev. Carl Addison assumed the position of Senior Pastor in August, 1990. Under Rev. Addison's leadership, a second Sunday morning service was added (8:15 a.m.) and Sunday evenings are now totally dedicated to prayer for the church, the community, our nation and world concerns. The Stafford Center, a multi-purpose "Family Life Center" and the newest addition to Tanner Street, was constructed during the late 1990's. *Submitted by Charlotte Johnson*

WESLEY UNITED METHODIST CHURCH

The Wesley United Methodist Church was established in 1956 as a satellite from the First United Methodist Church here in Sikeston, MO. The former Christian Church building at the corner of Trotter Street and South New Madrid Street was purchased by the First United Methodist Church to serve as the second church. The first pastor of the 48-member congregation was Rev. Chester Pullium.

The congregation moved to the American Legion Hall on South Kingshighway and then to a building at the Airport School which has since been razed.

The original section of the present building at Pine Street and Ables Road was started in 1962 and completed in 1963 at a cost of $75,000. Members and friends of the First United Methodist Church contributed about half of the original cost of the building.

Mr. L. M. Stanley and Mr. Robert Dempster, members of the First United Methodist Church, served temporarily on the Board of Trustees and as head of the liaison committee during completion of the new building. Other members of that committee were Dr. M. C. Mill, Dr. Leo Bruce, Mr. George Hale Jr., Mr. J. E. Harper and Mr. E. M. Allen.

The first service was held in the new building on Aug. 4, 1963. Prior to the service, the key to the front door was auctioned off. The family making the highest bid was given the honor and privilege of opening the doors of the new church and being the first to enter. Mr. and Mrs. John Houchin and family received that honor with their bid of $20.00. The key became their reminder of their part in that historical day in the life of Wesley Methodist Church.

A small, private service took place before the building was finished. Late in the afternoon of May 9, 1963 after the workers had left for the day, Dorothy and Clarence Templeton, sister and brother, and Peggie Murdock, cousin to the Templetons, were baptized and confirmed.

Our building may be built of brick and mortar, but "the church" is held together with love. The congregation is much more than a building full of people, they are a true family that holds you fast in a crisis and rejoices with you in triumph. They are a family waiting to expand and include the next person that comes through the doors.

In 1966, under the pastorate of Rev. J. Harmon Holt, the addition which now houses the office, nursery, and fellowship hall was built. The kitchen was added in 1974 in memory of Mrs. Beatrice Dempster. In 1986, the addition of the Family Life Center was started. Members of the congregation completed the majority of the interior of this addition, which includes an official size basketball court and classrooms.

The Family Life Center is now the center for any number of events, not the least of which are Pancake Day, Corn Beef and Cabbage Dinner, Ham and Bean Supper and the Salad Luncheon. All these dinners are sponsored by either the United Methodist Women or United Methodist Men. The Family Life Center has been well used over the years. There have been numerous church dinners, Boy Scout Courts of Honor, Sunday School Breakfasts and Rallies, Festival of Sharing Ingathering, and work for the Billy Graham Celebration 2000.

The Wesley United Methodist Congregation is well known for its good food and great fellowship. Everyone is welcome to join us for good food prepared by caring hands, and soul food presented by a caring congregation. These pastors along with dedicated lay persons and God's Spirit have made Wesley United Methodist Church what it is today. They are: Rev. Chester Pulliam, Rev. J. A. Wilson, Rev. John O. Enson, Rev. E. V. William, Rev. George Tait, Rev. Ron Bollinger, Rev. Bill Blackard, Rev. Ray Earls, Rev. Harmon Holt, Rev. Harold Norton, Rev. James Holt, Rev. Jim Phifer, Rev. Jerry Statler, Rev. Don Miller, Rev. Peter M. Soens, Rev. Rick White, Rev Mike Walters, Rev. Jerry Reynolds, Rev. Charles Moreland, Rev. Jay Ketsenburg and Rev. Rick Lasley.

The original church, the former Christian Church building.

Junior Band of Chaffee, Missouri, April 1936. Seated, left to right: Mary Blispinghoff, Dwain Dean, Richard Cookley, Rosa Lee Hobbs, and Coletta Slinkard. Standing: Tommy Lett, "B. Tight" Talley, Fred Cheek, Fred Blispinghoff, unknown, George Green, Bob Rosenquist, and Billy Mac Cress. (Photo courtesy of Tom Lett)

Morley High School Senior class, April 1941, on a one-day picnic to Arcadia. Kneeling in front: Velma Elsnerman and Mary Faye Dennis. Second row: Ruth Orr (leg up), Betty Watson, Jason Bearlslie, Bill Dennis, Margie Cannon, Margilee Andrews, and Edna Driver. Back row: James Hatley, Cletus Todt, Norma Jean Bryant, Jim Stowe, and E.G. Andrews. (Absent seniors: Eathel Vaughn and Hank May. Hank went into the Navy.) (Photo courtesy of Tom Lett)

Oran, Missouri. First row: Clara Stehn, Helen Driskell, Bertha Vogel, unknown, Helen Basel, and Kathleen Driskell. 2nd row: Alpha Lyons, Helen Oliver, Nora Shanks, Evelyn Miller, Lois Westcott?, Artinca Miller, Lora McCord, and Helen Bowman. 3rd row: Miss Spencer, Alice Driskell, unknown, Joe Glenn?, unknown Simpson, George Baxter Driskill, Earl Watkins, Earl Crater, and unknown teacher. (Photo courtesy of Tom Lett)

CHAFFEE NURSING CENTER

On Nov. 7, 1987 Richard Montgomery, Americare Properties, Inc. of Sikeston, MO, opened Chaffee Nursing Center located in Chaffee, MO at the north end of town on Highway 77. The facility opened with 18 skilled beds and 10 residential beds. This grand opening brought the total number of facilities for Americare Properties, Inc. to 15 skilled nursing facilities and 5 residential care facilities.

Chaffee Nursing Center provided skilled nursing services for the community. At its opening the facility provided a physician on call 24 hours daily. The nutritional care was directed by a dietitian. Other original services offered were a success oriented activity program for the residents, therapies to meet the needs of the patients and a Social Service Designee to work with the residents and families. All of these services were included in a new facility that was built to accommodate those who required skilled or resident nursing care.

Chaffee Nursing Center expanded its facility in 1988 with an addition increasing it to a 60-bed facility. The 18 residential care beds were converted to skilled nursing care beds at that time. Additional staff was hired to accom-

modate the expansion. In 1990 the facility expanded again. The addition of 11 more skilled nursing beds brought the capacity to 71 skilled nursing beds. It was at this time the facility received notification and approval that 10 beds were certified to care for patients with Medicare coverage. In 2000 and 2001 Chaffee Nursing Center was remodeled. New plans were drawn and implemented to update the interior, add an exterior storage and maintenance building, re-landscape the exterior grounds adding new fencing, a walking path, concrete patio furniture, and a sheltered entry for the south entry way. On Sept. 1, 2001, the facility received notification of approval from a previous request to certify all 71 beds as Medicare eligible.

The goal of Chaffee Nursing Center is to meet the medical, social, spiritual and emotional needs of our residents, yet consider significant individuals such as family members, in the lives of those entrusted to our caregivers. This facility's focus is to provide the highest level of care to ensure that each resident reaches their optimal level of health. Currently, Chaffee Nursing Center's onsite services include: licensed nursing care 24 hours daily; doctors of

Chaffee Nursing Center.

podiatry and psychiatry; a physician on call 24 hours daily; resident and family participation in the plan of care of the resident; rehabilitation services including physical, occupational and speech therapist; activities and social services; dietitian directed nutritional care; and spiritual care and services.

Chaffee Nursing Center has trained many employees over the years for jobs in the nursing field. The facility currently employs 60 people. Chaffee Nursing Center is known as one of the major employees in the town of Chaffee and is proud to be able to support its community.

FIRST NATIONAL BANK

When it comes right down to it, banking comes right down to service. At The First National Bank, our customers tell us that we go out of the way for them. But it's not out of the way for us. It's simply how we do business, and how we make our customers feel like they belong. If you'd like to experience The First National Bank approach to service, stop by."

Troy L. Wilson
- Troy Wilson, CEO

The First National Bank was originally chartered in 1903. Controlling interest in the bank was purchased in 1958 by Joel Mont-

gomery, Sr., a native of Sikeston, Missouri. Over the years, Mr. Montgomery's business interests have been in real estate development, as well as banking. Though now retired, the bank is still owned and managed by the Montgomery family.

As the largest privately owned bank in the State of Missouri our of 430, the bank has over $568 million in assets.

Since 1990, the bank has expanded throughout Southeast Missouri and into the St. Louis region. The First National Bank locations now include Cape Girardeau, Caruthersville, Chaffee, Jackson, Miner and Sikeston. In addition to the six Southeast Missouri branches, The

First National Bank has Financial service centers throughout the St. Louis region. Known as Montgomery First National Bank, these brnahces include Affton, Bridgeton, Chesterfield, Crestwood, St. Louis Hills and South County.

A community bank by tradition and design, The First National Bank branches are staffed with 189 individuals from the local community who are actively involved in local interest. Also, it is our unique style to provide quality customer service and noticeable friendliness to all our customers while at the same time embracing technological advances in banking-online banking, telebanc, etc.

THE FIRST NATIONAL BANK
EXPECTATIONS EXCEEDED *everyday*

1-800-455-2275
www.tfnb.com

Sikeston
One First National
Plaza
(573) 471-2275

Miner
2201 E. Malone
(573) 472-3447

First State Bank and Trust Co., Inc. of Sikeston

First State Bank and Trust Company, Inc. 750 South Main, Sikeston, Missouri. (573) 472-2424.

CRAFTMASTERS' KIDSMART

Founded by Nancy J. Craft July 1, 1988, Craftmasters' KidSMART occupies a 3,600 sq. ft. store in historic downtown Sikeston, Missouri. Customers marvel at how complete the business is with its extensive and diverse inventory of educational materials and supplies.

Children's literature, teacher's reproducible books, bulletin board sets, posters/charts, workbooks, toys, puzzles, games, software, music, and inspirational materials are among the variety of exciting products Craftmasters offers.

From their very beginning, Craftmasters' KidSMART has produced a newsletter to help communicate with its growing list of regular customers. Nancy Craft's husband Roger, heads the production of this full color, nationally recognized quarterly newsletter/magazine. It is read by an estimated 250,000 individuals with each seasonal edition.

"Educational News Quarterly" is published along with its sister publication, "Inspirational

Nancy J. Craft

News" and both are syndicated through a network of educational retailers nationwide.

Early in 2001, Craftmasters purchased an additional 10,000 sq. ft. building for warehousing, order processing and shipping/receiving. This building is also home to the graphic design, product ware-housing, and mailing/distribution departments, accounting, and general offices.

Craftmasters' KidSMART has been faithfully serving area parents, teachers and students for many years and they look forward to many "happy customers" for years to come!

Grand Opening Ribbon Cutting August 1, 1988. Front Row (L-R): Steve Forbis, Debbie Craft, Nancy Craft (owner, Craftmasters), Tara Phillips, Luke Phillips, Beverly Phillips, Vicki Rodgers, Cleda Curtis, Judy Beggs, Linda Mayfield; Second Row (L-R): Bob Blankenship, Mary Doggett, Roger T. Craft, R. Dennis Neal, Roger E. Craft, Glenna Shy, Jerry Shy, Julianna Gemeinhardt, Celeste Gemeinhardt, Margaret Waltrip, Julie Volk, Viola Statler and Hawkie Moore.

SEMO PORT

The Southeast Missouri Regional Port Authority (Semo Port) was formed in 1975 by Scott County and Cape Girardeau County under Missouri law. A nine-member board governs the port authority. Each county appoints four board members and a ninth member's position alternates between the two counties.

In the late 1970s, land was leased and a small dock was built on the Mississippi River, downstream of dike 47.9. Plans were made for a larger development including a slackwater harbor, and the Corps of Engineers confirmed the need in a 1985 study. To fund the project, local voters (by over 70%) passed a quarter-cent sales tax which began in 1986 and sunset in 1990. It generated $7.3 million for capital improvements at Semo Port. These local funds served as match for various Federal and State program grants, including construction of the slackwater harbor by the Corps of Engineers. The U. S. Department of Commerce provided partial funding for the general cargo dock, an access road (which is now Missouri Route K), and a connection to Scott City's water system.

The harbor and its industrial area are located south of Cape Girardeau, MO at Mile 48 on the Upper Mississippi River (above Cairo, IL). The county line between Scott County and Cape Girardeau County runs through the industrial area and the harbor. The mailing address is Scott City, MO. The railroad station name is Semo Port, MO.

The first land leases were signed in 1990. Girardeau Stevedores and Contractors, Inc., operates the Port's public terminal and general cargo dock. Midwest AgriChemico operates a fertilizer distribution terminal and grain elevator.

In 1994, the Semo Port Railroad, Inc. (SE) was formed and given approval by the Interstate Commerce Commission to operate as a common carrier switching railroad. The SE purchased from Union Pacific Railroad the six miles of track which extended from Capedeau Junction, MO (east of Scott City) to Cape Girardeau, MO. In addition to the UP, the SE connects with the Burlington Northern Santa Fe Railway (BNSF) in Cape Girardeau. A new one-mile track was built from the existing trackage into the harbor industrial area.

In 1994-1998, several projects in the harbor industrial area were completed with another USDOC grant; railroad trackage, roads, sanitary sewers, water lines, and a dock area for use during extreme flooding. Ameren UE extended additional electric service and a natural gas line.

The extension of Route AB from Interstate 55 directly to the harbor area was completed in 1997 by the Missouri Department of Transportation. Over one mile of it was built on a fill twenty feet in height, for flood protection. The same year saw the opening of a new grain elevator by Consolidated Grain & Barge and a hardwood chip mill by Missouri Fibre Corporation. In 1998, Riverport Terminals opened a grain and food products bagging plant.

By 1998, local taxpayer investment of $7.3 million had grown to over $17 million of assets through various grant programs. Moreover, private investment in the businesses at the Port had grown to $21 million, with room for more new industries in the future.

History & Families

SCOTT COUNTY, MISSOURI
ESTABLISHED 1822

1906 Sanders family reunion at the home of
Fillmore Sanders near Commerce, MO

Family Histories

ABLES – Lawrence Washington Ables was born Dec. 22, 1886 in Ballard County, KY, the son of Silas Washington and Mary Ann Ables. He married Etta Pearl Moore on Dec. 22, 1906 in Belmont, KY. In 1913, he moved his wife and three daughters, Pansy, Norene and Mildred, in their wagon with their cow tied behind across the Mississippi river on a ferry to Oran, MO. While living in Oran, he worked as an engineer for the Scott County Milling Company. In 1916, he moved his family to Sikeston, where he worked as an engineer at the City Ice Plant.

Lawrence W. Ables (sitting) with others working on the streets

During these years, four more children were born, two sons, Cline and Clennis, and two more daughters, Alma Gail and Lawrencetta. They were active members of the First Baptist Church and Mrs. Ables taught Sunday school there for many years.

When he started as Street Commissioner, Sikeston had a population of 3,500 people, one paved street, and no curbs or running water. By 1952, this had increased from 1-1/2 miles of paved streets to about 29 miles of paved and 97 miles of un-surfaced streets. In 1936, he was temporarily placed as the head of a 75-man WPA crew. Under his supervision, most of the present concrete streets were built. Under his supervision, the two barns that housed all the City street equipment were built.

Lawrence W. and Etta Pearl Ables

Mr. and Mrs. Ables celebrated their Golden Anniversary in 1956. He retired as Street Commissioner in 1957 and was honored with a surprise recognition dinner and given tribute by many of the city officials as well as members of the street department. They expressed their appreciation for his faithful service as a city employee as well as being a good citizen.

Mr. Ables died July 1, 1977 at the age of 90. Mrs. Ables died June 21, 1978 at the age of 92. Both are buried in Sikeston Memorial Park Cemetery. They were survived by six of their children, 19 grandchildren and a number of great-grandchildren.

ADAMS-PORTER – From 1939 to 2000, on a light post in the front yard at 342 Missouri Street in Benton, MO, hung the sign, "THE HESS POR-

TERS." Hess Porter (b. Aug. 25, 1913, d. Feb. 28, 2002) and Margaret Adams Porter (b. April 14, 1917) were married Nov. 15, 1939 and moved into this house they had built. Hess was employed as deputy treasurer in the office of then Scott County Treasurer, Emil Steck. In 1942 Hess was elected Treasurer of Scott County and remained in that position until his retirement in 1982. He served as Mayor of Benton for many years. Margaret worked in the Scott County Court House, Ray Lucas law office and in 1956 for then superintendent of Benton High School, Roy C. Hayes, continuing in that position at Kelly High School (Reorganized School District R-IV) until retiring in 1983.

Hess and Margaret are long remembered for their devotion to the youth in Epworth League and MYF at Benton Methodist Church. During their years of leadership, the youth designed, built, and furnished a chapel in the basement of the church for their own use. From this group, Willard Addison Spencer dedicated his heart and life to serving God as a full time minister in the United Methodist Church. "Bill" is the son of Addison and Betty Peal Spencer, and grandson of Probate Judge and Mrs. O. L. Spencer of Benton, MO.

Margaret Adams was born in Benton, MO to Ben Adams (b. March 6, 1892, d. June 20, 1979) and Norma Tirmenstein (b. Nov. 7, 1892, d. Oct. 27, 1986). Ben will be remembered as Benton's rural mail carrier and made his early deliveries by horse and buggy. Norma was a homemaker. Her sister, Leona Tirmenstein (b. Dec. 27, 1902, d. May 17, 1985) spent 29 years in the Benton Post Office, 11 years as a postal clerk and 18 years as postmaster. She retired from that position on Dec. 29, 1972.

Hess Porter was born in Morley, MO to W. C. Porter Sr. (b. 1887, d. 1963) and Floy Randol Porter (b. 1895, d. 1991). The family moved to Commerce in 1917 where they operated a café and gas station. In 1927 they moved to Benton and operated a restaurant and dance hall across from the Scott County Court House in the Ristig building, a gathering place for many teenagers learning the newest dance craze, the "Jitterbug."

Hess and Margaret are the parents of two children, William David Porter of Memphis, TN and Peggy Ann James of Norman, OK, and grandson Shannon Porter and a great-grandson, Devon Porter.

ADCOCK – John Anderson Adcock was born at Dahlgren, IL, near Mount Vernon, in Hamilton County. He was born July 26, 1873 and died Aug. 19, 1960 in Sikeston, MO. His parents were Isaac Franklin Adcock and Matilda Cross Adcock. His family came to Missouri in the late 1800s. They settled around the Portageville area. There he met and married Virgie Bowen. They had one daughter, Jannie Marie Adcock, born Feb. 20, 1900. Virgie died when Jannie was a small child. John moved back home so his mother could help raise his daughter. Jannie married Albert Gardner, and she died Dec. 23, 1992.

John later met his second wife Fanny Elizabeth Harrelson and married her Sept. 28, 1909 in Portageville, MO. Lizzie, as she was called, had presumably moved from Kentucky to Missouri. Her parents were James Harrelson and Maggie Marie Couch. Lizzie was born Oct. 19, 1890 and died Oct. 10, 1970 in Sikeston, MO.

John and Lizzie started their life in Portageville. He worked many different jobs to feed his family. His father was a carpenter and a farmer, so John learned to do both. He, with his brother Ira, built a lot of buildings in Portageville during this period of time. He was the town Marshall at one time, a deliveryman with his team of horses and even ran

a sawmill for a while. He moved to Scott County about 1930 to 1932 where he farmed in the summer and worked as a carpenter in the winter. John and Lizzie had eight children. They were in birth order:

Paul Mitchell Adcock who was born Aug. 20, 1910 and died May 11, 1911;

Fannie Maillian Adcock who was born Sept. 4, 1911, married Chester Stafford, and lived in Sikeston until her death on Nov. 25, 1998;

Myra Aliene Adcock who was born March 30, 1913, married Richard Hill, and also lived in Sikeston, until her death on Jan. 13, 1994;

J. D. Adcock who was born April 25, 1915 and died Dec. 30, 1916;

John A. Adcock Family. Standing: James Adcock, Marielian A. Stafford, Aliene A. Hill, and William Adcock. Seated from left: Beatrice A. Stanfill, Lizzie Adcock, John A. Adcock Sr., and John A. Adcock Jr.

James Franklin Adcock who was born March 6, 1917, married Frances Ivadelle Pulley, and eventually moved to Ohio, where he presently resides;

Nannie Beatrice Adcock who was born Nov. 11, 1920, and married Jesse Bert Stanfill, after having traveled over the United States for many years for Bert's job, they have retired in Kennett;

William Henry Adcock who was born May 4, 1923 and married Gearldean Hicks, they moved from Sikeston to Illinois.

John and Lizzie lived and raised their family in Scott County and both died in Sikeston, MO. They are buried in the De Lisle Cemetery in Portageville. *Submitted by Gary Adcock*

ADCOCK – William Henry Adcock was born at Portageville, MO on May 4, 1923. His parents were John Anderson Adcock and Fanny Elizabeth "Lizzie" Harrelson Adcock. His paternal Grandparents were Isaac Franklin Adcock and Matilda Cross Adcock. His maternal grandparents were James Harrelson and Maggie Marie Couch. The family moved to Scott County in about 1930-32. Their Dad was a farmer during growing season and a carpenter in the winter months. The family lived on several different farms over the years so the children attended different schools near their home.

From left: John H. Adcock, Lola Adcock, Gary Adcock, and William Adcock.

William had four brothers and three sisters. (See history of John Anderson Adcock)

William married Lola Mae Rettig on Sept. 5, 1944 at Blytheville, AR. He was 21 years old but Lola was only 17. Arkansas did not a waiting period so the couple eloped and were married there without her parent's permission.

Lola was born June 30, 1927 in rural Scott County. Her parents were Otto William Rettig and Bertha Caroline Wagoner Rettig. Her paternal grandparents were Fred Joseph Rettig and Anna Caroline Kreig Rettig. Her maternal grandparents were Allerson Alexander Wagoner and Sarah Frances Hamblin Wagoner. Lola attended Chaney Grade School and Blodgett High School.

Lola had three brothers and five sisters. (See history of Otto William Rettig)

William and Lola started their married life in Sikeston, MO. His first job was at the Sikeston Cotton Oil Mill earning 40 cents per hour and working seven days a week. As time passed he worked different places but spent 17 years working for Coca-Cola Bottling Co. in Sikeston. Lola worked 29 years as a seamstress. Seventeen years of this was working in the alteration department for Famous-Barr. She loved music and painting. Her favorite medium is oil.

William and Lola have two sons: John Henry Adcock was born Dec. 7, 1945. He attended Sikeston Grade and High School. He enlisted in the Army in 1966 to 1969. He spent one year in Vietnam. He married Brenda Kay Leyerle on June 7, 1969. They have two sons, John Jason and Mark Aaron Adcock. They live in Illinois.

Gary Lynn Adcock was born Aug. 22, 1949 at Missouri Delta Hospital. He attended Sikeston Grade and High School. He also attended Belleville Area College in Illinois and Southeast Missouri State College at Cape Girardeau. He first married Elizabeth Kay Vetter and they have one child, Kimberley Ann Adcock Andracsek. He is presently married to Cheryl Elaine Hicks Heller Adcock. Gary is a certified Real Estate Appraiser and lives in Cape Girardeau, MO.

William and Lola moved to Illinois in 1970. William worked for Nehi Bottling Company in Belleville, IL. Lola started working for Famous-Barr until she retired in 1990. William was already retired so they moved back to Sikeston where they now reside. *Submitted by John H. Adcock*

ANCELL – Edward Ancell was the first to arrive in America in about 1768. He married Sarah Catterton who was born in Calvert County, MD. They had ten children: Nancy, Henry, Robert, Edward, William, Michael, James, Elizabeth, Mary and John.

Henry Clay Ancell who was the second child of Edward Ancell married Nancy Beazley in Orange County, VA on Dec. 28, 1901. Several years after their marriage probably around 1810, Henry and Nancy moved their family in covered wagons to Todd County, KY. Henry worked as a brick mason until his death in about 1816. Henry and Nancy had seven children: Washington, Thornton, Pascal, Harriet, John, James and Henry.

In 1828, Nancy (Beazley) Ancell and her children moved to Scott County, MO near Kelso. Washington Catterton Ancell, her oldest son, was born on Nov. 21, 1803. On Nov. 19, 1929 he married Elizabeth Whitelaw. Elizabeth's grandfather James Beazley served for three years with the 2nd Virginia Regiment during the Revolutionary War. He participated in the battles of Brandywine and Germantown and was at Valley Forge. He later joined the Virginia Militia and participated in the Battle of Yorktown.

Washington and Elizabeth had five girls: Mary, Gabrielle, Minerva, Geneivieve and Josephine

and, twin boys Washington Durrett and Henry Clay who were born in 1842. Washington C. died in March of 1862 in Tiptionville, TN during the final days of the battle for Island Number 10.

The twin boys enlisted in the 8th Missouri Confederate Calvary, Company E. They participated in all of the major battles fought in Missouri during Price's 1864 Expedition. Washington D. was taken prisoner at Madison County, KS in October 1864 and served the remainder of the war in various prisoner of war camps. He was released in June of 1865 at Point Lookout, MD. When he returned to Scott County his mother had been forced to sell all of their land and possessions.

On Jan. 3, 1869, Washington D. married Isabelle Susan Goddard. They had two children who survived, Albert Clay, born Oct. 22, 1869, and Ralph Walter, born March 27, 1878. Isabelle died Jan. 26, 1897 and Washington on April 14, 1899. Ralph died on March 28, 1903 without any children.

Albert Clay married Anna Marie Moore on Nov. 20, 1895. They had eight children: Ralph, Clyta, Lynn and Leon (twins), Fred, Lillian, Harold Washington and Walter. Albert died on Oct. 19, 1912 and Anna supported her family by teaching at various one-room schools in Scott County. In 1920 she moved to Sikeston with her children and lived there until her death on Nov. 27, 1939. Her oldest son Ralph Leslie Ancell married Mary Slaten and had a son, Albert Clay, who married Kay Margraf on Nov. 25, 1966.

Harold Washington married Mary Dover on Oct. 8, 1942. He served for over three years in the South Pacific with the 12th Special Service Company. He has one son, Charles Dover Ancell who married Gale Skalsky on Aug. 16, 1969, and had a daughter Patricia Ann Bogue.

ANDERSON – Henry Orson Anderson was born Sept. 4, 1881 at Golconda, Pope County, IL, died Oct. 17, 1932, the son of George Washington Anderson and Eliza Bagley. He married Carrie Pinetta Bonnell born Jan. 14, 1884 in Golconda, Pope County, IL, died Feb. 1, 1957, daughter of Samuel and Caroline Stevenson Anderson.

To this union, these children were born: Opal Lois m. Lloyd R. Wentzell, b. Oct. 11, 1906, d. Oct, 11, 1998; Adrian J. Anderson m. Imogene, b. March 17, 1907; Bessie B. m. Joseph E. Lewis, b. April 3, 1909, d. Oct. 1, 1985; Glenn Ward Anderson m. Mildred Jones, died and buried in the Lutesville Cemetery; and Violetta m. Ralph McGee, b. Dec. 16, 1911 (?).

Henry was a farmer and owned and operated a thrashing machine. He and Carrie lived south of Sikeston until his death at a railroad crossing west of the farm by a Frisco Train. Carrie, enjoyed gardening both flowers and vegetables, she later had a house built at 324 Gladys Street, Sikeston, where she lived until her death. H. O. and Carrie are buried in the Garden of Memories Cemetery.

ALLEN – Pamela S. Hess Allen, daughter of Charles and Mary Hess was born on Dec. 14, 1970 on Linus Dirnberger, her maternal grandfather's, 65th birthday. She was raised on land west of Kelso, MO. As a toddler, she would visit her grandparents in New Hamburg. Her grandpa, Linus, would find some reason for them to take a walk and they would wind up at the store, where he would by her a candy bar and make sure it was eaten before they could get back to her brothers. Pam had his freckles and he even bought her overalls like his. Pam was seven when he died.

Pam spent a few days during some of the summers with her grandmother, Regina. Each morning, they would attend church and then work in

the flower gardens. Some days, Pam and her grandmother would take big, gorgeous bouquets of flowers to fill up the altar in church.

From kindergarten trough the eighth grade, Pam attended Kelso C-7 Elementary School in the heart of New Hamburg. Most classrooms held two class-years and one teacher. There were usually 10 to 15 students to a class. Not only did the teachers look out for all of the students, but also many of the upper class students seemed to make sure that the smaller ones stayed safe.

The beginning of Pam's first year at Scott City High School, she met Twylia (Gramm) Messmer who would be a friend forever. Everyone needs someone like her. With the guidance of math tutor Avelina Lichtenegger, Pam placed second in the State of Missouri in Geometry during her junior year and received first place in Trigonometry/ Algebra II. Inspired by Avelina, Pam began tutoring after high school to students of all ages.

Pamela Sue Hess with grandfather Linus P. Dirnberger, Dec. 1975.

She attended Southeast Missouri State University in Cape Girardeau, MO and graduated with a Bachelor's Degree in Business Administration with a major in economics.

Pam met Kelly Allen during her high school years and knew right away that it was meant to be. He is the son of Mearlin and Darlene Allen of Cape Girardeau, MO. After dating for more than two years, they married on March 10, 1990. He knew he was going to be a firefighter, just like his father and his grandfather before him. Since they were not going to hire family on the City of Cape Girardeau Fire Department and Mearlin was still employed there, he volunteered for the East County Fire Protection District. Pam soon followed and realized why Kelly needed to be a firefighter.

Finally, by way of a new chief and some influence by other firefighters on the department, Kelly was hired by the City of Cape Girardeau Fire Department. They have never been disappointed; in fact, he received the "Employee of the Year" award for the years 2001. He is now both a Career and a Volunteer Firefighter.

Pam and Kelly have one daughter, Sarene S. born Sept. 29, 1997. She has her father's determination and her mother's love of learning; she should go far. The family lives in the countryside in Cape Girardeau County.

ARNOLD – Marshall Arnold was born Oct. 21, 1945 in St. Francois County, MO and died June 12, 1913. He was a lawyer, admitted to the bar in St. Francois County, Mo and came to Commerce, MO shortly after the end of the Civil War. He was elected Prosecuting Attorney of Scott County, Mo and, according to his obituary, was given credit for driving the carpetbaggers out of Scott County and vigorously prosecuting criminals in the lawless years following the Civil War. He was elected to the Missouri Legislature and later to the United States House of Representatives, where he served two terms. He was the son of Elisha Arnold and Elvina Maria Calland Arnold, of St. Francois County, MO, both of whom were born in Virginia. He served a short time in the Confederate Army near the end of the Civil War.

Marshall Arnold married Ann Elizabeth Parrott, b. Oct. 22, 1856, and d. Nov. 6, 1933. She was the daughter of James W. Parrott b. Feb. 29, 1926, d. May 13, 1864 and Mary Maria Hunter b. Sept. 10, 1836, d. May 14, 1909. James W. Parrott was the son of Woodson Parrott, who came to Missouri from Virginia. Woodson Parrott's father was William Parrott and his mother was Susannah Turner, both of Virginia.

Mary Maria Hunter Parrott was the daughter of Joseph Hunter III, b. March 15, 1801 at Louisville, KY, d. July 18, 1840. Joseph Hunter III was the son of Joseph Hunter II, b. May 1760 at Carlisle, PA, d. December 1823 in Scott County, MO, and Katherine Phillips, b. April 3, 1770 at Louisville, KY, d. Aug. 18, 1813. Joseph Hunter II was the son of Joseph Hunter I, who was born in Pennsylvania, and Mary Ann Holmes Hunter, also of Pennsylvania. Joseph Hunter was a descendant of the Scotch-Irish people who were Scots who settled in Northern Ireland, and later migrated to Pennsylvania. Joseph Hunter II served under General George Washington in the Revolutionary War, and later in the Indian Wars in 1812. The mother of Mary Maria Hunter Parrott was Elizabeth Johnson b. Sept. 3, 1810, d. Jan. 22, 1883. She was born in Syracuse, NY. Her parents moved to New Madrid, MO where he father served as sheriff and they later moved to Benton, MO.

Marshall Arnold

James M. Arnold b. Oct. 1, 1883, d. April 24, 1966, was the son of Marshall Arnold and Ann Elizabeth Parrott Arnold. He married Mary Jeanette Adams in July 1918. She was the daughter of Thomas Jefferson Adams and Annie Barbara Miller Adams. Thomas Jefferson Adams was born in 1854 and died Dec. 25, 1933. He was the son of Daniel D. Adams b. March 10, 1823, d. Jan. 8, 1894. Annie Barbara Miller Adams was born March 23, 1872 and died June 1946. She was the daughter of Jessie J. Miller b. July 17, 1834, d. Nov. 9, 1906 and Mary A. Priest Lansmon Miller who died Nov. 6, 1896. Jessie J. Miller was the son of Alexander Miller (son of John and Ellen Miller of Calvert County, MD) and Mary Elizabeth Jones also of Calvert County, MD.

James M. Arnold and Mary Jeanette Adams Arnold had three sons: Marshall Arnold, an educator, born Sept. 7, 1920, who married Dorris McKee, both of whom reside at Henderson, KY. They have three children, Marshall McKee Arnold, Martha Arnold Ward and Russell Arnold. Thomas L. Arnold, a lawyer, who practiced in Benton, MO for 45 years. He married Betty J. Ramey and they had two children, Thomas L. Arnold Jr. MD and James S. Arnold. After the death of Betty J. Ramey Arnold, Thomas L. Arnold married Joyce E. Pack Owen, a lawyer. Jacks Russell Arnold, born Oct. 10, 1932, d. March 10, 1957. He married Janice Turk and had two children, Jack R. Arnold and Jeanette Arnold.

Seven generations of this family have lived continuously in Benton, MO.

BARNES – Elisha Darden Barnes settled on a farm in Scott County, MO about 1837. He had migrated with his family from Caldwell County, KY.

His family included his wife, Mary D. "Polly" Harrison, his children: Nancy H. born March 25, 1818, Phereby A. born in 1821, Sarah Green born in 1822, Diana Y. born in 1825, Lucy B. born in 1827, Philadelphia C. born in 1829 and Caroline born in 1831. His son, Albert Harrison Barnes, was born in 1838, shortly after the family's arrival in Scott County. Migrating with Elisha Barnes' family was that of his sister, Fereby Barnes Harrison, widow of John Harrison and their children: David, Esther Aramintha, Abner B., Nancy L., John S., and James. Elisha's youngest brother, John Barnes and his family (wife Diana Harrison and children) also made the move to Scott County from western Kentucky. Elisha's brother, Edwin, had moved earlier to the Scott County area.

Elisha Darden Barnes' parents were Joseph Barnes and his wife, Sarah "Sally" Darden. Elisha was born in Southampton County, VA in 1789, the first child born to his parents. His siblings were Edwin, Bennett, Fereby, and John. Elisha's father, Joseph, was the son of James and Ann Barnes of Southampton County, VA. Sarah's parents were Elisha and Fereby Darden, also of Southampton County, VA. Sometime in the early 1790s, Joseph and Sarah Barnes moved from southern Virginia and settled briefly in what became Robertson County, TN. Court records in Robertson County, TN indicate that Joseph and Sarah were active in selling land and other real property there in the mid 1790s. Sarah probably died in Kentucky shortly after her last child's birth in 1803.

Joseph Barnes died shortly after the family's arrival in Livingston County, KY in early 1809. The children remained together as a family, first with Edward Lacy as their guardian, and then Elisha assumed that role when he became 21 years old in 1820. Elisha Barnes married Mary D. "Polly" Harrison of June 26, 1817 in Caldwell County, KY. Her parents were John Harrison and his wife Nancy Gordon. Nancy Gordon's parents were John Gordon, a Revolutionary War patriot and his wife Anna Haynes.

The Barnes family prospered in Scott County, MO. Elisha Darden Barnes died in July 1857, according to probate files located in the Scott County records. His son, Abner Harrison Barnes, inherited the bulk of his father's estate.

Abner H. Barnes married Susan Walker in Scott County on Jan. 27, 1864. Her parents were Robert Lee Walker and Nancy Allen, both natives of Kentucky. Abner joined the Enrolled Missouri Militia and served several short tours during the Civil War. Their only child to survive to adulthood was Robert Lee Barnes, born March 27, 1867. Abner Harrison Barnes died on July 26, 1887. His wife subsequently married John A. Stone on Jan. 29, 1892, and after his death she married James Upshaw on Nov. 17, 1908. Susan Walker Barnes Stone Upshaw died on Sept. 20, 1917 in Scott County.

Robert Lee Barnes married Lily Cornelius Rose, daughter of John Matthew Rose and his wife Arminta Fox, on Nov. 23, 1892 in Jackson, Cape Girardeau County, MO. Their children were John Matthew Barnes, born May 21, 1894 and Jessie Lee Barnes, born Jan. 8, 1896. John Matthew Barnes married Grace Lillian Ireland on Nov. 21, 1919. Jessie Lee Barnes married Albert Esley Bentley on May 30, 1917 in Wickliffe, Ballard County, KY. They made their home in the town of Illmo in Scott County. To them were born three daughters: Jessiele, Alberta, and Rosemary. Albert and Jessie Lee Bentley farmed from their home in Illmo from 1920 through Albert's death on Aug. 1, 1949. Jessie Lee Barnes Bentley continued to live at their home until her death on April 24, 1980. Both Albert and Jessie Lee Bentley are buried at Lightner's Cemetery in Illmo.

Jessiele Bentley married William August Corvick in Falls Church, Fairfax County, VA on Dec. 21, 1945. William was born Aug. 1, 1920 in Scott County to William Michael Corvick and his wife Victoria Kern. William Corvick enlisted in the United States Army in 1942 and became a paratrooper, serving in the 517th Parachute Regiment Combat Team. At the end of the war he moved to McLean, Fairfax County, VA and took up heavy construction work with his cousin, M. J. Bles. William and Jessiele had three daughters: Rebecca Ann, who married Donald G. Quaintance on Jan. 19, 1947 and lives in Hannibal, NY with their daughter Katherine Elizabeth; Susan Elaine, who resides in Scott City, MO; and Carol Annette, who married Raphael J. LaPorte on July 15, 1983 and resides in Trenton, Clinton County, IL. William and Jessiele retired to Scott City, MO in 1977. William August Corvick died there on Dec. 3, 1987. He is buried at St. Augustine's Catholic Church Cemetery in Scott County. Jessiele continues to live at their home in Scott City. *Submitted by Carol A. LaPorte*

BENA – Saturna Bena, a Frenchman born Nov. 20, 1839 in Alsace Lorraine, immigrated with his parents, Claude and Maria Josephine Bena, and brothers, James, Eugene, Joseph, Leon and sister Mary and perhaps other children.

In 1861, at age 23, Saturna Bena was recruited at "Fornfelt, a country place near Commerce, Scott County, MO." He mustered in at St. Louis at the Jefferson Barracks as a Corporal on Sept. 6, 1861, where he joined Company B of the First Missouri Cavalry a month later. According to his service records he was five feet eight and one-half inches tall and had blue eyes, a light complexion and light hair. He gave his occupation as cooper or barrel maker. A scar on this U.S. Cavalryman's cheek later marked a war injury. When the war was over, he was at home ill and had not returned to his post and therefore was never eligible for a pension, or his wife for a widow's pension.

On April 17, 1964, while the Civil War raged on, Saturna, age 24, took for his bride, Maria Taylor, age 20. Maria was born on March 27, 1844 in Scott County, MO, just south of Cape Girardeau. She was the daughter of George Washington Taylor and his wife, Massa Parker Taylor. Perhaps the groom had worked on the George Washington Taylor plantation. Since all church activity had come to a standstill during this period in Scott County they were not married in a church.

Maria and Saturna were married instead, by the local Justice of the Peace, James Narrid, and quite possibly got in trouble with their families because Saturna was a Catholic and Maria most likely was Baptist. That was serious business back then! One child, Clara, was baptized at St. Vincent de Paul Church in Cape Girardeau.

An interesting note about the marriage certificate for this couple: The groom's name was "Saturnan Bernard" and since the war was not over, one wonders if it was to conceal his identity or simply a clerk's error. The bride was simply "Maria Taylor." In later years Saturna was a country doctor and said he had apprenticed at a Dr. Proffitt in Missouri. He also dabbled in various mining experiences.

The couple had ten children: Clara (Davidson), Augusta (Williams), Charles, Maggie (Albert R. Chapman b. July 15, 1871 McDonald County, MO, d. Sept. 25, 1949 Washington County, OR), Wallace and Adolphus (died young), Mildred (Madison), Grace (Jameson), Lyda (Leslie) and Sidney who died age 31 and left a widow, Elizabeth, in Colorado in 1918.

Saturna died at the age of 79 on his farm near Goodman, McDonald County, Mo on Nov. 6, 1918 and Marie passed away on July 23, 1928 at the age of 84. Marie may have become a Catholic sometime after her marriage but it is known that she converted to Methodism and was of that faith in her later years. Grandma Marie was beloved by all who knew her. *Submitted by Toni Martinazzi*

BLATTEL – George Blattel and his brother, Jacob, left Elz, Nassau, Germany and came to America in 1854. They were farmers in New Hamburg Community, homesteaded in Scott County, MO, cleared land, built a cabin and lived off the wild. He was born March 19, 1817 in Elz, the son of Johann George and Anna Maria (Michel) Blattel, and married Anna Maria Sabel on Dec. 5, 1843 at St. John's Catholic Church in Elz, Germany. She was the daughter of Wendelen and Anna Maria (Diefenbach) Sabel. Seven children were born to this union: the four oldest ones were born in the old country. John Blattel, born on Dec. 24, 1844, married Justina Reiminger, daughter of Anthony and Catherine (Heisserer) Reiminger, on Sept. 15, 1868 at St. Lawrence Catholic Church at New Hamburg. They had four children: Christine, Catherine, Jacob, and Anton. The mother died April 18, 1879. His second marriage was to Sophia Bosenmeier on Jan. 27, 1880. She was born on March 3, 1859, the daughter of Joseph and Dorthea (Lap) Bosenmeier. Nine children were born to this union: Charles, Philomena, Andrew, Caroline, Anna, Louis, Albert, Henry and Benjamin. John owned the land where part of the town of Kelso is located and donated three acres to St. Augustine Catholic Church. They were farmers in the community. Jacob M., who was born Oct. 4, 1850 and died May 12, 1926, married Philomena Glastetter on Nov. 23, 1880. He also learned the blacksmith trade. Conrad born Sept. 27, 1851 and died March 5, 1894, married Mary Reiminger on Feb. 7, 1873 at St. Lawrence Church in New Hamburg. Thirteen children were born to them: Simon, Mary, Anton Adelbert, Josephine, Anne Frances, Frank, Phillip J., Martin Florian, Leo Sylvester, Helena, Mary Catherine and Fredolin. Elizabeth, born May 9, 1853 and died Jan. 19, 1929 and is buried in St. Joseph's Cemetery in Advance, MO, married Bernard Kenkel on April 24, 1873 at St. Lawrence Church in New Hamburg. They had eight children, but the first three died in infancy: Bernard, Herman, and Frank; the other children were Mary Elizabeth, Regina, Frances, Theresa and Frank. Frank, born April 25, 1856 and died Dec. 12, 1908, married Mary Frances Gosche on Nov. 22, 1881. They only had one child named Annie M. and she married Otto Dannenmueller. George, born in 1858, died Oct. 25, 1971 at the age of 13 years and is buried in St. Lawrence Cemetery, New Hamburg. Joseph, born March 12, 1861, a native of Scott County and an enterprising young farmer, married Louise Margaret Heisserer, the daughter of John and Rosina (Glaus) Heisserer, on Oct. 26, 1887. He died Dec. 29, 1927 from blood poisoning, which developed from an infection in one of his feet. Eight children were born to them: Ortha Catharine; Paulina Rosina, who died at age 28 from influenza on Dec. 12, 1918; Celestina Catharina who died at age 4; Otto John who died Dec. 9, 1918 at age 23, also from influenza; Regina, Catharina, Herman William and Emil Louis.

Herman and Blanche (Hamm) Blattel

Herman William was born Jan. 5, 1903 and died Dec. 26, 1989, married Blanche Louise Hamm, the daughter of John and Emma (Diebold) Hamm, on Oct. 14, 1924 in St. Lawrence Catholic Church at New Hamburg. Four children were born to this union: Charles, Herbert Leon, their only daughter, Ramona Frances, and Cornelius John.

During the Civil War, George served as a Private in Company "C", Scott County, MO Home Guard Volunteer. He enrolled on May 1, 1861 and was discharged Aug. 5, 1861, and served under Captain Daniels. Several skirmishes were fought at New Hamburg. Sam Hilderbrand, a noted bushwhacker, claimed he was the leader of the Confederates. George died Sept. 10, 1874, and is buried at St. Lawrence Cemetery at New Hamburg, MO. *Submitted by Sharen Marie (Glastetter) Parker*

BLATTEL – Joseph Blattel, a native of Scott County was born March 12, 1861. He was an enterprising young farmer who bought his first 40 acres of land for $600 at the age of 22. There he homesteaded, cleared land and built a cabin. In 1887, he added another 40 acres. Two more plats were added in 1893 and 1896, all in Section 16 Township 29, North Range 14 East. On Oct. 26, 1887, he married Louise Margaret Heisserer, the daughter of John and Rosina (Glaus) Heisserer. He was regarded by the citizens of Kelso as a leader, demonstrating his practical nature by building up a profitable farm business, contributing much to the wealth of the community. He died Dec. 29, 1927 from blood poisoning, which developed from an infection in one of his feet. They were the parents of eight children. Ortha Catharine, born Nov. 1, 1888 and died Aug. 2, 1976, married Albin Bishop Marin on April 24, 1906. Six children were born to this union: Magdalena, Theon Otto, Edward Joseph, Arnold Edward, Hermina L. and Irene Regina.

Joseph and Louise (Heisserer) Blattel

Paulina Rosina was born Sept. 10, 1890 and died Dec. 12, 1918 from influenza at the age of 28. Celetine Catherine was born Aug. 20, 1892 and died Oct. 17, 1896 at the age of 4. Otto John was born Dec. 22, 1894 and died at the age of 23 years on Dec. 9, 1918, also during the influenza epidemic. Regina Frances, born April 10, 1897 and died March 27, 1957, married Louise Hahn on Aug. 17, 1915. They were the parents of five children: Arnold Joseph and Bertha Catharine died in infancy. Three living are Viola Caroline, Frances Alma and Lorraine.

Catherine, born Jan. 4, 1900 and died Feb. 29, 1980, was married to John S. Staebel on May 4, 1920. They were the parents of two children: Clarence Anton and Agnes Marie.

Herman William, born Jan. 5, 1903 and died Dec. 26, 1989, was married to Blanche Louise Hamm, daughter of John and Emma (Diebold) Hamm, on Oct. 14, 1924 in St. Lawrence Catholic Church at New Hamburg. Herman and Blanche were the parents of four children. Charles Louis, born Aug. 27, 1925 and died Aug. 24, 1973.

Herbert Leon, born Sept. 10, 1928, married Loretta Jansen on Oct. 27, 1951. They have four children: Herbert, LaDonna, Robert and Mary Jane.

Ramona Frances was born Jan. 22, 1929 and married Sylvester Benjamin Glastetter, the son of Paul and Anna Helen (Scherer) Glastetter, on May 7, 1949. They were parents of five children: Cornelius John, David Sylvester, Sharen Marie, Karen Marie and Ramona Louise.

In 1984 and 1987, Ramona and Sylvester traveled to France and Germany, visited the old Blattel homestead in Elz, Nassau, Germany and met some of their ancestors. Joseph's grandparents Johann George and Anna Maria (Michel) Blattel owned all the land where the town of Elz was started. They also visited with friends in Schirrhein, Alsace, France, the homeland of her grandfather, John Hamm.

Cornelius John, born April 19, 1930 and died Feb. 29, 1996, married Irene Urhahn on May 8, 1954 and they have three children: Darlene, Larry Joe and Mary Jo.

Emil Louise, born Jan. 22, 1908 and died Dec. 6, 1986, was married Estella Stockfisz in 1931. They were the parents of three children: Eugene, Sharon and Roger. Emil and his wife are buried in Resurrection Cemetery at Mount Clemens, MI. *Submitted by Dustin Paul Glastetter*

BLEVINS – James T. "Jim Blevins was born May 9, 1945 in Doylestown, PA. He was the only child of Thomas Elmer Blevins born Sept. 11, 1901 in Boone County, NC and Edith Ledford Blevins b. July 14, 1914 in Livingston, TN. She had resided in Morley, MO since 1978. On July 5, 1969 at First Baptist Church in Oran, MO he married Kathryn "Kathy" Phillips. She was born March 17, 1948 in Morley, MO to Vernon E. Phillips born Jan. 14, 1926 and Mary Ann Smith Phillips born Sept. 7, 1927 of Morley, MO.

Vernon's family came to Morley from Randles after moving from Lamar, AR. Vernon's father Lee A. Phillips was a laborer and carpenter. His mother was Sylvia Noe. Mary Ann's family was from Mississippi County, MO. Her father, Jake B. Smith, was a schoolteacher and graduate of the Normal School in Cape Girardeau. Her mother was Pansy Lane.

Kathy had two brothers. David Phillips, her oldest brother who died in an automobile accident in Ohio in 1981 and her younger brother Delbert Phillips who live in Scott City, MO.

Jim served in the US Navy from Sept. 12, 1965 until July 30, 1985 as an enlisted man with the rate of Tadevman. He served during the Vietnam War training

James T. Blevins Family. Back row: Sarah, Jim, and Tom. Front: Kathy and Phillip.

fighter pilots and working on shipboard computer trainers. This military obligation gave the family opportunities to live in many communities and share many experiences in the South and Eastern USA.

Kathy graduated from Oran High School in the class of 1966 and graduated from Baptist Memorial Hospital School of Nursing in June 1969. Shortly after her graduation they were married and moved to Jacksonville, FL.

They moved to Newport, RI in 1971 where their first son James Thomas II "Tom" was born on May 23, 1972. IN 1975 they moved to Meridian, MS where Sarah Rebecca was born on Oct. 27, 1975.

They moved to Virginia Beach, VA in June 1980 where Phillip Caleb was born on Nov. 4, 1980.

Jim retired in July 1985 and the family moved to Chaffee, MO. They moved in to a home built in 1905 by a railroad family, the Brandy's. The Blevins's became the fourth family to live in the home. The house was called the "Talley House" after the second family who lived in the house.

Kathy worked at Chaffee General Hospital for a while and later worked as a Community Health Nurse at Scott County Health Department. All three children graduated from Chaffee high School.

Jim graduated in 1988 from Southeast Missouri State University with a degree in Computer Science. He became employed with USDA as a computer specialist in 1988 and worked in a 22 county service area.

Kathy graduated from University of Texas Southwestern Medical School Ob/GYN Nurse practitioner program in 1990 and practices in Cape Girardeau. Tom works as a dispatcher for Chaffee Police Department and operated Topaz Computer Consulting. Sarah graduated in 1999 from Southeast Missouri State University after also studying at Oklahoma Baptist University, with a degree in Biology-Wildlife Management. Phillip is currently a student at University of Missouri-St. Louis studying Graphic Design. *Submitted by Kathy Blevin*

BOLLINGER – Bernie Emanuel Bollinger and Elsie Viola Crader were married in Marble Hill, MO in 1915. He was the son of Henry and Pernice (Cook) Bollinger. She was the daughter of Tom and Marada (Pierce) Crader. They lived near Benton, MO. Bernie was a self-employed farmer most of his life and Elise was a homemaker. In later years she moved to the Lambert neighborhood where she owned and operated "Bollinger's Store." Bernie passed away at the age of 59 and Elsie lived to be 92 years old. She died in 1990.

They were the parents of eight children.

Almeda married Addis Mayfield and they had three children, Doyle Ray, Addis Eugene, and Vernita. They left Scott County and lived near St. Louis. Addis passed away and Almeda is still in the St. Louis area.

Glenn, who married Alma Hooker, had one son Donald Lee. Donald Lee married Sandra Urhahn and they had one son Kevin. Although Alma and Donald Lee have both passed away, Glenn and Kevin's family still live in the Benton, MO area.

Bernie and Elsie Bollinger family, 1943. Front row: Mary Lou (Bollinger) Latham, Bernie E., Rosalie and Clyde. Back row: Glenn, Roy, Almeda (Bollinger) Mayfield, Ray and Dale.

Dale, who married Colleen Joyce, had four children, Linda (Bollinger) Harper, Judy (Bollinger) Vaughn, Frankie Dale, and Debbie (Bollinger) Wiggins. After Colleen passed away he and Rita Heisserer were united in marriage. Dale lived in the Oran, MO area until he passed away.

Ray married Leona Scherer. They left the area and lived near Alton, IL. They have four children: Gary Ray, Elsie May "Sissy" Hayes, Rodger Glenn and Vickie Lynn. Ray and Leona and three of their four children still reside near Alton.

Roy and Christine Stowers were united in marriage. They live in the Blodgett, MO area and have six children: Janet (Bollinger) Dirnberger, Peggy (Bollinger) Francis, Sandra (Bollinger) Ulmer, Kenneth Roy Bollinger, David Allen Bollinger, and Michael Duane Bollinger.

Clyde married Margaret Beeson of Commerce and they lived in the Cape Girardeau area where they had four children, Valerie (Bollinger) Davis, Lisa (Bollinger) Calvert, Jeff and Pete Bollinger. They now reside in Festus, MO.

Mary Lou and Robert L. Latham of the Blodgett area were married. They moved to the St. Louis area where they had two children, Carol Ann (Latham) Kapler, and Alan Lee Latham. They all reside in the St. Louis/St/ Charles area.

Their youngest daughter, Rosalie, lives near Benton.

Bernie and Elsie have around 100 descendants, several of them in the Scott County, MO area. *Submitted by Rosalie Bollinger*

BOUTWELL – William E. Boutwell was born on Jan. 6, 1846 in Scott County, MO. He was the eighth child of William E. Boutwell and Elizabeth Smith. His parents migrated west from Gallatin County, IL to Scott County shortly after 1840. His brothers and sister were Rachel, Marin, Stephen, John, Alexander K., James, George and Henderson.

On Oct. 10, 1962, at the age of 16, William Boutwell entered the Confederate Army. He served in Company H, 8th Regiment, Missouri Cavalry under Captain Alex Wright. He was involved in Price's Raids and the Siege of Vicksburg before his unit surrendered. He was pardoned in 1865 at New Orleans, LA.

Upon his return to the Scott County area he married Margaret Jane Wilson. She was the daughter of James and Permelia Wilson. To this marriage was born four daughters, Margaret, Permelia, Lillian and Katie. Only Katie survived to adulthood. The other three daughters died before 1880. Lillian is buried at the Sikeston City Cemetery. His wife, Margaret, passed away in early 1892.

On Oct. 5, 1892 William Boutwell married Harriet Elizabeth Hindman. She was the daughter of Matthew and Kittie Hindman. This marriage produced six children: John W., Matthew Kelly, Alonzo Clyde, Ruth Abby, Emma and Mary Lou.

William Boutwell was very active in various areas of the economic and religious influences of Scott County. He was a farmer, Justice of the Peace, Methodist Minister and Insurance Agent. In 1878 he was elected Mayor of Sikeston, MO and served in this position until 1885.

In the later 1890s he made his home in Oran, MO where he was a Circuit Minister for the Methodist Church. He continued his work in the Methodist Church up until the day he died. William Boutwell passed away on Sept. 2, 1928 in Oran, MO. He was buried at the family plot in Sikeston City Cemetery, Sikeston, MO. *Submitted by Steven Harris*

BOWMAN – William Chesley Bowman was born Sept. 7, 1859, in Oak Ridge, Cape Girardeau County, MO. He was the second of 13 children born to Benjamin Lee Bowman and Eliza Jane Ford, both natives of Virginia. His siblings were: Amy Sophia (1857), Charles Christopher (1861), Mary Lee (1863), Nettie (1866), Samuel Lee (1868), James Reed (1870), Thomas Ford (1872), Lou Ella (1875), Joseph Maple (1877), Wilbur Talley (1878), Anna (1880), and Franklin (1884).

When still a boy, "Billy" began to learn the milling business at the water-driven mill in Burfordville, Cape Girardeau County, as an ap-

William C. and Emma Bowman 50th anniversary grouping. Front row, left to right: Lee, Lyman, W.C., Emma, Joe, Sam, Paul, and Phil. 2nd row: Lee A., Byron, Eula Shanks, Mildred, Melvin Limbaugh, Jack, L.R. Jr., and Paul. 3rd row: John W., Verna, Margaret, Hita, Lida, Ila, and Ben. 4th row: Milem Limbaugh, Gene, Burnice Farmer, Ford Farmer, Elizabeth, Sam Jr., Adagene, Frances, and Margaret Emily.

prentice under the watchful eye of his uncle, Samuel Sterling Bowman. It was here he met Emma Estes, daughter of Joseph Estes and Lavina Limbaugh, descendant of Frederick Limbach, a German schoolteacher and early settler in Bollinger County, who did much to further the cause of education among the settlers in pioneer Missouri days. Emma was born Feb. 1, 1864, on a farm near Patton, Bollinger County, MO, but moved with her parents to Cape Girardeau County when just a small girl.

On Jan. 25, 1883, in Burfordville, William and Emma were married at the home of her parents by the Rev. William H. Welker, an uncle of W. C. Bowman by marriage and a Baptist minister. The first five of their children were born in Cape Girardeau County: Lyman Russell (Oct. 12, 1883); Eula Clippard (Nov. 11, 1885); Joseph (Jan. 3, 1889); Lee Reed (Jan. 25, 1891); and Samuel Schuyler (May 13, 1893). Five more children were born in Sikeston, Scott County, Mo: Arnold Paul (Feb. 15, 189); Robert Byron (Feb. 27, 1899); Melvin Emogene (May 26, 1901); Mildred Rebecca (Dec. 23, 1903); and William Chesley Jr. (July 21, 1907).

By 1882, William Bowman had taken charge of the Burfordville mill, eventually buying an interest in that mill in March 1887. In June 1893, he moved his family to Sikeston where he formed a business alliance with G. B. Greer and U. G. Holley. The company they organized, known as the G. B. Greer Milling Company, opened for business June 23, 1893, with Mr. Holley as superintendent of the plant, Mr. Bowman as head miller, and Mr. Greer as general manager. In June 1896 the business was reorganized as the Greer-Bowman Milling Company, with G. B. Greer, Charles D. Matthews, U. G. Holley, and W. C. Bowman as stockholders. In 1897 Mr. Holley retired from the company to accept the position of postmaster at Sikeston. In 1898 John D. Ebert acquired an interest in the company, becoming an officer and director, and the mill subsequently became known as the Greet-Ebert Milling Company. In 1899 Mr. Bowman sold his interest and acquired a flourmill at Dexter, MO, which was incorporated as the Dexter Milling Company. In 1902 W. C. Bowman and C. D. Matthews organized the Bowman-Matthews Milling Company and built the plant called Mill A in the west part of Sikeston. At the same time the Greer-Ebert Company built a plant at Oran, MO. In 1904 the Greet-Ebert Milling Company and the Bowman-Matthews Company were consolidated, and it was from this merger that the Scott County Milling Company came into existence.

In addition to his family and business responsibilities, W. C. was active in civic affairs. He served from 1912 to 1916 as a member of the Scott County Court, and was thereafter affectionately referred to as "Judge" Bowman. He was also a member and sometime president of the Sikeston Board of Education for many years and in every possible way helped to advance the educational advantages of the community's young people.

William Chesley and Emma Bowman were members of the Fist Baptist Church of Sikeston where he was ordained to the office of deacon in 1915. When it decided to build the new church, W. C. pledged that for every dollar raised by the congregation for the building fund, he would give another dollar. He kept that promise, and the first services were held in the new building on March 15, 1916. He considered it the best investment he ever made. He was also a mason of 32nd degree and was a member of the Masonic Lodge in Sikeston. Emma, in addition to her myriad of duties as the mother of a large family, was a member of the Order of eastern Star and the Women's Christian Temperance Union.

Emma Estes Bowman died on Jan. 5, 1938, following a year of illness caused by the complications of a fall. William Chesley Bowman remained active until just a few days before his death on April 22, 1950, at which time he was lauded in *The Sikeston Herald* as "Sikeston's First Citizen." *Submitted by Carol Jean Bowman*

BOX – Amos Box (b. August 1911) moved to Scott County in 1930 from Hagerville, Ark. Fay Newton (b. May 1914) came to Scott County in 1929, also from Hagerville. The two families lived in one large house and farmed. Amos and Fay married in 1932. They farmed in Crowder, Grant City, and Kewanee, MO areas until Amos' death in April of 1966. Fay moved to Sikeston following his death and worked for Missouri Delta Medical Center until her retirement in 1984. Amos and Fay had six children: Frank, J., Murline, Nadine, James and Deloris.

Fay Box in her garden.

Frank (b. April 1933) married Ruth Naney Slayton in September 1970. They have one daughter, Deanna (b. November 1980). She lives in Joplin, MO. Frank retired from the Missouri Highway Department in 1994. Ruth worked for Missouri Employment Office. They live in Dexter, MO.

J. (b. August 1935) married Barbara Richards, February 1956. He retired from Sikeston Motor Company in 1998, having worked there 40 plus years as body shop manager. She is a homemaker. They live in Sikeston, MO and they have two sons, Ricky and Randy. Rick (b. October 1957) married Myong Ye (Lee-Ann) November 1984. They have two children, Brandon (b. May 1986) and Amy (b. November 1990). He raced motorcycles, winning several trophies. He enlisted in the Army in 1977 and retired in 1997. He received the Meritorious Service Medal and several Army accommodations, including the Bronze Star for service in Desert Storm. They live in Clarksville, TN. Rick has two sons, Brice and Blake. Brice (b. August 1977) lives in Laurie, MO and works for a marina. Brice's son, Ethan Michael (b. October 1999) died in June 2000.

Blake (b. August 1980) married Karmin Keppel, October 1999 and lives in Eldon, MO. He works for Mr. Shower-Door at Osage Beach.

Randy (b. October 1961) married Jeannie Vines, August 1982. He went to work for Sikeston Motor Company while a junior in high school becoming body shop manager. Jeannie works for Nelson Equipment. They live in Sikeston and have two children, Erin and Andres. Erin (b. January 1986) is a student, active in church, school and sports. Andrew (b. April 1988) is a student, active in church, school and all sports.

Murline (b. April 1938) married Luther Mitchum in August 1958. She is a domestic housekeeper. He worked as a mechanic. They live in Arnold, MO. They have two daughters, Pam and Michele. Pam (b. December 1960) married Al Delgado. She has worked for Glass Company. He is a car salesman. They have one son, Chad (b. August 1991). They live in Granite City, IL. Michele (b. May 1973) has a daughter; Karyssa (b. May 2001) and they live in Arnold, MO.

Nadine (b. June 1940) married Gene Lucy in October 1961. She has worked for Home Health. He worked for the post office. They live in Sikeston, MO.

James (b. May 1945) married Faye Williams in April 1974. He served two years in the Army. He works for Noranda. They have one son, Brian (b. August 1980) who is in college. They live in rural Lilbourn, MO.

Deloris (b. 1947) married Perry Yount in July 1966. She works for Sikeston Public Schools. He works for Lanshire. They have one son, Brad (b. August 1977) who works for Larry Dewitt Company. They live in rural Bertrand, MO. *Submitted by Barbara Box*

BROCK – William Uriah Brock, a Revolutionary War Veteran (years 1775-1783), was born in 1759 in Virginia (he lied about his age to join the Army) died Nov. 15, 1845. He is buried in Old Lorimier Cemetery, Cape Girardeau, MO. His father was John Brock, and his grandfather was Auddy Brock. Uriah first married Martha Harrison in 1792. They had one child, Armstrong Brock who died 1846-1850. Uriah then married Elizabeth Marie Huskey in 1794 and they had six children.

Rebecca (b. 1794, d. 1845) married Moses Todd- her children: Mary and Malinda.

Elizabeth married Moes Judd- her children: Jonus and Joseph.

Mary "Polly" (b. 1801) married Benjamin Ogle (Benjamin was son of William Ogle who was killed in a duel with Joseph McFerron in 1807 in Cape Girardeau).

William (b. 1804) married Elizabeth Smith.

Malinda (b. 1808, d. 1856) married William A. Robertson (she is buried by her father in Old Lorimier Cemetery.)

Hartwell (b. 1804) married Delila Fowler. Hartwell was sheriff of Scott County in 1852. In 1862, he was appointed postmaster in Scott County. He was quite a politician.

Second generation: Hartwell Brock's children: George Cooper born 1837, Elizabeth married James Allen, Harriet Rebecca married Benjamin Allen (sons of Felix Allen, one of the first landowners in the town of Benton, MO) Uriah born 1848 had three children: Mary born 1866, Laura born 1868 and Endora born 1870 by his second wife Louvina Bowman.

Third generation: George Cooper Brock born 1837 married Anna Stevens born 1842. Their children were: Harriet "Hattie", Levi, Robert Cooper and Uriah. George served in the Civil War. He left Scott County for a while and lived in Fredericktown, Madison County, MO. Returning to Scott County when son Robert Cooper was 9 years old.

Fourth generation: Robert Cooper Brock was a share cropper and farmed land owned by the Allen's, Tom Scott, Ray Lucas and others. He was born Dec. 20, 1874. He married Amelia Stemile. Their children were: Vera (married Wade Miller), Georgia (married Claude Dirnberger), Wade Spencer (married Pauline Pattengill), Glen (married Geraldine LeGrand), Catherine (married Charles Henry), Robert Cooper (married Alma Brown), and William Uriah (married Ruth Ann Barton).

Fifth generation: Hattie Rebecca (married Claude Dirnberger in October 1931) had seven children: Lois Rebecca (married Joe Spalding), Claude Richard (married Mary Jo Ferrell), Janet Sue (married Vernon Vetter), David Cooper (married Dorothy Harris), Andrew (married Janet Bollinger), Glen (married Barbara Allen) and Vera Ann (married Alan Henneman).

Sixth generation: Lois Rebecca and Joe Spalding had four children: Joe Wayne, Rebecca Mary, Melissa Rose and John Daryl.

Seventh generation: Rebecca Mary (married Charles Schwartz) their children were: Suzanne Rebecca, Stephen, and Gregory. (You can see the family names handed down generation through generation.)

An 80-acre farm and eight lots in the town of Benton were part of the land owned by Felix Allen and inherited by his sons James and Benjamin who married Elizabeth and Hattie Rebecca Brock. Lois Rebecca Spalding now owns these. *Submitted by eighth generation, Suzanne Rebecca Schwartz a Scott County resident now attending Missouri University, Columbia, MO*

BROREIN – As my father and his brothers contributed through their lumber business to the development, clearing and draining Scott County farmland, I thought it would be of interest for the historical book of Scott County being prepared.

Enclosed is an article from *The Sikeston Herald* newspaper, March 29, 1951.

My father, David C. Brorein, came to southeast Missouri in 1904 to buy a veneer mill log processing business in Parma, MO. The timber being used came mostly from Scott County around Tanner and Crowder area. With his brothers Jake and William, he bought several large tracts of land covered with trees.

Arrangements were made with the Frisco Railroad Company to provide a spur for loading logs to be transported to Parma about 25 miles south. This spur was called "Carlston."

Most of the land was covered with water for a period of three to six months of the year but was good for lumber, which could be pealed to produce then sheets of wood called "veneer" which was used for furniture.

Most of the trees in the area were cypress and gum; some were so large that they were asked to send logs to the Worlds Fair in Chicago. There was no way to get whole logs out so they had to be cut into smaller pieces!

When my father, Mr. Brorein, came to southeast Missouri from Wapokoneta, Ohio on the train for the first time to the Sikeston area from St. Louis, the railroad tracks were on stilts about eight feet high most of the way as the land was covered with six feet of water. Marks on trees indicated water depth.

Drainage ditches were dug and trees cut so the farmland became some of the best anywhere as it was rich, black loam soil. Many stumps remained which damaged farm equipment. Dynamite was used to blow out the stumps. Mules were used to pile them for burning. Even during the last 50 years many plow points and disks had to be replaced because of stumps.

After the good timber was cut the land was

farmed by "sharecroppers" and managed by David Brorein who lived in Parma. He made regular trips on the Frisco train to Crowder and walked to the farms, as there was no roads except along ditch banks.

My husband, James W. Abernathy, farms some of the original tracts of land purchased by the Broreins and we have lived there since 1947.

There was only a sandy lane, which ended where our home was built on a ridge known as "Big Gum Ridge." The sandy land is now a beautiful blacktop, country Highway 470, where "Brorein Acres" stands today.

The Sikeston Missouri Herald Thursday, March 29, 1951:

At 12:04 yesterday morning, in a Cape Girardeau hospital, occurred the death of David Christian Brorein of Parma, one of the pioneer developers of southeast Missouri. He was aged 84 years.

Funeral services were conducted early this afternoon at the Parma Methodist Church, of which he had long been a member and devoted supporter. Burial will occur at Buckland, Ohio.

Survivors include his wife, Mrs. Clara Brorein of Parma; two daughters, Mrs. Wallace R. Knight of Poplar Bluff and Mrs. James W. Abernathy of "Brorein Acres" on rural route 1, Sikeston; five grandchildren, and one sister, Miss Mina Brorein of Wapokoneta, Ohio. The latter is now the only survivor of the Gilbert Brorein family of ten children.

David Christian Brorein was born in Auglaize County, Ohio in 1867. He came to Missouri in 1904 with two of his brothers, William G. and Jacob Brorein, and with them engaged in operating a large wooden veneer mill at Parma. The brothers also owned and operated large acreage of farmlands in the district, including "Brorein Acres" northwest of Sikeston, which is operated by Mr. and Mrs. Abernathy. The Broreins contributed materially to the development of New Madrid and adjoining counties during the past half a century.

Both William and Jacob Brorein passed away some years ago, the former in Tampa, Florida, where he was president of the Peninsula Telephone Company and the Florida state Fair Association. Another William Brorein, the son of Jacob, succeeded him as head of those two organizations.

The passing of David Brorein ended the activities of one of the few remaining men who made large contributions to the conversion of former southeast Missouri swamp lands into the fertile farms of today. *Submitted by Mary Margaret Brorein Abernathy*

BRUCKER – Clarence J. Brucker was born Aug. 21, 1925 at Perkins, MO. He was the son of Ambrose J. and Frances (Kirchdoerfer) Brucker and grew up around the Kelso, MO farm community. His brothers and sisters were: Pauline (Brucker) Uhrhan, Lawrence Brucker, Earl Brucker and Dorothy (Brucker) Quade.

On March 1, 1949, Clarence J. Brucker married Anna Marie Hennecke (b. Dec. 27, 1931) at St. Augustine Catholic Church, Kelso, MO. She was the eldest daughter of Walter J. and Hazel (Eakins) Hennecke. Her brothers and sisters were: Walter Lee Hennecke, Charles E. Hennecke, Frances (Hennecke) Hitt, William E. Hennecke, Connie (Hennecke) Myers, Donna (Hennecke) Voorhes and Bobby R. Hennecke.

A daughter, Darlene Ann Brucker, was born Nov. 4, 1951 and a son, Douglas J. Brucker, was born Nov. 13, 1952 at Cape Girardeau, MO.

Clarence rented and farmed land around Delta, MO for several years. In 1957, he purchased a farm just south of New Hamburg, MO

Clarence J. and Anna Marie Brucker, August 15, 1987.

and farmed and lived there until his death on Dec. 22, 1989. Also during his lifetime, he worked for several heavy equipment companies and construction companies. His wife, Anna Marie, worked all her adult life and retired from Thorngate, Ltd. in July 1996. Both Mr. and Mrs. Brucker were members of St. Lawrence Catholic Church at New Hamburg, MO.

Mrs. Brucker still resides on the family farm at New Hamburg and is survived by her daughter, Darlene (Brucker) Margrabe; son, Douglas J. Brucker; granddaughter, Jodi L. Margrabe; grandson Eric S. Margrabe; and twin great-grandsons, Dustin and Justin Deen.

BRUNS – Heinrich Christian Lewis Bruns was born April 15, 1873 in Kelso, MO and died Oct. 14, 1942 in Maplewood (now Cahokia), IL. He was the son of Pobst Bruns (b. July 1838 in Bremen, Germany and died Dec. 13, 1909 in Illmo, MO), and Elisabeth Ellermann (b. March 7, 1838 in Bremen, Germany and died Oct. 13, 1887 in Illmo, MO.) Heinrich Christian Lewis Bruns married Cora Eve Porter on May 6, 1900. Cora Porter was born Dec. 29, 1878 in Vienna, IL to William L. Porter and Louisa Brown. Heinrich and Cora had three children, Joseph Wilhelm (b. March 3, 1901 in Commerce, MO), Mary Alice (b. March 8, 1903 in Morley, MO) and Ruth Mabel (b. July 23, 1905 in Illmo, MO).

Heinrich had two brothers, Heinrich Christian Martin (b. Oct. 30, 1865 and died Sept. 14, 1880 in Illmo, MO) and Conrad Friedrich Wilhelm (b. Jan. 23, 1868 and died June 19, 1888 in Illmo, MO); and four sisters, Anna Johanna (b. July 17, 1870 and died Aug. 12, 1872 in Illmo, MO), Dorothea Sophie (b. May 29, 1875 and died July 28, 1877 in Illmo, MO), Marie Sophie Elisabeth (b. June 16, 1878 and died in 1909. She married Henry Sanders) and Emma Elisabeth (b. Oct. 12, 1880 and died July 30, 1959 in Belleville, IL). She married Joseph A. Sanders on Feb. 20, 1898. Joseph was born Aug. 12, 1874 and died Dec. 20, 1914 at his home. Heinrich was an engineer for the railroad in Scott County, MO and was said to have driven one of the locomotives onto the Thebes Bridge when they tested and dedicated the bridge on May 25, 1905. *Submitted by Ruth Bardot*

Heinrich Christian Lewis Bruns and Cora Eve Porter Bruns

BURGER – Alexander Anthony Burger Jr., born Oct. 23, 1927, was baptized at St. Augustine's in Kelso and attended school at Pleasant Hill. Vera Bertha Glastetter, born July 19, 1929, was bap-

tized at St. Lawrence Parish in New Hamburg, and attended school St. Lawrence and at St. Mary's High School in Cape Girardeau. Alex Jr. and Vera were married on May 28, 1946 at St. Lawrence at 8:00 a.m., followed by breakfast in the summer house where Alex grew up, with dinner, supper and dance at New Hamburg.

Alex, youngest of 10 children of Alexander Anton Burger and Clara Regina Georger, lost his mother when he was only 15. Vera, the second and younger daughter of Albert Joseph Glastetter and Cecilia Westrich, lost her mother at the age of 4.

They made their home at 307 Ball Park Road, Oran, where Junior farmed and Vera made a home for them and their five children. It is located three miles from Benton, New Hamburg and Oran.

Junior died on Oct. 24, 1992, one day after his 65th birthday, and is buried in New Hamburg. His son, Alexander Robin III, hosted a party for Junior at his house up the lane from them. All the children, the in-laws and grandchildren were there to help celebrate. When he died, there were so

Alexander and Vera B. (Glastetter) Burger

many people who wanted to pay their last respects, that not everyone could get in; it was one of the biggest funerals ever held in Benton.

Alex was a great softball pitcher, and he and his brother, Harold, made a talented pair in local games. He was a huge man, both literally and figuratively. He said that no one should every call anyone Junior, because when that person grew up, the name didn't fit anymore. He consequently didn't allow his children to be called Junior, or have any nicknames.

Vera was a great cook, and she spent a lot of her time cooking and playing "taxi" for their children. Together, they spent a lot of their time attending sports events for their children and grandchildren, which Vera still does. They also enjoyed hosting many parties at their home and played cards at home and away.

They had five children.

Jacqueline Diane (b. Nov. 12, 1946) m. Aug. 6, 1966, Steven Leon Griffith (b. March 24, 1943); children: Kelly Belinda (b. Nov. 10, 1970) m. July 23, 1994, Mark Allen Winder (b. Aug. 1, 1968); children: Jacqueline Belle (b. Aug. 8, 1998), child Blaise Griffith (b. April 30, 2002); and Deidre Diane (b. Nov. 5, 1975).

Daniel Raymond (b. June 24, 1949) m. Aug. 10, 1968, Patricia Lynn Margrave (b. June 21, 1949); children: Matthew Tyson (b. July 24, 1975) m. Dec. 5, 1998, Kristi Michelle Jenkins (b. Oct. 16, 1975); Blake Daniel (b. April 23, 1977) m. Feb. 9, 2002, Kimberly Michelle Riley (b. Nov. 5, 1979); Lyndsey Meredith (b. Dec. 18, 1979) m. Aug. 10, 2001, Justin Gregory Mosby (b. Jan. 3, 1976).

Alexander Robin III (b. July 25, 1952) m. May 6, 1972, Nancy JoElla Johnson (b. Feb. 6, 1952); children: Alexander Heath IV (b. July 1, 1973) m. Sept. 12, 1998, Karen Marie Riley (Dec. 6, 1972); children: Alexander Gale (b. March 8, 2000) and Riley Breann (b. Feb. 7, 200); Heather Suzanne (b. Aug. 2, 1978); Brett Thomas (b. May 16, 1983) and Mark Johnson (b. Dec. 9, 1990).

James Albert (b. Dec. 2, 1957) m. May 13, 1978, Sherry Jean Urhahn (b. Dec. 29, 1958); children: Vanessa Marie (b. July 23, 1979), Allison Anne (b. July 30, 1982), Celeste Elizabeth (b. Dec.

1, 1989, d. Dec. 1, 1989) and Paris Nicolette (b. Jan. 7, 1991).

Russell Lee (b. Oct. 6, 1963) m. Aug. 25, 1984, Stephanie Marie Westrich (b. Jan. 16, 1964); children: Alexander Major (b. Jan. 27, 1985), Kristain Dru (b. April 9, 1989) and Summer Mackenzie (b. Aug. 6, 1994). *Submitted by Jackie Burger Griffith*

BURGER – Anton was born Oct. 20, 1845 in Soufflenheim, France. Theresa was born Dec. 20, 1846 in Metz, France. They were married Nov. 13, 1871.

Anton fought in the Franco-Prussian War of 1870-1871. The Germans took control of Anton's homeland (the Alsace-Lorraine Region). So Anton and Theresa left France and sailed for the United States but settled in Toronto, Canada. Their first son, Ignatius, was born in Canada on March 20, 1873. Shortly after their sons birth, they came to Scott County to settle. Anton's occupation was farming. They had seven more children. Their names are as follows: Louis, Magadalena "Lena", Mary, Alexander, Louisa, Charles and Helen.

Anton died April 12, 1924 at the home of his daughter, Mrs. John (Mary) Schlosser, east of Kelso. Theresa died Dec. 23, 1925. They are buried in St. Augustine Cemetery at Kelso.

Their son, Alexander "Alex" was born Sept. 5, 1880. He married Clara Georger on Feb. 28, 1905 at St. Augustine Church in Kelso. Clara was born Jan. 20, 1885. They had 12 children. Their names are as follows: Ottilia "Tillie" Halter, Malonia "Lonie", Herbert, Leo, Rosalie "Rose" Hillman, Linda "Lindy" Ziegler, Antonilla "Ann" Thompson, Anton, Harold, Alma "Tootsie", Alexander "Alex" and Frances.

Alex died Aug. 18, 1963 and Clara died Nov. 3, 1942. They are buried at St. Augustine Cemetery in Kelso.

Alex's son, Herbert, my dad, was born Jan. 24, 1910 east of Kelso where Mrs. Harold (Louise) Burger still lives. He married Marie E. Held on June 1, 1940 at Cape Girardeau. He was a pilot with the Army Air Corps during WWII. He flew the Himalayan Mountains (Hump as it was known) carrying fuel, supplies and troops to the front lines. After the war he farmed and also had an excavating-timber clearing business for many years.

He died on June 24, 1992 and is buried at St. Augustine Cemetery in Kelso. Marie Burger is still living at their home in Scott County.

There were two children born to this union. Their names are Kenneth "Kenny" and Brenda. Kenny married Linda Ham on Sept. 20, 1969 at the Illmo Baptist Church. They have three children. They are Jarrett, Andrea and Aaron. Jarrett married Barbara Lee on June 25, 1990 at the Baptist Church in Benton. They have four children. Their names are as follows: Heather, Whitney, Madison and Hunter.

Brenda married James R. LeGrand on Nov. 6, 1971 at Eisleben Lutheran Church in Scott City. They have two children. Their names are Jeannette and Landon.

They Burger family still continues to farm and is now in the fifth generation of this occupation. *Information of this family history was provided by my cousin, Gary Ziegler, and submitted by Brenda (Burger) LeGrand.*

BURGER – Henry Adam Burger was born on Sept. 10, 1878 in Oran, Scott County, MO. His parents were Joseph Burger, born March 26, 1849 in New Hamburg, Scott County, with ancestry coming from Soufflenheim and Schirrhein, Alsace France, and Caroline Halter born June 22, 1850 in Alsace, France.

Henry Adam married Anna Jellin, born July 14, 1875 in Cape Girardeau, MO. Her parents were Jacob Jacques Jellin, born April 17, 1831 in Swit-

zerland and Marie Anna LeGrand, born July 1832 in Francorchamps, Belgium.

Henry Adam Burger and Anna Jelin Burger

Henry owned and operated Burger Bakery in Oran for a number of years. The two-story brick building is still there. The family lived both in Oran and on a farm near New Hamburg. The five children were baptized in either Guardian Angel or St. Lawrence churches. Their children were: Mary Loretto, William Henry (Dee Vandeven), Edward Joseph (Alma Hinkle), Joseph William and Agnes Camille (John Lee). Grandchildren were: James, Martha, Jeanette and William Vandeven, Mary Margaret Burger, Patrician, Allen, Richard, May, John, William and Francis Lee. There are many great-grandchildren.

One son, Edward Joseph, became a Trappist Monk and Joseph William is presently a Priest in Oklahoma.

The family moved to Cape Girardeau where they owned and operated the Burger Bakery as both a retail and wholesale business and continued to serve their customers in Scott County. With many relatives left in Oran and New Hamburg, they all returned to visit often. *Submitted by Mary Margaret Burger Kinnaw*

BURGER – James Albert "Jamie" Burger was born on Oct. 2, 1957, to Alexander Burger Jr. and Vera Bertha Glastetter-Burger of New Hamburg, MO. Jamie, the fourth born child, has one sister, Jacqueline Diane Griffith of Cape Girardeau, and three brothers, Daniel Raymond, Alexander Robin and Russell Lee, all of New Hamburg. Jamie married Sherry Jean Urhahn on May 13, 1978, at St. Denis Catholic Church in Benton, MO.

Sherry Jean Urhahn-Burger was born on Dec. 29, 1958, to Marvin "Curly" Zeno Urhahn and Ruth Ann LeGrand-Urhahn. Sherry, the fifth born child, has three sisters, Gail Ann Overbey of Cape Girardeau, Charlene Marie Camren of Benton, and Jacqueline Maria Rodriguez of St. Charles, MO, and two brothers, Richard Charles and Kenneth Raymond, both of Cape Girardeau.

Jamie graduated from Kelly High School in 1975. After graduation, he farmed with his father for two years. He was employed by Schneider Equipment Company in Cape Girardeau as a farm equipment salesman from December 1977 through August of 1983. Currently, he works as a shift foreman for Lone Star Industries in Cape Girardeau. In August of 2000, Jamie was elected 2nd district Commissioner of Scott County and is currently in the 2nd years of a four year term. He is also a basketball coach for the St. Denis Catholic grade school girls and boys teams and enjoys golfing in his spare time.

Sherry graduated from Kelly High School in 1977. She worked part-time at Hardware Wholesalers Inc. in Cape Girardeau while raising her daughters.

Jamie and Sherry Burger and family on January 2, 2001 at the Scott County courthouse after taking the Oath of Office for 2nd District Commissioner.

In 1988, she enrolled at Southeast Missouri State University. She received her nursing degree in 1994. She worked at Southeast Hospital in Cape Girardeau as a Registered Nurse on the Pediatric floor until 1996. She is currently employed full time at the Scott County Health Department in Benton and Sikeston, MO. Jamie and Sherry have three daughters. Vanessa Marie was born on July 23, 1979. She attended St. Denis Catholic Church Grade School for eight years. She graduated from Kelly High School in 1997 and went on to attend Southeast Missouri State University. She is currently employed by Schlumberger as a meter technician. She is engaged to be married on Nov. 30, 2002 to Gregory Heath Morgan of Benton.

Allison Anne Burger was born on July 30, 1982. She attended St. Denis Catholic Grade School for eight years, and graduated from Kelly High School in May of 2000. Allison is currently finishing her sophomore year at St. Louis (Jesuit) University where she is double majoring in Secondary Education and English. She is an active member of the Gamma Phi Beta sorority and has been named to the Dean's list.

Paris Nicolette Burger was born on Jan. 7, 1991. She is in fifth grade at St. Denis Catholic Grade School. Paris enjoys playing basketball, volleyball, and softball. She is a level 6 gymnasts at Class Act Gymnastics in Jackson, MO. She recently attended a gymnastics meet in Springfield, MO where she placed 8th in the state.

The Burger family resides at 190 Meyer Lake Court in Benton, MO and attends St. Denis Catholic Church in Benton.

BURKE – Evin Burke was born June 27, 1889 to Edmund Taylor Burke and Martha Moody Burke in Gipson County, TN.

When he was 10 years old he moved with his family to a farm approximately one mile west of Blodgett, MO. He grew to manhood there. In 1913, he married Mayme Deaton and to this union was born three children while living in the Blodgett Community. They are: Virginia, William and Marjorie. In February 1919, Evin moved with his family to a farm south and west of Vanduser, MO. Here a second son and fourth child were born named Jackson.

During the time spent here, Evin bought 400 acres of land. The major part of his life was spent farming. The land remains in the family.

Mayme Burke died Dec. 28, 1937 at age 47. Evin lived to the ripe old age of 91 years and 11 months.

The oldest child, Virginia, became a hairdresser. She married Maurice Armstrong and had one son, whom they named Bill. Bill grew to adulthood in Sikeston, MO. He married Kay Wright and to that union was born three children: Maurice, Susan and David. Maurice is a salesman and married Claudia Gatlin and they have two daughters, Anna and Allison. Maurice and Kay live in Nashville, TN. Susan, the daughter, is married to Dr. Frank Louthan and has one son, Michael. They live in Murphyfreesboro, TN where Dr. Louthan is a Pulmonologist.

David is married, works for Sears, and lives in Memphis, TN. Virginia died Aug. 13, 1992.

William also grew up in the Vanduser neighborhood. He became a teacher and then an insurance agent in Sikeston, MO. He married Wilma Batts and to that union was born three children: Dale, who lives in Monett, MO and is an Associate Circuit Judge. He married Sharon Grebe and they have four children. Randy is a Commander in the Navy and is assigned to nuclear submarines. He is married, but has no children. A daughter, Debbie, is a teacher in Springfield, MO, and is married and has one daughter, Erin. Another daughter, Lori, is a C.P.A., and lives in Monett, MO with her husband, Larry Welch, and their three sons: twins Dillon and Eric and son Ryan. A son, David, a mechanical engineer, lives in Dallas, TX.

A daughter, Joy, was born to William and Wilma. She became a teacher in Sikeston, MO and married Richard Leslie. They have two children: Stephen lives in Springfield, Mo. He is a computer expert and is married to Amber, who is a clinical psychologist. Then there is Laura, who lives in Jefferson City and is married and has one daughter, Kala. Joy and Richard Leslie live in Tulsa, OK.

A younger son, Terry, lives in Glennwood Springs, CO and is an audiologist. He married Vicki Cox and they have two children. Cody lives in Chicago and is planning to go to law school. Tara, their daughter, is at the University of Denver, pursuing a masters degree in architecture. William died April 2001. Wilma lives in Springfield, MO.

Marjorie, the second daughter of Evin and Mayme grew up in the Vanduser area. She became a teacher and taught for 36 years. In 1940 she married Cline Carter. They have no children and live in Sikeston, MO.

Jackson, the youngest son of Evin and Mayne was born on Feb. 5, 1922. He grew to manhood in the Vanduser community. While attending University of Missouri at Columbia, he enlisted in the Army Air Force and served during WWII. He returned after the war and reentered the University attending a Bachelor of Science degree in Agriculture. He met and married Sally Swank of Charleston, MO. They had two children. Jackson Jr. is a sales manager and lives in the Chicago area with his wife, Ginger. Jack and Ginger have two children, David Hilyard and Ryan Burke. Both are currently students at Missouri University, Columbia, MO. Then there is Mary Lee who lives in Manchester, MO with her husband Paul and two sons, Karl and Timothy. Mary Lee teaches high school mathematics in the Parkway School District. Son, Karl is attending Truman University and Timothy is a high school freshman in the Parkway Schools.

Many years of Jackson's life were spent farming. The last years he spent as Administrator of Mississippi County Health Department. Jackson died April 14, 1988.

This is but a very brief outline of the history of our family. We have been and are a close knit and religious family with a strong belief in Methodism.

BURNS – Fred Victor Burns was born Oct. 3, 1903 at Glen Allen, MO. His wife, Ruth Audrey Aldrich Burns, was born at Minfro, MO, may 3, 1903. They moved to Oran in 1935, then to Bell City before coming to Benton in 1938.

They have five children, all girls, born in Glenn Allen, MO. Girtrude Lillian (b. Aug. 9, 1925) married Herman Schwartz (b. Oct. 10, 1921. They were married March 23, 1941 at Ancell, MO. They had five children. Dorothy Jean (b. May 7, 1941) married Burnett O. Plumb Jr. They had two daughters, Shelia and Laura.

Darlene (b. Oct. 31, 1945) married John Ford with a daughter, Mechell Ford deceased and one son, Nathan. Her second marriage was to E. J. Urhahn on Jan. 31, 1998.

Belinda Juyce (b. Oct. 3, 1959) married Thomas Grisham.

Herman Louis Jr. (b. Nov. 13, 1959) married Phyllis Ann Keen at Morley, MO. There were three children: daughter to Herman by a previous marriage, Christina Anne, and Dustin Hermen and Dylan Xavier.

Terrance Charles (b. Nov. 15, 1965) married Phyllis G. Willard at Freeport, Bahamas. Terrance

has one daughter, Tasha Christana, and Phyllis has a daughter, Summer.

Marguriete Elizabeth (b. Nov. 28, 1925) married Glenn Orvil Proctor (b. May 15, 1921). They were married at Ancel, MO. They had one daughter Linda Charline, and raised a granddaughter, Amanda Nicole Drury.

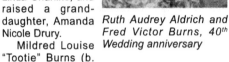
Ruth Audrey Aldrich and Fred Victor Burns, 40th Wedding anniversary

Mildred Louise "Tootie" Burns (b. Sept. 11, 1926) married Ray Joe Graham on Sept. 11, 1947. One son, Fred Joe Graham who is married to Katherine Lois Griffin. They have one son, Berry Thomas.

Georgia Mae Burns (b. Aug. 25, 1928) married Billie Lee Graham (b. Nov. 10, 1925). They had one son, Scott Lee Graham (b. June 7, 1953) who married Deborah Faith Estes Ourth. They had one daughter, Stephanie Leigh, who lived 21 days, a daughter, Madalyn Faith, and Deborah has a son, Jason.

Evelyn Aline Burns (b. Sept. 9, 1930) married William Albert Compas. They had three children. Charlotte Ann married Morris McCroy. She had a son by a previous marriage, Randol Stephen. Son Ronald is married and has two children and William Albert Jr. is married with three children.

Fred and Ruth Burns were farmers all their life. They had a root beer stand just north of the city limits, which was sold to the Bollinger family and they named it the M & M Drive Inn.

Buried at Forest Hill Memorial Garden near Morley. Deceased in the Burns family are:

Fred V. Burns Nov. 10, 1975
Billie Lee Graham Feb. 21, 1980
Ruth A. Burns Jan. 4, 1990
Stephanie Leigh June 10, 1984
William Albert Compas Nov. 25, 1997
Girtrude Lillian Schwartz Aug. 21, 1995, burial St. Denis Church Cemetery
Herman L. Schwartz Sr., Feb. 29, 2000, burial St. Denis Church Cemetery

Belinda Schwartz, (granddaughter) gave Fred Burns a little dog leash without a dog. It was stiff and you could walk it like it had a dog on the end. Our dad had so much fun with this dog leash; he walked it all over the grounds at Neighbor day. We all went to a Blue Grass show up in Bollinger County around Grassie and he walked it across the stage there. We had a great time. My father had cancer and this was his last big fling. He was such a humorous man, and was loved by all.

Our mother, Ruth Burns, baked such great homemade bread. We would all congregate when the bread would come out of the oven. What wonderful parents we had. *Submitted by Georgia Mae Graham*

BUXTON – Benjamine Raymond Buxton was born July 28, 1902 at Pocahontas, AR, the son of Ben and Lydia Buxton. He married Isabelle Tyler on Oct. 6, 1927. She was born Feb. 6, 1906 at Pocahontas, AR. They had two children.

Raymond and Isabelle with their children, Bill and Shirley, moved to Morley, MO from Pocahontas, AR in 1941. Raymond farmed for Chester Black for many years, until Mr. Black passed away. Then he farmed for Bill Black for several more years. Besides farming, he worked at the cotton gin at Morley and the alfalfa mill at Bell City.

Isabelle, a homemaker, made a large garden

every year and canned her own vegetables and did a lot of sewing for her and a few other people.

Raymond and Isabelle were members of the Church of Christ, as were their children when they were old enough. The Church of Christ met at Hickory Grove for several years and later on the members of the church built a building in Morley. Raymond and Bill helped work on the building.

Raymond worked as an elder for the church for many years.

Bill and Shirley attended Morley School. Bill graduated in 1948, Shirley in 1954. They had just built the new Morley High School in 1941.

Bill went in the Army in 1950 and had basic training at Fort Leonard Wood, then served as acting platoon sergeant for 11 months before spending over one year in Korea.

Shirley and Bill both married and moved to St. Louis. Bill and wife had four children, Gary, Larry, Debra and Eric. Shirley had two sons, Frank and Rich.

The Buxton's. Raymond, Isabelle, Bill and Shirley, 1947 in Morley, Mo.

Raymond and Isabelle moved to Oran in 1958. Raymond worked at the Cape Girardeau Golf Course. After retiring they moved to the St. Louis area where Raymond passed away in 1989 and Isabelle lived until 1995.

Bill was an over the road truck driver for Ralph and Ivern Isaccs before going into the Army.

Shirley retired and moved to Arkansas. Bill retired from American National Can Company after putting in 40 years. He now resides in Arnold, MO. *Submitted by Shirley Buxton Barrow*

BYRD – The Byrd's of Scott County descend from William Byrd of Virginia. William was a wealthy planter of colonial Virginia. He was a member of the House of Burgesses from 1677 to 1682, and became a member of the Council of State in 1684. Later, he served as auditor general of Virginia. His wide business activities included tobacco planting at Westover near Jamestown, slave trade with the West Indies, speculation in land and profitable trade with the Indians. He was born in London, and came to Virginia at an early age.

Horace Early Byrd migrated with his family from Lamar County, Alto Scott County around 1923. Horace was a farmer, and his sons, who grew to adulthood, were also farmers. He and his wife, Pearl Alma (Kemp) Byrd had 10 children in Alabama of which 7 living children migrated with them: Mattie Lou, Horace Eubanks, Daniel Kemp, Zelma, Minnie Lee, Aileen and Richard Dowen. Shortly after arriving in Scott County their 11th child, Billy Eugene was born, but only lived about a month and is buried in the Carpenters Cemetery near McMullin. Horace and Pearl are buried in the Garden of Memories in Sikeston.

Mattie Lou married Hoyt Holt in Scott County in 1931. After his death in 1936, she married Walter Lyons in Memphis, TN. They had one child: Vernon. Mattie and Walter are buried in the Garden of Memories in Sikeston.

Horace Eubanks married Margaret Robinson,

daughter of Henry and Hattie (Austin) Robinson, in 1939 in Sikeston. They had six children: Ramona Lee, Horace Jr., Harriet Jean, John Austin, Linda Ruth and Alan Joe. Horace is buried in the Garden of Memories in Sikeston, as is their son, Horace Jr. Margaret celebrated her 82nd birthday in 2001. John Austin and Alan Joe live in Sikeston.

Daniel Kemp married Sally Arizona Killian, daughter of Joseph and Leona (Neal) Killian, in 1939 in Scott County. They had two children: Danny Joe and Donna Kay. Daniel later married Madelyn Pryor and they had a child, Kimberly Dana. Subsequently, Daniel married Betty Pryor and they had a child: Barry Kemp. Daniel is buried in the Garden of Memories in Sikeston. Sally is buried in Memphis, TN. Danny Joe and Donna Kay attended Scott County Schools. Danny Joe married Nancy Lou George in 1962 in Sikeston. They had a child, Victoria Jane. Victoria married Darrel Dickey and they are the proud parents of Meredith Byrd, who was born in 1999, and brings a twinkle to Danny Joe's eyes. Donna Kay married Dudley Bridgforth and they have two children: Mary Dudley and Rebekah Byrd. Danny Joe is a businessman in Sikeston and is married to Reva June Hudson of the Scott County Hudson's.

Zelma died a few years after the Byrd's arrived in Scott County. She is buried in the Carpenters Cemetery at McMullin.

Minnie Lee married Robert Boone, son of William and Bess (Kemper) Boone, in 1938 in Sikeston. They have three children: Deborah Anne, Sheryl Lee and William Robert. Robert died in 1983 and is buried in Rolla, MO. Minnie Lee lives in Sikeston and will celebrate her 82nd birthday in 2001.

Aileen married Emerson Hill Laseter in 1938 in Sikeston. They had four children: Jerry Earl, Robert Hill, Michael David, and Tamrya Rae. Aileen and Emerson are buried in the Garden of Memories in Sikeston. Jerry Earl and his wife, Rita, live in Sikeston. So do Robert Hill and his wife, Wanda.

Richard Dowen married Loisel Young, daughter of John and Docia (King) Young. They had four children: Dixie Lee, Richard Dowens, Sandra Lois and Elizabeth Anne. Richard and Loisel are buried in the Garden of Memories in Sikeston. Dixie Lee (Byrd) Satterfield and Sandra Lois (Byrd) Sitzes live in Sikeston. *Submitted by Danny Joe Byrd*

BROOM – William Broom was one of the early pioneers of Scott County. Although his birth date is unknown, it is known that he lived in Scott County for years and died around 1838. William married Martha Strong and had at least one child, a daughter, Minerva, who probably preceded him in death. Minerva probably married William Hutson and they too, had at least one daughter, Louisa.

William Broom was a large land and slave owner. His business affairs are found in many county records. It has been reported that "On June 11, 1827 he (William Broom) deeded two Negro slaves to his daughter Minerva Hutson. And...is the earliest slave transaction on record in the county recorder's office in Benton."

Unfortunately it is rather difficult to trace his family in either direction because of the many variations that have been made when recording this family name. For example, when some indexes have been typed from the old handwritten documents, the name "Broom" was mistaken for "Brown" or other variations.

William Broom made a will on Feb. 28, 1838 before his death on Aug. 7, 1838. In it he names in addition to his wife, Martha, and Louisa, three other beneficiaries; Mary Jane Taylor, Elizabeth Shaw and

an infant namesake, William Broom Taylor, son of George Washington Taylor who witnessed the same will. The relationship between Broom and all these people is unknown. William Broom also mentions his own unnamed brothers and sisters. William's widow, Martha Strong Broom, remarried in 1839. The new husband was Charles Moore.

The will also makes interesting provisions for black family members. "6th Imprimis- It is my will and desire that my girl Sally shall be free at my wife's death, also the said Sally to have all the property: vis.-lands and tenements, household and kitchen furniture, also all the stock more or less, and Negroes (namely) Steve, Anthony, Reuben, Perry, Maria, Melinda, Mary, Rachel, to belong to her and her heirs forever after the death of my wife, but the said Sally shall not sell the land during her lifetime."

The following names are among those that have been found in Scott County records spelled "Broom": Sally Broom married Samuel Griffith Feb. 9, 1849. This could be the Sally mentioned in Broom's will. Then John Hall married Adaline Broom Nov. 2, 1869 (all "Colored"). The following marriages do not indicate race: Ruben Broom / Mary Edwards Jan. 7, 1877 with Anthony Broom witness; Archy Broom / Philis Daugherty with Asa Broom witness; Tobias Herring / Anna Broom Dec. 24, 1874; Annie Broom / Samuel Harper Jan. 30, 1890. Sarah Broom 36 and Darnzell Broom 13 were in the 1860 census.

Source: Scott County: Wills and Administrations Book E 1832-1848; Marriage; and Census records, Kelso Township. *The History of Scott County, Missouri Up to the year 1880*, by Edison Shrum. *Submitted by Toni Martinazzi.*

CALDWELL – Joseph Conrad and Margaret Jane Caldwell moved to this area and purchased the Tom Scott Farm in 1944. Joseph was Scott County Extension Agent. They had two children, Joseph "Joe John" and Dorothy. Joseph farmed and worked for the USDA as a statistician until his death in 1986. Dorothy resides in Las Vegas with her husband, Bill Pope. Joseph Conrad moved to Columbia after the death of his wife in 1947. He then became affiliated with the University of Missouri Foreign Exchange Program. He died in Columbia Feb. 17, 1966.

Joseph Caldwell family, 1945. Margaret Jane Johnson Caldwell, Dorothy Jane Caldwell Pope, Joseph Johnson Caldwell and Joseph Conrad Caldwell.

Joseph "Joe John" Johnson was drafted into the Army and completed OCS at Fort Campbell, KY. He then went overseas and served as a captain and field commission 2nd lieutenant serving in several campaigns. He met and married Marian who was a member of the British Royal Air Force. They returned to the United States and began a family in Scott County.

Joseph Johnson Caldwell (b. Oct. 12, 1921, d. June 23, 1986) married Marian Elizabeth Talbert-Jones on Jan. 7, 1947 in the Burrough of Kensington in the oldest Church of England. Marian was born

Feb. 24, 1926 and died July 2, 1967. The following children were born to this couple:

Jacqueline Jane Caldwell (Feb. 3, 1948) married to John Warren Merrick (b. Oct. 7, 1948) on July 19, 1969. Robert Caldwell Merrick (b. Aug. 3, 1971) married Dana Lynn Frederick on June 21, 1996; divorced February 2000. Born to Robert and Dana, Connor Joseph Merrick (Sept. 18, 1996) and Bryce Robert Merrick (Dec. 8, 1999).

Marion Elizabeth Caldwell and children, Anna (age 3), Janie (age 4), and Mary (age 2), April 1952.

Claudia Anna Caldwell (b. Jan. 24, 1949) married Galen Dewitt Harper (b. Jan. 2, 1948) on Sept. 10, 1966; divorced April 1990. Born were Gaye Lynne Harper (b. Oct. 3, 1966), Claudia Anna

Conrad Caldwell age 6, 1967.

Harper (b. May 13, 1970) and Rebecca Suzanne Harper (b. June 22, 1971). Gaye Lynne Harper married James Howard Gipson (b. May 25, 1966) on May 5, 1990. Born were Katelyne Elizabeth Gipson (b. March 25, 1992) and James Hunter Gipson (b. Dec. 9, 1996). Claudia Anna Harper married Joey Michael Little on Nov. 26, 1994. Born were Dawson James Little (April 28, 1998) and Harper Elizabeth Little (Oct. 11, 2000). Rebecca Suzanne married Larry Dale Standridge (b. Jan. 4, 1957) on Aug. 17, 2000. Born was Wyatt Caldwell Standridge on April 19, 2001.

Mary Elizabeth Caldwell (b. May 30, 1950) married David Eugene Hubbert (b. Aug. 9, 1950) on Sept. 30, 1969. Born were Elizabeth Ann (b. Sept. 22, 1970), Amy Suzanne (July 3, 1976) and Christina Leigh (b. Aug. 7, 1977). Elizabeth Ann Hubbert married Harold Douglas Menz (b. Oct. 10, 1966) on July 25, 1992. Born was Grant David Menz (Sept. 8, 2001). Christina Leigh Hubbert married Matthew Mark Hansen on July 25, 1997. Born was Brady Caldwell Jansen (Sept. 24, 1997).

Joseph Conrad Caldwell (b. April 1, 1961) married Teresa Kimbrough (March 30, 1960) on Jan. 14, 1988; divorced February 2000. Born were Joseph Johnson Caldwell (Oct. 10, 1988) and Jacqiyn Nicole (Jan. 18, 1990). Teresa had three children by a previous marriage. Adam Christopher Slaughter (b. July 23, 1978), Tosha Slaughter (b. March 26, 1980) and David Lee Abbott (b. March 23, 1985). Joseph Conrad remarried September 2001 to Melissa D. "Missy" Hoover.

CAMBRON – Benjamin Cambron was born March 10, 1874, in Perry County, MO, the son of Lewis and Julia Anna Mattingly Cambron. He and Cora Bell McFadden were married Nov. 23, 1903, in Benton, Scott County, MO.

Benjamin's parents, Lewis (1838-1877) and Julia Ann Mattingly (1844-18810 were married April 16, 1861, in Perry County. They had nine children, Benjamin being the sixth born. The families of both Lewis and Julia are listed in Timothy O'Rourke's book *Maryland Catholics on the Frontier.*

Benjamin was orphaned at an early age. From letters dated in the late 1890s with the family of his sister, Mrs. Robert (Mary Ann) Butler, in Benton, MO, it is obvious that he kept close contact with her family. Through visits with Mrs. Butler's family, it is assumed that he met the petite Miss McFadden.

Cora Bell McFadden (Benjamin's wife) was born in Scott County in 1882, the daughter of George and Mary Rhea McFadden. After their marriage, she and Benjamin lived in Scott County many years. Their children attended the school at Graysboro in the 1920s. They are in a picture of the Graysboro School students of 1924 in Edison Shrum's book *History of the Scott City Area*. The family later lived at Commerce in the home that is now the River Ridge Winery. Family legend has it that they believed this house was haunted. Ben was a farmer all his life, farming both in Scott County, MO and Hamilton County, IL, where they moved in the mid 1930s.

Benjamin and Cora Cambron

Benjamin and Cora had nine children: Mary "May" (1904-1910); Sylvester (1906-1925) who drowned in the Mississippi River near Ste. Genevieve; Lilly (1908-1990) m. Humbert Summers; Anna Lee (1910-1967) m. T. R. Zimmerman; Walter (1912-1912); James Herschel (1914-1995) m. Beulah Lance; Leon Dale (1916-1996) m. Lucy Mannina; Benjamin Jr. (1919-1989) m. Pauline Vineyard; Glenn Raymond (1923-1944) who was killed in Italy in WWII.

Benjamin and Cora both died in Benton, Franklin County, IL, but were brought back to Scott County for burial. They and four of their children are buried at Pollard Cemetery in Sandy Woods.

Their daughter, Anna Lee, made Scott County her permanent home. She and Theodore R. "T. R." Zimmerman (1904-1987), the son of William Lee and Sophronia Jane Pierce Zimmerman, were married May 4, 1927 at Benton, MO.

T. R. and Anna Lee had four children: LaVerne Mae (1928-1992) m. Ralph A. Gulley, son of Theodore and Opal Rubel Gulley; Lloyd Eugene (b. 1932) m. Willa L. Swindell, daughter of Freeman and Eloise Deweese Swindell; Vernon Edward (b. 1935); and Delnar Douglas Zimmerman (b. 1945) now living in Spokane, WA.

Their sons, Lloyd and Vernon, are presently living in Scott County, as well as LaVerne's daughters, Dianne Gulley Stephens (m. Michael Stephens, son of Charles and Violet Allen Stephens) and JoEllen Gulley Whitworth (m. Steven Marshall Whitworth, son of J. C. and Edith Sturm Whitworth).

T. R. worked for the Cotton Belt Railroad; he and Anna Lee are buried at Lightner Cemetery in Scott City, MO. *Submitted by Willa L. Zimmerman*

CANNON – Clarence W. "Doc" Cannon (born March 19, 1880, died June 13, 1961) was married to Lula Louise Wolsey (born March 14, 1888, died Feb. 22, 1980) on July 27, 1907. Daniel Cannon, father of "Doc," and his parents migrated to Scott County, MO in a covered wagon from the

state of South Carolina. The parents of Mrs. Cannon (the Wolseys), being of French descent, settled on Kaskaskia Island near Ste. Genevieve, MO.

The Cannons were farmers and lived on farms near Benton, MO, and later on a farm located on old Highway 61 between Morley and Benton for many years. This is where all the children grew up. They reared eight children, all of whom graduated from Morley High School.

Their oldest child, Clarence W. Cannon (born April 19, 1908, died Aug. 26, 1987) worked on the farm with his father and later, for many years, for the Scott County Highway Department. He was married to Nellie Griffaw Nelson (born May 8, 1909, died Nov. 1, 1973) on April 19, 1946. He later married Ethel Diamond Witt.

Julia Mae Cannon (born Dec. 28, 1909, died June 6, 2000) was married to Harold Nations, who died at the age of 42. She was a home maker and care giver of her parents in their old age. Julia Mae was a talented hobbyist leaving behind many beautiful crocheted items and quilts. She had no children.

Norval Lee Cannon (born Nov. 30, 1911, died Oct. 21, 1979) was married to Irene Sanders on Dec. 22, 1945. He was a long time educator in southeast Missouri having started his career as a teacher at Morley; principal of Benton Elementary School; principal of Diehlstadt High School from 1941 until 1957; math teacher and principal of Sikeston High School from 1957 until 1969. He taught at Central High School in Cape Girardeau, MO from 1969 until his retirement in 1976. He and Irene reared one daughter, Alice.

Neva Louise Cannon (born March 4, 1916, died Jan. 30, 1993) was married to Lloyd Franklin Stone on Oct. 14, 1936. They reared five children: Melba Joan; Jerry Lloyd; Nancy Louise; Betty Sue and James Stone. Neva worked in the maternity ward of Southeast Missouri Hospital in Cape Girardeau, MO for 33 years. She retired in 1989.

Paul Wesly Cannon (born March 12, 1918, died Dec. 23, 1987) was married to Annabelle Marshall from Commerce, MO. He was a CPA and worked many years for McKnight-Keaton Grocery Company in Sikeston, MO. Later he was the manager of the Governor Hotel in Jefferson City, MO where he retired. Paul and Annabelle reared two sons, Paul Robert and Daniel.

Clarence W. Cannon Family, July 25, 1957. Front row: Clarence, C.W. "Doc," Lula, and Paul. Back: Julia Nations, Marie Cope, Margie Williams, Norval, Jewel Harris, and Neva Stone.

Jewel Bridget Cannon (born July 16, 1920, died June 6, 1986) was married to Delbert "Shorty" Harris (born Dec. 12, 1914, died July 12, 1970) in 1940. She was a Certified Shorthand Reporter and worked as secretary to State Senator D. W. Gilmore. Later she worked as Court Reporter for the Workmen's Compensation Court for the State of Missouri for 20 years until her retirement. She and Delbert had one daughter, Mary Lou.

Margie Helen Cannon (born Jan. 30, 1923)

was married to Roy A. "Dick" Williams on May 23, 1942 (born Feb. 22, 1922, died Oct. 30, 1965). She worked 15 years in the Circuit Courts of Scott and Cape Girardeau Counties and later as Deputy Clerk in Charge of U. S. District Court in Cape Girardeau from 1970 to 1992. She retired after 22 years in that position. Margie and Dick reared three children; Gary Joe, Olivia Diane and Jeffrey Wayne.

Lillie Marie Cannon (born July 8, 1925) was married to Paul Edward Cope in Benton, MO. She worked as Deputy Recorder of Deeds of Scott County, MO for many years. She and Paul later moved to Eureka, MO where she worked as a secretary at an elementary school for more than 20 year when she retired. Paul worked as cashier and Vice President of Eureka Bank until he retired. They reared two children, Bruce Edward and Paula Kay.

CANNON – The Vincent Cannon family came to Scott County from Spartanburg County, SC in the fall of 1868. A number of other families also made the same journey, including the Bryant, Kirby, Deaton and Guthrie families. The families traveled by covered wagon and the journey was long and arduous. The Guthrie family continued to Arkansas, which was the original destination of some families.

While camping during the journey, when many individuals were sick, tired and discouraged, the group heard the hooves of a horse approaching. It was a Methodist minister who provided words of comfort and encouragement. Reportedly, that was the reason than many Cannon families became life-long Methodists.

Vincent Cannon (Nancy A. Dillard Cannon) first lived between Benton and Commerce on what became known as the Bill Weber farm. Their children included Sam, Roland, James, Hamlet, Daniel, Charity, Mary, and Madison. Vincent died in 1879 at the age of 52.

One of the sons, Daniel Ward Cannon (1851-1924) and his wife Luella "Lula" Virginia Bryant, raised their children on a small farm near the city limits of Benton, MO. Her parents were James Richardson Bryant and Adeline Caroline Kirby Bryant. The names of their children and spouses were: Clarence Ward "Doc" Cannon (Louise "Lula" Wolsey), Lena Caroline Cannon (Charles William Mowery), Ella Mae Laura Cannon (Richard Moses Williams), Ruth Cleveland Cannon (Golliher), Lloyd Thomas Cannon (Stella Mae Rapp), Charles Harry Cannon (Francis Randolph, Matilda), Lee Buren Cannon (Dorsey Dozier), and D. W. Cannon (died in infancy).

Clarence Ward "Doc" Cannon married Louise "Lula" Wolsey on July 27, 1907 in Benton, MO and raised eight children: Clarence Willard Cannon, Norval Cannon, Paul Cannon, Julia Mae Cannon, Neva Cannon, Jewell Bridget Cannon, Margie Cannon and Marie Cannon.

Clarence Willard Cannon remained a lifelong resident of Benton, MO and Scott County. He was a graduate and star athlete of Morley High School. He was inducted into the Army in December 1942. He was a corporal with an infantry unit at Camp Claiborne, LA. He was employed by the Scott County Highway Department for 32 years and superintendent of the department for 10 years. He retired in March 1973. After retirement, he did wood carving at his home.

Clarence Willard Cannon maintained an interest in Scott County and especially Benton until his death in 1987. He collected pictures and newspaper articles regarding many events and people connected to the Benton area throughout his life. Much of the information contained within this article came from material supplied by his wife, Ethel Witt Cannon.

There are many Cannons buried in the old Benton Cemetery on the south edge of town. *Submitted by Eugene Bullard, Grandson of Lena Cannon Mowery*

CANNON – As Mayor William "Bill" Cannon sits in this office at Chaffee, MO city hall; he feels a lot of pride for the town of 3,000 plus people that he serves. Not just because he serves the townspeople, but also because his family's heritage is here.

His grandfather, Carl Cannon, worked for St. Louis-San Francisco Railroad, and he brought his wife, Ruby (a Texas girl) and their children to Chaffee in 1926. It was a growing town and just beginning. The children were six in number, with a daughter, Dorothy, being born in Chaffee after they arrived. Four older ones born in St. Louis were Louie, whose family still resides in this area, Lillian, Mary, and Bill's father Elmer. His Aunt Thelma was born in Hayti and Aunt Marjorie in Hoxie, AR. They were a Frisco family in every sense. All attended Chaffee public School and it's still hometown, even though all but Louis and Elmer later moved to the state of Texas to raise their families.

Mary Cannon Sills, Margie Cannon Nelson, Elmer Cannon, Dorthy Cannon Larson and Thelma Cannon Teller at Elmer's home in Chaffee, 1999.

Bill's father married a Chaffee girl, Ethel Jefferies, also from a railroad family. Bill, with his brothers, Royce, spent most of their time at Grandma Jefferies' home on West Davidson Ave. A younger brother, Timothy, came along after Bill had entered the Army and was stationed in Germany. Bill returned to Chaffee in 1957 and married a Chaffee girl, Carolyn Ryan, and began his career as fireman and then an engineer on the Frisco Railroad retiring from Burlington Northern out of Chaffee. He later met and married Donna Smith from Delta, MO.

Ethel Jeffries Cannon and Elmer Cannon, in front, and sons, Bill, Tim, and Royce.

Bill has raised five children all of whom attended Chaffee Schools. He has twin girls, Kathi and Karen, two boys, Chris and Wade and one stepson, David Ivester II. Kathi and family reside in Cape Girardeau, MO. Karen and family reside in Springfield, MO. Chris and family reside in Cape Girardeau, MO. Wade attends college

majoring in art and resides at the family home on Clarman Drive in Chaffee, MO. Davie Ivester II grew up in the Cannon home and resides in Chaffee, MO. From his own graduation in 1955 until now he has been involved in the Chaffee School System and all that is a part of Chaffee in general.

Bill Cannon on right and youngest son Wade on left, May 2000.

When Bill retired, his interest in preserving history was foremost on his mind. With help from his wife Donna and a lot of good friends, they started the Chaffee Historical Society, which has been going strong since 1996. He also built his own railroad outside of town where he enjoys giving youngsters and oldsters a ride through the woods and over Heeb Creek.

Bill lost his father, Elmer, in May 2001 but the Cannon family holds a wealth of memories of Circle Park, Horstman Theater, Slaughters Café, Horman Field Swimming Pool, back to the old roundhouse where they repaired engines and the old hoop mill on north Main Street. There are a lot of good people who share their memories from 1926 until today in 2001.

The Cannon family invites everyone to visit Chaffee Museum, their railroad and their town of which they are very proud to share.

CARR – A. O. Carr of Crawford, County, MO was married in 1901 to Cora Elizabeth Sites of Red Bird, MO, daughter of Erasmus and Julia Harper Sites Reddick. The A. O. Carr family moved from Bland, MO where they operated a hotel and farmed, to Oran, Mo about 1930 where A. O. Carr farmed until he retired. His children married and stayed in the state. His oldest daughter Freda lived with them and taught school in Oran, MO for many years. Mr. and Mrs. Carr and Freda moved to St. Louis, MO where Freda taught school until she retired. They then moved to Festus, MO and lived until their death. Eula married Glen Maupin. They owned Maupin Funeral Home in Auxvasse and Fulton, MO. They lived in Fulton, MO until their death. Mayme married Rollo Stone, then Clay Moore, and lived in Kingdom City, MO until their death. Nell married Oley Stotts and lived in Sikeston, Mo where Oley was a bar-

Carr family of Oran, May 11, 1947. Front row: Clarence, A.O., Cora, and Herbert. Back: Chester, Mildred, Nell, Freda, Eula, Mayme, and Robert.

ber. They moved to Florida and lived until their death. Herbert "Hub" married Olive McCarty of Oran, Mo daughter of John P. and Lela Scott McCarty who owned McCarty Lumber yard in Oran, MO. Herbert and Olive bought a farm near Delta, MO where they lived and farmed until 1948 when he sold it and bought a farm at Auxvasse, MO, where they lived until their death. Mildred married John "Jack" Brooks and lives in Festus, Mo. Chester "Chet" married Irene Wagoner and lives in Oran, MO. Robert "Bob" married Velma McClelland and lived in Williamsburg until his death. Velma married Ambrose Elfrink of Oran, MO. They lived in Montgomery City, MO. From this family there was WWII soldiers, farmers, factory workers, Funeral Home Owners and teachers. All are respected and fine citizens. *Submitted by Jane Carr Griffith, daughter of Herbert and Olive Carr*

CARR – Sgt. Robert L. "Bob" Carr, 20, has experienced an eventful year in the service of his county. He was inducted at Jefferson Barracks on April 28, 1944, and trained at Camp Joseph T. Robinson, AR. After 17 weeks of basic training and a two weeks' furlough at home, he went to Fort Meade, MD.

With about 20,000 G. I.'s he crossed the Atlantic on the *H. M. S. Queen Mary*, said to be one of the fastest ships on the ocean. The crossing was made in five days and four nights, landing at Glascow, Scotland, on Oct. 15, 1944. From there he was sent to a camp in England, where he remained three days, then crossed the English Channel into Normandy, where he remained about a week.

Carr brothers, Spring 1946. Left to right: Clarence O., Chester R., and Robert Lee.

He was placed in Company I, 335 Infantry, 84th or Railsplitter's Division of the 9th Army under command of General Simpson. He was in action on the Western front from the last of October until taken prisoner in the battle of the Belgian Bulge on Dec. 24, 1944. Sgt. Carr has remarked that for security reasons he is not permitted to relate the circumstances, which led to his capture and release, nor any details of her period of imprisonment in Germany, even to his immediate family. He is under oath to safeguard all such military information both during his military service and later as a civilian.

On March 28, 1945, after 95 days in two different prison camps, he was among 250 prisoners who were freed when American ground troops overtook a train of box cars in which the prisoners were being moved from a camp near Limburg, further into Germany. He could not give details of the liberation except to say he lost 55 pounds and was too weak to walk. He was carried on a stretcher and placed on a C-47 evacuation plane and flown to an Army hospital in England.

When asked concerning the treatment he received in the prison camp, Sgt. Carr said that he could not say that he had not been mistreated physically by the Germans. Three days and nights was the longest period he had to go without any food. He praises most highly the treatment he received in the hospital in England. The Red Cross was at his side continually, and seemed they could not do enough for the boys.

His family in Oran had received news of his release on April 10, and on April 13, which was his 20th birthday; the Red Cross delivered to him a huge delicious birthday cake and also a birthday message from home. That was his first news from home since his capture on Christmas Eve. Following his period of recuperation in the hospital in England, he was sent home via Iceland and New Foundland in a C-54 transport plane and arrived in the States at an east coast airport may 18, the crossing from Scotland to the States requiring only 21 flying hours. He was sent to O'Reilley General Hospital at Springfield, MO, and from there arrived at his home in Oran Sunday, May 27.

Having been in service less than 13 months, he has had many and varied experiences. Looking well and virtually back to normal, Sgt. Carr had been very busy visiting friends and the members of his family. At a delayed birthday party held in his honor June 10 at the home of his sister, Mrs. Mayme Stone, of Jackson, he was the recipient of a wrist watch presented to him by his family. He is the youngest of nine children of Mr. and Mrs. A. O. Carr of Oran, and has often been called the caboose of the train of Carrs. Three other members of the family who are in the armed forces are St. Chester R. Carr, a tank commander who has served in Hawaii, on Leyte, P.I. and is now on Okinawa, Pvt. John W. Brooks, a brother-in-law, who served with the 42nd Infantry or Rainbow Division, of the 7th Army in Europe, and First Sgt. Clarence O. Carr, who also served with Gen. Simpson's 9th Army in Europe.

Bob is a member of the Methodist church and when asked his opinion of the power of religion, he replied: "The fact that I am alive and able to be at home again in not just a mere coincidence, but due to the prayers of my family and friends. For all these I am humbly grateful."

The following citation was awarded St. Chester R. Carr of Oran and award of the Bronze Star Medal, as follows: "By direction of the President under the provisions of an executive order a Bronze Star Medal is awarded by the Commanding General, 9th Infantry Division, to the following named personnel: Sgt. Chester R. Carr, 37132097, Infantry (Armored Division) Untied States Army. For heroic service in connection with military operations against the enemy on Okinawa Island from 1 April 1945, to 5 May 1945. Sergeant Carr, a tank commander, by his industriousness and control of his tank and crew, was of invaluable aid to his platoon, which was in support of an Infantry company's advance. On one occasion Sergeant Carr moved his tank into a forward position, exposing it to heavy anti-tank fire to provide the necessary protective fire to cover the evacuation of his wounded platoon leader from another tank. On 19 April, 1945, Sergeant Carr, after observing that his platoon leader's tank was immobilized, moved his tank along side to enable the platoon leader to use his tank for the control of the platoon. Sergeant Carr dismounted from his tank and while exposed to enemy fire, guided the remainder of the platoon past the disabled tank. He remained dismounted to affect the necessary repairs. Sergeant Carr's devotion to duty was a continual inspiration to all who witnessed his actions and is in keeping with the highest traditions of the military service."

Sergeant Carr is an older brother of St. Bob Carr, who recently arrived home from a German prison camp. The Carrs have a third son in the service, who is a sergeant also.

CLINE – Charles Floyd "C.F." Cline was born July 08, 1939 in Sikeston, Scott County, Missouri, son of Curtis Henry and Marie Price Cline. He graduated from Sikeston High School in 1957, had a distinguished career in the Air Force, and served in the 7th Air Force in DaNang, Viet Nam between 1966 and 1967 before receiving an Honorable Discharge. He then returned to Viet Nam and worked as a Station Manager for Continental Air Service between November 1967 and December 1970. Continental Air transported civilian passengers and civilian contractors who executed military construction for the U. S. Military in Viet Nam.

He married Kay Ireland January 23, 1972 in Sikeston, Missouri, daughter of Frank and Emma Potts Ireland. She was born September 11, 1946 in Poplar Bluff, Missouri and in August 1969, she graduated with a B. S. in Secondary Education from Southeast Missouri State University. In August *1975,* she received a Master of Arts in Teaching from Southeast Missouri State University, in 1989, attended Nova University in Fort Lauderdale, Florida, and obtained an elementary education certificate to teach in Florida.

C. F. was elected Missouri State Representative for District Number 159, covering parts of Scott and Stoddard Counties in 1972 and reelected in 1974 and 1976. He served as a member of Agriculture, Banks and Financial Institutions Committees and was Chairman of Miscellaneous Resolutions Committee. He was selected Missouri's Outstanding Young Men of America in 1973.

C. F, graduated with a Bachelor of Science degree in Education from Southeast Missouri State University in Cape Girardeau, Missouri in August 1976. He is a member of the Delta Scottish Rite Club, a Shriner and is a 32nd Degree Mason.

C.F. & Kay have two daughters: Susan Emmalea Cline, born August 24, 1974 in Sikeston, Missouri. She received a Bachelor of Arts in Fashion Merchandising from Mars Hill College, NC in 1986. Susan married Eric Marcell Jordan April 12, 1997 in Fairview, North Carolina. Eric was born February 21, 1972 in Ashville, NC, son of Harry Lee and Norma Ruth Ingle Jordan. They have one son, Jacob Zachary Jordan, born

C.F. Cline

March 26, 2002. Their youngest daughter is Karen Anne Cline, born March 23, 1980 in Winter Park, Florida. In 1996, she participated in a Youth Mission Project in Falmouth, Jamaica and in 1998 represented Charlotte County in the Miss Junior Florida Competition. She attended Edison Community College in Punta Gorda, Florida in 1999. Karen married James William Johnson, Jr. October 16, 1999 in Port Charlotte, Florida. James was born December 19, 1976 in Port Charlotte, Florida, son of James William and Tommie Lou Nix Johnson. They have one son, Andrew James Johnson, born November 16, 2002.

C. F. & Kay live in Port Charlotte, Florida. C. F. works for Sam's Club as special marketing representative and Kay is a teacher at Myakka River Elementary School in Port Charlotte. They are members of First Baptist Church of Port Charlotte. *Submitted by C. F. Cline, Port Charlotte, Florid*

CLINE – Curtis Eugene "Gene" Cline was born August 28, 1936 in Sikeston, Missouri. He is the son of Curtis Henry and Marie Price Cline. He married Jeanette Louise Ledyard on August 23, 1958 in Bryan, Ohio. Jeanette is the daughter of Richard and Genevieve Day Ledyard. She was born April 13, 1938 in Alvordton, Ohio.

Gene graduated from Sikeston High School in 1954 and graduated with a Bachelor of Arts in Music Education from Olivette Nazarene University in Kankakee, Illinois in 1959. It was there that he met his wife, Jeannette, who also graduated with a Bachelor of Arts in Music Education.

They have two daughters: Jeanitta Kay Cline, Born July 6, 1960 in Adrian, Lenawee County, Michigan. She received a Bachelor of Fine Arts degree in Graphic Communications and Advertising from Baylor University in 1982. She was active in Delta Gamma sorority and was chosen as a nominee for 1980 Homecoming Queen at Baylor. Jeanitta married David Upton Thomas, son of Clayton and Phyllis Butler Thomas, on August 16, 1986 in Tempe, Arizona. They have four sons. Their second daughter, Jeanelle Rene' Cline, was born April 8, 1966, in Chandler, Arizona. Jeanelle graduated from Arizona State University with a Bachelor of Arts in Organizational Communications in December of 1988, at Tempe', Arizona. Jeanelle married Andrew Shaw, son of Brian and Patricia Margaret Hurt Shaw of Yorkshire, England on October 5, 1996 in Tempe', Arizona. They live in Boston Spa, West Yorkshire, England and have one daughter.

Gene is a tenor singer and musician and Jeanette is an accomplished pianist. They travel the world each summer with the International Music Workshops. Gene is also an artist in the media of oil and pencil and studied and displayed in an art show in Lyons, France in 1994. They now live in Tempe', Arizona and after retiring from the public school system in Tempe' they continue to teach music from their music studio. They are members of Grace Community Church in Tempé, AZ. *Submitted by C. Eugene Cline, Tempé, A*

Gene and Jeanette Cline

CLINE – Curtis Henry Cline was born May 14, 1911 on a dairy farm near Morehouse, Missouri. He was the son of William Henry Cline, a native of Hickman County, KY and Nannie Lena Kline of New Madrid County, MO.

Curtis was respected in the community for his hard work, honesty and integrity. He owned and operated Cline Limestone Company from 1939 to 1949, and is best remembered as a horticulturist and owner of Cline Nursery between 1950 and 1989. He was an active member of the First Church of the Nazarene in Sikeston for over sixty years. Curtis was an optimistic person who kept his keen sense of curiosity and zest for living throughout his life.

He was united in marriage at Sikeston to Marie Ruth Price on November 2, 1935, in New Madrid County, MO, daughter of Henry Price, a native of Saline County, Illinois and Anna Caroline Rettig, a native of Vanderburg County, Indiana. Marie was devoted to her children and family and was happiest when

Curtis and Marie (Price) Cline

she was entertaining at home or when she was fishing. Marie died November 22, 200, after 65 years of marriage together.

Curtis and Marie had three children: Curtis Eugene "Gene" Cline, born August 28, 1936 in Sikeston; Charles Floyd "C.F." Cline, born July 8, 1939 in Sikeston; and one daughter, Margaret

Louise Cline Harmon, born July 4, 1944 in Cape Girardeau, MO.

Curtis and Marie (Price) Cline

When Curtis and Marie were in their 60s and early 70s, they purchased a camping trailer and lived in Florida in the cold winter months. Curtis sold the Cline Nursery when he was sixty-nine years old, but found that retirement was not for him, so he continued to do tree trimming and odd jobs until he was in his early 80s. Curtis died December 21, 2002.

In the twilight of their lives their health became frail and they resided in Clearview Nursing Center in Sikeston from December 1995 until their death. They are buried in Sikeston Memorial Park. *Submitted by Margaret Cline Harmon, daughter*

CLINE – Gazawell "Gaz" Cline was born July 27, 1903 in Morehouse, New Madrid County, Missouri. He was the son of William Henry Cline, a native of Hickman County, KY (1859) and Nannie Lena Kline of New Madrid County, MO (1870). He was named after his grandfather, Gazawell S. Kline.

Gazawell "Gaz" Cline

He married Bertha Klingel, daughter of Louis Herman Klingel and Mary Etta Stein Klingel, on May 7, 1930 in Morehouse, Missouri. Bertha was born February 17, 1911 in Madison County, Illinois. They had six children. Three sons and three daughters: Kenneth Harold Cline, born May 3, 1931 in Sikeston, who married Oleda Honeycutt in Alexandria, Louisiana and had two children, Alena Janel Cline and Darris Cline and then he married Dorothy Johnson on July 26, 1983 in Sikeston; Richard Arlen "Dick" Cline, born December 25, 1933 in Sikeston, who married Shirley Ann Richardson on September 20, 1958 in Salcedo, Missouri and they had three daughters, Toreia Kay Cline, Sherry Ann Cline and Hope Lynn Cline; Eileen "Sis" Cline, born August 15, 1936 who married Howard Ray Wyman on June 9, 1956 in Sikeston and they had four children, Penney Sue Wyman, Howard Allen Wyman, Cline Houston Wyman and another son, Stephen Ray Wyman was killed in an automobile accident on July 17, 1977 in Holly Springs, Mississippi; Robert Howard "Bob" Cline, born November 1, 1937 in Sikeston who married Carol Heckert on December 24, 1960 in Bertrand, Missouri and they had two sons, Kevin Lewis Cline and Keith Allen Cline (Keith died four days after birth due to complications during birth) and a daughter, Karen Lynette Cline; Barbara Sue Cline, born August 2, 1940 in Sikeston, MO who married Larry Lewis on April 4, 1959 in St. Ann, Missouri and they have two sons, Joseph Duane Lewis and Charles Dean Lewis; and Ruth Annita Cline, born December 7, 1945 in Cape Girardeau, Missouri and married Tony Wayne Clodfelder, Jr. on November 24, 1973 in Sikeston, Missouri and they have two daughters, Ruth Annita Clodfelder and Jane Cole Clodfelder.

Gaz was a farmer east of McMullen until 1954 when they moved to Bloomfield, MO where they purchased a farm. The family returned to Sikeston in 1958 and he went to work for the Missouri Highway Department until he retired. He was a member of Sikeston A.F. & A.M. Lodge #310 and served as Worshipful Master. He was an active Mason and lectured to help new members during their first months in the organization. He was a member of the shriners and was elevated to the 32nd degree.

Bert was a member of the Sikeston Eastern Star Chapter #137. She was a self-employed seamstress in Sikeston and was an excellent cook. She was well known for her sweet bread and candies.

Gaz and Bert were of the Methodist faith. Gaz Cline died November 1983 and Bert Klingel Cline died March 13, 1985. They are buried in the Sikeston City Cemetery. *Submitted by Annita Cline Clodfelder*

CLINE – Howard Cline was born April 8, 1891 on a dairy farm in Morehouse, Missouri the son of William Henry Cline, a native of Hickman County, KY and Nannie Lena Kline of New Madrid County, MO. He married Minnie Irene Null, daughter of William Scott and Mary Ann Hobbs Null of Hematite, MO, on July 24, 1913 and moved to Chaffee in 1917.

Howard Cline age 21, ca. 1911

Mr. Cline was employed as a conductor for the Frisco Railway Company and retired after 48 years of service in 1965. He was a member of A.F. & A.M. Lodge #615 and served as Worshipful Master. He was also Past District Deputy Grand Lecturer for the 49th District, a member of Brother of Roadroad Trainmen, and a member of the First Methodist Church in Chaffee.

Howard and Minnie had a son Howard Denton Cline, born November 30, 1914 in Chaffee. He married several times and had two daughters with Wilma Ruth Perry. One daughter died young and Howard and Minnie raised their granddaughter Betty Lou Cline. She married Morris Montgomery on November 17, 1957 in Chaffee. They had one grandson Howard Denton Cline Jr. who died young.

Howard Cline died January 11, 1967 at the Charleston Host House in Charleston, MO after residing at 211 W. Parker, Chaffee since 1917. His wife preceded him in death on April 8, 1955. They are buried in Union Park Cemetery, Chaffee, MO. *Submitted by Granddaughter Betty Cline Montgomery*

CLINE – William Edward "Ed" Cline was born March 7, 1899 in Morehouse, New Madrid County, Missouri. He was the son of William Henry Cline, a native of Hickman County, KY (1859) and Nannie Lena Kline of New Madrid County, MO (1870). He married Susie Smith Barnes, daughter of Robert W. and Nellie

William Edward Cline

A. Minner Barnes, on July 15, 1919 in Morehouse, Missouri. Susie was born June 16, 1896 in Crittenden County, KY. They had three children. A son, William Edward "Dub" Cline, born July 29, 1928 and he married Imogene Waggener and they had a daughter Debra Sue Cline and then he married Virginia Campbell and they had a son William Edward Cline III. Ed and Susie also had two daughters. Anna Sue Cline was born July 12, 1933 in Scott County and their youngest daughter is Betty Jo Cline, born September 04, 1936 in Scott County and she married Eddie Jobe of Bertrand on July 1, 1961 at McMullin, Missouri. They have one son, Mark Lee Jobe. Dub died November 21, 1991 and Anna Sue died May 31, 1998.

Ed was a prominent rancher and owned a general store in McMullin, Missouri, six miles north of Sikeston. He owned ranches in Scott, Perry and Bollinger Counties. He died on November 19, 1957 at St. Luke's Hospital in St. Louis as the result of injuries sustained in a traffic accident a short distance north of Sikeston on November 12, 1957.

Susie Barnes Cline was a retired school teacher in the Scott and Mississippi County School systems teaching over 55 years. She was a member of the Richwood Methodist Church and the McMullin Extension Club. She died July 20, 1984 in her home near Sikeston. Ed and Susie Cline are buried in Memorial Park Cemetery, Sikeston, MO.

CLYMER – Hixey (Garner) Clymer brought her family from Hickman County, TN, to Scott County, MO in 1857. Her husband, Andrew Clymer, had died in Hickman County in 1850. Andrew and Hixey had seven children: May, Charles, Nancy, John D., Samuel, James, and Lewis. This Clymer family's roots reach back through North Carolina and Virginia to Bristol, England.

John D. Clymer returned to Hickman County, TN in 1859. When the Civil War began, Clymer was forced into the Confederate Army. At his fist opportunity, he left the Confederate Army and joined the US Army, Company C. 12th Regiment, Tennessee Calvary. After the Civil War, John Clymer settled in Scott County, MO.

On Oct. 23, 1866, John D. Clymer married Elvira Evaline Hawkins, the widow of James F. C. Hawkins, the son of Rachael and Benjamin Hawkins. John and Evaline Clymer had two children, George Edward and Ida. After Evaline's death, John Clymer married Nancy Jane (Finley) Reynolds Lackey on Oct. 11, 1874. Nancy had children from her two previous marriages and she and John had children. Altogether, there were five sets of children. In the late 1880s John D. Clymer was the constable of Commerce. His granddaughter, Jennie Evaline, remembered his home as a log home with a large front room housing a very large fireplace.

George Edward Clymer was born Aug. 11, 1867. He was a jovial person who enjoyed singing and playing the accordion. He married Canzada Haden Penn Sept. 11, 1887. The children of George and Canzada were Alma, Piercie and Jennie. Clymer died in a logging accident on Jan. 9, 1905.

Canzada Haden Penn Clymer was born Jan. 20, 1863. She was the daughter of Mahala Jane (Kirk) Fleeman Penn and Joseph Penn. Joseph Penn was born in Tennessee, but the family was originally from Virginia and includes John Penn, signer of the Declaration of Independence. The Penn family was originally from England.

Jennie Evaline Clymer Caldwell

Jennie Evaline and Piercie Clymer, children of George Edward Clymer.

was born Feb. 7, 1896 in Commerce, MO. She was the daughter of George and Canzada Clymer. She married Guy Caldwell on Aug. 23, 1914 in Scott County, MO. Jennie and Guy had 12 children; however, four died as infants. Their children are: Mary, Jesse, Guy Jr., Geneva, Davis, Dean, Frank and Loretta.

Guy Caldwell was born Aug. 1, 1888 and died April 1, 1947 in Scott County. He was the son of Oscar Caldwell and Philomena Witt. Oscar Caldwell, the son of James Harvey and Sarah Caldwell, was born in New Madrid County on April 14, 1859. Oscar died Aug. 12, 1924, from injuries sustained after his team of mules bolted.

James Harvey was the son of David G. L. Caldwell who came to the Cape Girardeau District about 1805 from Georgia. Davis' father, William, was the son of David Caldwell and Anne (Harris) Caldwell of Mecklenburg County, NC. Beginning with the American Revolution, the Harris and Caldwell families have provided many American patriots. Both families are of Scottish ancestry.

Philomena (Witt) Caldwell was born Feb. 8, 1867, and died Feb. 5, 1948. She was the daughter of John Witt and Mary (Pobst) Witt. John Witt was born May 29, 1838 in Ohio. Born on Dec. 9, 1843 Mary Pobst Witt was the daughter of Joseph and Madeline (Pfefferkorn) Pobst. Mary died on Feb. 17, 1904. On June 20, 1905 John Witt sold 1800 acres of land to the Chaffee Real Estate Company of St. Louis for the establishment of Chaffee. John Witt died on Oct. 16, 1905. The Pobst, Pfefferkorn and Witt families were from the Alsace-Lorraine region of France. *Submitted by Mary Elizabeth Caldwell Young*

COLEMAN – Edwin Pope Coleman Jr. "E. P." was born on February 8, 1892 and raised on a family cotton plantation in Como, Mississippi. He attended Harvard Business School in 1910. While in the East he met his wife, Katherine "Kate" Hetherington from Canada. They were married in Boston in 1919.

E.P. Coleman

In 1923 the Coleman's moved to Sikeston, Scott County, Missouri with $50,000 from his father's Mississippi plantation. His father sent with him one of his own riding bosses, E. W. Wilson, so Coleman would not find trouble opening his farming venture. Coleman also brought a handful of Mississippi sharecroppers, most of who were black, to farm the enterprise he would build in Missouri. He was a forth-generation farmer and a businessman who entered agriculture in the 1920's to become one of the wealthiest landholders in the Bootheel of Missouri. Coleman was the first man to introduce large-scale cotton farming to the Bootheel region. In 1926 he built the Coleman Gin Co., a three slow speed Cotton Gin.

Coleman had acquired by good farming practices and investments 16,000 acres of farmland in the area by the outbreak of World War II. Besides being an astute businessman, Coleman was also very generous with his holdings. His sister, Ruth Coleman Gay, was widowed at an early age. To her he gave Tracts 10 & 58 in Scott and Cape Girardeau Counties respectively. To his niece, Mary Frances "Pam" Gay, he gave the 300-acre farm in Stoddard County. His other niece, Ruth Gay, received in Scott County 220 acres of land. His sister's only son, David, was given 17,500 acres in several

counties. He received more than twice the acreage of his sisters, evidence of a still-ruling patriarchy.

Coleman also set up several trusts for other relatives, which at one time or another also included his nieces and nephew. The E. P. Coleman Partnership gave 10 relatives a percentage of the profits from five farms in Scott County, totaling 1,170 acres. Pam, Ruth, and David were each given 10 percent of the partnership. Coleman also organized the Curry-Fitzgerald Trust with almost 1,200 acres on three farms, which he gave his sisters, Clara Coleman Curry and Miriam Coleman Fitzgerald.

John Hux Sr. was involved with Coleman's land enterprises from 1930's on. He continued to manage the land for several of the heirs after Coleman's death. Hux began working with Coleman in 1936 and was eventually adopted as a surrogate son' as Coleman himself was childless. Coleman sent him to law school, and the young man became the lawyer for the E. P. Coleman Company. Hux had two sons, John Jr. and James. The younger two Huxes have been involved with the Coleman land, with John Jr. managing the farmland and James providing the legal services.

In the early 1960's, Coleman donated a great deal of his time and money to the development of the Delta County Hospital in Sikeston, the first medical center in the area. During fundraising for the new hospital, he was the primary benefactor, with a donation in excess of $1 million matching community donations, He later gave 3,000 acres of land to that hospital.

When Coleman died, on September 7, 1972, his generosity with his land and farms continued. At his death he owned 9,000 acres of land in Scott, Cape Girardeau, Stoddard, and New Madrid Counties' collectively worth $6 million. The primary heir of his assets was his wife, Kate, who continued the generosity he practiced. In his will, Coleman passed land money to more than 50 people. However, Coleman's generosity and concern for others during his lifetime were also dominant parts of his personality. Although a capitalist entrepreneur, Coleman used his farms to ensure his family and friends were well taken care of and hoped at least part of land fortune would stay in the Coleman family line. *Submitted by John L. Wilson*

COMPAS(S) – Anton and Margaretha Compas(s) moved the family from the village of Luemschwiller, Alsace, France to the County of Waterloo, (now in the Province of Ontario, Canada) British North America in approximately 1832. Records indicate that two sons, out of a total of eight children, came with them; Morand, the oldest born in 1819 and Francis, born in 1825. In April 1845 Morand married Maria Josephina Hoffman at St. Agatha Church. They had three children: Mary Ann, Elizabeth and John. Per the 1851 census of British North America he owned and farmed 350 acres of land in Woolwich Township, Upper Canada. Francis married Catherina Cunemann in January 1850 at St. Boniface Church. It is not known what happened to Anton's other children.

Mary Ann married Christian Bechtel in an unknown year; Elizabeth married Frank L. Diebold in Kelso in May 1881; and John married Anna Mary Westrich in New Hamburg in February 1882.

In 1854, with father, mother and family, Morand moved to Scott County, MO where he purchased a farm of 80 acres three miles northeast of Kelso, at $6.25 per acre. Francis remained in Upper Canada to farm 125 acres in Woolwich Township. Morand's father was not satisfied with the new situation and returned to Upper Canada the next year. He then returned for the mother in the following year. Maria died in 1857. In 1858 he married Christina Gertrud Schlattmann (from Perry County, MO) on his farm. They had seven

children: Catharina, Rosina, Susanna, Henry, Joseph, Frank and Peter. In March 1883 Morand purchased an adjacent 40 acres of land.

Catharina married John N. Goshe in Cape Girardeau in September 1874; Rosina married Anton J. Diebold in Kelso in October 1879;

Morand Compas

Susanna married Joseph Welter in Kelso in April 1882; Henry married Philomena Joanna Bles in Kelso in May 1890 and then Regina Scherer in Kelso in November 1892; Joseph married Carolina Quellmalz in Kelso in September 1890; Frank married Amelia Dunger in Kelso in April 1891; and Peter married Magdalena M. Burger in Kelso in April 1894.

Morand was a farmer and reported to be a weaver of wool, cotton and flax. He is listed as a founding member of St. Lawrence Parish in New Hamburg in 1858. He enlisted to serve with the Home Guards during the Civil War. Mr. Compas is listed on the St. Augustine Church "Parish Family Tree- 1878, First 31 families." He is listed in the "Early Scott County Naturalization Records" as applying for citizenship from France, in 1882.

In February of 1903 (at age 84) he had three great-grandchildren per the *Scott County Kicker*. The paper goes on to print: He has always led an active life is a man of regular habits. Scrupulously honest and fair in his dealings with his fellow men, he enjoyed the confidence and respect of all who know him. In 1900 he fell and dislocated his hip joint, and now goes about on crutches. He had always been a reader of newspapers and kept well abreast of current events. He died at age 85, in February 1904. He and Christina are buried in the cemetery at St. Augustine Church, Kelso, MO. The burial location of Maria is unknown. *Compiled by David F. Compas, August 2001 in Indian Hills, CA*

COMPASS – As I came to the age of remembering things, my half brother Lawrence and my sister Emma were already married.

During the terrible snow storm of 1917, I was 4 years old and all I can remember was my brothers had dug tunnels (I don't know how deep) around the house to the barn, hen house and all the places they needed to get to. Snow from December 7th to March. I was told the people would go over the fields not knowing where the fences were. My brother Anton told me years later that he and brother Ben had their feet frozen, since they had to go to get and make wood nearly every day to keep all the stoves going.

As I grew older, my brothers Anton and Ed and sister Alvina had married and Clara and I were all that was left at home, so Clara helped Mom and I helped Dad. I knew how to harness the mules and hitch them to the plow, wagon, surrey, etc. I remember my Dad taking one mule (Beck) and a little one row plow to make the rows and I would follow with the other mule (Molly) with a one row planter to plant crops. I can't remember if we walked barefoot or wore some old shoes. We did a lot of hoeing those days.

In the fall, the corn would be gathered in the shucks and later we would sit out in the cold corn crib and pull the shucks off for the straw sacks for our beds. Each day the shucks would be stirred up to fluff up the bed. Can you imagine all the dust falling out and being under the beds (achoo)! The straw sacks were used in place of the inner spring mattress of today. On top of that we had the feather beds, which were made from the feathers that we had to pluck from the geese and ducks which we raised. I think about the only job I hated on the farm was plucking feathers. Those poor geese and ducks. It must have been hell for them, but after turning them loose, they seemed to enjoy the hair cuts.

Our home was part log and the rest added on. First floor consisted of Mom and Dad's room, a big hall and dining room when we had company and a spare bedroom in the front of the house. In back, was the girls' room and long kitchen. The boys slept upstairs and above the upstairs was a large attic. That is where we dried the feathers, made the feather beds and all the pillows. It was also a good hiding place for things around Christmas and Easter. With exception of the log room, our house was very cold. We used a lot of homemade quilts, comforters and sometimes even another feather bed to cover. Old pieces of rugs or rags were put to doors on the floor to keep the snow out.

No one was better at raising fruit than my Dad. We had two fig trees, two prune trees, at least six or seven kinds of peach trees, June peaches and some kind all summer until the Indian peaches in the fall. The same with apples. Early June red and yellow all summer until the winesaps in the fall, two kinds of pear trees. Also six or seven kinds of grapes. Some red ones were real late and lasted until frost. Dad knew how to prune grapes and trees. We also had goose berries, strawberries, dew berries and blackberry patches all over the farm. One year we picked 90 gallons. Can't remember for sure, but only got about 25 cents a gallon, I think. Not mentioning all the plum trees. They seemed to pop up everywhere in the fence rows. We would wrap apples and pears individually in catalogue papers and keep them in a room upstairs with very little heat and sometimes would have some yet at Easter time.

We raised a lot of sugar cane. My Dad cooked molasses. One year he cooked 2600 gallons; 25 cents a gallon for cooking for others and 50 cents if they bought ours. There was so much cane that year that people would have to put the cane in our barn until we were ready to get to it, so it wouldn't freeze. Dad cooked from early fall until Christmas.

Sorry so far I have written only about the working times, but that is about all anybody on the farm knew, just work. We didn't get to go anywhere, so I had a lot of cousins, who I never knew. We did get to go to the picnic at New Hamburg. The picnic was on the old picnic grounds which is north of the cemetery. Dad would give us each a quarter and when we would get there, he would buy us a soda. We were delighted. Clara and I would go fishing managed by the Nuns. I think they had nickel and dime fishing hooks. We usually fished twice, and on leaving, Dad would buy us an ice cream cone and we went home proud as a peacock because we had usually 15 cents left over to take home and call our very own.

When going to school, we walked three miles there and three miles back. No sidewalks or black top roads, but gravel and dirt roads. The dirt roads were easy to walk as long as it wasn't raining. Sometimes Mom would cut flowers for church and wrap a wet cloth around the stems and then wrap them in newspapers. They stayed real well. The Nuns would let us girls make bouquets for the Altars and sometimes go to certain places, like my Aunt Katie's house (she had a rose garden) to get beautiful roses and then is when I decided if I ever grew up and had my own garden, I would raise flowers for the altars. That is exactly what I did.

Later, Clara left to go to Cape to work. When I turned 16, Mom and Dad sold the farm, so I went to work, doing housework for a family of six. The

little girl had muscular dystrophy and couldn't do anything for herself. I worked six and a half days a week from 6 in the morning until sometimes 8 or 8:30 p.m., or even later, only Sunday afternoons off, and my wages were $5.00. I gave half of it home. Then came the great depression and the bottom fell out of everything. The wages went to $3.00 a week, and I still gave half of it home. *By Regina (nee) Compas, youngest daughter of Henry and Regina Scherer Weismueller Compas.*

COMPASS – John Compass was the son of Moran and Christina Schlatmann Compass. John married Mary Westrich Diebold Compass. John and Mary Compass had five children: Lawrence Diebold; Joseph; Leo; Alma and Johnny.

Joseph Compass (b. Dec. 17, 1882, d. Nov. 10, 1968) married Anna Marie (Bollinger) Hawkins (b. March 3, 1883, d. May 4, 1943) on Sept. 21, 1909 at St. Lawrence Church in New Hamburg, MO. Anna Marie was the daughter of John (b. March 20, 1858, d. May 4, 1938) and Marie Blattel Bollinger (b. July 28, 1861, d. Sept. 12, 1942). Anna Marie's father, John, was the son of Peter and Anna (Dirnberger) Bollinger. Her mother Marie, was the daughter of Jake and Margaritta (Schlitt) Blattel, had 12 children: Anna Rachel; Unknown; Victor; Theodore; Albert; Clara; Ida; Dora; Ameilia "Mely;" Hobard C. and John L.

Joseph and Anna Marie Bollinger Hawkins Compass had five children: Lorena Wesley Hawkins (b. Nov. 14, 1907, died Aug. 1, 1985); Edith (b. Dec. 25, 1911); Alma (b. Oct. 18, 1914; Theon (b. April 3, 1917) and Naomi (b. Nov. 20, 1919).

Mr. and Mrs. Monroe H. Lauck, May 28, 1942.

Naomi Regina Compass married Monroe H. Lauck (b. May 16, 1916, d. April 3, 1949) at St. Denis Church at Benton, MO on May 28, 1942. Monroe was the son of August Vincent and Frances Blattel Ourth Lauck. Naomi was the local telephone operator for many years for Southeastern Bell Telephone at her home in Benton. She also owned and operated the "Curve Inn Café" at Blomeyer, MO for over 30 years. Recently, Naomi retired from Chaffee Elementary School where she worked as a teacher's aide. She now resides in Chaffee. Monroe and Naomi Compass Lauck had two daughters, Charlotte (b. Feb. 12, 1944) and Jeanette "Jeannie" (b. March 9, 1949).

Charlotte Ann Lauck Surface married Roy L. Surface at St. Ambrose Church in Chaffee, MO on Feb. 13, 1965 and had two children. Melissa Ann Surface Lancaster (b. June 12, 1967, d. Sept. 19, 1993) and Todd Lee Surface (b. Dec. 17, 1975).

Melissa Ann Surface Lancaster had one son, Matthew Wayne Lancaster (b. Nov. 6, 1991) and Todd Lee Surface has one son, Damien Michael (b. May 25, 1999).

Jeannette "Jeannie" Lauck Stroder Chapman married Darrell A. Chapman Jan. 17, 1992. Jeannie has two children, Regina "Gina" Stroder Beggs (b. Dec. 19, 1973) and Clinton W. Stroder (b. Dec. 18, 1984).

Regina "Gina" Stroder Beggs married David L. Beggs and has two daughters, Courtney Ann (b. Sept. 16, 1994) and Karlee Marie (b. July 12, 2001).

CORVICK – Victoria Kern, born Sept. 20, 1889 in Scott County, MO, the daughter of John Adam

Kern (Oct. 27, 1849, Massillion, OH-April 20, 1911) and Mary Catherine Hess (Aug. 13, 1854-Nov. 24, 1944, both buried in St. Augustine Cemetery at Kelso, MO) and the granddaughter of Johannes Adam Kern (1811-Sept. 20, 1865, buried in St. Lawrence Cemetery) and Gertrude Eisemann (April 15, 1822-May 22, 1883, buried in St. Augustine Cemetery at Kelso, MO) was married to William M. Corvick on Oct. 9, 1908 in East St. Louis, IL. He was born Dec. 14, 1886 and died on his birthday in 1963. He was a retired engine inspector for the Cotton Belt Railroad. Seven children born to this union:

William M. and Victoria (Kern) Corvick

First child: Ethelyn Catherine Corvick (Oct. 5, 1909, St. Louis, MO-Jan. 21, 1949) m. James Fred Estes (Aug. 28, 1909-Oct. 21, 1985) on June 27, 1930. They have one son: James Edward Estes.

Second child: Thelma Anna Corvick (Dec. 18, 1911-Dec. 12, 1990, buried at Memorial Park Cemetery in Cape Girardeau) m. Werner Ressel (May 21, 1905-Nov. 29, 1998, buried in ST. Augustine Cemetery at Kelso), the son of Theodore Ressel and Mary Ann Diebold. He was owner of a small grocery store in Kelso. They divorced and she married Elmer Killian Glastetter (Sept. 26, 1926) on July 2, 1977 by Justice of the Peace in Benton. He is a retired farmer in the Rockview Community.

Third child: Helen Louvine Corvick (Nov. 2, 1917-Feb. 27, 1997, buried at Lightner Cemetery in Scott City) m. Albert Emil Martin in 1943 in Seattle, WA. He served in the Air Force during WWII, was reported missing in action; shot down during a bombing mission over Wessel, Germany on June 22, 1944. The body was never found. He was the son of Albert J. Martin and Nellie Maria Greer. One son from this union, John Albert Martin.

Helen's second marriage was to Woodrow Wilson "Bill" Davidson (born Aug. 14, 1917-April 20, 1984, buried in Lightner Cemetery, Scott City) on July 19, 1952 in Jonesboro, AR, the son of John Davidson and Rosa Powell. He was a retired locomotive engineer for the Cotton Belt Railroad.

Fourth child: William August Corvick (Aug. 1, 1920-Dec. 3, 1987) m. Jessilie Bentley on Dec. 21, 1945 at Falls Church, VA. He was a construction worker and had owned his own company. He was a paratrooper in the U. S. Army during WWII.

Fifth child: Laverne Corvick (Aug. 8, 1925) m. William Owen Rogers (Dec. 3, 1923) on May 29, 1948 in St. Augustine Church at Kelso, son of Owen Roger and Anna Welter. Celebrated their 50th wedding anniversary in 1998.

Sixth child: Lloyd John Corvick (June 2, 1928-June 5, 2002) m. Helen L. Webb on March 5, 1949 at St. Joseph's Parish rectory in Scott City. He was retired from Southwestern Bell Telephone Company. He served in the U. S. Marine Corp. Buried in Lightner Cemetery in Scott City. Four children to this union: Lloyd John Corvick Jr. (Dec. 9, 1948-Feb. 22, 2001) and three daughter,

Darlene, Marlene and Arlene (Nov. 27, 1949). Darlene died in 3 days old.

Seventh child: Elsie Darlene Corvick (June 26, 1934) m. James Samuel DeLong (April 8, 1934-April 8, 2001, buried in Warrensburg, MO) on March 21, 1954. Four children: James Samuel Jr. (Nov. 27, 1955); Kenneth Loren (Jan. 3, 1958); Debra Liane (March 25, 1959) and Kiesha Marie (July 20, 1984), a granddaughter they adopted. She was the daughter of Debra Liane DeLong m. Vincent Dewey Erzinger on June 26, 1977 at Patuxent River Air Base in Patuxent, MD.

Victoria Corvick died on Nov. 21, 1971 and is buried at Memorial Park Cemetery in Cape Girardeau, MO. Submitted by Elsie Darlene (Corvick) DeLong

DEASON – Bettie Lucille Kindred Deason was born June 8, 1930 in Sikeston, MO. The daughter of Nicholas Gilbert Kindred, born Dec. 21, 1894 near Blodgett, MO; died Feb. 18, 1979. Buried in Memorial Park, Sikeston, MO. He was a farmer and carpenter. He was in WWI, but did not go overseas. He married Anna Lucille Stubblefiled of McMullin, MO. She was born Nov. 30, 1901 and died July 15, 1935, of blood poisoning. Bettie was raised at McMullin, later called Grant City. From the time her mother died until she left home, her dad's parents raised her. On the farm was a wonderful place to be. The Kindred's were farmers and in the making of pottery. She grew up with uncles, aunts and cousins. Every summer there were family reunions. Bettie had a sister Francoise Kindred born Oct. 30, 1925; died Nov. 8, 1931 of Diphtheria at age 6. Buried in Carpenter Cemetery, off Highway 61, six miles north of Sikeston, MO. A brother William Thomas Kindred was born Oct. 9, 1932 six and a half miles north of Sikeston, MO. He was married first time to Mary Kathleen Spence and had a boy and a girl. Second time to Barbara Lee Ruiz; they have one boy. William lives in St. Mary's, GA. He graduated from Southeast Missouri State University. He received a Biology/Chemistry degree (Pre-Med). He served in Air Force for four years. Retired from Parke Davis after 36 years.

After Bettie's mother died her father married Mary Nell Rose of McMullin. Born April 3, 1914, died May 11, 1980. Buried Memorial Park, Sikeston, MO. Nicholas and Nell had one son, Gary Nicholas Kindred in Sikeston, MO. Born Nov. 24, 1944. He is married to Carol Reeves and they have two sons. Gary graduated from Scott Central High School. He is a salesman for Mid South Office Supply. Nicholas and Nell had one daughter Sandra Ann Kindred born April 14, 1945, lives in Sikeston, MO.

Bettie and Gordon were married Nov. 27, 1949, in Sikeston, MO. Gordon was born April 9, 1919 in Blytheville, AR. He was a farmer and worked for General Motors in St. Louis. Also his brother and he owned Deason's Grocery for several years and worked for MODOT. Died Jan. 6, 1970 of a heart attack. Gordon also was a veteran of WWII, serving in Guam and Japan. Bettie and Gordon had four boys. All of them were born at Missouri Delta Medical Center, in Sikeston, MO.

Gordon William Jr. born Aug. 6, 1950, went to Railroad school in Atlanta, GA, and then was inducted in the Army, served four years. He is a dispatcher for CSX RR, in Jacksonville, FL. He married Adrenne Benefield Fricia, born May 27, 1955, in Atlanta, GA. She is employed by Orange Park Schools. They have two daughters, Dixie Louise Fricia born July 4, 1978, in Atlanta, GA. Gordon Jr. adopted Dixie Jan. 2, 1986. She married Theron Golleher of Jacksonville, FL on June 12, 1999. They live in Jacksonville, FL. Theron is a police officer. Dixie is employed by Aetna Insurance Company, as a public relations

person. Their daughter, Anna Benefield Deason, born May 21, 1984 is a senior at Orange Park, FL. Her interest is in theater.

Bettie's second son is Randy Dale Deason, born Dec. 10, 1952 in Sikeston, MO. Married Connie Benson, they were divorced. They had one son Eric Darren Deason, born Feb. 25, 1974 in Cape Girardeau, MO. Connie married again to Eddie Workman; Eddie adopted Eric.

Bettie's third son is Terry Lee Deason, born Oct. 20, 1954 in Sikeston, MO. Terry had a carpet business in Benton, MO. He married Dorothy Marie Heuring born Dec. 11, 1955. She and Terry were married July 19, 1975. Dorothy is a graduate of Southeast Missouri State University. The Scott County School District R-IV as a special services coordinator employs her. They have three sons. Chase Matthew Deason, born March 1, 1984. A senior at Kelly High School; he wants to become a pharmacist. Kent Gordon Deason, born June 9, 1986 twin in Kendal Charles Deason; born at Southeast Hospital, Cape Girardeau, MO. They are both freshman at Kelly High School.

Bettie's fourth son is Paul Douglas Deason, born March 18, 1961 in Sikeston, MO. Married Melissa G. Blackburn July 31, 1982. They have three children, Joshua Paul Deason born February 1985 in Jacksonville, AR, Zachary Lee Deason born May 19, 1987 in Jacksonville, AR and Mary Katherine Deason born in Wichita, KS July 29, 1991. They attend Sikeston Schools. Paul was in the Air Force for 13 years. He and Melissa are divorced. Paul lives in Sikeston, MO. He is employed by Woodard District Company, Sikeston, MO. He also is in the National Air Force Guard in St. Louis, MO. *Submitted by Bettie Kindred Deason*

DEES – Avery and Dorothy Dees were married at 10:00 a.m. on Saturday June 17, 1950 at St. Ambrose Rectory, 418 South Third Street, Chaffee, MO by Father Thomas Gerayhty.

Avery, also known as "Harvey" because his name was incorrectly reported on his birth certificate, was born May 23, 1928 at Jackson, MO; the first child and only son of Claude and Emma Ellen "Ellie" Gobble Dees. He had three sisters, Winona, Dorinda and Terrie.

Dorothy, whose name is spelled Dortha on her birth record, was born May 26, 1933 east of Chaffee, Mo; fourth living child but sixth pregnancy of John and Bertha Lorene Lauck (also spelled Laux) Halter. Siblings are John Jr., Albert, Cecilia, Lorena, Elizabeth, Anna Mae, and Billy (William Leo).

Avery Dees family, 1967. Front row: Anthony, Joyce and Tom. Middle: Avery and Dorothy. Back: Debbie, Diane, Gary and Larry.

Avery and Dorothy met in 1948 briefly, introduced by a mutual friend. He, a tall, dark, handsome 20 years old marine in full dress blues. She a mousy 15 years old who hadn't started dating, but silently vowed she would someday marry the handsome young man.

He disappeared from her life. She turned 16.

Both had brief relationships, and then although he didn't seem interested at first, they began dating each other. They were both dedicated to the other, and fell in love. Dorothy often relates how she was infatuated, and by the grace of God, did fall in love in the process, a fact that she realized years later.

Only days after their marriage; when her dad, John Halter, and her Aunt Naomi Lauck were their witnesses, the couple left for Oakland, CA with his Aunt Cassie (Dees) Denman, and her husband Ivan, and their son-in-law and daughter, John and Jackie.

Later they came back to Chaffee, and on April 6, 1951 Gary Lynn was born. Followed by Diane Louise on Sept. 14, 1952, Larry Glenn, Sept. 23, 1953 and Debbie Lorene on March 27, 1955. All were born at the old St. Francis Hospital at Cape Girardeau except Debbie who was born at Borgess Hospital, Kalamazoo, MI.

In 1957 they returned to Chaffee from Michigan but soon moved to Oakland again. A family of six, with their possessions, packed into a car, with hopes and dreams of a new beginning.

Later they moved to Demin, NM, and then returned to Chaffee, again!

On March 5, 1962 Joyce Ann was born at the Chaffee Clinic, and Thomas Avery on March 31, 1963. In October 1964 the family moved to Scott City, and the family was complete when Anthony Albert was born Feb. 26, 1965.

On Oct. 11, 1969 Gary's car was struck by a train at the "Louie-Western" crossing in Scott City and he, with a friend, died instantly.

Diane married David Gramlisch, and raised two sons, Ron and Shawn. Ton served in the Marines and is now in the Navy. Shawn and Terri have Devon and Kinsey.

Larry married Melba Griffin and their son Brandon died on Sept. 1, 1994. They have Jessica and David living. A son, Jonathan, was born Dec. 30, 1982 and lived a short while.

Debbie raised her daughter Rhonda, who married Rob Coker and they have Daniel, Ashley, and Amy.

Joyce married Michael Weatherspoon and is the parents of Ryan, Chad, Ethan and Emily.

Tom married Angie (Razer) and has Elizabeth, Adam and Matthew.

Anthony married Wanda (Coleman) and has Randy.

Dorothy has lived alone since Avery died on April 12, 1996.
Submitted by Dorothy Dees

DIEBOLD – Dionysius "Dennis" Diebold was born March 7, 1820 in Ettlingen-weier West Germany, the son of Ignatius Johann and Katharina "Jung" Diebold. He married Magdalena Wanc/ Wantz in October of 1848 in Stark County, OH where they first homesteaded in about 1830, where the Alsatian settlement had been made earlier. They came to southeast Missouri in the mid 1850s. He had four brothers: Joseph, Peter, who married Maria Elizabeth Pirolth, then the second time to Catherina (Reece/ Rees) Menz; Bernard and Adam, both of whom died in infancy and are probably buried in Germany with their mother, who died of childbirth.

Dennis served in the Civil War as a private in Company "L" in the 10th Missouri Calvary Regiment and in Company "C" in Scott County Homeguard, commanded by Captain Robert H. Ruhl. He was discharged at Nashville, TN on Sept. 19, 1865.

Dennis and Magdalena were parents of eight children: John I. Married Josephine Kiefer; Josephine (never married); Frank L. married Mary Helena Hamm on Feb. 4, 1875 and she died in childbirth on Nov. 11, 1879. His second marriage was to Elizabeth Compas on May 3, 1881 and she died from typhoid fever on Oct. 7, 1881. His third marriage was to Mary Ann Wiedefeld on July 25, 1882 at New Hamburg. They were parents of 11 children: Frank, Peter L., Mary Ann, Louise R., Joseph, Magdalena (died in infancy), Clara, An-

Dennis and Magdalena (Wanc/Wantz) Diebold.

thony, Christine, Leo and Martha (died at age 4). Frank L.'s third wife Mary Ann died July 18, 1929 from stomach cancer and she is buried in St. Denis Cemetery at Benton, MO.

Leo (1854-1881) married Mary A. Westrich on Aug. 26, 1879. They had one child, Lawrence A. (Susanna Essner).

Anton (1857-1889) married Rosena Compas on Oct. 28, 1879. Four children were born to this union: William (Anna Roth), Regina (Herman Uelsmann), Carl and Paul both died in infancy.

Magdalena (1859-1937) married Michael Welter (1854-1942), son of Nicholas and Katharine (Gosche) Welter, on Feb. 16, 1882 in St. Augustine Catholic Church in Kelso, Scott County. They were the third settlers in Kelso and for 28 years he was a carpenter and was also in the undertaking business. They were parents of nine children: Leo P. (1883-1965) married Magdalena Buhs on Aug. 22, 1906 and had a family of two children: Gaylord and Woodrow; Rosalie died in infancy; Dora (1887-1967) married Emil Dohogne on Aug. 5, 1908 and they were the parents of five children: Walter, Marie, Olivia, Virginian and Alene; Albert (1889-1900); August (1891-1977) married Emma Schlosser on Aug. 17, 1915 and they were the parents of Germaine (Mose Schlitt), Vernita (Leon Urhahn), Cletus (Edveria Urhahn) and Elmer (Amy Martin); Edward married Elenora Pfefferkorn on Sept. 26, 1917 and they have three daughters, Doris (John S. Smith), LaVerne (Robert Rosenquist) and Laura Jean (Paul Robert); Pauline (1896-1983) married Edward Louise Menz on Aug. 24, 1944 at Kelso and had a daughter, Helen Welter (James Dumey); Agnes (1899-1965) married Andrew LeGrand on Oct. 12, 1921 and they were the parents of five children: Geraldine, Leon, Mildred (Gilbert LeGrand), Wilma (Theon Grojean Jr.) and Morris; Joseph (1903-1983) married Theresa Heuring on Jan. 26, 1926 and they were the parents of eight children: Jerome, Florence, Donald, Robert, Helen Ann, Gary, Sharon and Dale; Louisa (1860-1932) married Peter Welter on May 3, 1881 and nine children were born to them: Frank, Charles J. Alvina, Rosalia, Bertha, Lawrence I., Adolph, Anna and Josephine; Dennis and Magdalena's youngest child, Maria Louisa died in infancy.

Dennis died on Feb. 12, 1899 and in his will he expressed a wish that $1,000 of his estate and five acres of land be donated to the catholic congregation of Benton, provided the church be built with five years. Although the work was begun on the project, the people failed to build the church within the stipulated time. When Magdalena died in 1905 she made the same request, thus enabling the church to be completed. This second Benton Catholic Church was dedicated to God under the invocation of St. Dionysius in memory of Mr. Dennis Diebold. St. Denis as it is spelled today. *Submitted by Doris (Welter) Smith*

DIEBOLD – Ignatz/ Ignatius Diebold was born Aug. 3, 1838 near New Berlin, Stark County, OH,

the son of Ignatius John and Katharina (Martz) Diebold. The family came to southeast Missouri in 1856, homesteaded, cleared land and built a cabin west of Kelso. The Diebold's were among the pioneers who helped erect the first log church in New Hamburg, MO. They were farmers west of Kelso, MO.

Ignatz enrolled at Cape Girardeau, MO in Aug. 15, 1862 and served in the Civil War under Captain Christian Burkhardt as a Volunteer in Company "F" of the 29th Missouri Infantry Regiment as a corporal. He fought in the battles at Young's' Point and Millikin's Bend in Louisiana, Black River near

Ignatz Diebold in Civil War uniform.

Vicksburg and Corinth in Mississippi. He also fought in a battle at Bridgeport, TN. He was honorably discharged June 12, 1865 and returned home where he farmed in the New Hamburg-Kelso communities. Ignatz was married to Louisa Grojean on Jan. 9, 1866 in St. Lawrence Catholic Church at New Hamburg, MO by Rev. John Stroomberger. She was the daughter of Constantine and Dorothea (Oriente) Grojean. She was born Dec. 9, 1846 at Canton, Stark County, OH and died Oct. 24, 1931 in Cape Girardeau while living with a daughter, Emma (Diebold) and son-in-law, John Hamm. Ignatz died Aug. 8, 1917. They are both buried in St. Augustine Cemetery at Kelso, MO. They were the parents of six children: their first child died in infancy in 1867. Mary (b. Nov. 25, 1868, d. May 31, 1936) was married to George Blattel, the son of Jacob and Margaretha (Schlitt) Blattel on Nov. 28, 1886. They are buried in Prosperine Cemetery at Eldridge, MO. Six children were born to this union: Ignatz, Rosa, John G., Charles, George J., and Theon.

1898 Family Picture, Ignatz and Louisa Diebold and Children. By couple, from left: Louis and Dorothea (Bruenn) Diebold, Theodore and Frances (Dohogne) Diebold, Ignatz and Louisa (Grojean) Diebold, John and Emma (Diebold) Hamm, Charles and Theresa (Leible) Diebold.

Louis F., a farmer, (b. Oct. 7, 1870, d. Jan. 27, 1961) is buried in St. Mary's Cemetery in Pierce City. He was married to Dorothea Bruenn (b. Feb. 6, 1877, d. Oct. 16, 1971) on July 24, 1892 in St. Mary's Catholic Church in Pierce City, MO. They were the parents of 13 children; Leo Alonzo became a Benedictine Monk (Father Isadore) on Dec. 19, 1920, when he was ordained a Monk of Conception at the St. Pius X Monastery in Pevely, MO by Bishop Thomas Lillis of Kansas City, MO. He celebrated his Golden Anniversary as a priest on Dec. 25, 1970. The other children were: Theodore, Regina, John B., Lucille, Marie, Anna,

Pauline, Edmund J., Margaret J., Helen, Lawrence and Louis F. Jr. Theodore (b. Sept. 10, 1872, d. Dec. 24, 1944) married Frances Dohogne on Nov. 27, 1894. They were the parents of three children: Clara, Leo George (died in infancy) and George. Emma Clara (b. June 25, 1874, d. Nov. 16, 1944) married John Hamm; son of George and Catherine (Heisserer) Hamm on may 7, 1895. He was born Nov. 21, 1866 in Schirrhein, Alsace, France. Ten children were born to them: George married Colette Schlitt, then married Velma Arterfif Faulconer; Theodore married Ramona Gosche; Leo married Irmine Dannenmueller; Blanche Louise married Herman Blattel; Bertha and Joseph died in infancy; John I. married Alma P. Heisserer; Emma Theresa married Ralph McKeever; Clara Mary married James Scott and Charles Theon married Mary B. Coxon. Theodore, Emma Theresa, Clara Mary and Charles Theon left southeast Missouri and went to California to make their home with Uncle Joseph Hamm. John and Emma retired from farming in the New Hamburg community and moved to Cape Girardeau in the late 1920s. John died April 20, 1940 and they are buried in St. Lawrence Cemetery at New Hamburg, MO.

Charles Ignatius (b. April 14, 1877, d, Oct. 5, 1964) married Theresa Leible, the daughter of George and Mary Louisa (Riegert) Leible on Aug. 9, 1898. They were the parents of eight children: Theon married Mary Schott; Jacob married Bertha Grasser; Albert married Gladys Glueck; Joseph, Edward, and Raymond died from the measles; Leon married Marcella Stubenrauch; and Clara married Eugene Barks. *Submitted by Ramona Bess Blankenship*

DIEBOLD – Joseph Charles Diebold was born June 5, 1892 in Benton, MO. He is the son of Frank L. Diebold (1850-1934) and Mary Wiedefeld (1859-1928). Joseph Diebold was from a family of one half sister, six sisters and five brothers given here in order of their birth: Agnes, Mary, Peter, Frank, Louise, Martha, Joseph, Magdalina, Clara, Anthony, Leo and Christine.

On Sept. 28, 1915 Joseph Diebold married Coletta Susan Essner in the St. Denis Catholic Church in Benton with Rev. G. P. Fitzkam officiating.

Coletta Susan Essner was born June 25, 1893 in Benton. She is the daughter of Adam Essner (1857-1941) and Elizabeth Dirnberger (1862-1939). Coletta Essner is from a family of four sisters and three brothers given here in order of their birth: John, Regina, Lena, Coletta, Lawrence, Zetta and Leon.

Joseph Diebold and Coletta (Essner) Diebold have the following six children, all born in Benton: Bernice Elizabeth, born Feb. 19, 1918. She entered the Franciscans in Joliet, IL and after serving the order for 45 years as an educator she retired back to Benton.

Sylvester Joseph Diebold, born Feb. 3, 1920. He enlisted in the US Army Air Corp and was commissioned a 2nd Lieutenant. He served as a combat bomber pilot on a B-17 bomber. He was killed in a plane crash in Kearney, NE on Aug. 17, 1943. He is buried in the St. Denis Catholic Church Cemetery in Benton.

Quentin Charles

Joseph Charles and Coletta Susan (Essner) Diebold, September 28, 1915.

Diebold, born May 17, 1922 and died June 27, 1994. He was a WWII veteran. On June 30, 1949 he married Sirphenia Meier, born Feb. 16, 1925 and died Nov. 4, 1999. Both are buried in the St. Denis Catholic Church Cemetery in Benton. They have four children: Barbara (b. Jan. 10, 1951); Kathy (b. March 5, 1952); Kenneth (b. Feb. 19, 1957) and Keith (b. Nov. 20, 1958).

Joseph Diebold family, ca. 1942. Standing: Quentin, Jim, Sister Zita Bernice, Sylvester, and Francis. Sitting: Joseph, Gadys, and Coletta (Essner) Diebold.

James "Jim" Diebold, born Dec. 15, 1925 and died June 2, 1995 in St. Louis, MO. He was a WWII veteran. On Nov. 17, 1956 he married Geraldine Williams, born Aug. 22, 1931. They have three children: Diane (b. Aug. 25, 957), Nancy (b. June 27, 1959) and Cindy (b. Nov. 9, 1965).

Francis "Smokey" Loraine Diebold, born Sept. 6, 1927 and died March 9, 2000 in Wichita, KS. He was a WWII veteran. On Oct. 30, 1948 at St. Denis Catholic Church in Benton he married Patricia Hodgkins, born Aug. 5, 1930. They have three children: Carolyn (b. May 15, 1949 d. Feb. 13, 1983), James (b. April 29, 1953) and John (b. July 29, 1954).

Gladys Mary Diebold, born Dec. 15, 1930. On Nov. 17, 1950 at St. Denis Catholic Church in Benton, she married James Schumacher, born March 6, 1921 and died March 14, 1997. They have eight children: Mary (b. Oct. 9, 1952), Karen (b. Sept. 25, 1953), Joseph (b. Jan. 23, 1955), Mark (Feb. 11, 1956), Janet (b. Aug. 11, 1957), Jean (b. Dec. 31, 1961), Lynne (Sept. 7, 1963) and John (July 31, 1965).

Joseph Charles Diebold and Coletta Susan (Essner) Diebold lived their entire lives in Benton, in Scott County, MO. On June 9, 1947, at age 55, Joseph Charles Diebold died from a massive heart attack in Benton, MO. On Jan. 22, 1988, Coletta Susan (Essner) Diebold died at home at age 94. Both are buried in the St. Denis Catholic Church Cemetery in Benton, MO.

DIRNBERGER-DANNENMUELLER – Andrew Dirnberger and Catherine Dannenmueller are my paternal grandparents. Andrew's father, Michael Dirnberger, was born in Bavaria, Germany in 1835 and died in Scott County in 1908. At the age of 15 he had a job carrying mail on horseback between Benton, Sikeston, New Madrid, and Cape Girardeau. He married Regina Heisserer in 1857 at New Hamburg, MO. They owned a general merchandise store in New Hamburg and also farmed.

Catherine's father, Joe Dannenmueller, was born in Alsace-Loraine, France and came to Missouri at age 18 by way of Canton, OH. Catherine's mother, Martha Werle, came to Missouri from Baden, Germany alone at age 16.

Andrew was born in New Hamburg on Feb. 4, 1867 and died Feb. 15, 1929. He and Catherine Dannenmueller who was born March 17, 1872 and died Dec. 26, 1954, were married Nov. 14, 1889 at St. Lawrence in New Hamburg. Andrew owned

farmland and built his first home of logs on his father's homestead. This home and land has always remained in the Dirnberger family and is presently owned by a great grandson, Vincent Dirnberger. Besides farming, Andrew owned a general store in New Hamburg and built roads around the area for county government.

The following 12 children were born to Andrew and Catherine: Martha Regina married Arthur Vetter; Joseph Andrew married Mamie Scherer; Otilla Mary became a Nun of the Precious Blood Order; Michael Nicholas married Coletta LeGrand; Cyrill Adolph married Dora Heisserer; Leocadia married Philip Bucher; Theckla married William Schlitt; Sylvester Adam married Audrey Weinel; Sylvester Peter died at birth; Armella married Terry Alt; and Jerome married Dorothy Holder.

Claude William (b. Aug. 9, 1909) was my father. Claude was attending St. Louis University when his father passed away. He returned home to operate the general store for his mother. He later purchased the store and worked there until he retired and sold the store to a local boy. The store no longer remained in the Dirnberger family.

On Oct. 3, 1931 at Benton, MO Claude married Rebecca Brock (b. Oct. 11, 19090. Seven children were born to this union as follows: Lois Rebecca married Joe Amos Spalding; Claude Richard married Mary Jo Ferrell; Janet Sue married Vernon Vetter; David Cooper married Dorothy Harris; Andrew Michael married Janet Bollinger; Glen Albert married Barbara Huffman; Vera Ann married Alan Henneman. The seven children all remained in Scott and Cape County. Through the years every holiday and birthday was the occasion of a big celebration at the Dirnberger home with the seven children along with their spouses, 20 grandchildren and their spouses and 34 great-grandchildren all attending. Claude passed away May 19, 1996. Rebecca, age 92, is a resident of a local nursing home. *Submitted by Lois Dirnberger Spalding*

DIRNBERGER – Arthur Dirnberger was born on May 21, 1913 to Frank (b. Dec. 30, 1884; d. Dec. 6, 1980) and Ida Scherer Dirnberger (b. Oct. 25, 1885; d. March 12, 1949). Arthur passed away on May 11, 1992, ten days before his 79th birthday. He lived his entire life on the family farm that his dad bought in 1910 and sold to Arthur in 1945. This farm is located 1 1/2 miles northeast of Oran. Arthur had one brother, Robert, and two sisters, Viola and Anita. Robert married Viola Dannenmueller. Viola married Henry Brands. Anita married Denis LeGrand.

Evelyn Sietmann was born Nov. 2, 1917 to John (b. May 30, 1891; d. May 4, 1958) and Elsie Alsup Sietmann (b. July 17, 1896; d. Jan. 30, 1926). She lived near Oran until 1993, when she moved to her current residence on Church Street in Oran. Evelyn had one brother, John Edwin Sietmann, who married Ann Gabel.

Arthur and Evelyn were married on Feb. 3, 1937 in Guardian Angel Catholic Church in Oran. Arthur was a self-employed farmer. Evelyn was a stay-at-home mom. They raised two sons, Gerald "Jerry" and Lenard "Lenny".

Jerry was born Nov. 11, 1937. He is married to Carol Stoverink, who was

Evelyn Sietmann and Arthur Dirnberger

born Jan. 9, 1945. She is the daughter of Irene Thiele Stoverink of Jackson, MO and the late Alphonse Stoverink. Jerry and Carol reside on the family farm in the house that Frank and Ida Dirnberger built in 1917. Jerry and Carol are the parents of two daughters, Donna and Janis. Donna was born Oct. 16, 1967. She lives in Ballwin, MO. Janis, born March 9, 1970, is married to Dennis Gosche, son of Don and Alice Horrell Gosche of Chaffee. Their daughter, Amanda, was born Jan. 11, 2000. The Gosches live at New Hamburg, MO.

Lenny was born Oct. 11, 1947. He is married to Camilla Kiefer, who was born May 10, 1951. She is the daughter of Ellen Cody Kiefer of Oran and the late Frank Kiefer. Lenny and Camilla reside on the family farm in a house they built in 1980. Their son, Daniel, was born Jan. 15, 1981. He lives in Cape Girardeau, MO.

DIRNBERGER – Gerald "Jerry" Dirnberger and Carol Stoverink were married Sept. 10, 1966 at Immaculate Conception Catholic Church in Jackson, MO. Jerry was born Nov. 11, 1937 to Evelyn Sietmann Dirnberger (b. Nov. 2, 1917; resides in Oran, MO) and the late Arthur Dirnberger (b. May 21, 1913; d. May 11, 1992). Carol was born Jan. 9, 1945 to Irene Thiele Stoverink (b. March 18, 1922; resides in Jackson) and the late Alphonse Stoverink (b. Oct. 30, 1918; d. Aug. 27, 1998). Jerry and Carol are the parents of two daughters, Donna and Janis.

Jerry has lived his entire life at Oran - growing up on the family farm. After marriage, he and Carol lived in the town of Oran for 27 years. In March 1993, they moved to the Dirnberger farm, which has been in the family since 1910.

The Dirnbergers: Donna, Jerry, Carol and Janis (in front).

Jerry attended Guardian Angel Catholic School in Oran and graduated from Oran High School in 1956. He farmed with his father until March 1966, when he became a truck driver for Montgomery Ward in Cape Girardeau, MO. In March 1968, Scott County Milling Company of Sikeston, MO employed him as office manager and bookkeeper in the Oran branch. Cargill, Inc. bought the company in 1977. In October 1979, Jerry and Buster Bollinger, another former employee of Scott County Milling Company, formed a partnership known as BeeJay Supply. They leased the Cargill buildings and sold Gristo Feed. In 1980, Jerry took over ownership and changed the name to Dirnberger Feed Store. He sold Gristo Feed until it was no longer available, after which Nutrena Feed was the featured product. One of the services available at Dirnberger Feed Store included custom feed grinding and mixing. On July 31, 1999 Jerry sold his business to Animal Nutrition Center, where he continues to work part-time. Jerry became semi-retired in November 1999.

In the mid 1960s, Jerry and his brother, Lenny, formed The Varieties band, which later became the Dirnberger Brothers Band. Members of The

Varieties included, at various times, Rodney Roberts, Jerry Tindle, Mike Conrad, Randy Henley, Dale Patterson and Mike Kitchen as either drummer or bass player. Members of the Dirnberger Brothers were Jerry and Lenny, along with an electronic drummer. For 20-plus years, they provided music for various occasions such as public dances, weddings, anniversaries, picnics and Christmas parties. Their repertoire included waltzes, polkas, two-steps, country and light rock.

Carol attended St. John's School in Leopold, MO, for her first and second grades and Immaculate Conception School in Jackson during grades 3-8. She graduated from Notre Dame High School in Cape Girardeau, MO in 1962. Immediately after graduation, Carol worked at Jackson Hosiery Mill. That fall, Metropolitan Life Insurance Company employed her in Cape Girardeau. She became a stay-at-home mom in October 1967. Carol re-entered the work force in 1980 at Dirnberger Feed Store. From 1984 through 1989, she and Anita Brands Wubker produced the *Pride of Oran*, an insert in *The Chaffee Signal* newspaper. In 1989, Carol became a rural carrier substitute for the post office at Chaffee, MO and later at Oran. Currently, she is a full-time postal clerk at the Mail Processing Center in Cape Girardeau.

Donna Dirnberger, born Oct. 16, 1967, graduated from Guardian Angel School in 1982, Oran High School in 1986, and the University of Missouri-Columbia in 1990 with a major in computer science. She lives in Ballwin, MO and is employed as a senior program analyst by Maritz.

Dennis and Janis (Dirnberger) Gosche with baby Amanda, 2000.

Janis Dirnberger Gosche, born March 9, 1970, graduated from Guardian Angel School in 1984, Oran High School in 1988, and the University of Missouri-Columbia in 1992 with a degree in agricultural journalism. She works as an administrative assistant for the Missouri School Counselor Association in Jackson, MO. In February 1997, Janis married Dennis Gosche at Guardian Angel Catholic Church in Oran. Dennis was born June 12, 1966 to Don and Alice Horrell Gosche, of Chaffee. Janis, Dennis and their daughter, Amanda, born Jan. 11, 2000, live on the Gosche family farm in New Hamburg, where Dennis is a self-employed farmer.

DIRNBERGER – Money was so scarce when Linus Dirnberger and I were dating, it seemed like the only place we could afford to go was to dances. Admission 25 cents each. We didn't have money for an engagement ring and I picked the cheapest wedding ring I could find, so we would have money for some of the things we needed for the wedding. Our wedding day turned out to be another big depression. It started to rain at 6 a.m. Soon it was pouring. 8 o'clock Mass. The Good Lord must have stopped the rain while we were going in and out, at least I can't remember getting wet. It poured and poured. It started to snow and sleet and all that water was frozen in a solid sheet of

ice by evening. Some of the people went home early, but the others had stayed all night. We couldn't even have our wedding dance. We did take the tables out of the dining room and danced some there. We felt so cheated, so on our tenth anniversary we had a dance for relatives and friends. That is when Linus gave me a beautiful ring.

After the wedding, Linus had $20.00 left and I had $20.00 left. We needed a bedroom set so we went shopping. We found one; if we left the chest of drawers it would cost $39.50. They had it set up like a bedroom with two windows and curtains. We said if they would throw in the curtains, we would take it and they did. I don't know what we did with the curtains—our bedroom had three windows. We probably used them in the dining room. So we started out with 50 cents.

Before Linus and I got married, his parents and Angelica moved to Cape. Oscar wanted to stay on the farm, so the three of us lived on the farm. They had some hens which sure were good layers. We took a basket of 10 dozen eggs to the store and they didn't want them. Too many eggs. Four cents a dozen so we took them back home. Can you imagine all the eggs we ate and then later they tried to make us believe eggs weren't good for us. Guess I am living proof that eggs don't kill you. Beef sold at 1 cent a lb. and hogs were $5 a hundred weight. So for a 200 lb. hog we got $10.00.

Farmers practically lived off the farm, but we still had to buy flour, sugar, coffee and a lot of lemons so we could make lemonade to quench our thirst. No ice or cold drinks. Flour and sugar was bought by the 100 lbs. since we baked our own bread nearly every other day and always cake or pie, doughnuts or whatever every day. The stove was always going so the oven was always ready whenever we got to baking.

Money being so scarce, we started to milk a few cows and sold cream. With no refrigeration, we had to take the cream to the train station several times a week and so we had a small check coming several times a week, which always ended at the grocery store.

During the depression, meat, sugar, coffee and gasoline were rationed. We had our own meat, but with the sugar came a great problem, with all the baking, lemonade and canning and jelly making in the summertime using all the fruit. I usually made about 60 gallons of jelly and jams, sometimes cooked seven quarters of jelly at the time in the copper boiler. There was always plenty of syrup and so we had to learn to cook, bake, and can with syrup. To this day, I still enjoy making small batches of jelly and jams.

We always had a lot of people helping on the farm in the summer and making wood in the winter. Everyone stayed to eat. Some even stayed day and night all week.

God blessed our marriage with six wonderful children: Carnetta; Clyde; Germaine; Mary; Linus and Vernon. For our 25th and 40th anniversaries, the children surprised us with a cake, meal and gifts. That was very good since Linus passed away on our 45th.

We had several deaths in our family. My brother Lawrence's wife died from a miscarriage, leaving six children. Anton and Ora lost a 10 month old boy Wesley from pneumonia and Alvina and George lost a 22 month old girl Georgianna from colitis, and Linus and I lost our 15 year old son Clyde. He was 6 feet tall and was so good at everything. He loved the farm and it didn't matter if he was working with the horses or tractor. He was also good at wood work and I tried to console myself in thinking God needed him to build all those many mansions.

Tony lost a leg in a combine accident. He took

the shoe lace out of his other shoe and tied his leg so he wouldn't bleed to death. Somehow he managed to go through two fields and two gates and got to a neighbor's house. When he got there, he passed out.

Even though we had a lot of misfortunes, we also had our full share of blessings and we are thankful for all of them.

DIRNBERGER – Linus Phillip Dirnberger, born Dec. 14, 1905 at New Hamburg, was the youngest child born to John and Rosalie Heuring Dirnberger. He lived all his life on a farm, the home place of his parents, between New Hamburg and Oran until he moved to New Hamburg in 1962.

He married Regina M. Compas, daughter of Henry and Regina Scherer Compas on Nov. 15, 1932. They had six children: Carnetta Angelica, Germaine Nora, Clyde Marcus, Mary Margaret Alvina, Linus Robert and Vernon Francis. Linus and Regina shared their home with her mother, Regina Scherer Compas, for 14 years following the death of Henry in 1943.

Linus was a farmer and dairyman. When they were milking cows by hand, Regina alone milked as many as 12 cows one evening. They would sell the cream. After getting electricity and milking machines, they also sold the milk from as many as 32 cows.

They also raised hogs on the farm. While moving some of the hog's houses on June 2, 1951, a storm erupted and Clyde was struck by lightning and died. At that time, visitation was held in the home. Many friends and family members came to pay their respects. Linus and Regina had a statue of St. Lawrence dedicated to his memory and placed in St. Lawrence Catholic School. When the school became public, the statue was removed. It was later relocated to a gazebo in St. Lawrence Cemetery, where it now stands.

Linus had an accident one fall when they were shucking corn with mules and wagon. The wagon was loaded and when he jumped on the wagon tongue and grabbed the lines, the mules somehow got scared and ran. He slipped off the tongue, holding onto the lines so tightly that the steel shucking peg in his hand was bent. He was dragged across a large field, bumping his hip on every row right behind the mules and a wagonload of corn right behind him. A corn stalk had rubbed through his overall bib, but didn't hurt his chest.

Linus was co-owner with Charlie Wagoner of the Oran Feed Store. Linus would haul hogs to St. Louis and return with a load of feed for the store. During the summer, he would go to Florida for a load of watermelons.

In 1962, he sold the farm to Albert "Felix" Enderle, and Linus and Regina built a home in New Hamburg. The yard contains many beautiful flowers and shrubs, a life-long pleasure of Regina. She cut and arranged many bouquets of flowers from her yard and placed them on the church altars.

Linus drove the school bus for St. Lawrence Catholic School and Scott County School District C-7 for 12 years until his retirement in 1975.

He loved to play cards, especially euchre, pitch and pinochle. He and a number of friends would meet at the local gathering places to enjoy the games. He would rather play cards than eat.

Regina worked 14 years at the Holiday Inn in Cape Girardeau, from August 1966 until her retirement in 1980.

On their 45th Wedding Anniversary, Nov. 15, 1977, Linus passed away. Many people attended his funeral, including students of the school. They reminisced of the many times he had given them candy when he was driving the school bus.

DOGGETT – John Lesley Doggett, DDS and his wife Mary Louise (Wallis) Doggett, with their two children moved to Sikeston in the summer of 1953. Their two children were James Wallis (1951), born in St. Louis and Mary Laura (1952), born in Augusta, GA. John L. was born May 4, 1923 in Bollinger County, near Patton, MO. Mary L. Wallis was born in Blodgett, MO on July 25, 1928 at the home of her uncle, Elam J. Nienstedt MD and his wife Olive and daughter Louise. John L. was the son of John Columbus Doggett and Willie (Grindstaff) Doggett. Mary L. was the daughter of Hawn James Wallis and Carried (Nienstedt) Wallis of the Millersville Community, Cape Girardeau County. John L. and Mary L. were married in Cape Girardeau at Centenary Methodist Church on Aug. 18, 1946. After moving to Sikeston the Doggett family had two more children. They were Martha Jane (1954) and John David (1960). Both of them were born in the Sikeston Hospital.

John L. Doggett family, 1961. Left to right: Martha, John L., John David, James (in back), Mary, and Laura.

John L. had served in a Naval Construction Battalion during WWII and then attended Southeast Missouri State University and graduated from St. Louis University School of Dentistry, Class of 1951. Following graduation he served in the army Dental Corps during the Korean War. Upon moving to Sikeston, John L. established a Dental Office in Sikeston, first on Front Street, later moving to Center Street, and finally, with Dr. Howard Johnson, built an office on North Main Street. Sr. Doggett continued in his dental professional practice for 37 years, until his retirement in December 1989.

John L. was a Boy Scout Master for approximately 15 years and was active in the local PTA and the Southeast Missouri Dental Society, serving as president in both organizations.

The Doggetts joined the First Methodist Church in 1953, and continued as members of that church, later known as the First United Methodist Church.

Mary was a Girl Scout Leader for approximately 15 years, and also served in other capacities for the Cotton Boll council. Mary graduated from Southeast Missouri State University with BS degrees in 1975 and 1976. She was twice elected to the city Council of Sikeston (1977-1983) and in 1980, held the position of Mayor. Mary was active in the Republican Party, serving as an official both in county and the State Party. She taught in the Social Studies Department of the Sikeston Public Schools, briefly, before being hired as the Economic Developer for the Sikeston area. This position she held for five years (1985-19900, until retirement.

Vocations of the Doggetts' children follows: James – Registered Nurse; Laura- Real Estate Properties; Martha – US Forest Service; and John David – US Air Force/ Department of Energy.

John L. and Mary's six grandchildren are as follows: Jed (1981) and Tess (1985) Purcell (Laura's children); Colin (1984) and Alexis (1986) Doggett (James' children); and Cara (1989) and Hannah (1994) Doggett (John David's children).

Family hobbies and interests: Traveling, birding, wildflower ID, art, volunteering, stamp collecting and photography.

DOHOGNE – Dohogne Farm. Lone Rock is located between Chaffee and Oran on State Highway 77. It is thought to have been a trading post around the year 1821. The following excerpt regarding Lone Rock was taken from *The Story of Missouri* by Walter H. Ryle and Charles E. Garner. This book, published by American Book Company, was published in 1938. The excerpt, found on page 260, is as follows:

"An Old Lead Mine"

"There is a tale of an old lead mine down below Cape Girardeau between the modern towns of Oran and Chaffee. The Indians worked this mine and no one else knew where it was. Anyone wishing to buy lead would meet the Indians at a certain Lone Rock between Chaffee and Oran. You would bargain for lead and wait perhaps two hours, while the Indians returned to the mines and dug the lead and brought it to you. This ore in its native condition was so pure that it did not need refining. When the Indians left that part of Missouri, the entrance to the mine was closed up and as yet has not been discovered, even though many attempts have been made to locate it."

Dohogne farm house

The City Hall at Oran was built in 1937 from limestone rock taken from Lone Rock.

The farm on which Lone Rock is located has been owned by the Dohogne family for over 100 years. The Dohogne family came from Belgium to America around 1854. The farm was bought in April of 1893 by Joseph J. Dohogne. It was purchased from William and Amelia Heisserer and Mont P. Wade. In January of 1938, the farm was sold to his son, John Dohogne and his wife, Laura Dirnburger Dohogne. In 1917, John and Laura built a house on the farm that is still standing and in use. It was in this house that John and Laura Dohogne raised their two sons and four daughters. Following are the names of their children and grandchildren:

Lone Rock on the Dohogne farm

Bertilla was married to Arthur Pobst and they did not have any children. Lucy married Henry Caby and they are the parents of Henry Jr., John, Robert, Richard, Roger, Charles, Mary Ann, Barbara, and Donald (deceased). Lorena married Cletus Todt and they are the parents of James Wayne, Steven, Daniel and Brenda Sue. Anna married Melvin Glueck and they are the parents of Linda, Judy, Fred, Roger and Lana. John Jr. married Marilyn Davis and they are the parents of Kenny, John, Karen, Marica, Tina and Deborah (deceased). James married Mary McBride and they are the parents of Nancy, Cynthia, and David. At this time, John and Laura Dohogne are deceased as is Bertilla and Arthur Pobst, Henry Caby, and Melvin Glueck.

In the spring of 1958, John and Laura moved into a new home at Oran. James and Mary Dohogne currently reside on the family farm and purchased the farm and family home in 1967 from John and Laura. A "century farm" sign stands in front of the homestead marking 100 years that the Dohogne family had owned and lived on the farm.

DOLLINS – William "Bill" Dollins was born Feb. 27, 1935 in Bertrand, MO the son of Van Dollins and Addie Connelley. Van was the son of James D. Dollins and Thursy Burris, from Green County, AR. Addie was the daughter of Harry Connelley and Mary Foster from Pemiscott County, MO.

Bill moved to Morley, MO as a very young child, and then moved to Mississippi County, MO when he was a young teenage boy. There, his mother died in 1946. It was then when Bill had to drop out of school to help support the family of seven children. The siblings were: James (in the Korean War at the time), Mary, Jack, Burley, Deloris, Earnest, and Clara. It wasn't long after his mother's death when his father was hit by a car on the highway and broke his arm and wasn't able to work, so Bill, being the oldest at home, had to work on the farm at a few dollars a day to keep the family going until his father was able to help him again.

When Bill was 18 years old, he joined the Marines and was stationed in California until he went overseas to Japan during the Korean War. However, Bill didn't see much action as the war ended not long after he got to Japan.

Ina and Bill Dollins

In 1955 he came home on leave and then married Ina Russell (b. Dec. 11, 1940, in Portageville, MO). She is the daughter of Virgil Russell and Vesta Davis. Ina's family moved to a farm outside of Morley when she was 3 years old. She had two brothers and two sisters. One brother, Noel Joe died as an infant. Robert Don was born in 1935 in Lamar, AR and married Debra George.

One of Ina's sisters, Melba Russell, was born in 1929 in Lamar, AR. She married Carroll Edward Emerson in 1944. He was the son of Asberry Emerson and Elma Swaim.

Ina's other sister, Betty Russell, was born in

1937 in Matthews, MO. She married Bill Doty of Benton, MO. He was the son of Jess Doty and Anna Swan.

Bill and Ina have two daughters. Vicki was born on Nov. 24, 1956 and married Larry Caudle aka Rick Sinclair; they divorced. They had two daughters. Julee was born in 1976 in Riverside, CA and married Rev. Harold "Corky" Higgins. They have one son, Matthew, born Oct. 18, 2000.

Vicki's second daughter is Summer, who was born in 1981 in Riverside, CA. She is a Head Start Teacher, and will be going to college in the summer. Vicki is now married to Kenneth Newell of Patton, MO, where they make their home.

The second daughter of Bill and Ina is Donna, born April 7, 1960. She married Michael Mansker, son of Eula Mansker and Freda Fredericks. Donna and Mike divorced and she in now married to Danny Lefler.

Donna had three sons with Michael Mansker. Nicholas Mansker, born in 1977, married Thelma Bridwell; they have two children, Tristain and Trinity Mansker. Benjamin Mansker, born in 1980 in Cape Girardeau, MO married Tina Blackwell on Nov. 25, 2000. Geoffrey Adam Mansker, born 1982 in California, he is in the US Air Force, stationed in Texas. Donna and Danny Lefler have one daughter, Karyn Danielle Lefler, born 1993 at Sikeston, MO.

Bill and Ina attend the Morley Baptist Church, where both Bill and Ina both love singing in the choir and, on occasion, sing specials.

Bill is now retired but has worked at many things. Upon getting out of the Marines he returned to his hometown of Morley. He worked on a farm for a short time, and then went to work in the Morley grocery store for John Wheelen for a while. Before returning to Bakersfield, CA, where he worked on a ranch for a time, he went into construction work out of a union in Riverside, CA for a few years. He became homesick for Missouri and moved back to Missouri, where he trained to be a carpenter through his GI bill. Their girls went to high school at Scott Central High, Vicki graduating from there. Before Donna could graduate, Bill and Ina decided to move back to Riverside, CA where Bill could make more money. They lived there until Donna graduated from Riverside High. Both girls are married. They decided to move to Idaho with some friends and they lived there for about ten years on the Snake River in Buhl, ID. Then, when it got close to retirement time, Bill again decided to move back to Missouri, where he bought the Morley Café and ran it for about three years. *Submitted by Ina Russell Dollins*

DRURY – Charles Louis Drury was born Oct. 25, 1927 in Kelso, MO, son of Lambert Clements Drury (b. Aug. 12, 1902; d. April 2, 1979) and Lorraine Dohogne Drury (b. Oct. 7, 1904; d. Aug. 19, 1961). Shirley Jean Luebbers was born on May 26, 1935 in Cape Girardeau, MO, daughter of Winefared Daniel Luebbers (b. April 18, 1913; d. Jan. 6, 1993) and Hazel Eunice Stoffel (b. Dec. 20, 1914).

Charles and Shirley were married on June 11, 1955, at St. Mary's Cathedral in Cape Girardeau, MO. Their children are: Charles Louis II, Mary Jean, Joan Marie, Timothy Michael, Janice Ann, Jennifer Susan and Jacklyn Lorraine.

Charles Louis II was born Nov. 4, 1955 in Cape Girardeau, MO. He married Michelle Swenson (b. July 10, 1956) on April 128, 1979. Their children are: Charles Louis III "Charlie" (b. June 24, 1986) and Tommie (b. Dec. 2, 1989).

Mary Jean was born Oct. 22, 1956 in Cape Girardeau, MO. She married Fred Glueck in 1973. Jean and Fred's children are: Angela and Tamela (b. Oct. 15, 1973), April (b. April 5, 1978) and Casey (b. July 30, 1979). Jean and Fred are di-

vorced. Jean married Norman Tanner (b. Aug. 10, 1958) on Nov. 18, 1989. Their children are Katie (b. Aug. 10, 1987) and adopted by Jean, and Tabitha Nicole (b. march 24, 1997). Angela's daughter, Victoria Glueck Jones, was born June 8, 1993. Tamela's daughter, Taylor Glueck Hill, was born Oct. 6, 1998 and died Oct. 8, 1998. April married Jeff Bonham on July 7, 2001.

Joan was born Dec. 24, 1957 in Cape Girardeau, Mo.

Timothy Michael was born Dec. 1, 1958 in Cape Girardeau, MO. He married Cindy Cassady (b. Jan. 13, 1962) on May 22, 1993 in St. Louis, MO. Their children are: Kayla (b. Oct. 29, 1993), Timothy Michael (b. March 29, 1995) Brenna (b. Aug. 9, 1996) and Ethan (b. Jan. 20, 1998).

Janice Ann was born Nov. 22, 1959 in Cape Girardeau, MO. She married Jack Roupp (b. March 15, 1959) on May 5, 1984 at St. Augustine Catholic Church in Kelso, MO. Their children are: Rachel (b. April 19, 1986), Erica (b. Oct. 1, 1987), Megan (b. June 14, 1990), Jacklyn (b. April 9, 1992) and Graham (b. Nov. 14, 1996).

Jennifer Susan was born April 24, 1961 in Cape Girardeau, MO. Her daughter, Catherine Lorraine, was born Nov. 29, 1987.

Jacklyn Lorraine was born Aug. 16, 1963 in Cape Girardeau, MO. She married Mitch Pollvogt (b. Dec. 9, 1957) on May 30, 1987 at St. Augustine Catholic Church in Kelso, MO. Their children are Dalton (b. April 19, 1991) and Victoria (b. March 10, 1994).

The family was raised on the farm in Kelso, MO. The farm was purchased from the Monroe Wheeler family.

DUMEY – John Henry Dumey and wife Mary Anne Dohogne came to Scott County about 1848. John was born Jan. 11, 1811 and Mary Anne on Dec. 6, 1811 at Ster-Francorchamps, Belgium. They were married on April 14, 1836 at St. George Catholic Church at Francorchamps and immigrated to America about 1846. They first settled in Ohio but moved on to southeast Missouri. Land records show that John bought 40 acres of farmland near New Hamburg on April 10, 1849. John passed away on Feb. 9, 1974 and Marry Anne on Nov. 17, 1875. They are buried in St. Lawrence Church Cemetery at New Hamburg. Mr. and Mrs. Dumey were the parents of eight children, two having died young. The remaining six (in their original French) was: Justin-Joseph, Marie-Angelique, Joseph-Leopold-Paul, Jean-Baptiste, Marie-Therese, and Marie-Clementine Dumey.

Justin-Joseph Dumey was born Aug. 7, 1837 at Ster-Francorchamps. He was married on Oct. 21, 1860 to Catherine Diebold. They farmed west of Kelso. Justin served in the Civil War in the Missouri Volunteer Infantry and died on Feb. 23, 1919. Catherine died on July 7, 1936. They are buried at New Hamburg. Justin and Catherine were the parents of: Magdalena Ziegler, Rosa Koelzer, Charles, Matt, Frank, Cecelia Messmer, George and Frieda Dumey.

Mary Angeline Dumey was born Aug. 18, 1843 at Ster-Francorchamps. She was married to Michael J. LeGrand on Feb. 16, 1860. They were farmers in the New Hamburg-Oran area. Angeline died on March 5, 1908 and Michael on Dec. 17, 1890. Both are buried at New Hamburg. They were the parents of: Mary Welter, Emil, Frank, John, Joseph, Catherine Conklin, Mary Josephine Heisserer, Louise Heisserer Dohogne, William and George LeGrand.

Joseph Paul Dumey was born Dec. 15, 1844 at Ster-Francorchamps. He married Magdalena Diebold on Dec. 2, 1862. They farmed west of Kelso. Joseph served with the Missouri Volunteer Infantry during the Civil War and died Jan. 25, 1879. Magdalena died on Oct. 7, 1928 and is

buried in St. Augustine Church Cemetery at Kelso. Joseph and Magdalena were the parents of: Louise Thomas, Pauline Unnerstall, William, Leo and Joseph Dumey.

Joseph Paul Dumey, Civil War, 1862.

John Baptist Dumey was born March 12, 1848 in Ohio. He married Mary Felden on Feb. 14, 1871 and they farmed between Rockview and Kelso. John died on July 13, 1903 and Mary on April 12, 1906. Both are buried at Kelso. John and Mary were the parents of: Anna Lauck, Theresa Seyer, Ida Bertha Miller, Sybilla Lauck, Katherine Lauck, John Emil, Louis and George Albert Dumey.

Mary Theresa Dumey was born Aug. 23, 1850 in Scott County. She married Mathias Thomas on Nov. 21, 1871. They were the parents of George and Clara Thomas. Theresa died in childbirth on June 21, 1884. Mathias died on Nov. 14, 1928. Both are buried in Kelso.

Mary Clementine Dumey was born Oct. 7, 1854 in Scott County. She was married to John Baptist Menz on Nov. 12, 1872. They farmed between New Hamburg and Oran. Clementine died on Nov. 17, 1939 and John on April 6, 1920. They are buried in Guardian Angel Cemetery at Oran. Clementine and John were the parents of: John Martin Menz, Louisa Pobst, Mary Pobst and Matt Menz. *Submitted by Nick Dumey*

DYE – George L. Dye was born March 1, 1904 in Effingham County, Illinois son of George and Violia A. Parks Dye. His father was born in Owensburg, Indiana in 1860 and died in 1944 at Sikeston, Missouri near the end of World War II. His mother was born in 1865 in Effingham County, Illinois and died in Sikeston in December 1942. George and his family moved to Sikeston in 1911 to farm and was one of the builders of the Marshall Hotel in Sikeston. He had three brothers: Everett Adam Dye who married Vada M. Woody; Tanner C. Dye who married Cora Matthews and Frank P. Dye and one sister Etha "Nellie" A. Dye who married John H. Russell. George married Lena Grace Cline on February 15, 1929 in New Madrid, Missouri. She was born October 26, 1907 in Morehouse, MO, daughter of William Henry Cline, a native of Hickman County, KY and Nannie Lena Kline of New Madrid County, MO.

George and Grace lived in various places over their early years of marriage. They live in Morley, Missouri for many years. George was Mayor for a period of time and Grace was Post Master for twelve years in Morley. They were members of the First United Methodist Church in Sikeston. They had no children but many nephews and nieces. George L. Dye died in 1987 and his wife died in 1989 in Sikeston, Missouri. They are buried in Sikeston Memorial Park. *Submitted by their many nephews and nieces.*

EIFERT – Henry Eifert Sr, born 1814 in Dormstat, Germany, immigrated to the United States in 1852. Accompanying him was one son, David Karl, born 1838 in Rebeshain, Germany. They settled in New York. In 1853, Anna Maria Roth Eifert, Henry's wife, joined them bringing their four remaining children born in Germany. They were: Elisa, Sophie, Casper and Eva. They relocated in Kelso Township in Scott County, MO in 1854.

In 1855, a child named Julia was born but died the same year. John Eifert, born 1857 and Catharine Elizabeth born 1860 completed the family.

In 1846, Klamus Kettler, husband of Maria Kirchoff Kettler, from Minden, Germany, purchased 120 acres of property in Scott County, now Scott City. In 1849, he deeded two acres to the Evangelical Lutheran Church for a cemetery. This cemetery is now named the Little Eisleben Lutheran Cemetery and is located off Third and Lulu Streets in what is now Scott City. In 1862, Sophia Kettler, daughter of Klamus and Maria Kettler, married David Karl Eifert in his father's home. For a short time, the couple lived in the house of Mrs. Minnie Ruebel, at the corner of Seventh and Olive Streets in what is now Scott City. David built several rental houses as the city of Edna grew. He built a home for his family on the acreage of Maria and Klamus Kettler, his wife's parents. After the death of Klamus, Maria deeded 118 acres to David and Sophia. They had 11 children and they were: Karl Heinrich (1863-1929) farmer, married Anna Ristig; August (1864-1934) farmer and livery stable owner, Commerce, married Bertha Ristig; George (1865-1939) unmarried; Mary (1867-1961) seamstress, married Fred Ristig; Casper (1869-1950) married Bertha Hilleman; Ernst (1872-1872) died in childbirth; Elizabeth (1873-1945) married Albert Puchbauer; Daniel A. (1875-1950) farmer, married Pauline C. Will, 1903; John (1878-1969) farmer, Commerce Road, married Elda Koch; Emil Adolph (1881-1963) farmer, Commerce Road, married Meta Westerhold; and Lydia Sophie (1882-1983) seamstress, unmarried.

David later gave each of his children approximately one acre of land. In 1913, Daniel, his son, built a home for his family on this acre, which was considered at the end of the city limits of Fornfelt, formerly Edna. Lydia, his sister, built two houses next to Daniel's home. All three homes are presently *Henry and Anna Eifert, ca. 1906.* standing on North Lincoln Avenue in what is now Scott City. In 1925, Daniel purchased approximately 40 acres from his father's estate. In later years, he purchased from his brothers and sisters additional family farmland adjacent to his. At the present time, one son of Daniel and Pauline and two grandchildren live in homes on this acreage in Scott City. *Submitted by Elsie E. Eifert, daughter of Daniel and Pauline Eifert, Sept. 5, 2001.*

ELMORE – George Lee Elmore was born Nov. 2, 1858 to William Pinkney Elmore of North Carolina, and Elizabeth Angie (Lynch) Elmore of Tennessee. George died March 22, 1905, Morley, MO and is buried in the "Old" Morley Cemetery. His four sisters were: Eva, Sara, Minerva and Elizabeth "Betty". Paternal grandparents were John Elmore of North Carolina, and Henrietta (some spelled it Henryetta) (Lee) Elmore of Virginia (cousin of Robert E. Lee). Maternal grandparents were David Lynch, and Elizabeth (Smith) Lynch of Alabama. Maternal great-grandfather was John Smith, founder of Birmingham, AL. The Elmore's were pioneer families in Virginia, North Carolina, Alabama, Wilson, Carroll, and Benton Counties in Tennessee and Mississippi County, MO.

On Nov. 2, 1881 in Benton County, TN George Lee Elmore married Amanda Narcissus Rowe. Amanda was born March 16, 1862, in Hollow Rock (Carroll County), TN. She died Nov. 23, 1942, at

her home in Sikeston, MO and is buried in the "Old" Morley Cemetery. Her father was Elisha Rowe, who came from North Caroline to Wilson, Carroll, and Benton Counties in Tennessee, to Mississippi County, MO in 1883 and died there in 1886. Amanda's mother was Narcissus (Rogers) Rowe, born in Wilson County, TN and died in Tennessee in 1864.

George Lee and Amanda Narcissus (Rowe) Elmore, 1881.

George Lee Elmore and Amanda (Rowe) Elmore first farmed in Mississippi County, MO until 1903, when they moved to Morley, MO in Scott County. Following the death of her husband in 1905, Amanda continued to live and farm in Morley, along with her children and five grandchildren, whom she helped to raise. She later moved to Benton, MO with her daughters, Alma and Edith Elmore, and later with these daughters moved to Sikeston, MO where she resided until her death in 1942.

Children of George Lee and Amanda (Rowe) Elmore were: Olga Vernon born Aug. 1, 1882 Charleston, MO; Twins, unnamed, born April 22, 1885, died April 22, 1885 Charleston, MO; Claude Rowe Elmore born July 1, 1886 Charleston, MO; Blanche Elmore (died in infancy) born Feb. 20, 1889, died March 4, 1889 Charleston, MO; Guy Wilton Elmore born Oct. 6, 1890 Charleston, Mo and died 1963 St. Louis, MO; Alma Fern (Elmore) Burke (Mrs. Evin E. Burke) born June 15, 1896 Charleston, MO and died 1960 Sikeston, MO; Thelma Ruth (Elmore) Schubel (Mrs. Burnell L. Schubel) born May 2, 1896 Charleston, MO and died Feb. 26, 1987 Kansas City, MO; Erma Lucille (Elmore) Grant (Mrs. Elmer E. Grant Sr.) born Oct. 20, 1898 Charleston, MO and died June 15, 1997 Sikeston, MO; Edith Maurine (Elmore) Bomer (Mrs. C. D. Bomer) born Sept. 8, 1902 Charleston, MO and died 1990 Sikeston, MO.

EMERSON – According to *History of Our Branch of the Emerson Family*, it was in the year 1896 that Henry McDaniel Emerson and his wife, Almedia Self Foster, together with their four youngest children and all of their material possessions loaded into a covered wagon, left their home and relatives in Grantsburg, Johnson County, IL and headed for Missouri. Presumably, they crossed the Mississippi either at Cairo, IL or at Wickliffe, KY into Missouri.

Their eldest son, Henry Franklin, had preceded them to Commerce, MO to attend "The Commerce Seminary", preparatory to becoming a schoolteacher. He liked it so well that he sent for his brother, James Preston, who came to Commerce to follow in schooling and become a teacher. They both taught for some time before entering other fields of endeavor.

After Franklin and Preston were settled in their teaching carets, they sent for their eldest sister, Annie Jane, who came to Commerce to do housework for the family. Shortly after arriving in Missouri, Henry and Almedia, together with their children, Margaret Mae, Ura Alpha and Addye continued on to Morley, MO.

Thus, the Emerson's were in Scott County at the time it was known as "Swampeast Missouri" and many descendants of Henry and Almedia are still living in Scott County today. Henry and Almedia are buried in the Old Morley Cemetery.

Addye Marie married a Young and is buried in the old Sikeston Cemetery.

Henry Franklin married Ollie May Smith on March 10, 1896 in Scott County. They had four children: Henry Franklin Jr., Anne Janice, Jim Mac, and Joseph Kirby. After Ollie's death, Henry married Beulah Keesee on May 17, 1919 at Morley. They had one child named Camille. Henry Jr. married Sue Swaim. They had two children: Carolyn and Stephen. Anne married Franklin Edminston. They had one child named Franklin Jr. Jim Mac married Ava Evans. They had two children: James and Reda, who graduated from Scott County Schools. Jim served on the Morley High School Board of Directors for many years and as president of the Morley Alumni Association. Joseph married June Daugherty. They had one child who grew to adulthood, Judith. Henry and Ollie are buried in the Old Morley Cemetery. James lives in Scott County. His mother, Ava, still lives on the family farm near Morley. She celebrated her 88th birthday in 2001!

Annie Jane married Elmer Joyce. They are buried in the Old Morley Cemetery.

James Preston married Issie Mason on Jan .23, 1894 in Scott County. They had three children who grew to adulthood: Joyce F., Emory Mason and Norvell P. Norvell married Marie Reinemer and they are the parents of Congressman N. William 'Bill' Emerson who is buried in the Hillsboro Cemetery in Jefferson County, MO. His wife, Jo Ann, continues to serve the District as Congresswoman. His father, Norvell, is buried in the Old Morley Cemetery. Later in life, James married Ella Joyce. James, Issie and Ella are buried in the Old Morley Cemetery.

Asberry Garfield married Elmira Swaim on Dec. 19, 1891 in Scott County. They had seven children: James Raymond Sr., Drury A., John Mac, Geneva, Asberry B., Carroll Edward, and Ophia B. James married Ida Barker. They had four children: James Jr., Juanita, Kenneth and Anita. After Ida's death, James married Frances Stone. They had three children who grew to adulthood: Ray, Deborah and Rebecca. Drury married Mollie Pinkerton and migrated to California. John married Ossie Pratt. They had 10 children: Emma, John, Shirley, Melba, Jerry, Roxie, Edward, Joyce, Patrick and Elaine. Geneva married Barney White and migrated to California. Asberry B. married Armella Westrich and migrated to Illinois. They had two known children: Lawrence and Lee. Ophia married Roy Coy. They had three children: Faye, Ronald and Stephen. Asberry and Elmira are buried in the Old Morley Cemetery. Ray and Juanita live in Morley. Jerry lives in Sikeston. Kenneth lives in Advance.

Margaret Mae married Teve Griggs. They had two children: Herbert Redrick and Eileen. Margaret is buried in the Old Morley Cemetery.

Ura Alpha married Dora Elizabeth Levin. They had four children: Arlyn Lloyd, Anna Leona, Alpha Harley and Hurshell Melvin. Anna married Glenn Richardson. Hurshell married Mary McDaniel. They had two children: Charles and Elizabeth. After Dora's death, Ura married Esther Wright. They had three children: Bob, Jack and Jane. Ura and Dora are buried in the Old Morley Cemetery. *Submitted by Juanita Emerson*

EMERSON – The John Mac Emerson family of Scott County, MO has these direct Emerson forbears: Asberry Garfield, Henry McDaniel, Drury Willis, James (b. North or South Carolina, d. Illinois), Isaac and James "the Regulator" Emerson.

James "the Regulator" Emerson (sometimes spelled Emmerson) is so named because he was prominent in a tax rebellion in North Carolina where he fought to regulate and end tyranny at the famous pre-Revolutionary War "Battle of the Alamance" on May 16, 1771, was captured but later pardoned. Some believe colonial antecedents were Henry (wife Sarah) and William who arrived in Jamestown, Virginia Colony 1617 1618 aboard the *Sampson*, while others believe James came straight from England where he had wed Margaret Davis Jan. 1, 1761 at Barnard Castle, Durham. Either way, James definitely was married to a Margaret, died before Nov. 14, 1785 at Chatham, NC, was buried at Tick Cemetery.

John Mac Emerson (English extract, reputedly some Chickasaw blood) was born July 14, 1909 in Randalls, Scott County, MO; mother being Elma Mae Swaim (father James William, mother Sallie Edward Utterback). He wed Ossie Mae Pratt 1934 whose parents were George Washington Pratt (Irish ancestry) and Maude Mae (maiden name pronounced Crah-shaw, original spelling unknown but of French or Cajun origin) of Poplar Bluff. Offspring attaining adulthood were Shirley Maxine (Stidham), Genevieve Melba (Hicks), Jerry Mac, Roxie Mary (Stone), Edward Muriel, Joyce Mason, Patrick Maloy, and Elaine (Huey). Deceased in childhood were: twins John Michael and Elma Mae. Siblings attaining adulthood were: James "Raymond" Sr., Drury, Geneva, Asberry B "A. B.", Carroll Edward "Ed" and Ophia. Several later moved to Riverside, CA. Emerson-Swaim marriages go to early North Carolina. John Dick Swaim died for the Confederate States of America at Shiloh, April 8, 1862, unrecorded and in an unknown grave. Swaims were related to Arkansas' Governor James P. Eagle, entered Scott County from Kentucky. Some other families intertwined by blood or marriage and mostly also of Scott County, MO were: Blacks, Felkers, Vaughn's, Bausoms (Bascomb in England).

Henry McDaniel Emerson, wife Almedia Self (Foster) and their four youngest children entered Scott County, MO in 1896 by wagon. They were following sons Henry Franklin and James Preston Emerson, who had taken classes in Commerce near Benton to become teachers and later served as such even as other later Emersons have been southeast Missouri educators. Various Emersons also became large landowners, farmers and merchants, especially around Morley and Vanduser. Prominent was relative US Congressman William "Bill" Emerson. Author Ralph Waldo Emerson was of a New England branch possibly linked in England where a William Emerson was a famous scientist-mathematician, and Raffe Emerson received the coat-of-arms. J. Mason Emerson and Janice (Emerson) Edmiston were charter members of the Scott County Missouri Genealogy and Historical Society. Emerson may be Anglo-Saxon Emeric + son (Work + Kingdom + Son of) or, in Norman French, derive from Aimeric + son/sen, surnames unrecorded before the Middle Ages. Some references for serious genealogists are genfour.com, and *The English Emersons* by Peter Henry Emerson. DNA information should be enlightening.

ENDERLE – Leo Anthony Enderle was born Aug. 28, 1956 at Cape Girardeau, MO (old St. Francis Hospital) to Gladys (Koenig) Enderle and Elmer Paul Enderle. Glady's parents were Rosella (Horrell) and Tony Koenig. Elmer's parents were Dora (Glastetter) and Leo Enderle. Leo was the first born out of eight children. His other siblings are Wanda Blattel, Steve, Gail Walter, Dwayne "Butch", Tim, Shannon Chanley and one stillborn. Leo lived in Chaffee, MO and attended St. Ambrose Catholic Grade School and Chaffee High

School. After graduating, Leo worked fulltime with his father in the construction business. He married Connie Sue Gregory, May 14, 1983. She was born March 16, 1961 and raised in Advance, MO. She attended Advance Grade and High School. She is currently pursuing a BS in Economics and Accounting. Her parents are Vernon "Pruitt" Gregory and Glenda "Lucille" (Dellinger) Gregory. She was the only child. Her parents are divorced and she has stepbrothers and sisters. Pruitt married Becca (Young) Masters and Lucille married Teddy Ray "Ted" Walker. Stepbrothers and sisters are Ted and Tony Masters, Kathy Hopkins, Rob and Scott Walker.

Leo, Connie, Kristin and Katelyn Enderle, 1999.

Leo and Connie lived in Chaffee, Mo during the first two years of their marriage on the Leo Bisher farm until moving to Scott City, MO. They lived in Scott City until 2002 when they moved to rural Kelso/Chaffee.

Leo and Connie have two daughters: Kristin Elizabeth, born July 3, 1988, and Katelyn Nicole born Nov. 29, 1989. Both children attend St. Joseph Catholic Grade School. The whole family is very involved in the church, scouting and sports. Both girls attend band at Scott City Public School. Kristin plays flute and piano. Katelyn plays alto saxophone. They have been on the Scott City Swim team since 1985. The Enderle family tries to live by their faith and to put God and family first.

ENDERLE – Peter Enderle and Elizabeth Schneider, early farmers of Scott County, came to America from Germany in the early 1830s. Peter was born in 1800 and Elizabeth in 1807. They first settled in Stark County, OH, having purchased 61 acres of land in Perry Township. The birth records of their children are recorded in the Baptismal records of St. John the Baptist Catholic Church and St. Peter's Catholic Church, in Canton, OH. In November of 1850 they sold their land and moved to Missouri. Peter died on June 23, 1871 and Elizabeth died on Sept. 4, 1873. They are buried in the cemetery of St. Lawrence Catholic Church at New Hamburg. They were the parents of five children.

Joseph Enderle was born March 30, 1835 in Stark County, OH. He married about 1857 to Johanna Gosche. They were the parents of Jacob, Frank, John Baptist and Mary Elizabeth. Johanna died on March 26, 1866 and Joseph remarried on Feb. 5, 1867 to Frances Eichhorn. They had four children: Katherine; Rosina; Syvilla and Anna. Joseph passed away on Aug. 18, 1875 and Frances on April 18, 1912. Burials were in St. Lawrence Cemetery, New Hamburg.

Frank Enderle was born on Aug. 8, 1837 in Stark County, OH. He farmed with his brother, Joseph, until 1862 when he enlisted for duty in the Civil War. In 1864 he is reported sick at Vicksburg and died on March 31, 1864 at a hospital in Memphis, TN.

Jacob Enderle was born June 19, 1841 in Stark County, OH. He married Josephine Morper

on Sept. 18, 1866. They had nine children: Elizabeth; John B.; Leo Jacob; Magdalena; Louise; Joseph; Anna; Rosalie; and William. Josephine died on Jan. 17, 1887 in St. Louis. Jacob remarried Celestine Willmann on Nov. 19, 1887 at Kelso. They had five children: Benny; Alvina; Coletta; Otto and Frederick. Jacob was a farmer and served with the Missouri Volunteer Cavalry in the Civil War from 1862-1865. He died on Dec. 26, 1919 and is buried in St. Augustine Church Cemetery in Kelso.

Michael Enderle was born Sept. 20, 1844 in Stark County, OH. He married Mary Magdalena Riegert on Sept. 1, 1869. They had 10 children: Mary Theresa; Elizabeth; Peter; Jacob; Philip; Frank; Michael; Charles; Helen; and Joseph. After the death of his first wife on June 4, 1892, Michael remarried Maria Helena Schaefer on Jan. 9, 1893. Michael died on June 25, 1913 and is buried in St. Augustine Cemetery at Kelso.

John Enderle was born June 25, 1850 in Stark County, OH. He died on Jan. 29, 1872 and is buried in St. Lawrence Cemetery at New Hamburg. *Submitted by Steve Dumey*

ENGRAM – Soda cost five cents, movie admission was 20 cents, and a new Chevrolet coupe sold for $700.00. Times and costs were very different at the beginning of their lives together in the early 1940s for John Coleman Engram Sr. and Olivia McDonald. The young couple secretly eloped on Nov. 15, 1941, just a few weeks before the bombing at Pearl Harbor. Their first grocery bill, which consisted of two grocery carts full of food, cost $11.00, and their first home was a small four-room house located on a dirt road. They spent their first four years of marriage living in Stoddard County where they farmed and began raising a family.

The harvest from their first year of hard work was a very poor one due to flooding. Corn yielded 3-5 bushes per acre and cotton only produced half a bale per acre. In order to pay their grocery bill, the Emgrams picked cotton themselves to be debt free, which has been a goal of theirs to this day. Their first child, Joy Sue, was born in 1943, and their second daughter, Mary Janet, was born in 1945.

John and Olivia Engram

During the war years the young couple raised cotton, corn and beans. Olivia supplemented the family income by selling eggs, hogs and butter. They used ration books to obtain precious goods like gas, tires, sugar and other grocery items. They also canned their own garden crops and slaughtered their own hogs to provide food for the family.

In 1944, they obtained electricity which seemed "like a Christmas present" to them. In 1946, after WWII ended, the Engrams moved to Scott County and times seemed to improve. They purchased the first new refrigerator, wringer washer, and Oliver tractor, which arrived at Bell City following the conclusion of the war. They also purchased the first new Nash car, which arrived in Sikeston.

In 1952, their third child, Joann, was born, and modern conveniences- an International refrigerator, a telephone, and a black and white television entered the family's life. The next few years became even busier. John purchased his first farmland and became manager of the Vanduser Gin Company, in addition to his own farm responsibilities. Their fourth child, John Coleman Engram Jr. was born in 1957.

A major disaster faced the Engram's when their home and property were damaged by the historic tornado that hit Vanduser in May 1986. In addition, the Vanduser Gin was destroyed. Because it is the northern most gin in this area and because of its economic value to the town, John and the other gin directors decided to rebuild the facility, which was both an expensive and labor-intensive feat. After the gin's reconstruction and making sure it was operational, John retired from his position as manager on Dec. 17, 1987, after 32 years of service.

Over the years John and Olivia have made major improvements in their farming practices. They now own 750 acres of leveled and irrigated land and 335 acres in partnership with their son, John, who now farms the land.

Both John and Olivia have been classroom teachers at the Church of Christ at Vanduser, where they are members. In addition, Olivia has been active in PTA and Girl Scouts. John has received awards in recognition of farm management, is on the Extension Leaders Honor Roll at the University of Missouri, and was named Outstanding Conservation Farmer. He has been a member of the Scott County R-V School Board, Production Credit Association Board, Vanduser Gin Company Board, and 1st National bank Board of Directors.

Their family is now composed of: their daughter, Joy, who is married to John L. Whitten of Sikeston; their daughter Jan, who is married to John L. Wilson Jr. of Sikeston; their daughter Joann, who is married to Darrell W. Nichols, of Sikeston; and their son, John, who lives in Sikeston with his wife, Mary. They have seven grandchildren: John L. Whitten Jr., Jason Engram Whitten, Machelle Wilson Williams, Julie Wilson Reece, John L. "Trey" Wilson III, Elizabeth Anne Engram, and Isaac Coleman Engram. John and Olivia are also proud grandparents of six great-grandchildren.

During their 60 years of marriage, they have overcome the hardships of years with poor harvests, war, family illnesses, deaths, and even tornadoes. They look forward to life with excitement and anticipation and the loving bond with their family and friends.

ESSNER – According to my information the oldest ancestor I have information on now is Oswaldus Essner, who died before 1749 and was married to Magdalena Wohlfart. Their children were: Joannes Henricus, Joannes Theobaldus, Martha, Maria Catherina, Anna Magdalena and Anna Maria. They all lived in the Bourbach-le-Bas, Hauti-Rhin, France area.

Oswaldus and Magdalena Wohlfart Essner's oldest son, Joannes Henricus Essner, who died before 1790 and was married to Margaretha Sohnlen, had the following children: Mathias, Joannes, Maria Barbara, Catherina, Maria Margaretha, Stephanus, Maria Magdalena, Apolinaris, Magdalena and Joannes Theobaldus.

Joannes and Margaretha Sohnlen Essner's oldest son was Mathias, who died March 15, 1816 in Bourbach-le-Bas, Haut-Rhin, France and was married to Catherine Kippelen. Their children were: Catherine, Theobold (Thiebaut), Catharina, John Adam, Anna Maria, Anne Marie, Marie Therese, Sebastien and Mathias.

Leo and Rosa Uhrhan Essner family. Standing, left to right: Simon, Vincent, Herman, and John. Sitting left to right: Leo, Paul and Rosa

Thiebold Essner, born 1793 in Alsace, Germany (Bourbach-le-Bas, Haut-Rhin, France) and Maria Anna Nussbaum had seven children: Rosina, Ambroise, Nicolas, Thiebaut Jr., Martin (died March 21, 1831), Paul Essner, Jacques Essner (died March 9, 1831), Oswald T. and Marie Anne. Theobold and his wife Maria Anna and the above living children came to Baltimore, MD on Sept. 30, 1833. Theobold Jr. was not listed as coming to America with his family but probably that was an oversight. Two more children were born to this union after they arrived in America; Susanna Marie and Adam T. Nicholas and family came to Missouri in 1856. Oswald and his family settled in Michigan. Theobold Jr. and his family settled in Indiana. Apparently the rest of the Theobold Sr. family stayed in Ohio.

Nicholas Essner, son of Theobold and Maria Anna Nussbaum was born Dec. 11, 1823 and married Margaretta Rose Reece on Oct. 7, 1847 at St. Peters Church, Canton, OH. Nicholas and Margaretta Rose and their children: Oswald, Mary Ottilia, Andreas G., and Adam came to Missouri. Apparently, all of the Essners in this area are descendants of Nicholas, who according to a catalog of early settlers, arrived in Missouri in 1856. From an article in the *Scott County Democrat* dated Oct. 26, 1937, Adam Essner, a son of Nicholas, states that he was born March 10, 1857 in Ohio and came to Missouri in 1858. It is possible that Margaretta was pregnant with Adam in 1856 and stayed in Ohio until after the birth of Adam and in 1858 joined Nicholas in Missouri. Four additional children were born to this union after they arrived in Missouri: George, Frank, William and Susanna Margaretta.

I am proud of our Essner heritage. When I visualize Theobold and his wife and children leaving their homeland, knowing they will never see it again, and coming to America to experience the hardships they certainly did, to make a better life for themselves and consequently for me, words cannot express my gratitude. Then Nicholas and his wife and children leaving Ohio and coming to Missouri, was another new challenge. Mary Ottelia and John W. leaving their families and moving to Texas had to be a hard decision. *Submitted by John A. Essner, great-grandson of Nicholas and Margaretha Rose Essner*

ESSNER – Mary Ottilia Essner, born in Ohio Sept. 1, 1851, came to Missouri in 1858 with her parents and settled on a farm in the New Hamburg, MO area. On Nov. 16, 1869 Mary Ottilia married John Link. They had the following children while living in Scott County, MO: Andrew, Josephine, Maria Louisa, Susanna Margaretha, Katherine and Anna Maria. Katherine died while living in the New Hamburg, MO area and was buried in St. Lawrence Cemetery New Hamburg, MO.

On 1883, Mary Ottilia and husband John Link and the five surviving children left Missouri by covered wagon for Texas.

The family settled in Ellis County, TX in 1883 for two years, then moved to Anderson County, eight miles north of Palestine, TX. Wild turkey, deer, rabbits, and squirrels thrived among the beautiful hills, streams and woods of their settlement- a virtual paradise for hunter and fisherman John Link.

Another child Allean was born Jan. 26, 1886. In July 1887, Anna Maria and Allean died within a week of each other from diphtheria and were buried on the family farm. This began the Link Cemetery. This cemetery was dedicated in 1993 with a marker by the Texas Historical Commission. Marker reads: "Link Family Cemetery. This cemetery was established when John and Mary Otelia Link buried their young daughters Annie and Allean at this site within a week of each other in July of 1887. Both children died of diphtheria.

At that time no Catholic cemetery existed nearby and local tradition suggests the children were buried near their home because transportation of unpreserved bodies over a long distance in the heat was impractical.

John Link died in 1888 and was buried next to his daughters.

The Links practiced burial procedures commonly used in rural Texas in the 19th Century. The deceased was washed and laid out on a cooling board with bags of saltpeter or silver coins placed over the eyes in an undertaking shared by friends and neighbors. Pallbearers lowered the locally manufactured casket with the use of three traditional cotton straps.

Mary Ottilia Essner Link and John Link

After the burial, participants gathered at the home of the deceased to eat and express sympathy.

John and Mary's eldest son Andrew B. Link formally set aside the cemetery in a deed transferring family land to this youngest brother John F. Link in 1919. Of the 32 burials currently in the cemetery, 11 are of children under the age of 6. The Link family Cemetery is maintained by association of family members."

On Sept. 16, 1888, at the age of 40, John Link was killed in a water well accident. The story goes that a bucket of bricks being lowered into a well had a faulty rope, which broke, sending the cascade of bricks crushing down upon him. John joined the little daughters Annie and Allean, in what was to be from that time known as the Link Cemetery. John Jr. was born five months after his father's death. *Submitted by John A. Essner*

ESSNER – Nicholas Essner was born Dec. 6, 1823 in Alsace, France. He is the son of Theobold and Maria Anna (Nussbaum) Essner from Bourbach-le-Bas, Haut-Rhin, France. On Sept. 30, 1833, at 9 years of age, Nicholas Essner, along with his parents and several siblings, arrived on the ship *Palembaug* at the port of Baltimore, MD from Alsace.

The family then settled near Canton, OH where on Oct. 7, 1847 the marriage of Nicholas Essner and Margarete Ress was recorded in the St.

Peter's Church Wedding Registry. Margarete Ress born Jan. 15, 1824 in Bavaria. While living in Ohio four children are born to this union: Oswald (b. 1849), Ottilia (b. 1851), Andrew (b. 1854) and Adam (b. 1857).

In 1856 Nicholas Essner moved to Scott County, MO and by 1858 Margarete and the four young children joined Nicholas near Benton where, in the following years, four more children were born: George (b. 1859), Frank (b. 1861), William (b. 1864) and Susannah (b. 1868). Most of Nicholas's and Margarete's children married and raised their families in Scott County.

Nicholas Essner's tombstone

On May 31, 1878, at age 55, Nicholas Essner departed life and 29 years later, his wife Margarete died on July 20, 1907 at age 83. Both are buried at the St. Lawrence Catholic Church Cemetery in New Hamburg, MO.

Nicholas and Margaretha Rose Essner Children. Left to right: Cresenthia Scherer Essner, Margaretha Rose Essner (mother), Susanna, Frank, Mary Ottilia Essner Link, William, Adam, and Andrew.

During the Civil War Nicholas Essner served on the Union side in Company A of the Missouri Home Guard. He enlisted on May 5, 1861 and was discharged on Aug. 5, 1861. In 1891 Margarete (Ress) Essner, widow of Nicholas Essner filed for a Widow's Pension, claiming that her husband Nicholas died of disease of the lungs as a result of his Army service.

Nicholas owned several farms in the Benton and New Hamburg area and some of his property has been passed down from generation to generation and continues to be farmed by his descendants.

It is apparent that the Catholic faith and religion has always been very important to the Essner family as evidenced by the number of those who have served the Church as Priests and Nuns. Three of Nicholas's sons and one daughter were part of the 1904 original parish families of the St. Denis Catholic Church in Benton, and the rest of the family were members of the St. Lawrence Catholic Church in New Hamburg.

Members of this early Scott County family can be found as storekeepers in Chaffee, carpenter in Benton and woodcutter near Commerce. Although the early family members were predominantly farmers, their vocations quickly expanded and today they are found in almost every profession from laborer to judge.

Since their 1833 arrival in Baltimore from Bourbach-le-Bas, Haut-Rhin, France, the Essner family has spread far and wide. Today members of the Essner family may be found in all 50 states.

ESSNER – The Theobold Essner family arrived at the port of Baltimore, MD from Alsace, Germany on Sept. 30, 1833 (page 165, Passenger Arrivals, port of Baltimore). Their ship was likely named *Palembaug*. Listed was Theobold Essner, 40; Marianna (Maria Anna nee Nussbaum), 40; Rosina, 13; Ambrose, 11; Nicholas, 9; Paul, 5; Oswald, 2; Marianna, 2. There is no mention of Theobold Jr., 7 (error in record). Two more children, Susanna and Adam, were born later. The family settled in Stark County, OH, near Canon.

Records indicate all Essners in the Scott County, MO area are descendants of Theobold and Marianna's son, Nicholas (b. Dec. 6, 1823; d. May 31, 1878). He arrived in Missouri in 1856 (reference: catalog of first settlers). Oswald settled in Michigan. Theobold Jr. settled in Indiana.

Nicholas Essner served in the Missouri Home Guard during the Civil War on the Union side. He enlisted May 5, 1861 and was discharged Aug. 5, 1861.

Records conflict for the name of Nicholas' wife, Margaretha (b. Jan. 15, 1824 in Bavaria; d. July 20, 1907). One source states that Nicholas was married to Margaretta (Reece) Rose. New Hamburg, MO cemetery records state her name as Margareth Reise-Reece. Her declaration for Widow's Pension states that she was married under the name of Margarett Ress. A statement by her sister, Catherine Menz-Diebold, lists her sister as Margarett Essner nee Margaret Ress. An Oct. 7, 1847 entry in St. Peter's Church, Canton, OH Wedding Registry in Latin is interpreted, "I have joined Nicholas Esner and Margaret Res. Before me Theodore Esner and Susanna Red (Rev) T. H. Luhr."

Adam Essner, a son of Nicholas, was quoted in the *Scott County Democrat* newspaper (Oct. 26, 1937) that he was born March 10, 1857 in Ohio and came to Missouri in 1858. Conjecture is that Nicholas' wife, Margaretta, was pregnant with Adam in 1856 and stayed in Ohio until after Adam's birth, then joined Nicholas in Missouri in 1858. Probable route was down the Ohio River to Cairo, IL, then up the Mississippi to Commerce, MO then on land to Scott County, MO.

At the time of his death, Nicholas Essner owned a farm between New Hamburg and Benton, MO. This farm passed successively to his son, William Essner (1864-1923); to William's son, Leo William Essner (1892-1966), then to Leo's youngest son, Paul William Essner (1936-). When improvements to the original log house were no longer adequate, it was demolished by Paul on June 10, 2000. His family currently occupies a new house built on the same site. Paul's brother, John Essner, Cape Girardeau, MO preserved a 27" piece of log from the original structure. John recalled a large barn on the homestead that was built partly of logs with wood plank additions. He said, "I remember when I was young, we kept our cows in the bottom section of this log building. On cold morning, going into this cow stable to milk the cows, it was so much warmer inside." *Submitted by John Essner, Wayne Landis, and Karla Essner*

ESSNER – Theobold Essner's family arrived at Baltimore, MD from Alsace, Germany Sept. 30, 1833. All the Essners in this area are descendants of Nicholas Essner, the third of six Theobold Essner children. Nicholas settled in Missouri in 1856. He lived on a farm between Benton and New Hamburg. At the time of his death, the farm was passed on to a son, William. From William, the farm was passed on to a son, Leo Essner. Leo passed the farm to his youngest son, Paul, who resides there today. The old house was more than 150 years old. Paul recently built a new house where the old house stood.

Leo and Rosa (Uhrhan) Essner had five sons: Vincent, Simon, John, Herman and Paul. Paul was born June 4, 1936 at the family farm. He married Geneva Seyer, daughter of August and Minnie (Menz) Seyer, on April 19, 1958. They were married at St. Lawrence Church in New Hamburg. Paul and Geneva reside on the family farm. Paul farmed and Geneva worked at Buckstein's Pant Factory in Chaffee. In 1959 Geneva quit the factory to help on the farm and be a housewife.

Paul and Geneva Essner family

To their marriage was born eight children. Theresa, born March 25, 1959, never married. Gerard, born Jan. 10, 1963, married Carolyn Scherer on May 19, 1984. They have three children: Ashley, Zachary and Abby. Ronald, born Aug. 5, 1964, married Laura Riley on June 25, 1988. They had five children: Ryan, Lance, Kelsi, Ross and Seth. Kelsi Marie passed away Dec. 15, 2001 from cancer that started as a Wilm's tumor that was diagnosed in November of 1999. Kelsi is buried at St. Denis Cemetery at Benton. Sheila, born Feb. 3, 1967, married Ricky Harper on May 8, 1992. They have two children: Matthew and Whitney. Curtis, born Dec. 24, 1969 married Cheryl Miederhoff on Dec. 29, 1990. They have one son, Christian. Jeffrey, born May 19, 1973, married Gina Schiwitz on June 24, 2000. Melissa, born Jan. 28, 1977, married Justin Sullivan on April 17, 1999. Justin had a daughter, Ashley Sullivan. Justin and Melissa have one son, Austin. Jamie, born Jan. 22, 1979, married Emily Sander on June 9, 2001.

Paul is a farmer and worked at Lone Star Industries for 30 years. Geneva worked at Saint Francis Medical Center for 15 years. Gerard works at Mid-Way Trailers in Benton. Ronnie works at Lone Star Industries in Cape. Sheila works at Southeast Missouri Hospital in Cape. Curtis and Jeff work at Proctor and Gamble in Cape. Melissa works at Saint Francis Medical Center in Cape. Jamie works at Steward Steel in Sikeston.

Some of the grandchildren go to St. Denis School in Benton. Some attend Kelso C-7 in New Hamburg and one attends Kelly High School in Benton.

The Essners stay close by having many family gatherings.

ESSNER – Vincent Stephen Essner was born July 31, 1920, the eldest of five sons of Leo William Essner (b. Jan. 31, 1892; d. Sept. 25, 1966) and Rose Helen Uhrhan Essner (b. Oct. 26, 1892; d. Dec. 22, 1977). His birthplace was a white frame house on his maternal grandparents' farm, called the Kern farm in north Scott County, MO near New Hamburg.

Leo and Rose Helen's growing family (Simon Andrew, b. Oct. 1, 1922; and John Adam, b. Dec. 21, 1923) moved at least twice in five years into different houses in the area. They settled into a permanent home in 1925 where Herman Joseph (b. Sep. 1, 1926) and Paul William (b. June 4, 1936) were born. Paul's family occupied the house after his parents' retirement and relocation to town. The two-story white frame house was razed in 2000 for construction of Paul's new home.

Leo and Rose's family attended St. Lawrence Catholic Church, New Hamburg. Vincent and his brothers were educated through eighth grade in the parochial school taught by Sister Adorers of the Blood of Christ based in Ruma, IL. During Vincent's first year of school, classes were conducted in German.

Vincent married Lorena Mary Diebold (b. Sept. 28, 1922), daughter of Anton Joseph Diebold and Anna Theresa Ostendorf Diebold, on May 4, 1946 at St. Augustine Church, Kelso, MO.

The couple attended St. Lawrence Parish from 1946 to 1954, living in a house formerly owned by Leo Westrich in New Hamburg. There they welcomed three children; Anna Rose (April 19, 1947), Norman Simon (June 16, 1949) and Marilyn Kay (Oct. 24, 1951). Anna Rose attended first grade in St. Lawrence School before the family purchased an 81.5 acre farm and house near Kelso, MO in 1954 from Katie (widow of George) Scherer. The Essner family became members of St. Augustine Parish, Kelso.

The house burned just prior to the family's occupancy in March 1954. Their car was parked nearby, loaded with clothes that had not yet been carried inside. They moved into a hastily built framework on the same site. Their new house was completed in November 1954.

Over the years, the Vincent Essner farm raised barley, oats, corn, wheat, soybeans, beef, pork and seven children. Vincent and Lorena's children are: Anna Rose Essner Bles (b. April 19, 1947); Norman Simon Essner (b. June 16, 1949); Marilyn Kay Essner Friend (b. Oct. 24, 1951); Robert Paul Essner (b. May 19, 1955); Jerome Edward Essner (b. June 22, 1957); Shirley Ann Essner Hulshof Eftink (b. April 4, 1959); and Kevin Joseph Essner (b. Sept. 15, 1965).

Vincent Stephen Essner (center) with parents Leo William and Rose Helen (Uhrhan) Essner, New Hamburg, MO.

Anna Rose married Francis Eugene Bles on Aug. 8, 1970. Their four children are Michael Francis (Aug. 10, 1971); Kristie Ann (Dec. 17, 1972); Daniel Joseph (Nov. 24, 1974) and Lori Michelle (Oct. 1, 1977).

Norman married Dorothy Jane Stone on July 17, 1976. Their three children are Randy Vincent (Jan. 13, 1978), Leeanna Frances (Dec. 14, 1981) and Anton Gordon (Nov. 14, 1985).

Marilyn married Randal Dee Friend on May 24, 1980. Their three children are Aaron Blake (June 17, 1981), Todd Christopher (Aug. 2, 1983) and Chad Thomas (July 15, 1988).

Robert married Karla Susan Hahn on June 18,, 1977. Their three children are Nathan Robert (Feb. 7, 1981), Bonnie Sue (April 8, 1982) and Lee Timothy (March 21, 1986).

Jerome married Beverly Jo Seyer on July 8, 1978. Their five children are Scott Joseph (March 9, 1980); Amy Berth (June 13, 1982); Neal Edward (Oct. 15, 1983); Renee Catherine (Jan. 9, 1987) and Kyle Vincent (Nov. 20, 1988).

Shirley married Joseph Gordon Hulshof on Nov. 24, 1979. Their two children are Brian Henry (Aug. 27, 1980) and Michelle Ann (June 30, 1982). Gordon was killed in a farm accident on Jan. 3, 1984. Shirley married Greg Denis Eftink on July 31, 1993.

Kevin married Laurie Ann Holshouser on Sept. 26, 1987. Their three children are Brittany Nicole (Aug. 26, 1993), Madeline Rose (Sept. 12, 1997) and John Vincent (Oct. 7, 2001).

Vincent and Lorena have 23 grandchildren (through 2002).

As a young man, Vincent worked on his father' farm and was employed by a shoe manufacturer, Sports Specialty, Chaffee, MO. His first car was a black 1938 Chevy. As the car attempted to cross railroad tracks in 1942 between the towns of Ansell and Fornfelt (now combined as Scott City, MO), it became wedged on slipped planks. Vincent and his cousin, passenger William Klipfel, tried to free the car until an approaching train demolished it.

Vincent and Lorena (Diebold) Essner, 1991.

Vincent served in the U. S. Army (Oct. 21, 1942 to Dec. 21, 1945) during WWII as a veterinary technician T/5 with the 17th Veterinary Evac Hospital, caring for sick and wounded mules, horses and dogs. He was also a German interpreter for Col. Stevenson. He was awarded a Good Conduct medal and four Bronze Stars for campaigns in southern France, Rhjioneland, central Europe and Rome-Arno. Off-duty, he visited St. Peter's Basilica, Vatican City, Rome and witnessed a public balcony appearance by Pope Pius XII.

A farm accident in 1969 claimed three fingers from Vincent's right hand when they were caught in the pulley of a corn picker. Vincent was working alone in the field beside his barn when the accident occurred. He unhooked his tractor from the corn picker and drove it to the house, where he phoned Lorena, who was having corn ground at Kelso Milling Company a few miles away.

From 1945, through name and management changes until the shoe factory's closure in 1967, Vince worked at various production tasks in the bottoming (sole attachment) room. He bought and operated what had been the George Scherer farm outside Kelso, MO, beginning in 1954. He worked at Superior Electric from 1967 to 1982.

EVANS – Bartholomew Jenkins Evans, the second child of Enoch and Amelia Jenkins Evans, was born in Monongalia County, VA (now West Virginia) in 1799. In the spring of 1807, Enoch and Amelia Evans left Virginia for the upper Louisiana Territory, settling in Cape Girardeau District. Several years later Enoch moved a few miles south into what was to become Scott County, MO farming and serving as justice of the peace. The early years of Bartholomew Evans are not well documented, but the census of 1830 suggests he was still single and most likely living with his elder brother, John. Bartholomew married Mariah Lucinda about 1831 and by 1840 they were the parents of a growing family, including Mary Ann, John and George.

Shortly after the death of Enoch Jenkins in the mid 1840s, his children sold a parcel of land in Monongalia County that had been inherited by their late mother. At this point Bartholomew and two of his siblings and their families left Scott County for Texas. Bartholomew and Mariah Evans, along with James and Martha Evans, and George C. and Mary

A. Evans Anderson were in Rusk County, TX by 1847. The two Evans families and the Andersons bought land in Rusk County, but within a few years' time both Bartholomew and James Evans decided to move once again to Grayson County, in north Texas near the Red River. Perhaps the Evans brothers found Grayson County, with its large contingent of Missourians, more congenial then the east Texas county of Rusk.

Leaving the Andersons in Rusk County, Bartholomew and James Evans departed for Grayson County in late 1854 or early 1855. Shortly after the party arrived in their new home, James Evans died, followed with a few years by his wife Martha. By 1860, Bartholomew and Mariah Evans had bought a small farm northeast of Sherman in the Cherry Mound Community and were raising a substantial family in frontier conditions. Their eldest son, John, was elected sheriff of Grayson County in 1858.

The outbreak of the Civil War in the spring of 1861 disrupted life in the Evans household as Bartholomew's sons, John and George, enlisted in the Confederate Army, along with their brother-in-law John Reasonover, husband of Mary Ann Evans. The war years took their toll on the Evans's, as John died in the Indian Territory serving in the 22nd Texas Cavalry. John's mother, as well as his sister Mary Ann, also failed to survive the rigors of wartime hardship.

The census of 1870 showed the widowed Bartholomew Jenkins Evans and his youngest sons, age 11 to 21, continuing to work their 80-acre farm, adding cotton as a cash crop and bringing new land into cultivation. Bartholomew Evans was able in his early 70s to see that life above the primitive frontier level was possible as the long-sought railroad, with its promise of ready communication and access to distant markets, arrived in Grayson County in 1872.

The last of the children of Enoch and Amelia Evans, Bartholomew Evans, died in 1875 and was buried in Cherry Mound. His youngest sons, Jink and Simpson, operated the farm for a few more years before leaving to pursue careers in the city. *Submitted by Bob Taylor*

FELDEN - Louis William Felden, of Rockview, was born on Sept. 5, 1887, son of Frank Felden and Mary Unnerstall. He married Clara Irene Haynes on Feb. 2, 1910 at St. Ambrose Catholic Church in Chaffee. Clara was born on Feb. 19, 1893 at Gravel Hill, daughter of William Campbell Haynes and Mary Jordan. L. W. Felden was a farmer at Rockview who raised vegetables and took them to merchants in nearby towns. The family homesteaded in Keiser, AR from 1915-1923. They cleared the land, built a log cabin, and farmed. They moved back to Rockview when the children were old enough to be enrolled in school. In the 1940s they sold their hill farm and moved to another farm on the Bend Road, north of Cape Girardeau. Friends and neighbors at Rockview got together and gave them a "good-bye and best of luck" dinner. About 1954, L. W. and Clara retired from farming and later moved to a home on Sprigg Street in Cape Girardeau. L. W. died on March 3, 1974 and Clara on Jan. 1, 1980. They are buried in St. Mary Catholic Church Cemetery at Cape Girardeau. They are the parents of eight children.

Norman Felden was born Dec. 3, 1910. He was first married to Rachel Halter and then Wanda Fisher. He had two children Mary and Billy Felden. Norman died on Feb. 28, 1976.

Agnes Cecelia Felden was born on April 16, 1913 and married Frank Leo Dumey on Sept. 14, 1932 at Chaffee. They are farmers near Delta and have three children: Pauline, Donald and Joan.

Lawrence Edward Felden was born Feb. 17, 1916 and died on Nov. 9, 1976. He was a veteran of WWII and had worked for the Shell Oil Company at Wood River, IL.

Phillip Gregory Felden was born on March 16, 1922 and died on June 28, 2000. He resided with his parents and worked as a farm laborer.

Louis W. Feldon and Clara Haynes wedding photo, February 2, 1910.

Elizabeth Bernice Felden was born Jan. 6, 1924 and was first married to Ralph Hoots. Ralph died in a drowning accident on July 10, 1950. She married a second time to Lavern Goodwin. Lavern died on Oct. 10, 1997. Elizabeth had three children: Linda, Rick and Tracy.

Paul William Felden was born Aug. 26, 1927 and passed away at Rockview on March 16, 1935 of complications from an ear infection.

Marie Dorothy Felden was born Jan. 13, 1929 and married Don Lenhart on July 18, 1953 at Jackson. Don passed away in April of 1985 at Elkhart, IN. They were the parents of four children: Don, Dana, Darla, and Diane.

Lucy Margaret Felden was born Aug. 1, 1930 and married Thomas Schwartz on Sept. 7, 1963. They lived for many years in the St. Louis area. *Submitted by Don Dumey*

FINNEY – Dr. W. O. Finney was a well-known and respected physician in Chaffee and the surrounding areas for many years. He was one of the last physicians in the state to continue to make house calls to his patient's homes.

Dr. Finney was born in Laflin, Bollinger County, MO on July 13, 1886 to Dr. William B. Finney and the former Martha E. Clippard. Dr. Finney's father was also a physician and a large landowner in Kennett, MO.

Dr. Finney attended school in Kennett, and then went to what is now Southeast Missouri State University for his undergraduate studies. After graduation from college he taught in the Kennett High School before leaving to attend medical school at St. Louis University. At St. Louis University

Dr. William O. Finney

he received his medical degree, graduating magna cum laude from the university. After graduation from medical school, he also taught at the medical school for a brief time.

Later, he moved to Chaffee to set up his medical practice in 1910. In 1955, he was honored as Chaffee's Outstanding Citizen for his civic and professional contribution to the city. At that time he was recognized for having brought over 2,500 children into the world since his practice began. He was very active in working for good roads, schools, libraries, and better businesses in Chaffee and Scott County. He also furthered the work of the Boy Scouts and was a charter member of the Chaffee Chamber of Commerce and was one of the first members of the Rotary Club. He served on the school board for nine years and was active in the Masonic Lodge and the American Legion. He was a member of the Democratic Central committee for many years and served as a director and president of the Building and Loan Association in Chaffee.

Dr. Finney was an organizer of the Scott County Health Association and a founder of the Well Baby Clinic in Chaffee. He was also an organizer of the Scott County Medical Association. He served as Division Surgeon for the Frisco Railroad Medical Group and was a member and president of the Missouri State Board of Medical Examiners. He was also a member of the Missouri Medical Association and the American Medical Association. He was instrumental in helping secure several prominent Chaffee sites such as factories, and the city swimming pool at Harmon Field. Dr. Finney was also very involved in the work of the National Foundation of Infantile Paralysis (March of Dimes) in the late 1940s and early 1950s. He was the Scott County medical officer and made many trips to Benton to treat prisoners at the county jail. A lifelong Democrat, Dr. Finney was active in Scott County politics for a number of years.

On April 22, 1941 Dr. Finney married Mardell A. Masters of Chaffee who had two children, Betty Jane Warner Bauerscah and William R. Warner. Dr. and Mrs. Finney had three children, Kathryn S. Finney Stewart, Walter B. Finney and Norman W. Finney.

Dr. Finney died on May 29, 1970.

FOSTER – On Dec. 20, 1910 James Columbus Foster married Sarah Adeline "Addie' Joyce. James and Addie represent three Scott County families: the Foster, Joyce and Finley families. James was the son of Carter Foster and Ellen "Ella" Miller Foster and grandson of Jessie Miller, Frederick McClain Foster and Barbara Allen Ragsdale Foster. Addie was the daughter of William Edward Joyce and Sarah Adeline Foster Joyce and granddaughter of Wilson Foster and Julia Riggs Foster and Robert Joyce and Lucinda Thompson Joyce. She is the great-granddaughter of Edward Joyce and Hannah English Joyce. Addie's mother died soon after her birth and the Finley's became her foster family.

Although not blood relatives, there was a family connection to the Finley's. Upon the death of their spouses Addie's grandmother Julia Riggs Foster and Robert Wood Finley were married. Julia and Robert brought young children into the marriage and Addie's mother became part of this blended family. Years later Addie's mother placed her into the care of her good friend Nannie Elizabeth Stone and her new husband, stepbrother Richard Montgomery Finley, and the Finley's forever became a part of our family history. Grandmother Julia Riggs Foster Finley lived her entire life (110 + years) in Scott County. She has been referred to as one of Scott County's proud and industrious women. Julia Riggs Foster Finley raised not only her own children but also 19 foster children.

James and Addie Foster had four children: Joyce Richard, died in infancy; Mildred; Mabel and Ella "Lucille" Foster. Two of the girls, Mildred and Lucille, married brothers Audie and Eskell Sneed. The Sneed families farmed and remained in the Benton Sikeston area. Lucille and Eskell had no children. Audie and Mildred had two children: Sally and James. Sally is now married to David Lott and living in Mississippi. They have two daughters: Elizabeth Grace and Anna Joyce. James is married to Sue Beggs and they have two sons James and Jonathan. James also has a daughter Katherine from a previous marriage. James still farms in Sikeston. The third daughter Mabel followed members of her mother's foster family, the Finley's, to Michigan. There she married Francis McCracken. They had two children: Joyce Anna and Francis Foster. Joyce Ann is married to James Ogden and lives in California. She was previously married to Richard Hlava they had two children: Jeff and Nicole. Jeff is a lawyer married to Kate and living in Chicago. They have two children: Jack and Quinn. Nicole is a doctor doing her residency in Boston.

Francis Foster married Jo Ann Reay and they have two children: Amy Marie and Steven Francis. Amy lives and works in Florida and Steven is married to Lori and working in the family business in Michigan. Like so many families the descendants of James and Addie moved from

Addie and Jim Foster, 1910

an agrarian lifestyle and have spread out over the USA representing a variety of occupations. However, the families' roots proudly represent approximately three generations of Scott County Missourians. *Submitted by Jo Ann Reay McCracken*

FOSTER – Frederick Carter Foster (1858-1940) and Ellen Miller Foster (1862-1899)

Carter Foster's ancestors traced back to Scotland and from there to Pennsylvania, to southern Illinois and up the Mississippi River to the general area where they resided for about one year while the men began to seek farm land in the area of Cape Girardeau, MO.

Ellen Miller Foster's ancestors traced back to 1730 and moved to Cape Girardeau County (MO) in 1813. They came from Calvert County Maryland to Cairo, IL by way of a Koll Boat, then by boat to Cape Girardeau. The family purchased what was to become the County Poor Farm.

Carter Foster and Ellen Miller were married Sept. 3, 1884 at Cape Girardeau. They had five children: Mamie, Nolea, James, Marie, and William Allen.

After the death of Ellen in 1899, Frederick married Frankie Stowe and they had two children: Annie and Carter Foster Jr.

The first wheat threshing machine in S.E. Missouri belonged to Carter Foster, ca. 1900.

Carter and wife purchased a farm three miles south of Benton in the late 1880s. Carter, besides farming, brought to Scott County the first steam engine and threshing machine. Wheat threshing season ran from the latter part of June through August. He also had a pea huller and hay baler and installed a gristmill on the farm. People brought their corn to be ground for corn meal.

The season of wheat threshing was looked forward to. It brought neighbors together to help each other harvest grain. Normally there were 20 to 30 men involved at each farm to bring the wheat to the threshing machine. The women also gathered to prepare a huge sumptuous feast for all.

The first steam engine had no way to move themselves so they had to be pulled by a team of oxen. It was quite a chore to move the engine, the thresher, pea huller and hay baler from one farm to the other. Sometimes the machinery was located at one farm and neighbors brought their grain to the site to be threshed and bagged. A travel route was established so each farmer knew when to make preparations for his grain.

Carter established a route extending from Cape Girardeau through Scott County on south to below Matthews, Mo in New Madrid County. Sons of Carter were: James Foster married Addie Joyce and located in Benton, MO. He was a carpenter. His children were: Mildred, Mable and Lucille.

William Foster married Beula O'Neal and settled in Morley, MO. Their children were: Robert, Paul, Billy, Geneva, Clara, Vonda, Don and Dale.

William served in WWI. At age 15 he helped dig St. Johns Ditch. In 1926, he worked for EP Coleman who bought Cook Gin in Morley. Over the years he built a total of 31 cotton gins in the Bootheel. At the start of WWII he installed the entire water system at Fort Leonard Wood in Missouri.

FROBASE – Frank Gotliep Froboese was born in Hamburg, Germany. He immigrated to America in the 1860s. In 1865 he married Sophia Maria Bruns, also from Hamburg, Germany. They had three children: Henry George, Joseph H. and Annie D. In 1874, they moved to Morley, MO where Frank operated a restaurant and confectionary. Joseph and Annie each married, but no children survived. Henry married Emma Marie Noble in 1887. The spelling of the family name was changed to Frobase. They had four children: Frank J., Mayme S., Chester J. and Myron N. Henry moved his family to St. Louis, MO in 1910, where he operated a "Show House" in the days of silent movies and illustrated songs. In 1915, they returned to Benton, MO to build and operated the Frobase Restaurant and later the "Annex" beside the restaurant that featured patent drugs, sundaes, and a soda fountain. This was also the Greyhound Bus stop. After Henry's death in 1929, the three brothers operated the restaurant from his brothers, tore it down and built the "Frobase Theatre" in 1944. He operated it until he closed it in 1955. It is now the site of the Amick-Burnett Funeral Chapel. Myron operated the Annex until 1954, when he closed the business and moved to San Antonia, TX. R. R. and D. H. Enterprise now own the building.

In 1960, Chester H. Frobase and his son Thomas W. purchased the Moore-Harris Abstract of Land Title Company from Judge O. L. Spencer. They operated the business until selling it in 1972. Later, Thomas W. returned to college, where he earned a degree and became a Registered Nurse, specializing in emergency and trauma.

Frobase Theatre and Annex Building, 1944.

Frank J. Frobase married Alma Widman and they had one daughter named Virginia, who married Paul Shindler. They had two sons. Mayme S. married Maurice Van Harris, and they had three daughters: Mary Virginia, Martha Emma and Nadine Catherine. Chester H. married Etta M. Pitman and they had two sons: Chester J. Frobase Jr. who was never married and was killed in an auto accident in 1955, and Thomas W. Myron N. married Nina Bernice Hearn and they had one

daughter, Betty Marie, and adopted another daughter, Betty Ruth, who was married, but died without having any children. Betty Marie married William H. Hall in 1953. They have six children: William B., Nina K., Randolph K., Jana R., Justine R., and James R. They are retired and live in Pueblo, CO. Thomas W. married Judith Wills in 1956. They had two daughters, Debbie L. and Sally L. They were divorced in 1963 and Thomas raised the children. He married Gloria D. Haney in 1978. They are now retired and live on a farm near Benton, MO.

GEORGER – Daniel Georger, a farmer in the Kelso-New Hamburg area, was born Aug. 11, 1852, the son of Joseph and Caroline (Burger) Georger. He was married to Regina Morper, born Sept. 20, 1858, the daughter of Johann Michael and Gertrude (Eck) Morper, on June 6, 1879 in St. Lawrence Church at New Hamburg, MO. Daniel died Jan. 15, 1926 and Regina died Sept. 11, 1917 and both are buried in St. Augustine Cemetery at Kelso. They were parents of seven children:

Daniel Georger Jr. (b. June 5, 1888; d. May 14, 1963) married Bertha R. Blattel (b. May 26, 1880; d. Feb. 18, 1935) on April 2, 1910 in St. Augustine Church at Kelso. She is the daughter of Jacob M. and Philomena (Glastetter) Blattel. A daughter was born to them; Lorena Regina Georger married Theodore Joseph Berghoff (1905-1987) on Nov. 13, 1933.

Robert Georger (b. Sept. 16, 1883; d. Feb. 9, 1937) married Bertha Helen Schoen (b. Sept. 27, 1892; d. Feb. 10, 1969) on Oct. 27, 1910. To this union, seven children were born. William D. Georger (Anita Kiefer); Helen Marie Georger; Omer Charles Georger; Camilla F. Georger (William Peter Seyer); August; Louis Robert died at age 13; and John Wendolin (Ruth Patsy Neely).

Clara R. Georger (b. Jan. 20, 1885; d. Nov. 3, 1942) married Alexander Burger on Feb. 28, 1905. Ten children were born to them: Leo Emil Burger (Florence Hahn); Linda Marie Burger (Joseph J. Ziegler); Otillia R. (Otto Halter); Anton Alexander and Helen Marie were stillborn; Herbert Daniel; Antonella Catherine; Harold Joseph (Louise Scherer); Alexander Burger Jr. (Vera Glastetter); Alma Cecilia Burger and Malonia Burger.

Charles Georger (b. April 23, 1887; d. Jan. 7, 1972) married Louise Otillia Schoen (b. Jan. 18, 1889; d. Aug. 14, 1974) on Aug. 20, 1912 in St. Augustine Church at Kelso, MO. Nine children were born to them. Mat August Georger (b. July 15, 1913; d. Dec. 24, 1998) married Rosalia D. Tuccy on Aug. 20, 1955 in St. Joseph Catholic Church in Chicago, IL. Joseph Robert Georger (b. Dec. 22, 1914; d. July 18, 1953) was killed in a car accident at Grant City near Sikeston, MO; Augustine Catherine Georger (b. July 17, 1916; d. Jan. 6, 1999) became Sister Augusta in the Order of the Sisters of St. Francis in Wheaten, IL. Funeral services were held in St. Augustine Church at Kelso and burial was at St. Mary's Cemetery in Cape Girardeau, MO. Lucas Georger (Dorothy Mae Lowes) lives in Advance area; Regina Maria Georger died in infancy; Coena Dorothea Georger (b. June 16, 1921; d. Feb. 21, 2002) (Benjamin A. Damback). She was buried at Memorial Park Cemetery in Malden, MO; Anna Theresa Georger became Sister Elaine in the Order of the Sisters of St. Francis in Wheaten, IL; Alvina Lillian Georger (Donald Lett) and Marina Rosalia Georger.

Otillia Georger (b. Oct. 17, 1889; d. Nov. 17, 1936) died from pneumonia, was married to Herman Joseph Miller (b. Dec. 104, 1889; d. Jan. 26, 1972) on July 14, 1914. To this union, six children were born: Clara Maria Miller (George Schafer); Estella Josepha Miller (b. May 8, 1917; d. Nov. 8, 2001); Edward Joseph Miller (Edith

Braden); Pauline Henrietta Miller (Samuel Gibbs); Anna Cecelia Miller and Donald Herman Miller.

Ida Mary George (b. Aug 28, 1894; d. May 6, 1943) was the second wife of Anthony Halter on July 9, 1918. Ida Mary is buried in St. Augustine Cemetery and Anthony is buried in New Guardian Angel Cemetery at Oran, MO.

Wendelin Anton Georger (b. Sept. 3, 1898; d. June 20, 1974) married Bertha Layne. Wendelin is buried at Memorial Park Cemetery in Cape Girardeau, MO. They have one daughter; Shirley Georger (b. Nov. 15, 1935) married Dean Patt (b. Jan. 6, 1931 Deluge, MO) on April 8, 1961 in St. Joseph Rectory in Clayton, MO.

GLASTETTER – Joseph Glastetter was born Aug. 15, 1826 and his brother, Fredolin, along with their father, John Joseph, immigrated to Scott County in 1848 from Ettlingen, Baden, Germany. They lived in the wilds of southeast Missouri where they cleared land to build a cabin. Their mother Josepha Haller, died in Germany. Joseph became a citizen on April 10, 1854 in Scott County. They had to live in the United States for five years and one year in the state of Missouri. He died Aug. 5, 1877 and is buried in New Hamburg.

Joseph married Louisa Glaus on Aug. 17, 1852 in St. Mary's Catholic Church near Benton. She was born Nov. 1, 1833 and was the daughter of John Glaus and Louisa Martin from Schirrhein, Alsace, France.

Joseph served in the Civil War as a private in Company "B" in the Home Guard, commanded by Constantine Grojean. He and 12 others were taken prisoners by Jeff Thompson, "The Confederate Swamp Fox," the later part of July 1861 and remained prisoners for three weeks. After that time, they had to swear that they would no longer bear arms against the south and were released.

Elizabeth (Enderle) and Joseph Glastetter holding Paul and Rosalia, 1898.

They were the parents of ten children: Pauline (b. March 2, 1853) died in infancy; Engelbert (b. Nov. 17, 1854; d. Nov. 22, 1925) never married; Leo S. (b. Dec. 26, 1856; d. Feb. 6, 1917 from cancer) married Louisa Eck, who was the daughter of Lawrence and Mary (Kern) Eck on Jan. 17, 1893. Louisa was first married to Andrew Halter on Sept. 22, 1885. He was born Dec. 13, 1860 and died Sept. 26, 1890 and was the son of Nicholas and Magdalena (Heisserer) Halter.

Appolonia (b. Feb. 9, 1859; d. April 10, 1917) was married to John Bles, the son of George Bles and Salome Wilhelm on Nov. 25, 1879.

Amelia (b. Sept. 23, 1861; d. Feb. 18, 1888) married Herman Joseph Telker on April 26, 1887 in St. Henry's Catholic Church in Charleston, MO. Frances (b. March 8, 1864; d. Aug. 4, 1944) married John B. Gosche on Sept. 20, 1887.

Anton (b. Nov. 2, 1866; d. June 17, 1930) was married to Laura Katherine Heuring, the daughter of Frank and Anna Maria (Westrich) Heuring, on May 30, 1893. She died May 13, 1897. Anton's second marriage was to Regina Heuring, daughter of George and Theresa (Scherer) Heuring, on April 23, 1901.

Rosalia (b. April 4, 1869; d. Dec. 4, 1948) married Charles Henry Dumey on April 24, 1900. His parents were Joseph Justin and Catharina (Diebold) Dumey.

Joseph (b. Sept. 13, 1871; d. March 19, 1943)

married Elizabeth Enderle on April 17, 1894 at St. Augustine Catholic Church in Kelso. She was the daughter of Michael and Mary Magdalena (Riegert) Enderle. Joseph and Elizabeth were the parents of 11 children: Rosalia; Paul, married Anna Helen Scherer; Pauline; Benjamin died in infancy; Joseph L.; Mary Elizabeth; Bernard F.; Zeno Martin; Leon William; Clara Catherine; and Colette Louisa.

Martin J. (b. Oct. 23, 1874; d. May 23, 1947) married Bertha Theresia Gerst on Nov. 17, 1896. She was the daughter of Andrew and Amelia (Heuring) Gerst. *Submitted by David Sylvester Glastetter*

GLASTETTER - Paul Glastetter, farmer east of Kelso, was born Jan. 6, 1897, the son of Joseph and Elizabeth (Enderle) Glastetter and died Nov. 26, 1969. He married Anna Helen Scherer, the daughter of Donat and Otillia (Schoen) Scherer, on Aug. 17, 1920.

Paul was called to the service of his country during WWI. He was inducted on Aug. 27, 1918 in the 3rd Company 2nd Bn. 164th Depot Brigade to Dec. 10, 1918 and was given excellent character on his discharge certificate at Camp Funston, KS. Paul and Anna were raised on small farms in Scott County and lived in the Kelso Community.

Paul and Anna Glastetter wedding picture, August 17, 1920.

They are the parents of ten children. 1. William Joseph (b. May 18, 1921) married Bertha Backfisch on Jan. 9, 1945 and they were the parents of six children: Gerald Andrew, Linda Kay, Edward Marion and Laverne Marie (twins), Gary William and William Gerard.

2. Sylvester Benjamin (b. June 27, 1922) was called to the service of his country during WWII. He served 39 months with 18 months overseas. He married Ramona Frances Blattel on May 7, 1949 in St. Augustine Catholic Church in Kelso. Five children were born to this union: Cornelius John, David Sylvester, Sharen Marie and Karen Marie (twins) and Ramona Louise.

3. Delphine Bertha (b. Sept. 24, 1923; d. June 28, 1997) died from cancer and is buried in St. Denis Cemetery at Benton. She was married to Charles Backfisch on Sept. 14, 1943. They were the parents of 12 children: Paul Joseph, Robert A., Sylvester, Norma Jean, Joyce, Mary Lou, Vernon, Ruth Ann, Dennis, Carol Marie, Karl and James Noel.

4. Aureilia Marie (b. July 25, 1925) married Edwin Martin Muster on Nov. 2, 1963 at the Courthouse in Jackson. They have a son, Alan Paul.

5. Louis Paul (b. Aug. 2, 1926) married Anna M. Bucher on March 28, 1951 at St. Lawrence Catholic Church in New Hamburg. They were the parents of eight children: Thomas Louis, Helen Ann, Anna Mary, Lorita Agnes, Nancy Sue, Robert Gerard, Jane Louise and Bonnie Theresa.

6. John Zeno (b. Sept. 29, 1929) married Dorothy Vandeven on Jan. 17, 1953 at St. John's Church in Leopold. Their six children are: Michael John, Diane Marie, Mary Helen, Carol Ann, Steven Joseph and James Maurice.

7. Rita Clara (b. May 9, 1932) married Alfred Joseph Kluesner on June 25, 1955. they were the parents of five daughters: Charlotte Sue, Patricia Ann, Nancy Marie, Betty Lou and Marlene.

8. Colette Clara (b. Jan. 16, 1934) married Philip W. Eftink on Nov. 20, 1954 and he died April 18, 1963. They had three children: Phillis Ann, Shirley Louise and Daniel Paul. Her second marriage was to David Neff on Feb. 13, 1971 and they have one child, Sally Ann.

9. Helena Louisa (b. march 21, 1935) married Alvin Vandeven in Aug. 8, 1953 in St. John's Church in Leopold. They were the parents of eight children: Alvin, Elaine M., John, Ronald Lee, Gary Lynn, Larry, Gerard and Edward Charles. Alvin passed away on June 28, 1996.

10. Bertha Anne (b. Feb. 16, 1937) married James Joseph Seyer on June 21, 1958 and they have five sons: Herbert Joseph, Michael James, Kenneth Lee, Jeffrey Alan and James Patrick. *Submitted by Sylvester Benjamin Glastetter*

GLASTETTER – Edward "Shorty" Glastetter (b. Aug. 15, 1905; d. Dec. 3, 1996) a native of Scott County and farmer in the New Hamburg community, the son of William Fredolin "Fritz" and Anna Catherine (Leible) Glastetter married Coletta Glaus (b. April 16, 1906; d. Oct. 27, 1971) on Feb. 1, 1926 in St. Lawrence Church at New Hamburg, MO, the daughter of Michael and Mary (Bisher) Glaus. They also raised sugar cane and cooked molasses. They were the parents of five children:

Marcella Mary Glastetter (b. July 5, 1926) married Arnold Kapfer on June 3, 1946. Four children born to this union: David, Jane Ann, Daniel and Donald.

Clyde Raymond Glastetter (b. Dec. 28, 1950) married Shirley M. Holtkamp (b. June 7, 1930 in St. Louis, MO) on Feb. 20, 1950. Parents of five children: Clyde Ray, Judy, Nancy Ann, Kenneth James and Ted Louis. Retired farmers in New Hamburg community.

Alice Alma Glastetter (b. June 17, 1931) married Lucas John Ressel on May 30, 1952 at St. Lawrence church at New Hamburg, MO, son of Otto Joseph and Lorena T. (Schlosser) Ressel. Farmers in Kelso community and also did electrical wiring. "Luke" as he was known served with the Army during WWII. He was inducted on Nov. 14, 1944 at Jefferson Barracks, MO. He served as a TEC 4 in Company K 123rd Infantry. He was in the battle at LUZON as an automotive parts clerk and received Asiatic-Pacific Theater Ribbons W/1 Bronze Star- Philippine Liberation Ribbon W/1 Bronze Star- Victory Medal – Good Conduct Medal – Army of Occupation Medal, Japan. He also received a Lapel Button and two Overseas Bars. He was discharged on Nov. 15, 1946 at Fort Sheridan, IL. They are the parents of 13 children:

Bradley Lucas Ressel (b. Sept. 19, 1953) married Sandra Kay Springs (b. Feb. 19, 1955) on June 9, 1973. Two children to this union: Jason Bradley (b. Feb. 27, 1977) and Matthew Lee (b. July 23, 1981).

Second child: Diane Marie Ressel (b. Sept. 26, 1954) married Kenneth Wayne Page (b. Feb. 10, 1954) on Nov. 22, 1973. Seven children: Christie Anne Page (b. May 16, 1974) married Donald "Andy" Rodgers – a son, Andrew Riley Rodgers (b. July 2, 2001). Amy Marie Page (b. June 25, 1975) married Stephen O'Brien on June 27, 1997, a son, Landon Cole O'Brien (b. Jan. 18, 2002). Jennifer Lee Page married Ivan "Norman" Brant on Sept. 16, 2000 in St. Joseph Catholic Church in Scott City, MO. Pamela Susan Page (b. Nov. 1, 1982); Wesley Lucas Page (b. Nov. 4, 1985); Kassie Elizabeth Page (stillborn May 25, 1989) buried St. Joseph Cemetery at Scott City, MO; Cody Wayne Page (b. June 22, 1990). Third child: Linda Susan Ressel (b. Nov. 3, 1955) married James Lynn Wade (b. June 8, 1955) on Nov. 30, 1974. Two children: Jeremy Lynn Wade (b. Feb. 2, 1977) and Wendy Susan Wade (b. Sept. 24, 1979) married Christopher Holt

on Aug. 5, 2000. Daughter, Kaylie Susan Holt (b. Jan. 30, 2002). "Jim" is a sales manager for Jarvis Motor Company in Sikeston, MO. Fourth child: Elaine Mary Ressel (b. Jan. 11, 1957) married Tracy Howard Estes on Aug. 7, 1978. Two children: Travis Lee Estes (b. Sept. 21, 1977) and Trenton Dale Estes (b. Feb. 8, 1984). Fifth child: Patrick Dale Ressel (b. April 21, 1958) married Penny Rebecca Estes on Sept. 6, 1980. Three children: Ryan Ellinger (b. Sept. 25, 1976 – son of Karen Ellinger) married Stephanie Baker on Dec. 28, 1996. A son: Cole Ryan Ellinger (b. Sept. 4, 2001) Jacob Patrick Ressel (b. June 30, 1982) and Megan JoAnn Ressel (b. July 28, 1984). Sixth child: Sharon Kay Ressel (b. July 16, 1959) married Wesley Lee Urhahn (b. Aug. 8, 1957) on Sept. 17, 1977. Two children to this union: Lori Ann Urhahn (b. June 25, 1978) married Wesley Short on July 8, 2000, and Eric Urhahn (b. July 19, 1996). Seventh child: Kevin Joseph Ressel (b. Nov. 7, 1960) married Yvonne Denise Lesh (b. Nov. 25, 1964) on Nov. 25, 1988 in St. Paul the Apostle Church in Memphis, TN. Eighth child: Dennis Wayne Ressel (b. Jan. 16, 1962) married Brenda Kay Westrich (b. May 29, 1962) on April 26, 1986. Three children: Joshua Michael Ressel (b. April 29, 1981); Derek Wayne Ressel (b. May 4, 1987) and Madelyn Ressel (b. Sept. 14, 1989). Ninth child: Brian Edward Ressel (b. March 24, 1963) married Connie Leigh Jacobs (b. Dec. 9, 1963) on June 15, 1985. Connie's parents died and they took into their home her little brother, Herman "Joey" Jacobs and raised him. Tenth child: Vickie Faye Ressel (b. Dec. 5, 1964) married Curtis Wayne Hall (b. Dec. 1, 1961) on June 6, 1987. Four children to this union: Curtis Wayne Hall Jr. (b. July 3, 1988); Clayton Alan Hall (b. Aug. 2, 1995); Macy Elizabeth (Aug. 2, 1995) and Marisa Hall (b. July 21, 1997). Eleventh child: Jeffrey Allen Ressel (b. Sept. 14, 1966) married Amy Marie Dover on May 2, 1992; one child: Caleb Ressel (b. April 7, 2001). Twelfth child: Douglas John Ressel (b. March 29, 1969) married Karen Elizabeth Lampe on July 24, 1999; one child, Tyler (b. Aug. 26, 1997). Thirteenth child: Craig Anthony Ressel (b. Nov. 8, 1970) married Tamara E. Steger on Dec. 7, 1991. Two children: Lindsey Elizabeth (b. May 21, 1992) and Alex Anthony (b. Oct. 4, 1994). Luke and Alice Ressel celebrated their Golden Anniversary in May of 2002.

Roy Lawrence Glastetter (b. March 18, 1939) married Julie Marie Phelps (b. April 15, 1943) on April 20, 1963 in St. Mary's Church in Cape Girardeau, MO. They are owners of several IGA Stores in the Heartland. They have three children: Lisa Marie Glastetter (b. Feb. 11, 1964) employed at Wal-Mart in Cape Girardeau, MO; Robert Scott Glastetter (b. July 3, 1965) married Jacquelyn Lee Clubb (b. Oct. 12, 1965) on Oct. 26, 1985 in St. Mary's Church in Cape Girardeau, MO and Steven Scott Glastetter (b. Feb. 13, 1969) married Deborah Darlene Akins (b. Nov. 29, 1958), they have a son, Christopher Scott (b. July 4, 1990). Robert and Steven helped and worked in the business. They also started the Glastetter Rock and Roll Band in 1981. Bob taught himself how to play guitar when he was 14 and Steve at 12 learned to play the guitar from brother, Bob. By 1986 and 1987, they started to write their own songs. In late 1990, the band broke up.

Gary Frank Glastetter (b. Dec. 15, 1942) married Mary Ann Kern (b. Aug. 10, 1944; d. Sept. 28, 1972- died from cancer and is buried St. Lawrence Cemetery at New Hamburg, MO) on May 11, 1963 in St. Ambrose Church in Chaffee, MO. One child: Shelia Glastetter (b. Aug. 18, 1964). Gary Frank's second marriage was to Carma Jean Hicks (b. Dec. 24, 1949) on Sept. 24, 1974 at New Hamburg, MO. Farmers in the

Chaffee-New Hamburg area. One child: Venus March Mary Glastetter (b. Dec. 15, 1975). *Submitted by Mrs. Lucas (Alice Glastetter) Ressel*

GLASTETTER – Sylvester Benjamin Glastetter, a native of Scott County was born June 27, 1922, the son of Paul and Anna Helen (Scherer) Glastetter and was called to the service of his country during WWII. He entered on Nov. 12, 1942 as a private and took basic training at Camp Roberts, CA. The 265th Field Artillery Battalion was constituted on Jan. 25, 1943 as a 105 mm Howitzer Battalion. It was made active March 1, 1943 at Camp Shelby, MS as the 3rd United States Army. When the unit made a permanent change of station to Fort Bragg, NC the armament was changed from 105 Howitzer to 240 mm Howitzer. Then they arrived and occupied a position near Plabennec in the Brest, France area, they were reassigned from Third Army to Ninth Army on Sept. 5, 1944. Cannoneer was a member of a 240 mm Howitzer Gun Crew and assisted in moving, emplacing, firing and with drawing the piece in combat operations. He spent 39 months in the service of his country, 18 months overseas. He received three Bronze Stars for battles and campaigns in North France, Rhineland and Central Europe and received a Good Conduct Medal. He was also entitled to wear American, European African Middle Eastern Theatre Campaign ribbons and three overseas bars. He was discharged Jan. 23, 1946 at Jefferson Barracks, MO. After returning home, Sylvester farmed with his father for a year and then went to work for Lambert Drury as a hod carrier. Later he became a plasterer and was employed by the Drury Company for 33 years, working in many of the Motels, Churches and Schools in the area. On May 7, 1949 he married Ramona Frances Blattel, born Jan. 22, 1929, the daughter of Herman William and Blanche Louise (Hamm) Blattel. Ramona, a native of Scott County is a historian and Missouri Archivist specializing in Scott County Research. They bought a home in Ancell, now Scott City, and lived there nine years. In 1957, they bought a farm, which is part of the Parrott Plantation in North Scott County. (James Parrott, a Major in the Confederate Army during the Civil War died in 1863 in Little Rock, AR. The body was brought back on a boat to Commerce and a slave was sent there to bring it to this part of the Plantation for burial.) In August of 1999, Tom Arnold moved the tombstone to the Benton City Cemetery without our knowledge. In 1981, they bought a home in Kelso. Sylvester and Ramona celebrated their Golden Anniversary in May of 1999. They were the parents of five children:

Cornelius John was born March 26, 1951 and died May 26, 1963 at the age of 12.

David Sylvester was born Aug. 9, 1953 in Cape Girardeau and married Denise Catherine Schlosser on Dec. 30, 1978 at St. Denis Catholic Church in Benton. She is the daughter of William Eugene and Patricia (Uhrhan) Schlosser. David is broker-owner of ERA Cape Realty in Cape. Denise teaches in the Jackson School District. They have two sons: Kurt David, born Aug. 4, 1982, is a sophomore at Southeast Missouri State University in Cape Girardeau and Dustin Paul, born Oct. 8, 1986, is a

Sylvester Glastetter World War II, Nov. 12, 1942 - Jan. 23, 1946.

freshman at Notre Dame Regional Catholic High School in Cape.

Sharen Marie, born Oct. 1, 1954, married William Ronnie Parker on June 8, 1991 at St. Vincent's Catholic Church in Cape Girardeau. She was an art teacher and is now a housewife and Ronnie works for the State Rehabilitation Office.

Ramona and Sylvester Glastetter, 50th Wedding anniversary

They have a daughter; Maris Elizabeth Parker born Aug. 1, 1995 is in kindergarten at St. Vincent Catholic School in Cape.

Karen Marie, her twin sister, married Cary Hou on March 11, 1987 in the District Court of Taipei, Taiwan. She is a registered dietitian with the Los Angeles County Hospital in California. Cary is a tour guide for air travelers, making many trips to Alaska. They have a daughter, Ellen Ramona Hou born Feb. 3, 1989 in Taipei, Taiwan – Republic of China.

Ramona Louise, born June 11, 1957, married Bruce Edward Blankenship on April 30, 1977 in St. Augustine Catholic Church at Kelso. He is the son of Alvin E. and Margie (Watson) Blankenship. She is employed at Blair Industries at Scott City and Bruce at Do It Best, formerly HWI on Nash Road. They have two children: Ramona Bess, born Feb. 2, 1985, a junior at Notre Dame Regional Catholic High School and Louise Maria, born Oct. 21, 1989, a sixth grade student at St. Augustine Catholic School at Kelso. *Submitted by Ramona Blattel Glastetter April 10, 2002.*

GLUECK – Franklin Thomas Glueck "Frank" was born Jan. 12, 1960 and lived near New Hamburg, MO. He is the son of Joseph August Glueck (b. Dec. 15, 1926; d. Oct. 26, 1979) and Marie Ida Menz (b. Feb. 4, 1926; d. May 13, 2000) married on May 14, 1951. Joseph was the son of August Glueck (b. Aug. 27, 1896; d. March 4, 1983) and Pauline Glastetter (b. Nov. 15, 1898; d. Oct. 27, 1976). The parents of August were Joe Glueck and Margaret Seyer. The parents of Pauline were Joe Glastetter and Elizabeth Endele. Marie was the daughter of Leo Menz (b. Dec. 28, 1892; d. Dec. 28, 1972) and Emeline Urhahn (b. Sept. 11, 1896; d. Dec. 24, 1995). The parents of Leo were Casper Menz and Rosa Westrich. The parents of Emeline were John Urhahn and Rosa Glasser.

Frank has five brothers and two sisters. Patricia Ann "Pat" was born on April 10, 1952. Anthony Joseph was born May 19, 1954. Michael Davie was born Oct. 7, 1955 and was killed in an automobile accident on Jan. 11, 1978. Stephen Raymond "Steve" was born Oct. 31, 1956. Kathy Marie was born Sept. 13, 1958. Paul Edward was born Aug. 9, 1961. William Eugene "Bill" was born Feb. 18, 1963.

Cynthia Marie Vetter "Cindy" was born June 25, 1960 and lived near Benton, MO. She is the daughter of Vernon Linus Vetter (b. Feb. 2, 1935) and Janet Sue Dirnberger (b. Dec. 20, 1939) married on Oct. 11, 1958. Vernon was the son of George Vetter (b. March 17, 1899; d. Nov. 14, 1983) and Alvina Compas (b. Jan. 20, 1906; d. Nov. 29, 1990). The parents of George were John Vetter and Rosa Scherer. The parents of Alvina were Henry Compas and Regina Scherer. Janet was the daughter of Claude Dirnberger (b. Aug. 9, 1909; d. May 9, 1996) and Hattie Rebecca Brock (b. Oct. 11, 1909; d. Jan. 12, 2002). The

parents of Claude were Andrew Dirnberger and Catherine Dannenmueller. The parents of Rebecca were Robert Brock and Amelia Steimle.

Cindy has one sister and two brothers. Victoria Ann "Vicky" was born July 13, 1959. James Andrew "Jim" was born July 8, 1961. Jeffery Gerald "Jeff" was born July 27, 1965.

Frank and Cindy were married on May 2, 1982 in Benton, MO. They have two children: Adam Francis was born on Dec. 19, 1985. Hannah Marie was born on April 14, 1989. They reside in New Hamburg and attend St. Lawrence Catholic Church.

GODDARD – William Demetrius "Bud" Goddard was born Sept. 20, 1853 in Craighead, AR. He died Sept. 29, 1898 in Sikeston. He was the son of Thomas J. and Hannah Goddard. He had three sisters: Mary Goddard (b. 1849 in Alabama); Sarah E. Goddard (b. 1855 in Arkansas) and Martha J. Goddard (b. 1857 in Arkansas). He and

William Goddard before he married Molly Greer, ca. 1905.

his siblings came to Scott County in the 1860s with his father and stepmother, Susan.

He farmed as his father before him. He married his first wife, Missouri Harvey, Sept. 17, 1882 in Sikeston, MO. He married his second wife, Mary Ellen Messer, Aug. 5, 1884 in Sikeston, MO. They had five children: Jennie Goddard (b. 1885); William "Willie" Samuel Goddard (b. Nov. 21, 1888); Charles "Charlie" Goddard (b. December 1891); Oscar Goddard (b. March 1894); and Reese Goddard (b. July 1897). He was listed as member #20 in the earliest membership record of The First United Methodist Church.

Left to right: William Goddard holding Mary Black, Andrew Black, and Mary Ellen Goddard holding Jenny Goddard.

William "Willie" married Molly Lavinia Greer, Nov. 27, 1906 in Charleston, MO. They had seven children: Beulah Irene Goddard (b. Aug. 26, 1907 in Sikeston); Muriel Cecil Goddard (b. June 13, 1909 in Sikeston; d. April 18, 1986 in Yuba City, CA); Janet Lucille Goddard (b. Jan. 29, 1911 in Sikeston); William "Dub" Samuel Goddard Jr (b. Aug. 30, 1914 in Sikeston; d. Sept. 5, 1993 in Yuba City, CA); Allene Goddard (b. Jan. 21, 1917 in Sikeston; d. March 12, 1917 in Sikeston); Maxine Goddard (b. Jan. 28, 1918 in Sikeston; d. Feb. 3, 1918 in Sikeston); and Betty Quinn Goddard (b. Sept. 24, 1923 in Illmo).

William "Willie" and Charlie ran the baker shop in Chaffee for many years.

After William S. died, Molly moved her family to Lilbourn. When their family was grown and married, they all moved to California.

GOSCHE – As written and narrated by their eldest son, John Gosche of Oran, MO, at the Tony Gosche Family Reunion on May 29, 1988 in Oran MO.

Our forefathers came from Alsace-Lorraine, a province between France and Germany. Both countries had possession of this province at different times through the years, so we do have some French in us. According to the records, the coat of arms of the family name, Gosche, of Germany was granted in 1629 (359 years ago).

Anton (Tony) Gosche's father and mother were John and Mary Dannenmueller Gosche. He was only four years old when his father, John, passed away. John Gosche was born July 2, 1841 and died March 25, 1885. Mary Gosche was born Feb. 19, 1844 and died April 14, 1913. Mary's parents were Nick Dannenmueller, born Dec. 22, 1861 and died July 22, 1949, and Mary Dannenmueller born May 2, 1866 and died Oct. 13, 1951. Mary's grandfather Joseph Dannenmueller was born May 14, 1836 and came to the U.S. Jan. 1, 1856. Her great grandfather (also Joseph Dannenmueller) was born Sept. 26, 1795. Her great great grandfather Benoit (Benedict) Dannenmueller I (the first) was born in 1725. Her great great great grandfather Philippe was born about 1700. The later four were born in Schirrhein, Alsace-Lorraine, France.

Tony Gosche, second youngest child of John and Mary Gosche, was born Nov. 2, 1881. Ida Dannenmueller, oldest daughter of Nick and Mary Dannenmueller, was born April 18, 1886. After a courtship, they decided to get married. Tony got up enough courage to ask Nick and Mary Dannenmueller for Ida's hand in marriage. They both consented, so on Sept. 12, 1905, Reverend C. Moenig united Tony and Ida in Holy Matrimony in St. Lawrence Church in New Hamburg, MO. Tony was a prosperous young farmer. Tony took his young bride to an 80-acre farm near Bleda, MO, which he had rented from his brother, August Gosche, to start their new married life. Caney Creek, a mean stream of water in times of hard rains, bordered the farm in Bleda. It was levied and, during a time of high water, the farmers would patrol the levees, watching for weak spots that might appear. Ida would become frightened, especially at night when Tony would be out on the levees. She was not used to high water, so if for any reason she had to get up out of bed, she would put her bare foot on the floor to find out if any water was in the house. Their first child, Irmina May, was born on Aug. 1, 1906.

On Jan. 31, 1908, another daughter arrived, Elenora Susan. In 1909 they decided to own their own farm and purchased the adjoining farm from Mrs. Mary Amrhein, a widow. It contained 100 acres. May 14, 1910, a son named Nick arrived. He weighed 11 or 12 pounds...almost big enough to go to work.

Leona Clara was born July 1, 1912. She passed away as an infant on Jan. 1, 1913. On Nov. 14, 1913, Corona Rose popped up. Zeno Louis started crying Sept. 21, 1916. Nov. 27, 1918, Wilhelmina "Wilma" Amanda made her appearance one year after the family had moved into a new home. That made six living children. On Sept. 2, 1921, Harold Joseph appeared.

The children were all educated in the Bleda School, which was a one-room house of studies. Another room was added later. The school building is still standing. The children attended Guardian Angel Parochial School in Oran for one year when they reached the age to make First Solemn Holy Communion.

The Liquor Prohibition Amendment was ratified in 1919. So, no more saloons. As we all know, the German people have a great taste for beer, so they started to make Heim Gemach, also known as Home Brew. The more sugar you added, the stronger it was. Some of it was so strong, it would almost kick you over into the adjoining county. In those days, when someone in the neighborhood had a birthday, the married couples would play cards and the younger set would have a barn dance in warm weather. So Heim Gemach and wine were the prevailing refreshments.

John Nick recalled at the age of 21, making an extra supply of refreshments for a barn dance. Tony and Gus Seyer, two boys that worked in the neighborhood as hired hands were to play the music. One had a fiddle, the other a guitar. Everybody was having a great time. The Heim Gemach took a little extra effect on the band. The two boys were laid in the hayloft. Early the next morning, Tony called the two families who employed boys and told them they would not report for work until around noon. So the boys left about that time, still wondering what happened.

In 1925, a young prosperous farmer, Paul Pobst, mustered enough nerve to ask for Irmina's hand. The marriage took place on Oct. 19, 1926 in Guardian Angel Church in Oran, MO. They moved to a farm southwest of Bleda and started housekeeping. To this union, five girls were born: Laverne, Marietta, Dorothy Marie, Doris Lee and Carolyn June. Dorothy Marie died as an infant July 13, 1937, and Doris Lee died as an infant March 5, 1940. Paul passed away Sept. 17, 1955.

Nora, Tony and Ida's second daughter, married Matthew Pobst on April 23, 1929. They moved to a farm north of Bleda and, in later years, purchased a farm near Chaffee. To this union, three sons were born: Clifford, Norman and Larry. Matthew passed away Nov. 17, 1962.

In early 1941, Zeno told his parents he was going to make a stab at married life with a twin girl named Berneda Pobst, sister to Irmina's husband. They married on May 24, 1941. Zeno owned and operated the Gosche Supermarket (Gosche Store) at Caney, previously known as Bleda. Zeno was called into the armed forces in WWII. The store was closed during his time in service and then reopened upon his return. To this union, two children were born: Stephen and Nancy. Berneda passed away March 12, 1971. Zeno then married Fannie Davis on March 9, 1979. Zeno passed away Sept. 6, 1985.

Wilma and Jerome Metz tied the knot on May 27, 1941, just three days after Zeno's wedding. Jerome was employed with the Postal Department in Oran. Jerome also entered the armed services of WWII. Jerome and Wilma retired from the Postal Service with 70 years of combined employment between them. They have one son, Donald.

Corona married Herman Feuerhahn, from the Gordonville area, on Sept. 12, 1941. He was a mechanic in heavy equipment and later became involved in sales work. They now reside in Hudson, OH. Two children were born to this union: Myron and Nina. Myron passed away at the age of 33 on July 18, 1978.

In the spring and summer of 1932, Tony furnished the mules and equipment and John Nick plowed, cultivated and shucked 10 acres of corn on a neighbor's farm. He received one third of the crop – 127 bushels of corn at 19 cents per bushel = $24.13. In January and February of the same year, two other neighbor boys and John had a chance to clean up 10 acres of land where the trees had been cut, leaving the tree tops and sprouts to be burned. They lived in a one-room log cabin for those two months and worked six days a week; were paid $100.00 and split it three ways. John started work for Standard Oil Company in 1935 in Oran. Then in 1937, he and two others founded Scott County Oil Company. Some years later, John became the sole owner and operator. On April 26, 1945, John married Almerette Leible. One son, William, was born to this unit. Almerette passed away on Feb. 14, 1988. John sold the company and retired in 1976.

Harold Gosche and Leona Heisserere were united in marriage on May 3, 1946. They lived with his parents until April 9, 1947, when they moved to Oran into their new home. To that union, five children were born: Donna, Ronald, James, Marlene and Douglas. Harold passed away Nov. 11, 1986. Harold's youngest child, Douglas, is now farming the home place, making Doug the third generation to proudly operate the farm in Caney.

Tony and Ida Gosche celebrated their Golden wedding anniversary on Sept. 11, 1955. Ida passed away Aug. 23, 1956 at the age of 70.

Irmina moved back home to care for her dad, Tony, on Oct. 11, 1956 as her husband, Paul, had passed away in September of 1955. She took care of him until his death on Jan. 29, 1972 at the age of 90. *Submitted by Marlene Gosche Bell*

GRAHAM – The Graham's were from England.

W. O. and Lena Graham lived at Blodgett, MO. They had 14 children.

Blodgett was the Watermelon capital of the world at one time. The trains would stop there, and people from all over that area would come with their watermelons and load the boxcars. W. O. and Lena owned their own farm east of Blodgett. They also grew cantaloupes and other crops.

W.O. and Lena Graham

The children always loved to shoot firecrackers at Christmas time. The Christmases are times to remember with such a large family. There was always plenty of food on the table. In the summer time we always had a baseball game out in the front yard. There is so much good fun to remember.

Grandchildren and great-grandchildren
Mark Lesley Nov. 19, 56
Sherrie Owens Feb. 1, 56
Whitney Lyn Feb. 11, 81
Mark Adam Oct. 14, 83
Kelly Jean Baker May 8, 59
Ronnie Eugene Dec. 8, 57
Ross Edward Sept. 15, 87
Beverly Colley Aug. 11, 57
Celeste Lauren Sept. 15, 86
Kathryn Anne Feb. 17, 89
Fred Joe Feb. 2, 48
Kathy Griffin
Barry Thomas Dec. 28, 79
Scott Lee June 7, 54
Debbra F. Estes Dec. 21
Jason O.
Stephanie L.
Madalyn F. Jan. 8, 1987
Debbie Pittman June 27, 1955
Cliff Pittman Aug. 10, 53
Matt May 3, 82
Andy Dec. 30, 89
Charles Evert Aug. 30, 42

Mary Ann Masters Dec. 12, 43; died Oct. 9, 2000, (Last name Stevens)

Charles Edward I June 12, 49
Shirley Maronay
Charles Edward II March 28, 71
Chris Wayne June 21, 72
Larry Jean Nov. 14, 77
Steven Jan. 1, 87
Kerry Wayne born 1959-July 3, 92
Micha and Marshall Graham
Sept. 14, 87 July 3, 92
Died Victoria Teria
Randy Bohannon
Julie Norton
Brittney March 30, 88
Blair Oct. 2, 91
Ross Oct. 10, 93
Angela Helen William Dec. 26, 59
Nicholas Chanalas Aug. 9, 90
Michael Chanalas Aug. 20, 93
Tammy Rogers Feb. 20, 62
Den Rogers
Graham Lee Dec. 4, 88
William Rogers Oct. 11, 94
Louis Michel Williams Dec. 4, 57
Eugene Lee Rudd married
Lil 2000
Birthday In Laws
William Dietz Dec. 23, 1903
Evertt Masters March 19, 1916
Charles Maronay Feb. 21, 1926
Willy Williams (Harald) March 12, 1930
Gene Rudd March 26, 1932
Clayton Bohannon Oct. 30, 1926
Imogene Eaton Sept. 17, 1922
Mildred Louise Burns Sept. 11, 1926
Georgia Mae Burns Aug. 25, 1928
Kelles Leasley Wade Jan. 23, 1935
Married
Benita and William Watkins April 24, 1946
Helen and Evertt Masters March 8, 1941
Paul and Imgoene Graham June 10, 1942
Bill and Mae Graham Jan. 18, 1947
Ray and Mildred Graham Jan. 18, 1947
Emela and Charles Bohannon Jan. 20, 1951
Hazel and Bill Dietz June 20, 1953
Louise and Willie Williams July 27, 1955
Sue and Gene Rudd Sept. 10, 1955
Jean and Kelles Wade Dec. 18, 1955
Lena and W. O. Graham Jan. 17, 1915
Mom's mother and father
George Franklin Lewis
Lula Leota Thompson Lewis
Dad's mother and father
William Oscar Graham
Willa Crawford Graham
The Grahams came from England
Birthdays
W. O. Graham Dec. 5, 1893 Grahamville, KY
Lena Leota Graham Sept. 20, 1897 Doniphan, MO
Willie Benita March 25, 1916 Blodgett, MO 1988
Hazel Marie Oct. 23, 1917
Lewis Alonzo June 11, 1919 1944
Paul Crawford Nov. 3, 1921 1976
Helen Mae Nov. 3, 1923
Billie Lee Nov. 10, 1925 1980
Clay O June 21, 1927 1933
Ray Joe June 21, 1927
Ruby Leota march 25, 1929
W. O. Jr. March 25, 1929
Enela Aug. 19, 1930
Myron Louise April 25, 1933
Mary Sue Aug. 24, 1934
Martha Jean July 3, 1937
Deaths
W. O. Graham Sept. 5, 1959 age 66
Lena L. Lewis G. Feb. 1, 1987 age 90
Lewis Alonzo July 5, 1944 France age 25

Paul Crawford Dec. 4, 1976 age 55
Billie Lee Feb. 24, 1980 age 59
Benita April 30, 1988 age 72
Charles Maroney Jan. 3, 2000

GRANT – E. E. "Chuck" Grant, III was born July 19, 1942 in Sikeston, MO. He is the son of E. E. "Gene" Grant Jr. and Freda Lambert Grant. They lived in the Sikeston area where he graduated from Sikeston High School in 1960.

On Aug. 16, 1963 he married Joan Crities. She was born in Lutesville, MO and is the daughter of Avery R. and Freda (James) Crities. Chuck and Joan have two sons. E. E. "Chip" Grant was born on Sept. 5, 1965 and graduated from Sikeston High School in 1983. He earned his B.S. from Anderson University and an M. A. in Choral Conducting from New England Conservatory. Bart Allen Grant was born on July 9, 1973, and graduated from Sikeston High School in 1991. He earned his B.S. degree from Southeast Missouri State University with a major in economics. On May 11, 1994, he married Angela B. Williams. They have one son, Cooper Allen Grant, who was born on Jan. 2, 1999 and are expecting their second child in November 2002. In 1996 Bart joined A. G. Edwards and Sons, Inc. as a financial consultant and was appointed Branch Manager in 2002.

Chuck was in the banking business in Sikeston for 19 years with Security National Bank and First Federal Savings and Loan. He has been a financial consultant in the brokerage business with A. G. Edwards and Sons, Inc. since 1985 and has earned the title of Trust Specialist and Vice President – Investments.

GRANT – Jasper Newton "Jap" Grant was born Feb. 3, 1858 in Van Buren, AR to William Newton and Pynthia (Bean) Grant. His family had come from Scotland to North Carolina, to Arkansas, to Everton (Dade County) MO and to Scott County, where they lived and farmed around Oran, Morley, and Vanduser areas. On Nov. 12, 1879, Jasper N. Grant married Margaret Ellen Hinkle, who was born Feb. 4, 1863, to Isaac Hinkle (b. March 30, 1840; d. March 19, 1872; buried Carpenter Cemetery, 6-1/2 miles north of Sikeston, MO), and Nancy (Hinton) Hinkle Carpenter (b. May 8, 1843; d. Oct. 31, 1928), buried in Carpenter Cemetery. Jasper Newton and Margaret Ellen Grant farmed south of Morley, MO; behind present day Scott County Central School District, and in the Vanduser, MO area. Jasper N. died at his farmhouse south of Morley, MO on Dec. 15, 1926. Margaret Ellen Grant later moved to Sikeston, MO with her daughter, Lucy, where she died March 15, 1947. Both are buried in Carpenter Cemetery.

Jasper Grant family, 1898. Front row: Jasper Ernest, Louisa Caroline, Margaret Ellen holding Oscar Newton, Jasper Newton holding Elmer Eugene, and Lucy Naomi. Back: Ida Myrtle, Lutie Ethel, and William Isaac.

Children of Jasper Newton and Margaret Ellen (Hinkle) Grant were: Louisa Caroline (Grant) Thacker (Mrs. Marshall Thacker) born Jan. 27,

1884, died Jan .8, 1936. Buried in "Old" Morley Cemetery. William Isaac Grant "Will" born Oct. 23, 1886, died March 4, 1911. Buried in Carpenter Cemetery. Lucy Naomi Grant (unmarried) born March 3,1888, died July 30, 1977, Sikeston, MO buried Carpenter Cemetery. Lutie Ethel (Grant) Mason (Mrs. Reese Mason) born 1889, died 1975 Sikeston, MO. Buried Garden of Memories Cemetery, Sikeston. Ida Myrtle (Grant) Mason (Mrs. Emory Mason) born 1891, died 198- Oran, MO. Buried Forest Hills Cemetery, Morley, MO. Jasper Ernest Grant born 1893, died at his farm south of Morley, MO in 1946. Buried Memorial Park Cemetery Cape Girardeau, MO. Elmer Eugene Grant born Feb. 15, 1895 Vanduser, MO, died May 8, 1949 Sikeston, MO. Buried Memorial Park Cemetery Cape Girardeau, MO. Johnny Marvin Grant (died in infancy) born Jan. 12, 1897, died Jan. 29, 1897. Buried Carpenter Cemetery (Hinkle Family Plot). Oscar Newton Grant (Unmarried) born Jan. 13, 1898, died Oct. 3, 1924. Buried Carpenter Cemetery. Effie Ellen (Grant) Sutherlin (Mrs. Grover Sutherlin) born 1901, died 19—, Charleston, MO. Buried Charleston, MO.

GREENLEE – Edith Ivy Greenlee was the fifth child of Jesse W. Bean and Louisa Cordelia Hinkle Bean. She was born on Jan. 16, 1901 in New Madrid, MO and grew up in and around Sikeston. On May 25, 1918 in Canalou, MO she married Homer John Greenlee, son of John and Ever Elizabeth Brasher Greenlee. Homer was born Dec. 19, 1896 in Fredonia, KY and died March 28, 1985 in Lubbock, TX.

The family moved to Odessa in 1951 during the oil boom so Homer could build houses and except for short stays in Lubbock and Fort Worth, she lived there to the end of her life. She died May 15, 2001.

Edith was the granddaughter of Isaac and Nancy Hinton Hinkle of Morley, MO. Isaac and his brother owned the livery Hinkle and Brother.

She was preceded in death by her parents, three brothers: Clarence William, Cecil Isaac and Otto Orval; and three sisters: Alma Bean, Helen Bean Drake and Lula Mae Bean. One sister of Sikeston, MO survives her: Veda Muriel Bean Craig. She is buried at Sunset Memorial Garden in Odessa, TX. Edith was a life long member of the Church of Christ.

Edith was known by her family to be a wonderful cook. She was loved and is missed by all of her descendants.

Edith Ivy Bean b. Jan. 16, 1901 in New Madrid, MO; d. May 15, 2000 in Odessa, TX

Homer John Greenlee b. Dec. 19, 1896 in Fedonia, KY; d. March 28, 1985 in Lubbock, TX; m. may 25, 1918 in Canalou, MO

Zelma Edith Greenlee b. Jan. 23, 1920 in Charleston, MO; d. Oct. 16, 1997 in Odessa, TX

Louis Cyrus Couch b. April 23, 1917 in Gloversville, NY; d. Aug. 8, 1982 in Odessa, TX; m. Sept. 14, 1939 in Charleston, MO

Phillip Ray Couch b. Jan. 9, 1941 in Sikeston, MO

Suzanne Wright b. May 5, 1949 in Fort Worth, TX; m. Sept. 6, 1968 in Fort Worth, TX

April Denise Couch b. May 6, 1917 in Swedish Hospital Denver, CO; d. May 6, 1971 in Swedish Hospital Denver, CO

Aaron Michael Couch b. Dec. 3, 1971

Brandi Ackmann m. Oct. 23, 1999 in Amarillo, TX

Faith Ann Couch b. July 13, 1942 in Sikeston, MO

Luther Alvin Neal Jr. b. Aug. 6, 1936 in Fort Worth, TX; m. Aug. 1, 1958 in Northside Church of Christ, Odessa, TX

Valerie Ann Neal b. Feb. 14, 1961 in Fort Worth, TX

Tony Daniel William b. Nov. 11, 1959; m. June

15, 1979 in backyard parents home, Crowley, TX

Brandon Roy Williams b. March 8, 1985 in Forth Worth, TX

Brittiny Renee William b. July 8, 1988 in Forth Worth, TX

Nathan Todd Neal b. Jan. 21, 1964 in Forth Worth, TX

Lisa Carole Beustring b. Jan. 6, 1967; m. July 16, 1994 in First Methodist Church Forth Worth, TX

Ever Elizabeth Neal b. May 11, 1995
Elliott Todd Neal b. April 26, 2000
Mark Andrew Neal b. May 31, 1966 in Fort Worth, TX

Amy Rachael Wiley b. Aug. 27, 1970; m. March 6, 1993 in Robert Carr Chapel Fort Worth, TX

Paxton Landreth Neal b. March 10, 1997
Avery Anne Neal b. April 16, 2000
Craig Alan Neal b. Dec. 10, 1968 in Fort Worth, TX

Ashley Wilemon b. May 4, 1976; m. March 16, 2000 in University Christian Church Fort Worth, TX

Stephanie Renee Neal b. May 22, 1970 in Fort Worth, TX

Andrew Harper Brownlow b. July 20, 1970 in San Angelo, TX; m. March 25, 1996 in North Richland Hills Church of Christ Fort Worth, TX

Blaze Harper Brownlow b. Oct. 13, 1997
Beaux Neal Brownlow b. June 26, 1999
Rodger Wayne Couch b. Dec. 12, 1946 in Sikeston, MO

Beth Cantell m. Dec. 12, 1972 in parents house Odessa, TX

Michael Lewis Couch b. Dec. 31, 1976
Second wife of Rodger Wayne Couch:
Alicia Inez Grottie b. Feb. 3, 1948 m. Feb. 17, 1980 in mother's house Bowie, TX

Phillip Edward Couch b. Feb. 1, 1981 in Fort Worth, TX; d. Feb. 16, 1981 in Fort Worth, TX

Jessica Ann Couch b. Dec. 21, 1982
Second husband of Zelma Edith Greenlee: William McColloch b. Oct. 4, 1909 in Oklahoma; d. March 22, 2000 in Odessa, TX; m. Oct. 6, 1984 in Lubbock, TX

Elmer Henry Greenlee b. Nov. 28, 1921
Virginia Stout m. November 1945
Ronald Greenlee b. June 16, 1946
Jeannie Boren b. Aug. 18, 1946; m. Feb. 18, 1967

Brian Greenlee b. Nov. 22, 1967
Kristy Riley m. May 2, 1992 in Sikeston, MO
Madison Greenlee b. October 1995
Lauren Greenlee b. March 2000
Scott Greenlee g. Dec. 27, 1967
Second wife of Elmer Henry Greenlee:
Betty Joan Bailey b. April 8, 1920; m. Oct. 8, 1958

Charlotte Jean Greenlee b. Sept. 3, 1932 in Scott County, MO

James Alan Lynn b. March 28, 1928 in Fornfelt, MO; d. April 4, 2000 in Lubbock, TX; m. Feb. 18, 1949 in Missouri

Don Cornel Lynn b. Oct. 30, 1949
Linda Lovett b. Nov. 15, 1947; m. Nov. 14, 1970 in Lubbock, TX

Don Alan Lynn b. Nov. 15, 1970 in Odessa, TX

Glenna Clark b. Nov. 16, 1972
Second wife of Don Alan Lynn:
Debbie b. Aug. 20, 1967; d. July 17, 1996; m. Aug. 20, 1994

Daren Lynn b. June 1, 1971
Allan Dale Lynn b. July 10, 1954 in Odessa, TX

Kimberly Lynn Wilson m. June 1978
Second wife of Allan Dale Lynn:
Geri Lynn Dunlap b. Sept. 29, 1954; m. June 1, 1983 in Austin, TX

Laren Nicole Lynn b. Jan. 16, 1992

Stephen Dewayne Lynn b. Sept. 23, 1959 in Odessa, TX; d. Sept. 26, 1959 in Odessa, TX

Eric Homer Lynn b. Jan. 4, 1962 in Odessa, TX

Pam Morgan
Second wife of Eric Homer Lynn:
Lisa Tijerina Luper m. July 12, 1997 in Lubbock, TX

Katrina Luper b. June 25, 1994
Madison Lynn b. Aug. 25, 1997
Dane Allie Lynn b. Jan. 4, 1962 in Odessa, TX
Martha Brumelow b. May 9, 1960; m. Oct. 8, 1983 in Lubbock, TX

John Christopher Lynn b. Aug. 12, 1985
Haley Ann Lynn b. June 25, 1992
Holly Ann Lynn b. Dec. 28, 1995
Derek James Lynn b. Jan. 4, 1962 in Odessa, TX

Teresa Simphins b. May 9, 1969; m. Jan. 23, 1996

Chloe Simphins b. April 17, 1992
Hayden Simphins b. Sept. 3, 1993
Louise Annette Greenlee b. Oct. 14, 1937
Bobby J. Stephens b. Oct. 28, 1963; d. Nov. 26, 1983 in Odessa, TX; m. Dec. 18, 1959 in Odessa, TX

James Gregory Stephens b. Feb. 1, 1961 in Odessa, TX

Kristy Kay Williams b. Nov. 29, 1966; m. May 10, 1987 in Odessa, TX

Bobby James Stephens b. June 6, 1988
Jordan Michelle Stephens b. July 14, 1991
Jeffrey Scott Stephens b. Aug. 27, 1963 in Odessa, TX

Charlotte Anne Rundle b. Sept. 26, 1968; m. Aug. 9, 1992 in Crowley, TX

Ashley Neejia Stephens b. Dec. 14, 1992
Alyssa Ann Stephens b. May 30, 1996
Julie Annette Stephens b. Nov. 22, 1968
Tommy Lee Jones
Second husband of Julie Annette Stephens:
Frank Jones b. Nov. 6, 1963; m. 1988 in Corpus Christi, TX

Ryan Wilson Jones b. June 27, 1992
Robin Annette Jones b. May 22, 1995
Casey Robert Jones b. April 9, 1999
Second husband of Louise Annette Greenlee:
James Fred Gunter m. Nov. 1, 1989

GREER – Green Berry Greer was born Aug. 16, 1808 in Virginia and moved to Scott County in 1825. He died in 1852, and is buried in Carpenter Cemetery near Sikeston. Green Berry and his first wife, Jane Hutson, had five children. Their middle son, Calvin Greer, was born July 26, 1833. Calvin married Frances Turner on Nov. 9, 1854 and had six children. Calvin Greer's descendents still reside in Scott County.

Calvin Greer was at one time Judge of the County Court of Scott County, and later, the Police Judge. In addition, he was the third Mayor of Sikeston, serving from 1895-1896, and then again, from 1898-1902. His six children were: twin girls, Jane "Jennie" and Rebecca; Elizabeth; twins John Bell and Martha; and Green Berry. Jennie married Frank M. Sikes; Rebecca married Charles D. Matthews Sr., Elizabeth also married Charles D. Matthews Sr. after her sister's death in 1874; John Bell married Louisa Mason; Martha died as an infant; and Green Berry married Mary Alice Moore.

Green Berry Greer II, known as Green Greer, was a mill owner, banker, and landowner. He and Mary Alice had two children, Green Moore (born 1887) and Juanita (born 1889).

Their son, Green Moore, married Rose Esther Marshall, and they had three children, Green Moore Jr. (Moore Jr.), Green Berry III (G. B.) and Esther Jane.

G. B. Greer III married Peggy Tatum, and they

raised their three sons in Sikeston: Green B. IV (Barry); David Tatum; and John Calvin. Barry and his wife, Susan, have two daughters, Emily Tatum and Lyndsay Ellen, and live in Huston, TX. David and his wife, Elizabeth Ann, have a daughter, Alecia Ann, and reside in the Atlanta, GA area. John and his wife,

G. Moore Greer and his sister, Juanita.

Christine, have a daughter, Meredith Martin, and live in St. Louis. Mrs. G. B. Greer lives in Sikeston.

Esther Jane Greer married Charles E. Brooks Jr. and moved to Kingsport, TN. They had five children: Charles E. III, Greer; Dorothy Helen; Andrew; and Rebecca.

Moore Jr. died in 1970, G. B. in 1987, and Esther Jane in 2000.

Green Greer's daughter, Frances Juanita, married Frank W. Van Horne. They had two children, Frank W. Jr. "Bill" and Alice Greer. Bill Van Horne was killed as a WWII Marine pilot in 1943.

Alice married William S. Huff "Bill", and they still reside in Sikeston where they raised their three daughters: Rebecca Greer (Greer); Patricia Van Horne; and Stephanie Alice. Greer died in 1980. Patricia married Josiah D. Bill, and they live with their three children Sarah Greer, Catharine Phelps, and Josiah D. Jr. in Sikeston. Stephanie resides in San Francisco, CA and St. Louis. *Submitted by Alice Van Horne Huff*

GREER – Greenberry Greer was born Aug. 16, 1808 in Davidson County, TN. He died in Sikeston, Scott County, MO March 29, 1852 and is buried in Carpenter Cemetery near McMullin in Scott County. He moved to Scott County about 1825 from Davidson County, TN and bought several pieces of land from the Seminole Indians. The Greer family had always been involved in farming. Greenberry married Jane Hutson about 1828. They had five children: Isaac; Ben Harrison; Calvin; Thomas Nathaniel; and Martin.

Greenberry then married Elizabeth Stanley on July 23, 1843 in Scott County. Elizabeth was born in Illinois, Oct. 30, 1813. He and Elizabeth had seven children: Amanda, Delilah, Albert, Susan, Lilbourn "Dock", Mary C., and Nancy M.

William Berry Greer and Lilbourn "Dock" Greer.

Lilbourn married Catherine Woods July 22, 1873. They had two children: Johnny and Lucy Greer. On Aug. 9, 1880 "Dock" and Druzilla Louisa Pratt married in Scott County, MO. "Dock" was born Jan. 23, 1850 in Scott County and died sometime in the fall of 1923 and is buried in Hart Cemetery. Druzilla was born Feb. 18, 1860 in Scott County, died Jan. 25, 1917 and is also buried in Hart Cemetery in Sikeston. They had ten children: Molly Lavinia; William Berry; Green Alfred;

Mamie; Myrtle; Janet; Rebecca; Dock; Ethel Jane; and Lida Bell. All were born in Scott County. Molly Lavinia married William Samuel Goddard Nov. 27, 1906 in Charleston, MO. Molly and William lived in Chaffee had seven children: William Samuel Jr. "Dub"; Beulah Irene; Muriel Cecil; Janet Lucille; Allene; and Maxine (all born in Sikeston); and Betty Quinn born in Illmo. After William's death in 1927, Molly Greer Goddard moved to Lilbourn, MO. She then went to California in the late 1940s with her oldest son Muriel, where she died in 1956 in Yuba City, CA.

GRIFFITHS – One of the families who lived in Scott County for many generations was the Griffiths. David Griffiths, wife Catherine, came to Scott County from Kentucky in 8100s. David's death was around 1833. His will was recorded on Aug. 30, 1833. Christopher Houts and Charles Griffiths were the executors.

David on 94 acres in the New Philadelphia, Scott County with Catherine and six children. David and Catherine Griffiths' children:

1. William (born July 25, 1804, Kentucky) married four times.
2. Charles.
2. Louisa "Lovie" married Mr. Lovel.
3. Anna.
4. Elisabeth "Betsy."
5. Rebecca, born 1809, Kentucky, married before 1833 Richard Finley.

William's (David) first wife's name is unknown. They raised six children and farmed in the Commerce area.

Elizabeth (William, David) "Betsie," born 1827, Missouri, (named after her aunt Elizabeth) married March 7, 1847 Milton Fowler.

David L., (William, David) born about 1828, Missouri, (became a minister) married Sarah J. Wheeless Greer.

Catherine, (William, David) born about 1830, Missouri, married March 3, 1852 George W. Frickie. Stephen, born about 1831, Missouri, married Sarah Melvina (last name unknown).

Charles, (William, David) born about 1833, Missouri.

Archibald P., (William, David) born about 1836, Missouri, married Mary Price.

After William's first wife died, he married three more times. The second wife's name is unknown, third marriage was on July 8, 1848 to Leah Malinda McElmury, who had at least two children she brought into the marriage, along with the four below they had together.

Alvin Cook, (William, David) born about 1848, Missouri, married Marthy E. Head.

Elmina, (William, David) born Sept. 11, 1856, Missouri, married William Bell.

Nathaniel, (William, David) born between 1859-1862, Missouri.

Jefferson Davis, (William, David) born about 1864, Missouri, married Katherine Billings.

The fourth marriage of William Griffiths was on Jan. 22. 1869 to Aurela McKaney/McCain. It is not known if these two children were from a previous marriage, however they went by the name of Griffiths.

Charles F., (William, David) born about 1869, married Lizzie (last name unknown).

Cora Ann, (William, David) born about 1870.

In the 1840 Federal census, William owned 17 slaves. They worked the acreage, planted crops, tended chores. By 1850 the number of slaves was nine. Some of the slaves took the last name Griffiths.

William died Dec. 26, 1878, buried in the Old Commerce Cemetery/Anderson Cemetery, Commerce, MO.

David L. (William, David) and Sarah Wheeless Greer had two known children: James Frederick,

(William, David, David) born about 1866, married Aug. 19, 1893, Edna Shoulders, Scott County, MO.

James Frederick Griffiths (David, William, David) and Edna Shoulders' children:

Nellie, (James, David, William, David) born 1897, Missouri, married Lewis Phelps.

Marie Phelps (Nellie, James, David, William, David).

Betty Phelps (Nellie, James, David, William, David).

Sallie, (James, David, William, David, born 1898, married Mr. Jones.

Laura (James, David, William, David), married Ed Springer; one daughter.

Cline F., (James, David, William, David), born Aug. 13, 1915, married Aug. 22, 1936, Rosetta Bennett. Cline died in 1945.

Katherine Elmina (David, William, David) "Kate," born 1871, Scott County, MO, married three times. All the marriages took place in Scott County.

First Arch. W. Fizer Jr., married Sept. 16, 1885 with no children from this marriage.

2nd Robert "Brownhorse" L. Branon, married Oct. 24, 1890, two children from this marriage.

Katherine Elmina "Kate" Griffiths and Robert "Brownhorse" L. Branon's children:

Marie "Mame" Nacoma, (Katherine, David, William, David) born July 29, 1891, Scott County, MO, married twice:

First Lawrence Felix Herzog, married July 6, 1905, Scott County.

Marie "Mame" Nacoma Branon and Lawrence Felix Herzog's children:

Leo, born 1906/1907 Scott County, died infant, buried in Benton, MO.

Pearl, born 1908/1909 Scott County, died infant, buried in Benton, MO.

Vadys Mary Josephine (Marie, Katherine, David, William, David) born Oct. 2, 1910, Scott county, MO, married May 19, 1925 Louie Edward Bloom, Ste. Genevieve, MO.

Cy George William (Marie, Katherine, David, William, David) born Jan. 31, 1912, Farmington, St. Francois, MO, married Elnora M. Grissom Aug. 21 1933, St. Francois County, MO.

Raymond Franklin Lawrence (Marie, Katherine, David, William, David) born Aug. 9, 1914, St. Francois County, MO, married Doris Younger, Memphis, TN.

Henry Thomas Weber (Marie, Katherine, David, William, David) born Jan. 11, 1917, St. Francois County, MO married Dorothy Bishop, Jan. 17, 1924, Blytheville, AR.

Second Frank Anthony Heckinger. No children from this marriage. Mame died Jan. 28, 1948 Memphis, Shelby County, TN.

William "Bill" James Branon (Katherine, David, William, David) married Audie Ellen Bloom April 28, 1918, Farmington, St. Francois, MO and had nine children with four living to adulthood:

William Thomas (William, Katherine, David, William, David) born Nov. 13, 1921, Farmington, MO.

Edna Maxine (William, Katherine, David, William, David) born June 3, 1923, Farmington, MO.

Billy Joe (William, Katherine, David, William, David) born April 10, 1931, Farmington, MO.

Jerry Dale (William, Katherine, David, William, David) born Aug. 18, 1934, Farmington, MO.

Katherine (David, William, David) married third Abraham Vaughn on Jan. 22, 1895, Scott County, MO.

Katherine Elmina "Kate" Griffiths and Abraham Vaughn's children:

Ethel (Katherine, David, William, David).

Franklin (Katherine, David, William, David) born July 1897.

Joseph S. (Katherine, David, William, David) born June 1894.

This family has spread to many states in the United States carrying on the bloodline of the first forefathers that came to Scott County, MO.

GROJEAN - Constantine Grojean (b. Aug. 25, 1817 near Paris, France) came to America in 1833 with his parents, Constantine and Josephine (Martean) Grojean, first homesteading in New Berlin near Canton, Stark County, OH where the parents died. He became a citizen of the United States after living here for five years and one year in the State of Ohio. He married Dorothea Oriente/Rinder, the daughter of Lawrence and Dorothea (Gaubner) Oriente, on Nov. 10, 1844 in St. John's Catholic Church at Canton, OH. They came to southeast Missouri in 1849. They were the parents of 11 children, the first four born in Ohio. John H. (born Aug. 16, 1845) died Jan. 12, 1905 and is buried in Riverside Cemetery in Farmington, ME.

Louisa (b. Dec. 8, 1846; d. Oct. 24, 1931) was married to Ignatz Diebold on Jan. 9, 1866. Their living children were: Mary Emilia; Louis Franc; Theodore; Emma Clara married John Hamm; and Charles. Mary Margaretha (b. July 6, 1848; d. Feb. 8, 1933) was married to Frank Diebold, known as "Smoka Franz" on Oct. 1, 1867. Charles (b. Nov. 22, 1849; d. June 30, 1905) married Mary Metz on Nov. 21, 1876 and they had seven children: Bertha; Frank; Lawrence; Benjamin Leo; Theon; Marcella; and Benjamin John.

Henry Jose (b. Sept. 26, 1851; d. July 10, 1939) married Anna Mary Scherer on May 23, 1881. Six children were born to them: Helen; Emma; Clara Mary; Joseph; Emanuel; and Anna Olivia. Josephine (b. Feb. 10, 1853) entered the Order of the Sisters of St. Francis in Joliet, IL and took the name, Sister Mary Constance. She died June 8, 1933 and is buried in St. John's Cemetery in Joliet, IL.

Back row: Mrs. Ignatz Diebold (Louisa Grojean), Leo Grojean, and Mrs. Frank Diebold (Mary M. Grojean). Back: Henry, Constantine, and Charles Grojean.

Constantine (b. Dec. 28, 1854; d. April 8, 1927) married Margaretha Bucher, the daughter of Louis and Elizabeth (Morper) Bucher, on April 13, 1880. Their children were: Theodore, Leon, Maria, John, Mary, Louis, Amelia, Olivia, Constantine, and Stella Agnes. They left this area in 1895 and moved to Hanover, PA as their youngest daughter was born there in 1902.

Sometime after that, they moved to Kit Carson, CO and in 1914 to White Church, Howe County, MO, where they farmed. They are buried in St. Joseph Cemetery in White Church, MO near West Plains. Amalia "Emma" (b. Sept. 3, 1856) married Nicholas Heisserer, the son of Anthony and Katharina (Hahn) Heisserer, on Nov. 21, 1876. Shortly after their marriage, they moved to Commerce and went into the grocery business. Nick heard about Pierce City, which had been established only a few years previously. The railroad had now reached the city. It was a natural crossroad for the wagon trains going west where people stopped to get supplies, so they packed up and moved to Pierce City with three small children, Bertha, Alexander, Dorothea, and a fourth child, Theodore who died in infancy. Opening a grocery store there and the business prospered. After a time the railroad moved their division point from Pierce City to Monett and this created a hardship on the townspeople. Many of them worked for the railroad and moved to Monett. Their other children: Leo Ben, Alphonso, Otto Alonzo, Edmund and Raymond were born at Pierce City. In 1913, Nick and Emma moved to Minneapolis, MN. There they lived in semi-retirement until Nick died in 1928. He is buried in St. Francis Cemetery in Minneapolis. They celebrated their 50th Wedding Anniversary with a trip back to Missouri to visit the relatives. Rosalina (b. Sept. 25, 1858; d. Sept. 30, 1889) married Frank Bles on Jan. 8, 1881. Five children were born to them: Regina, Henry Joseph and Emma Louise died young; Bertha; and Alvina. Frank (b. Dec. 4, 1861) died in infancy.

Leo (b. Dec. 8, 1861; d. May 8, 1929) married Caroline Walter on Aug. 25, 1885. They were parents of six children: Louisa "Lucy", John Joseph died at age 5, Gregory Frank, Clyde Anton, Dorothea, and Rowena died as an infant.

Constantine died Nov. 17, 1872 and is buried in St. Lawrence Cemetery at New Hamburg, MO. *Submitted by Louise Maria Blankenship*

HAIRSTON – Vic was born May 2, 1954 in St. Louis, MO to Thomas Burton and Alice O'Dean "Dean" (Mason) Hairston. The Hairston's and the Mason's, being originally from Arkansas, moved to the Kewanee, MO area as teens to work in the fields. They moved to St. Louis in 1953 where Tom owned and operated

Caryl Maria (Joyce) and Thomas Victor Hairston, 25th Wedding Anniversary

service stations until 1972. In 1972 the family of four, Mr. and Mrs. Hairston, Vic, his brother Mark (b. July 9, 1959), and sister Sue (b. Dec. 13, 1955) moved to the Matthews area, living at the corner previously known as Horseshoe, owned by Tom's parents, Everette and step-mother Dorothy (Featherston) Hairston. The Hairston lineage can be traced back to Peter "the immigrant" Hairston, who came to America in 1729 from Scotland.

Vic and his siblings attended public schools and he graduated from Matthews High School in 1972. After graduation he enlisted in the US Marine Corps, serving four years as an aviation electrician with the Harrier program.

On Aug. 27, 1976 he married Caryl Maria Joyce at the First United Methodist Church in Sikeston. They made their home at Cherry Point, NC until this discharge in February of 1977, and then returned to Sikeston.

Vic attended Southeast Missouri State University, then transferred to Control Data Institute technical school in St. Louis and studied computer technology. Then they returned to Sikeston where he went to work for Superior Office Products, owned by Henry Dirnberger of Benton until the business sold in 1995. At that time Vic started his own business, AA Copier Service and Sales, which he and Caryl operated from their home just outside of Sikeston.

Caryl Maria was born July 24, 1955 to Margaret and Carl Joyce in Sikeston. She attended Sikeston schools graduating in 1973. After graduation she attended Southeast Missouri State Uni-

versity in Cape Girardeau for five semesters. She worked at the Malone Theater during school and then at MoDelta Medical Center in the x-ray department until their marriage. After the couple returned to Sikeston, she worked at various retail jobs until 1984 when she went to work at Buckner Ragsdale. After it closed she worked at Garden Lane Nursery for her husband.

She was a member of the Girl Scout; Red Pepper, Job's Daughters, American Business Women's Association, and is presently a member of the Scott County Historical Society, holding the position of Secretary. She does genealogy as a hobby and the Joyce lineage is traced back to Edward Joyce of Catahoula Parish, LA. Her fourth grandfather came to Scott County from Cape Girardeau County n the early 1800s.

Vic and Caryl are the parents of two sons: Joshua Skye (b. Aug. 12, 1979 in Sikeston) and Mitchell Wade (b. July 18, 1985 in Sikeston). Josh is a 2001 graduate of Lambuth University in Jackson, TX where he played soccer and was a member of the Kappa Sigma fraternity holding various offices. Mitch is presently a sophomore in Sikeston High School, plays soccer and races dirt bikes as hobbies.

The Hairstons are members of the First United Methodist Church in Sikeston.

HALL – Eugene Brenkenridge "Gene", son of William E. and Mary Farmer Hall was born July 26, 1882 near Tebbetts, MO and Delilh Irene "Lila" Link was born Oct. 19, 1887 near Holts Summit, MO. They were married April 4, 1909.

They had one daughter, Edith Mae, born Sept. 3, 1912 at Jefferson City, MO. She married Roy William Richards on Jan. 7, 1933. Gene farmed and Lila taught school in a one-room schoolhouse. Gene also owned a grocery store at Jefferson City.

They moved to Kansas City, MO where Gene worked in a laundry and Lila worked in a shoe store, both within walking distance of their home. Edith Mae went to kindergarten there. In 1920 they moved and bought a farm near Cote Hill, at the edge of the Missouri River.

They moved back to the Jefferson City area where he farmed and raised cattle and hogs. Later they rented more land to farm. They moved to southeast Missouri in 1936, first to a farm in Diehlstadt, MO, then to the Hubbard farm on Champion Lane, south of Sikeston, MO.

They went to the Methodist Church in Sikeston. They retired from farming in 1959. Their grandson, Larry Richards, took over the farm. They bought a house in Sikeston and lived there until Gene's death on July 4, 1966.

Lila sold the house in 1975 and moved to her daughter, Edith Mae's, who lived on her farm between Matthews and East Prairie, MO until her death on Sept. 6, 1984.

Gene and Lila Hall with three grandchildren: R.L. Richard, Lary, and Barb, 1944.

Gene had six brothers and three sisters. One of the brothers, Buck Hall, moved to Scott County also.

Lila had three brothers and one sister. Two of her brothers moved to Scott County: Cecil Link and Herschel Link. Another brother, Church Link, lived here for a short time.

Cecil and Minnie Link owned and operated El Capri Motel several years. *Submitted by Barbara Box, August 2001*

HALTER – Alfred Adam "Andy" Halter was born Aug. 19, 1914 in Benton, MO. He was the son of Andrew Edward and Lena Margaret (Essner) Halter, and grandson of Andrew E. and Louise (Eck) Halter and Adam and Elizabeth (Dirnberger) Essner of Benton. On Sept. 2, 1947, he married Mary Helen Wagner, daughter of Roy Henry and Blanche Delia (Jones)

Alfred Halter and Sylvester Felter's graduation from St. Dionysus Grade School in Benton, MO., June 9, 1929.

Wagner of Sikeston, and granddaughter of Alfred Neal and Hannah Elizabeth (Long Haskett) Wagner and Telimicus and Mary Emma (Cavaness) Jones of Lutesville, MO.

Alfred Halter graduated from St. Dionysus Catholic School in 1929 and from Benton High School in 1933. He was active in sports and enjoyed hunting. During WWII, he served with the US Army from 1941 to 1945 in Hawaii, Iwo Jima and the Philippines. He returned to Benton after his military service, and was a founding officer in Benton's' American Legion Post 369 in 1945.

In 1947 Alfred was recommended to the Governor by the Scott County Democratic Party to fill the vacancy of Scott County Assessor, which he assumed until 1973. Alfred was the first president of the Benton Chamber of Commerce in 1957, a charter member of the Elks Club in Chaffee, and a member of St. Denis Catholic Church. Alfred passed away Sept. 26, 1978.

His wife, Mary Helen, was a 1940 graduate of Sikeston High School and attended Southeast Missouri State University. Mary Helen had been active in Girl Scouts, serving as Brownie Leader and Neighborhood Chairman. She served the town of Benton as the City Collector for 25 years, and the District Clerk at the Scott County Soil and Water Conservation District office from 1976 to 1999.

Alfred and Mary Helen have three daughters, all born and raised in Benton. Mary Ann is married to Don Johnson, son of Andy and Betty Johnson of St. Louis, MO. They reside in Oakville, MO. They have two children: Rebecca Elizabeth, a Public Relations Specialists who is engaged to Brian Krueger of

Alfred "Andy" and Mary Helen (Wagner) Halter, September 2, 1947.

Harrisonburg, VA; and son, Andre Loren of Oakville, MO, an EMT student and future firefighter. Mary Ann is a manager for Great West Life Insurance. Don is an account representative at Eastern Metals Supply.

Elizabeth Jane is married to Daniel Scherer, son of Cletus and Celeste Scherer of Benton. They live in Fairview, TN with their three children: Jesse Erin, Sarah Elizabeth, and Aaron Daniel. Elizabeth is the early childhood special education teacher at Fairview Elementary School. Daniel is a department manager at A-1 Appliance Company.

Emma Lou is married to Eddie Brewer, son of James and Elizabeth Brewer of Benton. They live in Frankfort, KY with their two daughters, Jamie Lynn and Katie Ann. Emma is an office manager for the law firm of McBrayer, McGinnis, Leslie and Kirkland. Eddie is a general manager at Flying J Travel Center. *Submitted by Emma Brewer*

HALTER – John Anthony Halter was born June 17, 1901 at Oran, Mo., to the late Leo and Theresia Halter. On November 19, 1924, he married Bertha Lauck at St. Henry the Emperor Church in St. Louis.

John A. Halter of Route #1 in Chaffee, Mo. then again with his daughters (photo at right), counterclockwise: Cecilia, Lorena, Anna Mae, Elizabeth, and Dorothy. Taken in 1945, the home was later razed for the current Elk's Park and Lake. The lake was named Lauck Lake for the A.V. and Frances Lauck family, who had resided there for years.

He was a member of St. Ambrose Catholic Church.

His wife Bertha preceded him in death on July 23, 1940. John A. died at age 72 in the Chaffee General Hospital on August 27, 1973. He had been admitted 12 days prior after falling in his home. Death, however, was due to an apparent heart condition.

He was survived by three sons: John V. Halter, Albert L. Halter, and William L. Halter; five daughters: Cecilia Walton, Dorothy Dees, Lorena Halter, Elizabeth Stubbs, and Anna Mae Meyer; two brothers: Joseph Halter and Theon Halter; two sisters: Christine Brockmeyer and Katie Miller; 24 grandchildren, three step-grandchildren, and five great grandchildren. *Submitted by Dorothy Ds*

HARMON – Thomas Ralph Harmon, Jr. was born June 12, 1942 in Lamar, Johnson County, Arkansas, son of Thomas "Ralph" and Sally Arebell Cater Harmon. He married Margaret Louise Cline, daughter of Curtis and Marie Price Cline, on October 31, 1959 in Ft. Leonard Wood, Missouri. She was born July 4, 1944 in Cape Girardeau, Missouri. They have a daughter, Tina Loise Harmon, born April 8, 1960 in Sikeston. She married Robert Earl Harvard Jr., son of Robert and Mary McKey Havard, on March 26, 1983 in Baton Rouge, Louisiana. They have one son, Rob-

Tom and Margaret Harmon, March 26, 1983

ert Earl "Trey" Havard III, born December 23, 1984.

Tom moved with his parents to Scott County in 1946 with a group of related familie of Harmon, Holman and Chronisters, all from Johnson County, Arkansas. The families settled in various counties of southeast Missouri.

Tom enlisted into the regular Army on September 11, 1959. He served in La Chapelle St. Memi, France, Fort Ord, Calif. And he attended Personnel Management Specialist School at U. S. Army Adjutant General School, Fort Benjamin Harrison, Indiana in 1965. He was then assigned to the Panama Canal Zone before transferring to 180th Transportation Battalion Headquarters, Fort Hood, Texas in February 1967. He was honorably discharged in 1968. Tom was employed with Brooks Erection and Construction Company in St. Louis after retuning to civilian life and was Warehouse Foreman through 1976. In January 1977, he was promoted to Purchasing and Office Manager of the new Southern Division of Brooks Erection and Construction in Baton Rouge, Louisiana. He also did remodeling of homes on week-ends.

Margaret graduated from Sikeston High School in 1963 and then attended Draught's Junior College in Memphis, Tennessee. She also attended Louisiana State University in Baton Rouge between 1978 and 1990. Margaret was employed with Ethyl Corporation April 1977 through November 1993 as Supervisor of Private Trucking Operations and then was Travel and Relocation Coordinator. Margaret was featured as "Monday Woman" on August 19, 1985 in the *Baton Rouge Advocate* for her respected work as a meeting planner, videographer and genealogist.

Due to corporate downsizing, Tom and Margaret relocated to Little Rock, Arkansas in December 1993 for brief employment. In 1995 they moved to Cape Girardeau to assist with their aging parents needs. Tom opened a successful home inspection business – Homebuyers Inspection, Inc. Margaret began to write historical and cemetery articles and in September 1997 she began working for Southeast Missouri State University as a Senior Secretary. The position allowed her to write in the evening and on weekends, keep books for Homebuyers Inspection, and look after their parents in Sikeston. Tom retired in December 2000 for health reasons. In the fall of 2002 Margaret started to college full time in Historic Preservation. *Submitted by Margaret line Haon*

HARMON – Vyrn G. Harmon lived all of his life in Scott County, with the exception of the five years of World War II. This account begins with that era. Vyron had been a member of the 140th Infantry Band since high school days; his instrument was the trumpet. Because of problems overseas, the National Guard was mobilized in 1940. He was sent to Camp Robinson at Little Rock, AR., on Dec. 23, 1940 for one year of training with the 35th division. Here they engaged in intensive war maneuvers. During this time a six-week march, under cover of darkness, was made from Little Rock to Louisiana. Their division was divided into the Red and the Blue. They marched and fought mock battles en-route. Because America was not prepared for war, wooden guns were used in battle; also, with no summer uniforms available, they were forced to wear woolens in the heat of the Southland.

The shocking event of Dec. 7, 1941 sent the 35th division to San Diego, CA. immediately instead of returning home as was promised after one year of training. His long-time sweetheart, Lillian Boehme, followed, and they were married July 10, 1942. For a few months life was great - playing in the band at street parades and at ship

departure times. His Army Band days ended when a Major called Vyron out of band formation inquiring about his knowledge in electronics. After a short conversation, the Major asked, "What the hell are you doing in a band?" Vyron was ordered to report immediately to 115th radio Intelligence at the Presidio in San

Vyron G. and Lillian Harmon's wedding, July 10, 1942

Francisco. Actually this was a fortunate break for Vyron as he remained on the West Coast for the duration of the War building, improving, and servicing equipment for copying Japanese radio messages. After approximately two years he was transferred to Ft. Lewis, WN, to build another intercept station. This was because Allied forces were moving north and another intercept station was needed so Japanese messages could be copied from shorter range. Vyron remained at this location until peace was declared.

His lifetime desire was fulfilled when he opened a furniture and appliance company in Illmo, MO. on September 26, 1946. He accomplished the seemingly impossible with only $1,500.00 that he had saved by working after army hours for local radio shops in both San Francisco and Olympia, WN. Since able-bodied men had all been called into active duty, radio repair personnel was not available. This gave Vyron the opportunity to repair many radios in off duty hours. With much ingenuity and hard work he turned this $1,500.00 into a successful business. A salesman for a furniture outlet company in St. Louis helped a great deal. He had so much faith in Vyron that he filled his new store with furniture and scarce merchandise that was available post-war. His comment was, "I know you will pay when you get the money." After 30 plus years he turned his business over to his daughter.

Vyron's retirement years were spent traveling this continent in a motor home. During these 20 years he visited and photographed 50 governors, obtaining their autographs, along with security patches from capitol police. Likewise, travel through Canada provided visits and photos of most Premiers.

yron Harmon was born in Chaffee, MO., on July 27, 1918. His wife, Lillian, was born in Jackson, MO., on April 10, 1920. His first daughter, Mrs. William Joiner (Martha), was born in San Francisco, CA., on March 18, 1943. His other daughter, Mrs. James Suttle (LaDonna) was born in Cape Girardeau, MO., on October 2, 1949. *Submitted by Lilian Harmon*

HARRIS – Dr. Clarence D. Harris, affectionately known as "Little Doc," was born in Morley, MO on Jan. 6, 1875 and died in Morley on July 4, 1933. He married Mary Howle, who was born June 9, 1876 in Wickliffe, KY and died Aug. 8, 1960 in Rolla, MO. The couple was married March 1, 1896 in Ellis Grove, IL by the bride's father, Rev. James Howle, Southern Baptist Preacher.

Some Harris genealogy is included in *The Browns of Obion County, Tennessee*; a book complied by a cousin, Rev. Ralph Dodson. Ancestry is traced back to John Chappell, born in 1752 in Amelia County, VA, and died in 1812 in Halifax County, VA. He married Ann D. de Graffenried April 27, 1789. Birth and death dates are unlisted.

According to family history, Clarence and Mary began courting in their early teens. Clarence's parents objected because the Howles were not financially affluent. When Clarence wanted to attend medical school, his father told him that he would finance the education if he would give up his courtship of Mary. Otherwise, Clarence could foot the bill. Clarence and Mary postponed marriage plans until he graduated from medical school.

The day he left Morley on the train, he told his parents goodbye, then walked through the coach to the back of the train where Mary waited. After their farewells, she hurried away before the train moved on. On Clarence's return from medical school, he went into his father's office and said, "Papa, I am going to get married." His father asked, "Who to?" He replied, "Mary Howle." The father looked up at his son and said, "If you are determined to have that damn little girl, go ahead."

Dr. Clarence D. Harris and Mary Howle Harris wedding picture

Their offspring were: Harold, (b. June 12, 1897; death date unlisted) later became a doctor, married Ollie Broach and had three children: Mary, Nancy and Ann. He lost both legs resulting from WWII injuries but continued practicing medicine in Troy, MO as one of only three doctors ministering to 15,000 patients in Lincoln County.

Ruth (b. March 5, 1899; d. April 30, 1988) married Paul Finney, pharmacist, on Aug. 9, 1920. Their children were: Paul Jr. (b. June 7, 1921; d. April 18, 1929), John Marshall III "Jack" (b. July 7, 1924; d. Dec. 26, 1988) Mary Sue (b. July 22, 1929). Ruth was well known for her excellent piano playing, school teaching, and social service work. When teaching school in Morley, if students became restless or bored, she would say, "Let's close the books and sing awhile." With that she would go to the piano and start entertaining. Former students still recall their favorite "Miss Ruth" stores.

Jim Van, pharmacist, (b. Dec. 25, 1901; d. Jan. 1, 1951) married Georgia Brock and had one daughter, Kathleen who is deceased.

Mayme (b. March 5, 1905; death date unlisted) married Roy Kilmer and had two sons, Clarence Aaron, deceased and Van, who lives in Sikeston.

Clarence Jr., pharmacist, (b. May 25, 1915, deceased) married Lila Fisher. Their offspring were William King and Clara Lou.

The Harris home still stands in Morley; built 1905.

HEISSERER – John Heisserer was born Dec. 21, 1839 in Schirrhein, Alsace, France, the son of Anthony and Katharina (Hahn) Heisserer. The family came to America on the ship *John Cadmus* from Le Harve, France, landing at New Orleans, LA on Oct. 20, 1847, with seven children. John was 7 years old and the youngest one was only 9 months old. He married Rosina Glaus (1845-1871), the daughter of Johann and Louise (Martin) Glaus, on Nov. 23, 1865 at St. Lawrence Catholic Church in New Hamburg.

John served in the Union Army during the Civil War as a private of Company "C" 2nd Regiment

Missouri Volunteers. He was enrolled on July 28, 1861 at Cape Girardeau for three years and commanded by Captain Charles Fueller. He was promoted to 8th Corporal on April 9, 1863 Regiment Orders. He fought in the Battle of Chickamauga, one of the most desperate engagements. The battlefield is now a National Park. He was honorably discharged Sept. 27, 1864 in St. Louis, MO. In 1926, the *Scott County Newspaper* stated that after the Civil War he established the first mail service between Cape Girardeau and New Madrid, carrying the mail on horseback, the trip taking him a full day.

He was a farmer in Kelso Community. He and other parishioners donated much time and many hours in order to get St. Augustine Church built in 1878. He donated the statue of St. John to the church. John and Rosina were parents of three children: Adam (1866-1935) married

John Heisserer in Civil War uniform

Catharina Ellinger; Louisa Margaret (1868-1931) married Joseph Blattel, the son of George and Anamariah (Anna Maria Sabel) Blattel; Bernard married Helen Scherer. On Feb. 23, 1873 John married Elizabeth Himmelsbach, the daughter of Sebastian and Rosina (Hoffman) Himmelsbach at New Hamburg, MO. Eight of their nine children grew to adulthood. Ulrick Charles and Appolonia Josephina died in infancy. Rosina Katharina (1874-1944) married Clemens Westrich. Celestine (1876-1937) married Bernard Baudendistel. Solomon John (1880-1970) married Sophia Blattel, daughter of Jacob M. and Philomena (Glastetter) Blattel; Caroline Elizabeth (1882-1911 died from typhoid fever). Otto Charles (1884-1951) married Emma Louise Scherer. Aloys (1886-1966) married Mary M. Scherer, sister to Emma Louise both were daughters of Theophil and Mary M. (Glastetter) Scherer. August (1890-1969) married Clara Bucher, daughter of Lawrence and Vernocia (Scherer) Bucher on Oct. 12, 1915 at St. Lawrence Catholic Church in New Hamburg. They were the parents of six children: Joseph P. (1916, still living) married Coletta Glastetter, daughter of Joseph and Elizabeth (Enderle) Glastetter and sister to Paul; Herman Andrew and Zita Anna both died in infancy; Linus A. (1919, still living) married Frances Sietman; Harold Michael (1921-1995) remained single; Lawrence (1923, still living) married Mary Wilma Beard; Clara died in 1925. August's second marriage was to Rosalia Glastetter (1895-1949), sister to Paul and Coletta, on Jan. 24, 1927 at St. Augustine Catholic Church in Kelso. Their children were: Coletta Paulina and Helen Coletta both died in infancy; four grew to adulthood, Mary Elizabeth (1929) married LeRoy Dannenmueller. Their children are: Donald, Mary Margaret, Richard, Cletus, Robert, Dale, and Lynn Rose.

Rita (1930) married Ervin Eichhorn, Army Veteran of the Korean War. They are the parents of five children: Rose Ann, Laura Jean, Randall, Lester and Jerome.

Bernard A. (1932) Navy Veteran of the Korean War married Alta James, and they were the parents of five children: John, Deborah, Paula, and Missy; Rex Wayne was stillborn.

Cletus (1936) married Ernestine Klingler. They have two children: Victoria and Michael.

John Heisserer, the old pioneer farmer died Jan. 9, 1928. He was blind the last two years of his life and is buried in St. Augustine Cemetery at Kelso.

Surname found several ways: Heisserer, Heiser, Hyser, Hauser. *Submitted by Maria Elizabeth Parker*

HEISSERER – Ralph and Mary Louise were married May 8, 1948 at Saint Augustine Church in Kelso, MO and are farmers north of Oran, MO.

Ralph was born June 1, 1925 at Oran and served in the US Army in Korea during WWII. His parents were Raymond George and Alma Catherine Dirnberger Heisserer. Raymond was the son of George Heisserer and Louise Legrand Heisserer (Dohogne). Alma was the daughter of Michael Dirnberger and Mary Bucher. The Heisserer's are descendants of Anthony Heisserer and Katherine Hahn who came to America Aug. 15, 1847 and settled in Scott County, MO. Ralph has four sisters: Margarita Louise Heisserer of Saint Peters, MO; Joan Eleanor Busche of Poplar Bluff, MO; Helen Antonette Walker of Middleburg, VA; and Margaret Ann O'Neill of Maplewood, NJ.

Mary Louise was born May 12, 1927 in Chaffee, MO. She later moved to Kelso, MO with her parents, Paul Joseph and Coletta Philipmena Bles Enderle. Paul worked for Frisco Railroad Company in Chaffee, MO. Paul Joseph was the son of John B. and Louise Logel Enderle. Coletta was the daughter of John and Amelia Quellmalz Bles. The Enderles are descendants of Peter Enderle and Elizabeth Schneider, who came to America between 1835 and 1838. They settled in Stark County, OH, later coming to Scott County, MO. Mary Louise had two sisters, Georgianna Ressel of Kelso, MO and Cecilia Amelia Arnold of Jonesboro, IL, and one brother Paul John Enderle of Scott City, MO. Paul John passed away Aug. 9, 1995.

The Ralph S. and Mary L. Heisserer Family, August 5, 1978. Melvin Ray, Dolores Ann, Ralph Simon, Mary Louise, and Karl Michael Heisserer.

Ralph and Mary Louise grew Certified Seed for the University of Missouri for over 50 years. Ralph lived his entire life on the farm his father, grandfather, and great-grandfather farmed north of Oran. He graduated from Oran High School and attended Southeast Missouri State University at Cape Girardeau, MO. Mary Louise attended Saint Mary's High School at Cape Girareau, MO.

Ralph and Mary Louise have three children: Karl, Melvin and Dolores.

Karl Michael Heisserer (Feb. 21, 1952) married Barbara D. Curtis. He is the owner of HBA Associates of Indianapolis, IN. They have six sons: Robert Konrad (b. Aug. 12, 1976) who married Sandra Hartman on June 30, 2001; Curtis Lee (b. March 30, 1978); Joseph Paul "JP" (b. May 17, 1979); Eric Allan (b. July 1, 1983); Michael Ryan (b. July 15, 1987); and James Karl (b. March 5, 1991).

Melvin Ray Heisserer (b. April 1, 1954) married Shirley Kaye Hanstein. He is a Quality Control Engineer for Dynegy of Decatur, IL. They have three sons: Christopher Aaron (b. Feb. 25, 1984); Brian Conrad (b. April 9, 1986) and Lucas Simon (b. May 2, 1988).

Dolores Ann Heisserer married Robert Steven Andersen. Dolores is pursuing a Bachelor of Science degree at Southeast Missouri State University of Cape Girardeau, MO. They have two children: Louise Marie Anderson (b. March 14, 1990) and Shane Robert-Thomas Andersen (b. April 6, 1992). *Submitted by Ralph and Mary Louise Heisserer*

HELD – It was in the small farming community of Besebruch that "Fritz" Held was born on Thursday, Oct. 8, 1829. Besebruch was one of several farming communities that made up the village of Mennighuffen, which is now located in the northeastern part of the German state of Nordrhein-Westfalen, but which was then part of Prussia. The people of this area spoke the Ravensberger dialect of Low Germany. He was baptized in the local Lutheran Parish as Carl Friedrich Phillipp Held, and was the only child of Heinrich Philipp Held and Anne Marie Wilhelmine Louise Kottkamp. Heinrich Philipp died at the young age of 27, when Fritz was only 2 months old. No subsequent records for Anne Marie have yet been located.

Carl Friedrich Philipp "Fritz" and Katharina Elizabeth (Eifert) Held, ca. 1890.

Family tradition indicates that his paternal grandfather, Carl Wilhelm Held, reared "Fritz." Carl Wilhelm was actually the biological son of Johann Albert Voegeding or Voegding and Anne Marie Louise Kellermeier, but was reared by and assumed the name of his stepfather, Johann Hermann Held. Interestingly the Held line appears to have originated with an ancestor in the late 1600s who changed his name from Reinking to Held. At that time the family had come from the village of Gohfeld to Mennighuffen. From the German, Held translates to "hero."

In October 1849, 20 year old Fritz was required to serve three years in the Prussian army, and afterwards was required to be a reservist for life. This was at the tail end of the 1848-1849 Revolutions which had swept through Europe. Afterwards, times were hard; he went to the Ruhr valley where he sought work in the mines, and later to Holland, where he worked as a thrasher. He made application to emigrate while living in the town of Dunne. His official discharge document (Number 1734, C.I.) as a Prussian citizen was granted on Tuesday, July 22, 1856. He traveled to the port city of Bremen, where he boarded the steamship Hermann, and was listed as "Passenger 193, C.F.HELD." He was 27 years old at the time.

The Hermann arrived on Friday, Oct. 24, 1856 in New Orleans, where Fritz boarded a steamship and traveled up the Mississippi to St. Louis. There, he may have been assisted by the Lutheran Church-Missouri Synod with food, clothing and accommodations, and possibly went to Carlyle, Clinton County, IL where other emigrants from his home area had settled. He later went to Scott County, MO and was first listed in the Eisleben Lutheran Church records in 1859 as attending services and receiving communion. He served in the Scott County Home Guard during the Civil War, during which, at the age of 32, he was married to 19 year old Katharina Elisabetha Eifert. Pastor Erhardt Riedel conducted the ceremony, which was witnessed by Elisabeth's parents, on Saturday, April 12, 1862 in the parsonage of the Cape Girardeau Lutheran Church. Elisabeth was born on Tuesday, Nov. 14, 1843 in the village of Engelrod-Rebgeshain, near Ulrichstein, in the Germany state of Hessen-Darmstadt. She was the third of 10 or 11 children born to Johann Heinrich Eifert and Anna Maria Roth, who immigrated to Scott County around 1852. It's possible that Fritz served in the Union Army during the entire Civil War, as we have limited records for him during this period.

Wedding picture of David F. and Emilie (Sander) Held, August 16, 1903.

Before the war started, in 1860, he bought an 80-acre farm south of Illmo from the Sneiman and Sickman families. He also owned land east of Illmo (near Miller's Peach Orchard). After their marriage though, Fritz and Elisabeth lived near Kelso, and didn't move to their farm until around 1880. The farm was later given to their sons David and Fritz, with the stipulation that the parents would be taken care of in their old age. After 141 years, the farm is still in the family and owned by their granddaughter, Marie (Held) Burger and family. It was on Monday, Sept. 9, 1872 that Fritz went to Commerce and made a formal declaration to become an American Citizen. Two years later, on Tuesday, Oct. 20, 1874, Fritz was officially a proud American! The following children were born to Fritz and Elisabeth: Katharina Elisabeth, Oct. 22, 1866, who married Fritz Weisenstein; Heinrich Theodor, May 6, 1869, who married Christina Sander; Maria Elisa, Feb. 26, 1871, who married August Schaefer; David Friedrich, March 5, 1873, who married Emilie Sander (great-grandparents of the author of this biography); Johanna Elisa, March 19, 1875, who married John Martin Sander (brother to Christina listed above); Sophie Marie, April 12, 1877, who died at 2 months; Casper Georg, May 23, 1878, who died at 2 months; Johann Heinrich, about May 29, 18u9 and died July 19, 1879; Fritz Jr., Aug. 28, 1880, who never married; Emma Marie, Jan. 4, 1883, who died at 18 months. After nearly 70 years of life, Elisabeth Held died on Thursday, Dec. 5, 1912 and was buried in the Eisleben Cemetery. Carl Friedrich Philipp Held lived to be one month shy of 89 years old, and went to his Creator on Tuesday, Sept. 3, 1918. He is also buried in the Eisleben Lutheran Cemetery in Illmo, MO. *Submitted by John L. Maurath*

HELD – Carl was known to the family as Friedrich and was born on Oct. 8, 1829 (according to church records) in Ostcheid, Westfalen, Prussia (Germany). As a young man he worked in the coal mines near his home. He married Katharina Elizabetha Eifert on April 12, 1862 at a Lutheran Parsonage in Cape Girardeau. She was born Nov. 14, 1843 in Rebgeshain, Hessen-Darmstadt-Germany.

They lived on a farm east of Illmo (Scott City) that adjoins the Frank Lindsey farm. Carl and Katharina had six children. Their names are Henry, David, Katie, Mary, Elizabeth and Fritz.

Friedreich died Sept. 3, 1918 at Illmo (Scott City). Elizabeth died Dec. 5, 1912 at Illmo (Scott City). They are both buried in the Eisleben Lutheran Church Cemetery at Illmo.

Their son David, my grandfather, was born March 5, 1873 on a farm east of Illmo (Scott City). He married Auguste Emilie (Amelia) Sander. She was born July 23, 1883 in Fornfelt (Scott City). They lived on a farm about two miles south of his parents' house where Marie (Held) Burger lives today. To this union, the following children were born: their first child was a son who died at birth; next was Herman; then Alvin "Tiny;" along with Irma Uelsmann-Bryant; Edna Hagan; Irene "Renie" Sanders; Clarence "Butch;" Marie Held-Burger; and Vera Mae Smith-Lohmann.

David's occupation was farming, as was his father's before him. He also raised strawberries. He would load them onto the Gray's Point Ferry just east of Illmo (Scott City) and sell them in Thebes, IL.

David died on Dec. 29, 1948 in Illmo. Amelia died Feb. 22, 1959 in Cape Girardeau. They are buried at Eisleben Lutheran Church Cemetery in Illmo.

Their daughter, Marie, was born May 6, 1922 on the farm southeast of Illmo, where she still lives today. She married Herbert D. Burger on June 1, 1940 in Cape Girardeau. She enjoys working in her flower beds and vegetable garden. The pleasure and enjoyment in raising flowers can be seen throughout her family and ancestors.

Herbert died on June 24, 1992 in Cape Girardeau and is buried at St. Augustine Cemetery in Kelso. Marie (Held) Burger is still living at her home in Scott city.

There were two children born to this union. Their names are Kenneth "Kenny" and Brenda. Kenny married Linda Ham on Sept. 20, 1969 at the Illmo Baptist Church. They have three children. They are Jarrett, Andrea and Aaron. Jarrett married Barbara Lee on June 25, 1990 at the Baptist Church in Benton. They have four children. Their names are as follows: Heather; Whitney; Madison and Hunter.

Brenda married James R. LeGrand on Nov. 6, 1971 at Eisleben Lutheran Church in Scott City. They have two children. Their names are Jeannette and Landon. *Information gathered by Bill Held and Marie (Held) Burger and submitted by Brenda (Burger) LeGrand*

HESS – Charles Peter Hess, son of Joseph M. and Zita O. Schaefer Hess, was born Jan. 6, 1944, in Scott County, MO, second son and third child in a family of seven children. He was a graduate of St. Augustine Catholic Grade School in Kelso and of Illmo-Scott City High School in 1962. After graduation, he worked for Kelso Milling Company at Kelso and Scott City for nearly 38 years. He joined the National Guard in 1963 and served for six years. In 2000, Charles went to work for Russ Mothershead at First Missouri Terminals at the Southeast Missouri State University Port. There he unloads grain trucks, loads fertilizer trucks and oversees the operation on the shore for the terminal.

On Jan. 9, 1965, Charles and Mary Margaret Dirnberger were married at St. Lawrence Church in New Hamburg. Four children were born to this marriage: Kevin Charles Hess (b. May 6, 1966), Timothy Scott Hess (b. May 2, 1967), Steven Ray Hess (b. June 23, 1968) and Pamela Sue Hess (b. Dec. 4, 1970).

Mary was born March 7, 1946, the daughter of Linus P. and Regina M. Compas Dirnberger.

She was a graduate of St. Lawrence Catholic School in New Hamburg and of Thomas W. Kelly High School, where she was valedictorian of her class. While still in high school, Mary worked part time for Moore-Harris Abstract Company in Benton, MO. She left the company in 1966 and worked a short time with DLH Services in Cape Girardeau and wrote for the *Scott County Democrat* in Benton and the *Jimplicute* in Illmo while raising her family. In 1975, Scott County Abstract Company and Moore-Harris Abstract Company were merged and in 1976, Mary returned to title work with Scott County Abstract Company, now Southeast Missouri Title Company where she is vice-president.

Hess Spring Place, home of Charles and Mary Hess family, West of Kelso, MO, 1968-76.

After living in Scott County for three and a half years, they moved to Hess Spring Place, on June 23, 1968, the day their third son, Steven, was born. This two and a half acre tract was formerly known as the John A. Glueck home place, one-half mile west of Kelso, MO. John was a great-uncle to Mary Hess, Mrs. Johanna Glueck being the sister of Regina Scherer Compas, her maternal grandmother.

The spring had provided water to residents and passersby since at least 1904. Years ago, many children would stop on their way home from school to get a drink from the ever-flowing spring. The spring still provides the only source of water through a system whereby the water is piped into the home.

The house was two-story brick with sandstone foundation. The west and north walls were three bricks deep but the south and east walls were only two bricks deep. Originally, the home contained two roms downstairs and two upstairs, with the kitchen, porches, summer kitchen, and cellar added later.

The property also held a chicken house, barn, and springhouse, which covered the cream trough. Overflow from the spring (through the cream trough) provides water for the livestock. The family raised baby chickens for laying hens and sold the eggs. The children enjoyed raising the baby calves, which they bottle-fed. Other animals included pigs and even rabbits. The children had a dog named Peppy and a number of cats and kittens.

Fruit trees provided cherries, apples and pears for pies and jellies. The garden provided strawberries, blackberries, potatoes, lettuce, radishes, tomatoes, onions, peppers, corn and sweet potatoes. Pecans were gathered, cracked and shelled by all family members.

In the spring of 1976, the barn was torn down to make room for the new house built that same year. After moving into the new house, the old house was removed and a barn built in its place. Later, the old springhouse was replaced and the chicken house received the same fate.

While living in the old house, the smell of smoke had the family searching for its source with never discovering any. When the stairway in the house was demolished, a number of burnt boards were uncovered. Boards replaced in the stairwell had hidden the damaged area from an old fire.

In 1994, a 24 x 30 foot room was added to the house to accommodate a growing family. This room has seen many a celebration, including family reunions, seating as many as 50 guests. This room was designed by Steve Hess, son of Charles and Mary, and built with the help of many family members, neighbors, and friends.

Kevin Charles Hess married Carrie Robinson Dixon on June 28, 1997, at First Baptist Church in Jonesboro, IL. Children of the couple are Alexis Dixon and Lance Dixon, twins born April 3, 1991, and Olivia Brehanne Hess, born Dec. 15, 1997.

Timothy Scott Hess married Diane Marie Claspill on Oct. 26, 1991, at Immaculate Conception Catholic Church in Jackson, MO. Children of the couple are Mindy Gene Bryant, born Aug. 7, 1979, and Lawrence Eugene Bryant, born May 9, 1982. Children of Mindy are Jordan Abraham, born Aug. 8, 1996, Trinity Lee-Ann Bryant, born Sept. 26, 2000, and Ronnie Abraham III born Oct. 1, 2001.

Steven Ray Hess married Christy Kay Brougher on April 23, 1994 at Immaculate Conception Church in Jackson.

Pamela Sue Hess married Kelly Dewane Allen of Cape Girardeau, MO on March 10, 1990 at St. Joseph Catholic Church in Scott City, MO. They have one child, Sarene Christen Allen, born Sept. 29, 1997.

HESS – The story of the Nicholas Hess family in southeast Missouri centers around a farm located about two and a half miles west/ northwest of Kelso, MO.

Nicholas Hess was born Aug. 28, 1812 in Alsace Loraine, France, son of Nickolas and Catherine Jacobi Hess. On Aug. 31, 1852, he married Maria Theresa LeGrand, daughter of Henry J. and Mary Ann (Marianne) Colin LeGrand, in St. Mary's Church of Scott County, MO. Five children were born of that union: Joseph J. Hess (b. Aug. 4, 1853); Mary Catherine "Katie" Hess (b. Aug. 13, 1854); Francis "Frank" Hess (b. Oct. 18, 1857); John B. "Johannes" Hess (b. Jan. 18, 1860) and Nicholas Hess (b. March 14, 1862).

Nicholas Hess purchased an 80-acre farm from John and Mary G. Beardslee, his wife, on Sept. 3, 1872 for $1200.00, where he raised his family.

Nicholas Hess died Oct. 8, 1882 in Kelso, MO, survived by his children. Joseph Hess and his wife Victoria Leist Hess, Catherine Hess Mirgaux (Mirgeaux) and her husband Henry, John Hess and Nicholas Hess conveyed their interest to Frank Hess in 1883. Frank Hess and his wife, Louise Haas Hess, conveyed the property to Joseph Hess in November 1883 who then in 1887, conveyed it to John Hess.

The Gray's Point Terminal Railway purchased a right of way through the property in 1897, which connected the railroad towns of Ancell, Edna and Illmo with Rockview and Chaffee. For years, there was a double set of tracks; however, only one set of tracks remains.

Up until the 1920s, the northern portion of the farm was bottomland, a swampy area not conducive to tilled crops. The Little River Drainage District began construction of some ditches to drain the swamp in 1914. In 1921, work began on the Sals Creek diversion channel and levee and in 1922; the Little River Drainage District acquired a 100-foot wide strip through the Hess land, which divided the farm between the hills and the swamp. In the summer of 1952, the Little River Drainage re-dug Sals Creek. In August of that year, while

the drainage district was still working on enlarging the creek, a 10-inch deluge resulted in water cascading over the levee in several places and the bridge to float away. This was later replaced.

John and Matilda (Fischer)Hess and children, 1901. Left to right: Adeline, Matilda (Fischer) holding Rosalia, Anton, John B., and Louis.

John B. Hess died in a log cabin on the family farm on June 8, 1939. Five year old Elsie Corvick (now DeLong) along with her mother, Victoria Kern Corvick, daughter of Mary Catherine "Katie" Hess and John Adam Kern, and niece to John B. Hess, visited him while he lay on his deathbed. Elsie remembers his two-legged bed to be in a corner of the room and attached to the wall. He had the prettiest blue eyes with white beard and hair. He called her Rosalie, which was the name of one of his daughters. (Told to Charles Hess by Elsie Corvick DeLong.)

The heirs of John B. Hess were Adeline Blattel, Louis Hess, Matilda Peetz, Leona Hess, Elfreda Hess Blattel, Joseph Hess, Helen Hess Welter, and Edward Hess Bles. These heirs, along with their spouses, conveyed the farm to Joseph Hess and Zita Schaefer Hess, his wife, in 1940.

Joseph and Zita Hess had seven children: Lillian, James, Charles, Alice, Aleen, Betty, and Earl. Joseph Hess died Sept. 9, 1976 and Zita Hess continued to live on the property until 1980, when she purchased a home in Kelso and sold the farm in 1981 to her son, James Hess, who still retains ownership. The homestead property, with slight modifications, has remained in the Hess family for four generations and more than 125 years.

HESS – Kevin Charles Hess was born May 6, 1966, oldest son of Charles Peter and Mary Margaret Dirnberger Hess. At that time, the family lived at 1100 Perkins Street in Scott City, MO. When Kevin was 2, they moved to land known as the Glueck place, west of Highway 61, purchased from Monroe and Helen Hess Raines.

Kevin was a graduate of Kelso C-7 Elementary School at New Hamburg, Scott City High School, and Vo-tech school in Cape Girardeau, and was a member of St. Joseph Catholic Church in Scott City. When Kevin was 16, he became employed at Economy IGA at Scott City, owned by Clara Mae Dillow.

While a junior at Scott City High School, he pre-enlisted in the Navy. In July 1984, he left for naval training in Florida and upon graduation, was assigned to Meridian, MS for schooling. His permanent assignment was in Maine, with overseas deployments at Kadena Air Base in Okinawa; Roda, Spain; the Azores, Portugal; Iceland; Greenland; Puerto Rico; and Korea. He flew into Africa among other places and while overseas, visited France and Germany. He was an aviation storekeeper, ordering part for the aircraft P3. (Part control) He was Honorably Discharged July 16, 1990.

Kevin married Carrie Robinson Dixon, daughter of Kathy and Ellison "Fuzz" Knight, in

Jonesboro, IL on June 28, 1997. Carrie was born May 29, 1962. Twins Lance and Alexis Dixon were born April 3, 1991 to Carrie Dixon by a previous marriage. Olivia Brehanne Hess, daughter of Kevin and Carrie Hess, was born Dec. 15, 1997.

Carrie is a teacher at Jonesboro Elementary School and Kevin is a salesman for Heartland Distributing of Cape Girardeau.

HESS – Mary Katherie Hess (b. Aug. 13, 1854; d. Nov. 24, 1944), daughter of Nicholas Hess and Theresa LeGrand, married Henry M. Mirgeaux (b. Jan. 5, 1842; d. Nov. 17, 1886), the son of Lawrence Mirgeaux and Mary Kemp, on Feb. 19, 1878 in St. Lawrence Church in New Hamburg, MO. Three children were born to this union.

First child: Joseph Mirgeaux (b. Nov. 11, 1879; d. Jan. 29, 1969) was a bricklayer. He married Alice Cecilia Rosemersky (b. April 14, 1885; d. Dec. 22, 1972 St. Louis, MO) on Aug. 23, 1904 in St. Augustine Church in Kelso, MO. Five children were born to this union: Vernal Catherine and Vernon Charles, twins (b. June 16, 1914); Joseph Lee (b. Jan. 23, 1917); William Kent (b. March 9, 1924); and James (b. Feb. 24, 1925), who married Velaria Ressel.

Second child: Mary Katherine Mirgeaux (b. Aug. 29, 1883; d. May 7, 1974) married Nicholas Menz (b. April 5, 1881; d. Oct. 10, 1967), on Nov. 21, 1904 in Bostwick, FL. Both are buried in St. Joseph Cemetery at Scott City, MO. Nicholas is the son of John Menz and Josephine Dannenmueller. Nine children were born to this union: Opal Menz (married Arnold Ressel); Monroe; James H.; Amanda; Silverius Frank; Martha Lucille; Charles; Mary Josephine; and Villa Marie.

Third child: Henry Mirgeaux (b. July 1887; d. Sept. 2, 1911) married Mary Philomena Buhs (b. July 15, 1887), the daughter of George Buhs and Justine Miller, on May 14, 1907 in St. Augustine Church in Kelso. They have three children: Evelyn, Sherill and Ross.

Mary Katherine Hess' second marriage to John Adam Kern Jr. (b. Oct. 27, 1849; d. April 20, 1911), the son of John Adam Kern Sr. and Gertrude Eisemann, on July 17, 1880 in St. Augustine Church in Kelso. Four children were born to this union.

First child: Victoria Kern (b. Sept. 20, 1889; d. Nov. 21, 1971) married William M. Corvick on Oct. 9, 1908 in East St. Louis, IL. Seven children were born to them: Ethelyn Catherine; Thelma Anna; Helen Louvine; William August; Laverne; Lloyd John; and Elsie Darlene.

Mary Kathryn (Hess) Mirgeaux Kern

Second child: August Otto Kern (b. March 2, 1892; d. Aug. 1, 1987) married Dosha Butler (b. Feb. 2, 1899; d. May 29, 1984). Both are buried in California. They had four children: Agnes Lorraine Kern (b. Nov. 16, 1916); Ruth Ellen Kern (b. Jan. 2, 1926); John Dale (b. March 7, 1935); and Charles Stanley (stillborn Feb. 16, 1930).

Third child: Katherine Mary Kern (b. Aug. 4, 1894; d. Jan. 9, 1990) married John Frederic Glasser (b. Feb. 21, 1886; d. Nov. 16, 1970), son of Stephen Glasser and Elizabeth Unnerstall, on Feb. 3, 1914 in St. Augustine Church in Kelso, MO. Three children were born to this union.

Catherine Glasser became Sister Claudia in the Order of the Most Precious Blood in O'Fallon, MO. She entered the convent in 1950. She is an Occupational Therapy Technician and is employed at St. Francis Medical Center in Cape Girardeau, MO.

Wilfred Lloyd Glasser (b. Sept. 15, 1924) married Mary Elfrink, daughter of Benjamin Elfrink and Christine Beel, on June 7, 1949 at St. Ambrose Church in Chaffee, MO. They had eight children: Kenneth; Mary Louise; Wilfred John (married Karen Heuring); Rose Marie; Mildred Ann; Catherine Sue; and Susan Christine.

Dorothy May Glasser (b. Feb. 27, 1929) married Benjamin Abbott on Sept. 23, 1950 in St. Augustine Church in Kelso. They have three children: Kathryn A. Abbott (b. Aug. 1, 1952) married Gary Huckstep; Donna M. Abbot (b. July 17, 1953) married Tom Jones; and David M. Abbott (b. Jan. 19, 1955) married Rhonda F. Ruch.

Fourth child: Leo Aloysius "Peggy" (b. Jan. 6, 1897; d. April 2, 1962). He is buried in St. Augustine Cemetery at Kelso. On June 7, 1911 at the age of 14 _, he was riding a mule next to the wheat binder, cutting wheat for Mr. Andy Heisserer on his farm southwest of Kelso. There was a good breeze blowing and the reel picked up some straw and blew it on the five mules, frightening them and they ran out of control. The mule Leo was riding stumbled and threw him right into the path of the sickle. It drug him for about 90 feet then passed over him cutting his right leg almost off. It chewed his leg up from his foot to about four inches from his knee. He also had a large hole cut out of his left thigh and the calf of his left leg, and the flesh was torn from his shoulder to his elbow on his left arm. His right leg was amputated just below the knee and he became known as "Peggy Kern" from then on. He lived to be 65 years old. He made painting and wallpaper hanging as his life's work.

HESS – Mary Margaret Dirnberger Hess was born March 7, 1946, the daughter of Linus Phillip and Regina Compas Dirnberger, at the family home located between New Hamburg and Oran, MO. My brother, Clyde used to play farm with me when I was small. We would use wooden clothespins, making X's with them, for the fences to keep in our play animals. He was very tall, even as a young teenager; so tall in fact, that he had to bend to enter the kitchen door. He not only played farm with me, he was a big help to my dad on our farm. Then, when he was 15, lightning killed Clyde during a storm while he was moving houses in the field. I remember seeing him there in the hog house, where they laid him and I remember all the people coming to our house for the viewing. That was the first time I saw my daddy cry.

Playing house with my dolls and dressing up in play clothes were two of my favorite things to do when I was a small girl. During the summer, mom and dad had a playhouse for me. When my friends came to visit or whenever I wanted to play with my dolls, a trip across the back porch and through the smoke house led to the playhouse where I had a table and chairs, doll beds and all the wonderful things a young girl needs to play house. In the winter, all my playthings would be moved to the attic.

My grandmother, Regina Scherer Compas, lived with us. Together, we spent many hours playing cards. (I think she let me win most of the time.) Grandma peeled many potatoes for our meals. It took many potatoes because we fed the workers who helped on the farm. One of these was Joe Fiser, a very kind man. He even took care of us when mom and dad had to go to town.

I remember my mother teaching me to can vegetables from our large garden. We also canned fruits that we bought from the orchard. I remember sitting on that back porch with bushels of peaches. Mom let us eat as many as we wanted. She said the more we ate, the less she had to can.

A ride on the school bus would take me to a very interesting new world. Usually there were two or three grades in one classroom. But when I was in the fifth grade, there were four classes in my room due to a shortage of teachers. One day when I was in the eighth grade, my teacher asked me to go to the first and second grade room for a short time while their teacher had to be absent. It was then that I thought I'd like to be a teacher. Though I never became a schoolteacher, I have trained a number of people in the title insurance industry.

While attending Thomas W. Kelly High School, my love for mathematics, typing and other office work developed. I received many awards on the school and district level in these areas. I was editor of the school yearbook my senior year under the direction of the business teacher, Mrs. Hortense Watkins. Mrs. Watkins recommended me for a position with Moore-Harris Abstract Company in Benton, MO, and I worked there the summer prior to my senior year and then after school and Saturday mornings. The courthouse where we fathered information was a fascinating place with the smell of old books and the wonder of history they hold. Abstracting has now developed into title insurance and, since I still work in that area, I credit Mrs. Watkins with knowing me better than I knew myself.

On Jan. 9, 1965, Charles P. Hess and I were married at St. Lawrence Church in New Hamburg. We have four children, Kevin, Tim, Steve, and Pamela. They have given us wonderful grandchildren and great-grandchildren.

HESS – Steven Ray Hess was born June 23, 1968, third and youngest son of Charles Peter and Mary Margaret Dirnberger Hess. At that time, the family lived at 1100 Perkins Street in Scott City, MO, but the day Steve was born, Charles moved the family to land known as the Glueck place, west of Highway 61, purchased from Monroe and Helen Hess Raines.

Steve was a graduate of Kelso C-7 Elementary School at New Hamburg, Scott City High School, and Vo-tech school in Cape Girardeau, and attended Southeast Missouri State University. He was a member of St. Joseph Catholic Church in Scott City.

Charles and Mary Hess family, 1975. Timothy, Mary, Steven, Kevin, Charles, and Pamela.

Steve loved to help with chores, especially those that took him outdoors. He would help haul hay and mow yards, clean the barns, fix fence, help the neighbor farm, cut firewood, and feed the chickens. One of his favorite things was to bottle feed the calves. He loved to play such games as basketball, baseball and wrestling. While in high school, Steve worked for Scott City Bakery and later, for Gil Robert's restaurant at Benton, MO.

His Vo-tech class built a home in Cape Girardeau over a two year span, giving him his life training. During that time, Steve competed and won one state and two district awards through Vocational Industrial Club of America (VICA).

In 1986, he perfected his carpentry skills by working for David Sanders for three years and in 1989, he became employed by Mike Glastetter at Glastetter Drywall, Inc. Glastetter Drywall built Eagle Ridge Christian School and Christian Faith Fellowship. Steve also built some background scenery for the Easter Pageant held there. His wife, Christy, and her niece, Angie, performed in the pageant.

On April 23, 1994, he married Christy Kay Brougher, at Immaculate Conception Catholic Church in Jackson, MO. Christy was born June 23, 1968, the daughter of Felix and Lois Brougher. Steve and Christy have the same birthday. They were born 13 hours and several states (Missouri/Alabama) apart. They live in Gordonville where, in 2001, Steve built a shop for his woodworking and a beauty salon for Christy, who is a beautician and owner of "About Styles" beauty salon.

He is a volunteer firefighter and in 2002 became a building maintenance officer for the Gordonville Fire Department.

HESS – Timothy Scott Hess, the second son of Charles Peter and Mary (Dirnberger) Hess, was born May 2, 1967. He lived in Scott City, MO one year, and then moved to Hess Spring Place one-half mile west of Kelso.

He went to Kelso C-7 then on to Scott City High, graduating in 1985.

What I remember most about growing up in Scott County was the chores we did growing up. There were always chickens to feed, work to do in the huge garden mom and dad put out every year, cutting grass and other yard work. As we got older, the chores changed to fit our ages. Somehow we always managed to have fun while we worked.

While the new house was being built, we would get off the school bus and couldn't wait to see the progress from the day before. After all, not too many kids get to watch their new house getting built any time of the day. They new house took the place of the old barn.

When the house was done, we got to help tear down the old house, brick by brick, literally! Kevin, Steve and I would get our first lessons with sledgehammers during this time, knocking walls down, while Pamela stacked bricks. This area of land was to be the new barn. We all got a chance to work on this project as well.

While in Scott City High School, I started working at Scott City Bakery at the age of 17. I would go to work at 5 a.m., work until 7:30 or so and then off to school. Later, after graduation, I went to work full time at the bakery until I was 23 years old.

At age 24, I married Diane Claspill on Oct. 26, 1991, at Immaculate Conception Church in Jackson, MO. Diane had two children so I became an nstant father the same day, with no regrets; they are Mindy Gene Bryant (b. Aug. 7, 1979) and Lawrence Eugene Bryant (b. May 9, 1982).

After we married, we moved to Cape Girardeau, MO. When the kids got out of school and on their own, we re-located to Memphis, TN, where we currently live.

Mindy had made us grandparents three times: Jordan Marie Abraham was born Aug. 8, 1996; Trinity Lee-Ann Bryant was born Sept. 26, 2000; and Ronnie Abraham III was born Oct. 1, 2001.

Though we miss our families and friends, we still manage to go home on a regular basis and keep in touch by phone and e-mail. We try to never miss family reunions and holidays. I have come to cherish the holidays more so because of this.

HEUISER – Jasper Heuser and his wife, Catherine, were born in Darmstadt, Kuhressa, Germany. They operated an inn there prior to their departure for America in 1855. They arrived at a New Orleans port after an 18-week voyage. From there they made their way to Alhambra Township, IL, where Catherine's half-brother, Henry Seibert, farmed. Jasper rented land nearby, but in a short time developed malaria and died at age 50. He was buried in Ellison Cemetery north of Marine, IL, now abandoned.

In 1866, Catherine and her children bought a 120-acre farm near Fruit Station, IL where they lived in a log house. Catherine developed typhoid fever and pneumonia, and then died in August 1873, before she was able to move into her new home. She was buried in the Fruit Station Cemetery, now abandoned. Two of their children died in Germany and one child died in America. Until his death, the farm was owned and operated by a grandson, Gilbert Dankenbring. Heuser was the original spelling of the name in Germany but was changed by the younger brother due to difficulty in pronunciation.

Heuiser Family. First row, L to R: Levina Gottman, Minnie Boda Heuiser, Charlie Heuiser, Livley. 2nd row: Verna Pratt, Irene Hodges, Myrtle Fletcher, Elma Alcorn, and Ella Schuchart. 3rd row: Alvin, Charlie, Fred, and Arnold.

Catherine's half brother, Henry Seibert, born in 1827 in Germany, came to America before 1855. He was in the Civil War, developed pneumonia and died in a hospital in Gravely Springs, AL in 1865. In his will he left an endowment fund of $7500 to the Seibert School, located on his land between Marine, IL and Alhambra. He also left $7000 to the poor of Madison County, IL, $50 to his sister, $50 to Catherine, and $200 to his mother.

Jasper and Catherine had five children: Casper, Mary, Conrod, John and Henry.

John Heuiser was born Feb. 21, 1849, and died in October 1925. He married Henrietta Miebaure on March 26, 1874. She was born June 27, 1850 and died Oct. 14, 1929. They had seven children: Charlie, Matilda, Anna, Lena, John, Henry, and Rosa.

Charles Heuiser was born on Jan. 3, 1875, and died Jan. 3, 1946. He married Minnie Boda on Oct. 18, 1899. She was born Jan. 11, 1875, and died May 20, 1943. They had 12 children: Arnold, Alvin, Charlie, Fred, Irene, Myrtle, Albert, Ella, Verna, Elma, Linley and Levina. Albert died as a child. Ella Matilda Heuiser was born June 29, 1911 and died April 30, 1999. She was afflicted with Alzheimer's for over 10 years. She married Sylvester "Wes" Schuchart on April 23, 1935, at the priest's home of St. Francis Xavier parish in Sikeston, MO. She and Wes had been married 64 years at the time of her death. To this union was born four children: Donald, Barbara, Daniel and John.

Ella's father, Charlie, lived in Madison County, IL where his first ten children were born. He read about land for sale in Scott County, MO, which he

subsequently purchased from Noah Randolph in 1913. Before his death, Charlie sold each son a portion of his land and each daughter received cash.

The Seiberts owned what is now Schuchart Farms, north of Morehouse, MO. Eventually, the Seiberts sold their land to Rudolph P. Schuchart Sr. through Dale Alcorn Real Estate. In 1942, Sylvester R. "Wes" Schuchart purchased his land, at Salcedo, through the Heuiser relatives. *Submitted by Barbara A. Schuchart R.O., B.S.N., N.S.N. in memory of Ella Heuiser Schuchart*

HEURING – Joseph "Joe" Lawrence Heuring was born March 21, 1933, son of Lawrence and Clara Gosche Heuring. He was born on the family farm southwest of New Hamburg, MO. He attended St. Lawrence Catholic School in New Hamburg for eight years. He started to work at the Sports Specialty Shoe Factory in Chaffee, MO at the age of 16. He was drafted into the Army on April 28, 1953. He served with the 5th Army Engineers in Fort Leonard Wood, MO and Fort Riley, KS. He was discharged April 28, 1955 as a corporal.

Joe has three brothers and one sister: Charles John, born Feb. 25, 1919, married Lucille Josephine Westrich, have six children; Elmer George Heuring, born June 11, 1923, married Alene Scherer, have three children; Sylvester born march 30, 1933, died Oct. 16, 1998, married Dorothy Ann DeBrock, have two children; and Lorena Clara Heuring, born Dec. 1, 1938, married Henry Beussink Jr., have two children.

On January 10, he married Margaret Alma Chapman, daughter of Billy Sunday and Gladys "LaRue" Scism Chapman. She was born west of Bloomfield in Stoddard County, MO at the home of Lewis and Lora Scism Hopkins. Margaret attended schools in Gray Ridge, Leora, and Blomeyer and graduated from Delta High School in 1956. Margaret has two sisters and four brothers: Mary Alice Chapman, born March 21, 1940, died Dec. 16, 1992, married Gerald Kinder and has two sons; Billy Dale Chapman, born Aug. 13, 1941, died April 2, 1983, married first Billie Jean Wren, had one son and one daughter, married second Victoria Glastetter, had two daughters; Kenneth Edward Chapman, born Feb. 12, 1944, married Lois Menz, has two sons; Gale "Norman" Chapman, born Oct. 19, 1945, married Sharon Kay Ackman, has one daughter; Larry Hugh Chapman, born July 27, 1948, married first Bonnie Sue Bowers, has two daughters and one son, married second Shelly Jacobs, has one son; and Sharon LaRue Chapman, born July 6, 1953, married Larry Bowen, has two daughters.

Father Thomas Doyle married them in the St. Lawrence Catholic Church. They have three children; Sheila Renee Heuring, born Oct. 24, 1961, married Cameron Ferrell Beggs, Dec. 29, 1980 (divorced) have three daughters, Ashley Brooks, born May 9, 1981, Megan Summer, born April 19, 1983 and Whitney Ferrell, born June 17, 1987; Kenneth Joseph Heuring, born March 5, 1964, died June 2, 1999, married first Jacqueline Michelle Wiginton (Oct. 30, 1982) have two sons and one daughter, Christopher Brooks, born April 26, 1983, Brant Joseph, born Dec. 19, 1985, and Brittney Elizabeth, born July 18, 1989, married second Sharon Dunn; and Dean Patrick Heuring, born July 24, 1973.

Joe and Margaret (Chapman) Heuring

Joe Heuring worked at the Sports Specialty Shoe Factory in Chaffee and at Homestead Distributing Company in Sikeston, Mo for 32 years retiring in 1996. Joe played men's fast pitch softball for 22 years beginning at age 16 for New Hamburg, MO. He was a member of the Schindler's Fastpitch Softball Team that won the state championship in St. Joseph, MO in 1967. He also coached fast pitch softball for several years. Joe is a past president and member of St. Joseph Men's Sodality of St. Lawrence Catholic Church in New Hamburg, MO.

Margaret worked at Sports Specialty Shoe Factory, Buckstein Pants Factory and as bookkeeper/secretary for the Kelso C-7 School in New Hamburg for 31-1/2 years retiring in 2001. She is a member of St. Ann's Sodality of St. Lawrence Church in New Hamburg, Mo, former 4-H Leader, past President of Kelso C-7 School PTO, past president of New Hamburg Homemakers Club and member for 25 years, past president of Scott County Homemakers Extension Club, served one term on Scott County Extension Council, member of Mis-Sco-Deau Office Personnel, and past president of Mis-Sco-Deau Office Personnel 1980-1982.

Joe and Margaret have resided in New Hamburg, MO their entire married life.

HINKLE – The Hinkle families of Scott County and surrounding areas are descendants of Reverend Anthony Jacob and Elizabeth Dentzer Henckel. He was born in Mehrenberg, Germany and baptized Dec. 27, 1668 in the Evangelical Lutheran Church. He married Maria Elizabeth Dentzer, daughter of Reverend Nicloaus Dentzer, Lutheran pastor at Birkenau, Germany. They were the parents of 12 children.

On June 3, 1717 he immigrated to the province of Pennsylvania. William Penn, after hearing of the conflict between the Catholic authorities and the Rev. Henckel and his congregation, personally invited them to immigrate to the new land.

In Pennsylvania he reorganized a local New Hanover Lutheran Church and founded the St. Michael Lutheran Church at Germantown, PA. After coming to America, the family changed the spelling of the name to Henkel. Anthony Henkel III changed the spelling of the name to Hinkle.

Jacob Anthony Henckel came to Pennsylvania with his father. He married Anna Margaret, maiden name unknown. They had nine children. Of their children, a son and his wife, Charles and Elizabeth Johnson Hinkle and other families moved to Lincoln and Rowan Counties in North Carolina. There they had adjoining farms and were wheelwrights and blacksmiths. Charles became a captain in the Revolutionary War. He hauled ammunition, food, clothing, and served as assistant quartermaster. His son, Casper Hinkle was a private in the same militia. He fought and captured the Tories, guarded prisoners taken at Cowpens. Besides assisting in the capture of other Tories and British in Rowan County, he rode express between revolutionary camps in North Carolina.

Casper Hinkle married Fanny Robertson and had several children. In 1814 the family moved to Shelby County, KY where his brother, Charles, had previously settled. In 1823 he moved to Perry County, MO and applied for a war pension. He died about 1839. Isaac, one of Casper's sons, would follow the family to Cape Girardeau County at a later date.

Peter Hinkle, a first cousin, moved to Cape Girardeau County in 1816. Catherine Hinkle, his daughter, married John Welker. In July 1825, Isaac, Casper's son, married John Welker's sister, Catherine "Kitty" Welker. They moved to Scott

County and Isaac became a prosperous farmer. He also owned land in Missouri and Arkansas. Isaac and Catherine's known children were: Casper Hinkle married Maryann; Mary Hinkle married Charles Ellis; Francis Elizabeth married James Trotter; John Hinkle married Mahala "Molly" Worley; Isaac Hinkle married Nancy Hinton; Louis Hinkle married Pharody E. Hareson; and Louisa Hinkle.

Jesse Bean, husband of Lula Cordelia Hinkle, and daughters, Veda and Lula Mae.

In 1849, Isaac and a group of men invested in a venture to build a road connecting Cape Girardeau and Scott Counties. The Turnpike Road Company failed but was later built in 1851 and called the Rock Levee Road. The road was completed before the Civil War and continued in use until Highway 61 was completed in the early 1920s.

After Catherine died Sept. 21, 1851 Isaac married Zulema Morrison and they had a son, William H. Hinkle. Both William and his mother are buried in the Cobb-Ingram Cemetery in Scott County, MO. Isaac died April 14, 1856. He is buried next to Catherine. Henderson Winchester was the administrator of the estate of Isaac Hinkle.

Some of Isaac's sons were businessmen and farmers. Two of his sons, Casper and Isaac, were both farmer and together owned a livery business in Morley, MO. The partnership for the livery, Hinkle and Brother, was dissolved by the death of Isaac. Isaac met and married Nancy Hinton of New Hamburg, Mo about 1862. She was the daughter of Paul and Panthea Payne Hinton. Isaac died March 19, 1872 and is buried beside his parents in Carpenter Cemetery. Known children of Isaac and Nancy: Margaret Victoria Hinkle married Jasper Grant; John Hinkle married Soaf Brizeal; Lewis Hinkle; and Louisa Cordelia Hinkle married Jesse W. Bean.

Many of the Hinkle descendants still live in the Scott County area. The Hinkle family was a pioneer family. The *Hinkle family genealogy, 1500-1960* has much more to be learned about this family of Reverend Anthony Jacob Henckel.

HINKLE – Isaac Hinkle (Casper, Captain Charles, Jacob Anthony, Anthony Jacob, George, Matthias, Casper) was born April 9, 1802 in Rowan County, NC. He was the son of Casper and Fanny Robertson Hinkle and the great-great grandson of the Reverend Anthony Jacob Henckel. The Reverend Anthony Henckel came to Germantown, PA and established the first Lutheran Church in 1728.
Isaac married

Lula Cordelia Hinkle, daughter of Isaac and Nancy Hinkle.

Catherine "Kitty" Welker, daughter of Daniel Welker, July 18, 1825 in Cape Girardeau, MO. He owned land in Arkansas as well as in Missouri and was involved in a failed road-building venture that would have linked Scott and Cape Girardeau Counties. After Catherine died Sept. 21, 1851, Isaac married Zulema Morrison and they had a son, William H. They are buried in the Cobb-Ingram Cemetery in Scott County. Isaac died April 14, 1856. Catherine and Isaac are buried together in the Carpenter Cemetery, Scott County, Mo. Henderson Winchester was the administrator of the estate of Isaac.

Isaac's descendants were farmers and businessmen. Two of his sons, Casper and Isaac both were farmers and had formed a partnership to run a livery business in Morley, MO. There, Isaac met and married Nancy Hinton of New Hamburg, MO in 1862. Isaac died March 19, 1872 and is buried in the Carpenter Cemetery. Nancy married William Carpenter in 1877. William and G. W. Carpenter sold their land to Scott County for the Carpenter Cemetery hence the name Carpenter Cemetery.

Three of the known children of Isaac and Nancy are Margaret Vick, John and Lula Cordelia.

Margaret Vick married Jasper Grant and their children are Louisa, Lutie, Myrtle, Lucy, Effie, Elmer, Earnest, and William.

John married Soaf Brizeal and their children are Grace and Stella.

Lula Cordelia married Jesse W. Bean and their children are Clarence, Cecil, Otto, Alma, Edith, Helen, Lula Mae, and Veda.

Homer and Edith Bean Greenlee, daughter of Lula Hinkle Bean, married May 25, 1918.

Another son, John, married Mahala Worley, daughter of James Worley. Their son Charles J. married Nettie Hurst, living and farming around Morley. William C., son of Charles married Bessie Reed and they were farmers in Scott and Stoddard Counties.

Many of Isaac Hinkle's descendants are living in the Scott County area. Some, but not all, of the surnames are Bean, Greenlee, Coffey, Crains, Grants, McConeyhay, Drake and Trotters.

Veda Bean Crain of Sikeston, the keeper of Isaac and Nancy's family history has been the inspiration to family members to carry on the search for all of Isaac Hinkle's descendants. Alma Bean Coffey, Otto and Barry Bean, daughter, son and grandson of Otto Bean, Annette Greenlee Stephens, daughter of Edith Bean Greenlee, and Faith Ann Neal, granddaughter of Edith Bean Greenlee are all working on the research of the Hinkle family.

HIRSCHOWITZ – Mr. and Mrs. Max Hirschowitz moved to Oran in the year 1909 from St. Louis. Max was born in Lithuania, Russia, of a family of 14. Life was so very difficult in Russia that Max, as a young man, decided to come to America. Being poor, he had to book passage of a very low class – down where the livestock was kept.

After arriving in Philadelphia he stayed awhile,

but not being able to grasp the ways of the New World, he decided to go back home. In the year 1904, he returned to America, and this time settled in St. Louis where he knew of some kinfolk.

The year 1904 he came to Oran because his brother Morris was down in this vicinity buying iron, bones, and hides. Max stayed with his brother awhile, but he returned to St. Louis and went to work in a Junk Yard. Having a good knowledge of horses and mules, he waited for the opportunity to go in that business.

He met his wife Mary who encouraged him to go back to Oran Community. She lent him a few hundred dollars and he went down the river on a cattle boat to Commerce, MO, where from this point he began his new business venture. In 1909 Mr. and Mrs. Max Hirschowitz became residents of Oran.

A year later, Max's brother Ben came to Oran, and the two of them went in business. The big reason for going in business in Oran was that it was a German-speaking community, and Max and Ben could speak and understand the language. The brothers formed a business partnership known as Hirschowitz Brothers, Max and Ben, Dealers in Horses and Mules. In the year 1922, Ben sent for his family whom he had left behind in Lithuania. That year they took up as residents of Oran, bringing two girls and one boy from Russia.

The community was good to the brothers, and they expanded their business to Senath, MO where they bought a barn and started in the Horse and Mule Business. In later years, they expanded their business to farming and other livestock buying.

The stories have been told that Max and Ben would saddle their horses and drive their mules to Senath, MO, which is about 100 miles from Oran.

Mary Hirschowitz was born in Paris, France, but her family moved to Santiago, Chile, then to Caracas, Venezuela to homestead a section of land. The South American Government gave the early settlers money to build a log cabin, which Mrs. Hirschowitz said was very crude. The land was so far back in the interior, it was not safe to live because of the Native South American Indians being hostile to white settlers. After three years on the farm, her parents decided to give up farming and moved to San Salvador in El Salvador in Central America. Mrs. Hirschowitz's father contacted yellow fever and died. The rest of the family moved back to Paris, and Mrs. Hirschowitz came to St. Louis. There she married Max Hirschowitz in 1908, and moved to Oran in 1909 to raise their family—Anna, Philip, Abram and Louie. (One other child died in early infancy.)

Mrs. Hirschowitz said today, "Oran is like any other part of the world—same skies and stars. Life is how you live and make it. Oran has been good to us."

HITT – Grover Benjamin Leander Hitt and his family became residents of Scott County, MO in February 1929 and farmed near the Oran, Blodgett and Commerce Communities. In 1940 the family purchased land located on the Commerce-Charleston Road, Route N, and built their home on this land. They continued to live here and Grover farmed this and additional rented land until his retirement in 1955. In the 1940s and early 1950s, the

Grover Benjamin Leander Hitt, 1948.

family owned an exceptional Durham cow. She bore three sets of twin calves, which is somewhat of a record in the bovine world, making 12 calves for the 11-year-old cow.

Grover Hitt was born April 3, 1885 on his parent's farm in Bollinger County, MO. He was the son of William Benjamin and Mary Elizabeth

Esther Ellen Snider Hitt, 1944.

(Zimmerman) Hitt. He was of German heritage. His ancestors arrived in the colony of Virginia in the spring of 1714 from Nassau-Siegen, now Province of Westphalia, West Germany and were miners or ironworkers.

They settled in the Germanna Colony on the Rapidan River in Virginia. They arrived in Missouri territory in 1806, first settling in the Cape Girardeau area and later moving to Bollinger County.

On Feb. 17, 1914, in Bollinger County, Grover married Esther Ellen Snider, daughter of George Franklin and Sarah Elizabeth (Proffer) Snider. Esther's ancestors came to Missouri territory from Lincoln County, NC in 1811. They settled in Cape Girardeau County, which later became Bollinger County, near Laflin. Her father was a farmer and landowner in southwest Cape County near Whitewater. The oldest house still standing in the eastern part of Bollinger County is the brick home built by Andrew Snider in the later 1840s. Andrew's slaves made the bricks from clay mined and fired near the site. Andrew Snider was a great-great uncle of Esther Snider Hitt.

Grover and Esther were parents of 11 children.

Herschel Milford Hitt who married Mary Kelly Bradshaw

Cecil Matthew Hitt who married Leona (Steele) Rouse

Leon Elwood Hitt who married Thelma Virginia Miller, and after her death he married Kay (Bom) Gibson

Leathal "Leatha" Elizabeth Hitt who married Ebert Gerald Rister

Eugene Franklin Hitt who died at age 22

Roby William Hitt who married Vernetta Maxine "Babe" Vaughan

Myrtle Irene Hitt who married Edward "Ed" Reed Jr.

Marie Allene Hitt who married Charles Gary Stalon

Earnest Benjamin Hitt who died at age 4 weeks

Herman Poletious Hitt who married Peggy Joyce Gross

Paul Leroy Hitt who married Mary Jean Koch

Five of Grover and Esther's sons served n the US Army. Herschel, Cecil, and Roby served during WWII, Herman during the Korean War and Paul Leroy during peacetime. The family attended St. Paul United Methodist Church at Commerce.

After Grover's death Dec. 11, 1960, Esther lived in their home until her death Feb. 11, 1967. Both are buried in Oakdale Cemetery near Commerce. *Submitted by Paul Leroy and Mary Jean Hitt, family history researched by Marie Allene Hitt Stalon*

HOEFLER – Lawrence August Hoefler was born in Scott County, Jan. 20, 1891 the first son of Louis and Regina (Dannenmueller) Hoefler. Lawrence's maternal grandparents Louis and Veronica (Schlosser) Dannenmueller came to Scott County in the 1830s from Schirrhein, France. They were married on May 3, 1847 in a home near New

Hamburg. Their marriage took place during the time when persecution at St. Mary's Catholic Church at Benton forced church services to be held in private homes. Louis opened one of the first businesses in Kelso, a saloon. By 1867, Louis had expanded his business, in his original location, which was now known as Dannen-muellersville, to include a dry goods store, saloon, grocery store, stables and offered just about everything to accommodate the needs of the local community as well as the traveling public. During the Civil War, Louis served in the Missouri Home Guard at New Hamburg.

At age 16, Lawrence married Emma Messmer on Nov. 24, 1907. Emma was born Jan. 6, 1890 in Scott County, the daughter of Frank and Veronica (Swan) Messmer. Emma's maternal grandfather, John R. Swan, served in the Union Army during the Civil War. He was born in Gibraltar, Spain but was a British citizen and lived in London, England until he came to the US in 1847. He first settled in Pennsylvania, where he met and married Mary Ann Brabender. In about 1855, they moved to Scott County, MO.

Lawrence A. Hoefler family, 1943. Back row: Bernice Hoefler Ulett, Naomi Hoefler Ulett, Robert Edward Hoefler, Lucille Hoefler Lee, and Raymond Hoefler. Front: Lawrence August Hoefler Jr., Lawrence August Hoefler Sr., Emma Messmer Hoefler, and Dolores Hoefler Shcrick.

Lawrence and Emma purchased a farm about one-half mile south of Kelso, known as the Dannenmueller Farm, on Messmer Road (where the Diebold Orchard was later located). He purchased the farm from Kasimer Martin on April 4, 1912. Lawrence worked hard on the farm and did hauling for individuals and businesses. He owned one of the first automobiles in Kelso- a 1910 Ford.

Lawrence built a large barn with a wood floor and, on Saturday nights, held public "barn dances" which became very popular.

Lawrence and Emma had nine children, five of whom were born in Scott County. They were: Raymond Frank (b. Aug. 20, 1908); Florence Caroline (b. Aug. 18, 1908); Lucille Veronica (b. Sept. 10, 1911); Robert Edward (b. Oct. 6, 1913); and Naomi Marie (b. March 10, 1916). Florence died on Jan. 12, 1912 at age 2-1/2 years, from diphtheria.

Lawrence worked hard to make the farm and his hauling business prosper, but by 1916 he was experiencing financial difficulties. He decided to lease the farm and move his family to St. Louis. After several odd jobs, on Aug. 14, 1916 at age 25, he went to work for the St. Louis Public Service Company. He spent the rest of his working years as a streetcar operator and motorman.

They lived in the city of St. Louis for several years. Lawrence Harry was born there in 1917 and so was Bernice Harriet, on her father's birthday, Jan. 20, 1919. Harry died when he was 6 months old from a sudden attack of pneumonia.

In 1919 they purchased a home at 1637

Vassier Street in St. Louis County where two more children were born. Lawrence August on Dec. 30, 1921 and Dolores Emma on Oct. 15, 1926.

Lawrence died on June 2, 1968. Emma died on July 21, 1978. Both are buried in Calvary Cemetery in St. Louis, MO. Most of their descendants live in the St. Louis area. *Submitted by Dolores Hoefler Schrick*

HOWELL – Wiley Howell (1788-1859) married Tabitha Howell (1792-1851). They were the parents of Thomas Howell (1824-1896). He married Nancy Howell (1832-1862). They were all natives of Tennessee. They came to Missouri with their parents, first moving to Scott County, then to West Plains, MO. Thomas fought in the Civil War. After the war, in 1865, Nancy and Thomas moved back to Scott County. Nancy bore eight children. They were: Martha (Woodside); Mollie (Robertson); Jane (Jenkins); William Howell; Sally (McMullin); George; Millie (Congleton); and infant Nancy. Upon the birth of the youngest child, Nancy, the mother passed away, in 1865. After a few years, Thomas was remarried to Eliza Hall, a widow. They lived in Blodgett, MO. William Howell remained with his parents until 1875. He bought some land four miles north of Oran and became a stock farmer.

William Howell was married to Martha Montgomery, daughter of L. D. and Elisabeth Montgomery of near Chaffee, MO. They had four children: Minnie Howell (Halter); Maude Muller Howell (Slinkard); George Howell; and William Ross. William and his wife were devoted members of the Methodist Episcopal Church South. William was a county judge and a member of A.O.U.W. Martha passed away in 1887. In 1890, William remarried to Frances Evangeline Dennis. She had lived with her parents James and Emily and two brothers, Lee and Lafayette, in Poplar Bluff, MO. When her father James Dennis, passed away in 1873, the Dennis family moved to a farm two miles north of Oran, MO. James Dennis, the father, had been a lawyer and Prosecuting Attorney in Poplar Bluff. To the marriage of William and Frances came Thomas, Beatrice Howell (Hancock), Ulmont, Anna Lucille, Mable Howell (Estes), Preston and Presley (twins), Roy Wallace, and Mildred Howell (Carter). Two of William's daughters, Beatrice and Mable raised their children in Scott County.

In the year 2001, William's children have all passed away leaving a host of grandchildren and great-grandchildren. *Submitted by Patricia Howell Uptain, daughter of Ulmont R. Howell and granddaughter of William Howell*

HUDSON – The eight children of Newton Bishop Hudson and his wife, Alice Maud Goodman, were born in Ripley County, MO but several were Johnny-come-latelys to Scott County. They arrived several years after "swampeast Missouri" was drained and added many acres to its farming industry.

Newton was a farmer. He was also a fiddler and played for barn dances. Several of the children picked guitars and the Hudsons were known for their hoedowns when family and friends gathered. The children of Newton and Alice: Mabel Gertrude (1898-1962); Edna Nora (1900-1965); Charlie Barton (1902-1989); John Burton (1904-living); Bessie McClellan (1907-1975); Chester Goodman (1909-1974); Blanche Marie (1912-1992); and Hubert Richard (1914-1982).

Mabel, John, Chester, and Hubert migrated to Scott County. John is still living in Scott County. Mabel, Chester and Hubert are buried in Scott County. Charlie and Blanche lived in Scott County for a while. Charlie migrated to the St. Louis area and Blanche migrated to the Detroit area.

Mabel married William Verley McArthur (1896-1973), son of Henry Columbus McArthur and Laura Ann Pender, on Oct. 9, 1918 in Ripley County. They had seven children: Willie Verlene; Buford Lacy; Shirley Attalee; Theola Alice; Con Leon; and twins Choleta Fay and Chloene May. Mabel and Verley migrated to Scott County in the late 1930s. Verley farmed near Vanduser. Their children graduated from the Vanduser and Morley High Schools. Willie married Ruben Manual Blankenship. They had two children: Sharon Reigna and Larry Dale. Burford married Norma Emogene Hampton. They had one child: Donna Ka. Shirley married Dorothy Juanita Cherry. They had two children: Brenda Sue and Shirley Wade. Theola married Arnold Chester Miles. They had one child, Mary Alice. Con married May Jane Gibbs. They had three children: Sandra Kay, Robert Duane and Linda Ann. Choleta married Theodore Orville Martin Jr. They had two children: Annah Lea and Sherri Lyn. Chloene married Wiley Archie Alliston Jr. They had two children: Terry Lee and William Alan. Con and Mary live in Morley. Chloene lives part-time in Sikeston. Mabel and Verley are buried in the Forest Hills Memorial Gardens near Morley.

Charlie married Alice Florence Thomas (1907-1996), daughter of George Melville Thomas and Alice Florence West, on Oct. 31, 1924 at Corning, AR. They had two children: Viva Dean and Modean Alma Jean. Charlie and Alice migrated to Scott County in the early 1940s. Modean graduated from Vanduser High School. Charlie farmed near Vanduser and later east of Morley. Charlie and Alice migrated to the St. Louis area in the 1950s. Viva married William Oliver Boatmon. They had five children: Linda Jean; Charles Lindell; Mary Marlene; Teresa Elaine and Dana Sue. Modean married Hubert Franklin Killian. They had two children: Sandra Lynne and Dennis Bruce.

John married Thelma Christeen Hart (1917-1992), daughter of Arphus Jasper Hart and Margaret Rebecca Mae Lamb, on Sept. 28, 1935 at Corning, AR. They had four children: Mae Dean; Austin Ray; Harley Odell and John Richard. Mae and Harley died in infancy. John and Thelma migrate to Scott County in 1941. Austin and John graduated from Scott County schools. Austin married Loretta Jean Reyes. They had five children: Austin Jr., Michael Eugene; Monica Jean; John David and Ernest Burton. John married Marian Evelyn Boid. They had one child: Mychelle Lynn. Later, he married Rose Mary Wilson. They had one child, John Jr. Thelma is buried in the New Morley Cemetery. John celebrated his 97th birthday in 2001.

Chester married Pearl Gracie Wampler (1917-1996), daughter of William Oscar Wample and Martha Jane Mitchell, on July 14, 1934 at Corning, AR. They had four children: Glenna Dene Pearl; Conrad Loren; Reva June and Charles Eugene. Chester and Pearl were the last to migrate to Scott County. They arrived in 1946. Chester farmed east of Morley. All of their children graduated from Morley High School. Glenna married Ronald Lee Pulliam. Glenna and Ronald had two children: Steven Lee and Dana Lynn. Glenna subsequently married Dominic Santangelo and later Jerry Carlton May of the Scott County Mays. Conrad married Bette Jo Brame. They did not have any children. He then married Joan Elizabeth Fisher. They had two children: John Patrick and Julie Elizabeth. Reva married Robert Lee Penrod. They did not have any children. Reva subsequently married Danny Joe Byrd of the Scott County Byrds. Charles married Sharon Kay Rickman of the Scott County Rickmans. They had two children: David Loren and Derek Kent. Glenna and Jerry live in Morley.

Reva and Danny live in Sikeston. Chester and Pearl are buried in the Forest Hills Memorial Gardens near Morley.

Blanche married Samuel Earl Hill (1915-1992), son of James R. Hill and Mary E. Watson, on Aug. 22, 1933 at Corning, AR. They had two children: Betty Evelyn and Mary Joann. Blanche and Samuel migrated to McMullin in Scott County during the early 1940s, but moved on to the Detroit area during the war years. Betty married Frank Edwards Hayden. They had two children: Frankie Edward and Robert Stephen. Mary married Harold Thomas Rodibaugh. They had two children: Victoria Lynn and Kelly Marie.

Hubert married Hulda Belle Clark (1914-1993), daughter of John Clark and Effie Parrish, on Nov. 6, 1937 at Corning, AR. They did not have any children. Hubert and Hulda migrated to Scott County shortly after they were married. Hubert farmed east of Morley. Hubert and Hulda are buried in the Forest Hills Memorial Gardens near Morley. *Submitted by Conrad Hudson*

HUNTER – The Hunter family originated in Scotland. Joseph Hunter I, came to America around 1730 to Carlisle, PA, and later to Missouri in the 1770s. Joseph Hunter II is the progenitor of the Hunters of southeast Missouri. From 1811-1812, he moved his family to Big Prairie, now Sikeston.

Joseph II's son, David, is buried on the farm at LaForge, which is still owned by J. Clay Hunter. David had a son, Samuel, and he had a son, Albert. Albert's son was Henry Clay Hunter, who married Elvena Latimer of Marston. There were two children born of this marriage, J. Clay and Mary Ella.

Jackson Clay Hunter

Jackson Clay was born Jan. 20, 1945. He attended schools in New Madrid, MO; New Birnswick, NJ; Newfoundland, Canada; St. Louis and Mexico, MO. He is an alumnus of Missouri Military Academy.

In 1962, Jackson Clay enlisted into the United States Air Force working security in the Minuteman Missile System. He was honorably discharged in 1966 and enlisted in the Air National Guard, and later in the Navy Seabee's. In 1966, he was employed by City Finance Company of Memphis, TN, prior to entering Technical College. Clay graduated from State Technical Institute in Memphis in 1969 with an associate degree in architectural engineering technology. He completed his Bachelor of Science Degree in construction engineering technology in 1971 from Memphis State University in Memphis, TN. He received his masters in education in 1989 from Southern Illinois University, and also continued his PhD work there.

Clay worked for Missouri Department of Transportation and BWF Architects and Engineers.

He married Martha Marcotte in Sikeston, and had a son, Jackson Clay II. Jackson Clay II is a graduate of Washington University in St. Louis, and presently resides with his wife, Katie, in Massachusetts, while attending Harvard University MBA Program.

Jackson Clay I is a teacher for Sikeston Public Schools, and also teaches for Southeast Missouri State University. Jackson Clay resides in Miner, MO. He still operates the family farm in LaForge, MO, dating from 1805. His hobbies include art, motorcycling, scuba and skydiving.

He was discharged from the Navy Reserve

Seabees in 1996. He is a member of Hunter Memorial Presbyterian Church, Masonic Lodge, Scottish Rite, Shriner, and a life member of the Jaycees, serving as local and regional director. Clay is a member of Missouri Vocational Association, Sikeston Teachers Association, Missouri Trade and Technical Association of Professional Auctioneers Association, National Auctioneers Association (serving as Board Member and President, respectfully). He has served 13 years as Insurance Chair and two years as Chair of Legislative Committee.

Clay will be retiring from teaching in 2005, after which he plans to return to auctioneering and real estate.

Great-great-great grandfather, Joseph Hunter (b.1760; d. 1823) buried Sikeston, MO Hunter Memorial Presbyterian Church Cemetery.

Great-great grandfather, David Hunter (b. 1798; d. 1837) buried LaForge, MO.

Great grandfather, Samuel Hunter (b. 1828; d. 1864) buried in North LaForge, MO.

Grandfather, Albert B. Hunter (b. 1855; d. 1930) buried New Madrid, MO Evergreen Cemetery.

Father, Henry Clay Hunter (b. 1881; d. 1948) buried New Madrid, MO.

Son, Jackson Clay Hunter I (b. 1945).
Child Jackson Clay Hunter II (b. 1976).
Child Heath Scott Hunter (b. 1983).

JANSEN – Bernard William Jansen was born Dec. 17, 1890 near Leopold, MO to Joseph Gerhardt and Mary Thedora Jansen, the eighth child of ten in the Jansen family. They were members of St. John's Catholic Church where Ben was baptized in the old log church. His father, on the committee to construct a new church, involved all the members of his family old enough to help. Formal education in those days was competed in three or four years for many including Ben. His teacher, only six years older than he, was a strict disciplinarian and although they were cousins it in no way affected the teacher-student relationship.

When they became of age Ben and his brothers left home to find employment in Oran, MO. It was after this that their mother died, August 1917, in Leopold and their father bought farms east of Oran, one of the first from Leopold to buy land there.

The Theodore Brockmeyer family including a daughter, Christine, also lived near Oran. A friendship developed between she and Ben, but the unsettled conditions in the world interfered as the World War began. It began for the United States April 6, 1917 and men between the age of 21 and 30 were required to register for the draft.

Ben was inducted into the Army on July 18, 1918 at the age of 27. He was sent to France Nov. 19, 1918 after serving at Camp McArthur, TX with Company A, 4th Bn. Infantry and then with Company D 329th Infantry attached to the 15th Recruit Company GSI. Ben would not say much about his military service, except for one memory of having nothing to eat for three days but a farmer's winter supply of apples they found. He was honorably discharged on Feb. 13, 1919.

Upon returning, Ben settled again in Oran. His friendship with Christine developed into a serious relationship and his mustering out payment was used to purchase an engagement ring. They were married in Guardian Angels Church on Nov. 25, 1919, one of the first marriages in the new church.

In 1923 Ben and Christine moved from Oran to Cape Girardeau where he worked at the shoe factory for 14 years. The family moved back to Oran in 1938 farming the place known as the Hulshof farm until 1945 when a farm west of Kelso, MO was purchased.

The Ben and Christine Jansen family, 1956. Front row, left to right: Irene, Ben, Christine, and Corena. 2nd row: Herman, George, Martin, Paul, Leon, and Lucille.

Nine children were born to them including Leon, (spouse Bernice Dirnberger); Herman (wife Rita Klipfel); Paul (Juanita Brantley); Lucille (Joe Klipfel); Martin (Mary Jane Drury); George (Louise Sobba); Irene (Joe Klueppel) and Corena (Elmer Obermann) (LeeRoy Berkbigler). One son Raymond died at age 2 of pneumonia.

Bernard died at age 81 on Nov. 24, 1971 and Christine at 82 Aug. 17, 1981, leaving five sons, three daughters, 39 grandchildren and 25 great-grandchildren. They left their family a legacy of love, integrity, faith, and a strong work ethic. Their lives were spent doing the best they could for family, church and community. *Submitted by Mrs. George P. Jansen*

JANSEN – In an area near the Holland border in the village of Rees on the Rhein, Rees, Esserden, Germany lived the Gerhardt Jansen family. He and his wife, Carolina, were born in that area in 1811 and 1813 respectively. Carolina died after an illness within a year of the marriage. Gerhardt then married Johanna Gissing also from that Northern Rhein community. To this union were born Joseph Gerhardt, the subject of this history, Karolina, who died at an early age, Bernadina, who married Anton Hulshof, and Louis, who married Bertha Holzum.

Joseph Gerhardt Jansen family, ca. 1900. Front, left to right: Henry, Joseph, Mary Theodora, and Bernadine. Back: Gerhardt, Louis, Carolina, and Bernard.

Political conditions in Germany were factors in the immigration to America, and Gerhardt and Johanna were among those deciding to leave their homeland for a new country. They homesteaded near Cincinnati, OH until they could join other German and Dutch families who had settled in Leopold, or Vineland, as it was called at that time, in Bollinger County, MO two years earlier in 1858.

Joseph was about 8 years of age when his father bought a farm two miles west of Leopold, but Gerhardt did not get to enjoy his new country very long. He died apparently of appendicitis in April of 1861 leaving his wife and four small children. The Civil War affected the little village of Leopold and many of its residents left the com-

munity to escape the danger. Johanna took her children to live for a number of years in St. Louis with relatives. Thereafter, she married Ben Brummer and the family settled once more in Leopold on the Jansen farm. It adjoined another farm on which the Poor Farm was located. For those who had no home or means of support it was a place to live and work for their keep.

Joe, at age 27, married Mary Thedora Brauer April 30, 1879 in Leopold. Life was difficult in those times with many hardships to bear. Four of ten children died in infancy and one son, Louis, drowned at the age of 25 in Lake Kilarney where he was a lifeguard. The remaining children were Gerhardt, who remained single; Caroline, who joined the School of Sisters of Notre Dame; Bernard, whose wife was Christine Brockmeyer; Bernadine, married to Joseph Linneman; and Henry, who married Caroline Arnzen.

Several families from the Leopold area moved to Oran where land was better, and Joseph was the first to buy farmland there. The Jansen sons, Gerhardt, Ben and Henry, left the Leopold home earlier and moved to Oran, Scott County, MO to find work. Their mother, Mary, died in 1917 and Joseph was left alone. In 1926 he left Leopold to live with his son, Gerhardt, on one of his Oran farms.

Joseph Gerhardt Jansen had lived a full life caring for his family, farming. Fully involved with his community and his church, he died January 1929 at the age of 77 at his home near Oran and was buried in Old Guardian Angel Cemetery on the hill. Many descendants were left to carry on the family name. *Submitted by Mrs. George P. Jansen*

JEFFRIES – Willie Edward Jeffries was born on June 18, 1891 in Littleville, Colbert County, AL. His parents were Edmond S. Jeffries and Safronia McClellan Tharp. He married Cynthia Margret Crittenden, daughter of Lafayette F. and Octimee Ellen Webb Crittenden, on May 25, 1914 in Colbert County, AL. Cynthia was born on March 25, 1893 in Spring Valley, Colbert County, AL.

Willie Edward worked for the Southern Railway Company from April 1910 to April 1913 in Sheffield, AL. Then he got a job with the River Division of the St. Louis and San Francisco Railway Company (also known as the Frisco Railroad) in Chaffee, Scott County, MO, where he worked until he retired in 1950. After he married, he moved his wife to Chaffee. Willie Edward's mother had a brother, Will Tharp, who also worked on the railroad and was already living in Chaffee. Willie Edward had many jobs for the railroad including carpenter, brakeman, and his last and longest was conductor. Cynthia would take him his lunches when the train was scheduled to pass through Chaffee. During the Great Depression, the railroad kept all employees working, but did cut their pay. Cynthia, who had learned to sew at an early age, took in sewing and also made Willie's clothes and the clothes of her children. In his retirement years, he drove a taxi to meet the trains. They are both buried at Memorial Park in Cape Girardeau.

Cynthia and Willie Edward lived at 324 West Davidson in Chaffee where they raised two children. Their first-born was Orvel Sigler, born Oct. 4, 1915, but he died before he was a year old on Aug. 18, 1916. Willie Edward took the baby back to Alabama for burial in a family plot in Osborn Hill Cemetery in Littleville, AL. Next was Ethel Louise, born on Jan. 25, 1917 in Chaffee. She married Elmer Andrew Cannon, son of Carl Combs and Rubie Lee Skinner Cannon, on May 4, 1935. Elmer was born Dec. 2, 1916 in St. Louis, MO.

Elmer and Ethel Jeffries Cannon had the following children: Royce Venable born Sept. 16, 1936 in Chaffee, MO. He married Sandra Napp Showers Sept. 16, 1967. Sandy was born Nov. 8, 1938 in Pennsylvania. Royce retired from the Air Force and also United Services Automobile Association. Royce graduated from Chaffee High School. William Macklind was born Oct. 9, 1937 in Chaffee, MO. He married first Carolyn Sue Ryan Nov. 7, 1959 and divorced in 1978. He next married Donna Smith. Bill served in the US Army, worked for the railroads, and now serves as Mayor of Chaffee. Bill graduated from Chaffee High School. Timothy was born Aug. 23, 1955 in Chaffee, MO. Timothy married Brenda Budde Sept. 13, 1986 in Overland, MO. He works at Jeffco College in Hillsboro, MO.

W.E. and Cynthia Margaret Crittenden Jeffries.

The third child of Willie Edward and Cynthia Crittenden Jeffries was Opal Marie Jeffries who was born on April 21, 1919 in Chaffee, MO. Opal married Barney Oldfield Green Nov. 16, 1941 in Marion, Crittenden County, AR. Barney was born Oct. 9, 1919 in Caruthersville, Pemiscot County, MO. His parents were Joseph Calicutt and Eunice Shrum Green. Both Opal and Barney graduated from Chaffee High School in 1937. Opal attended William Jewel College for three semesters and transferred to Southeast Missouri State Teachers College in Cape Girardeau, MO, where she graduated in 1940. She taught in the Chaffee Schools for a couple of years before she got married. Barney had joined the US Navy and served in WWII. Opal got a job with the Treasury Department in St. Louis during the war. Barney retied from the Navy in 1961 and died July 25, 1972. Opal died July 4, 1988 in Huntsville, AL. They are both buried in Arlington National Cemetery.

W.E. and Cynthia Jeffries

Barney and Opal Jeffries Green had two children. Linda Lou was born Sept. 12, 1946 in Cape Girardeau, MO. Linda is a retired Lieutenant Colonel US Army, a published author, and currently works on a missile defense program. Barney Edwin was born June 17, 1959 in Bethesda, MD. Barney Edwin married Sharon E. William Aug. 26, 1981 in Petersburg, VA. He owns his own computer consulting business. They had one son, Andrew Jeffries Green, born Dec. 19, 1995 in Raleigh, NC. Barney and Sharon are divorced. *Submitted by Mrs. Elmer Cannon*

JENKINS – Reverend Albert B. Jenkins was born March 10, 1899 at Tanner, Mo and died Aug. 10, 1985. He was the son of Francis Marion and Ada Belle (Morris) Jenkins, a share-cropper farmer. To this marriage were born Ella Frances, who married Henry Mangold and moved to Peoria, IL where they raised their family; Clarence Layton, a farmer, who married Lola Berry and lived in Lilborn, MO then later in East Prairie, MO where they raised their family; Joseph Washington, a mill worker at Hemmelburger Harrison in Morehouse where he retired, who married Lottie Spurlin in Morehouse, where they lived until their death and raised their families; Ike, who married Ophia Barker and made their home and later moved to Falfurrias, TX (he was a mechanic in the Ford Motor Company there for many years), then on to the Bells, TX where they raised their families. Grover, who worked at Ford Motors and retired there, married Lydia Knight and moved to Falfurrias, TX, then to Raymondsville, TX, where they raised their families; Albert B. was a twin to Alfred who died at the age of 1-1/2 years. Albert married first May Everett and a son, Joseph, was born. He joined the Navy and married a lady from England, settled in San Diego, CA. He married second Mary Jane (Vanover) Jenkins, daughter of Richard Vanover and Grace Whelchel of Jackson, IL, born Dec. 30, 1904 and died Dec. 3, 1987, and later moved to Scott County, MO.

Albert and Mary Jenkins holding John R. and Jack E. Jenkins.

Children born to this marriage are: Albert Fay, born Aug. 13, 1927 and died April 9, 1984, worked at Ford Motors in Sikeston and later owned his own shop. He was married to Margaret Marie McCormick who died in July 1987. They raised three girls. Francis Richard, born Jan. 13, 1933 and died March 17, 1999. He worked for McKnight and Keaton, Malone and Hyde, Potlatch Inc. where he retired. He married Lillian Hubbard. They had three boys and one girl and lived in Sikeston, MO. He organized a gospel-singing group "Jubileers." He raised his family there.

Jackie Dale, born Dec. 20, 1934 and died November 1999. He worked for Carr Roofing, played guitar, and sang gospel music. He married Lola Mae Burton and raised his family in Sikeston. He had three boys and four girls.

Betty Sue (Jenkins) Long, born Feb. 10, 1937, married Lester Eugene Long (b. Feb. 21, 1927 and died June 1997) in Washington. She was a nurse aide at Sikeston Convalescent Center and retired. Seven children (five boys and two girls) were raised in Scott County, MO.

Albert, as a young man worked for the WPA and helped build the Sikeston Armory. He had an old horse and wagon that he used to haul coal, wood, and corncobs to the folks who needed it for heating their homes.

In years to come he became a minister and pastor for 40 plus years and built the church known for many years as the Community Church of God on Second Street in Sikeston, MO. In the old days he would carry coal and wood down to warm the building before service each night that there was services. It was here a number of ministers were called to preach. Several others started their lives in gospel music, one being their son, who started the Gospel Jubileers involving the family members. *Submitted by Betty Jenkins Long (daughter)*

JONES – Charles Franklin Jones (1896-1978) and Clemmie Agnes (Boze) Jones (1898-1984) came to Missouri in 1935. They settled for a while in New Madrid County then moved to Scott County. Later they bought a farm in Scott County on Highway 91, between Bell City and Morley. Here they remained until their death.

Charles and Clemmie Jones family. Ollie, Ernie, Neva, Floyd, Charles Jr., Imogene and Frank.

Charley was the son of Robert James Jones and Mary Bell (Ross) Jones. Charley's grandparents migrated from Georgia in 1871 and some of them settled in Arkansas. Others moved to Oklahoma and Missouri. One of his grandfathers fought in the Civil War with the Confederate Army. He was captured by the Union soldiers and died in a prison camp.

Clemmie was the daughter of Marshall Boze and Lucy (Whitten) Boze. The Boze family came to Missouri circa 1848. They settled in Oregon County, MO. They originally came from Cornwall and Wales, England. Some of the Boze men served in the Revolutionary War and some fought in the Civil War.

Charley and Clemmie had seven children: Ollie; Ernie; Neva; Floyd (deceased); Charles Jr. (deceased); Imogene and Frank.

Ollie married Roy Eugene Sindle (deceased). He lived in the Hooe Community area. They had seven children: Charles; Jerry; James; Kathy (deceased); Steve; Ronnie and Rena. They lived in Scott County most of their lives.

Ernie married Odessa Miller of Crowder. They lived in Scott County most of their lives. They had six children: Peggy; Larry (deceased); Linda; David; Albert and Brian.

Neva married Robert Willard Harris (deceased) of the Hooe Community area. They later moved to Illinois. They had four children: Patsy; Jane; Nina and Michael.

Floyd (deceased) married Alma Reynolds (deceased) of the Hooe Community area. They later moved to Perkins, MO. They had three children: Carol (deceased), Brenda and Gregory.

Charles Jr. (deceased) married Viola Woods of the Vanduser area. They moved away for a while, but later returned to Scott County. They had four children: Phyllis, Douglas (deceased); Patricia Ann; and Vicky.

Imogene married William Albert Harris (deceased) of the Hooe Community area. They later moved to Illinois. They had three children: Jeannie, Billy and Sharon.

Frank married Evelyn Miller of the Bell City area. They live in Bell City. They had two children, Donna and Pamela.

There was someone from each of the families that served in the service of their country; from WWII to the present day.

JOYCE – Carl was born Carl Thurman Joyce May 5, 1928 to Pearl Lyman and Ruth Ione (Wallace) Joyce in Sikeston. He is the Great-great-great grandson of Robert and Lucinda (Thompson) Joyce who donated and are buried on the land where the Mt. Zion Cemetery in Scott County is located. The Joyce's arrived in Cape Girardeau County along with Robert's grandmother, Hannah (English), who married Edward Joyce in Louisiana, and her family and parents, Thomas and Jane (Wicker) English, on land they obtained and settled on at the time of the Louisiana Purchase.

Carl's father was one of seven children born to Robert James and Bertha Divinity (Mason) Joyce.

The children are: an infant son and daughter who did not survive; Pearl, born Feb. 24, 1904 and died June 7, 1950; Cecil "Ted" born Dec. 2, 1905, married Margaret "Willie" Hamilton, and died Sept. 6, 1968; Opal, born July 26, 1907, married and divorced Bob Robertson of East St. Louis, IL and died Sept. 25, 1971; Ava "Gyp", born Sept. 28, 1909, married Charles Eaker, and died July 4, 1975; and Karl "Rex," born Jan. 10, 1914, married Velda Bridges, and died June 11, 1976. The entire family resided in and raised their families in Sikeston.

Margaret, Carl, Trent, and Bertha Mae Joyce.

Bertha was the daughter of Joshua and Martha E. (Miller) Mason of Morley, MO. She had ten brothers and sisters. They were: Charles J., born July 22, 1877 married Robert's sister, Ida Armenta Joyce, and died Aug. 4, 1914; Edwen F., born Jan. 18, 1878 and died Sept. 3, 1884; James William, born March 19, 1880; Bertha, born Dec. 4, 1881 and died March 7, 1921; Francis Luther, born Dec. 18, 1883 and died Feb. 28, 1900; Issie, born Dec. 31, 1885, married Ralph McCullough and died Aug. 1, 1943 in Leadwood, MO; Reese Franklin, born Jan. 5, 1886, married Luttie Grant, and died June 19, 1956; Lina Jane, born Jan. 1, 1888, married Ernest Minner, and died Aug. 11, 1969; Emory Clinton, born Aug. 11, 1890, married Myrtle Grant, and died March 15, 1968; Pearl W., born Aug. 30, 1893 and Feb. 3, 1894; and an infant boy, born and died Aug. 11, 1895. The majority of these families also resided in Scott County.

Robert had three sisters: Ida, born Sept. 29, 1875 and died Jan. 28, 1951; Mary Ellen, born March 27, 1881, married James Preston Emerson, and died Aug. 20, 1901; and Eunice May, born March 6, 1885, married William Mason and died Aug. 5, 1926. A brother, Thomas Eugene, was born May 17, 1889 and died May 23, 1889. The parents of these were Thomas English and Sarah Ann (Hill) Joyce. He also had a stepsister, Eve Eugenia, born July 1, 1895, married Joseph Robert Abernathy, and lived and died in California in January of 1994. Her mother was Mary Rosella (Spann) who was first married to a Mr. Mills from Kentucky.

Carl attended Sikeston schools and resided with his mother and sister, Bertha Mae. His father left Sikeston when he was a child to work construction and was killed in New Orleans June 7, 1950 in a construction accident. His mother was sick during their childhood and at times the children lived with their grandfather, Robert, and step grandmother, Minnie (Freeze) Joyce, in Chaffee, and with Robert's brother James "Jim" and his wife, Annie, in Vanduser.

On June 6, 1948 Carl married Margaret Marie Miller, daughter of Arlen and Blanche (see story) at the home of the bride in Sikeston. Then on Nov. 29, 1951 Carl, was drafted into the Army and served until Aug. 31, 1953 in Korea. Upon his discharge he returned home and entered the Army Reserve National Guard and served as sergeant over the motor pool until his retirement on May 4, 1988. He was employed by the Missouri Highway Department until he retired in 1989. After that he worked in the family owned business, The Buckner Ragsdale Store /company.

Margaret, born Sept. 2, 1930 in Sikeston, grew up on the family farm just south of Diehlstadt and graduated from Diehlstadt High School in 1948 when she went to work at The Buckner Ragsdale Store then owned by Mr. and Mrs. George Lough. When Mrs. Lough died in 1980 her sister-in-law, Bertha Mae, bought the store and operated until December 1991, when they closed the store.

They are the parents of four children: twin boys, Larry and Garry, born and died March 14, 1954, Caryl Maria (see Thomas V. Hairston), and James Trent, born April 13, 1960, married and divorced Angela Sue Lathum, then married and divorced Theresa Carmack. Trent and Angela are the parents of Brandy Sue, born June 8, 1977. His daughter, Stacy, was born July 28, 1979 to Theresa. He also has a daughter, Brittani, born Sept. 18, 1989 to his partner, Karen Danneger. They reside in St. Louis.

Margaret and Carl are active and well respected members of the community, being involved in various organizations, members of the FUMC, scout leaders, and Margaret was chosen Sikeston's Woman of the Year in 1988. Since their retirement, though Carl has Parkinson's disease, they enjoy travel and are a vital part of their children and grandchildren's lives.

JOYCE – Robert James Joyce was born June 1, 1878 in Scott County, MO, the son of Thomas English and Sarah (Hill) Joyce. Robert attended school in Vanduser and on March 22, 1900 in Scott County, married Bertha Divinity Mason, the daughter of Joshua and Martha Ellen (Miller) Mason. The Joyces lived and farmed in the Vanduser area where they raised a family of five: Pearl Lyman (see story); Cecil "Ted" born Dec. 2, 1905, married Margaret "Willie" Hamilton; Opal, born Aug. 26, 1907; Ava "Gyp" born Sept. 28, 1909 who married Charles Eaker; and Karl "Rex" born Jan. 10, 1914, who married Velda Bridges.

Bob farmed until the 1930s after which he went to work at the roundhouse in Chaffee for the railroad. The Joyces lived on Black Street in Chaffee until Bob's death on Aug. 8, 1949. He is buried in the Old Morley Cemetery.

Bertha passed away March 7, 1921 in Vanduser and is buried in the Old Morley Cemetery. After her passing, Bob married Minnie (Burger) Freeze of Cape Girardeau.

They Joyce's enjoyed life, even though it was a hard life, and their home was the scene of many family gatherings. They attended the Baptist Church at McMullin, and always had a large garden, which they shared with the neighbors and raised chickens and hogs.

JOYCE –Pearl Lyman was born Feb. 24, 1904,

the son of Robert and Bertha (Mason) Joyce in the Richwoods Community in Scott County, MO. The family of seven farmed the Vanduser area for many years. He attended the Hunter and McMullin Schools, and then completed his schooling at Vanduser in 1921, after which he went to work on the farm.

On Jan. 12, 1926 he married Ruth Wallace, the daughter of James Franklin and Ida May (Smith) Wallace in Charleston, MO. They made their home in Sikeston, going to work at the International Shoe Company where they worked for several years. In 1941 Pearl left the shoe factory and went to work in the construction field. He worked on the Alaskan Highway in Canada and around the country, finally ending in New Orleans, LA where he died in a construction accident on June 7, 1950. He is buried in the Sikeston Memorial Park Cemetery. Ruth was born Dec. 16, 1905 on a farm near Blodgett, the oldest of 16 children. Her parents were itinerant farm workers. The children were: Kermit, born Sept. 6, 1907; Dallas, born March 26, 1909; Harold, born July 27, 1910; Cecil, born March 8, 1912; Elvis, born Aug. 25, 1913; Esther and Lester, born Oct. 17, 1915; Margaret, born Jan. 13, 1918; Marvin "Buddy", born Jan. 2, 1920; Helen, born April 18, 1921; Hazel, born May 18, 1922; Junior, born Aug. 5, 1923; Thomas, born July 23, 1925; Leo, born 1927 and Billy, born May 9, 1934.

Pearl and Ruth are the parents of two children, Carl Thurman (see story) and Bertha Mae who was born Nov. 24, 1929 both in Sikeston.

Bertha Mae has never married and lives in the home her parents purchased on Helen Street. She attended school in Sikeston, graduating in 1947. She went to work for the Gristo Feed Company located downtown, next to the Bank of Sikeston and part time at the Malone Theatre. She retired from the feed company in 1980, after which she and her sister-in-law bought the Buckner Ragsdale Store, which they operated until 1990.

Bertha Mae also serves her community in many ways, having been a Girl Scout leader and active in many organizations, such as the American Cancer Society. She is a member of the First United Methodist Church. *Submitted by Bertha Mae Joyce 314 Helen, Sikeston, MO*

KENKEL – Herman Francis Kenkel was born in 1830 to Bernard and Maria Ann (Worsemann) Kenkel. He married Anna Mary Heuring on Jan. 30, 1866 in New Hamburg. They had a son, Bernard (b. Oct. 20, 1867; d. Dec. 12, 1940) and a daughter, Catherine (b. March 11, 1870; d. May 4, 1870). Bernard "Barney" married Rosa Baumann (b. May 14, 1873; d. June 9, 1930) in New Hamburg, MO on April 18, 1893. They had a son, John (b. May 29, 1894; d. May 29, 1894) and a son, Frank (b. April 17, 1905; d. Oct. 6, 1951). Rosa died of elephantiasis in 1930. Barney was a farmer for many years. He lived near New Hamburg until he bought 40 acres near Randles about a year before he died of influenza and heart disease. He is buried in Union Park Cemetery in Chaffee. An article about his death in the *Scott County Democrat* said that he was "a good neighbor and everybody had great respect for him" and the "he always had a true heart for the poor class of people and many a time people who were in need always went to Barney and nevr went away without help."

Frank, who had married Linda Bertha Westrich (b. March 6, 1909; d. Feb. 17, 1989) on April 9, 1929, lived on the family farm near New Hamburg. Frank and Linda had seven children: Bernard, Rose, Paul, Caroline, Doris, Elmer and Lawrence. Bernard died at birth on Jan. 23, 1932. Frank was killed in an automobile collision on

Highway 61 south of Kelso on Saturday, Oct. 6, 1951. His car was hit by another car that swerved out of control. Linda and Paul, who was 15, each sustained a broken arm and cuts. Frank is buried at St. Lawrence Cemetery in New Hamburg. Linda continued to raise her family on the farm, but moved to town in 1973. She died at Miner Nursing Center on Feb. 17, 1989.

Easter1967, Linda Kenkel and children. Doris, Paul, Linda, Larry, Rosie, Elmer, and Caroline.

Elmer married Glenda Schlosser on Aug. 14, 1971. They have three daughters: Michelle, Jennifer, and Julie. Elmer lives near Scott City, but still farms the family farm, which he bought in 1981. The farmhouse, built of hand-hewn logs, was in the process of being dismantled and reconstructed at a new location in 2001. *Submitted by Linda Phillips*

KERN – Jacob Westrich (b. March 7, 1822; d. March 26, 1885) married Katherine Steinmetz (b. Nov. 9, 1833; d. Sept. 21, 1917) on Jan. 11, 1853. Jacob was born in Prussia and Katherine in France. They came to the US prior to 1854. Their children were: Phillip, Catherine, Francis, Jacob, John, Leo, Louis and Joseph. Joseph (b. April 10, 1869; d. May 1952) married Sophia Gosche (b. Jan. 4, 1872; d. Oct. 21, 1927) April 21, 1896 at St. Augustine Catholic Church, Kelso, MO. Their children were: Mary "Mamie" (Scheeter); William "Willie" Kasper died at 11 months of age; Raymond "Cappie"; Johan "Cletus"; Agnes (Glastetter); Paul Theon; Cecilia (Glastetter); Rosalee "Sullie" (Kern); Anna (Glastetter); Michael; Antoinette (Dirnberger) killed in a tragic accident on Highway 61 with her husband and two sons, Gerald and Herman on April 4, 1959.

Aloysius Kern was the son of George Kern and Caroline Grasser. George (b. Sept. 1, 1851; d. March 23, 1927) married Caroline Grasser (b. Aug. 29, 1856; d. Jan. 2, 1926). They had six children: John A., Mary, Frank, Bill (Wibertum), Alyosius and Simon. Aloysius (b. June 2, 1895; d. June 7, 1960) married Rosalee "Sullie" Westrich (b. July 16, 1911) on Sept. 9, 1932 at St. Lawrence Catholic Church, New Hamburg. Al served in the Us Army during WWI as Missouri Private Company 163 Depot Brigade WWI. Al was a carpenter by trade and his wife Rose was a homemaker and an avid bingo player. They are the parents of: Jo Ann; Georgianna (George); Elmer "Cotton"; Robert "Duke"; Barbara "Gin"; Charlene; Carol; Aloysius "Otto" Jr.; and Donald "Donnie". Jo Ann (b. Jan. 8, 1933; d. Feb. 12, 1934 from complications from childhood diseases); George (b. May 7, 1934) married Richard "Curly" Bennett, (Missouri A2C US Air Force) b. Jan. 20, 1943; d. Dec. 19, 1967 from cancer, they were married May 7, 1966 at St. Lawrence; Elmer (b. Feb. 25, 1937) married Patricia "Pat" Landewee (b. June 6, 1942) on Sept. 16, 1962 at St. Ambrose, Chaffee, MO; Robert (b. April 25, 1939) married Rosalee Gloth (b. Jan. 9, 1942) at St. Lawrence July 29, 1963; Barbara (b. Nov. 28, 1940); Charlene (b. Feb. 18, 1943) married Shelby "Skip" Steger (b. April 10,

Bernice and Al Kern family

1960) Feb. 14, 1976 at St. Lawrence; Carol (b. Nov. 5, 1945) married Floyd Klipfel (b. March 26, 1947) July 29, 1967 at St. Lawrence; Aloysius (b. Oct. 13, 1948) married Bernice Landewee (b. Feb. 12, 1952) April 15, 1972 at St. Ambrose Chaffee. Two brothers married two sisters so when the sisters get mad at one anther they claim to be in-laws instead of sisters.

All of the Al and Rose Kern family reside in New Hamburg and attend St. Lawrence Parish and did attend the elementary school there. Two streets in New Hamburg bear the Kern name: Kern Street and Rose Lane.

Bernice and Alyosius had four children: Shawn (b. Aug. 23, 1973) graduated from Southeast Missouri State University, with a BSN degree. He is presently employed as a traveling nurse in Miami, FL. He had practiced in New Jersey, North Carolina, Virginia, West Virginia and Houston, TX. Denitra (b. April 4, 1976) graduated from Southeast Missouri State University with a BSN degree and works for S.E. Hospital, prn, and Visiting Nursing Association. Torey (b. Nov. 11, 1980) is presently a junior attending Southeast Missouri State University majoring n social work. Aloysius "Bradley" III (b. June 4, 1987) is a freshman at Kelly High School.

Aloysius "Otto" was drafted into the US Army Jan. 29, 1969 discharged Jan. 28, 1971. He served during the Vietnam War. While stationed at Fort Leonard Wood, MO he had the privilege of pitching softball against the nationally well known softball team, "The King and His Court." He was known for his softball pitching abilities by area and statewide softball teams. Al has been working for the Chaffee Postal System for 28 years. In his spare time, he enjoys repairing small engine motors and cutting wood. Bernice has been the longest employee of the Riverside Regional Library. She has been serving the people of Benton, MO for 27 years. She is active in community affairs, a 4-H leader and church organist.

KERN – John Adam Kern Sr. (b. 1811; d. Sept. 20, 1865) married Gertrude Eisemann (b. April 15, 1822; d. May 20, 1965). Parents of six children.

First child: Mary Catherine Kern, born 1847 married John Halter (b. Jan. 15, 1845; d. June 5, 1872) on July 28, 1868 in St. Lawrence Church at New Hamburg, MO. He is the son of Mathias Halter and Theresa Martz. They had two children: Mary Theresa Halter (b. July 27, 1868; d. March 1, 1898) married Aloysius Louis Felter on Oct. 19, 1886 at New Hamburg. A farmer in Scott County, he was born Nov. 5, 1863 at Kauffenhiem, Alsace, France, the son of Joseph Felter and Louise Broman. He died Nov. 17, 1918, and is buried in St. Augustine Cemetery in Kelso, MO. Their second daughter, Emma

Gertrude Catherine (Eisemann) Kern Petz, wife of John Adam Kern, Jr.

Halter (b. May 20, 1870; d. Aug. 8, 1871) is buried in St. Lawrence Cemetery at New Hamburg, MO.

Second child: Mary Ellen Kern, born 1848 in Ohio married Bartholomew Schaefer (b. Sept. 23, 1845; d. March 23, 1890), the son of Andreas Schaefer and Mary Ann Volk, on Oct. 24, 1967. They were farmers in Scott County. They had nine children: Mary Catherine Schaefer (b. Nov. 26, 1868; d. Aug. 19, 1873) buried in St. Lawrence Church at New Hamburg, MO; Adam Schaefer (b. May 18, 1872; d. June 13, 1941) married Rufina Schlosser (b. Jan. 7, 1873; d. Oct. 30, 1949) the daughter of John Schlosser and Rufina Steinmetz on Oct. 3, 1893 at Kelso. To this union ten children were born: Coletta Caroline; Mary Matilda; Joseph Eric; Michael E.; Zeno Joseph; Charles Ervin "Peanuts"; Hilda P. (Edward S. Enderle); Zita O. (Joseph Hess); Cora Leona (Peter Seyer) and Eleanora (Fred Enderle). Rosena Rosa Schaefer (b. April 10, 1873; d. Oct. 22, 1948) buried in Lightner Cemetery at Scott City, married Nicholas Robert (b. Sept. 16, 1871; d. Aug. 11, 1894) buried at St. Augustine Cemetery at Kelso; second Ludonus Robert (b. Sept. 1, 1867; d. Oct. 27, 1953) buried in St. Denis Cemetery at Benton, MO; Katharina Marie Schaefer (b. Aug. 25, 1875; d. Sept. 9, 1880) buried at New Hamburg; Louis Schaefer (b. Nov. 16, 1877; d. May 25, 1922) married Sara Philomena Weber (b. Feb. 8, 1882) on Sept. 24, 1901; William Adam Schaefer (b. June 20, 1880; d. Jan. 11, 1946) farmer in Scott County married Josephine Blattel Ourth on April 21, 1924 in St. Ambrose Church at Chaffee, MO; Mary Gertrude Schaefer (b. June 16, 1882; d. June 24, 1883); Frank George Schaefer (b. Feb. 2, 1884; d. July 22, 1956) married Ortha Heisserer on Sept. 9, 1905 at St. Augustine Church in Kelso. The youngest child, Andreas Schaefer (b. Aug. 24, 1886).

Third child: John Adam Kern Jr. (b. Oct. 27, 1849; d. April 20, 1911) married Mary Katherine Hess on July 19, 1880 at Kelso. Four children were born to this union: Victoria Kern married William Corvick; August Otto Kern married Dosha Butler; Katherine Mary Kern married John Frederic Glastetter and Leo Aloysius "Peggy" Kern.

Fourth child: George Kern (b. Sept. 1, 1851; d. March 23, 1927) farmer in Scott County married Caroline Glasser (b. Aug. 29, 1856 in Germany; d. Jan. 2, 1926) in Ohio at the age of 20 years. Both are buried in St. Lawrence Cemetery at New Hamburg, MO. This was a family of ten children: Mary Julia Kern (b. Oct. 25, 1877; d. Oct. 13, 1940) married Adelbert Blattel (b. Oct. 11, 1879; d. March 16, 1955); John Adam Kern (b. Jan. 18, 1883; d. July 5, 1953) married Mary Schitter on Sept. 5, 1905, married second wife, Mary V. Dirnberger, on June 16, 1933; Dennis, Bertha Cornelia, Alvina Caroline George and Oswald all died in infancy or at a young age; Simon never married; William Kern (b. June 24, 1887; d. Oct. 31, 1965) married Bertha K. Schlitt on Aug. 21, 1912. This was a family of five children: Elmer Frank Kern (b. Oct. 13, 1913; d. Sept. 13, 1996) carpenter, married Marie Ellen Morie (b. April 3, 931) daughter of Peter Morie and Cecilia LeGrand on June 29, 1953. Second son, Clarence Simon Kern (b. June 6, 1915; d. Feb. 12, 1992) married Velma Mae Nelson (1931-1982) on Sept. 5, 1953. Both are buried in Rockford, IL. Sylvia Emma Kern (b. Dec. 10, 1919) married Bernard F. Steimle (b. May 29, 1923; d. Dec. 23, 1967 in an auto accident) son of Frank Steimle and Bertha Goshe. Vernita Kern (7 Sept. 1921) married Jesse Hardy Gettings (b. 1914-1989 buried in Union Park Cemetery at Chaffee; William Kern died in infancy. Aloysius Kern (b. June 2, 1895; d. June 7, 1960 of a heart attack) married

Rosalia Anna Westrich (b. July 16, 1911) on Sept. 6, 1932. This is a family of nine children: Joanne Cecelia (b. Jan. 8, 1933; d. d. Feb. 12, 1934) Georgia Anna (b. Nov. 12, 1934); Elmer Joseph (b. Feb. 25, 1937); Robert Harold (b. April 25, 1939); Barbara Jeanne (b. Nov. 28, 1940); Charlene Sylvia (b. Feb. 18, 1943); Carol Ann (b. Nov. 5, 1945); Alyoysius Otto (b. Oct. 13, 1948) married Bernice M. Landewee on April 15, 1972 at St. Ambrose Church in Chaffee, MO and Donald Bernard Kern (b. Nov. 4, 1951).

Fifth child: William Kern (b. March 16, 1859; d. May 31, 1873).

Sixth child: Philip Kern (b. Feb. 26, 1862; d. July 26, 1862). Both William and Philip are buried in St. Lawrence Cemetery at New Hamburg, MO.

KIELHOFNER – Peter Kielhofner was born June 19, 1853 near Alsace-Lorraine, France. His parents were Louis and M. (Goetz) Kielhofner. Peter immigrated to the United States between 1871-1880. He lived with Ignetz Goetz and his family on June 4, 1880, working as a farm laborer in Moreland Township, Scott County, MO. Peter married Catherine Messner in Formosa, Bruce County, Ontario, Canada around 1887-1888. Catherine's parents were Wendelin and Theresa (Helmer) Messner. Catherine was born in Soufflenheim, Alsace, France on April 1, 1864. She immigrated to North America on the ship *Ile de France* in 1887.

Peter and Catherine settled on a farm near New Hamburg, MO in 1888. His occupation was farming. Together, they had ten children: Eugenia Katherine (b. Dec. 5, 1888); Wendelin Louis (b. Feb. 21, 1891); Clotilda Ottilia (b. April 18, 1892); Theodore (b. July 14, 1894); Pauline (b. Dec. 15, 1897); Andrew (b. April 17, 1899); Mary Rosalia (b. Feb. 27, 1901); Charles Leo (b. June 23, 1903) and Rose Josephine (b. March 18, 1908).

Peter and Catherine Messner Kielhofner

On Saturday, July 15, 1911, Peter drowned fishing in the Hubble Creek in Scott County, MO. Peter's sons Wendelin, Theodore and Andrew were on the bank watching the others fish. Peter, Dennis Grasser and son, Leo Morrie, Ed Backfisch and a Mr. Prindle were in the water "hogging" catfish, catching fish with their hands. Peter stepped into a hole in the stream and was unable to save himself. He was buried on Sunday, July 16, 1911 in the St. Lawrence Catholic Church Cemetery in New Hamburg, MO. He was 59 years old and left a wife and nine children behind. *Submitted by Teresa Kielhofner Jansen*

KLUEPPEL – The first Klueppel family to arrive in Scott County was August Joseph and his wife, Mary Augusta Hercules, along with four children: Mary, John, George and Frank. A fifth child, August Jr., was born after the family settled here. In 1901 they came down the Mississippi River on a boat with all their belongings and arrived at Commerce, MO where they loaded the household items onto a wagon.

August and Mary were born in St. Louis, MO. He was the son of John Henry Kluppel who was an immigrant from Prussia, now known as Germany. The family home along with other family members remain today in the village of Dornholthause. In Germany the name is spelled Kluppel and in America it i spelled Klueppel. His

mother, Catherine Dausch, was from Bavaria. Henry migrated to St. Louis around 1852 and became a citizen of the United States in 1856.

Henry and Catherine were married at St. Peter and Paul's Church in St. Louis on Aug. 24, 1854. They were the parents of 14 children. Many of the children died very young or were stillborn. Only four lived to reach adulthood. Two sons, Louis and August, married and raised a family. A daughter, Josephine, lived to the age of 101 years. Another son, Johann, lived to be only 27 years old.

August Klueppel family. Left to Right: George, August , Frank, Mary, John, and Mary (standing in back).

August operated the August Klueppel Grocery located on the corner of Soulard and Seventh Streets in St. Louis. He was both a wholesaler and retailer of grocery, wine, liquor and feeds. This building stands today and currently houses another business. It is believed that the family lived on the second floor above the business. Upon arrival in Scott County, August purchased a farm of 120 acres on the Benton-Oran County Road.

Three of his children; George, Mary and August Jr., remained on the farm until their deaths. George died in June 1969, Mary in March 1981 and August Jr. in March 1993.

Frank married Dorothy Martha Scherer and raised three sons, Frank Jr., Joseph and Charles on a farm just north of Benton on Highway 61. John and his wife, Martha Essner of Benton, returned to St. Louis where he was employed by the postal service. They raised six children, John, Martha, Mary, Josephine, Albert and Cresence.

George and Frank both served in the United States Army during WWI. George remained in the United States and Frank was sent to serve in France.

August had no experience in farming when he arrived in Scott County. He worked hard to learn the latest techniques and was successful in raising various crops that included fruits. August and Mary lived on the farm until their deaths. He died in April 1945 and she died in May 1948. *Submitted by Frank and Carolyn Klueppel*

KLUEPPEL – Frank was born Sept. 22, 1932, the son of Frank and Dorothy Scherer Klueppel. He attended St. Denis Grade School until the 8th grade and graduated from Benton High School in 1951. He grew up on a farm just north of Benton and at a very young age helped the family with the operation of their dairy farm. While in grade school, he would assist with the milking of cows before and after school. In the summer months, he would help with baling hay and the planting and harvesting of the crops.

After graduating from high school, he served in the United States Army from February 1953 to February 1955. He took his basic training at Fort Leonard Wood, MO. After basic training he was stationed at Fork Polk, LA until the unit was transferred to Fort Hood, TX. While in the Army he

Left to right: Frank, Christy holding Abby, Carolyn, Cathy, and Jim.

served as company clerk for Company B of the 35th Engineer Group.

Shortly after returning from service he moved to Cape Girardeau, MO and was employed by Oz-Arc Gas Equipment and Supply as office manager and accountant.

On Nov. 16, 1963 he and Carolyn Eileen Hinton were married. She is the daughter of George Dewey and Eileen Spain Hinton.

In November 1965 they founded Plaza Gifts and Office Supplies. They operated the business until 1988 and, at one time, had locations in Cape, Sikeston and Carbondale. The business was developed into one of the largest office products dealerships in the Midwest. They were also one of the largest Hallmark Card dealers in the St. Louis Region.

They raised three children. James Vincent was born in 1970. He is married to Jennifer Marie Maxwell and they are living in Hillsboro, MO. Jim is employed as an Onshore Resource Analyst for United Van Lines and Jennifer is a Probation and Parole Officer.

Christine Eileen was born in 1973. She is registered nurse working in a St. Louis Hospital. She married Todd Alan Dohogne and they have a daughter, Abigail Christine. They make their home is Eureka, MO. Todd is a computer programmer for Maritz in Fenton, MO.

Catherine Ann was born in 1974. She is an Occupational Therapist working in Jefferson City, MO. She married Michael Alan Best and they make their home in Ashland, MO. Mike is a Tele-Communication Specialist for State Farm Insurance in Columbia, MO.

Frank is now working as an insurance agent. Carolyn is retired. They have traveled throughout the United States, Canada and Mexico. *Submitted by Frank and Carolyn Klueppel*

KLUEPPEL – In 1901, Frank Vincent Klueppel Sr., came to Scott County with his parents, brothers and a sister. He was born April 1, 1894. The family had lived in St. Louis, MO and came down the Mississippi River by boat to start a new life on a farm between Benton and Oran.

In May of 1918 he was inducted into the Army and served with the 313th Engineers in Nice, France during WWI. He returned home in June 1919.

Frank worked several years following the wheat harvest through Kansas, Oklahoma, Nebraska, North Dakota and South Dakota. He worked for a time polishing chrome for an automobile plant in Detroit, MI. He purchased a farm near Swinton, MO. In 1931 he purchased a farm north of Benton along Highway 61.

He and Dorothy Martha Scherer were married in May 1931. She was born Sept. 26, 1902. She was the daughter of Theophil and Mary Glastetter Scherer. Before their marriage, she worked as a stenographer for the Scott County Farm Bureau. Prior to that she was employed as an assistant cashier at the Bank of Benton.

Dorothy earned many ribbons at Neighbor Day for her canned fruits, vegetables, breads and flowers.

Their children: Frank Jr., Joseph and Charles, were born and raised on the farm. Frank Jr. married Carolyn Eileen Hinton and they raised three children: James, Christine and Catherine. Joseph married Irene Bertha Jansen and they raised four children: Robert, John, David and Janet. Charles married Angela Clarissa Kluesner and they raised four daughters: Sondra, Linda, Cheryl and Diane.

Frank and Dorothy (Scherer) Klueppel, Charles, Frank, and Joe.

Living and working on a dairy farm required many long hours as the milking was done twice a day by hand. The cream was separated from the milk and sold. They hauled hay with a team of horses and a wagon. A wood stove provided the heat to keep them warm during the winter months and also served for cooking. They raised all their food and it was canned and stored for the winter. They butchered hogs and cows and the meat was cured and smoked. Dorothy baked homemade bread at least three times a week.

Around 1943 electricity became available. At that time they switched from selling cream to selling milk on a milk route. They bought their first tractor in 1945. In 1948 threes off the farm were cut into logs and hauled to the sawmill where they were cut into lumber to build a new barn. In 1950 a hay baler was added. Milking machines meant they no longer had to milk by hand. A cistern provided water until a well was drilled. The well made it possible for indoor plumbing and supplied water to they dairy barn.

Frank and Dorothy farmed until they retired in 1962 and moved to Benton. They sold the farm to Joe and Irene.

Frank died Dec. 24, 1992 at the age of 98. Dorothy passed away Jan. 15, 1994 at the age of 91. *Submitted by Frank and Carolyn Klueppel*

KOCH – Heinrich Ernst Christian Friedrich "HECF" Koch immigrated to the USA aboard the sailing ship *Bremen*, and arrived in New Orleans on June 13, 1855 from Bremen, Germany. He was born Oct. 31, 1833 in Beulshausen, Kreis Gandersheim, Braunchweig, Germany, the eldest of six known children of the farmer Johann Christian and Johanna Marie Wilhelmine Christiane Koch nee' Kasten. His ancestors had lived in Beulshausen since 1750 when they had moved from nearby Bruchhof parish. His mother was born in Woltershausen, Hannover, Germany in 1813. His father died in 1846 and his mother married Heinrich Andreas Sander who farmed the Koch land.

After arriving in Cape Girardeau, MO, HECF Koch worked at a rock quarry and farmed in Cape Girardeau County. On Dec. 31, 1857, he married Hannah Johanne Caroline Wilhelmine Amalia Soesemann, eldest of four daughters, of Andreas Heinrich Christoph and Wilhelmine Soesemann nee' Steinhoff at Dissen, Cape Girardeau County in a ceremony performed by E. Riedel, Ev. Lutheran Pastor. Christopher had emigrated with his family from the port of Bremen and landed at New Orleans on June 2, 1857 aboard the ship *O'Thyen*. His occupation was listed as linen weaver. Amalia's ancestors were from the area of Sudheim, Hannover, Germany. During the Civil War Christoph is believed to have served the

Union cause under the name Christopher Suesemann. He enlisted Jan. 27, 1862, in Cape Girardeau and was mustered in on Feb. 20, 1862. He served as a private in Company D, 12th Regiment, Missouri State Militia (MSM) Cavalry Volunteers under Captain Flentge. This unit became the 5th Regiment Cavalry MSM where he

Heinrich Ernst Christian Friedrich Koch

served as a Company Cook. He was discharged at Cape Girardeau on Dec. 12, 1863 at the admitted age of 54.

HECF Koch also enrolled at Cape Girardeau on Jan. 27, 1862 likely in the same 12th MSM Cavalry unit as his father-in-law. He subsequently served in Company K, 5th Regiment MSM Cavalry, commanded by Captain William Flentge. He was disabled in October 1863 from an injury sustained when rebels fired on the Scout and his horse fell when jumping a ditch. He was discharged on March 9, 1864 at Rolla, MO. After the war he lived and worked as a laborer in Cape Girardeau. Also, he visited and sought medical care in Germany for a few months.

On Jan. 28, 1868 HECF Koch purchased 80 acres of land in Kelso Township, Scott County. The land was situated on SE Qr. Of the NW Qr. And NE Qr. Of the NW Qr. of Sec. P, Twp 29N R14E. Here he and Amalia farmed and resided until his death on March 2, 1904. Amalia continued to live on the farm until Feb. 25, 1911 when she sold it. On March 7, 1911 she purchased Lots 15 and 16 in Block 7 in Murphy and Wall's addition to Illmo. Amalia died there on Oct. 31, 1912. Both she and HECF Koch are buried in the Eisleben Church Cemetery.

HECF and Amalia Koch were parents of ten known children: Heinrich Christoph Friedrich Wilhelm Koch whose marriages were to Elisa Eifert, who died Aug. 16, 1887, Anna Bretzel who died Aug. 18, 1906, and Susan Angeline Raines nee Teal; Heinrich Christian Koch who married Margareta Rosina "Rosa" Bretzel; Adelheid Anna Minna Catharina Koch who died at an early age; Emma Johnne Wilhelmine Koch who married W. M. Reckewey; Dorothea Marie "Mary" Koch who married Anthony Julius Brennecke; who all died at an early age; Johann Otto Koch/Cook who married Mary Schaefer; and Elda Katharine Elisabeth Koch who married John Eifert. *Submitted by Mary Jean Koch Hitt*

KOCH – Martin Wilhelm Friedrich Koch was born in Kelso, MO Sept. 4, 1884, twin son of Heinrich Christoph Friedrich Wilhelm and Elisa (Eifert) Koch. His twin brother, Johann Heinrich, died at age 1 year, 5 months, and 2 days. Other siblings were Dora Marie Anna Koch (b. Nov. 7, 1882) and Eduard Carl Heinrich Koch (b. June 26, 1887). Eduard died at age 1 year and 7 days. Martin was of German heritage and his grandfather Henrich Ernst Christian Friedrich Koch came to America in 1855 from Beulshausen, duchy of Branschweig, Germany. His grandmother, Johanne Wilhelmine Caroline Amalia Soesemann, emigrated from Sudheim, near Northeim, Hannover, Germany with her family in 1857. His Eifert ancestors came to Scott County around 1852. His grandfather, Johanan Heinrich Eifert, was from Rebgeshain, grand duchy of Hessen, Darmstadt, Germany. His grandmother, Anna Maria Roth, was from Engelrod and Rebgeshain.

On Feb. 5, 1914, Martin married Bessie Estelle Raines, daughter of Joseph J. and Susan Angeline (Teal) Raines. Bessie was born Nov. 3, 1895. Her family came to Scott County from Alexander County, IL between 1900 and 1904.

Martin and Bessie lived in Scott County their entire lives, with the exception of about four years, living near Jacob, IL. They farmed near Kelso, MO, Jacob, IL and north of Commerce, MO purchasing a farm in Sec. 13 Twp 29 R14E in 1947. Martin and Bessie were parents of five children.

Marion C. Koch married Katherine Thelma Miller, daughter of John C. and Bertha (Ash) Miller. Marion worked for the now Southwestern Bell Telephone Company 43 years and was an engineer at retirement.

Joseph O. Koch married Dorothy Lee Doughty, daughter of Harry and Louise Agnes (Meyer) Doughty. Before entering the Army Air Force in 1942, Joe was a lineman for Southeast Missouri Telephone Company. He was serving overseas during WWII at the time of his death Feb. 15, 1944, while on a bombing mission in New Guinea. He was a 2nd Lieut, 499th Bomb Squadron, 345th Bomb Group (M).

Martin Wilhelm Friedrich Koch and Bessie Estelle Raines Koch, 50th wedding anniversary, 1964.

Albert Fredrick Koch married Pauline Vee Carlton, daughter of John T. and Emma (Harris) Carlton. His career was with Southwestern Bell Telephone company 22 years, then organizing a partnership company, Tel Line Inc. serving as president from 1964 to 1981. Albert died Aug. 14, 1985.

Golda Virginia Koch married James Thomas Johnson, son of Thomas F. and Connie Z. (Phelps) Burford Johnson. Farming and Homemaking was their occupation.

Mary Jean Koch married Paul Leroy Hitt, son of Grover Benjamin Leander and Esther Ellen (Snider) Hitt. Farming, a career with the Missouri Division of Employment Security, and secretarial work was their occupation.

The family attended St. Paul United Methodist Church at Commerce. Martin and Bessie celebrated their 50th Wedding Anniversary there in 1964.

After Bessie's death March 1, 1965, Martin sold the home place to Golda and Jim Johnson and moved to Scott City, MO live with his son Marion. Martin died May 3, 1975. Both he and Bessie are buried in Forest Hills Cemetery at Morley, MO. *Submitted by Mary jean Koch Hitt*

LANDIS – Wayne M. Landis was born Dec. 19, 1945 in Madisonville, KY. He is the son of Delmer Landis (1916-1973) and Pearl (Sisk) Landis (1920-1964). Wayne attended first grade in a two-room school at Pleasant Ridge Grade School, Union County, IL. The second through the eighth grades were at Lick Creek Grade School in Union County and he graduated from Anna-Jonesboro High School in 1963. Wayne attended Southern Illinois University at Carbondale, IL for two years. In 1965 he moved to Benton in Scott County, MO.

Bernadette "Bernie" L. Meyer was born Dec. 14, 1946 in Cape Girardeau, MO. She is the daughter of Ben Meyer (1906-1996) and Lorena (Essner) Meyer (1914-1989) of Benton, Scott County, MO. She attended St. Denis Catholic Grade School in Benton, MO for eight years and graduated in 1960. She graduated from Kelly High School, Scott County, MO in 1964.

After four years of dating and engagement, Wayne and Bernie married on Nov. 23, 1968, first in Pleasant Ridge Baptist Church in Union County, IL and some years later they repeated their vows in St. Joseph Catholic Church in Scott City, MO.

Clockwise from left: Tracy, Wayne, Jason, and Bernadette Landis.

From 1966 to 1978, Wayne was employed in various fields of highway construction, and Bernie worked in various local factories. From 1968 to 1972 they lived at 608 R. Main Street, Scott City, MO. In 1972 work took them to Brandon, Pearl County, MS where on Dec. 19, 1973 their first child, a daughter, Tracy Dawn Landis was born in the Baptist Hospital in Jackson, MS. What a great birthday present for her dad. In 1975 the family moved back to Scott City, MO where they bought a home. Work soon took them to Troy in Lincoln County, MO where they lived during the summer construction period. They moved back to Scott City during the winter months. In 1977 the family moved to Potosi, MO still following highway construction, but by the summer of 1978 Bernie moved back to Scott City, pregnant with child. Wayne bought and lived in a 19-foot camper trailer while he finished the 1978 construction season. They had their second child, a son, Jason Ryan Landis born Sept. 19, 1978, in Southeast Missouri Hospital, in Cape Girardeau, MO. In early 1979 Wayne and Bernie bought a small café in downtown Benton, MO just across the street from the County Courthouse. After a year they bought a second café only 150 feet from the first. They owned and operated both café's for a few years and then combined the two into one operation named Bernie's County Seat Café at 211 Winchester, Benton, MO. They are currently in the 24th continuous year of operation at this location. They are known for their homemade pie and homemade kettle beef along with a wide variety of other meals. Their motto is "We haven't sent anyone away hungry in 24 years and we won't let you be the first."

LASETER – Emerson Hill Laseter was born Nov. 21, 1906 at Winfield, AL, and died Dec. 8, 1976, the son of James Ward Laseter and Mary Pannell. He married Aileen Byrd, the daughter of Horace Early Byrd and Pearl Alma Kemp, on July 3, 1938. She was born Oct. 1, 1921 and died Nov. 7, 1973. They had four children: Jerry Earl, born May 21, 1939; Robert Hill, born Aug. 8, 1941; Michael David, born Feb. 13, 1945 and Tamrya Rae, born May 8, 1960.

Emerson farmed in southeast Missouri many years; Aileen worked at the shoe factory and was active in the Miner Baptist Church until her death in 1973 from injuries in a car wreck. Aileen's mother and father were charter members of the Miner Baptist Church.

Emerson and Aileen are buried in the Garden of Memories Cemetery, Sikeston, MO.

LASETER – Jerry Earl Laseter was born May 21, 1939 at Sikeston, MO, the son of Emerson Hill Laseter and Aileen Byrd. He married Rita Jean Lewis on Aug. 12, 1960 at the First Christian Church in Sikeston. She was born Jan. 17, 1942, the daughter of Joseph Earl Lewis and Bessie B. Anderson. They had two children, Jerry Earl, born Dec. 2, 1961 and Rita Jo, born Oct. 10, 1965.

From the time Jerry was very young and living near Brooks Junction where he watched the trains go by, he has been infatuated with trains. In 1956, after he graduated from high school in Sikeston, MO, he attended Union University in Jackson, TN until his enrollment in a Telegraph School in Pueblo, CO. His Uncle Walter Lyons was a telegrapher on the railroad and honed Jerry's skill in telegraphy, thereby enabling him to get a job with the Cotton Belt Railroad as an Agent-Telegrapher in November 1957. Then on June 20, 1960, he was employed by the Missouri Pacific Railroad and later what became the Union Pacific Railroad Company. In 1985 to 1992, Jerry was instrumental in the merging of the Missouri Pacific Railroad with the Union Pacific Railroad, serving in St. Louis as Assistant General Director of the Union Pacific Railroad Company. He retired Feb. 29, 1996 as Director of Transportation, Little Rock, AR.

In 1950, at age 8, Rita's picture was made for a Texaco advertisement, with her horse "Bill" rearing for the photographer, which featured her dad, Joe Lewis and the local Texaco dealer. The advertisement came out in the 1952 February issue of the Farm Journal. As a child she was active in 4-H. She graduated

Jerry E. and Rita (Lewis) Laseter

from the Matthews High School and attended college at Arkansas State at Jonesboro, AR. As an adult she was a homemaker and active in the PTA, the Girl Scouts, served as Secretary of the Junior Babe Ruth Organization, and enjoyed riding and showing horses. She participated many years in the Sikeston Rodeo; first posting flags for the Grand Entry and later on, posting the winners flag for the Coca Cola and Pepsi Corporations. Rita was a member of the Bootheel Archeological Society and had won awards for her archeological finds. She is a member of the King's Highway Chapter NSDAR Daughters of the American Revolution.

Jerry and Rita are members of the First Christian Church in Sikeston, MO. They have two grandchildren: Joseph Scott, age 9 and Layla Laseter, age 2.

LAUCK – Parents of August Vincent Lauck were Bernard "Barney" John and Cecilia (Mattingly) Lauck. Parents of Frances Lauck were Conrad and Mary (Reiminger) Blattel. Barney was the son of Louis and Julia Lauck. He was born Sept. 18, 1850 in Germany. Cecilia was born Dec. 16, 1847 at Perryville, MO, daughter of Leo and Theresa (Miles) Mattingly. Leo was the son of James and Catherine, and grandson of William Mattingly Sr. He was born about 1741. His mother was Anne (Manning), daughter of John and Anastasia (Ormsby).

Conrad Blattel was born to George (b. March 19, 1817 in Nassau, Germany; died Sept. 18, 1874) and Anna Marie (b. 1820; d. Oct. 15, 1861). Cecilia was a descendant of William, born about 1741 in Maryland, and died in 1819. Ignatius was born in 1704 in Maryland, and died 1789. Thomas II was born in 1650 in England and died in 1714 in Maryland. Thomas I was born in 1630 in England and died in 1664 in Maryland.

Children of A. V. and Frances Lauck were: Bertha Lorene; Oscar Simon; Leo Barney; Anthony John; Marcus Vincent; Monroe Henry; and Augusta Lucille.

August Vincent was born Aug. 18, 1879 at Perryville, MO.

He married Anna Frances Blattel Nov. 25, 1903 at St. Augustine's Church in Kelso, MO. He died March 5, 1973 in Cape Girardeau, MO. He is buried at Oran, MO.

Anna Frances was born Jan. 21, 1882 at Kelso, MO and died May 16, 1980 at Cape Girardeau, MO. She is buried at Oran, MO. *Submitted by Dorothy Dees*

LAWRENCE – Alexander "Alec" and Addison "Addie" Lawrence were brothers, sons of John Butler Lawrence, an emigrant from England, and Sarah Jane Davis Stone, a widow. Both were born in southern Illinois at Karber's Ridge near Rosiclare; Alec on Dec. 4, 1877 and Addie on April 21, 1879. They spent their lives together. Alec married Izora Sneed and Addie married Ethie Patton, a niece of Izora. Alec and Izora had no children. Addie and Ethie had five children: Nigal (1907-1909), Fay Loretta (1910-1955, married Elmer Sanders), John Thanet (1911-1974, married Georgia Lee Miller), Emal Coil (1914-1983, married Marcella Albers) and Guy Vernon (1918-1980, married Frances Young and then Dorothy Powell). Alec and Addie moved to southeast Missouri about the turn of the century to cut ties for railroad tracks. They cut the cypress and then farmed a homestead at Yarboro in northeastern Arkansas near Blytheville. Alec and Addie returned to Missouri in 1927. Addie purchased 80 acres on the Ditterline Ditch and lived there until Ethie died. He sold the place and moved to the Dodge place in Commerce and rented that farm for several years. He then purchased half of Alec's 80 acres south of Commerce on the inside of the levee and the two brothers farmed together. Ethie died Aug. 25, 1932, Alec died May 28, 1971, Addie died March 11, 1974, and Izora died Sept. 26, 1973. Their only descendants living at this time in southeast Missouri are Kenneth Vernon Lawrence and Bruce Allan Lawrence of Sikeston, sons of Vernon and Dorothy Lawrence, and their families.

LAWRENCE – John Thanet Lawrence (b. Aug. 18, 1911; d. Sept. 3, 1974) and Georgia Lee Miller (b. April 22, 1913) were married Jan. 26, 1935 in Commerce. John T. was born in Catron, Stoddard County near Sikeston, the son of Addison Lawrence (b. April 21, 1879; d. March 11, 1974) and Efie Patton Lawrence (b. Nov. 8, 1888; d. Aug. 25, 1932) who came from Karber's Ridge in southern Illinois. His parents homesteaded near Yarbro, AR for several years before moving to a farm south of Commerce in 1927. Georgia Lee was born near Illmo (now Scott City), the daughter of Henry David Miller (b. Oct. 26, 1885; d. July 29, 1963) and Laura Anna Koch Miller (b. Sept. 20, 1888; d. Oct. 28, 1954) who were both born in Scott County.

John T. completed high school in Benton in 1930. He received a B.S. from Southeast Missouri State College in 1940 and a M.Ed. from the University of Missouri in 1943. Immediately after completing high school, John T. began teaching in a one-room school in Rockview at the age of 19. He then taught in Commerce, Cardwell and Potosi before becoming high school principal at Bell City. He was superintendent of schools at Bell City, Hornersville, and Bloomfield from 1942-1962. Subsequently he worked with the State Department of Education in Jefferson City until he retired in 1973. He was a 32-degree Scottish Rite Mason and Worshipful Master of the Bloomfield Masonic Lodge.

Lawrence family, 1947. John Thanet, Addison Lee, John Miller, and Georgia Lee (Miller) Lawrence.

Georgia Lee attended grade school at the Macedonia School from 1918-1926 and, after several years' absence, attended high school in Commerce and then Benton where she was graduated in 1933. She worked as a secretary. She was Worthy Matron of the Bloomfield Chapter of the Order of the Eastern Star and Noble Grand of the Rebekah Lodge in Bloomfield. She has resided in Tampa since 1979.

Their older son, Addison Lee, was born Dec. 19, 1935 in Cape Girardeau. He was graduated from Bloomfield High School in 1953, and received his B.S. from Southeast Missouri State College in 1956 and his M.A. and Ph.D. from the University of Missouri in 1958 and 1962 respectively. He taught one year at Westminster College (1962) and then at the University of Houston (1964-1979). Since 1979, he has been Director of the Texas Agricultural Experimental Station and a professor in the Department of Wildlife and Fisheries Science at Texas A&M University where he is a Regent Professor. He is a world authority on the aquaculture of shrimp.

Their younger son, John Miller, was born Oct. 11, 1937 in Cape Girardeau. He was graduated from Bloomfield High School in 1955 and received his B.S. from Southeast Missouri State College in 1958, his M.A. from the University of Missouri in 1960, and his Ph.D. from Stanford University in 1966. He was awarded the title *Docteur honoris causa de la Universite' de la Medite'rrane'e (Aix-Marseile II)* in 2000. He has been a professor in the Department of Biology at the University of South Florida since 1965. He is a marine biologist specializing in echinoderms. *Submitted by John Lawrence*

LEE – Charles Andrew Lee (b. March 29, 1908; d. Oct. 5, 1977) was born in Chaffee and married Elnora Seabaugh (b. Feb. 18, 1914). Charles is the son of Edward H. Lee (b. December 1886; d. Jan. 11, 1931), born in Olney, IL and married Pauline May Klein (b. December 1887; d. July 6, 1932). Edward is the son of George Lee and Lucinda Decker. Edward had seven children and George had 11 children.

Charles and Elnora had four children born in Chaffee. Shirley Jean Lee (b. Feb. 23, 1932) single. She moved to St. Louis in 1951 after graduating from Chaffee High and worked at small loan companies, as a stockbroker, at asphalt pav-

ing company, and Dow Chemicals. She retired from Dow in 1988, and continued working until late 1995. She moved back to Chaffee in 1999.

Charles and Elnora Lee

Charlene Lee Horton (b. May 10, 1934) worked at Bank of Chaffee and GFC Loan. She married Carroll L. Horton April 16, 1955. They reside in Lexington, KY and have three children: Vicki Lynn Whitehead, Lee Sanders Horton, and John Allen Horton.

Charles G. Lee "Sonny" (b. Nov. 3, 1935) married Margie Lee Miller (Marble Hill). They have three children: Michael Charles Lee, Cathy Sue Graham and Sandra Michelle Bogle. Sonny runs a garage and wrecker service in Chaffee.

Ronald Wayne Lee (b. Nov. 7, 1946) married twice, no children. He runs a garage outside Chaffee.

Charles farmed most of his life, also worked on WPA and helped build Chaffee swimming pool. Also worked on an oil pipeline, as a bartender, a butcher a Groser Shy. He was also a substitute mail carrier for John Metz. Elnora worked at Thorngate for 35 years. Charles also lived in Harrisburg, AR and traveled to Chaffee in a covered wagon. *Submitted by Shirley Lee, daughter of Charles Lee*

LEE – Edwin Jean Lee Sr. was born in Swinton, MO Jan. 24, 1941. At the age of 6 years, his parents, Jimmie and Sylvia Morris Lee, moved outside of Commerce on the Lee Tull's farm. Edwin has five sisters and one brother. On July 14, 1961 he married Delores Faye Knight, born Jan. 5, 1944, daughter of Roy Lee and Isabelle Knight; she has four brothers and one sister. Delores and Edwin live in Commerce, MO. Edwin Sr. is a Captain on the M/V Sheryl owned by Luhr Bros. Construction. Delores is a homemaker.

They are the parents of four children: Edwin Gene Lee Jr. married Sharon Roth and they live in Scott City with their two children, Ashley Nicole Lee and Shawn Christopher Lee.

Edwin J. Lee Sr. family

Brenda Kay Lee married Douglas Morton, and they live in Lakeside, CA. They have three children: Jessica Leigh Morton, Michael Terry Morton (deceased) and Jeffrey Douglas Morton.

Timothy Scott Lee married Rosa Marie Griffith, and they live in Cape Girardeau, MO. They have four children: David Van Pelt; Megan Ann Lee; Tammie Marie Lee and Brooke Michelle Lee.

Barbara Helen Lee married Jarrett Michael Burger, and they live in rural Scott City, MO. They have four children: Heather Danielle Burger; Whitney Paige Burger; Madison Nicole Burger and Hunter Michael Burger.

LEGRAND – The LeGrands in Scott County all descend from two brothers, Nicholas and Henry J. LeGrand, who came to the US in 1846 from Ster, commune Francorchamps, Belgium. They arrived at New York and then went to Massillon, Stark County, OH a few years before coming to New Hamburg, MO.

Henry J. LeGrand was born Feb. 8, 1795 and married in 1818 Mary Ann Collin. They came to Scott County in 1849 with their five children: John; J. Francis; Hubert J.; Teresa; and Mary Josephine. John married Barbara Job, but died during the Civil War leaving no known descendants. J. Francis married Mary J. Charlier. His biography is in *Goodspeed's History of Southeast Missouri, 1888.* Their children were: Louis (married Mary Hakes); Nicholas (married Regina Westrich); Mary (married Adam Dirnberger) and Leo (married Mary Dirnberger). Hubert J. LeGrand married Catherine Bucher and their eight children were: Teresa (married Simon Reiminger); Elizabeth (married Andrew Menz); Louise (married Anton Amrhrin); Rosalia (married Balthazar Menz); Anton (married Susanna Essner); Magdalena (married William Essner); Louis A. (married May Scherer); and Katherine (married Louis Gangel). Teresa LeGrand was married in 1852 to Nicholas Hess (born 1812 in Belgium). Mary Josephine LeGrand was married in 1850 to Diece Donne Charlier, also from Belgium. Henry J. died Jan. 17, 1858 and Mary Ann died Aug. 29, 1867.

There is no evidence that Nicholas LeGrand survived to come to Missouri, as the early Scott County land records are in his wife's name. Nicholas LeGrand was born June 26, 1784 at Ster and married Marie Jeanne Quirin Jean. Their children were: Peter, Michael, and Mary Ann, who was married in 1858 to Jacob Jelan.

Peter LeGrand, born May 3, 1822 at Ster, died in Scott County in 1899. He married first Catherine Jango and had three children: Leo (married Palina Sledge); August (married Millie Cox); and Mary. In 1870 he married Josephine Boyer and had five children: Julia (married Oswald Kapfer); Margaret (married Oswald Kapfer); Frank (married Anna Lee Schanks) and Annie.

Michael LeGrand was born Feb. 22, 1825 at Ster and was married at New Hamburg Feb. 16, 1860 to Angeline Dumey (b. Aug. 18, 1843) also from Ster, daughter of John H. Dumey and Mary Ann Dohogne. Twelve children were born to them, and ten survived. Mary married John Welter. Josephine was Frnk Heisserer's first wife. Louise married George Heisserer and second Joseph Dohogne. Kate went to San Francisco, survived the earthquake of 1906 and later married Guy Conklin. The six sons of Michael and Angeline were: Emil, Frank, John, Joseph, William and George. Emil moved to the Oklahoma Territory in the 1890s and died unmarried. Frank married Rosa Diebold; John married Magdalena Scherer; William married Lucy Grojean; and George married Edith Witt. Michael LeGrand was in the Home Guard during the Civil War and died Dec. 17, 1890. His beloved Angeline survived until Aug. 5, 1908.

My grandfather, Joseph LeGrand, was born Oct. 2, 1868 decided to leave the hills of New Hamburg for the flatlands. In 1896 he married Clara Witt and settled on the first farm south of present day Chaffee. John Witt,

Clara Witt and Joseph LeGrand

Clara's father, owned most of the land where Chaffee is and sold it to the Chaffee Development Corp in 1905. Joe and Clara's three children were: Steve, Edith and Cornelius. Steve married Ruth Sandefur and their only daughter, Imogene, married Cornelius Heisserer. Edith married Russell Gibson. Joseph LeGrand died Jan. 4, 1947 and Clara died April 7, 1939.

My father, Cornelius LeGrand, was born Sept. 27, 1909 and was married May 14, 1942 to Christine King (b. Feb. 16, 1910) at Thebes, IL. Their four children are: Joanne, Bob, Larry and Bill. Joanne lives in Chaffee. Bob is an avid genealogist and researched the family origins in Belgium in 1970 after visiting Francorchamps. Larry married Evelyn Harbison and their son is Jason. Bill married Teresa Duff and their children are: Natalie, Stephen and Valerie. Natalie is married to Chris Dittmer and they have a daughter, Anna. *Submitted by Bob LeGrand*

LETT – Thomas Harddie Lett Jr. was born April 12, 1924 in St. Louis, MO. His parents were Thomas Hardy Lett Sr. and Evelyn Pauline Miller. Thomas Hardy Lett Sr. was born Nov. 13, 1892 in Bertrand, MO and died June 5, 1961 in Mt. Carmel, IL. He married Evelyn Pauline Miller, daughter of Sylvester Glynn Miller and Lucenda Sefried on July 15, 1923. Evelyn Pauline Miller was born March 19, 1898 in Mill Sholes, IL and died Sept. 7, 1979 in Cape Girardeau, MO. Thomas Sr. and Evelyn are buried in Memorial Park, Cape Girardeau, MO.

Thoms Harddie Lett Jr. was the only child of

Thomas H. and Mary Lou Lett

Thomas Sr. and Evelyn. Thomas Harddie Lett Jr. married Mary Lou Caldwell, daughter of Earnest Caldwell and Edith Lightner, on Dec. 14, 1952 in Piggott, AR. She was born June 17, 1927 in Cape Girardeau, MO. Children of Thomas Jr. and Mary Lou are: Thomas Hardy Lett III, born Aug. 2, 1953 in Cape Girardeau, MO. (He died of cancer Jan. 7, 1994 in Cape Girardeau, MO); Scarlett Lynn Lett, born July 6, 1957 at Cape Girardeau, MO. (She married Henry Charles Puls, June 11, 1983 in Cape Girardeau, MO); Charles, born Sept. 24, 1959 in Cape Girardeau, MO; Paul Allen Lett, born Oct. 30, 1967 at Fort Belvoir, Fairfax County, VA. He married Dina Marie Dempsey-Santos, child of Mitchell and Diane Santos, Aug. 3, 1998 in Fort Walton, FL. She was born May 6, 1977 in St. Maries, ID. Selina Marie Lett, born Oct. 26, 1999, daughter of Paul and Dina Lett.

Military service: enlisted U. S. Navy, July 1942, V-5 Program Cadet. Kirksville, MO Civilian Pilot Training, received Pilot License 1942. Pre-Flight School, Iowa University, Iowa City, IA. Primary Flight Training, 1943, Hutchison, KA. Instrument Training and Advanced Training, Corpus Christi, TX and Kingsville, TX. Received Wings and Commission as Ensign November 1943, Corpus Christi, TX. Fighter Pilot Training, Sanford, FL. Feb. 10, 1944 crashed in a F-4-F at an outlying field. February-April 1944, Jacksonville, FL Naval Hospital, April – Brooklyn Naval Hospital,

Averell Harrison Hospital, NY, Sea Gate Convalescent Hospital, Brooklyn, St. Allens Naval Hospital, Long Island. November 1945 retired U. S. Navy.

LETT – Thomas LaFayette Lett, born July 8, 1871, Bertrand, MO; died April 7, 1944, Bertrand, Mississippi County, MO, married second on July 4, 1911 to Minnie Evelyn Golightly, born Feb. 13, 1877, Charleston, MO, died March 16, 1977. Children:

Martha Virginia Lett, born April 1, 1912, Bertrand; died Sept. 2, 1996, Sikeston, married Richard Otto DeWeese.

Robert Anthony Lett, born Nov. 22, 1913, Bertrand, married Jean Scott. Children: Robert Anthony Lett Jr., Richard Lett, David Lett, Fred Lett.

Evelyn Marie Lett, born Oct. 15, 1915, Bertrand, died June 1989, Granite City, IL, married Lindell Patrick. Children: Bruce Wilson Patrick and Sharron Ann Patrick.

John Lett, born Sept. 6, 1917, Bertrand, died June 18, 1992, Memphis, TN, married Rose Marion Stallings. Children: Mary Evelyn Lett, Demaries "Debbie" Lett, Lynda Lett.

June Elizabeth Lett, born June 21, 1919, Bertrand, married Melvin A. Couch. Children: Jane Lett Couch, Betty Lou Couch, Tandy Couch.

Mary Jane Lett, born July 18, 1921, Bertrand, married Charles J. Lucas. Children: George J. Lucas, Marilyn J. Lucas, Charles J. Lucas Jr.

Hattie Nell Lett, born May 22, 1923, died Sept. 7, 1931.

Leota Lucille Lett, born Nov. 25, 1926, Bertrand, married on Aug. 26, 1943 at Charleston, MO to William Wesley Jackson. Children: William Lett Jackson, born July 16, 1944, Sikeston and Elizabeth Lett Jackson, born March 11, 1959, Cape Girardeau.

Thomas Ann Lett, born Jan. 27, 1930, Bertrand, married Wilford Stanley Britt. Children: Thomas Ann Britt and Jane Stanlee Britt.

LEWIS – Joseph Earl Lewis was born Dec. 23, 1907 at Dulaney, KY and died July 7, 1980, the son of William Zephaniah Lewis and Dealy Eller Tirey. He married Bessie B. Anderson, on April 9, 1929. She was born April 3, 1909 and died Oct. 1, 1985. She was the daughter of Henry Orson Anderson and Carrie Pinetta Bonnell. They had four children: Shirley Joe (born and died June 1935); Larry Joe (b. Aug. 8, 1937); Rita Jean (Jerry Laseter) (b. Jan. 17, 1942); and Judith Kay (Jim Carins) (b. Dec. 18, 1947).

During their younger years Joe and Bessie

Bessie (Anderson) and Joe Lewis

lived on Murray Lane in Sikeston. While Joe worked for the Standard Oil Company, Bessie worked at the Sikeston Shoe Factory. When his father Zeph, retired from farming, they moved to the farm south of Sikeston, MO, where they continued the farming operation over 44 years, retiring in 1979. Joe was known to be one of the best farmers in southeast Missouri. He raised cotton,

soybeans and corn. His crop yields were consistently high. Over 100 Bu. Corn was raised before irrigation systems were part of farming. He also raised Hampshire hogs, Hereford Cattle, lespedeza and alfalfa hay.

Joe served on the Fairview School board and was instrumental in the organization of the Fairview 4-H Club. He also bought and sold several farms, owned real estate in Sikeston and Miner, MO, and owned stock in the Sikeston Gin Company. Joe enjoyed fishing and hunting and made many trips to Iowa to hunt Pheasant.

In 1950, with support from the Texaco Company, Joe put together three individual Vetch planters on a crossbar behind his Allis Chalmers C tractor, thereby saving time, labor and fuel. He could plant 40 acres a day. It was a time when Vetch was planted between the cotton middles, to put Nitrogen back into the soil and for soil cover. The Texaco Company featured Joe with his idea and the local Texaco distribution man, Barney Cunningham, in a full page Texaco ad, in the February 1952 issue of the Farm Journal.

Bessie was active in the Fairview Extension Club, taught school at Fairview and took US Census as well as serving with Joe as voting judges. Bessie raised a few chickens for family use and she enjoyed sewing and gardening, both flowers and vegetables. Both Joe and Bessie belonged to a Canasta club where they enjoyed their many friends. She worked for the J. C. Penny Company many years and in July 1966 Bessie was voted the "Friendliest, Most courteous Woman Employee" in Sikeston, MO, sponsored by *The Daily Standard*. Later Bessie co-owned and operated a dress shop called Mode O Day in the Mid Towner Village Shops. She was also a member of the King's Highway Chapter NSDAR Daughters of the American Revolution.

Joe and Bessie were long time members of the First Christian Church in Sikeston and are buried in the Garden of Memories Cemetery, Sikeston.

LEWIS – William Richmond Lewis was born May 10, 1905 at Dulaney, KY and died on Feb. 24, 1985. He was the son of William Zephaniah Lewis and Dealy Eller Tirey. He married his wife, Thelma Jane McCarver, on Jan. 17, 1924. She was born July 20, 1905 and died Feb. 1, 1965. They had three children together: Martha Jane (Ralph Boyer), Helen Janet (Veryl Riddle) and William Richmond Jr.

William Richmond Lewis and Thelma Jane McCarver probably met at Dogwood School, which they both attended. Richmond graduated from the 8th grade and Thelma from the 10th grade.

After W. R. "Rich" Lewis and Thelma Jane Lewis were married in January 1924 in East Prairie, they first lived and farmed between

Thelma Jane McCarver and William Richmond Lewis, 1923.

Matthews and East Prairie near the "Yellow Dog" community. During the Mississippi River flood of 1927 they lost everything, including their house. In 1928 they were fortunate to move to the Corrigan Farm across from the Fairview School south of Sikeston on the Sikeston Ridge. All three children were born in this house. Martha Jane on June 21, 1928; Helen Janet on April 27, 1934 and William Richmond Lewis Jr. on Nov. 15, 1937.

Mr. Lewis made several good crops with mules

and also threshed neighbor's crops with a steam-powered engine.

In 1937 when tractors became available Mr. Lewis opened an Allis-Chalmers Farm Equipment dealership in Sikeston and also traded for a 400-acre farm on the western outskirts of Sikeston, where the family moved in 1941. In 1943, not being able to get anything to sell because of WWII Mr. Lewis sold the Allis-Chalmers dealership to E. P. Coleman Jr. Mr. Lewis later had an Allis-Chalmers dealership in Dexter and also New Madrid in partners with Roy Shelby. He was a pioneer in irrigation and dug the first well in 1954. He also introduced the chisel plow to southeast Missouri with a group of local investors was instrumental in drilling the first and only oil well ever drilled in Scott County.

Mr. Lewis retired from farming in 1967 and sold

William R. and Thelma Jane Lewis with children: Martha Jane, Helen Janet, and William R. Jr.

the farm equipment store shortly afterward.

Mr. Lewis was a member of Masonic Lodge #310 of Sikeston and was a 32-degree Shriner Moolah Temple and was an active member of the Southeast Missouri State University Shrine Mounted Patrol. He was a member of the First Christian church of Sikeston. Rich Lewis bought a place in Ft. Meyers, FL and died there Feb. 24, 1985. He is buried in Garden of Memories Cemetery in Sikeston.

Thelma Jane was a homemaker. She enjoyed sewing and gardening, both flowers and vegetables. She won many ribbons for her flower arrangements at Garden Club activities. She served many years as a Grey Lady at the hospital. She was a very active member of the First Christian Church.

William R. Lewis in Shrine Patrol uniform

Thelma Jane Lewis was murdered at her home Feb. 1, 1965 and is buried in Garden of Memories Cemetery in Sikeston, MO.

LEWIS – William Richmond Lewis Jr. was born Nov. 15, 1937, in New Madrid County at home across from the old Fairview School.

He moved with the family to Scott County west of Sikeston in 1941. Mr. Lewis attended South Grade School and graduated from the former Sikeston High School on Tanner Street in 1955.

While in high school, Bill Lewis participated in football, playing some quarterback and full time defensive safety. He was co-captain of the undefeated 1954 Sikeston Bulldogs.

Bill Lewis enrolled in the University of Missouri at Columbia in the fall of 1955, then transferred to University of Mississippi in Oxford. In 1956 he

went back to the University of Missouri for another year.

In the spring of 1957 Mr. Lewis rented 80 acres south of Sikeston. 1957 was one of the most wet years on record and he lost the whole crop.

Disgusted with college and farming and broke, Mr. Lewis joined the Missouri National Guard in March 1958 and spent 6 months active duty in Fort Leonard Wood, MO and Fort Ord, CA. While at Fort Leonard Wood, Bill Lewis made the highest score in the training regiment of 1200 men on the rifle range and received a 3-day pass, which was greatly appreciated at the time. He remained in the Missouri National Guard for 5-1/2 years.

William R. Lewis, Jr.

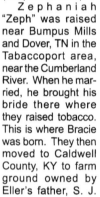

Meredith Jane (Lewis) MacAulay and William R. Lewis III.

In 1959, Bill Lewis rented the 400-acre "home place farm" from his father and farmed for the next 35 years. He retired in 1994 after having back surgery. He also bought a hill farm in 1973 and raised cattle before selling the ranch in 1986.

On Aug. 10, 1966 William Richmond Lewis Jr. married Kristin Meredith Dahlby in Groton, CT, whom he had met while she was attending Southeast Missouri State University in Cape Girardeau. They were divorced on May 24, 1982.

Two children were born of the marriage, William Richmond Lewis III on March 20, 1967 and Meredith Jane Lewis on Oct. 27, 1970. William Richmond Lewis III is now living in Hilo, HI. Meredith Jane married John MacAulay and they live in Sydney, Australia.

In 1959, Bill Lewis became involved in politics and served as, Democrat Committeeman, Richland Township, Chairman of Scott County Democrat Committee and Chairman of the 8th Congressional District Democrat Committee.

In 1965, Bill Lewis was appointed an honorary Colonel of the staff of Governor Warren E. Hearnes. In 1968, Mr. Lewis was appointed by Governor Hearnes to Judge of the Scott County Court 1st District to fill a vacancy.

Bill Lewis worked in Jefferson City from 1977 until 1981 in the administration of Governor Joseph P. Teasdale, serving as Deputy Director of the Missouri Department of Agriculture.

William R. Lewis Jr. is a lifetime honorary member of the Sikeston Jaycees, American Legion Boosters Club Post 114, Fraternal Order of Eagles Aerie 3319 and Charter Member Elks Lodge #2319.

Bill Lewis is also a member of Sikeston Masonic Lodge #310 and the First Christian Church of Sikeston. He lives in Sikeston.

LEWIS – William Zephaniah Lewis was born Jan. 27, 1871 in Stewart County, TN and died Sept. 18, 1942 in Sikeston, MO. He was the son of James Lewis and Josephine Earle Harris Williams Lewis. He married Dealy Eller Tirey on Dec. 23, 1894. She was born March 14, 1877 in Hopkins County, KY and died Dec. 27, 1961 in Sikeston, MO. She was

the daughter of Samuel Jackson Tirey and Martha Purdy Tirey. To this union seven children were born: Harmon Bracie Lewis (b. March 31, 1896); Thomas Jefferson Lewis (b. September 1899); Ruby Lewis Ralph (b. Feb. 7, 1901); William Richmond Lewis (b. May 10, 1905); Joseph Earl Lewis (b. Dec. 23, 1907); Virginia Mabel Lewis Wallace (b. Jan. 24, 1911) and Marie Lewis McGill (b. April 17, 1915).

Zephaniah "Zeph" was raised near Bumpus Mills and Dover, TN in the Tabaccoport area, near the Cumberland River. When he married, he brought his bride there where they raised tobacco. This is where Bracie was born. They then moved to Caldwell County, KY to farm ground owned by Eller's father, S. J. Tirey. This is where Tom and Ruby were born. They then moved to Delaney Gap, KY to raise tobacco and other crops. This is where Richmond and Joseph were born. The family then moved to New Madrid County near the "Yellow Dog" area, which he always referred to as "White Oak Ridge." This is where Mae and Marie were born, and where Zeph had a farming operation. Zeph farmed until the flood of 1927. They then moved to Sikeston Ridge to a farm rented from Joseph Matthews. Here he farmed until c.a. 1934, turning the farming operation over to one of his sons, and bought a farm east of Sikeston and a little south of Bertrand. He lived here about a year, until his health failed. He then sold that farm and bought a house at 219 East Kathleen Street in Sikeston, MO, where he lived until his death.

The story is told that the reason for William Zeph Lewis moving to southeast Missouri from Kentucky is that he wouldn't agree to sell his tobacco to the large tobacco companies at their offered price. He preferred to market his own tobacco. In the middle of the tobacco crop year, what were then called "Night Riders" came and rode their horses through their tobacco field and destroyed the crop and recommended that he leave the area.

Eller was a housewife and wonderful grandmother and lived to be 84. A story told on "Grandma Lewis" was: when the first time she saw the Aurora Borealis or Northern Lights, she dressed her children in their Sunday best and awaited what she thought was the Coming of the Lord and the end of the

William R., William R. Jr., and William Zephania Lewis

Samuel Jackson Tirey, father of Dealy Eller (Tirey) Lewis, and a scout in Co. A, 8th Regiment Johnson's Commandery of the Confederate States Army.

Dealy Eller (Tirey) and Willaim Zephania Lewis.

world. Eller's father, S. J. Tirey served as a Scout in Company A 8th Regiment in Johnsons Commandery of the Confederate States Army. After the Civil War, he was paroled at Paducah, KY and took an oath of allegiance to the government of the United States of America.

Zeph and Eller are buried in the Memorial Park Cemetery in Sikeston, MO.

LOGEL – Ignatius Logel and his wife Julia Ann (Halter) Logel were born in 1828-1830 in Schirrhein, Alsace, France. They emigrated to New Hamburg, Scott County, MO in 1852. Their eldest children were Charles Sr. and Josephine Logel. Ignatius' trade was a schoolteacher who turned to farming. Ignatius helped in the building of St. Lawrence Church in New Hamburg with his labor and money.

Donald L. Logel and mother, Alvina (Thomas) Logel, September 1950.

On Aug. 11, 1862, Ignatius volunteered in the 29th Missouri Infantry Volunteer Regiment as a private and served in the Union Victory of the siege at Vicksburg, MS. He served until June 12, 1864, when he marched in the Grand Army of the Republic in Washington, D.C., where he was discharged. Around 1875 he and his family moved to Kelso, Scott County, MO, where he is listed as one of the founding fathers of St. Augustine Church.

Ignatius' son, Charles Logel Sr. married Louise (Felden) Logel in Kelso. They had six children. Charles Sr. died at age 41 when he was accidentally shot in the leg while hunting. He left his wife Louise and six children, of whom the oldest was Charles Logel Jr., age 12 years. His wife, Louise (Felden) Logel, assumed his business, a restaurant and butcher shop. She was a very good businesswoman and the business thrived.

Louise Logel owned the first local phone company in Kelso and sold her interest to emerging larger county systems. When she died, she left much more than her husband had left her. Louise and her son, Frederic Logel, ran the Kelso, MO post office for some 30 years total.

Her son, Charles Logel Jr. married Alvina (Thomas) Logel in 1904 in Kelso, MO. Alvina was the daughter of Matthias Thomas of Kelso, MO, who was a one time State Representative, County Judge and Justice of the Peace, besides being a grain merchant in Kelso and Ancell, MO. Louise (Thomas) Logel's mother was Madgelena Diebold Dumey. Charles Logel Jr. and his wife, Alvina, and five children moved to St. Louis, MO in 1922; where their last child, Donald Logel, was born. Charles Logel Jr. and his wife, Alvina Logel, are buried in Calvary Cemetery in 1941 and 1975. Of their six children, only two remain: Valeria Roy and Donald Logel, both of St. Louis. Logel relatives now live in Cape Girardeau, Defiance, and Jefferson City in Missouri.

Donald Logel served in the US Army in Korea in 1950-1952 and is retired. Valeria Roy is a grandmother and retired. *Submitted by Donald L. Logel*

MAEVERS – Mary Ann Elizabeth Schreckenberg Maevers was born in Leopold, Bollinger County, MO on May 30, 1937 to Ben and Mary (Jansen) Schreckenberg. Her father's grandparents came from Germany in the 1830s. Dad's great-uncle went to California during the Gold Rush. His

grandfather, a blacksmith, along with several other men, was captured by guerrillas during the Civil War.

The guerrillas found out Great-Granddad's occupation and ordered him to shoe their horses and do other blacksmith work. As a reward, they turned him loose and he came back home. The other captives were shot.

Her mother's family came from Reiss, Germany in 1856. The Leopold farm, where her great-grandparents settled, is still owned by Mary Ann, her brother Joe, and sister Patsy. The original land-grant is signed by President Franklin Pierce.

Mary Ann graduated from Ursuline Academy High School in Arcadia, MO. After receiving a B.S. and Masters Degrees in Education, she began teaching fourth grade in 1959 at old South Grade and later at Southwest Elementary in Sikeston. She retired after 30 years of service.

In 1972, Mary Ann married Arlen Maevers, a widower with two teen-age daughters—Sheri and Ellen. The daughters have given them 5 grandchildren.

Arlen was born in Tilsit, Cape Girardeau County, but was raised in Jackson. His parents, August and Amanda (Nagel) Maevers, had five children named Mildred Lohmann, Norman, Jerlene Hutteger, Arlen and Lester.

Arlen is a registered land surveyor. He worked as senior construction inspector for Missouri Department of Transportation District 10 in Sikeston. One of his assignments was as senior construction inspector of the Mississippi River bridge at Caruthersville.

Arlen volunteers as an AARP tax aide and is on the board of SEMO Youth Camp, Wappapello. He has served on the Board of Directors of his church for years, holding many officer positions.

While teaching, Mary Ann served on numerous committees, was grade-level chairman, was president and vice-president of Community Teachers Association, and was a charter member of the KSAM Program. She served on KSAM writing conferences from which several *How-to Make Science and Math Exciting* books resulted.

Arlen L. and Mary Ann Maevers

Mary Ann was chosen for "Who's Who in American Education" for 1989-1990. She was honored in 1994 by the MSTA Southeast District with the Meritorious Service to Education Award. Mary Ann is a life-time member of Missouri State Teachers Association, Missouri Retired Teachers Association, Beta Sigma Phi Sorority, and Bollinger County Historical Society. She is a member of Scott County Historical Society, Missouri State Historical Society, SEMO Area Unit of RTA, Daughters of Isabella, and Laureate Chapter of Beta Sigma Phi. She has held numerous offices. She has been president of SEMO Unit RTA since 1991. She serves as the RTA Region 12 Director and is a member of the State RTA Executive Board. Mary Ann volunteers as a tour guide at the Sikeston Depot Museum and gives talks on Missouri history to schools and clubs. She is busy with church activities and teaches a Parish School of Religion class once a week. *Submitted by Mary Ann Maevers*

MANSFIELD – William (Lord) Mansfield was born about 1679, Buslem Staffs, England. His wife, Jane was born in 1683, also in Buslem Staffs,

England. Their son, Joseph Mansfield, (born 23 Jan. 1711, Buslem Staffs, England) immigrated to America during the time that Captain John Smith's (1580-1631) life was allegedly saved by Princess Pocahontas (1595-1617).

Joseph Mansfield's son, also named Joseph, was born near Williamsburg, VA. This Joseph also had a son named Joseph who married Frances Harrison.

Joseph and Frances had a son, John Mansfield (b. 1760 – d. 10 Sept. 1843 in Scott County, MO) who married on 22 Dec. 1790 in Albemarle County, VA to Mary Smith (b. 1772, Virginia – d. 1830-40, Missouri). Her father was Stephen J. R. Smith. Her stepfather was William Flint. Mary's mother was Agatha Durrett.

The Mansfields moved west from Virginia to Christian and Todd Counties in Kentucky.

James Smith Mansfield (born 14 Jan. 1786, Virginia), son of John and Mary, fought in the War of 1812 battles at Tallushatekes and Tallandega. On 10 March 1819 in Christian County, KY, James married Mary A. Gillum (born 30 Sept. 1800, Virginia), daughter of E. D. Gillum. James died 18 Sept. 1868 and was buried at Mt. Zion Cemetery, Scott City, Scott County, MO. Mary Gillum later moved to Thebes, IL to be near her daughter, Susan E. (Mansfield) Wilkerson Lightner. Mary died 28 April 1889 and was buried in Thebes, IL cemetery.

Susan E. Mansfield, born 17 May 1828, Todd County, KY, was married first to George Wilkerson and had one son, George, born 1843, Louisiana. She later married (in 1848) in Scott County, MO; Judge Levi Luther Lightner, and crossed the Mississippi River to make her home in Thebes, IL. Levi and Susan had seven children: E. Julia Lightner who married Roy Breeze; James C. married Josephine Stewart; Euginia Lightner married Albert Brawn; Eleanor died as an infant; and Nathaniel William Lightner; Levian "Lilly" Lightner married C. P. Spann at Thebes, IL; Pearl Naomi Lightner, born Thebes, IL, died as an infant.

Nathaniel William Lightner (4 July 1861, Thebes, IL – died 25 March 1949, St. Louis, MO) married Mattie Belle Boles (born 24 Feb. 1867, Georgia or Tennessee – died 4 June 1934 at McClure, IL, buried Thebes, IL) on 22 Oct. 1882, Thebes, IL. Mattie was the daughter of Charles Boles and mother's maiden name was Gordon. They had nine children.

Edith Lyle Lightner, daughter of Nathaniel and Mattie, was born 16 April 1883, Thebes, IL and died 14 Feb. 1980, Cape Girardeau, MO. Edith was married on 12 April 1905 in Cairo, IL to Ernest Caldwell (born 30 Dec. 1880, Delta, IL – 18 April 1934, McClure, IL). Both are buried at New Lorimier Cemetery, Cape Girardeau, MO. They had eight children.

Mary Lou Caldwell, eighth child of Edith and Ernest, was born 17 June 1927 in Cape Girardeau, MO. She was married in 1952 to Thomas H. Lett Jr. *Submitted by Mary Lou Caldwell Lett*

Susan E. (Mansfield) Wilkerson Lightner, Sarah (Mansfield) Asher, and unknown.

MANSFIELD – Joseph Mansfield, son of Joseph Mansfield, was born near Williamsburg, VA and married Frances Harrison. Their children were: George, who died young; John married N. Carr; Sam married L. Schelton; William married S. George of Alamoles, VA; Robert married M. Clark; Lawrence married E. Jefferson; John (born 1760, VA-10 Sept. 1843, Scott City, Scott County, MO) married on 22 Dec. 1790 to Mary Smith (1772, Albermarle County, VA – d. 1830-40, Scott City, MO).

John and Mary (Smith) Mansfield had the following children: James Smith Mansfield (born 14 Jan. 1786, Virginia or Tennessee – d. 18 Sept. 1868, Scott City, MO); Mary Mansfield married Mr. Baldwin; Mildred Mansfield married Thomas Harrison Price; Joseph G. Mansfield married Joanna M. Wilson; Nancy Mansfield married first Mr. Stone, second William Ashley; Pauline Mansfield married William Daugherty; Emily Mansfield married John Strong Thompson; John L. Mansfield married E. Moore; William A. Mansfield (1 April 1821, Kentucky – 16 Sept. 1882, Mississippi County, MO) married on 20 Feb. 1845, Cape Girardeau, MO to Martha Jane Joyce.

James Smith Mansfield married on 10 March 1818 in Christian County, KY to Mary A. Gillum (born 30 Sept. 1800, in Christian County, Virginia-29 April 1889, Thebes, IL). Their children were: Alvin Mansfield (born 1820 in Todd County, KY); Martha Mansfield (born 1822 in Todd County, KY) married B. Head; Ellen Mansfield (born 1824 in Todd County, KY) married first J. Rawinson, married second F. Stephene; Emily Mansfield (born 1826) married first J. Brady, second A. Numan and third B. Head; Susan E. Mansfield (12 May 1828 in Todd County, KY– December 1905, McClure, Alexander County, IL, buried Thebes, IL) married first George Wilkerson, married second on November 1848 to Levi L. Lightner; Robert D. Mansfield (born 1830); John H. Mansfield (born 1832); Francis Mansfield (born 1835) married first G. Riggs, second S. Boon; Eliza Mansfield (born 1837 in Scott County, MO) married M. J. Stephson; Sarah (Aunt Pet) Mansfield (born July 1839 in Scott County, MO – 11 Sept. 1911) married E. Asher; and George Mansfield (born 1846 in Scott County, MO). In 1836, James Smith Mansfield moved his family from Todd County, KY to Scott City, Scott County, MO where the last three children were born. *Submitted by Mary Lou Caldwell Lett*

MARGRABE – Darlene (Brucker) Margrabe was born Nov. 14, 1951 at Cape Girardeau, MO, the daughter of Clarence J. and Anna Marie (Hennecke) Brucker. She has a brother, Douglas J. Brucker, born Nov. 13, 1952. She attended St. Lawrence Catholic Elementary School and graduated from Thomas W. Kelly High School in May 1970, where she was active in Beta Club, Student Councill, Band and FHA. Upon graduation, she attended Southeast Missouri State University in Cape Girardeau, MO.

Larry S. Margrabe was born Jan. 29, 1951 at Poplar Bluff, MO, the son of Herman J. and Beatrice (Houseman) Margrabe. He has a sister, Patricia Lynn (Margrabe) Burger. He attended St. Ambrose Catholic

Darlene Margrabe family. Back: Darlene A. and Eric S. Front: Jodi L. holding Justin W. (right) and Dustin J. (left) Deen.

School in Chaffee, MO and graduated from Chaffee High School in May 1969, where he was active in football and tennis.

Larry S. and Darlene A. Brucker were united in marriage April 17, 1971 at St. Lawrence Catholic Church in New Hamburg, MO. A daughter, Jodi Lynn Margrabe, was born Sept. 18, 1975 and a son, Eric Steven Margrabe, was born March 20, 1979, both at Cape Girardeau, MO. Larry and Darlene divorced in January 1986.

Darlene has resided at the family home at Sikeston, MO since May 1976. She worked at Berry-Patmor & Co, CPAs for eight years. She has been a Missouri State Licensed Preschool and Daycare provider since October 1985. She is a member of St. Francis Xavier Catholic Church, Sikeston, MO, serving as Eucharistic Minister, Lector and Vice-President for the Region 8 Catholic Leadership Council. She is the grandmother of twins, Justin Wayne and Dustin John Deen, also of Sikeston, MO.

MARSHALL – The Marshalls are Sikeston proud and we come from a long line of black people that migrated to the Scott County area in the 1940s.

Matthew L. Marshall was born March 8, 1953 in Rich, MS to Edgar and Almeter Marshall. His father's parents were Robert and Murlee Marshall who also became citizens of Sikeston in the early 1940s. Edgar was the oldest of his siblings (Robert, Quincy, Louis, Johnnie Mae, Jessie and Samuel). He was a sharecropper. Matthew remembers quite vividly life on the plantation with siblings: Edgar Lee Jr.; Henry Lee; Richard Lee; Johnny Lee; Leroy Lee; Matthew Lee; Monroe Lee; Lessie Mae; Jimmy Lee and Roy Lee. Being raised in the fields is what he remembered most. Work was chopping cotton, then picking cotton. That was the way of life. One night they were awakened by their parents. All siblings were awakened at one time for there were as many as seven to a bed in those days. Quietly, the family furniture was loaded onto a large, long bedded truck that had pulled up close to their shotgun house. We all jumped in with the furniture. After hours of driving, which seemed to be an eternity, "Lord and be HOLD," they had arrived in Sikeston, MO. Later, Matthew was told by his older brothers that they were free. All family members started shouting, "glory Helle lu ah" "We were free."

He was 8 years old in 1960 when the family arrived in Sikeston. His parents quickly found out that it was mandatory for children to attend school. They were accustomed to working the fields and schooling was only of a secondary nature in the south. Matthew started his school year in the fourth grade at Lincoln Elementary in the Sunset neighborhood, known as the black area of town. Lincoln Elementary was an all black school. He could not speak the English language well when he began. When he did try to talk, his language was not interpretable. Today, they call it Ebonics and anyone listening closely can interpret the language well.

Although he could not speak well, he vividly remembers black teachers impressing upon him the need to always try to do the best that he could. That long lasting impression of knowing that someone cared for his inabilities remains with him each day. He feels blessed to have overcome such inadequacies.

From segregation to integration, it happened to us in 1965. All Sikeston Public Schools became one system. Matthew graduated from Sikeston Senior High School in 1971.

He enlisted in the US Army in March of 1972 and did basic training at Fort Leonard Wood, MO. After basic training he was sent to Fort Gordon, GA to train as a Radio Relay Operator. Immediately, after 16 weeks of training, he was shipped to Frankfurt, Germany for an extended tour of duty. Matthew was honorably discharged from military duty Jan. 9, 1975 at Fort Jackson, SC.

He returned to Sikeston, enrolled into SEMO University utilizing the GI Bill the fall of 1975. He graduated in 1981 with a Bachelor of Science Degree in Industrial Education.

Marshall Family. Sitting, left to right: Almeter, Edgar Lee, and Lessie Mae. Standing: Edgar Lee Jr., Henry Lee, Richard Lee, Leroy, Matthew Lee, and Monroe.

After graduation he returned to Sikeston, to marry Shirley Ann Baker, the daughter of Sylvester and Ida Murphy of Sikeston. During this union, Matthew Lee Marshall Jr. was born. In April of 1982 Matthew began employment with the Sikeston Power Station as an electrical apprentice and worked through the apprenticeship program achieving the title of journeyman electrician. He was employed with Sikeston Power Station for 18 years. In March of 1999 he had to retire due to a job-related injury.

In conclusion, all honor is given to Edgar and Almeter Marshall for our upbringing. They celebrated their 56th anniversary Dec. 17, 2001. Thanks to them, we have become responsible citizens of the United States of America by becoming Professional Businessmen, Train Conductors, Vietnam Veterans, Home Makers, Professional Photographers, Retired Factory Workers, School Teachers and Preachers. Life in Scott County has not been all bad.

MARSHALL – William Marshall was born in Ireland in 1747. He came to the new country at a very early age, first locating in North Carolina, then traveling on the wilderness trail to Bullit County, KY. He married soon after arrival in what became the United States, to a German born Elizabeth Lewis. They had seven children including James Henry Marshall (1791-1868). Around 1830 James Henry moved to Missouri and settled on what is now known as the Sikeston ridge, about 3 miles north of where the town of Sikeston was founded. James Henry Marshall and his wife, Elija Adams (1795-1875), had eight sons and two daughters. Their fourth son, Samuel (1827-1910), moved about a half mile northeast of his childhood home where he bought 115 acres for $300 from John and Catherine Sikes in 1853 and cleared the land. The farm was very fertile and he named it the Richwoods farm. This farm was located on the famous El Camino Real, the Kings Highway. This farm is still in the Marshall family today. Sam had three wives, Martha Ann Turner (1831-1874),

Samuel Marshall, Sr.

Sarah Womack (1852-1878) and Mrs. John B. Austin (1849-). All together they had 15 children: Mary Jane; Sarah Frances; Samuel Jr.; John E.; Nannie; Charles; William; Benjamin F.; Sterling; Issac; George; Joseph; Cyrus and Reece.

Sam served in the Civil War on the side of the South in the Special Scott County Confederate Unit D. His younger brother, William, served in the same war in the Union army. It is not known if they ever faced each other in battle but family dinners must have been real interesting. In the spring of 1862 during the Union General John Pope's raid down King's Highway to New Madrid the Yankee troops stopped at Sam's home and confiscated his horses.

Several of Sam's children lived full lives. Becoming merchants, landowners, and one son, John E., became a State Senator. *Submitted by Mike Marshall*

MARSHALL – In this essay, I am writing about Benjamin F. Marshall and his family. Benjamin Franklin Marshall was born on the Richwoods farm north of Sikeston in 1867. He married Florence Austin (1874-1961) who was the daughter of Mr. and Mrs. John B. Austin. John Austin died early in life and Mrs. Austin later became the third wife of Sam Marshall, as a result Florence was a stepdaughter of Sam Marshall and a stepsister to Ben F. Marshall. At an early age Ben F. Marshall started acquiring land in the county. He purchased land and harvested timber off his land, processing it in the several saw mills in the area which he owned. He built a large general store in Blodgett which was the largest of its kind in the area. People say that you could purchase anything from sewing needles to a threshing machine. The second floor of the store was the furniture department and also a fine display of caskets could be seen. Undertaking accommodations were available, complete with a horse-drawn hearse. The J. F. Nunnelee family worked in this area of the store, later going out on their own. In 1927, fires destroyed the Marshall Mercantile Store.

While the mercantile business was good for the enterprising young man, he was not satisfied with this. He was active in the town of Blodgett's prosperity serving as mayor for several years. In 1901, he started the Blodgett Bank. Over the years, Marshall purchased a vast amount of land totaling over twenty thousand acres. But what Ben F. became most famous for was the watermelon business that he began in 1888. Around the turn of the century, Blodgett became known as the Watermelon Capital of the World and Ben F. Marshall was the King. Marshall's watermelons won a blue ribbon at the St. Louis World's Fair of 1904. According to a report by the Missouri State Board of Agriculture in 1913, "over the past 25 years, Marshall has shipped an average of 1,000 rail cars a season. This means 25,000 carloads of melons. As from 900 to 1,300 melons are required to fill a car, it is safe to say that Mr. Marshall has handled not less than 25,000,000 melons." Marshall, in addition to handling so many melons on commission, is also an extensive grower. During the busy season of 1908 Marshall's firm shipped in a three-day period, 253 carloads of watermelons at an average of $110 per car.

Ben F. and Florence had two children, Ben F. Marshall Jr. (1902-1966) and Elizabeth Marshall (1907-1984). At an early age Ben F. Marshall Sr. developed TB. Due to this illness Marshall made plans for his estate. He intended to put twenty thousand acres on the market in January 1917, however he died November 1916 before his land could be sold. According to county records his will was filed in the probate court in Benton. Florence Marshall, according to the will, is to receive one-half of the net income of the farms, which at that time constitute a tract of more than 10,000 acres, and each of the two children an annual allowance of $2,000. The other half of the estate was placed into a trust with the First National Bank Trust Company in St. Louis. This trust is still in existence today.

Benjamin F. Marshall, Sr.

Ben F. Marshall Jr. was only 14 when his father died. He grew up to be a landowner and Banker and served as president of the Blodgett Bank. Following the Bank Moratorium in 1933, when all banks in the United States were closed by order of President Franklin D. Roosevelt, the Bank of Blodgett was the first of only two banks in Scott County allowed to reopen for business. It continued to serve the Blodgett area until the year 1938 when it was moved to Oran and became the Oran State Bank. In 1926 Ben F. Marshall Jr. married Catherine Mooney (1907-1998) of St. Louis and moved her down to Cape Girardeau and later to Blodgett. They had three sons: Ben F. III, Thomas Austin and John Burke. *Submitted by Mike Marshall*

MARTIN – John Martin, my great grandfather, was among the first four families to arrive at Prices Landing in Scott County, MO, in the spring of 1840.

Louis Martin, my grandfather, born Dec. 21, 1828, was only 12 years old at the time they came from Davis County, KY, to Scott County, MO. According to our family Bible, record has it that Louis Martin married Alice Noyes, Jan. 29, 1854. She died and Louis married the second time to Elizabeth (Huff) Davis, Oct. 20, 1863, to which there were born six children, one being my father, Charles Dunning Martin, March 19, 1874. My dad talked about his father (or grandfather, I'm not sure), going to California during the gold rush. He was so hungry, he bought a moldy piece of pie for $5.00, scraped off the mold, and ate it. While there, he went into an establishment, saw it was a den of thieves, and backed out. He was told by an onlooker that he was the first man to come out alive. Everyone else had been robbed and killed after being dropped through a trap door in the floor. We assume he never found any gold. He was the only survivor in the group to come home. The rest of the wagon train got sick and died in the desert.

Charles and Clara Martin with Rosa Lee Martin Fluegge

I think Joseph Martin was my dad's great grandfather's name, but I'm not sure.

Charles Dunning Martin was born March 19, 1874 (died March 27, 1963) to Louis and Eliza-beth Susan Martin near Price's Landing, which is now called Lusk, where he farmed and raised seven children, one of whom is writing this. *Submitted by Rosa Lee (Martin) Fluegge*

MASTERSON-MYERS – Maggie Masterson was born Feb. 8, 1856 in Sikeston, MO. She was the daughter of William Squire and Mary (Marvin) Masterson, who were married on Oct. 3, 1844 in Scott County, MO. After their marriage they continued to live and raise their family in Commerce, MO. William was a "River Boat Gambler" and traveled from Commerce to New Orleans and back. When Maggie was about a year old, her mother was shot and killed by a group of renegades who were after her father. William was then married to Mary Shephard. William was shot and killed on Nov. 4, 1873 in Commerce, MO by Mary's sister's husband, Travis Harris.

Maggie married William Jennings Myers, who was born in Lancaster County, PA on Feb. 6, 1852 and was the son of Dr. Jonathan and Elizabeth (Beers) Myers. The Myers family moved to Iowa in 1860.

Maggie and William were married in 1881 and lived in Anthon, IA where their children, William (1883), Alfonzo (1884), Link (1886) and Lettie (1888) were born. In 1895 they moved to Niobrara, NE where two more sons, Jay (1896) and Frank (1899) were born. While living in Niobrara, they

William and Maggie (Masterson) Myers, 1895.

farmed and raised cattle. In 1902, for health reasons, they and their two youngest boys moved south to Okmulgee County, OK, where they managed a creamery. They then moved to Cauthron, AR in 1905. It was there that they lived their remaining years, raising cotton, sheep and cattle. William, a 32nd Degree Mason, died on Dec. 22, 1927 and Maggie died on Jan. 27, 1946. They are both buried in the Old Cauthron Cemetery. *Submitted by Janice Myers*

MATTHEWS – The first Matthews to arrive in what is now southeast Missouri, was Edward Matthews. Edward was born in Virginia, circa 1760. He fought in the Revolutionary War at Fort Jefferson along the banks of the Mississippi River. After the war, he went to The Falls of the Ohio (Louisville, KY), married, and began to raise a family. He and his wife Drusilla, had five sons: Charles (1785); Edward N. (1787); Joseph (1789); James (1791); and Allen (1793). In 1800, Edward's wife, Drusilla, passed away, and Edward, along with his five sons, left Louisville and came to the Louisiana Territory. They settled in what was known as Saint Charles Prairie (near the present site of Charleston, MO), but would become known as Matthews Prairie. In 1812, four of the five sons fought in the War of 1812. After the conclusion of the war, they all returned to Matthews Prairie and began raising families of their own.

The Charles D. Matthews family descends from Edward's first son, Charles, and then through his son, Edward. Charles D. Matthews was born Jan. 11, 1843 on the family farm in New Madrid County, approximately ten miles south of the present day Sikeston. Charles found farming a precarious occupation after his father died. He and his brother, Felix Edward, remained there with their mother, raising barely enough corn to keep the family fed. His mother, Elvira, and brother both died in 1867, at which time Charles moved to Sikeston. In Sikeston, he clerked at the Stringer & Co. general store, reporting to work at 5 a.m. and working until 10 at night. Charles also became involved in trading grain through the Hunters of New Madrid, along with buying and selling

Charles David Matthews

small parcels of land. Within two years of moving to Sikeston, Charles had saved enough money to buy Stringer's store, and changed the name to Matthews Mercantile Company.

Charles began trading and buying farmland, and over the years that followed, he became an extensive landowner. Then came the drainage and clearing of the land in the district, and he profited. His holdings made him a fortune, and he reinvested it in land that again turned his money several times. In 1887, he founded the Bank of Sikeston, which remained in the family for more than a hundred years. He was also a founder of the Scott County Bank in Morley (1891), and the Peoples Bank of New Madrid (1892). He was a partner in the Matthews-Greer Grain Company, the Greer-Bowman Milling Company, and a founder of the Scott County Milling Company. In 1901, Charles Matthews founded the Farmer's Supply Company, which became the largest mercantile concern in Sikeston. During the early 1900s, he had interest in the Holley-Matthews Lumber Company and the Baker-Matthews Lumber Company, with extensive land holdings in Missouri, Mississippi, Tennessee and Illinois.

He was first married to Rebecca Greer in 1872, to which union one daughter was born. The daughter, Hallie, along with Rebecca died in 1874. He married his wife's sister, Bettie Greer, the following year, to which union were born three children: Charles Jr.; Edward "Ned;" and a baby that died at birth. After the death of his second wife, he married Mrs. Betty McMullin Sikes, to which union one child, Joseph, was born. Charles D. Matthews died Oct. 17, 1917. The descendants of his three sons still live and work in Sikeston. *Submitted by Edward C. Matthews Jr.*

MATTHEWS – John Andrew Matthews, the son of Mr. and Mrs. Charles Matthews, was born at McMullin on June 17, 1864. Joanna "Annie" Hatcher, daughter of Mr. and Mrs. Benjamin F. Hatcher, was also born at McMullin on May 14, 1868. Soon after their marriage on Dec. 3, 1890 they moved to Sikeston and lived at what is now 211 Greer.

Eight children were born to this union, seven of whom survived. They were: Glenn Andrew, who married Clara Cox; Ben Oscar, who married Jennie Watts; Ben Oscar's twin died; Andrew Jackson "Jack," who married Esther Brumfield; Cora (Mrs. Tanner C. Dye); Maggie (Mrs. Wilbur W.

John A. and Joanna (Hatcher) Matthews

Ensor); Fred, who married Helen Copeland; and Lena Matthews who still resides at 211 Greer.

For more than 40 years Mr. Matthews was one of Sikeston's most prominent and prosperous farmers. He was gifted with a good mind, retentive memory, and exceptionally good business judgment. He did not keep books, as he accurately held the details of his affairs in his mind and remembered every little account. He farmed a large portion of the land now occupied as part of Sikeston south of the railroad, across the ridge up to what was known as the lake, including the land on which the old high school and the old highway building stood, and from the Slapout School west to the edge of the ridge. He also operated the Wagon Yard, located on the corner of Greer Avenue and South Ranney.

He watched the development of the country, witnessed the draining of the swamps, saw the forest cleared, and the population increase. He was one of the hardest workers of the county.

In his business dealings he was thoroughly honest, dependable and trustworthy. His word could be trusted. He always kept his word and expected others to do the same. He was a man of unimpeachable morality. He taught his children four things: (1) Be honest in all things; (2) Tell the truth; (3) Pay your debts and (4) Follow your convictions, regardless of what others think. These principles he not only taught his children, but practiced. His was a happy home and a congenial family.

He died March 15, 1934 and is buried in the Sikeston City Cemetery.

Mrs. Matthew's mother died when she was 4 years old. A request made by her mother shortly before her death was carried out. She was taken into the home of Dr. and Mrs. William Lennox, and lived there until her marriage.

She was a faithful and devout Christian and her church and her family were her consuming interests in life. The quiet force of her personality radiating Christ-likeness will live long in the memory of those who were privileged to know her. "Always Good" was an appropriate term applied to this Christian gentlewoman.

She died on March 21, 1932 and is buried in the Sikeston City Cemetery.

This information was taken from their obituaries on the front page of the *Sikeston Standard*.

MAY – Abraham May was born in Germany, probably about 1840. Abraham was in Indiana at the time of the Civil War. In 1865, he enlisted in Company I of the 145th Regiment Indiana Volunteers. He attained the rank of Corporal and was on duty in Georgia. Abraham married Charlotte East on Oct. 27, 1859 in Monroe County, IN. Abraham and Charlotte had three sons: Jasper; Alex; and Frank. Abraham arrived in Scott County probably a few years before his death on Aug. 18, 1889 and is buried in the Old Morley Cemetery. After Abraham's death, Charlotte married Peter Maxley in Scott County.

Jasper married Lizzie Howle, daughter of the Reverend James Lewis Howle and Amanda Polk. Jasper and Lizzie had six children who grew to adulthood: Maud; Creal; John; Luther; Georgia; and Hugh. Maud married William Daugherty. They had five children: Leda; Maxine; June; Sara; and Will. Creal married Clara Carlton on May 29, 1920. They had seven children: George; Charlie; Ellen; Donald; Mollie; Jerry; and Thomas. John married Virginia Halley. They had five children: Leah; Carolyn; Elizabeth; James; and Howard. Luther married Bertie Graves on June 1, 1919. They had four children: Glenda; Joseph; Lois; and Richard. Georgia married Forrest Watson on Ma y26, 1919. They had six children: Betty; William; Mary; Dara; Tommy; and Robert. Hugh married Ruth Kaiser. Jasper and Lizzie are buried in the Old Morley Cemetery, as are Maud and William, Creal and Clara, and Georgia and

Forrest. Luther and Bertie are buried in Frost Hill Memorial Gardens at Morley. The May, Daugherty and Watson children graduated from Morley High School. Jerry lives in Morley.

Alex and his wife, Mary, had one child that grew to adulthood, Lex. Alex and Mary are buried in the Old Morley Cemetery.

Frank and his wife, Minnie, did not have any children who grew to adulthood. They are buried in the Old Morley Cemetery. *Submitted by Jerry May*

MAY – Clara Elva was born April 20, 1899, one month after her father, Thomas Carlton, died on March 17, 1899. Her sister, Clennie, was born in 1896 at Greenbriar, Bollinger County. The 1900 Scott County Census shows Clara's mother, Leona Leta Brendel Carlton and second husband, James Henry Graves, living in Morley with Clara (8 months) and Clennie (4 years). Three children were born to Leona and James: Bertie Graves, May 1902-1975; Pearl Graves Leonard, 1905-1949; and Adolph Graves, 1908-1970. Leona died around 1910 when Clara was about 10 years old. Clara spent the next several years baby-sitting her stepbrother and sisters. Clennie married Joe James, who owned Hotel-Restaurant in Brownwood. Clara worked in restaurant at Brownwood.

In 1920 Clara was a waitress in Morley when she met Jasper Creal May (1893-1968) who had returned from WWI. They were married May 29, 1920.

Thomas Carlton's grandfather, William Carlton, was born in 1800 in North Carolina. The Carltons were early immigrants from England. William moved to Jackson County, AL (west of Chattanooga). Thomas' father, Lowry, was born there before moving to Castor River Valley, MO. The three Carlton men were returning home from the Civil War when William E. Carlton died two miles from home.

Clara (Carlton) May, 1979.

Lurena Carlton (1839-1902) married into the Perkins family and lived near Zalma where Perkins Creek enters Castor River. Perkins kept a daily diary for two years during the Civil War. A copy is at Stars & Stripes Museum, Federal Cemetery at Bloomfield. Colonel Jefferes and Captain Wilson's companies camped on General Watkins' farm near Morley from Aug. 17 – 26, 1861. The campsite was south of General Watkins Cemetery. These men went north several times toward Cape Girardeau and engaged the north. On Aug. 27, they camped at Sikeston. On Sept. 1, the Cavalry went to Charleston and took $57,000 of northern money from the bank. On Sept. 10, General U. S. Grant's gunboats came down from Cairo and shelled their camp at Bellmont. Shells exploded in treetops without damage. The Confederates had erected a chain across the Mississippi that failed to stop the gunboats. On Sept. 26, brother Jesse Perkins was injured and later died from wounds received in the engagement with the North at Belmont.

Leona's grandfather, Frederick Brendel, was born in Weimer, Saxony, Germany in 1813. Frederick's mother, determined not to lose her second son to the German military, sent her teenaged son to America. He met the Gunkle family in Pennsylvania and married Marie Gunkle. The families moved westward, living in Morgan

County, IN where most of their 14 children were born. The oldest child that lived was Leona's father, Lewis Adam Brendel. The families moved on to Lyon County, Emporia, KS. Before 1860, Frederick moved his family to Greenbriar, Bollinger County, MO. Frederick was a Captain and son, Lewis, a Corporal in the Union Army and served in the Cavalry with the Fremont Rangers.

In 1861, Lewis Adam Brendel married Mary A. Crites at Greenbriar. Mary Crites' family was on the historical wagon train from North Carolina that crossed the frozen Mississippi at Ste. Genevieve in 1800. Ste. Genevieve was the only settlement west of Mississippi. Nine of Lewis Brendel's children were girls. Most married in southern Bollinger or northern Stoddard counties. Their eighth child was Clara's mother, Leona Leta Brendal. Clara died May 23, 1996. *Compiled by Don May*

MAY – Abraham May was born in the wilderness of southwest Missouri in 1839. He died in 1889 in Morley and is buried in the Old Morley Cemetery. Abraham's great grandfather, Jacob May, was born in Bavaria, Germany in 1730 and came to America around 1750. Jacob and family were living in the Tygart Valley of Virginia during the Revolutionary War. His eldest son, also named Abraham (1762-1840) served in the Virginia Militia during the war and was marching on Richmond when Cornwallis surrendered.

After the war, Jacob moved his family to Ashe County, NC where he died in 1800. Abraham's grandfather, William May, was born in 1769 in Randolph Count, VA and died in 1855 in Monroe County, IN. Abraham's father, Simon May, was born in 1809 in North Carolina and died in 1889 in Monroe County, IN. Simon May lived in Tennessee, Kentucky and Indiana before moving into the wilderness of southwest Missouri in 1838. According to Newton County history, at Trail's End, he built one of the few cabins in Newton County at that time. He and his family show up on the 1840 Newton County, MO census. Simon's third child, Abraham May (1839-1889), was born there. One day when the May men were away, some Osage Indians stole their axe, saw and tools. The men caught up but were badly outnumbered and severely beaten. Simon then traded his cabin and improvements for a yearly colt to M. R. Ritchey, the author of this story in the History of Newton County, and made the long journey back to Monroe County, IN. He shows up on the 1850 Monroe County, IN census.

Jacob May descendents: Don, George, Tom, Ellen, Charlie, Jerry, and Molly at Cousin's Reunion in Morley, MO. Children of Clara and Creal May.

Abraham married Charlotte East on Oct. 27, 1859 in Indiana. My grandfather, Jasper Hannigan May (1861-1921), was born in Monroe County, IN. Also his brother, Alex May (1863-1906), and Frank May (1867-1954). The three brothers are buried in the Old Morley Cemetery in Morley, MO. Abraham served the North in the

Civil War in Company I, 145th Indiana Infantry and was hospitalized in Macon, GA. After the war, he moved his family to Ballard County, KY. His neighbors were the Minister James Lewis Howle's family of five girls and four boys. Both families moved to Scott County, MO in about 1888. Jasper Hannigan May married Lizzie Howle (1863-1957) and had two daughters and four sons that lived. They are: Maud (1891-1947); Jasper C. (1893-1968); J. Howle (1885-1967); Walker (1898-1957); Georgia (Watson) 1902-1980); and Hugh (1905-1975). Maud married William W. Daughtery (1885-1921) who was killed by a Frisco Train near Brooks Junction when he was planting cantaloupes with his father-in-law, Jasper H. May. While going for water he was struck and killed and Jasper H. May died of a heart attack on the spot. Walker May was shot in the neck during WWI and received a pension. My father, Jasper Creal May, served in the Navy on the Battleship *Oregon* during WWI and received a pension for disabilities. Jasper Creal May married Clara E. Carlton after the war. Two girls and five boys were born from this union. They are: George B. May (1921-); Charlie Frank May (1923-); Ellen May (1927-); Donald May (1929-); Molly Lou May (1933-1996); Jerry Carlton May (1935-); and Thomas F. May (1939-). All five boys served in the military. Charlie Frank was at Pearl Harbor on Dec. 7, 1941. Ellen also worked for the Navy during WWII in Hawaii. *Compiled by Don May*

McCARTY – John Parks McCarty was born on March 28, 1867 in Mason, OH. He died on May 7, 1946 at his home near Oran, MO.

His parents were Peter A. McCarty and Hannah Hawthorn.

John was first married to Fannie Ross. From this marriage three daughters were born: Mary Ellen McCarty Green; Sarah Etta McCarty Swanagon; and Ruth A. McCarty. He then married Lela Rowena Scott on April 1, 1905. To this union four daughters were born: Honora Jane McCarty; Olive Rowena McCarty Carr; Grace Alice McCarty McCallister; and Clara Eudora McCarty Graviett.

In January 1908, when Honora was 2-1/2 years old, and Grace was 2 weeks old, they moved from South Lebanon to Spring Valley, OH. While living in Spring Valley, John was a dairy farmer. In the morning, they had to get to the barn and milk, and separate the cream in time to get the ten gallon can of cream down the long hill for the trolley that ran to Dayton. He also managed an ice cream factory.

In 1913 John sold a herd of registered Jersey cows, hogs and beef cattle, and the farm on a Saturday, then moved to Oran, MO.

The furniture, two horses, one cow, one dog and a crate of chickens were brought to Missouri in a freight train car. John and a farm hand were in the car to water the stock. Lela brought the girls on the train by herself, arriving in Oran on March 4,1 913 around noon.

That spring John started a concrete business, making house basements, culverts and bridges. He purchased several homes and moved them onto the concrete basements. He was one of the first pioneers in basement construction. He built sidewalks and some of the store buildings in Oran.

Also he built roads through some of Scott County. He contracted and helped build the rock base road from Oran to Perkins to replace the Corduroy Pole Road. He cut steep grade to make Friends Hill Road on the way to Benton. Also he contracted and helped build the Rock Road from Oran to Caney Creek along the Frisco Railroad.

In 1923, John organized the JP McCarty Lumber and Coal business, which he operated with the help of his daughters until he had a stroke.

Olive helped the longest and continued to run the business.

Mr. McCarty was active in the Republican Party and was often a committee man, and was very patriotic. His daughter, Grace, was my mother. *Submitted by Evelyn Duncan*

McCONNELL – Athel Edward McConnell was born Nov. 16, 1905 at Boydsville, Weakley County, TN, the son of Edward "Eddie" Cleveland (born May 10, 1886, Boydsville, Weakley County, TN and died May 10, 1971, Dexter, Stoddard County, MO) and Beulah Gale (Stephenson) McConnell (born April 3, 1889 in Tennessee and died April 13, 1944, Sikeston, Scott County, MO). Both are buried at Sikeston Memorial Park.

Our subject married Maggie Viola Reynolds on April 26, 1925 at Piggott, AR. She was born Feb. 22, 1907 at Aquilla, Stoddard County, MO, daughter of Albert Logan Reynolds (born 1866, Bloomfield, Stoddard County, MO and died 1944) and Etta Bell (Reed) McConnell (born 1875 and died 1926).

They were parents of 10 children: L. C. (born March 11, 1917, Fulton, Hickman County, KY); Dortha Bell (born July 14, 1929, Morehouse, New Madrid County, MO); Basil (born November 1930, Morehouse, New Madrid County, MO and died July 5, 1958); Ama (April 21, 1932); Earl Dwain (Feb. 7, 1934, Bernie, Stoddard County, MO); Athel Edward Jr. (Sikeston, Scott County, MO); Martha Louise (Sept. 28, 1937, Sikeston, Scott County, MO); Gerald Oscar (Oct. 29, 1939, Scott County, MO); Harold Lee (July 3, 1941, Sikeston, Scott County, MO: died Aug. 15, 1941); Brenda Mac (Oct. 15, 1946, Sikeston, Scott County, MO).

They moved from Bernie, Stoddard County, MO to Sikeston, Scott County, MO in 1934. He was a farm laborer and worked for the Missouri Sate Highway Department. During WWII, he worked at the Parks Air Force Base in Sikeston, Scott County, MO, then went to work for Fabick Brothers Equipment Company, where he was a mechanic for 28 years. He retired in 1967.

Athel died at his home in Sikeston, MO on April 22, 1985. Maggie died at the Missouri Delta Medical Center, Sikeston, MO on Feb. 17, 1989. Both are buried at the Bernie Cemetery, Bernie, Stoddard County, MO. *Submitted by Norma Faye (Sams) McConnell*

McCONNELL – Earl Dwain McConnell was born Feb. 7, 1934 in Bernie, Stoddard County, MO, the son of Athel Edward and Maggie Viola (Reynolds) McConnell. He came to Sikeston, Scott County, MO with his parents in 1934.

While in high school, he played on the Sikeston Bulldog Football team, was the President of the Diversified Occupations Club, and graduated in May of 1953. On July 25 1953 he married Norma Faye Sams from Diehlstadt, Scott County, MO at Cornith, Alcorn County, MS. They have two sons; Harold Dwain (born Aug. 13, 1954) and Larry Dale McConnell (born Dec. 18, 1956). They also have 10 grandchildren and one great-granddaughter.

Growing up in Sikeston, Scott County, MO, his first job was picking cotton in the cotton field where his home is built today. He worked at the Sikeston Standard, Dick's Bar B Q Inn, The Colonial Inn, Wal-Green's, Missouri State Highway Department and worked for Palmer TV for 17 years before he and his brother, Gerald O McConnell, opened McConnell Bros. TV in July 1967 in Sikeston, Scott County, MO. He retired Feb. 7, 1991 due to an accident. He was a member of the Sikeston Volunteer Fire Department and the Sikeston Voluntary Rescue Department from Jan. 1, 1968 until July 23, 1983. He was the first one in the Sikeston squad to use the Jaws of Life. At the time of retirement he held the rank of Captain. He was a

Little League coach and worked with Troop 43 Boy Scouts of Sikeston, Scott County, MO. He was a member of the Sikeston Lions Club, a voluntary member of the Sikeston Depot, Scott County, MO and a member of the First Baptist Church, Sikeston, Scott County, MO. *Submitted by Norma Faye (Sams) McConnell*

McCONNELL – Norma Faye (Sams) McConnell was born Sept. 9, 1935, Berkley, Carlisle County, KY, the daughter of Raymond Hershell (born Nov. 13, 1908, Crosno, Mississippi County, MO; died Oct. 2, 1979 at Bardwell, Carlisle County, KY, buried in the Berkley Cemetery, Berkley, Carlisle County, KY), son of James A. Sams (born Sept. 26, 1881, Berkley, Carlisle County, KY, died April 25, 1963 at Bardwell, Carlisle County, KY) and Lula Bell Nolen (born March 11, 1882, Carlisle County, KY; died June 7, 1944, Berkley, Carlisle County, KY, buried Berkley Cemetery, Carlisle County, KY) and Margaret Louise (Fields) Sams (born Feb. 17, 1914, Wyatt, Mississippi County, MO; died Oct. 14, 1955 in a auto and truck accident), daughter of Albert Eugene (born June 8, 1888, Mississippi County, MO, died Jan. 12, 1929, Wyatt, Mississippi County, MO), and Bertha Elizabeth (Mayson) Fields (born June 5, 1894, Mississippi County, MO, died Aug. 4, 1942, Wyatt, Mississippi County, MO).

Our subject moved from Kentucky about 1937 to Wyatt, Mississippi County, MO; then in 1945, she went to live with her uncle Elbert "Ike" and Dorothy Marie (Fields) Jackson at Diehlstadt, Scott County, MO and graduated from Diehlstadt High School, Scott County, MO in May 1953. She married Earl Dwain McConnell from Sikeston, Scott County, MO (see story).

She was a member of the First Baptist Church of Sikeston, Scott County, MO, a volunteer at the Sikeston Depot, Sikeston, Scott County, MO; member of Scott County Historical Genealogy Society, Benton, MO; the Stoddard County Genealogy Society, Dexter, MO; the Mississippi County Genealogy Society, Charleston, MO; the Ballard-Carlisle Historical and Genealogy Society, Wickliffe, KY; the Commerce Historical and Genealogy Society, Commerce, Scott County, MO; the Genealogy Society of Southern Illinois, Carbondale, IL; the Genealogy Society of Butler County, Poplar Bluff, MO; the Graves County Genealogy Society, Mayfield, KY; the Tennessee Genealogy Society, Brunswick, TN; the Fulton County Genealogy Society, Fulton County, KY; the Mountain Press, Signal Mountain, TN; the Pemiscot County Historical Society, Caruthersville, MO; the Henry County Genealogy Society of Tennessee, Paris, TN; and the Weakley County Genealogy Society, Martin, TN. *Submitted by Norma Faye (Sams) McConnell*

McFERRON – One of the most prominent men in the Cape Girardeau District, during the early period, was Joseph McFerron. He was an Irishman who came to America in early life and was a man of fine sense and possessed a superior education. He was reserved in manner and peculiar in appearance. He was the first clerk of the courts of the Cape Girardeau District and held the position for a number of years.

In 1807 Joseph McFerron and William Ogle fought a duel on Cypress Island opposite Cape Girardeau. Before accepting the position with the court he was a merchant in Cape Girardeau. For some reason there arose difficulty between the two men and Ogle challenged McFerron to a duel. It seems that McFerron had never even fired a pistol, but he accepted the challenge. Ogle was killed, while McFerron was unhurt. After his duel with Ogle, McFerron resigned from office, but public sentiment was such that he was re-elected and held the office until his death in 1821.

Joseph McFerron (born about 1780 in Ireland, died Feb. 5, 1821 in Cape Girardeau County, MO) married on Feb. 6, 1810 to Eve "Effie" Tyler (born in 1792, died May 30, 1857 in Clarksville, Red River County, TX), adopted daughter of Christopher and Eve Hayes. They had six children: Erin McFerron (born 1811, died after 1867 in Stoddard County, MO); Columbia McFerron (born 1812 in Missouri, died about 1892); Erina McFerron (born July 30, 1814 in Cape Girardeau County, MO, died March 4, 1874 in Clarksville, Red River County, TX); Columbus McFerron (born Sept. 20, 1816 in Kelso, Scott County, MO, died Jan. 4, 1865 in Kelso, Scott County, MO); Enaminodas McFerron (born 1819 in Kelso, Scott County, MO); and Joseph J. McFerron (born Nov. 20, 1820 and died November 1848 in Cape Girardeau County, MO).

Erin McFerron (born 1811, died after 1867 in Stoddard County, MO) married Myra English (born 1822 in Louisiana)—no children. Second marriage to Sarah Ann (Knott) Raney (born Feb. 12, 1822, died Dec. 11, 1886), daughter of John and Louisa Bartles Knott of Maryland, and widow of Johnson Raney (died March 11, 1855). She had five children with him who may have lived with her and their step-father, Erin. They had one child together. He had another marriage to an unknown person, and a fourth to Matilda Glover on Jan. 22, 1867.

Columbia McFerron (born 1812 in Missouri, died about 1892) first married Joseph English (born about 1796, died Nov. 4, 1834) on May 10, 1829—they had no children. She then married Rev. Thomas W. Anderson on Oct. 4, 1836—they had six children, but names are unknown.

Erina McFerron (born July 30, 1814 in Cape Girardeau County, MO, died March 4, 1874 in Clarksville, Red River County, TX) married Simeon J. English (born July 22, 1798 in Washington County, GA, died Jan. 14, 1887 in Clarksville) on April 26, 1832. Their children were Thomas McFerron English; Effie Jane English; Joseph McFerron English; Elizabeth English; Hanna Louisa English; John English; Simon Robert English; Margaret English; Amelin English; and Martha English.

Columbus McFerron (born Sept. 20, 1816 in Kelso, died Jan. 4, 1865 in Kelso) married Nicey Jane Kinnison (Born Jan. 30, 1820 in Cape County, died Aug. 6, 1897 in Kelso) on Nov. 5, 1843. They had seven children: Erina Louise (b. Sept. 13, 1844); Abner Jason (born March 25, 1846); Eve "Effie" Jane (born Aug. 17, 1848); Simeon Joseph (born Dec. 1, 1851); Columbia Elizabeth (born April 27, 1854); Margaret Matilda "Maggie" (born Nov. 9, 1856); and Martha Agnes (born Dec. 18, 1860).

Erina Louise McFerron (b. Sept. 13, 1844, d. July 16, 1919) first married William Taylor. They had two children, Louisa (b. about 1860) and Elizabeth (b. about 1865, d. after 1933) married Charles W. Pruitt. She married Thomas Carrol Welch and they had one son, Albert.

Abner Jason (born March 25, 1846, d. Feb. 4, 1921) married Maria J. Foster (b. April 11, 1851, d. Feb. 6, 1881). They had seven children: Edgar R. (b. about 1870, d. 1949, married Ada Ancell Dec. 12, 1890); Anna Gertrude (b. Nov. 7, 1871, d. Nov. 9, 1872); Arthur (b. Feb. 20, 1876, d. October 1939) married Viola Kelly—13 children: Edna Marie; Henry Curtis; Myrtle Blanche; Louis Kelly; Ada Minta; Howard Jason; Lester Carl; Edwin Fort; infant; Thomas James; Harold Eugene; Marjorie Ruth; and William Ray; Asa (b. Jan. 18, 1875, d. Feb. 8, 1875); Clara A. (b. about 1878); Rosella; and Williams.

Eve Jane (b. Aug. 17, 1848, d. Oct. 4, 1935)

marred William M. Jeffords—they had six children: William; James; Joseph; Lillie; Viola and Martin.

Simeon Joseph (b. Jan. 1, 1850, d. March 4, 1935) married Sarah Ancel—they had four children: Addi; Nina; Ralph and Estelle.

Columbia Elizabeth (b. April 27, 18954, d. June 12, 1880) married Chelsley D. McCallister—they had one child, Columbus Gail.

Margaret Matilda (b. Nov. 9, 1856, d. Oct. 10, 1950) married William Daniel Jones—they had 12 children: Columbus Hill; Florence Edith; Columbia Elizabeth; Eva Jane; Louisa Violet; Simeon Jason; William Ray; Mark Osborn; Pearl Margaret; James Paul; Leona Elsie; and Mabel Grace.

Enaminodas McFerron (b. 1819) married Suzanna ? (b. 1837)—one child, Nancy.

Joseph J. (b. Nov. 20, 1820, d. November 1848).

McGAHEY – Hazel "Mac" McGahey was born in 1914, in Glass County, a rural area in Obion, TN. His parents were Nicholas and Hallie (Halloway) McGahey. Hazel had three brothers and one sister. His parents died while Hazel was a youth. He lived with relatives until crossing the Mississippi River to Caruthersville, MO in 1931. This was during the Great Depression years. He found work as a day laborer. He met Virginia Shy from New Madrid, MO and they were married in 1932. Their daughter, Charlotte, was born in 1933, and Peggy Jo in 1936. Peggy died from colitis at 17 months.

Mac McGahey in his barber shop. The customer is Mac's nephew, Rodney Shy of Oran, Mo.

Hazel was not accepted in the armed services during WWII, due to medical reasons. He wanted to better himself, so he enrolled in the Moler Barber College in St. Louis in 1940. After barbering in New Madrid and Sikeston for 7 years, he bought the corner building at the corner of Kingshighway and Front Street in 1948. The building had been constructed in 1931 as a sandwich shop. As Mac's Barber Shop, Hazel became known as "Mac" the barber. He barbered over 50 years, loved his work, the people and the community.

Hazel moved his family to Sikeston in 1942. Charlotte was in the fourth grade and attended Bailey School. During Junior High, she met her future husband, Gene Johnson. They both graduated in the class of 1951.

Gene's parents were George and Laura Lee Johnson. Both were born in 1900. George was from Blandville, KY, while Laura Turner's family came from Hannibal, MO in 1910. They were married in 1921. Their children were Betty, Gene and Rose Marie. They resided on Center Street with Johnson's Garage built behind the house in 1935. Laura Lee died in 1974 and George died in 1985.

Franklin E. "Gene" Johnson was born in 1932. He and Charlotte were married in 1953. Charlotte graduated from Southeast Missouri State College with a B.S. degree and an M.A. degree in education. In 1957 she began teaching at the Sikeston Airport School, which was renovated from the Harvey Parks Airport.

She then taught at Southeast Elementary, retiring in 1900 with 37 years. She was a member of Delta Kappa Gamma Society, an organization for women educators.

Gene joined the US Air Force in 1953. He

spent 2-1/2 years in the states and 1-1/2 years in French Morocco. Returning to Sikeston 1957, he worked in the family garage and drove the school bus several years. His dream was to have a farm with horses. Although he never lived on a farm, Gene did custom farming and later bought Tanner Grain Elevator. He sold the grainery in 1999 and semi-retired. Gene was a 32 degree Freemason in the Sikeston Masonic Lodge. He was a member of the Scott County Sheriff's Mounted Posse.

Gene and Charlotte's daughter, Susan, was born in 1959. She met her future husband, Allan Davidson, during high school. They both graduated in 1977 and attended Southeast Missouri State University. They were married in 1978 and made their home in Sikeston. Allan worked for Southwestern Bell Telephone, and Susan worked as a church secretary. Their children were Chris and Laura, both of whom graduated from Sikeston High School and attended college.

All family members were members of the Tanner Street Church of God in Sikeston.

Gene Johnson died on June 18, 2000. Virginia McGahey died on July 6, 2000.

McRILL – Lois Ann (Miller) McRill was born Oct. 24, 1935 in Sikeston, Scott County, MO to parents Henry Arlen Miller and Serena Blanche (Moody) Miller. I was the third child, with one brother – Donald Roy Miller, and one sister, Margaret Marie Miller. A young sister – Linda Mae Miller, was born 2 years 5 months later.

The Miller family resided in Sikeston until 1936 when we moved to a farm in Mississippi County, northeast of Bertrand. There, the younger child, Linda, was born. We resided there until April 1944 when our house burned to the ground, leaving nothing but ashes. Daddy then moved our family to a small apartment in Diehlstadt, where we lived several months, then moved to a small house located where the Drury Inn is now located in Miner. The town was known then as "Miner Switch." Daddy bought a house in 1945 on Matthews Street in Sikeston, where Linda still resides.

My father, H. Arlen Miller, was born Nov. 20, 1902 and died March 13, 1985. Mother was born May 9, 1906 and died July 7, 1985, only three months after Daddy's death. My eldest sibling, Donald Roy Miller, died Oct. 16, 1998.

I married Chandos Irvin McRill on June 1, 1969. We purchased the home at 555 Park Avenue in Sikeston just prior to our marriage, and moved in shortly after our wedding....I continue to reside there. My husband, Chandos, was born Oct. 20, 1922 and died June 9, 1991. We were married on what would have been his mother and natural father's 50th wedding anniversary. Chandos died on what would have been his mother's 90th birthday.

Chandos' father, Samuel Irvin McRill, died when he was a mere baby, as the result of injuries received in WWI. His mother, Alta Ruth Crites McRill, born June 9, 1901, later married Lee A. Jackson on March 23, 1925. Lee Jackson was the only father Chandos every knew. His mother, Alta, died Aug. 31, 1978. His stepfather, Lee, died July 10, 1989.

Chandos McRill had two adopted daughters, Anita Faye McRill, born Jan. 25, 1951 and Rebecca Jean McRill, born Oct. 24, 1955.

Anita McRill married at an early age and became the mother of James Feverston Jr. born Aug. 27, 1969. Anita's second son, Chandos Eldon Humphries, was born Nov. 21, 1975 and she had a daughter, Misty Erica Humphries, on Feb. 21, 1977. Anita was married and divorced twice, then married Edward Zimmer Oct. 18, 1980. Edward adopted Chandos and Misty following their mar-

riage. All three of Anita's children are married and have children of their own, now living in Texas.

Rebecca Jean McRill resides in Reno, NV. Her first husband, George Arthur Parr Sr. was killed in a motorcycle accident Sept. 25, 1976, leaving her with a baby, George Arthur Parr Jr., born Dec. 1, 1973. She remarried and divorced twice. Then she married Rodney Robert Walker Sr. She has a son, Jeremy Walker, born Jan. 16, 1977, and a son, Rodney Robert Walker Jr., born March 4, 1980 of that marriage.

I have lived in Sikeston most of my life. I attended grade school at South Grade School, which was located on School Street in Sikeston, where the City now has a low rent housing project. I graduated from Sikeston High School, located on Tanner Street, where the City swimming pool and YMCA are presently located. The YMCA facility is the old Gymnasium, where I received my high school diploma in May 1953. The City demolished both schools several years ago....calling it "progress."

I began working in the office of the Buckner Ragsdale Store Company on East Front Street in Sikeston in May 1950 at the age of 15. I continued working there until June 1953. I then worked for Mr. Harry J. Harty in his Real Estate and Farm Loan Association until ill health forced the closing of his office a year later. I returned to the Buckner Ragsdale Store Company, where I remained until May 1969. My soon-to-be husband was in the life insurance and investment business, so I decided to assist him in his work after our marriage. A few years later, I returned to the Buckner Ragsdale Store Company as the need became evident for help in their office.

Ownership of the Buckner Ragsdale Store Company changed, due to the death of the original owners. I left work there in January 1983 and began working with the Sikeston Regional Children's Services, a center for abused/neglected children, and the Scott County Juvenile Office. I continued working as Administrative Assistance for SRCS until we were forced to close the center due to funding. I then remained with the Juvenile Office, where I continue to work as Administrative Assistant/Office Manager.

Scott County is a great county to live and work in!

MEHR-MIER – An early settler of what was once known as Bleda and now known as Caney, was Mr. Johannas John Mehr-Mier, who was born Nov. 10, 1830 in Prussia, Germany. His father's name was Phillip Mehr and his mother's name was Elisebeth Gruderkemper. He was of German and French descent. The Kaiser was putting the boys in the Army over there, so at a very early age he came to America as a stowaway on a freighter which left the port of Hamburg, Germany and docked at New Orleans, LA. A gentleman by the name of Mr. McDillian reared him until he was a young man. He then came up the Mississippi River and landed at Commerce, which was at one time a docking point for most of the river traffic. From Commerce he came to New Hamburg, MO. There he met Katharina Metz. They were married in the St. Lawrence Catholic Church in New Hamburg, MO in 1861.

John fought in the Civil War on the Union side (1860-1865). In his early 30s he came to Bleda and homesteaded the land that was at that time a wilderness. He bought 80 acres of land to start, cleared it and built a house, and farmed the new ground. John and Katie had 13 children, of which nine survived. Through the years, another 240 acres was added to the original 80 acres. The old home stood until 1964, when a new one replaced the original.

John died Jan. 3, 1902 at age 72 of typhoid

fever. Katie died May 24, 1902 at the age of 62. They are buried in the old Catholic Cemetery on the hill in Oran, MO.

The Miers are one of the five older families of the Caney District. Leroy Mier still lives on the original land where the old home stood. The barn that is there was built in 1907 by John Pobst, Lucia Mier's husband. Bertha Katharina Mier and her husband, John Stephens, ran the store at Caney for several years after they got married. The mail was delivered by horse and buggy for 77 years. The windmill that was used on the farm was 55 feet high and the original parts are still in the barn. Early Scott County naturalization records: John Mier, Prussia, 1859.

MEYER – Frances Bernard Meyer, known and loved as "Ben," was born 13 Nov. 1906 in St. Genevieve County, MO. He is the son of Henry Jacob Meyer (1879-1970) and Regina Louise Guethle (1881-1926). Ben is the grandson of Joseph Peter Paul Meyer (1856-1899) and Mary Pfaff (1856-1949) and the great grandson of Jacob Meyer (1827-1901) and Helena Baechle (1828-1880) from Baden, Germany. As a young man, Ben moved to Stoddard County, MO and from there to Scott County, MO around 1934. On 23 Oct. 1934 in the St. Denis Catholic Church in Benton, MO, Frances Bernard Meyer married Lorena Christina Essner. Lorena was born in Scott County, MO and she is the daughter of Eugene Essner (1889-1966) and Clara Diebold (1894-1973). She is the granddaughter of Frank Essner (1861-1946) and Crescent Scherer (1863-1949) and the great granddaughter of Nicholas Essner (1823-1878) and Margarete Ress (1824-1907).

Photo ca. 1968. Front row left to right: Eileen, Laverne, Ben, Lorena, Rita, Jane, Denise. Middle row left to right: Bernie, Margie, Helen, Carolyn, Marie. Back row left to right: John, Charlie, Gene, Tom

Ben and Lorena spent their entire married life together in Scott County, MO where they owned and operated a 120-acre farm just outside the north edge of Benton in Scott County, MO. Their farm life consisted of raising cattle, hogs, sheep, chickens, and row crops and hay fields along with a huge vegetable garden. Ben and Lorena were faithful members of the St. Denis Catholic Church in Benton where Ben served as bell ringer and custodian for many years while Lorena kept the church linen spotless.

Ben and Lorena are the parents of the following 14 children: 1) Marie, born 23 July 1935; 2) Lavern, born 1 Aug. 1936; 3) Rita, born 9 Aug. 1938; 4) John, born 13 Dec. 1939; 5) Helen, born 6 April 1941; 6) Eugene "Gene," born 23 June 1942; 7) Margaret "Margie," born 17 Sept. 1943; 8) Carolyn, born 29 Sept. 1945; 9) Bernadette "Bernie," born 14 Dec. 1946; 10) Jane, born 25 Feb. 1948; 11) Thomas "Tom," born 1 Feb. 1950; 12) Charles "Charlie," born 19 Feb. 1952; 13) Eileen, born 16 March 1953; 14) Denise, born 18 June 1954.

At the age of 74 Lorena died on 15 March 1989 and at age 89 Ben died 2 Oct. 1996. Both are buried in the St. Denis Catholic Church Cemetery in Benton, MO.

MHOONS – The Ivery D. Mhoon clan migrated to Scott County in the late 1960s from neighboring Pemiscot and New Madrid counties. Originally from Clarksdale, AR, Mr. Mhoon, son of Mr. and Mrs. Adolphus Sr. and Bessie Ward Mhoon, and grandson of Mr. and Mrs. Charlie and Clora Mhoon, from Tunica, MS, met and later married his bride, Dursilla Anderson, daughter of Reverend and Mrs. Asberry and Sally Anderson of Osceola, AR on March 15, 1939.

Ivery (born Jan. 1, 1919) and Dursilla (born Jan. 26, 1923) celebrated their 63rd wedding anniversary. There were 13 children of the marriage: Lorene (Coleman); Roscoe; Ivery Jr.; Asberry (Anderson); Atha; Wil Ella died 1960; Edward; Eddie; Charles Earl; Willie Gene; Melvin Lee; Annie Laura; and Linda Rene.

For many years Ivery carried on the tradition of his father and grandfather by farming the land. His father, Adolphus, who both owned and rented acreage, taught him the necessary skills to carve a living from the harsh conditions. Ivery would need these same skills to provide for a growing family of 13. The often uncertainty and unpredictability that plagued farming prompted him to try his hand at other vocations.

Ivery left his family while he worked for a two-year span as a special trained railroad team laying rail in Ste. Genevieve County. This required him to be away from his family for long periods of time. He sent money home weekly to support the family.

Ivery also worked cutting logs at a sawmill, Barnes Hospital in maintenance, McCord Seed Company, Sikeston Cottonmeal Company and Malone and Hyde where he retired in 1985 after 14 years of service.

Dursilla, in addition to raising 13 of her own children, would often welcome and take in extended family for lengths of time with no expectation of compensation. It is estimated that besides her own 13, she has easily raised 30 additional children. One son remarked that she never knew how to cook small portions but always had lots of food. Another son tells a story of her opening her home to a drifter that wandered the train track and "just looked hungry." Although by nature Dursilla was very gentle and mild mannered, this lady commanded the attention and respect of her family.

In reflection, Mr. and Mrs. Mhoon stated that when it comes to measuring a life or leaving a legacy, they have done both as they stand in the middle of the road looking to what has been and towards all that will be.

MICHAEL – Robert "Bob" Charles Michael Jr. was born June 21, 1937 in Blytheville, AR. He was the son of R. Charles Michael (born April 19, 1914) and Bernice Lorraine Hooper (born Feb. 11, 1912). They were married April 7, 1934 in Booneville, MS. After her death (Oct. 7, 1960), Charles married June Belk on Dec. 9, 1962.

In his life (Aug. 16, 1991) of farming, Charles learned of the good and bad of his vocation. During the depression, his farm family lost their land in Mississippi and moved to Arkansas to share-crop.

Charles and Bernice welcomed their first-born, Bob, in 1937 in their tenant home. About 1938, the family moved to their Benton, MO homestead and purchased about 70 acres originally, thus beginning a reign of hard, but productive years which resulted eventually in the ownership of approximately 1500 acres, and the ability to rent an

additional 1500 acres. Much of this rich land was on Big Island (near Commerce or in the bottoms behind his home).

A second son, Joseph "Joe" Lee, was born Dec. 8, 1942. Joe graduated from the University at Columbia and later taught VO-AG for years.

On March 1, 1959, Bob married Sandra "Sonnie" K. Cotner (born March 1, 1940) of Cape Girardeau, MO (daughter of Virgil J. and Edna May (Heuschober) Cotner) at Maple Avenue U.M.C. They lived in Benton 12 years and had three daughters: Shauna Kay (June 19, 1961, died after birth); Rhonda Shea (April 29, 1962); and Leslie LeAnn (May 3, 1965). Both girls graduated from Kelly Schools and SEMO University.

On Jan. 26, 1985 Rhonda married Don M. Painton at Maple U.M.C. where her parents and grandparents had married. They have two sons, Michael Charles (born July 26, 1985) is a tenth grader at Bell City High, honor student, drummer, pianist, and is completing his Eagle Scout project and is a member of St. Paul U.M.C. Marcus Don (born Jan. 17, 1989) is a seventh grader at Bell City Junior High, honor student, drummer, Life Scout, and a member of St. Paul U.M.C. Rhonda teaches at Bell City Elementary school.

Leslie has worked for the USDA for 14 years and was appointed to Jefferson City, MO (April 7, 2002) as Assistant State Conservationist. After being raised in a farm family, she continues in Ag related field.

Bob Michael Jr. family, October 2001. Leslie, Michael, Sonnie, Donnie, Rhonda, Marcus, and Bob.

In February 1971, Bob purchased the Ed Johnson farm at Commerce and the family has resided there since, with the majority of the land located on Big Island.

The family attends the 113 year old St. Paul U.M.C. (established 1889), two blocks from the mighty Mississippi River. However, during the 1993 flood, the church remained high and dry.

Bob belongs to Unity Baptist Church, Masons, O.E.S. and is former President of Big Island Levee Association. He was instrumental in rebuilding the levees after the 1993 and 1995 floods.

Sonnie has served as Church Board Secretary for 30 years, sings in the choir and is a 40-year member of Benton Homemakers, O.E.S., and member of St. Paul U.M.C.

On Nov. 29, 1990 they were honored as Scott County Farm Family at the annual Farm Recognition Banquet at Sikeston.

Family Time – Farming – and Focus on God continues to be important factors for their lives! *Submitted by Sandra K. Michael*

MILLER – Henry "Arlen" Miller was born Nov. 20, 1902 in Henry County, TN to Warren and Mittie Salina (Biggs) Miller, who married in Blodgett March 20, 1897.

He was one of a family of five children: Ollie, born Feb. 6, 1898 in Scott County and married Charles Alexander; Elva Mae, born July 15, 1900 in Henry County and married Clayton Wood;

Lessie Marie, born May 5, 1906 married Jack Watson; Arvel Roy, born April 24, 1911 in Scott County, married Grace Patrick; and Charles, born Nov. 20, 1915 in Scott County and died Sept. 3, 1916. His mother, Mittie, died in the flu epidemic in Scott County, Dec. 20, 1917 and is buried in the Silent Hill Cemetery along with other members of the family. His father lived until 1954 and died at the home of Elva and Clayton Wood in Sikeston.

Arlen attended school at Pleasant Valley and Boardman Chapel in Scott County through the sixth grade when he went to work in the fields. At the age of 4, Arlen and his family returned from Tennessee during the winter, crossing the Mississippi River in a wagon on the frozen ice.

Arlen and Blanche (Moody) Miller, 1974.

On Dec. 28, 1924 in New Madrid, MO at the courthouse he married Serena "Blanche" Moody of Scott County, daughter of Thomas Williamson and Eliza Belle Murrell Moody of Blodgett. Blanche was also one of five children: Margaret Lucille, born 1896, married Aubrey Davis of Scott County; William Murrell, born 1900 in Scott County; Ethel Ann, born 1903, wife of Orlando Shrum of Mississippi County; and Thomas Harold, born 1909 who married Beatrice Davenport.

The Moody family were active in establishing the Methodist Church in Blodgett and were active members of the community.

Arlen and Blanche bought a farm just south of Diehlstadt in 1935. Arlen went to work at the International Shoe Factory the day it opened (December 1923) and continued to work until his retirement in December 1967. The house on the farm burned, and he moved the family to Sikeston, buying the house where his youngest daughter still resides.

The couple parented four children: Donald Roy, born Aug. 10, 1928 in Sikeston, who married Elizabeth Wanda Arbaugh, she preceded him in death and he married Shirley Davenport; Margaret Marie, born Sept. 2, 1930 and married Carl Joyce; Lois Ann, born Oct. 24, 1935 and married Chandos McRill; and Linda Mae, born March 8, 1938 has never married. Lois and Linda graduated from Sikeston High, working and residing in Sikeston their lifetime. Lois worked at the Buckner Ragsdale Store and presently works for the Scott County Juvenile Court.

Linda went to work at the Missouri Highway Department after graduation where she worked until her retirement.

Arlen passed away March 11, 1985 at the Missouri Delta Med. Center and Blanche passed away July 7, 1985. They are buried in the Sikeston Memorial Garden Cemetery.

The Miller's were lifetime members of the Bertrand Methodist Church, though Arlen was raised in the Baptist Church. Blanche was active in the Methodist Women, taught Sunday school and babysat for several Sikeston families. Linda and Lois sang in the church choir, taught Sunday school and Linda played the church organ. They were well thought of and highly respected in the Sikeston, Blodgett and Bertrand communities.

Linda and Lois are presently active members of the First United Methodist Church in Sikeston and are volunteer hosts at the Sikeston Depot Museum. *Submitted by Linda Miller*

MILLER – Dennis Ferrell Miller was born on June 26, 1944 in rural Sikeston to Ferrell Miller and Willine Rettig Miller. His paternal grandparents were James Madison Miller and Rose Etta Hale Miller. His maternal grandparents were Otto Rettig and Bertha Wagoner Rettig. He had three brothers: Ronald; Lyle and Roy, and one sister, Sharron Miller Mallot.

Dennis went through the Sikeston School system, where he graduated in 1962. He attended part of two years at SEMO State. He went to work for the Missouri Highway Department in 1965. He enlisted in the National Guard in 1965 and trained for six months in North Carolina and in Ft. Lewis, WA. He returned to work for the Highway Department almost 30 years as draftsman and a highway designer. He died of cancer on Sept. 26, 1994, a few months short of retirement. He lived his entire life in Scott County.

Kerri, Dennis, Jan, and Darin Miller

On Oct. 1, 1965 in Sikeston, he married Jan Nicholas. She is the daughter of Clyde Nicholas and Alma Corlew Nicholas. Jan worked as secretary to the school system; 25 years at the Kindergarten Center.

They had two children: Kerri Denise Miller, born July 5, 1970 and Darin Blake Miller, born March 15, 1972.

Dennis loved to bowl. He was the first to bowl a 300 game at the Sikeston Bowling Alley. He loved to hunt, especially deer, and to fish. He was active in the bowling league as well as Little League Baseball. He helped plan and construct the gym at First Church of the Nazarene. *Submitted by Jan Miller*

MILLER –Ferrell Miller was born in Knowville, AR on Feb. 28, 1919 to James Madison Miller Jr and Rose Etta Hale Miller. His paternal grandparents were James Madison Miller Sr. and Ellen Burrow. His maternal grandparents were Thomas Jefferson Hale and Malinda Clark. He had three brothers: Collie; Gladys and Odel and four sisters: Connie Havener; Jewell Bennett; Odessia Jones and Novella Yates.

Back row: Ronnie, Dennis, Sharron, Lyle, and Roy. Seated: Willine and Ferrell Miller.

His parents were farmers in the Arkansas River Bottoms. When a dam broke during the flood of 1927 on the Arkansas River, they had only hours

to get out. They lost all their farming equipment and belongings. After living there a few more years in Arkansas, they migrated to Wardell, MO and on to Crowder in Scott County, where the family still farms. He attended school in Crowder. In 1937 he joined the CCC camps for 30 months. He was stationed at New Madrid and Delta camps. He had to help the 1937 flood refugees find shelter in schools and churches. In 1940 he joined the Missouri National Guards in the 140th Infantry of the 35th Division. He left for training in Little Rock, AR in January 1941. He later trained at Camp Hood, TX and spent nine months in the Philippine Islands. He was discharged in April 1946. He returned to Sikeston and spent 36 years working for Pepsi-Cola, 33 year as manager, before retiring in 1983. He loves hunting and fishing and spending winters in Okeechobee, FL.

On Nov. 24, 1940 at Charleston, he married Willine Rettig, who was born on Feb. 14, 1922 near what is now Grant City, MO. Her parents were Otto and Bertha Wagoner Rettig. Maternal grandparents were Alexander Wagoner and Sarah Hamblin Wagoner. Paternal grandparents were Fred Rettig and Anna Caroline Krieg Rettig. Anna and Fred's parents came from Germany. Willine had three brothers: Sherman; Laverne and Harold. She had four sisters: Cleo Davis; Sadie James; Lola Adcock; and Dorothy Broderick.

Willine graduated from Chaneyi Grade School and from Blodgett High School in 1939. She was a homemaker basically, but did direct Kiddieland Nursery School for 14 years for Eastside Church of the Nazarene. She also worked 15 years for H. and R. Block.

They had five children: James Ronald Miller, born Aug. 19, 1942; Dennis Ferrell Miller, born June 26, 1944 and died Sept. 26, 1994; Sharron Rose Miller Mallot, born Dec. 27, 1947; Lyle Douglas Miller, born Sept. 22, 1949; and Roy Leslie Miller, born Oct. 8, 1953.

Ronnie Miller served three years in 1961-64 in the Army at Fort Lewis, WA and Alaska. Dennis Miller served six years in the National Guard with camps in North Carolina and Fort Lewis, WA. Lyle spent three years in the Army, training at Fort Knox, KY and Brooks Army Hospital in San Antonio, TX. *Submitted by Ferrell Miller*

MILLER – James Madison Miller Jr. and Rose Etta Hale Miller first came to Scott County in January 1934. They lost all their farming equipment and household goods when the Arkansas River flooded in 1927.

The depression came before they were able to start farming again. They migrated to Pemiscott County in the fall of 1933. They came on to Scott County where they started to share crop on a farm outside of Crowder. In 1945 they moved to Sikeston. J. M. worked at the REA until he retired. He died in 1968 and Rose followed him in 1969.

J. M. was the son of J. M. Miller Sr. and Ellen Burrows. J. M.'s great grandfather came to this country from Ireland.

Rose is the daughter of Malinda Clark Hale and Thomas Jefferson Hale. She is of French and Indian descent.

J. M. and Rose married in Arkansas on June 8, 1908. They raised eight children to adulthood. They are: Collie C.; Connie; Gladys C.; Jewell; Ferrell; Odessa; Novella; and Odell.

C. C. married Bonnie Marie Holcomb of Cardwell, MO. They resided in Cardwell until they retired. Then they moved to Jonesboro, AR. They had four children: Jerry Lee; Joe Allen; Glenn Dale; and Bonnie Jean.

Connie married Dock Bradford Havener of Hartman, AR. They lived in the Sikeston area most of their lives. Dock passed away in 1993.

They had six children: Calvin (deceased); Gerald; Alyne; Barbara (deceased); Brenda and Fannie (deceased).

Gladys (Huck) married Wanda Warpeha of California. They resided in California most of their lives. They had three children: Mary Francis; Jean Delores; and Linda Rose. Wanda passed away in 1976 and Gladys in 1991.

Family of J.M. and Rose Miller

Jewell married Chester Troy Bennett "Jack" of Crowder, MO. They resided in Sikeston until sometime in the 1950s when they moved to the St. Louis area. They had three children: Roger Wayne; Kathy and Chester Troy Jr. Jack passed away in 1988.

Ferrell married Willine Rettig of the Sikeston area. They lived in Sikeston. They had five children: James Ronald; Dennis Ferrell; Sharron Rose; Lyle Douglas; and Roy Leslie.

Odessa married Ernie Jones of the Oran area. They lived in the Oran and Morley area most of their lives. They had six children: Peggy Lucille; Larry Robert (deceased); Linda; David; Albert; and Brian.

Novella married Robert A. Yates Jr. of New York. Robert passed away in 1979. Novella moved back to Sikeston in the 1980s. They had three children: Constance Joy; Lawana; and Barbara Ann.

Odell married Betty Jane Davis of Sikeston. After living in Illinois and Maryland, they moved back to Sikeston in the 1980s. They had two children: Terry Odell (deceased) and Janie Renee. Odell passed away in 1998.

MILLER – James Ronald Miller was born at Sikeston on Aug. 19, 1942 to Ferrell Miller and Willine Rettig Miller. His paternal grandparents were James Madison Miller and Rose Etta Hale Miller. His maternal grandparents were Otto Rettig and Bertha Wagoner Rettig. He had three brothers: Dennis; Lyle and Roy and one sister, Sharron Miller Mallot.

He grew up through the Sikeston Public School System where he graduated in 1960. He enlisted in the Army Aug. 20, 1961, training first at Fort Leonard Wood, MO and later stationed at Fort Lewis, WA, and from there he spent six months in Alaska.

Ron Miller Family

He returned to Sikeston in 1965 and was employed by Pepsi-Cola for 34 years. He started as a route man and later as assistant manager and trainer. He retired from Pepsi in 1998 and presently lives in Pella, IA.

He was first married to Gail Harbin in 1968. They divorced in 1974 and he married Aimee Hammock Sailors on July 11, 1975. She had a daughter, Janey Elizabeth Sailors, whom he raised. He and Aimee had one son, Jason Ronald Miller, born Jan. 5, 1977. Aimee worked several years for Southwestern Bell and was a secretary for the Girl Scouts when she became sick. She died of cancer on Aug. 27, 1991. Ronnie and Aimee had one foster son, who was later adopted. Travis Ray Masterson, who was born May 13, 1979, was adopted in February 1992. Ronnie married Dorothy Cathey Kelley on March 20, 1993. She had two daughters, Vicki and Lisa Kelley.

He loves to cook, especially to try new recipes, to travel and take pictures. *Submitted by Ron Miller*

MILLER – Roy Leslie Miller was born Oct. 8, 1953 at Sikeston to Ferrell Miller and Willine Rettig Miller. He was the grandson of Madison (J. M.) Miller and Rose Hale Miller and of Otto Rettig and Bertha Wagoner Rettig. He had three brothers: Ronnie; Dennis; and Lyle and one sister, Sharron Miller Mallot.

He attended all 12 of his school years in the Sikeston Public Schools, graduating in 1972. He attended the National Business School in Kansas City in 1972 and Space Age Careers. He started work with First National Bank in Sikeston, then First National Bank of St. Louis in Cape Girardeau. In 1989 he went to work for First Security State Bank in Charleston, MO as Data Processing Manager Compliance Officer and Purchasing Officer.

He first married Trudie Stephenson in 1979 and they divorced in 1980. He later married Linda Armstrong Courtois on Aug. 23, 1996. She has three daughters: Amber Greer; Brittany; and Mallory Courtois.

He is an avid hunter and fisherman. He has several deer head

Roy and Linda Miller

mounts in his family room and big fish pictures, one of a 40-pound catfish from the Mississippi River which was caught on a rod and reel. He enjoys sports of all kind and plays volleyball and softball in the leagues. *Submitted by Roy Miller*

MOORE – A long-time resident of Sikeston, Alfred Joseph Moore Sr. was born Feb. 19, 1874 on his father's farm in New Madrid County, near the community of Noxall on the Sikeston to New Madrid Road, formerly called "Kings Highway." His parents were Franklin "Uncle Doc" Moore (1847-1931) and Sarah Ann Knox (1848-1923), both of New Madrid County. Alfred Moore's paternal grandparents were William Franklin Moore (1812-1866) and Nancy Stoker (1813-1923), who had come by wagon from Henry County, TN in 1832 and had homesteaded the very farm of Alfred's birth. The maternal grandparents were William Harrison Knox and Elizabeth Knox, also of New Madrid County. Not raised to farm work, Alfred Joseph Moore graduated from Christian Brothers College in St. Louis and afterwards attended Bryant and Stratton Business College in Louis-

ville, KY. There he completed a certified course in public accounting. Returning to Sikeston, he worked briefly at the Citizens Bank and then entered the employ of the Bank of Sikeston, where he remained until his death nearly 40 years later. Although his official title was assistant cashier, Alfred Moore was a trusted

Alfred J. and Grace Ann (Schumate) Moore, December 2, 1915.

advisor and true friend to many hundreds who patronized the bank. On May 10, 1899 he was united in marriage with Grace Ann Shumate, daughter of Dr. John L. Shumate and Lucinda Jane Magee of Sikeston. Grace Shumate attended Hardin College in Mexico, MO. The couple resided at 517 Park Avenue in Sikeston, where all three of their children were born. Alfred Joseph Moore Jr. was born on July 6, 1903 and was educated in the Sikeston public schools. He attended the University of Illinois for 2-1/2 years before accepting a position as clerk in the Senate House in Jefferson City. "Joe" Moore underwent surgery for the removal of kidney stones at Baptist Hospital in St. Louis, but he did not survive the operation and died on July 13, 1929. A second son, John Franklin Moore, called "Franklin,," was born on March 11, 1906. Franklin also attended the Sikeston schools and later worked as farm manager of the C. D. Matthews Estate. Franklin Moore, who was unmarried, died unexpectedly on July 20, 1946. The last child, and only daughter, born to Alfred and Grace Moore was Camille Henrietta Moore, born Oct. 6, 1915. Unfortunately, Grace Moore did not survive childbirth, and she died on Dec. 2, 1915. In 1920 Alfred J. Moore Sr. married his wife's older sister, Henrietta "Etta" Shumate McMullin, who was previously the wife of deceased John Perry McMullin of Scott County. Alfred Moore predeceased his second wife on May 3, 1937, while Etta Shumate Moore passed away on May 12, 1944. They are all buried in the Sikeston City Cemetery. Camille Henrietta Moore, called "Henrietta," was likewise educated in the Sikeston schools. She attended Fairmont Junior College in Washington, D. C. and graduated from the University of Missouri in 1937. On May 31, 1941 she married Capt. Charles Berton Root, United States Army Air Corps, a native of Madison, SD, who was then commander of the Air Corps Training Detachment at the Harvey Parks Airport in Sikeston. Henrietta Moore Root died on March 13, 1976 while her husband, Maj. General Bert Root, lived until Nov. 8, 1998. General and Mrs. Root are survived by their children: Tom Moore Root; James Franklin Root and Nancy Ann Sheppard, all of Mobile, AL; and Carl Joseph Root of Seattle, WA. *Submitted by Tom Moore Root*

MOORE – Herbert "Herb" Franklin Moore was born June 5, 1968 at Missouri Delta Medical Center in Sikeston, MO.

He is the only child of the late Larry Dale Moore (May 6, 1946-March 11, 1999) and Brenda Sue Abernathy Moore (July 29, 1948). Brenda resides in Sikeston, MO.

Herb is the grandson of the late Hunter "Tab" Moore and Pauline Moore, formerly of Laforge, MO, and the late Herbert Abernathy of Morehouse, and Cordia Abernathy, who still resides in Morehouse, MO.

Herb attended Sikeston Public Schools, gradu-

ating in 1986. As a teenager he was in the Cadet program with the Sikeston Department of Public Safety and active in the Martial Arts. After graduation, he chose a musical career as a professional percussionist.

The first band Herb played for was the Larry Swift Bank. He later played for Manitou, and is currently with Neon Nite. These bands have opened shows for several well-known entertainers. Too numerous to mention them all by name, but one for instance, would be the late great Keith Whitley.

On Sept. 10, 1997 Herb married Coye Lyn Dueitt, the daughter of the late Pamela Henley Luttrull (March 9, 1953-Aug. 29, 2000) and Ronald Lee Dueitt (March 24, 1948, residing in Brenham, TX).

Together Herb and Coye have two children; a son, Shaddow Hawk Moore, born Dec. 12, 1996 and a daughter, Heaven

The Moore's. Herb, Meagan, and Christy; Heaven, Coye, and Shaddow.

Lee Moore, born Sept. 10, 2001. Herb also has two older daughters, Meagan Christina (born Feb. 8, 1988), residing in Brookpark, OH; and Christy Lynn (born April 4, 1988), residing in Jackson, MO.

Herb and his wife, Coye, are known locally for their appearances on the Kenny Rogers Cerebral Palsy Telethon, where they are asked to perform annually. Each of them have great vocal talent.

Coye is presently enjoying being a wife and mother. In addition to Herb's music, he is also an employee for the Food Giant Warehouse in Sikeston, MO. Herb is also very talented in art and special effects. Some of his artwork includes portraits of country music artists, such as George Strait, whom in fact has some of these portraits displayed in his home. *Submitted by Brenda S. Moore*

MOORE – The earliest record of my great grandmother, Jane A. Latham, in Scott County, MO was her marriage to George Washington Moore on Dec. 14, 1853 in Scott County. They lived in Richland Township at that time. In February 1860, George W. Moore died of pneumonia in New Madrid County. The 1860 census shows Jane as a widow in New Madrid County. The census showed three children: Sarah E.; Martha C. and Robert M. Shortly after 1860 Jane moved back to Scott County to be near her older sister, Martha Latham Badget, who had moved to Missouri from Kentucky between 1855-1859. Also, a younger sister, Catherine Caroline Latham, had married William Bowman about 1853 and they settled in Scott County.

Shortly after arriving in Scott County, Jane Latham Moore met Sion Bray who had drifted to Missouri from North Carolina. Sion had left home at about 15 years of age and has no record until arriving in Missouri. Aug. 9, 1863 Sion and Jane were married in Scott County, MO. Prior to this time, Jane's son, Robert M. Moore, appears to have died.

The Bray farm and property were located about midway between Benton and Sylvania (now Oran). Their first child, my grandmother Laura Bray, was born Aug. 9, 1864; the only daughter of this union. She did have several brothers.

About 1882 Jane died and was buried on the family farm. A young son and some stillborn babies were also buried there. Sion Bray died in

1899 and is buried on the family plot. In 1983 I was able to locate the family cemetery. The owners of the farm remembered a family burial plot in what was called Kieffers' woods. The trees are gone so we put a marker on the curve of the old wagon road that marked the old family cemetery. This wagon road curve is about one-half mile south of the old road between Benton and Oran. A hundred years ago the curve was several hundred feet east of the farm house and turned right toward Morley and left toward a connecting road to Sylvania.

The Brays had also built a large two-story house in Morley for a granddaughter of Jane, who they raised after the death of her mother, Sarah E. (Moore) Edmundson. This granddaughter, Mary Edmundson, married Albert Engle. The house in Morley is still standing just south across the street from the railroad tracks in the northwest part of Morley. Besides this property, the Bray family also owned some lots in old Sylvania.

About 1908 a banking crisis arose and all property of this family was lost. However, these early people were a hardy lot and even though they lost their worldly goods, they rebuilt their lives and proved to be useful citizens of Scott County and other areas to which some of them relocated. *Submitted by Ted Armes*

MOORE – The children of Ruth Mae Moore and John Byrd Pippin had their first family reunion in Sikeston, MO in July 1983. They visited their childhood homes in Oran and Morley, the cotton gin where they delivered cotton, the Hooe School site, the old swimming holes, the school and the Baptist church they attended in Oran, and the sites of the farms they worked on. Following the reunion, Leon and Emily Pippin, son Brett, daughter Jeanne, and grandson Daniel, remained in Sikeston. They were determined to solve the family "mystery" and find out who the parents of Ruth Moore were.

Over the years, bits and pieces of Ruth's ancestry were passed around among the children. She was an orphan; she had lived with many families as a house servant; she had lived with Nellie Abernathy for several years. But they had been told that none of the families she lived with were *Ruth Mae Moore Pippin* any relation. Emily and Jeanne decided to dig until they found some good hard evidence about who this little orphan really was.

They went door to door, asking if anyone knew anything about Ruth Moore. No one knew anything, but each would refer them to another individual. They searched the Courthouse records in Benton and were overjoyed to find the marriage license of Jon and Ruth, who were married on Oct. 6, 1918 in Oran by Rev. Wm. Boutwell. They found the names of both sets of parents. Ruth was the daughter of Ida May Guthrie and George Moore. They found Ida May and George's marriage certificate showing they were married on Feb. 8, 1896 by a Justice of the Peace in Benton. But who was Ida May Guthrie?

Finally, on the third day, almost ready to give up, they asked someone about Nellie Abernathy and Ruth Moore. That someone told them Mrs. Mary Shuffit in Benton had a story by Beulah O'Neill Foster called "Little Tex" that mentioned Ruth Moore. They rushed to her home. Sure enough, Ruth was mentioned on page 18: "A short

time after we moved, my Aunt Allie wrote a letter to Mother and wanted to come live with us, as she was ill and there was no one to care for her, except her little Granddaughter, Ruth Moore, who was only nine years old. So Mother took Aunt Allie and Ruth into our home and cared for them until Aunt Allie passed away. A few months later, mother's niece and husband, Nellie and Clarence Abernathy, took Ruth and kept her until she married."

Jubilation set in for they had found Ruth's grandmother, her great aunt, and realized that she had lived with a niece of her great aunt. They learned more. Ruth was the daughter of Ida May and George Moore, the granddaughter of Barbara Alabama Bryant and George Guthrie, great granddaughter of Caroline Kirby and James Richardson Bryant, the great great granddaughter of Jemima Dillard and James Bryant and the great great great granddaughter of William Briant and Sarah Tolleson.

They located Ruby Abernathy, daughter-in-law of Clarence and Nellie, and spent the day talking with her. Ruby's husband, Ralph, had gone to school with Ruth Moore.

The Pippin family returned to their home in Fort Wayne, IN, excited and satisfied. Leon's mother Ruth had a family, a history and a heritage – and so did he. *Submitted by Jeanne Marie Pippin Hicks, granddaughter of Ruth Mae Moore*

MORPER – Michael Johann Morper, an early settler at New Hamburg, was born on Nov. 8, 1809 at Trimberg, Unterfranken, Bavaria, Germany. He was a son of Michael Morper and Margaretha Spahn. He came to America about 1838 and first settled in Ohio. His wife was Mary Anna Brandt, born June 9, 1812 in Bavaria, Germany. The family moved to Scott County about 1847. Michael Johann died on Dec. 7, 1867 and was buried in St. Lawrence Catholic Church Cemetery at New Hamburg. In 1878 Mary sold her farmland and moved to Jackson County, IL with three of her children. She died on June 23, 1894 and is buried in St. Andrew's Cemetery at Murphysboro, IL. The family over in Illinois spell the surname Morber. Michael and Mary were the parents of seven children: Mary; Caroline; George; Josephine; Katherine; Magdalena and Elizabeth.

Mary Morper, born in 1840, first married Martin Bollinger on Feb. 14, 1860. They had a son, Joseph. After the death of Mr. Bollinger, she remarried to Henry Baehre. They had two children, Nora and Anna. Mary died on April 29, 1919 and is buried at Cape Girardeau. Caroline Morper, born in 1843, married George Wiegand on July 16, 1863 at New Hamburg. She passed away on July 5, 1873 and is buried in St. Mary's Cemetery in Cape Girardeau. George J. Morper/Morber was born Sept. 1, 1846 in Ohio. He married Elizabeth Jarrett on Dec. 24, 1880 in Jackson County, IL. They were the parents of: John; Mary; Charles; Albert; Katie; Elizabeth; Lena; Peter and William. George died on Sept. 13, 1906 and is buried in Mt. Joy Cemetery, Jackson County, IL. Elizabeth Jarrett died on April 8, 1923. Josephine Morper was born Jan. 17, 1848 in Scott County. She married Jacob Enderle on Sept. 18, 1866 at New Hamburg. They were the parents of: John B.; Magdalena; Louise; Joseph; Anna; Rosalie and William. Josephine was taken to St. Louis for an illness, and she died there on Jan. 17, 1887. She is buried in St. Peter and Paul Cemetery in St. Louis. Jacob Enderle died on Dec. 26, 1919 and is buried in St. Augustine Cemetery at Kelso. Katherine Morper/Morber was born Sept. 25, 1853 and married John Adam Young on Aug. 20, 1871 at Murphysboro, IL. They were the parents of: Emma; Ab; Mary; Charles; Lora; Gus; Louie and Ben. Katherine died on March 14, 1938 and is

buried in Oakwood Cemetery in Carterville, IL.

Magdalena Morper/Morber was born Aug. 7, 1854 in Scott County. She married on Nov. 9, 1877 in Jackson County, IL to Thomas Calvin Jackson. They were the parents of Anna, A. D., Edmont, William, Henry and Lawrence. Magdalena died on March 5, 1944 and is buried in Oakwood Cemetery in Carterville, IL.

Elizabeth Morper was born Oct. 7, 1855 in Scott County. She was married on May 23, 1872 to Francis Tenkhoff. She had a daughter, Mrs. Louis Hopper, of Cape Girardeau. Elizabeth died on July 19, 1939 and was buried in St. Mary's Cemetery at Cape Girardeau. *Submitted by Steve Dumey*

MORRIS – Children of Isaac and Allice Morris were:

Phoebe Ann Morris, b. June 17, 1875, Bloomfield, MO, Stoddard County, died Sept. 25, 1941, Bloomfield, MO, buried Carpenter Cemetery, Scott County, MO.

Ada Belle Morris, b. May 1876, Vandouser, MO, Scott County, died Nov. 5, 1916, Scott County, MO.

Mary Morris b. September 1881, Missouri, died Dexter, MO, Stoddard County, buried Hagy Cemetery, Dexter, MO.

George Lafe Morris, b. April 10, 1886, Oran, Scott County, MO died June 19, 1934, Vincennes, IN. Buried Fairview Cemetery, Vincennes, IN, Knox County.

Eva Morris, b. March 1894, Oran, Scott County, MO. Died 1918 during flu epidemic. Buried Scott County, MO.

Phoebe Ann married June 21, 1901 to John Robert McCormick. Children:

William Robert Isaac McCormick, b. Dec. 12, 1899, Stoddard County, MO. Died Aug. 2, 1979. Buried Morley, MO, Scott County, buried Forest Memorial Cemetery, Morley.

Ada Mary McCormick, b. 1907, Stoddard County, MO. Died 1907, stillborn.

William Robert Isaac "Ike," married Feb. 5, 1930, Scott County, MO to Helen Stallions. Children:

Geneva Mae McCormick b. Feb. 5, 1930, Scott County, MO. Died May 1930, Scott County, MO.

Mary Lee McCormick, b. Nov. 1, 1931, Morehouse, MO, New Madrid County. Mary Lee married first 1947 Scott County, MO to Carl E. Burgess. Children: Carl Robert Burgess; Bernice Sharon Burgess; Julius Fredrick Burgess; Kennie Bayen Burgess; Doyle Derwin Burgess; Charles Burdett Burgess; Pamela Sue Burgess. Mary Lee married second 1975, Scott County, MO to Charles Edward Williams.

Mary Morris, married April 16, 1901 Scott County, MO to Oliver Anthony Davis. Children: Oliver Anthony Davis Jr., b. 1906, Missouri and Frank Davis, b. 1908, Missouri, died in St. Louis, MO.

George Lafe Morris married first April 18, 1912, Scott County, MO to Clevie Belle Baker. Children: Alfred Desmel Morris, b. July 10, 1912, East Prairie, MO, Mississippi County and Lyman Lester Morris, b. Nov. 2, 1913, Oran, Scott County, MO.

George Lafe Morris married second Nov. 21, 1925 to Hazel Belle Cornwell, parents William W. Cornwell and Mary Emily Denton. Children: Mary Deveda Morris, b. Nov. 21, 1927, East Prairie, New Madrid County, MO. Sherman Lee Morris, b. March 27, 1930, East Prairie, New Madrid County, MO, died April 12, 1989, Vincennes, IN, Knox County, buried Fairview Cemetery, Vincennes. Betty Fern Morris, b. Sept. 28, 1932, East Prairie, New Madrid County, MO. Georgia Helen Morris, b. March 1, 1935, Vincennes, IN, Knox County.

Mary Deveda Morris, married Nov. 23, 1946

to Gilbert Merrill Goldman, son of Benjamin Ernest and Martha Gertrude Kelly Goldman. Children: Richard Eugene Goldman, b. Jan. 13, 1947, Vincennes, IN, Knox County. Gilbert Merrill Goldman Jr., b. Oct. 14, 1948, Vincennes, IN, Knox County. Betty Joann Goldman, b. Jan. 30, 1950, Vincennes, IN, Knox County.

Richard Eugene married Dec. 11, 1966, Houma, LA, Terrebonne Parish to Mary Lee Manor, daughter of Douglas and Lily Perry Manor. Children: Kristie Dawn Goldman, b. Nov. 9, 1970, Houma, LA. Rickie Elizabeth Goldman, b. April 8, 1978, Houma, LA. Rickie married April 18, 1998, Alexandria, LA Masonic Temple Church to Charles Jason Carney, son of Charles Carney and Vickie Bankston. Child, Victoria Elizabeth Carney, b. Aug. 31, 1999, Walker, LA.

Gilbert Merrill, married Aug. 28, 1968, Big Springs, TX, Webb A/F Chapel to Maria Alizara Gomez, daughter of G. O. Gomez and Maria Sanchez. Children: Sherrie Marie Goldman, b. March 6, 1969, Big Springs, TX. Wendy Suzette Goldman, b. Feb. 9, 1970, Houma, LA, Terrebonne Parish. Gilbert Merrill Goldman III, b. Aug. 21, 1974, Houma, LA. Jessica Deveda Goldman, b. Feb. 9, 1978, Big Springs, TX. Timothy Joshua Goldman, b. Nov. 10, 1979, Baton Rouge, LA. Sherrie married first June 18, 1988, Liberty, MS, Amite County, to Steven Perry. Children: Darcy Renee Perry, b. Aug. 25, 1989, Liberty, MS, Amite County. Diane Marie Perry, b. Aug. 25, 1989, Liberty, MS. Nancy Elaine Perry, b. May 6, 1991, Liberty, MS. Donna Ruth Perry, b. May 22, 1992, Liberty, MS. Sherrie Marie married second Jan. 22, 2000, Liberty, MS to Karl Vincent Conger, son of Marvin Conger and Elizabeth Dupre.

Wendy Suzette married first Dec. 10, 1988, Liberty, MS to Brian Anthony Lester. Child, Ryan Anthony Lester, b. March 23, 1989, Liberty, MS, Amite County. Wendy Suzette married second April 26, 1997, Las Vegas, NV to Anthony Michael Gambone III. Child, Anthony Michael Gambone IV, b. Dec. 15, 1995, Las Vegas, NV.

Jessica Devada married May 4, 1996, Houston, TX to Patrick James Baxter, son of Timothy Baxter and Marion Stabb. Children: Maria Elizabeth Baxter, b. March 21, 1998, Houston, TX. Kaley Alyssa Baxter, b. Oct. 12, 1999, Houston, TX.

Betty Joann married in Houma, LA, Terrebonne Parish to Daniel Paul Blanchard, son of Wilmer and Aline Portier Blanchard, graduate of Nichols College B.S. Children: Elizabeth Ann Blanchard, b. Feb. 9, 1970 in Frankfurt, Am Main, Hessen, Germany, graduate of U.S.L.-B.S., Teacher. Daniel Paul Blanchard Jr., b. Oct. 26, 1973 in Houma, LA; graduate of L.S.U.-B.S. Electrical Engineering and Computer Science-Lockheed-Martin in Houston, TX. Michael Joseph Blanchard, b. Aug. 10, 1975 in Houma, LA, graduate of U.T.I.-Associate Degree, Houston, TX-Mercedes-Benz-New Orleans, LA.

Elizabeth Ann married Sept. 2, 1989 in Houma, LA to James Lafayette Gaither, son of James and Mary Dunklin Gaither. Children: Ashton Elizabeth Gaither, b. June 17, 1992 in San Francisco, CA. Kodi Alyce Gaither, b. June 4, 1999 in Jenerette, LA. Sidni Claire Gaither, b. Feb. 14, 2001 in Jenerette, LA.

Sherman Lee married May 21, 1947, Lawrenceville, IL to Betty Lou Abel. Children: Sherman Lee Morris Jr., b. Jan. 6, 1948, Vincennes, IN, Knox County, died on Jan. 6, 1948 in Vincennes, IN, buried Fairview Cemetery. Robert Eugene Morris, b. Jan. 6, 1949, Vincennes, IN, Knox County. William, b. Dec. 17, 1949 in Vincennes, IN, Knox County.

Robert married first Carolyn McGregor, Sept. 12, 1969, Vincennes, IN. Children: Robert Eugene Morris Jr. b. March 2, 1970 in Vincennes,

IN. George Allen Morris, b. April 14, 1971 in Vincennes,, IN. Rickie Lee Morris, b. June 9, 1972 in Vincennes, IN.

Robert married second to Lisa Smith. Children: Matthew Shawn Morris, b. Oct. 31, 1986, Vincennes, IN. Rebecca Lynn Morris, b. April 29, 1988, Vincennes, IN.

William Lee Morris married July 15, 1967, Vincennes, IN to Bonnie Evans, daughter of Floyd Evans and Henrietta ?. Children: Bonnie Lou Morris, b. 8, 1967, Vincennes, IN. Bobbie Lynn Morris, b. Aug. 30, 1968, Vincennes, IN. William Lee Morris Jr., b. Oct. 3, 1969, Vincennes, IN.

William Lee married second ca., 1976 to Sheila Willis, Vincennes, IN. Children: Deborah Lee Morris, b. Feb. 22, 1978, Vincennes, IN.

Betty Fern married Nov. 15, 1956 to Joseph M. Witteried, son of Hirman and Anna Poe Witteried. Children: Joseph M. Witteried Jr., b. Dec. 23, 1957, Vincennes, IN, Knox County. Herman George Witteried, b. Jan. 2, 1959, Vincennes, IN. Christina Marie Witteried, b. March 3, 1965, Vincennes, IN, Knox County, died March 11, 1965, buried in Memorial Park Cemetery in Vincennes, IN. David Lewis Witteried, b. May 8, 1968, Vincennes, IN.

Joe married Dec. 30, 1985, Henderson, KY to Dhondra Peach. Children: LaTosha Lynn Witteried, b. July 2, 1980, Vincennes, IN, Knox County, married B. J. Dunham, 1999, Vincennes, IN. Shania Mae Witteried, b. Oct. 30, 1995, Vincennes, IN. Robert Edward Dunham, b. April 20, 2000, Vincennes, IN. Kaylie Jo Witteried, b. Jan. 5, 1986, Vincennes, IN.

Herman George married 1988, Vincennes, IN to Cynthia Ann Pruitt. Child: Holly Witteried, b. Sept. 10, 1979, Vincennes, IN. She married Aug. 10, 1999 in Vincennes, IN to Randy Pethtel, divorced. Graduate of Vincennes University, degree in Criminal Law-Parole Officer.

Herman met Regina Evans and they have a girl named Christina Marie Witteried, b. July 15, 1992, in Vincennes, IN, mother is dead.

Georgie married April 12, 1952, Vincennes, IN, Knox County, to Ralph Eugene Wininger, son of Wilber and Elizabeth Young Wininger. Children: Hazel Elizabeth Wininger, b. Dec. 27, 1952, Vincennes, IN. Steve Eugene Wininger, b. July 19, 1954, in Vincennes, IN. Jerry Lee Wininger, b. Oct. 3, 1955, Vincennes, IN. Ralph Eugene Wininger, b. Nov. 19, 1956, Vincennes, IN. Terry Jean Wininger, b. June 11, 1959, Vincennes, IN. Gary Dean Wininger, b. June 11, 1959, Vincennes, IN. Mary Fern Wininger, b. Oct. 16, 1960, Vincennes, IN. Helena Loretta Wininger, b. Oct. 17, 1963, Vincennes, IN. Julia Andra Wininger, b. July 9, 1966, Vincennes, IN. Stacie Lynn Wininger, b. Aug. 4, 1968, Vincennes, IN.

Hazel married Feb. 12, 1971, Vincennes, IN to Ellis Fields, son of Blythe Fields and Ella Peach. Children: Ellis Lee Fields Jr. b. Dec. 13, 1985, Vincennes, IN. Crystal Lynn Fields, b. March 1, 1974, Vincennes, IN. Crystal married ca., 1993, Vincennes, IN to Ronald James Allen, children: Cody James Allen, b. Jan. 5, 1994, Vincennes, IN and Brittney Paige Allen, b. Jan. 13, 1997, Vincennes, IN.

Steve Eugene married first Nov. 24, 1984, Vincennes, IN to Theresa K. Laslie. Children: Kimberely Ann Wininger, b. Sept. 17, 1985, Vincennes, IN and Amie Nicle Wininger, b. Feb. 9, 1988, Vincennes, IN.

Steve married second ca. 1994 to Jackie ?. Child: Stephanie Jean Wininger b. 1995, Vincennes, IN.

Jerry Lee married 1983 Vincennes, IN to Cynthia Fuller, daughter of Charles and Madeline Stengle Fuller. Child, Violet Jo Wininger, b. Sept. 7, 1984, Vincennes, IN.

Ralph Eugene married first 1978, Vincennes,

IN to Patsy Lynn Theriac. Children: Amber Michele Wininger, b. March 23, 1979, Vincennes, IN and Joshua Eugene Wininger, b. March 13, 1980, Vincennes, IN.

Ralph Eugene married third Feb. 14, 1997, Vincennes, IN to Kathy Jo Hill, daughter of Harold and Kathy Phillips Hill. Child, Ralph Eugene Wininger Jr., b Jan. 2, 1998, Vincennes, IN.

Terry married unknown. Children, Jeremy Scott Wininger, b. Jan. 7, 1977, Vincennes, IN and Jamie Lee Wininger, b. Feb. 10, 1979, Vincennes, IN.

Terry married June 23, 1980, Vincennes, In to Richard Pollack. Children, Curtis Wayne Pollack, b. Feb. 12, 1980, Vincennes, IN and Bobbie Jo Pollack, b. April 14, 1982, Vincennes, IN.

Gary Dean married first 1979, Vincennes, IN to Cindy Lucas. Child, Phillip Harrison Wininger, b. Jan. 21, 1980, Vincennes, IN. Gary married second 1984, Vincennes, IN to Elaine Miller. Child, Gary Dean Wininger Jr., b. Oct. 21, 1988, Vincennes, IN. Gary married, Vincennes, IN to Lisa Smith. Child, Shyene Helen Elizabeth Wininger, b. Feb. 3, 1995, Vincennes, IN.

Mary Fern, married unknown. Children: Adam Joseph Wininger, b. May 14, 1977, Vincennes, IN. Kellie Jo Wininger, b. Jan. 23, 1980, Vincennes, IN. Melissa Sue Wininger, b. April 21, 1981, Vincennes, IN.

Mary Fern married Sept. 2, 1988, Vincennes, IN to Larry Melvin Lemons.

Helena Loretta married Oct. 17, 1963, Houston, TX to Samer Fakri Tanib, son of Fakbri and Noel Hasser Tanib. Children: Rema Rasheda Tanib, female, b. April 12, 1984, Vincennes, IN, Knox County. Rushed Samer-b-Fakri Tanib, male, b. Dec. 10, 1993, Baton Rouge, LA. Samya Samer Fakri Tanib, female, b. Dec. 2, 1994, Taulkarm, West Bank, Palestine. Laith Samer Fakri Tanib, male, b. Aug. 13, 1995, Taulkarm, West Bank, Palestine.

Stacie Lynn married Jan. 30, 1989, Henderson, KY to Abrahim Khalil Eljirby, son of Khalil Eljirby and Huda ?. Children: Aishah Andra Eljirby, female, b. March 16, 1990, Vincennes, IN, Knox County. Yasmin Ibrahim Eljirby, female, b. March 23, 1992, Terre Haute, IN. Khalil Ibrahim Eljirby, male, b. July 9, 1995, Saudi Arabia.

Eva Morris, married May 27, 1911, Scott County, MO to William Parker. Eva died during the 1918 flu epidemic and I was told William and two of the children died also. Children: Raymond Parker, b. 1912, Scott County, MO. Irene Parker, b. 1914, Scott County, MO, died 1918 with the flu. Infant Parker, b. 1918, Scott County, MO, died 1918 with the flu.

MUEHLSIEPEN – Johannes Muehlsiepen and his wife, Sophie Kleinhoff (Little Yard) bought the estate of Tusan 1742 from Joseph Larow Von Beweun on the Marsian Lansbaug for 600 Thalen. From this marriage came four children: Marie Catherine; Maria Agnes; Maria Gertrude and Johannes Henrikus.

Johannes Henrikus Muehsiepen took over the Tusan Estate from his widowed mother in 1772 for 700 Thalen. His wife was Elizabeth Ferbowen. From this marriage came three children, Johannes, Ludgerus, Elizabeth and Helena.

Johannes Ludgerus Muhlsiepen married Elizabeth Weidkamp in 1809. They had three children, Johannes, Peter and Wilhelm.

Johannes Ludgerus married Katherin Pfeifer. From this marriage came seven children: Heinrich; Gertrude; Christina; Elizabeth; Sophia; Gretchen and Maria.

Elizabeth married Peter Scherfen. They had no children.

Helen married Joseph Hagan. They had two children, Joseph and Helena.

Peter, son of Johannes Ludgerus and Elizabeth Weidcamp, married Kathy Mehrkamp. They had four children: Wilhelm; Katherin; Gretchen and Elizabeth.

Wilhelm, son of Johannes Ludgerus and Elizabeth Weidkamp, married Elise Terbogan. They had three children, Fritz, Josephine and Henrich.

Johannes Ludgerus's wife, Elizabeth, died in 1817. He married Katherina Schersam in 1819. They had six children: Herman; Bernard; Elizabeth; Gertrude; Gretchen and Heinrick.

Herman, son of Johannes Ludgerus and Katherine Schersam, married Katherina Klaus. They had nine children: Elizabeth (Grandma Keusenkothen); Maria; Kristina; Johann; Gertrude; Anna; Heinrick; Gretchen and Katherina.

Bernard married Katherin Brauns. They had one son, Wilhelm.

Elizabeth married Peter Bohn. They had five children: Maria; Herman; Johann; Eda; and Wilhelm.

Gertrude married Wilhelm Brums. They had five children: Maria; Herman; Johann; Eda; and Wilhelm.

Gretchen married no one and became the housekeeper for Pastor Laungan Schurf in Boslar.

Heinrick was born Sept. 5, 1834 and was ordained to be a priest in St. Louis on Dec. 5, 1857 by Archbishop Kenerick. In 1868 he was promoted to General Vicar on the 15th of May. Pope Leo 13th gave him honor with title of Monseigneur. He died in St. Louis, MO on July 21, 1903.

Elizabeth, daughter of Herman and Katherine Klaus, was born May 7, 1858 and died Nov. 7, 1938. She married John C. Keusenkothen on Nov. 17, 1895 in Oefte by Kettwig in Germany. They had three children, Mary, John and Joseph.

Maria, daughter of Herman and Katherine Klaus, entered the order of Franciscan in Archen, and took the name of Sister Gilla. She was born September 1860 and died Nov. 1, 1937.

John H., son of Herman Muehlsiepen and Katerina Klaus, was ordained Aug. 10, 1890 and made pastor at Kelso, MO on Sept. 9, 1910. He was born April 9, 1862 and died Sept. 21, 1940.

Maria, daughter of Herman and Katherina, was not married. She lived in Hoesel on the Thusen and died at 50 or 60 years of age from a stroke.

Gertrude and Anna, daughters of Herman and Katerina, both died at age 17 of scarlet fever or typhus.

Heinrich, son of Herman and Katerina, married and had five children: John; Elizabeth; Anna; Maria and Greta.

Greta and Katherine, daughters of Herman and Katerina, came to the U.S.A. to housekeep for their older brother, Father John H., at Kelso. They are buried at Arcadia.

Bernard, son of Johannes Ludgerus and Katherine Schersam, married Katherin Bruns. They had one son, Wilhelm.

Henrick, son of Johann Muehsiepen and Katherina Pfeifer, married Kathy Millandorf. They had eight children: Ammalia (married Lambert Schmalback-four children); Johann B. (born Sept. 23, 1865, ordained in San Antonio, TX as redemptorist Pastor, died July 26, 1936); Maria (married Joseph Allkott); Bertha (married Ferdinand Weiselburg); Katherin; Joseph; Lehnchen and Gretchen.

Johannes Keusenkothen (born Oct. 30, 1822 in Oefte, Germany) married in 1856 to Margareta Catharina Preutenborbeck (born Jan. 20, 1836 in Holstergausan, Germany). He was guard for Kaiser Frederick William IV, King of Prussia. King Frederick was a friend of the Preutenborbeck family and baptismal sponsor for Margareta's older brother, also named Frederick William. Their children were: Emilie (Jan. 17, 1858-Nov. 3, 1923); Johann C. (Dec. 6, 1858-July 28, 1943); Bernardine (Jan. 3, 1860-Sept. 21, 1926); Berta (1863-1865); Frederick (May 25, 1865-March 22, 1949—married Mariechan Eggebrecht (Aug. 4, 1863) on Aug. 22, 1904—buried at cemetery in Borbeck, Hulsmann Street—was a soldier—no children); Agnes (Jan. 10, 1867-?—Sister Makrina); Eda (Dec. 25, 1868-1873—drowned in water lilly pond); Mariechen (April 7, 1870-?—Sister Seruatia); Katarina (March 10, 1872-May 23, 1933—Sister Erasma); Clemens (Nov. 25, 1876-July 21, 1896—he was a hunchback due to a fall from a wing or while climbing a tree).

Johann C., son of Johannas and Margareta C. Preutenborbeck, married Elizabeth Muhlsiepen Nov. 27, 1895. She was born May 7, 1858 and died Nov. 7, 1938. They had three children, Mary Gertrude, John Ludger and Joseph F. In July 1912 Johann C. and Elizabeth, with their three children, came to Kelso, MO in the U.S.A. where Elizabeth's younger brother, Johann Muhlsiepen, was pastor.

Mary Gertrude, daughter of Johann C. and Elizabeth Mulsiepen, was born March 15, 1898 and died Sept. 12, 1968. She was the housekeeper for her younger brother, MSGR. Joseph, where she became well known among neighboring priests for her elaborate meals. She would also have a feast for her brother, John, his wife, Genevieve, and ten children for Christmas and Easter.

John Ludger, son of Johann C. and Elizabeth Mulsiepen, was born July 17, 1900 and died July 14, 1977. He married Genevieve Marie Diebcold on June 24, 1929 at St. Augustine, Kelso, MO. They had 12 children: Mary Genevieve; John Joseph; Joseph Aloysius; Paul Anthony; Hubert Francis; Bernard Florian; Eugene Louis; Robert Vincent; Marianne Elizabeth; Richard Michael; Mary Therese; and Frederick Stephen. John Ludger lived in Kelso and attended college at Quincy, IL and later at St. Louis University in St. Louis, MO where he received his law degree. He began a law practice at Illmo, MO and later at Cape Girardeau,, MO. Genevieve, his wife, attended an all girl's academy and later attended business college in Cape Girardeau, MO. She was bookkeeper at her father's flour mill and later for Kelso General merchandise, owned and operated by John Schumacher.

Mary Genevieve (born April 25, 1930, died Dec. 7, 1977—buried at Ripa) became Sister Marie Bernadette (School Sisters of Notre-Dame) on Aug 1, 1949 at Ripa, St. Louis, MO. Sister Bernadette taught music in many schools in Missouri, also in Illinois, Iowa, Kansas, Nebraska and California. She played the organ for the inaugural of Governor Joe Teasdale.

John J. (born Sept. 1, 1931) married Annabell Gilder on Aug. 23, 1958 at St. Mary's in Cape Girardeau, MO. They had five children: John Daniel; James Joseph; Michael Richard; Lisa Marie and Mary Beth. He was administrator of Saint Francis Medical Center in Cape Girardeau. John D. (born March 10, 1960) married Kathy Shrum (born Sept. 12, 1983) at Immaculate Conception in Jackson, MO—children are John and Joseph. James J. (born Nov. 27, 1961) married Kim Wiedefield June 10, 1983 at St. Mary's Cathedral in Cape Girardeau, MO—children are Joshua, Jennifer and Justin. Michael R. (born Aug. 5, 1963) married Kara Shrumm—children are Michael and Eric. Lisa M. (born May 8, 1966) married Jeff Unterreiner—children are Anna and Evan. Mary Beth (born July 17, 1968) married David Hercules—children are Elliott and Sophia.

Joseph A. (born Jan. 7, 1934) is a repair technician for office machines in St. Louis.

Paul A. (born July 4, 1934—died March 21, 1935). He was a "blue" baby and died with a bad heart.

Hubert F. (born June 11, 1936) became Brother Thomas Marion (CFA). He took vows on Jan. 16, 1959 at Grisham, WI. He was assistant administrator and senior lab technician at Alexian Brothers Hospital in St. Louis. He held these positions at Alexian Brothers Hospital at Elizabeth, NJ, Chicago, IL and San Jose, CA. He is presently president and CEO for Alexian Brother's Health Systems.

Bernard F. (born Sept. 27, 1938) married Mary Kathleen Murphy on Dec. 30, 1962. They had five children: Caroline Ann; Paul Francis; Edward John; Diane Marie and Thomas Patrick. He is owner and chief engineer for Derkin Equipment Co. in St. Louis. Caroline Ann (born June 2, 1963) married Sarob Luwate—children are Paul and Bridgette. Paul Francis (born Aug. 2, 1964) married Frannie—one child, John; Edward John (born July 17, 1966) married Heidi; Diane Marie (born June 13, 1969) married John Devrey—one child, William; Thomas Patrick (born Jan. 25, 1973) married Colleen—one child, Margaret.

Eugene L. (born Jan. 12, 1940 married Laverne Cecilia Klipfel on May 8, 1965 at St. Lawrence, New Hamburg, MO. They have four children: Stephen Eugene; Patricia Ann; Mark Anthony and Gail Marie. He is a product design engineer at Federal Mobul Piston Plant at Malden, MO. Stephen Eugene was born Jan. 31, 1966. Patricia Ann was born April 25, 1967 and married John Straus—children are Sean, Isaac, Gabe and Lianna. Mark Anthony was born Sept. 10, 1969 and married Susan Stark. Gail Marie was born July 23, 1974.

Robert V. (born May 24, 1942) married Rose Marie Clay on July 22, 1972 at St. Mary's, Helena, AR. They had two children, Robert Kenneth and David Thomas. He is an electrical engineer for Technicon Corp, and maintains hospital lab test equipment in St. Louis and surrounding cities. Robert Kenneth was born April 9, 1974. David Thomas was born Feb. 5, 1980.

Marianne E. was born Aug. 6, 1943. She is Sister Genevieve in Daughters of Charity—vows Sept. 12, 1959 at Marillac in Normandy, MO. She taught school for some years before receiving her nursing degree in Dallas, TX. She is a nurse at DePaul Hospital in St. Louis and is presently archivist for the Daughters of Charity in St. Louis.

Richard M. (born May 10, 1945) married Kathy Ann Ross on Aug. 11, 1973. He graduated from Quincy College in 19696. He was drafted into the army and served in Vietnam from September 1968 to September 1969. He works at Chrysler as relief man for any positions on the line.

Mary Therese was born March 17, 1947 and died March 17, 1947.

Frederick S. was born June 8, 1948 and is a seminarian at Springfield, MO, Little Rock, AR and Dubuque, IA. He worked as a professional visiting nurse for the elderly at Dubuque, IA. He is presently working at Missouri Botanical Garden, Research Division, Web Group, imaging technician, in St. Louis.

MURPHY – Francis "Marion" Murphy and Grace Portis were married in Scott County on March 30, 1905. "Marion" was born there on 4 Feb. 1878. Grace was born at Marble Hill, Bollinger County on Sept. 24, 1885. Her parents were William Joseph and Mary Hannah (Davenport) Portis. The Portis family moved to a farm near Benton, Scott County in 1886.

Marion and Grace Murphy were the parents of six children: Norman M. Murphy, born Feb. 6, 1906 in Benton, died in Sikeston, Scott County on Feb. 8, 1963.

Norman, called "Buster" or "Turk," married Angie Woodward of Vanduser. Norman and Angie lived at Morley. They had one child, Karen Francis Murphy, born in Morley on Feb. 27, 1949.

Mary Elizabeth Murphy, born/died about 1908.

Harold Clinton Murphy, born May 5, 1912 in Morley, died Feb. 24, 1980 in Cape Girardeau, married Lucille LeGrand, no children.

Joseph Riley Murphy (called JR), born Oct. 21, 1913 in Morley, died Feb. 7, 1996 in Cape Girardeau. He married Edna F. Irvin of Morley in 1941. Three children were born to this union: Betty Joe Murphy, born June 17, 1942; David Frank Murphy, born Nov. 30, 1946 and Ronald Dean, born March 18, 1953.

Marian "Louise" Murphy, born in Morley on 26 Feb. 1917 married Clarence P. Black Jr (called "Junior") of Sikeston on May 15, 1949; no children. Louise was a teacher at schools in East Prairie and Sikeston. "Junior" had a car dealership in Sikeston.

Anna "Lora" Murphy was born Dec. 5, 1920 in Morley. She married Donald Eugene Jacobs Sr. of Morley on June 5, 1943. They were the parents of three children; Donald Eugene Jacobs Jr., born March 29, 1947; Sharon Ann Jacobs, born Jan. 9, 1949 and Katheryn Louise Jacobs, born Nov. 17, 1952. Donald Sr. passed away in 2001 and Lora lives in Cape Girardeau. *Submitted by Betty-Jo (Hart) Wagoner*

MURPHY – Francis "Marion" Murphy was born Feb. 4, 1878 in Scott County. He was the son of Riley and Betsy (Dewrock) Murphy. He married Grace May Portis on March 30, 1905 in Benton, MO. They lived in Morley, MO most of their lives. They had six children, with five surviving into adulthood. The five surviving children were: Norman M. Murphy (Buster or Turk); Harold D. Clinton Murphy; Joseph Riley Murphy (called J.R.); Marian Louise Murphy Black; and Anna "Lora" Murphy Jacobs.

Francis Marion and Grace May (Portis) Murphy

Marion was a gentleman of many talents, including being an excellent trumpeter. He organized a band that included his brother, Charles Murphy. Charles played the slide trombone and was one of the original members of the band. When the children were old enough to learn to play an instrument, they all learned at least one musical instrument. Lora, the youngest child, accompanied her father in the band, playing the saxophone. The band played at functions such as homecomings, school activities, and community-business company picnics. Marion's "quiet time" was to teach music. Grace, a spunky little lady, liked to quilt, crochet, and play Chinese checkers with her friend, Mrs. Lee. Grace spent many hours reading her Bible and clipping poetry out of newspapers and magazines.

Marion sold insurance and home appliances, selling the first Maytag washing machine in Scott County. He built a platform on the front of his coup to deliver machines and other merchandise. Marion died July 28, 1963 and Grace died Jan. 31, 1979. They are buried in Old Morley Cemetery, Morley, MO.

Descendants of Francis Marion Murphy and Grace May Portis:

Norman M. Murphy (Buster or Turk) born Feb. 6, 1906, died Feb. 8, 1963, married Nov. 27, 1935 to Angie Woodward. Children – daughter (no name) born/died 1939 and Karen Francis Murphy, born Feb. 27, 1949.

Mary Elizabeth Murphy, born/died about 1909.

Harold Clinton Murphy, born May 5, 1912, died Feb. 24, 1980, married Feb. 27, 1960 to Lucille LeGrand.

Joseph Riley Murphy (J.R.), born Oct. 21, 1913, died Feb. 7, 1996, married to Edna Frankeline Irvin. Their children: Betty Joe Murphy and her children, Sheri Raye Denham; Mary Edna Denham; Raymond Perry Denham III. David Frank Murphy and his children: David Scott Murphy; Christopher Allen Murphy; Timothy Brian Murphy; and Ronald Dean Murphy.

Marion Louise Murphy, born Feb. 26, 1917, died May 31, 1977, married to Clarence P. Black.

Anna Lora Murphy Jacobs born Dec. 5, 1920 married June 5, 1943 to Donald Eugene Jacobs Sr. Her children, Donald Eugene Jacobs Jr. His children, Holly Christine Jacobs and Donald Eugene Jacobs III; Sharon Ann Jacobs and children, Spencer Allen Williams and Morgan Leigh Williams; Katheryn Louise Jacobs, and her children: Marcus Nathaniel Spain; Jonathan Andrew Spain; Allison Louise Spain and Joseph William Spain.

Anna, called Lora, was one of those "Murphy kids" that played in her Dad's band. She played piano, saxophone and clarinet. Her husband, Gene, was in the Navy during WWII. After discharge he was employed by contractors (one contractor constructed the Gateway Arch in St. Louis.) Lora and Gene reside in Cape Girardeau, MO.

MURRELL – William Dockery Murrell was born May 2, 1869 in Kentucky to Henry Harden Murrell (b. Feb. 7, 1821 in Adiar County, KY, d. Au. 6, 1898 in Harrisburg, AR) and Margaret Frances (Marple) Murrell (b. April 7, 1843, d. Feb. 5, 1907 in Blodgett, MO).

In the late 1800s the southern part of Scott County was forest and swamp. The Indians were still living in the forest area. Because of the growth of the area, the demand for lumber used for new homes, and for business, made the lumber business an important job. W. D. Murrell was reported to be a riding boss for the Marshall Land Co. W. D. "Uncle Billie" made friends with the Indians. He often stayed with them overnight when he was too far away to reach home at night. Blodgett was being settled and several Murrell related families settled in and near Blodgett. His mother, Margaret Murrell, lived in Blodgett. Will Murrell lived with his mother and worked as a builder. He helped build the present Methodist Church in 1921. It was reported that when the large stained glass windows were being uncrated someone said, "Oh what if they won't fit?" Uncle Billie said, not bragging, just with confidence, "They will fit, 'cause I measured them." He lived with his mother until her death in 1907. Then on Nov. 8, 1908 he married Minnie Mae Riley (b. Oct. 15, 1872, d. Feb. 10, 1958 in Blodgett). They had two daughters, Ruby Marie (B. Oct. 5, 1914, d. dec. 12, 1999) who married Corwin Looney in Thayer, MO on Dec. 13, 1939 and Thelma (b. October 1917, d. Sept. 29, 1991) married Ward Enterline and lived in Doniphan, MO).

Will had five sisters: Dovie Ann (married Henry Shamley); Eliza Bele (married Thomas Williamson Moody); Harden Muir (married Joe Hughes); Tula Love (married Ernest Vaughn) and Cora Estella (married Lemual Strayhorn).

Several of Will's sisters married, and their families were, and still are, active in the growth of Scott County.

Dovie's (one of Will's sisters) husband, Henry Shamely, was an Inn Keeper and one of the signers of Incorporation of Blodgett in 1900.

Ruth Murrell Miner, and husband Richard Minner, were early settlers, as was Bell Murrell and husband, Tom Moody. Bell was a charter member of the Blodgett W.M.U. A grandson of

Bell and Tom was Robert Davis, who was appointed Scott County Deputy Sheriff in 1958, and served until 1963. From 1967 to 1970, he served as second district judge of Scott County.

Lula Murrell married Ernest Vaughn and they moved to East St. Louis.

Cora Murrell and husband, Lem Strayhorn, were successful farmers. Their sons, Wesley and Winfred Strayhorn, continued to farm, and they were active in livestock sales until their deaths. One of Cora's daughters married Dennis James. Another daughter, Zelma Strayhorn Carroll, lives in Blodgett. She and her late husband, Clayton Carroll, have been responsible for keeping records of the Blodgett Cemetery and other community activities.

MYERS – Peter Caverno Myers was born on Jan. 4, 1931 in Racine, WI, the son of Margaret "Peg" Caverno Myers and Samuel Peter Myers, who at the time was a lawyer in Racine. Peter's paternal grandfather, Peter Jacob Myers, was a farmer and lawyer in the Racine area. Peter J. was married to a farm girl, Eda Hansche, and together they had three sons and two daughters. Peter's maternal grandfather was Judge Xenophon Caverno, who was the son of a Methodist circuit-riding preacher in Wisconsin. Judge Caverno married Louise Lay in Kewanee, IL where they owned the Kewanee Municipal Electric Power Plant. The Judge sold the power plant in 1905 and purchased land in New Madrid County, MO. He was one of the original landowners who formed the Little River Drainage District, which is the largest privately funded drainage project in the world. Judge Caverno and the other landowners' original intent was to pay for the land by selling timber as the land was drained, but the depression of the early 1930s made this very difficult. He became a farmer as the land was drained and cleared. The abstract on his farmland reads like a financial history book as the Judge borrowed and paid back many loans during the tough financial years of the 1930s.

Peter C. Myers married Mary Williamson in September of 1952. Together they completed Peter's degree in Agriculture at the University of Wisconsin in Madison, WI and then moved on to Peter's two-year Army career in Maryland and Texas. In late 1955 they moved to the Canalou, MO area and began farming on 80 acres of the original Caverno land. Peter rented this land from a partnership formed by himself and his two sisters, Margaret Louise Megowen of South Dartmouth, MA and Judith Lay Myers of Spokane, WA.

Peter and Mary Myers

Mary Williamson Myers was born in Racine, WI on Sept. 10, 1933, the daughter of Everett Williamson and Lillian Taft Williamson. Everett, an accomplished baritone soloist, spent his life as an employee of the J. I. Case Tractor Company in Racine. Everett and Lillian raised Mary and her two sisters, Mitzi W. Ivanoski and Joan W. Wittmann, in modest homes in Racine. Mary graduated from Racine Horlick High School, where she met Peter and eventually they moved to southeast Missouri.

Peter and Mary later purchased the 400 acre Caverno homeplace from his cousin, Ellen Caverno Burnett, which was later sold to their daughter, Kristina, and her husband, Tim

Coppage, who was from nearby Charter Oak. Kristina and Tim have three sons: Timothy Gordon Jr.; Samuel James and Daniel Peter; and Mark by Tim's first marriage. Peter and Mary adopted five children including: Joseph William; Peter Caverno Jr.; Kristina Morrill; Ann Gretchen; and Jon Eric. Joseph's children are Erin and Joe Jr.; Ann Gretchen and Jonathan Maloyed have two children, John Ross and Emma Marie. Jon's children are Sarah Elizabeth and Jon Eric II.

In 1982 Peter Sr. and Mary, together with Gretchen and Jon, moved to the Washington, D. C. area when Peter was appointed the Chief of USDA's Soil Conservation Service. In 1985 Peter was promoted to the position of Assistant Secretary of Natural Resources and Environment and later in 1986 became the USDA's Deputy Secretary of Agriculture.

They returned to Sikeston in 1990 where Peter started Myers Land Management Company and Mary continued her volunteer work as President of Adopt A Farm Family, Inc., a nation-wide Christian ministry to farm and ranch families; especially those in difficult situations. In 1998 Peter was elected as State Representative to the Missouri House from Scott County.

NORTON – Daniel "Dan" Smith Norton was born July 14, 1934 in St. Louis, MO. He is the son of Hugh Kipper Norton (born Aug. 29,1907; died April 1, 1970) and Irene Mary Kendall Norton (born May 20, 1905; died Dec. 17, 1994). They lived in St. Louis, MO until Dan moved to Sikeston, MO to practice law in 1957. Dan had one brother, Richard Neil Norton, born Dec. 3, 1929, who died November 1996. He has one brother, Donald Jean Norton, born May 20, 1932, who has retired and lives in Williford, AR.

Dan has a son, Hugh Kipper Norton II, born May 22, 1956 who lives in Columbia, IL; a daughter, Nancy Adrianne Norton Sallee, born June 3, 1958, who lives in Kansas City, MO; a son, Daniel Fenton Norton,, born March 28, 1960, who lives in Sikeston, MO and practices law with his father; and a daughter, Cynthia Dianne Norton Newell, who lives in St. Louis, MO. Dan married Linda Jo Freeman, born June 17, 1943 on Dec. 30, 1966 in Florissant, MO. She is the daughter of Charles Lee Freeman (Oct. 17, 1924-1983) and Clara Pearl Freeman (March 15, 1923), who lives in Sikeston, MO. A daughter, Alexandria Jo Norton, born July 6, 1977, lives in Springfield, MO; and a son, David Andrew Norton, born Oct. 2,1978, lives in Sikeston, MO with his wife, Jamie Susie Laymon (July 12, 1981). Linda has a brother, Danny Lee Freeman, born April 10, 1946, who lives in Jefferson City, MO and a sister, Charlene Chambers, born June 25, 1952, who lives in Sikeston, MO.

Dan has practiced law in Sikeston, MO since he graduated from Washington University Law School in 1957. He has been very active in his church and community, to-wit:

1. Junior Chamber of Commerce – President.
2. Jaycee Bootheel Rodeo – Board of Directors.
3. Municipal Board of Utilities – Board of Directors.
4. St. Paul's Episcopal Church – Vestry Member, Senior Warden and Stewardship Chairman.
5. Scott and Mississippi Counties Juvenile Department – Legal Advisor.
6. Sikeston Regional Children's Services – President and Board of Directors.
7. Sikeston Public Schools Advisory Board – Member.
8. Sikeston Community Arts Council – Chairman.
9. Scott County Multiple Sclerosis Society – Chairman.
10. American Cancer Society – Relay For Life Member.
11. Kenny Rogers Children's Center – Board of Directors.
12. Lee Hunter School – PTA Officer.
13. Sikeston Community Choir – Member.
14. Department of Public Safety Advisory Board – Member.
15. Sikeston City Attorney – 1982-2000.
16. Bootheel Counseling Services – Board of Directors.
17. Missouri and American Bar Associations – Member.

OLLER – Joann Taylor was the twelfth child and the seventh daughter born to George Washington Taylor and Massa Parker Taylor. Joann was born on the same farm where eight of her siblings had been born in what is now Illmo by Scott City. She was born sometime between 1853 and 1854. Joann married Henry C. Oller, who was born about 1848, when she was quite young. When she was still 17 years old, Joann already had a 1-year-old son, Elmer H. Oller.

This little family was living with her mother, the widowed Massa Taylor, in the old family home when the census taker came by in 1870.

Source: Federal Census 1860 and 1870; Scott County Probate records. *Submitted by Toni Martinazzi*

PATTENGILL – W. C. and Nellie (Pray) Pattengill moved from Cape Girardeau in April of 1933 to a farm three miles northeast of Benton on the Benton and Commerce road. The Pattengills farmed and had a dairy farm. There were 13 children in the family. They reared 11 of the children. They rode the school bus to school at Benton. Joe Spalding Sr. and Bob Cannon were bus drivers through the years. Mr. H. L. Jackson was School Superintendent. He had all the children's interest at heart and wanted the students to apply themselves to get a good education. George Hilpert and Marshall Jackson were also High School Superintendents for several years.

W.C. and Nellie Pattengill family. Front row: Lawrence, Nellie, W.C., Evelyn, and Gladys. 2ⁿᵈ row: Alice, Pauline, Paul (Bud), Ruby, and Marie. Back: Lee, Rex, and Ralph.

In 1944 the Pattengills moved into Benton, across the street from the Grade School. Several of the family members still live in southeast Missouri. Mr. Pattengill passed away in May of 1954 and Mrs. Pattengill passed away in November of 1965.

PEACOCK – Eugene Aldin "Gene" Peacock was born Jan. 8, 1953 in Mt. Clemens, MI, to parents Ralph and Joyce Peacock. He has two older brothers – Jim Peacock (Michigan) and Carl Peacock (Texas) and one older sister – Karen Zilkie (Arizona). Gene was in the US Marine Corps, serving in Viet Nam. He moved to St. Francois County, MO in 1985. He has two children – Ed in Alpena, MI and Suann in Valles Mines, MO. Gene is dispatch officer at Scott City Police Department.

Martha Jane (Gard) Peacock was born May 19, 1955 in Pontiac, MI to parents Arthur Vernon (Oct. 31, 1914 to Feb. 6, 1995) and Gladys Lorene (Steward) Gard (May 7, 1913 to Dec. 16, 1990). The family moved to Dexter, MO in 1959. Jane has three older brothers: Bill and Sharon Gard in Pontiac, MI; Dave and Donna Gard in Bloomfield, MO; and Don and Barbara Gard in Dexter, MO. She has one older sister, Pam and David Millsaps in Athens, TN. After graduating from Dexter High School in 1973, Jane moved to Memphis, TN and attended one year at Draughon's Business College, majoring in Accounting/Computer programming. She lived in Memphis for eight years, moving back to Missouri in 1982. Jane worked as a computer operator for 12 years before going to work for the US Postal Service in 1986. She began her postal career in Sikeston, MO as a clerk and was promoted to Postmaster in Kelso, MO in June of 1991. She remains at Kelso as Postmaster today.

Gene and Jane met while he was working as a gospel radio disc jockey at Marble Hill, MO. They put some music together for a puppet ministry skit at church. They began attending church together and were married Nov. 16, 1997 at Clearview General Baptist Church in Scott City, MO, where they still attend. They lived in Kelso, MO until May 2001, when they moved to Scott City, MO. *Submitted by Gene Peacock*

PEETZ – The history of the Heinrich Peetz family began with our early settlers from Schlewecke, Germany, Kingdom of Hannover, who came to America and settled in Tilsit, MO.

Johann Heinrich Gottlieb Patz (Peetz) was born Nov. 12, 1812 and died April 28, 1892. He married Johanna Sophie Henrietta Bolm on April 30, 1843. She was born on Nov. 28, 1818 and died Dec. 6, 1906. Both are buried in St. James Church Cemetery, Tilsit, MO. Their children are: Heinrich; Carl; Marie; Henrietta (Jacob Brennecke); Caroline (Charles Dralle); August (Caroline Meier); and William (Augusta Meier) all of Cape Girardeau County, MO.

Their son, Heinrich Peetz was born on Sept. 28, 1843 in Kingdom of Hannover and was 7 years old when he came to America. He married Wilhelmina "Minnie" Meier on Sept. 2, 1869. They settled on a 60 acre farm two miles northwest of Kelso in Scott County, MO in a seven room log house. Heinrich died Feb. 8, 1912; Wilhelmina died Nov. 22, 1930. Both are buried in the little cemetery (Margrabe-Dannenmueller), north of Kelso, MO. Their children are: Charles; Heinrich Jr.; Wilhelmina; Emma; Anna; and Mary Peetz. Only three of these children lived to adulthood: Heinrich Jr.; Wilhelmina and Mary.

The Scott County Peetz family was associated with the Lutheran Church. They were traditionally of the Republican political party. The children attended the Lutheran School located at the church in Illmo, MO. Since they would have to walk several miles to school, the children often stayed with the Lutheran pastor during the school term. Henry was a farmer and Minnie was the typical housewife and "farm hand" of those days. When they died, the farm was divided equally among the children. Minnie and her husband, Adolph Sprenger, lived on their portion and also purchased Anna's part when she and her husband, William Sander, moved to Cape Girardeau, MO. Henry and his wife, Mary Roth, remained on their 20 acre portion of the farm.

Charles Peetz, born Dec. 3, 1869, died Nov. 22, 1883; buried in the little cemetery at Kelso, MO.

Henry and Mary Peetz Family. Front row: Manda (Peetz) Dunger, August Peetz Jr., Wilhelmina (Mary Roth) Peetz, and Bertha (Peetz) Heuring. 2nd row: Marie (Peetz) Kinder, Henry J. Peetz, Pauline (Peetz) Reeves, George Peetz, Otto Peetz, and Neta (Peetz) Raines.

August Heinrich William Peetz Jr., born March 22, 1873, died Feb. 21, 1962, married Wilhelmina Elizabeth Maria Roth on April 19, 1897. Mary, as she was called, was born Jan. 19, 1878 to Johann and Anna (Soessmann) Roth and died Dec. 20, 1942. Both are buried in Eiselben Lutheran Church Cemetery (Illmo) Scott City, MO. They remained on their portion of the family farm after his parents' death. Their children were: Otto, married Augusta "Lady" Walter. Their children are: Walter (Wanda Pritchard) and Gale (Gene Dale). George married Mathilda Hess. Their children are: Ruby (David Friedrich); Norma (Merrill Simmons); Joann (Warren Pollock); and Martha (Johnny Holzum). Manda married William H. Dunger. Their children are: William Jr. (Francis Bailey); Charles (Thelma Kinder); Clarence (Doris Wacker); Ida Marie; Dorothy (Leander Drury); and Shirley (Dennis Schroeder). Louis, born Oct. 10, 1903, died Oct. 15, 1907. He is buried in the little cemetery in Kelso, MO. Pauline married Rev. Oggie Reeves. They were foster parents of Larry and Sanford Porter. Ida, twin sister of Neta, died before she was 2. Neta married Leslie Raines. Their children are: Alice (Austin Getz); Wilford (Sharon Steger); Marvin (Bonnie Hawn); and Gladys (John Z. Smith). Marie married Ross Kinder. They had no children. Henry Peetz married Lillian Enderle. They had one child, Linda (Charles Frey). Bertha married Henry C. Heuring. Their children are: Henry Jr. (Laverne Ziegler); Lavada (William Schlegel); Larry (Pam Essner); and Jerry (Elaine LeDure).

Wilhemina Peetz, born Dec. 1, 1874, died Oct. 12, 1948, married Adolph Sprenger Nov. 24, 1892. Both are buried in Eisleben Cemetery. Their children were: William; August; Gustav; Lydia; Emil and Adolph "Eddie" Sprenger.

Emma Peetz, born Aug. 18, 1877, died Jan. 8, 1878, buried in little cemetery, Kelso, MO.

Anna Peetz, born Nov. 28, 1878, died July 7, 1951, married William Sander Feb. 11, 1902. Both are buried in Memorial Park Cemetery, Cape Girardeau, MO. Their children are: Frieda; Ruby; Alwine and Edna Sander.

Mary Peetz, born Nov. 2, 1881, baptized Feb. 12, 1882, died Aug. 11, 1883, buried in little cemetery (Margrabe), Kelso, MO.

Henry and Mary Peetz were farmers and hard workers. The family built a two-story house with a summer kitchen. They loved to dance and have fun. Wheat thrashing would bring neighbor helping neighbor.

Henry and Mary's portion of the farm was sold to Les Raines, who in turn sold it to Ray Bennett. He sold it to Leroy Reinagel. He sold it to Bob Kielhofner.

Henry and Mary Peetz' family were members of Eisleben Lutheran Church, Illmo, MO. There are grandchildren, great-grandchildren; great-

great grandchildren, and great-great-great grandchildren of the first Heinrich Peetz who settled in Scott County who are still members of Eisleben Lutheran Church today. *Submitted by Gladys Raines Smith*

PERSON – Ellis Person was born January 1825 in Baden, Germany. Family tradition states that his father drowned in the Rhine River while going for a swim after a day's work cutting timber on its bank.

According to census records, Ellis came to America in 1845. He entered the country in New York. Nothing is known of his life from that time until 1860. His name appears in Hamilton County, IL in the 1860 census. He lived in that area until moving to Cape Girardeau, MO sometime around 1880. By 1900, he and his family were in Scott County, MO.

Ellis served in the 87th Illinois Infantry, Company E during the Civil War.

Ellis apparently was first married to a woman named Mary. They were the parents of a daughter, Julia. Julia was born Aug. 5, 1858. She married Joseph Herbst on Oct. 24, 1882 in Cape Girardeau, MO. Julia died April 16, 1916 in Cape Girardeau.

Ellis married Anna Stacia Heilzlee Specht on Aug. 21, 1861 in Hamilton County, IL. Anna was also of German descent. She had a son, Joseph Specht.

Ellis and Anna were the parents of at least six children. 1. Mary was born in 1863. Nothing else is known of her. 2. Stephen, June 16, 1866-Sept. 8, 1937, was first married to Clementine Diebold on May 1, 1800 in Scott County. After her death, he married Louise Castain. 3. Ellis E., March 10, 1868-Feb. 23, 1938, married Clara Rosa Schoen on April 24, 1890 at New Hamburg. 4. Gustaf was born about 1869. Nothing else is known of him. 5. Theresa, July 4, 1871-April 22, 1933, married Charles H. Stutsman. 6. Valentine N., Jan. 8, 1873-Aug. 2, 1955, married Alma Kneezel on Jan. 2, 1892 at Benton. He was also married to Anna Lee Morrow, Jennie Stowell and Mary Shaver.

Ellis died May 27, 1901 in Scott County. In the years following his death, the family moved away from the area. Some of the family moved to White County, AR. The rest of the family moved to Ojai, CA. Anna Stacia died Feb. 25, 1909 at Ojai, CA and is buried there. *Submitted by Roberta McReynolds*

PFEFFERKORN – Mathias Pfefferkorn (May 30, 1855-Nov. 14, 1904), son of Andreas and Mary Magdalena (Schlosser) Pfefferkorn, married Carolina Georger (June 28, 1860-Dec. 18, 1924), daughter of Joseph and Carolina (Burger) Georger, on May 14, 1878 in St. Lawrence Catholic Church at New Hamburg, MO. They were farmers east of Kelso and both are buried in St. Augustine Cemetery at Kelso. Seven children were born to this union.

1. Emma Louise Pfefferkorn (May 2, 1879-June 6, 1940) married Charles Joseph Blattel (Nov. 3, 1880-Aug. 11, 1925) on Jan. 13, 1903. He is the son of John Blattel and Sophia (Bosenmeier). Their five children are: Wilmer Theodore Blattel (Kathryn Mesitich); Edwin A. Blattel (Celine Glueck); Estella Blattel (Charles Hahn); Lloyd Mathias (1910-1918) and Theodora Blattel (Albert Butler).

2. Theodore John Pfefferkorn, born March 20, 1881, married Emma Mary Welter on Oct. 10, 1905 in St. Augustine Church in Kelso, MO. She is the daughter of Joseph and Susanna (Compas) Welter. While working on a hay baler, he got his hand caught in the machinery and it was so badly lacerated the doctor had to amputate the thumb

and index finger. (SCD-Nov. 30, 1911.) Later the doctor severed the arm above the elbow, but blood poison set in and resulted in his death on Dec. 9, 1911 (*Scott County Democrat* – Dec. 14, 1911). A child was born to them, Bertha Pfefferkorn (Curtis Laven), divorced.

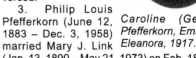

Caroline (Georger) Pfefferkorn, Emma and Eleanora, 1917.

3. Philip Louis Pfefferkorn (June 12, 1883 – Dec. 3, 1958) married Mary J. Link (Jan. 13, 1890 – May 21, 1973) on Feb. 18, 1908. She is the daughter of Andreas and Frances (Weber) Link. They are buried in St. Joseph Cemetery in Scott City, MO. They were parents of six children: Anna C. Pfefferkorn (Bill O'Brien); Earl Mathias Pfefferkorn; Edward Theodore Pfefferkorn; Ellen Marie Pfefferkorn; Irma Frances Pfefferkorn (Earl Clayton); and Paul Andrew Pfefferkorn died in infancy.

4. Albert Lambert Pfefferkorn lived eight days and died in 1886.

5. Andrew Pfefferkorn (Jan. 27, 1887-May 31, 1907) married Alvina Logel on Nov. 9, 1909 at St. Augustine Church in Kelso, MO, but later divorced. Four children were born to this union: Alveretta M. Pfefferkorn; Aurelia M. Pfefferkorn; Dorothea Louise Pfefferkorn and Oscar Clarence Pfefferkorn.

6. Louis Pfefferkorn (April 18, 1890-Sept. 16, 1953) married Cecelia Logel on June 28, 1910 but later divorced. She is the daughter of Charles and Louise (Feldon) Logel. One child was born to this union, Viola Pfefferkorn.

7. Benjamin Pfefferkorn (Jan. 17, 1893-Aug. 24, 1894) is buried in St. Augustine Cemetery, Kelso, MO.

8. Eleanora "Elly" Pfefferkorn (Aug. 8, 1898-July 4, 1983) married Edward Welter (March 21, 1894-June 6, 1975) on Sept. 26, 1917 in St. Augustine Church at Kelso, MO. He is the son of Michael and Magdalena (Diebold) Welter. They owned and operated the Kelso Milling Co. from 1937 to 1959. Three daughters were born to them: Doris Marie Welter (John "Jack" Smith); Laverne Caroline Welter (Robert Rosenquist) and Laura Jean Welter (Paul Robert).

PHILLIPS – Vernon Euman Phillips, son of Lee A. and Sylvia Noe Philips, was born in rural Lamar, AR on Jan. 14, 1926. He had brothers, Vernie, Velmer, Vance, Verlon, Vick and Vester. His sisters were Arzella and Izola. His family moved to Randles, MO in 1938, where he went to school. In 1946 his parents bought the old Sullivan Hotel at Morley, tore it down and built a house where it stood. Vernon drove a truck, did farm labor, and worked in Grant Andrew's service station. (This is where he met his bride-to-be.)

Mary Ann was born in Charleston, MO and soon moved to rural Blodgett, MO, where she went to school her first nine years. Her family moved to Morley in 1942, where her father took a job as bookkeeper for the Black Gin Company. She has sisters Wanda Mae, Ruth Jean, Lillian, and Shirley, and two brothers, John Earl (died in WWII), and Henry. She finished high school at Morley in 1945.

She worked at International Hat Company and on July 5, 1947, she and Vernon were married at Morley. Rev. B. G. Corn officiated.

Vernon worked for Texas Eastern for 37 years. To this union were born the following children: James David Phillips (Dec. 31, 1946-Dec. 9,

1981). He married Linda Patterson and then Carol Jean Kaushakis. He had no children.

Kathryn Ann Phillips (March 17, 1948-) married James Thomas Blevins July 5, 1969. They have three children; James Thomas Jr. (May 22, 1972), Sarah Rebecca (Oct. 27, 1974) and Phillip Caleb (Nov. 4, 1980). Kathryn is a Nurse-Practitioner. Her husband spent 20 years in the Navy and now works for the Department of Agriculture. Young Tom is dispatcher for Chaffee Police Department, Sarah is working in a National Park teaching children about nature, and Phillip is near finishing his degree in Art.

Vernon and Mary Ann Phillips family, 1953. Children, left to right: Kathryn Ann, Delbert, and David Phillips.

Delbert Earl Phillips (Dec. 16, 1951) is married to Sondra Elaine Mayfield (Sept. 2, 1952). Delbert worked for Lone Star at Cape for nearly 20 years and Sondra works at the SEMO University. They have two children; Hollie Elizabeth (July 28, 1978) and Heather Elaine (Aug. 7, 1981). Hollie reads meters of the electric company and Heather works for Wal-Mart. She married Cody Mayberry June 2000.

PIPPIN – Joseph F. Pippin (b. April 23, 1856, Jackson County, TN; d. Feb. 16, 1930, Sylvania Township) was the tenth child of William M. Pippin and Sina Finn. Joseph married Mary Alice Slagle Dec. 25, 1878 in Putnam County, TN. In the 1880s, words like "the opening," "stake a claim," "free land," began to sift through to Tennessee. Joseph and Sarah, along with Joseph's sister and brother-in-law, Marion and Lucinda (Pippin) Grimes, loaded up covered wagons, headed for Kansas, and lived near the border of Oklahoma territory until the land opening on April 22, 1889. Both families staked claims in Kingfisher, OK. Tragedy struck the first year. Mary Alice died on April 22, 1890 and was the first person buried in the Grimes Cemetery in Kingfisher. Oklahoma Territorial Census, June 12, 1890, lists Joseph, Annie 9, Etter (daughter) 6, Arther 4, Louie (daughter) 2, in Oklahoma 13 months. Joseph, discouraged, relinquished his land and returned to Tennessee.

The Pippin family. Back row: J.C., Imogene, Dean, Maxine, Ruth Moore Pippin, Wilma, and John Byrd Pippin. Front: Richard, Leon, and Glenn.

Joseph married Sarah J. McBroom on Jan. 5, 1892, and about 1900 moved his second family from Putnam County, TN to Scott County, MO. Their four children were: William (b. May 29, 1893, d. March 30, 1958, Sikeston, MO); Florence Lucille (b. July 1894, d. after 1953, buried Tunica, MS); Magdelena "Lena" (b. August 1896, Tennessee, d. Feb. 12, 1969, Hillsboro, IL); and John Byrd (b. March 17, 1898, Double Springs, TN; d. Oct. 2, 1981, Shelbyville, IN). William remained in Scott County until his death. Florence married first Frank Cartwright and second Warny Garland. Lena married Zeno S. Westrich.

While caring for his ill daughter, Florence, in Dunklin County, Sarah Pippin became ill with flu during the WWI epidemic. Joe went to get her but she died before he arrived. Distraught, Joe returned home and Frank Cartwright arranged to have Sarah's body sent to Scott County. Joe died 12 years later from burns he received while warming himself by the stove. Sarah and Joseph Pippin are buried in Old Morley Cemetery, Lot 31, according to a letter from Jim O'Neal, Mayor of Morley, MO, dated Nov. 14, 1988.

John Pippin married Ruth Mae Moore, daughter of Ida May Guthrie and George Moore, on Oct. 6, 1918 in Oran. To this union were born 10 children: Wilma Henrietta (b. July 9, 1910, d. Jan. 3, 1987, Grand Rapids, MI); Eileen Mae (b. April 28, 1922, d. May 6, 1922); Norma Maxine (b. April 14, 1923); Wiladean (b. Dec. 14, 1924); JC (b. Sept. 14, 1926, d. Sept. 29, 1998, Colorado); Elizabeth Imogene (b. July 30, 1928); Glenn Edward (b. Sept. 12, 1930); Donald Leon (b. Jan. 30, 1934); Richard Denzil (b. Oct. 24, 1935, d. May 6, 2001, California); and CP Pippin (b. and d. Sept. 15, 1939).

In 1947 John and Ruth Pippin and their three youngest boys, Glenn, Leon and Richard, moved from Scott County to Nashville, MI and remained there until Ruth's death. One daughter, Imogene Pippin Whorton, still lives and works in Scott County. *Submitted by D. Leon and Emily L. Pippin*

POPE – James Arthur Pope was born in Madison County near Fredericktown in 1905 to Lina and Noah Pope. He was an ordained Baptist Minister. He also farmed and worked in timber. He married Rua Ethel Brown Sept. 1, 1927 and they lived in St. Louis where he was a streetcar driver. They had four children.

Their first child, Norma Patricia, was born in St. Louis July 19, 1928. Their second child, Arthur Eugene, was born Oct. 28, 1930 in St. Louis.

The family moved back to the Marquand area after Arthur lost his job due to the Great Depression.

Their third child, Raymond Kenneth, was born in Marquand Jan. 27, 1934.

In 1939 the family moved to the Bell City area where their fourth child, Carolyn Ruth, was born Dec. 13, 1940.

The family moved to a farm west of Oran where the children attended Bryeans country school.

In 1946 they moved to Bell City again and in 1952 again back to Oran.

Arthur went to work for the city of Oran and Ethel worked at the hat factory.

Arthur helped start the Benton Missionary Baptist Church at Benton. He taught Sunday School and served as a Deacon in his church in Oran.

On May 20, 1959 Arthur was taking Ethel to work and was hit by a Frisco train. She was killed instantly and he lived in a coma for eight weeks and died July 8, 1959.

The oldest daughter, Patsy, married Delane McCulley of Bell City in 1946. They had two sons,

James Alfred born July 2, 1949 and Roger Dale born Oct. 15, 1952 and died 1993.

Delane died of a heart attack in 1968. Pat then married Jess Reddick of Scott City in 1970. They live in Jackson, MO.

Arthur and Ethel Pope

Eugene joined the Air Force in 1951 and retired from the service in 1974. He married Virginia Ullom in 1954 in Rapid City, SD. They have four children: Terry Eugene, born in 1955 and died in infancy; Cynthia Kaye, born Dec. 18, 1956 in Riverside, CA; Cheryl Ann, born March 23, 1960 in Fort Worth, TX; and Todd Eugene, born Nov. 5, 1963 in Orlando, FL.

Eugene and Virginia were divorced in 1982. He then married Madeleine Burger in 1988. They live in San Bernardino, CA.

Carolyn married J. C. Caudle in 1959 in Oran. They have two children, Pamela Kay, born June 24, 1961 and James Allen, born June 29, 1964. They all live in the St. Charles-Winfield area.

The second son, Kenneth, married Viva Jean Eakin, daughter of Ardis and Gussie Freeman Eakin, Aug. 28, 1953 at Garden Ridge Baptist Church near Bell City.

In April 1953 Kenneth went to work for Missouri Utilities. In August 1956 he was drafted into the Army and served two years, which he spent at Fort Lewis, WA.

After returning to Bell City after service, they had a daughter, Kimberly Ann, born June 8, 1959.

In 1962 the family built a house and moved into Oran. Ken continued to work for Missouri Utilities.

The family attended First Baptist Church and were active members. Ken has ushered, taught Sunday School, served as Sunday School superintendent, and trustee at his church. Viva has taught Sunday School, taught and worked in Bible School and is active in WMU.

Kenneth Pope family of Oran. Back row: Marty Pope, Jordan Fitts, Kenneth Pope, Adam Pope, Viva Pope, Abbie Pope, and Allen Fitts. Front: Carla Pope, Elizabeth Fitts, Kim (Pope) Fitts, and Daniel Fitts.

Ken is an active member of Morley Masonic Lodge, belonged to the Lion's Club, is a board member of North Scott County Transit Company and was on the school board for 12 years.

Ken and Viva are both members of Morley Eastern Star. Viva worked as a supervisor for Thorngate Ltd. From 1968 to 1988.

On June 6, 1963 a son, Martin Kenneth Pope, was born at Sikeston hospital, as was Kim. Both children graduated from Oran, Kim in 1977 and Marty in 1981. Kim also graduated from SEMO in 1981 as a Speech Pathologist.

Kim married Jim Allen Fitts on July 21, 1984

at Oran First Baptist Church. She teaches in the Dexter schools. Allen works for Monsanto Seed Co. at Sikeston and farms part-time. They live at Dexter and have three children and attend First Baptist Church of Dexter. Elizabeth Anne was born Feb. 2, 1990 and twin boys, Jordan Allen and Daniel Kenneth, were born April 7, 1994.

Marty married Carla Jean Bollinger June 4, 1988 at St. Marys Catholic Church in Cape Girardeau, where they still attend.

Marty works at Schnuck's and Carla teaches at Nell Holcomb School. They live in Cape Girardeau and have two children. Abigail Jean was born July 4, 1993 and Adam Kenneth was born March 10, 1997.

Ken retired from Ameren Electric in 1994 after 41 years. They will be married 50 years in 2003. They still live in the same house and are still active in their church. *Submitted by Viva J. Pope*

PORTIS – Corinne Melvina Portis was born near Benton in Scott County on July 26, 1898. She was the daughter of William Joseph "Joe" and Mary Hannah (Devenport) Portis. Corinne married Monroe Hardin on Sept. 26, 1917 at the Benton courthouse. They lived at Commerce until Mr. Hardin's death in the early 1920s. Corinne then moved to St. Louis to be near her parents. On Sept. 14, 1923 she married Edward Gilliam Hart Sr. in St. Charles, MO. They were the parents of three children; Betty-Jo, Edward Gilliam Jr. and Rosemary. Corinne died in 1988.

William Joseph and Mary Hannah (Devenport) Portis were married on Nov. 23, 1884 in Cape Girardeau County and moved to Scott County shortly thereafter. They moved to St. Louis in 1917. Joe was a carpenter and supplemented his income by farming.

William Joseph Portis was born Aug. 17, 1862 in Graves County, KY and died Sept. 14, 1946 in St. Louis at the home of his daughter, Corinne. He was the son of Samuel David and Manourva Melvina (Frizzell) Portis. His grandparents were William H. and Elizabeth (Johnson) Portis and John and Rebecca Frizzell. The Portis and Frizzell families were originally from North Carolina. In the early 1850s they moved to Bedford County, TN where Samuel and Manourva were married Feb. 13, 1856. They relocated to Graves and Calloway Counties, KY and in 1874 settled in Cape Girardeau County, MO.

Mary Hannah Devenport was born Aug. 11, 1867 in Cape Girardeau County, the daughter of Francis Monroe and Frances Ann (Gilliland) Devenport. She died Sept. 28, 1934 in St. Louis. Her grandparents were Joab A. and Jane (Wilkinson) Devenport and Hiram Alexander and Rebecca (Primm) Gilliland of Cape Girardeau County. The Devenports, Gillilands, Wilkinsons and Primms also were from North Carolina.

Joe and Mary's other children were:

Grace Portis, born Sept. 24, 1885, married Francis Marion Murphy on March 30, 1905 in Scott County. They lived in Morley until 1940 when they moved to Cape Girardeau. Marion Murphy was the director of the Morley town band for a number of years, playing the coronet. Their children were: Norman; Harold; Joseph Riley (JR); Louise and Lora.

William M. Portis, born March 14, 1887, married Iva Hopson and resided in Hayti, MO. They had one daughter, name unknown.

Corinne M. Portis, 1916.

Martha Jane Portis, born March 7, 1891 married Charles Rauh and resided in Cape Girardeau. Their children were Viola, Mabel, Lottie, Charles Jr. and Leo.

Charles L. Portis, born July 19, 1892 married Lula Mae Johnson in Scott County on Nov. 1, 1916. Charlie was a barber. They lived in Benton until 1927 when they moved to St. Louis. Their children were VanDean, Irvin and twins Donald and Ronald.

Juanita Portis, born June 23, 1902 married Orville Nettles in St. Louis and had three children; Dorothy, Virginia and James.

Mary Blanche Portis, born July 26, 1904 married Benjamin McNeal in St. Louis and had four sons: Russell; Robert; Kenneth and Lowell. *Submitted by Betty-Jo Hart Wagoner*

PROPST—Melvin Benjamin (Ben) Propst was born December 14, 1964, in Poplar Bluff, Mo. He is the son of Melvin Dean Propst (born June 26, 1941; resides in Bloomfield, Mo.) and Ora Francis Putney (born January 27, 1935; resides in Dexter, Mo.) They lived in Mt. Morris, Michigan, a suburb of Flint, on a farm

Clockwise from left: Ben, Ashley, Brandon, and Sabrina Propst.

until the fall of 1976, when they moved to Advance, Mo. In the summer of 1979, they moved to Dexter Mo., where Ben started his freshman year at Dexter High School and graduated in 1983. Ben had one brother, Martin Darrell Propst, born December 6, 1961, and died June 15, 1974, in Mt. Morris, Mi., by a bicycle accident involving an automobile. He has one sister, LaWanda Gail Propst Durham (born July 20, 1960). She married Larry Dewayne Durham II of Dexter, Mo. They have 3 children; Larry Dewayne III, born April 4, 1992; and the twins-Sarah Elizabeth and John Anthony, born August 24, 1995. Ben married Sabrina on June 30, 1990, at the Gospel Assembly Church in Sikeston, Mo. where they were attending.

Sabrina June Brown was born February 15, 1967, in St. Charles, Mo. She is the daughter of Raymond Charles Brown (August 26, 1941-June 25, 1993) and Lana June Bohannon (born November 13, 1948), who resides in Dexter, Mo. and has a business (Taxes Unlimited and Bohannon Insurance Agency). In the fall of 1982, Sabrina moved to Dexter, Mo. where she started her sophomore year at Dexter High School and graduated in 1985. Sabrina has two sisters, Anissa Rae Raymer (three children, Christopher Clay, born April 9, 1990; Amber Michelle, born February 2, 1994; and Erica Violet, born November 26, 1995), Karen Diane Robertson (two children, William Cody, born August 20, 2000, and Brianna Michelle, born November 23, 2002), and one brother, Raymond Charles Brown II (twins, Jordan Charles and Devin Ray, born March 30, 1998).

Ben and Sabrina have two children. Ashley Nicole (born February 1, 1991) and Brandon Martin (born December 6, 1993). They were both born at Missouri Delta Hospital in Sikeston, Mo. Both children are homeschooled, although Ashley attended Scott County Central her kindergarten year. Ashley is currently in 6th grade while Brandon is in the third. Both are members of the Sikeston Area Christian Home Educators and enjoy organized sports.

Ben gained experience while working for his

father (Propst Pools, out of Dexter, Mo.) for many years. Due to this experience, in June of 1997, Ben chose to start a construction company (Propst Pool Construction) specializing in swimming pools and concrete work. He enjoys serving the Southeast Missouri area as far north as Perryville and Fredericktown, Mo.

Ben and Sabrina lived in Dexter, Mo. until 1996 when they moved to Morley, Mo. in Scott County. They attend the Church at Morley in Morley, Mo. Ben plays a trombone and bass guitar in the church band and Sabrina plays an alto saxophone. Their family enjoys church activities, music, and time together. *Contributed by Sabrina Propst*

RASMUSSEN – Rasmus George Rasmussen was born in 1870 in Stensved, Denmark to Johan and Dortea Jorgensen Rasmussen. To avoid conscription he came to the USA at age 21. He entered through Ellis Island. Shortly after arriving here, he became involved in the dredging business, becoming Vice-president of Timothy Foohey Dredging Company. Eventually, he wound up in western Missouri (Bates County, MO). There he met and married Alice Maude Short, born in 1892, the daughter of Thomas and Anice Andrews Short. The Rasmussen's were married in 1911 and came to Scott County, MO in approximately 1914, where he was involved in many of the early dredging operations here, including Little River Drainage.

Mr. Rasmussen invested in farmland near Vanduser, MO which his heirs still operate today. Mr. and Mrs. Rasmussen are both buried at Memorial Park Cemetery in Cape Girardeau, MO.

They were parents of two children, born in Scott County, MO; a son, George Thomas Rasmussen, born in 1915, and a

George and Alice (Short) Rasmussen, ca. 1912.

daughter, Mary Elizabeth Rasmussen, born in 1923. Both children graduated from Oran High School, Oran, MO. George graduated from SEMO State University and served in WWII as a Navy Lieutenant. George was a sales representative of Merck Sharp and Dohme for 32 years before retiring. He died in 1984 and is interred at Memorial Park, Cape Girardeau, MO.

George Thomas Rasmussen married Mary Lee Reed (daughter of Aquilla Simpson and Maude Jane Dellinger Reed) in 1946. They had two daughters, Reed Ann Rasmussen, RN, born in 1958 married Burl Lee Reynolds in 1979 and they have two daughters, Paige Leann Reynolds and Faith Alyssa Reynolds. Their second daughter, Jane Ellen Rasmussen was born in 1963 married Timothy Allen Kurre and completed her degree in Finance from SEMO State University. Reynolds and Kurre are co-owners and operators of Rhyno Performance Motorsports, LLC in Cape Girardeau, MO.

Mary Elizabeth Rasmussen became a registered nurse by attending Jewish Hospital School of Nursing in St. Louis, MO. She married Irwin Charles Alsdorf (born in New York) in 1948. Alsdorf was a civil engineer with Brown and Root. They spent their married life in Houston, TX and were parents of three sons; Michael David, Charles William and Alan Andrew, and one daughter, Mary Beth. They all reside in Pasadena, TX. *Submitted by Mary Reed Rasmussen*

REGARD – Jacob Riegert/Regard, farmer, born about 1824 in France, was the son of Jacob and Magdalena (Martz) Riegert. He married Mary Bucher on Jan. 20, 1946 at St. Vincent's Catholic Church in Cape Girardeau. She was born Dec. 6, 1828 in Schirrhein, Alsace, France, daughter of Wendolin and Mary Magdalena (Halter) Bucher.

Jacob and Mary were the parents of nine children: Louis P. (1846-1915); Mary Magdalena (1848-1892) married Michael Enderle; Jacob (1850-1916) married Maria Eva Menz; Catherine E. (1852-1861); Lawrence Wolfgang (1854-1893) married Paulena Dellas; Mary Louise (1857-1937) married George Leible; Caroline Gertrude (1859-1948) married John Goetz, second time to Joseph Walter; Regina (1861-1883) married Edmund Halter and Theresia (1863-1886) was the second wife of Edmund.

Jacob Regard's tombstone

Jacob Reigert/Regard enlisted for a period of three years in the Civil War as a Private on Oct. 28, 1862 at Camp Magazine, MO in Company "L" 10th Missouri Cavalry Regiment commanded by Captain C. Henrick. He deserted Dec. 23, 1862, and returned to his regiment on Feb. 23, 1864. He was restored to duty by Special Order NO 104, dateline "Headquarters, Vicksburg, MS April 24, 1864 with loss of pay during absence."

On Nov. 2, 1864 a letter was written to his wife and children by Jno King –by request of husband. "I am now nine miles from Memphis badly wounded. I was sent out on a Scout, fell in with the Confederates about three miles above Raleigh at Union depo. I was shot through the right side above the hip. I pray God may take care of you all and BLESS and provide for you."

On Nov. 4, 1864 another request was written by Jno King —"that he was taken to a citizens house by the name of Roberts. A doctor attended to him there and he died later that evening." He was buried at Memphis National Cemetery in Memphis, TN.

Michael and Mary Magdalena (Riegert) Enderle were the parents of 11 children. Those living to adulthood were: Elizabeth (1871-1947) married Joseph Glastetter; Peter Joseph (1873-1958) married Katherine Rosalia Gosche; Frank Anton (1880-1965) married Anna Pfefferkorn; Helen Mary (1885-1959) married William Pfefferkorn; and Joseph (1892-1964) married Louise Schlosser.

Elizabeth and Joseph Glastetter (1826-1877), the son of Joseph Glastetter and Louisa Glaus were parents of 11 children: Rosalia (1895-1949), wife of August Heisserer; Paul (1897-1969) married Anna Helen Scherer; Pauline (1898 - 1976), wife of August Glueck; Benjamin (1900-1901); Joseph L. (1902-1967) married Coena C. Calliotte; Bernard Frank (1906-1989) married Anna Westrich; Zeno (1908-1980) married Lenora Warren; Leon William (1910-1971) married Clara Backfisch Litzler; Clara Catherine (1913-1973), first wife of Lawrence Westrich. Coletta (1916-still living), wife of Joseph Heisserer. *Submitted by Karen (Glastetter) Hou*

REIMINGER – Antoine Reiminger, son of Joseph Reiminger and Marie Ann (Kess) Reiminger, was born June 6, 1813 in Bischwiller, Bas-Rhin, Schirrhein.

Antoine served in the 13th Division, 60th Regiment of the French Army in Brest, France. He was honorably discharged on June 1, 1841. At the time of his discharge, he had not been wounded. He was single and not widowed.

Antoine and family, consisting of wife Katharine (Heisserer) and children Justine, Simon and Mary, immigrated to the United States from LeHavre, France aboard the *S/S Sea Queen*. They arrived in New Orleans on Nov. 7, 1853.

Antoine applied for and received his citizenship from the Probate Court of Scott County in Benton, MO on July 22, 1859. This is recorded in Book A, Pages 66 and 67.

On Aug. 1, 1860 Antoine received a Land Patent for 80 acres in Scott County, MO from the General Land Office of the United States. The land was described as follows: The North half of the Northwest Quarter of Section Twenty-Seven in Township Twenty-Nine, North of Range Thirteen, East.

Antoine and Katherine had three children; Justine, Simon and Mary.

Justine (b. March 8, 1847, d. April 18, 1879) married John Blattel (b. Dec. 24, 1844, m. Sept. 15, 1868, d. Aug. 31, 1926) and their four children were: Maria Christina (Aug. 31, 1869) married Frank Enderle; Katharine (Sept. 21, 1870) married John Lipps; Jacob P. (Jan. 8, 1872) married Mary Agatha Scherer; Anton Francis (March 18, 1873-April 28, 1873). After Justine died, John married Sophia Bosenmeier and they had nine children.

Simon (b. Feb. 18, 1851, d. March 9, 1939) married Mary Theresa LeGrand (b. Jan. 16, 1855, m. Nov. 12, 1876, d. July 10, 1930) and their 10 children were: Antoine Joseph (Sept. 13, 1877) married Corena Eva Mier; Katharine E. (Oct. 23, 1878) married August Sebastian Schlosser; Rosalia (June 3, 1880-Nov. 19, 1899); Johannes (July 31, 1882-July 31, 1898); Mary Magdalene (Aug. 15, 1884) married Theodore Jacob Strebler; Anna T. (Aug. 26, 1886-Sept. 4, 1886); Carolina (Jan. 14, 1888-July 4, 1888); Leo William (Jan. 25, 1891) married Clara Helen Weber; Regina (Dec. 12, 1893-Jan. 17, 1897); Lawrence (May 2, 1896) married Christina Gertrude Weber.

Mary (b. April 10, 1853, d. Aug. 20, 1898) married Conrad Blattel (b. Sept. 27, 1851, d. March 5, 1894) and their 13 children were: Simon F. (Feb. 5, 1874) married Caroline C. Hahn; Maria Justine (Sept. 25, 1875) married Henry Westrich; Anon J. (Dec. 28, 1876) married Regina L. Diebold; Mary Katharine (Feb. 13, 1878) married Martin Hoffer; Adelbert (Oct. 11, 1879) married Mary Julia Kern; Josephine (Nov. 8, 1880) married Jacob Ourth; Anna Frances (Jan. 21, 1882) married Theodore Ourth; Frank (Nov. 27, 1883) married Ollie Virginia Stallings; Phillip J. (Jan. 22, 1885) married Mary Julia Hahn; Martin Florian (July 27, 1886) married Mary Theresa Seitman; Leo S. (May 18, 1888) married Anna C. Schoen; Helena (Feb. 17, 1889-July 2, 1897); Fredolin Jacob (April 17, 1891) married Mary Elizabeth Collie. *Submitted by Ralph Reiminger*

RESSEL – Otto Joseph Ressel, a native of Scott County, farmer and carpenter, born May 21, 1899 at Benton, the son of Theodore and Mary (Diebold) Ressel, married Lorena T. Schlosser on Nov. 21, 1922 at St. Augustine Church in Kelso, MO. She was born Dec. 9, 1899, the daughter of John Schlosser and Mary (Burger) Schlosser.

"O. J.," as he was known, died July 27, 1990 and Lorena died March 4, 1995; both are buried in St. Augustine Cemetery at Kelso. Before retiring they built a new home in Kelso. They had a family of nine children:

Marcus Frederick Ressel (July 3, 1924) married Georgianna Enderle Oct. 9, 1948. They are owners and operators of Kelso Sales & Service.

Four children born to them: Stephen Leslie (April 8, 1950) married Sandy Buchheit on May 8, 1981; Annetta Marie (Jan. 30, 1953); a twin sister, Colette Mary married Paul Hendrickson; and Mark Gerard (March 14, 1957) married Jane Ellen Schlosser on June 21, 1980 at St. Joseph Church in Scott City, MO, daughter of Theon and Patricia (Drury) Schlosser. Their children are: Anthony Mark; Jonathon Paul; Katie Suzanne; Alex Joseph and Grant Michael. Their sons, "Steve" and "Mark," work in the business with them.

Lucas John Ressel, farmer and electrician born Nov. 13, 1925 married Alice Alma Glastetter on May 30, 1952 at St. Lawrence Church in New Hamburg, MO, daughter of Edward "Shorty" and Coletta (Glaus) Glastetter. Thirteen children born to this union: Bradley Lucas; Diane Marie; Linda Susan; Elaine Mary; Patrick Dale; Sharon Kay; Kevin Joseph; Dennis Wayne; Brian Edward; Vickie Faye; Jeffrey Allen; Douglas John and Craig Anthony.

Valeria Genevieve Ressel, born April 30, 1927, married James Mirgeaux on Oct. 18, 1949. Their children: James J. (Terry Blackwell); David Carl (Beverly Dawn Shaffer) and Rene Susan (Edwin K. Phillips).

Mary Ann Ressel (April 26, 1929-July 15, 1995) buried St. Augustine Cemetery at Kelso, MO, married Richard Weber on April 4, 1951. Three children: Richard Jr. (Charlene McClain), Carol Ann (William Howard Morrow) and Mary Jane (Daniel Slaten).

Gertrude Mary Ressel (Aug. 14, 1931-Jan. 18, 1986) married Otis Williams (March 27, 1935-July 4, 1987), both buried at St. Mary's Cemetery in Cape Girardeau, MO.

Leona Mary Ressel (Feb. 25, 1933) married Jimmy Jones on Sept. 26, 1959. Mary Kimberlee is their only child.

James Joseph Ressel (Feb. 8, 1939) married Ester Brooks on Sept. 23, 1961 at St. Mary's Church in Cape Girardeau, MO. They have three children: Roberta, Eric and Michael.

Joann Maire Ressel (April 4, 1938) married Joseph Gleasson on Sept. 26, 1964. Parents of four children: Laura, Timothy, Thomas and Leslie.

Judith Marie Ressel (Nov. 30 1941) married Lawrence Stevens (Jan. 12, 1935-Sept. 20, 1997) buried St. Augustine Cemetery in Kelso, MO. They have four children: Gary Christopher; Sandy; Sherry Ann; Cindy Elizabeth.

RETTIG – Fred Joseph Rettig was born Dec. 2, 1868 in Louisville, KY. He passed away Nov. 15, 1946 in Sikeston, MO. His parents were Louis Rudolph Rettig and Elizabeth Milch. Fred's parents came to America from Germany.

Fred Joseph Rettig

Fred met and married Anna Caroline Krieg. She was born Feb. 22, 1867 in Terre Haute, IN. Her parents were George Krieg and Caroline Fisher. Her parents also came from Germany. Fred and Anna met in Evansville, IN and began their life there.

Their children were:

Otto William Rettig was born Nov. 24, 1892 and died Aug. 9, 1987 in Sikeston, MO. He was married to Bertha Caroline Wagoner.

Anna Caroline Rettig was born Sept. 24, 1894 and died May 19, 1963 in Sikeston, MO. She first married Henry Price, then William Clyde Austill.

Katherine Bloom Rettig was born Sept. 3, 1898 and died July 3, 1976. She married Isca "Ike" Brummitt.

Fred George Rettig was born Sept. 6, 1901 and died Feb. 12, 1969.

Lorene Rettig was born April 5, 1908 and died Oct. 3, 1985. She married Hess Perrigan.

On Feb. 18, 1911 the family loaded all their possessions, wagons and livestock onto a boxcar and they rode passenger on the train arriving at the Sikeston, MO Depot. Their destination was a farm southwest of Blodgett, MO.

Family of Fred Rettig, from left: Caroline R. Austile, Otto Rettig, Katherine R. Brummitt, Fred George Rettig, and Lorene R. Perrigan.

At some time, Fred and Anna moved to Dorena, MO where Anna died in April 1922. Dorena was flooded at that time so they had to take her across the river to Hickman, KY to be buried there in Brownsville Cemetery.

Years passed and Fred became old and feeble. His son, Otto, in Sikeston moved him to his home where he lived until he died Oct. 15, 1946. He is buried in Memorial Park Cemetery in Sikeston. *Written by William Adcock*

RETTIG – LaVerne Rettig was born in rural Scott County on Oct. 24, 1918. His paternal grandparents were Fred Joseph Rettig and Anna Caroline Kreig Rettig. His maternal grandparents were Allerson Alexander Wagoner and Sarah Frances Hamblin Wagoner. He attended different grade schools and finished up going to Chaney Grade School in Scott County.

LaVerne had two brothers and six sisters. (See history of Otto William Rettig).

LaVerne married Deloris Greenlee Jan. 31, 1940 at Benton, MO.

Deloris was born Nov. 23, 1921 to Leonard Greenlee and Della Alberson Greenlee. Her paternal grandparents were Ever Elizabeth Braiser and John Henry Greenlee. Her maternal grandparents were Laura Alice Marker Alberson and James Henry Alberson.

LaVerne and Deloris started their married life on the farm working with his Dad. In a few years they moved to a farm in Essex, MO, then south of Morehouse, MO. They farmed here for 34 years and raised their two children.

Their two children are:

Gayle LaVerne Rettig was born Jan. 12, 1943 in Sikeston, MO. He attended Morehouse Public Schools. He married Audrey Faye Ross Aug. 9, 1963 at Morehouse, MO. Gayle entered the Army Air Defense Command, working with Nike Missiles. He served four years from 1966 to 1970. He spent one year in Korea. They had one son, Gayle LaVerne Rettig Jr., March 27, 1971. Audrey died Nov. 12, 1983. Gayle is now married to Patsy Hill Rettig.

Shelia Jo Ann Rettig was born Aug. 1, 1958. She attended Morehouse Public Schools and Nursing School in Sikeston. She worked in hospitals in Sikeston and Cape Girardeau, MO. She is school nurse for Sikeston Public Schools. She

married J. Lynn Ray Oct. 14, 1978. They have three daughters: Lynda Jo Ann Ray born April 9, 1980; Ashley Di Ann Ray born April 1, 1985; and Kasey Le Ann Ray born Aug. 7, 1988.

LaVerne farmed during growing season and worked as a carpenter in the winter months. They are retired and live in Sikeston, where he enjoys working with

Seated: LaVerne Rettig and Deloris Rettig. Standing: Gayle L. Sr. and Shelia Rettig Ray.

wood and gardening. Deloris enjoys making her quilts and cooking delicious meals.

They now have a great grandson, Gayle LaVerne Rettig III. This makes four living generations of Rettigs. *Submitted by Deloris Rettig*

RETTIG – Otto William Rettig was born Nov. 24, 1892 in Evansville, IN. He passed away Aug. 9, 1987 in Sikeston, MO. His parents were Fred Joseph Rettig and Anna Kreig Rettig. Their parents had migrated to America from Germany. Otto was the oldest of five children. His brother and sisters were:

Anna Caroline Rettig was born Sept. 24, 1894 and died May 19, 1963 in Sikeston, MO. She first married Henry Price, then William Clyde Austill.

Katherine Bloom Rettig was born Sept. 3, 1898 and died July 3, 1976. She married Isica "Ike" Brummitt.

Family of Otto W. Rettig. Seated, from left: Lola R. Adcock, Otto Rettig, Bertha Rettig, and Sherman Rettig. Standing: Willine R. Miller, Sadie R. James, Harold Rettig, LaVerne Rettig, Dorothy R. Broderick, and Cleo R. Davis.

Fred George Rettig was born Sept. 6, 1901 and died Feb. 12, 1969;

Lorene Rettig was born April 5, 1908 and died Oct. 3, 1985. She married Hess Perrigan.

When Otto was 7 years old, the family moved to Louisville, KY. They lived there 10 years. Then they moved back to Indiana, staying there approximately 11 months before moving to Missouri. They settled southwest of Blodgett, MO in about 1911. The family moved from Indiana by train. They brought all the family possessions, including their livestock, by train and arrived at the depot in Sikeston, MO. They were farmers, as had been their fathers before them.

Otto met his future bride and married Bertha Caroline Wagoner March 21, 1915. She was born July 27, 1895, the daughter of Allerson Alexander Wagoner and Sarah Frances Hamblin Wagoner. Her family came from Austin Springs, TN. She died Oct. 22, 1971.

Otto and Bertha lived and raised their children on a farm in Scott County. Their children are:

Sherman Alexander Rettig, who was born Oct. 24, 1912 and died April 1, 1975. He married Nell Cook;

Rose Lee Rettig was born and died in 1916;

LaVerne Rettig was born Oct. 24, 1918. He married Deloris Greenlee;

Berniece Cleo Rettig was born Oct. 19, 1920. She married Lowell Davis;

Dora Willine Rettig was born Feb. 14, 1922. She married Ferrell Miller;

Sadie Marie Rettig was born Sept. 9, 1924. She married Mitchell James;

Lola Mae Rettig was born June 30, 1927. She married William Henry Adcock;

Dorothy Lee Rettig was born July 29, 1931 and died Sept. 2, 1997. She married William Broderick;

Harold Otto Allan Rettig was born Jan. 10, 1937. He married Mary Beth McAnulty.

Otto and Bertha lived on a farm with a big yard and many shade trees. Many Sundays were spent with their children and grandchildren. They enjoyed playing baseball, horseshoes, singing and having big dinners.

Otto loved the land and was a good farmer. Otto and Bertha are buried in Memorial Park Cemetery in Sikeston, MO near his father, Fred Joseph Rettig. *Written by Lola Rettig Adcock*

RICHARDS – Roy William, son of Albert A. and Maymie Hubbert Richards, was born Jan. 7, 1913 at Mooreland, OK. His great-grandmother came from Ireland. His great-grandfather came from Holland and settled in Pennsylvania. In 1830 he moved to Ohio, then to Kansas. Grandpa Hubbert made the run from Kansas when Oklahoma Territory was opened in 1900. The family came in covered wagon and homesteaded about five miles from Mooreland, OK.

Roy's Dad went to Oklahoma in a cattle car in 1900 and homesteaded. Roy was born there and went to school. At age 17, he went to Independence, MO to work and live with his brother, Carl. In 1932, he went to Calloway County in his "Ford roadster with rumble seat" to help his sister on their farm.

He married Edith Mae Hall in January 1933. They moved to southeast Missouri in 1936. They bought a farm between Matthews and East Prairie and moved there in 1939.

They had three children; R. L., Larry and Barbara.

They moved to Sikeston in 1945. The children went to South Grade School. In third grade, Larry wanted to live on a farm, so he went and lived with his grandparents, E. B. and Lila Hall, and went to school at Matthews, MO.

Roy Richards, Gene Hall, and unknown man hauling logs in 1933.

Edith Mae worked at the Parks Airport during the time the cadets were training. She worked for Kroger Store (there were three at one time), then for El Capri Motel as cashier.

In August 1971, on their way to the farm, they had a wreck on AA Road, south of Miner. Roy lived a month and died in the hospital on Sept. 23, 1971. Edith sold the house in town and moved to the farm in 1972. Her mother sold her house in town and lived with her until her death in 1984. Edith moved back to Sikeston in 1995 until her death in August 2000.

R. L. farmed the homeplace after his marriage to Jeno Silverthorn. They moved to Sikeston in 1977 and started Reliable Freight. Larry farmed his grandparents' farm after their retirement and his marriage to Liz Haynes. Then they moved to the family farm until he retired from farming. He now drives for Reliable.

R. L. has two sons: David, who runs Reliable, and Michael, who farms and owns EM-CAL Trucking Company. David has two children, Derek and Danielle. Michael has two daughters, Emily and Callie.

Larry has two children, Bryan is a RN, CDMS, CCM and fieldcase manager and supervisor.

Cindy is a probation officer.

Barbara married J. Box and has been a homemaker. Barbara has two sons - Rick and Randy.

Rick retired after 20 years in the Army. He owns and leases a truck. Rick has three sons; Brice, Blake and Brandon, and one daughter, Amy.

Randy is manager at Sikeston Motor Company Bodyshop. Randy has two children, Erin and Andrew. *Submitted by Barbara Box*

ROTH – Johannes Casper Roth (June 13, 1792-May 26, 1867) and his wife, Anna Katharina (Kimpel) Roth (Sept. 11, 1797-Oct. 3, 1876), came with their son, David (Dec. 3, 1826-Aug. 31, 1899), and his family to America around 1851. When Casper married Katharine of Rebgeshain on Aug. 25, 1813, he was a farmer and baker in Engelrod. Casper, a devout Lutheran who left Germany for religious freedom, assisted in organizing many area Lutheran churches. The 1860 census shows Casper and Katherine living with David and his family in Illmo.

David, a shoemaker born in Rebgeshain, married Anna Juliana (Boss) Roth (Jan. 23, 1819-Sept. 5, 1892) of Lauzenhain on Feb. 24, 1848. David and Juliana had seven children, two born in Germany and the rest in Missouri: George; Katherine; Casper; Marie; Johann, Sophia and Elizabeth. On Nov. 22, 1854, David Roth purchased 200 acres of land on the main road leading to Commerce, which was a thriving river town. By 1875, he had 570 acres. In 1868 he sold some land to Eisleben Lutheran Church, on which the present church is located. David, a farmer, was a trustee of the church and a home guard during the Civil War.

David built the Roth house southeast of Illmo, but the year it was built has not been proven. Ernest Roth (Nov. 4, 1901-Dec. 30, 1989), grandson of David, said his father, Johann, was 9, putting the date around 1866. The Roth home is a German-style farmhouse built of handmade bricks baked in a nearby kiln. The Thebes sandstone smokehouse is thought to be considerably older than the house. The wooden bank barn, built on a bank so the animals could live in the basement and machinery and equipment could be stored on the ground level, has a basement made of unmortared Thebes sandstone.

Johann Roth (Dec. 9, 1857-Aug. 11, 1945) purchased the home and 173 acres from his father, David. He married Justine Sophie (Luecke) Roth (Jan. 10, 1861-Aug. 2, 1926) on Nov. 3, 1881. They had 12 children: Martin; Ida; Erna; Rosa; Martha; August; Edna; Oscar; Arthur; Alma; Ernest and Herbert. Johann farmed and ran a molasses mill. He was an active church worker, played the organ and fiddle, and enjoyed entering his farm products in the Neighbor Day fair in Benton.

Roth House

Ernest purchased the land and home from his father, Johann, and farmed the land. He and Anna Marie (Walter) Roth (March 2, 1913-July 28, 1995) married on Sept. 5, 1936 and had six children: Richard; Ralph; Rose; Frank; Don and Ernestine. Richard, Ralph and Frank purchased land from Ernest and live near the old homestead. Don, who owns Roth Hardware, purchased the house from his father, Ernest. After the death of his mother, he sold the house to his niece, Linda, who is the daughter of Richard and the great-great-granddaughter of David. Richard married Doris (Kenkel) Roth on Dec. 24, 1961. They had two sets of twins: Karen and Sharon, and Linda and Brenda. Linda married Donnie Phillips on Oct. 4, 1986. Their children, Chelsea and Travis, are the sixth generation to live in the Roth home. *Submitted by Brenda Roth*

SANDERS – "Big apple, lil' apple, Suzy-Q, come on Illmo, we're rootin' for you!" This was just one of those cute little ditties she would sing to us kids as we were growing up. It was one of the chants she had learned as an Illmo High School cheerleader in 1947. Looking back on it all

Evelyn Sanders age 16.

now, she was a fun Mom to grow up with, while still being a disciplinarian. She is probably one of the sweetest ladies you could ever meet. Here's her story.

Maurath Family, 1980s. Back row: Jacqueline Marie, Evelyn Sue, Elmer Richard, Gregory Richard, and Joseph Justin. Front: John Louis, Cheryl Ann, Connie Louise, and Linda Irene.

It was a cold day in January 1932 that she was born to Irene (nee Held) and John Mack Sanders on the David and Emilie (pronounced Amelia) Held family farm, just south of Illmo. John Mack's uncle, Doctor George Thomas Dorris, came out from Illmo to deliver the baby. She was christened in Eiselben Lutheran Church by Rev.

George Hilpert as "Evelyn Sue" and the godparents were her uncle and aunt, Harry and Erma (nee Held) Uelsmann. They lived with her grandparents on the farm until she was about 7, and then around 1939 they moved to a house near Eiselben, next door to Gus and Mary Miller. It was around this time in 1938 that they saw the "great light" in the sky, or "Aurora Borealis," which had been pre-

Evelyn Sue Sanders and Elmer Richard Maurath, January 28, 1953

dicted at Fatima, Portugal in 1917. Then they moved to Fornfelt, to the home of Fritz "Pa" and Elizabeth ("Ma"-nee Wolter) Sander, who were the parents of her grandma, Amelia Held. They then moved to 411 Scott Street. Interestingly, there were no street signs. During this time, she met her best friends, Dorothy Jane Crow (who was like a sister), Thelma Dunger, Joanne Brazel, Othella Bean "Beanie" and cousin Gloria Rose Held. She attended Fornfelt High School in her freshman year 1946, and Illmo High School in her sophomore year 1947. It was at this time she was nominated the Illmo "Queen of Hearts." Her parents also moved to an 80-acre farm, where they built their home themselves, with the help of uncles, James Richmond Sanders and Louis Sanders. She said these were some of the best years of her life, as they had so much fun on the farm together and learned to be very self-sufficient. She said her parents and brother, Richard, were the greatest, and her Mom was her very best friend. Interestingly, some strange things happened on the farm, including frequent sightings of UFOs. In 1948, the high schools consolidated as Illmo-Fornfelt High School, where she attended junior and senior years. Her boyfriend was Billy Dale Hopke, who later married Goldie Hale. After graduation, she went to St. Louis with her aunt and uncle, Jennie (nee Sanders) and Don Schmitt, to find work. It was at this time that she met the love of her life, Elmer Richard Maurath, who was the attendant at "Cook's Service Station" on Chippewa and Macklin in St. Louis, where Jennie and Don frequented. After a few months though, she became very homesick and moved back home, where she got a job in the Ely-Walker Garment Factory with her parents. Coincidentally, Elmer had taken a job with his brother's waterproofing company, and happened to be in Cape twice, and Evelyn just happened to see him by chance and they talked. They were still in love. She moved back to St. Louis in 1951 with friend, Shirley Dunger, and got a job with her Aunt Jennie. Elmer found out she was back in town, and they started dating. He was drafted into the Army during the Korean War. They were so much in love that she joined the Catholic Church, and he obtained special permission to come back home in order to be married. His orders to go to Korea were delayed and eventually dismissed. They were married in the New Cathedral in St. Louis on Jan. 28, 1953 and then went back to New Jersey to finish out his tour of duty with the Army. There they met Army friends, Rudy and Betty Clapp, with whom they remained friends throughout the years. They moved back to St. Louis, where they raised seven children, with frequent visits back home to Scott County. They had a good, fun, productive life together. Suddenly, at the young age of 65, Elmer died unexpectedly of a rare lung disease. She was crushed and very lonely, but with God's grace, was able to cope, and eventually remarried to Rudy Clapp, who has been a good companion and soul-mate, and always listens with interest to the many stories she tells about the love of her life. Mom, you have been the greatest, and everyone who knows you, loves you! We, your children, love you, and dedicate this to you! So, from an old ballad: "Every sorrow and care in the dear days gone by, was made bright by the light of the smile in your eye. Like a candle that's set in a window at night, your fond love has cheered us, and guided us right. We love the dear silver that shines in your hair, and the brow that's all fuddled and wrinkled with care, we kiss the dear fingers so toil-worn for us.....oh, God bless you and keep you, forever with us!" *Submitted by John Maurath*

SANDERS – Two of the most wonderful people were my parents, John Mack Sanders and Irene Held. Daddy was born Nov. 28, 1914 on a farm north of Commerce, and is the son of Henry Wilson Sanders and Hulda Franziska Sander. Grandpa Sanders, who had eyes as blue as the sky, was the son of John Mack Sanders I (or Senior)and Mary Mathilda "Molly" Miller. John Mack's parents were Richmond and Mary (nee Raspberry) Sanders, who came to Scott County from Tennessee. Grandma Hulda was the daughter of Adam Daniel Sander and Magdalena Conradena Uelsmann. Daddy, who still lives in Scott City at age 87, was a very good fiddle player in his younger days and played at barn dances. He was a handsome young man. Country music is his hobby and joy, and he is also fond of playing the guitar, banjo and other instruments. My mom, Irene Held, was not only the best mother a girl could have, but she was also my best friend. She was born March 2, 1914 on the Held family farm south of Illmo, and was the daughter of David Held, whose parents came from Germany, and Emilie (Amelia) Sander (who was no relation to Grandma Hulda Sander) listed above. Not only was Mom so pretty with her dark hair and eyes, but she was also a very nice, sweet person to everyone – and, she could do just about anything. Mom and Daddy met at a barn dance, and after they were first married, lived on Grandma and Grandpa Held's farm before moving into town (Illmo). After a while, they bought their own 80-acre farm near Grandma and Grandpa. My brother, Richard, and I, and our parents had so much fun on the farm. They both worked at the Ely-Walker clothing factory in Illmo, from where they both retired. Mom was a sewer and Daddy was a pattern-maker. After retirement, they moved back to Illmo and then to Scott City, where Mom died on Jan. 13, 1991. This was the saddest time for me. We were members of Eisleben Lutheran Church in Illmo, where Mom is buried and where Daddy will also be buried. We were a very close and happy family, and I look forward to seeing my Mom in Heaven, while worshiping our God. *Submitted by Evelyn Sue (nee Sanders) Maurath-Clapp*

John Mack and Irene (Held) Sanders, 1943.

SANDERS – Isaac Sanders was the son of William and Sarah Sanders, who were living in the Camden District of Richland County, SC. Around 1797, the Sanders and several other families migrated to the area of Robertson County, TN, that later became part of Cheatham County. Among this pioneer group was Isaac's son, William Sanders and his wife, Mariah, who were the parents of 12 children. After the death of William around 1830, the Sanders, along with other families, migrated to Williamson County, IL, except for one son, Richmond Sanders.

Richmond was born March 20, 1813. His marriage to Mary Raspberry (b. March 23, 1814) was recorded as Jan. 3, 1836 in the Davidson County, TN clerk's records, entry #491, page 154. Mary was the daughter of William Raspberry and Siniah Hooper, both families having also migrated from South Carolina to Tennessee. Some of Mary's relatives later migrated to Scott County, MO.

Hulda Franziska Sander, daughter of Adam Daniel Sander and Magdalena Konradena Uelsmann. Henry Wilson Sanders, son of John Mack Sanders, I and Mary Mathilda "Molly" Miller. Ca. 1908.

And so, some time in 1842, Richmond and Mary traveled in a covered wagon with three small children to Scott County. They settled on 40 acres between Commerce and Illmo, near Mary's relative George Raspberry. They finally received a preemption certificate (#17333) for this land in 1856, signed by President Franklin Pierce himself. The land is still in the family, and the Sanders Family Cemetery is located on this land, where Richmond and Mary and many of their descendants are buried. It is a quaint, picturesque, and well-maintained family cemetery.

The children of Richmond and Mary are: 1) Miriam Adeline, born 1837 in Tennessee, and married to David Spradlin, a Civil War veteran; 2) Churchhill born 1839 in Tennessee. "Church" was married twice and was a Civil War veteran; 3) James K. Polk born 1841 in Tennessee, and died in the Civil War in 1861; 4) Martin Van Buren born 1845 in Missouri, married twice, to Mary "Molly" Griggs and Leonor R. Smith. Martin was a Civil

1906 Sanders family reunion at the home of Fillmore Sanders near Commerce, MO. First row, left to right: Charlie Sanders, unknown, unknown, Algie Sanders (Tude), Fillmore S. Jr., Mack Sanders, Claude Sanders, Archie Sanders, unknown, Iola Weaver, Viola Weaver, Lucille Sanders, Ara Miller, Iena Sanders, Cordia Sanders. 2nd row: Addie S. Edmonds, Belle Garvey, unknown Spradlin, Jennie Sanders, Mollie Sanders Bretzel, Jessie Sanders, Mary Sanders, Mrs. Henry Sanders (Mary S. Bruns), Emma Sanders (Bruns), Joe Sanders (holding Glen), Charlie Weaver (holding Grace). 3rd row: Tom Matthews, Lum Lern, Rose Garvey, Fannie Belk (Miller), Mr. Bruns (Emma S.'s father), Geo. Miller (holding ?), Mrs. Ed Garvey (holding Hugh), Bea Miller, Jess Odom (behind Aunt Bea), Grand Archie Odom. 4th row: Allen Sanders, Martin Sanders, John Mack Sanders, Fillmore Sanders Sr., Jim Sanders (from Illinois side), Mrs. Jim Sanders, Pete Wile, Elsie Wise, Emma Wilkerson, unknown, Yancey (with fiddle), unknown, Leona Sanders (with unknown), Alice Sanders, Richmond Sanders, Sara Sanders (holding unknown), Roy Sanders, Susan Miller, Alice Weaver (holding unknown), Fred Weaver, Mollie Sanders (in doorway). The children held by Charlie and Leona are possibly Ida and Hugh Brewer infants.

War veteran; 5) Allen Brasell born 1847 in Missouri, married twice, to widow Elsie Ann House-Beckman and widow Sarah Russell-Francis. Allen was a Civil War veteran; 6) John Mack I born 1849 in Missouri, and married to Mary Mathilda "Molly" Miller. He was a Civil War veteran, having only served in the Scott County Home Guard as a teenager, and often told the story of how he was shot at one day by a sniper, while walking across the family farm. He was the grandfather of this author; 7) William S. born 1851 in Missouri and died as an infant; 8) Fillmore born 1852 in Missouri and married Sarah Alice Odom; 9) Mary Richmond born 1858 in Missouri, and no other information.

John Mark Sanders, I, son of Richmond and Mary Sanders, his wife, Molly (nee Miller), and his son Mack Sanders. Ca. late 1890s, early 1900s.

Richmond died May 27, 1882 and Mary died Sept. 25, 1896. The Sanders are well known for being musically inclined, specifically with the fiddle and have played at many a barn dance in the county. This author still has the 175-year-old fiddle brought by great-grandpa Richmond from Tennessee to Missouri. The story of this family is detailed in the book *The Sanders Family: An American Odyssey* by Holden E. "Gene" Sanders. *Submitted by Jack Mack Sanders II and his grandson, John L. Maurath*

SANDERS – Louis E. Sanders was born Sept. 27, 1917 on a farm near Commerce, MO. He is the son of Henry Sanders and Hulda Sander Sanders-Hilleman. He is the great-grandson of Scott County pioneer settler Richmond Sanders.

Louis was educated in the public schools of Commerce, finishing his education by graduating from Commerce High School.

As a boy, Louis worked on his father's farm, along with his four brothers and five sisters. (Three of those siblings failed to live to maturity.) As a young man, he joined his father in doing carpentry work in the Scott County area.

Louis served in the U. S. Army during WWII, seeing action in France and Germany. After the war, he returned to the Scott County area. He soon hung up his tool belt and went to work for International Shoe Company, later Florsheim Shoe Company, in Cape Girardeau, MO. He remained with that company until he retired in 1980.

He married Frances M. Stehr of Cape Girardeau on May 28, 1956, at St. Mary's Catholic Church in Cape Girardeau. She was born Aug. 17, 1923 in Cape Girardeau, the daughter of Raymond Stehr and Clara Glaus Stehr, both natives of Scott County.

Frances and Louis continue to live in the Cape Girardeau home they bought when they first married. They have four children: Susan Sanders; Jean Sanders Hermsdorfer; David Sanders; and Sharon Sanders, all of Cape Girardeau. Jean is married to Paul Hermsdorfer.

The couple also has two grandchildren, Katherine F. Mayer and Laura R. Hermsdorfer, both of Cape Girardeau. *Submitted by Sharon Sanders*

SANDERS – Heinrich Sander (born 1798) and wife Henrietta (born 1804) immigrated to the United States from Gross Ruden, Hannover, Germany between 1846 and 1850. They left Germany under the rule of Frederick Wilhelm IV, a time of threats of war and religious persecution. As so many before them, they came to America to pursue a new life for them and the only child we have record of, Carl.

Their Port of Entry was New Orleans, where they took a paddle wheel boat up the Mississippi River to Missouri. They first settled in Cape Girardeau County and then on to Scott County, where they were members of Eisleban Lutheran Church. Henrietta Sander died Aug. 29, 1872 and Heinrich Sept. 11, 1874 and both are buried in the Eisleban Cemetery.

Their son, Carl or Charles J. Sanders, was an adventurous, debonair, carefree man. He married Mary Henrietta Grumbrecht June 26, 1853 and had one son, August Sander. After the death of Mary Henrietta, Charles married Henrietta Vogelsang on May 30, 1856, and had six more children. The other children, Frederick, Carolena, Aguste, Dorthea, Henry and William, lived most of their adult lives in Scott county, either as farmers or wives and mothers.

Both Heinrich and Charles were volunteers in the Missouri Militia (Union) during the Civil War and have had descendants who lost their life in WWI, WWII and the Korean War.

The eight generations in America of Heinrich and Henrietta Sander have produced farmers, merchants, ministers, CEOs, lawyers, doctors, RR men, bankers, accountants and engineers. Many of these descendants still live productive lives in Scott County. Proud Americans all. *Submitted by Christina Schaefer*

SCHAEFER – Rufina Schlosser was born Jan. 7, 1873 to John and Rufina Steinmetz Schlosser in Germany. She came to America with her parents when she was 7 years old.

Zita, Cora and Hilda Schaefer in the strawberry patch.

Adam B. Schaefer was born May 18, 1872 in New Hamburg, MO to Bart and Mary Kern Schaefer.

Adam B. Schaefer and Rufina Schlosser were married Oct. 3, 1893 in Kelso, MO. To this union were born: Mary Eleanor "Nora" who married Fred "Fritz" Enderle; Coletta Caroline who married George Thomas; Mary Mathilda "Mattie" Schaefer; Joseph Erich "Slim" who married Rose; Michael Amiel Schaefer who died at the age of 3 months; Zeno Joseph Schaefer who died at the age of 2 years; Edwin Charles "Peanuts" Schaefer; Hilda Philomina who married Edward Enderle; Zita Ortha who married Joseph Marion Hess; and Cora Leona who married Peter Bernard Seyer.

They lived for a while on a farm near New Hamburg, and then resided at Kelso for 19 years. In 1897, Adam purchased a lot in Kelso and, in 1905, he acquired adjoining property, all on Blattel Street. Adam was a carpenter and also had a butcher shop in Kelso.

In 1916, Adam purchased land on a hill east of Chaffee, near Rockview. Here they grew strawberries, apples and sweet potatoes among other fruits and vegetables.

On Friday, Sept. 21, 1934, Zita Schaefer was bitten on the top of her left foot by a large snake while working with her father in a field. The limb swelled and she was in intense pain. After receiving treatment from a Chaffee physician, she was brought to St. Francis Hospital in Cape Girardeau for a serum treatment. Though not definitely known as to what type of snake inflicted the wound, it was believed to have been a poisonous cottonmouth moccasin. (Information taken from *Southeast Missourian* Sept. 22, 1934 edition.)

SCHATZ – Henry was born March 22, 1858 in Cape Girardeau, MO, the son of German immigrants who arrived in the United States in 1856. As was the custom of the German people, Henry was sent at an early age to become an apprentice and learn a trade. Henry chose to be a wagon maker and apprenticed three years to become a "Graduate Wagon Maker." After finishing his apprenticeship, he moved to Commerce, Scott County, MO, and set up a blacksmith shop.

In September of 1879, he traveled back to Cape Girardeau and married his childhood sweetheart, Caroline "Lena" Sander. They set up a home in Commerce and raised nine children. All but one of the children were born in Scott County.

Henry was a pleasant, affable man known as "Uncle Henry" to all the children and younger people. As well as the blacksmith shop, he and his sons, Bill and Ed, had a lightening rod business. He made the lightening rods and they installed them on barns and houses in the community. In the years before electricity was installed in the home, this was a common practice. He, along with Bill and Ed, played in a Brass Band; Henry played the Bass Horn. They performed in parades and at parties along with their neighbors.

At times Henry followed the timber and would set up temporary blacksmith shops to repair broken saws and wheels as the men cleared the timber, and shoe horses. While he was away, Lena remained at home with the children and oversaw the farm. The oldest son, Bill, often went to help his father and Ed stayed at home to do the chores and raise the garden. One of the younger sons, John, would take produce and eggs to town in a wagon and sell it to those who had no garden. At one of the out-of-the-area blacksmith jobs, Lena took John and Edith with her and they set up a temporary boarding house for the timber workers. Edith helped cook and John waited tables.

Henry and Lena raised their nine children with a sense of God and duty, expecting them to be respectful, hard working, productive citizens. Henry would bribe his children with gifts. On his son, John's 18th birthday, he gave him a gold signet ring not to smoke. It worked.

Henry had what was known then as consumption (TB) for a number of years, dying of a lung hemorrhage on Feb. 4, 1913. Some of the children married and continued to live in Scott County. Edith, who married Aubrey Shipman, was one of them. John lived in Scott County until 1927 before moving to Michigan, and Bill and Ed both lived in Scott County for a number of years. Nell lived in the county for a number of years before moving to Cape Girardeau. Matt, Irene and George all moved away after they were married. *Submitted by Christina Schaefer*

SCHERER – Donatus Scherer, born Feb. 12, 1891 in Baden, Germany, the son of John and Mary (Ziegel) Scherer, was first married to Sophia Stuppy on March 27, 1845 in Canton, Stark County, OH. Sophia was born Sept. 10, 1823 in Schirrhein, Alsace, France, the daughter of John and Elizabeth (Willwohl) Stuppy. Donatus and a brother, Valentine, came to southeast Missouri in 1846. Two other brothers followed, Benedict in 1852 and John Baptist in 1853, all farmers. They settled in the wilderness south of Kelso, clearing land, building a cabin and living off the wild. They had seen this section rise to a finely settled and improved farming county. The area was called Schererville District. They were among the founders of St. Lawrence Catholic Church and did much work to help build the church and the town of New Hamburg. During the Civil War, the church was burned by the guerillas.

Mrs. Scherer's death was the first one recorded in St. Lawrence Catholic Church records, where services were held and burial was in the church cemetery. Her remains were hauled by Dennis Diebold and the brush had to be cut out to let the wagon through. Her monument is 7 feet high. The stone was hauled with oxen from the quarry at Cape Girardeau and Benedict Scherer was the sculptor. Only such tools as are common to the farmers were used, such as a hatchel, chisel, etc. The lettering is as good as to be found on any modern stone and tells the story that Mrs. Scherer died on Oct. 5, 1847 at the age of 24 years.

Donatus' second marriage to Mary Magdalena Bucher/Bohart (1832-1901) was April 24, 1848 and they were one of the first couples married in St. Lawrence Log Church, built in 1847. She was the daughter of Wendolin and Mary Magdalena (Halter) Bucher/Bohart, who donated three acres of land for church property. They were the parents of 13 children: Anton; John G.; Mary Theresa; Leo; Theophil; Catherine Regina; Elizabeth; Donat married Otillia Schoen; Wendolin; Mary Magdalena; Louisa; Martin Leo; and his twin brother, Phillip.

Donat Scherer, a Scott Countian born Dec. 26, 1861 in Schererville District south of Kelso, married Otillia Emma Schoen (1868-1937), daughter of Henry and Katharina (Cooper/Cupper) Schoen, in 1886 at New Hamburg. Eight children were born to this union: William Andrew (1887-1914); Bertha Caroline (1888-1957); and the youngest son, Louis Theophil (1905-1968) were never married. The other

Otillia (Schoen) and Donat Scherer, New Hamburg, Mo., 1927.

children were: Pauline Magdalena (1891-1970) was the wife of Alphones Charles Chatman and had five children, three living to adulthood; Celeste E. (1915-1996), remaining single; Hermina C. (1917-is still living) married Raymond Gosche and their children are: Raymond Donald; Geraldine Ester; James Elroy; Robert Louis; Marjorie Anne; and Lillian Marie. Twins Clara Ann and Maria Anna died in infancy.

Clara Philomena (1893-1967) and her husband, Edward Bles, were the parents of seven children: Louise Coletta; Thomas; Bertha Mildred; Irene Gladys; John Edward; Margaret Ann; and Mary Catherine, known as "Babe."

Genevieve M. (1896-1957) married Phillip August Weber on Sept. 25, 1917 in St. Augustine Catholic Church in a double wedding with sister, Clara Philomena and Edward Bles. It was the first double wedding to be held in the church at Kelso. Phillip and his wife were parents of five children: Louis William; Alma Emma; Loretta Bertha; Mary Frances and Dorothy Ann (married John James Forgione and they live in Wilmington, DE).

Anna Helen (1898-1990) married Paul Glastetter on Aug. 17, 1920 in St. Augustine Catholic Church at Kelso. All of their ten children grew to adulthood: William Joseph; Sylvester Benjamin (married Ramona Frances Blattel); Delphine Bertha; Aurelia Marie; Louis Paul; John Zeno; Rita Clara; Coletta Clara; Helen Louise; and Bertha Ann.

Anton Otto (1901-1960) and Martha Lalumandiere have two daughters, Lucy Katherine (married Edward Leo Klipfel) and Rosalie (married Raymond Joseph Urhahn). *Submitted by Kurt David Glastetter*

SCHERER – Theophil Scherer and Mary Magdalena Glastetter were married Nov. 18, 1884 in Kelso, MO. He was born June 29, 1856 and was the son of Donatus and Mary Bucher Scherer. They were the parents of the following seven children.

Ida Alvina, Oct. 25, 1885; Emma Louise, Feb. 12, 1887; Mary Magadeline, Jan. 10, 1889; Fredolin Joseph, March 18, 1892; Bernard George, March 4, 1894; Victor, Oct. 22, 1895; and Dorothy Martha, Sept. 26, 1902.

Ida married Frank Dirnberger, they were the parents of four children. Viola, Aug. 18, 1908, married Henry Brands. Anita Katherine, March 8, 1911, married Denis LeGrand. Arthur George, May 21, 1913, married Evelyn Seitmann, and Robert Frank, June 4, 1915, married Viola Dannenmueller.

Emma married Otto Heisserere, they were the parents of four children. Raymond August, June 4, 1909, married Frances Wilhelm. Leona M., Sept. 21, 1910, married George Diebold. Corona Anna, March 17, 1913, married Dr. Arthur Fuerth. Theon, June 20, 1922, married Jettie Hinkle Buchheit.

Mary Magdaline married Aloys S. Heisserer, and they were the parents of five children. Leon O., Sept. 3, 1909. Johnny T., March 11, 1911. Corina Clara, Jan. 4, 1913. Lorraine Marie, Dec. 28, 1914, married Norman Rainey, and Bernice, Oct. 10, 1919, married Charles Franz.

Fredolin Joseph married Mary Elizabeth Sanders and they were the parents of nine children. Melvin David, May 30, 1912, married Avanell Hill. Benjamin Franklin, March 4, 1914. James Martin, Dec. 25, 1915, married Evelyn Jones Dorothy Elizabeth, March 2, 1918, married Harvey Myers. Mary Ada, Feb. 2, 1920. Fred Lincoln, July 4, 1922, married Alice Matthews; Sarah Alice, Feb. 3, 1924, married Hugh Schott. August John, Aug. 31, 1928, married Opal Turnbo, and Robert LeRoy, Aug. 3, 1933, married Mona Jones.

Bernard George and Mary Eftink were the parents of eight children. James Theophil, Aug. 8, 1916, married Nora Brands. Richard George, Nov. 14, 1918, married Viola Klipel. Gilbert Warren, Nov. 2, 1920, married Florence Brands. Veronica Mary, Oct. 29, 1922. Edna K., Jan. 26, 1925, married Joseph Christian. Bernard John, Feb. 8, 1928, married Pricilla Sandler. Georgia Rose, June 12, 1919. Mary Jane, July 15, 1931, married Herman Clark.

Victor and Pauline Welter were the parents of seven children. Mary Ann, May 22, 1921, married Benjamin Scheffer and then married Leo Bruenderman. Jerome Jacob, July 20, 1922, married Rosalia Duenne. Victor Jordan, Dec. 2, 1923. Ralph Andrew, April 28, 1925, married Ann Vetter. Geneva Katherine, Jan. 13, 1927, married Cornelius Dirnberger. Gregory Beno, Sept. 24, 1929, married Mary Louise Scherer, then married Georgia Guinn Grady. Wilma Hermina, Sept. 28, 1931, married Celestine August Martin.

Dorothy Martha and Frank Vincent Klueppel Sr. were parents of three sons. Frank Jr., Sept. 22, 1932, married Carolyn Hinton. Joseph Raymond, Sept. 20, 1934, married Irene Jansen. Charles Edward, Oct. 25, 1935, married Angela Kluesner. *Submitted by Frank and Carolyn Klueppel*

SCHLOSSER – Charlotte Kathryn Schlosser was born on July 1, 1951 in Cape Girardeau, MO. Her parents were Theon John and Ella Irene (LeDure) Schlosser. Theon was born on April 3, 1906 in Kelso, MO, son of Emil Schlosser and Helen Anne Burger Schlosser. Ella Irene was born on Oct. 25, 1912 in Kelso, MO, daughter of August Pius LeDure and Anna Maria Martin LeDure. Ella and Theon had 14 children; seven were boys and seven were girls. Charlotte was the ninth child in the family. Her brothers' names are Theon Louis; William Eugene; Maurice Charles; Franklin Joseph; Marion Dale; Richard Anthony and Joseph August. Her sisters' names are Helen Ann; Ella Theresa; Doris Emma; Diana Marie; Mary Elaine and Juanita Marian. At the time of this writing, Ella and Theon had 58 grandchildren, 83 great grandchildren and 2 great great grandchildren.

Charlotte married Robert Eugene Hooper (born on Aug. 30, 1950 in St. Louis, MO) on Jan. 24, 1970 in a double wedding ceremony at the St. Augustine Catholic Church in Kelso, MO. Her sister, Diana Marie and Ira Thomas Judd, were married at the same time. Charlotte and Robert were later divorced on Jan. 25, 1979.

Robert's parents were William Charles Hooper and Pansy Farmer. William was born on May 14, 1921 in Johnston City, IL, son of Thomas Hooper and Ethel Bryant. Ethel was born on May 18, 1902 in Johnston City, IL. Pansy Farmer was born on Sept. 2, 1921 in Bell City, MO, daughter of Tom Farmer and Nette Cook.

Four daughters were born to Charlotte and Robert: Christine Marie, born Aug. 20, 1970;

Cheryl Ann, born July 14, 1971; Rebecca Mae, born Jan. 9, 1976; and Sara Ella, born Oct. 10, 1978.

Christine Marie married Clint Allan Estes on June 17, 1989 at St. Augustine Catholic Church in Kelso, MO. Their children are: Caleb Allan, born on Sept. 13, 1989; Zachary Robert, born on Oct. 21, 1993 and Abagail Christine, born on April 16, 2000.

Cheryl Ann married Barry Dale Stone at St. Joseph Catholic Church in Scott City, MO (later divorced). Catrina Ann Stone was born on June 7, 1989. Ryan Michael Brock was born on July 6, 1994, son of Cheryl and Michael Brock. Cheryl married Timothy Lynn Tucker on May 29, 1998.

Rebecca Mae married Carmon "Allen" Collier on June 6, 1998 at St. Augustine Catholic Church in Kelso, MO. Their child is Alivia Mae, born on Jan. 19, 2001.

Sara Ella has a child who was born on June 28, 1996, Dominic Michael Hooper. His father is Lee Eads, who was from Scott City, MO.

Family is an important part of our heritage. Be proud of who you are and where you came from. Enjoy life and always remember that family is here for you. *Submitted by Charlotte Hooper*

SCHLOSSER – John Schlosser was born Nov. 3, 1836 or 1838 in Alsace, Lorraine, France. He married Rufina Steinmetz, who was the daughter of Sebastian Steinmetz and Marie Mosser. They settled on a homestead south of what is now known as Scott City. They had seven children: John; Joseph; Rufina; Caroline; Sebastian; Emil and August.

John Schlosser was my grandfather and the oldest of the seven children. He was born May 17, 1869 in Alsace-Lorraine, Germany. He came to the United States around the age of 11. John was married to Mary Burger, who was born May 29, 1879 in Kelso, MO. John and Mary stayed on the family homestead and raised seven children: Louise; Edmund; Lorene; Anton; Ervin; Pius and Henrietta. Later, Edmund bought the farm and John and Mary moved one-half mile west from the family homestead. John was an avid winemaker and a grape arbor that he planted still produces many grapes. Later, they moved to Kelso, MO and Mary died at their home on June 5, 1956. John then moved back to live with Edmund and Ida, where he died at their home on July 6, 1959.

John Schlosser family. Back row: John Schlosser, Rufina Schlosser Schaefer, Caroline Schlosser Linnerstall, and Joe Schlosser. Front: Emil Schlosser, Mother Rufina Stemmetz Schlosser, and August Schlosser.

Edmund and Ida Schlosser were my parents. My father was born Oct. 9, 1901. He was well known to be the first in the area to purchase the latest in farming equipment. He also had a love for coon hunting and carried on the tradition of winemaking. On Jan. 5, 1990, he passed away at the age of 89. My mother, Ida Westrich Schlosser, was born Jan. 19, 1906. She was a helpmate to my Dad, as they often worked side by side on the farm. She died on July 7, 1996 at her home at the age of 90. They had four children: Vernon, Wesley, Betty Lou (deceased) and Glenda.

Vernon and his wife, Revella, are the fourth generation now living on the family homestead. They have three children: Patricia, Gary and Brenda.

Wesley and his wife, Louise, live between Randles and Perkins, MO on a farm originally owned by great-uncle Joe Schlosser. They have six children: Donna; Daniel; Cathi; Douglas; Richard (deceased) and Connie.

Glenda married Elmer Kenkel and resides on the family farm once owned by Grandpa John and parents Edmund and Ida Schlosser. They have three daughters: Michelle, Jennifer and Julie. A granddaughter, Alyssa Nicole Mohney is the fifth generation now living at the present residence once occupied by great-great grandparents John and Mary Schlosser, her great grandparents Edmund and Ida Schlosser, and her grandmother Glenda. *Submitted by Glenda Schlosser Kenkel*

SCHLOSSER – John Schlosser, a farmer, was born Nov. 3, 1838 in Schirrhein, Alsace, France, the son of Michael and Madeline (Hagenback) Schlosser married Rufina Steinmetz in France. She was born Feb. 26, 1837, also in Schirrhein, the daughter of Sebastian Steinmetz and Marie Ann (Mosser) Steinmetz. Five children were born in France. The family arrived at the Port of New York, New York in January of 1880 aboard the vessel *France*. The reason for leaving their home land was the Franco-Prussian War. Alsace was fought for across the Rhine River between France and Germany. It was Germany part of the time, then France, back and forth during the War, stayed with France in the end. John and Rufina's children: Joseph, born March 7, 1868 married Katharina Schott on Sept. 24, 1895 and they were the parents of six children: August John; Anna Emilia; Joseph William; Otto Leo; Adam Felix and Andreas Pius.

John, born May 17, 1869, married Mary Burger on Nov. 9, 1897 and died July 6, 1959. Five children were born to this union: Louisa; Lorene Theresia; John A.; Henrietta; and Pius Joseph.

Rufina, born Jan. 7, 1873, married Adam Schaefer on Oct. 3, 1893 and died Oct. 30, 1949. This was a large family of 10 children: Coletta; Michael; Zeno; Matilda; Joseph; Edwin; Hilda; Zita; Cora; and Eleanora. Caroline was born March 12, 1875, married William Frederic Unnerstall on May 3, 1898 and died Nov. 4, 1968. Seven children were born to this union: Emil; Benjamin; August; Ervin; John; Juliana and Dorothy. August Sebastian, born Jan. 26, 1878, married Katharina Reiminger on April 28, 1903; their children are: Emil T. Schlosser, born July 12, 1880 at Kelso and married Helen Burger, the daughter of Anton and Theresa (Haas) Burger, on Feb. 14, 1905. They were the parents of three children: Theon John, born April 3, 1906, married Ella Ledure, the daughter of August and Anna (Martin) Ledure, on Oct. 27, 1931. Theon and Ella were farmers and had a family of 14 children: Theon Louis, born Nov. 1, 1932, married Patricia Ann Drury, the daughter of Lambert and Lorraine (Dohogne) Drury, on Nov. 5, 1955.

William Eugene, born Jan. 6, 1934, married Patricia Ann Urhahn on Nov. 20, 1954 (first marriage to take place in the new St. Denis Catholic Church at Benton). She is the daughter of Theon and Lorena (Hawkins) Urhahn. "Bill" and "Pat" are the parents of four children:

Denise Catherine, born Sept. 19, 1956, married David Sylvester Glastetter, the son of Sylvester Benjamin and Ramona Frances (Blattel)

Glastetter, on Dec. 30, 1978. They have two sons, Kurt David, born Aug. 4, 1982 and is a freshman at Southeast Missouri State University in Cape Girardeau, and Dustin Paul, born Oct. 8, 1986, is a freshman at Notre Dame Regional Catholic High School, also in Cape.

Denise and David Glastetter with their boys, Dustin Paul and Kurt David.

Their son, Ronald William, born Feb. 25, 1958, married Maryilyn Kay Blattel, daughter of Earl and Virginia (Sater) Blattel, on Oct. 4, 1980. Their children are Tyler Channing and Miranda Alexis.

Carla Jean, born Feb. 27, 1959, married David Robert, son of Gilbert and Mary Ann (Glastetter) Robert, on Oct. 29, 1977. Three children were born to Carla and David, David Aaron, Natalie Suzanne and Mindy Renee.

Alicia Ann, born Jan. 11, 1965, married David Nathaniel Yant on Sept. 26, 1987. Their children are Madison Brooke, Mallory Ann and Mitchell Nathaniel.

Theon and Ella's other children were: Helen Anna; Franklin Joseph; Maurice Charles; Ella Theresa; Doris Emma; Diane Marie; Charlotte Kathryn; Mary Elaine; Juanita Marian; Marion Dale; Richard Anthony and Joseph August. Emil and Helen's daughter, Irene Clara, was born Dec. 12, 1907 and died Jan. 23, 1990. She married Eugene Robert, the son of Charles and Ida (Holmann) Robert, on April 24, 1935. They had two children, Wade and Dorothy. The infant son of Emil and Helen was stillborn. *Submitted by Denise (Schlosser) Glastetter*

SCHLOSSER – Theon John Schlosser was born April 3, 1906 in Kelso, MO. He was the son of Emil Schlosser and Helen Anne Burger Schlosser. Ella Irene LeDure was born on Oct. 25, 1912 in Kelso, MO. She was the daughter of August Pius LeDure and Anna Maria Martin LeDure. Theon and Ella were married on Oct. 27, 1931 at St. Augustine Catholic Church in Kelso, MO.

Theon and Ella had 14 children. Theon Louis Schlosser was born on Nov. 1, 1932. He wed Patricia Ann Drury on Nov. 5, 1955. Their children are Jane, Joan, Lori, Marianne, Theresa, Patrick, John and Elizabeth. John and Elizabeth were twins who died at birth. William Eugene Schlosser was born on Jan. 6, 1934. He wed Patricia Ann Urhahn on Nov. 20, 1954. Their children are Denise, Ronald, Carla and Alicia. Maurice Charles Schlosser was born on May 21, 1935. He wed Margie Ann Burton on Oct. 27, 1956. Their children are Kathy, Timothy, Randy and Sandy. Helen Ann Schlosser was born on Aug. 13, 1936. She wed Rudolph "Buster" Kluesner on April 20, 1955. Their children are Wanda, Dale, Charlene, Donna, Kenneth, Kevin, Dewayne and Todd. Franklin Joseph Schlosser was born on Nov. 7, 1940. He wed Mary Kay Dohogne and divorced later. Their children are Bradley, Darryl, Sheila and Michelle. Ella Theresa Schlosser was born on Sept. 14, 1942. She never married. She died on Sept. 12, 1992. Doris Emma Schlosser was born on March 30, 1947.

She wed Daniel Moore I on Dec. 27, 1966. Their children are Daniel II, Donald, Dawn, Danette, Douglas, Debra and David. Diana Marie Schlosser was born on June 15, 1949. She wed Ira Judd on Jan. 24, 1970. Their children are Diane, Pamela, Angela, Melissa, Ira, Susan, Brian, Shane and Alan. Charlotte Kathryn Schlosser was born on July 1, 1951. She wed Robert Hooper on Jan. 24, 1970 and later divorced on Jan. 25, 1979. Their children are Christine, Cheryl, Rebecca and Sara. Mary Elaine Schlosser was born on Oct. 17, 1953. She has never married and is living on the home place, which is pictured. Juanita Marian Schlosser was born on Oct. 19, 1954. She wed Jack Dannenmueller on Nov. 22, 1975. Their children are Michael, Misty, Nicholas, Curtis, Jack and Mark. Marion Dale Schlosser was born on Sept. 15, 1956. He wed DeRhonda Ward on May 6, 1978 and divorced later. Their child is Chad Schlosser. Richard Anthony Schlosser was born on April 14, 1958. He wed Karen Ella Buchheit on Feb. 19, 1977. Their children are Rachael, Derrick and Cory.

Aerial view of Theon Schlosser farm.

Our family was raised in rural Scott City, MO. Pictured is the farm that we were raised on. It was originally owned by Emil and Helen Schlosser. The farm does not look the same and time changes for all of us. A lot of happy memories are there of celebrating birthdays, anniversaries and other occasions. Our parents believed in family gatherings. If there was work, we did it together. *Submitted by Charlotte Hooper*

SCHLOSSER – William "Bill" E. Schlosser was born Jan. 6, 1934. He is the son of Theon Schlosser Sr. and Ella LeDure Schlosser. He was raised on a farm near Kelso, MO. He had 13 sisters and brothers. He attended the St. Augustine Grade School through eighth grade. At the age of 18 he joined the National Guard, and was a member for approximately eight years. Bill married Patricia Ann Urhahn (born Feb. 23, 1936), daughter of Theon and Lorena Urhahn of Benton, MO. They were married Nov. 20, 1954 at St. Denis Church, the first couple to be married in the new church. Their first home was in a farm house on the Pfefferkorn place near Kelso. After two years, they moved to a farm on what is now County Hwy. 325. Bill's brother, Maurice, lives there now. Bill and Pat moved to Benton in 1962, where they built a house on Diebold Drive. From 1954-1960 Bill was a dozer operator for Herbert Burger. He then started his own business, Schlosser Construction Company, which specializes in dozer work and excavating for farmers in southeast Missouri and southern Illinois. He has been in this business for 41 years. Pat is the secretary/bookkeeper for their business.

Bill and Pat have four children, 10 grandchildren and one great-grandchild. Denise Catherine was born in Cape Girardeau Sept. 19, 1956. She married David S. Glastetter, son of Sylvester and Ramona Glastetter of Kelso, on Dec. 30, 1978 at

St. Denis in Benton. Denise is a Reading Recovery/Remedial Reading teacher at Orchard Drive Elementary in Jackson. David is broker/owner of ERA Cape Realty. They have two children. Kurt David was born Aug. 4, 1982 and is a sophomore at SEMO. Dustin Paul was born Oct. 8, 1986 and is a freshman at Notre Dame. They live in Cape Girardeau.

Family of William E. Schlosser. Back row: Ronald Schlosser, Pat Schlosser, and Bill Schlosser. Front: Alicia Yant, Denise Glastetter, and Carla Robert.

Ronald William was born Feb. 25, 1958 in Cape. Ron married Maryiln Blattel, daughter of Earl and Virginia Sater Blattel, on Oct. 4, 1980 at St. Ambrose Church in Chaffee. He is a technical specialist for the City of Cape Girardeau. Maryiln is director of the University Child Enrichment Center at SEMO. They have two children. Tyler Channing was born March 5, 1984 and is a senior at Kelly High School in Benton. Miranda Alexis was born June 3, 1988 and is a seventh grader at St. Denis School.

Carla Jean was born Feb. 27, 1959. She married David T. Robert, son of Gilbert and Mary Ann Glastetter Robert, on Oct. 29, 1977. Carla is an administrative assistant with a law enforcement agency. David is a Lone Star Alternative Fuels Division technical supervisor. They have three children and one grandchild. David Aaron was born Jan. 29, 1978 and is a contractor with West Vaco Paper Mill in Benton. Natalie Suzanne was born July 17, 1981 and is a nursing student at SEMO. Natalie has one son, Peyton James Eftink, born July 24, 2001. Mindy Renee was born Nov. 9, 1987. She is in the eighth grade at St. Denis.

Alicia Ann was born Jan. 11, 1965. She married David N. Yant, son of John and Mary Hamlett Yant, Sept. 26, 1987 at St. Denis. Alicia is an OB Nurse at Missouri Baptist Hospital in St. Louis. David is an Anheuser Busch corporate storeroom manager. They have three children. Madison Brooke was born May 19, 1991 and is a fifth grader at St. Paul in Fenton, MO. Mallory Ann was born April 15, 1993 and is in the third grade. Mitchell Nathaniel was born Feb. 27, 1997 and attends pre-school. *Submitted by Denise Glastetter*

SCHOEN – Andrew Schoen was born Oct. 7, 1833 in Hesse-Darmstadt, Germany, the son of Conrad Schoen and Magdalena Lab. He came to America with his parents in 1845. He married Susanna Dirnberger, daughter of Adam Dirnberger and Anna Susanna Lallen. She was born Dec. 26, 1840 in Bavaria.

Andrew and Susanna were the parents of 12 children: 1. Catherine, June 9, 1859-July 10, 1887, married Andrew Essner on Nov. 21, 1878; 2. Andrew J., Feb. 12, 1860-Oct. 17, 1909, married Rosena Kuhn on Feb. 21, 1889; 3. Maria, Feb. 19, 1862-Sept. 28, 1862; 4. Michael, Oct. 11, 1863-Oct. 23, 1919, married Frances Salome Glaus on May 9, 1899; 5. Peter, March 12, 1866-

Feb. 19, 1907, married Matilda Oberlie Aug. 12, 1890; 6. Regina, April 27, 1868-April 10, 1905, married Solomon Diebold May 6, 1890; 7. John, April 2, 1870-Oct. 27, 1872; 8. Anna Catherine, Feb. 7, 1872-July 31, 1908, married Charles Strack on Oct. 30, 1894; 9. Clara Rosa, Nov. 18, 1872-Feb. 23, 1938, married Ellis Person Jr. April 24, 1890; 10. Louise Philomena, Oct. 23, 1876-Sept. 4, 1880; 11. Leo John, Dec. 27, 1878-??? married Lena Miller on Nov. 11, 1925; 12. Theresa, March 7, 1883-Sept. 18, 1949, married Frank Kuhn, brother of Rosena Kuhn, on June 21, 1904.

Andrew was a farmer in Scott County. During the Civil War, he served in the Missouri Home Guard. He was a Justice of the Peace in Scott County for 30 years.

Andrew died on June 10, 1900. He is buried at St. Lawrence Cemetery, New Hamburg, MO. Susanna died Feb. 26, 1884 of cholera. She is also buried in St. Lawrence Cemetery. *Submitted by Roberta McReynolds*

SCHOEN – Henry Schoen, born Dec. 2, 1829 in Hesse Darmstadt, West Germany and came to America with his parents, Conrad and Magdalena (Lab) Schoen, in 1845. He married Katharina Cooper/Cupper on April 13, 1852. She as a native from Germany who came to America at age 16. Her parents were Mathias and Mary Ann (Amann) Cooper/Cupper. Religion was very important in the life of the early settlers; they would walk four miles from their farm home to attend Mass at St. Lawrence in Hew Hamburg.

Henry and Katharine bought 80 acres of land in July of 1852, the west one-half of the southeast one-quarter in Section 14, Township 29, Range 14; located east of Kelso. They worked hard in clearing 20 acres in order to build a cabin. For food, they lived off the land by killing wild animals (such as deer, turkey, etc.) for meat. They also picked polk greens and berries.

Carmen Diana and Ella Marie (Hamm), 1998

Henry served in the Civil War, as a Pvt. In Company "G" for a period of three months in the Home Guard. The days of war were trying ones for the people of this section as both northern and southern soldiers were in the area. The guerillas and bushwhackers made conditions trying and dangerous. Fathers of families would hide out and valuables would be buried or secreted in out of the way places. The soldiers took horses, cattle, hogs and sheep as well as flour, meal and other edibles. Henry and Katharina were parents of seven children, five growing to adulthood.

Mary Magdalena (1855-1897) married Ferdinand Heisserer, and they had four children: John; Joseph William; Caroline and Ida.

Andrew H. (1857-1942) married Louise Schitter in 1884. She died in 1894. Four children were born to this union: Frank Louis served as a Pvt. in Missouri Company "G" 329 Infantry during WWI; Ida Paulina; Rosa died in infancy; and Mary Carolina, who entered the convent of the Sisters of the Most Precious Blood at Ruma, IL on Dec. 31, 1908 and took the name of Sister Mary Louis.

Andrew H. married June 2, 1898 to Anna Schlitt, the widow of Andrew Vetter and the daughter of Jacob Schlitt and Mary Ann (Wahl). They had two children, Johann and Leo Gregor.

William George (1860-1925) married Marie Springer in 1886 at Cape Girardeau. They were the parents of eight children: John Alex; Louisa Otillia; August Leo; Bertha Helen; Anna Catherine; Katharine W.; and Ida and Adam M. (twins). Marie died in 1902 and in 1905 William George married Theresa (Gibbear), widow of Mr. Schwepker. Five children were born to this union: Anton Henry; Robert Donat; Otillia; Victor L.; and Marie Bertha.

Louisa Dorothea (1865-1933) married John Schlitt in 1884. They had a family of seven children: Emma Louisa; Leo Joseph; Bertha Katharine; Caroline Mary who entered the convent, the Order of the Most Precious Blood at Ruma, IL in 1909. (She died from TB in 1917 at Carlsbad, NM); Louis August; Coletta Anna (1901-1954 died from a stroke) married George Hamm on April 26, 1921, the son of John and Emma (Diebold) Hamm and they had one daughter, Ella Marie, who married Carmen Diana whose parents were Andrew J. and Anna C. (DeGregory) Diana, who came to America from Italy and lived on the East coast. Ella and Carmen were parents of Andrew J. and John W. They also had a daughter, Mary, twin to John W. who was killed in an automobile accident while in high school in Tucson, AZ at the age of 16; William Nicholas, the youngest child, married Theckla Louisa Dirnberger.

Otillia Emma (1868-1937) married Donat Scherer, the son of Donatus and Mary Magdalena (Bucher) Scherer in 1886. Eight children were born to this union: William Andrew; Bertha Caroline; Pauline Magdalena; Clara Philomena; Genevieve; Anna Helen married Paul Glastetter, son of Joseph and Elizabeth (Enderle) Glastetter; Anton Otto and Louis Theopil; Eva Catharine; and John who died in infancy.

The surname was spelled three ways: SCHOEN – SCHANE – SCHAIN. *Submitted by Ellen Ramona Hou*

SCHOEN – Otto P. Schoen and his twin brother, Charles, were born May 30, 1892 in New Hamburg, MO to Peter and Mathilda Oberle Schoen. They were two of four children born in this German-American family. The oldest son, Theon, became a priest and the daughter became a Catholic nun. Otto and his brothers and sister attended the parochial school in New Hamburg. Otto was first employed at Tony Baudendistel Hardware Store in New Hamburg, then established Baudendistel-Schoen general dry good store in Fornfelt.

During WWI, he served in France with the United States Ordnance Department. In 1920 Otto Schoen was married to Miss Edna Quickley and in 1924 they had a daughter, Mary Margaret Schoen. Edna Schoen died shortly after the birth of their daughter, so Otto and his young daughter lived with his mother, Mathilda, who helped raise Mary Margaret. His father, Peter Schoen, died in 1907 and is buried in New Hamburg.

After he returned from his military duty, he became interested in politics in Scott County. Mr. Schoen served as a member of the Scott County Democratic Committee and was for a time its chairman. Older Scott Countians tell me that if anyone wanted to be elected in Scott County in the 1920s through the 1950s, they had to get the support of Otto Schoen if they wanted to get the vote in northern Scott County.

He was a successful egg inspector for the Missouri Department of Agriculture, an investigator for the State Tax Commission and a member of the staff of Secretary of State Dwight Brown.

In 1947 he was appointed United States Marshall for the eastern Missouri District. He was a close friend to President Harry Truman and served as United States Marshall until 1953, when the Republican administration of President Dwight D. Eisenhower took over. He "resigned" when the administration changed to Republican. He then accepted a position in Attorney General Dalton's office, which he held until the time of his death on June 25, 1959 in St. Louis. *Information furnished by his daughter, Margaret Schoen Fulton, prior to her death on Feb. 20, 2001 in Kansas City, MO*

SCHOTT – Leo Schott Jr. was born Nov. 18, 1868 near Alsace-Lorraine, France. His parents were Leo and Victoria (Brucker) Schott. Leo immigrated to the United States as a young child. His ship arrived in Norfolk, VA. Leo Schott's family settled near Oran, MO. He married Theresa Dohogne on April 10, 1894 at St. Lawrence Catholic Church in New Hamburg, MO. He acquired farmland near Perkins, MO and became a successful farmer. Leo and Theresa had four children: Lawrence, born Jan. 12, 1895; Catherine, born Sept. 14, 1896; Mary Magdalina, born Feb. 9, 1904; and Christine Cecilia, born Jan. 13, 1909.

Leo Schott Jr. Family

Leo was married for 23 years until Theresa died at the age of 43. Leo and his family were members of Guardian Angel Church in Oran, MO. He made contributions to the church by purchasing the St. Joseph altar and a stained glass window with his family name on it. Later in life, he developed diabetes and lost a leg to the disease. He died May 21, 1950 at his home in Perkins, MO. Leo and Theresa are buried in Old Guardian Angel Cemetery, Oran, MO next to his parents. *Submitted by Leon Kielhofner*

SCHUCHART – Rudolph Peter "R. P." Schuchart, one of 13 children, was born June 6, 1884 at Eureka, MO to John Schuchhardt and Theresa Pheiffer, who immigrated from Germany in the late 1860s. The spelling of Schuchhardt, through translation, became Schuchart. The family moved to Moselle, MO in the early 1900s. R. P. met and married Wilhelmina Hanneken on Feb. 9, 1909. They began life together on a small farm living in a log cabin where John Henry, 1910; Sylvester "Wes" Rudolph, 1912; Martha Wilhelmina, 1913; Emil "Flip" Jacob, 1915; and Alice Frances, 1917, were born. He then built a 13-room house which still stands today on the "old Schuchart" farm. Another son, Rudolph Peter Jr. "Doc," 1919, was born there. The county road leading to Union, MO is named Schuchart Road.

With the advent of four sons, R. P. decided he needed more acreage so he moved to Leslie, MO. There, Robert "Bob" Lee, 1921, and Ada Louise, 1923, were born. Farm land here was not very profitable so upon looking around, a decision was made to move to southeast Missouri. He settled on a rented farm near Morehouse, MO. Here the ninth child, Stella, 1926, was born. A year later, he bought a farm in Scott County. As years went on, he purchased more and more land, forming the Schuchart Farms Corporation.

R. P. Schuchart died in January 1966 while visiting his daughters in Arlington, VA. His wife preceded him in death in January 1961. They are buried in Garden of Memories Cemetery in Sikeston. The sons all continued as farmers and dairymen in the Sikeston area.

The Schuchart Family. Back row: John, Wes, Emil, Doc, and Bob. Front: Stella, Ada, Minnie, R.P., Alice and Martha.

John died January 1997. He was married to Mary Elizabeth Rennier. They had three children; Linda, Brenda and Donna. Sylvester "Wes" was married to Ella Heuiser, deceased. They had four children: Donald, deceased; Barbara; Daniel and John, deceased. Emil "Flip," who died in January 1988, was married to Alma Branum, deceased. They had five children: Shirley; Sharon; Emil Jr.; Joseph, deceased; and Marilyn. Rudolph "Doc," who served in the military during WWII, is married to Alberta Kyle. They have three children, Trent, Theresa and Lisa. Robert "Bob," who died Sept. 8, 2001, was married to Grace Streeter, deceased. They had two daughters, Connie and Bonnie.

One daughter, Martha, was an elementary teacher before serving 27 years in Army Intelligence. She retired with rank of Lieutenant Colonel, then married Abner Sachs, now deceased. Alice also taught school before marrying Kenneth Howard and moving to Los Angeles, CA. Their children are Tom and Janice. Ada was a nurse in WWII Pacific area and later married Azro "Hap" Johnson, deceased. Stella, former Morehouse school teacher, married Cleborne Dean "Bill" Foster, deceased. They had six children: Cleborne Dean Jr.; James; John Carter; Nancy; David and Amy.

The Schucharts were members of St. Frances Xavier Catholic Church in Sikeston. *Submitted by Martha Schuchart Sachs*

SCHUEMER – "Barney Schuemer Plans to Raise the Medical Plants on Big Scale"
Scott County Democrat – Aug. 14, 1913 – Page 1.
One morning last week a string of six wagons passed through Benton loaded with lumber. Again in the afternoon the same wagons went through similarly loaded. The curiosity of the Democrat man was aroused to ascertain what was being done with all this lumber, so we interviewed one of the men, who had a few minutes to rest and get a drink of Benton's deep well water. Fortunately we struck the right man, who was fully competent to give the required information. He said his name was Barney Schuemer, proprietor and manager of Excelsior Ginseng Garden, New Hamburg, MO.
In answer to inquiries he stated that he went into the ginseng business about two years ago. He got his start of plants by going to the woods and digging roots and setting them out in ground previously well prepared for the purpose and that he had now about one and a half acres set out and growing well. He is preparing now to set out one and one half acres more. The lumber he was having hauled was to make sheds, as the ginseng cannot bear the hot, direct rays of the sun beaming continuously upon them, but must have protection.

Mr. Schuemer has never yet dug any of the precious roots and placed them upon the market but he thinks he will dig some this fall if he has time. He is more interested in increasing his acreage just now. He has no doubt about the market being ready to absorb all his offerings at anytime and at a good price. The Chinese are great consumers of ginseng. They ascribe wonderful medicinal properties to this pleasant aromatic shrub. The present market price is about $9 per pound for dried ginseng. The supply is wholly inadequate to the demand. The price is likely to advance.

The Excelsior Ginseng Gardens, New Hamburg, Barney Schuemer, Proprietor.

Ginseng once grew very abundantly on the hills of Scott County but it is no longer plentiful enough to make the gathering profitable. Mr. Schuemer is investing a great deal of money and labor on this venture and seems to have no fears about results. *Submitted by George and Louise Jansen*

SCHUEMER – Henry Schuemer was born Dec. 1, 1830 to Franz and Anna Maria Mertens Schuemer. He and his family immigrated from Stockum, near Arnsberg, Westphalia, Germany by way of the port of Bremen, Germany on the *U. S. Humbolt*, arriving in New Orleans, LA on Dec. 16, 1845. He married Maria Anna Grothoff, daughter of Antonio and Christina Miederhoff Grothoff. Maria gave birth of Louise, John and Frank but died with the birth of their fourth child, Mary Anna Josephine. He and his second wife, Christine Miederhoff, who was born Jan. 11, 1852, were married in Applecreek, MO Feb. 15, 1876. She was the daughter of Frank and Anna Mary Klueppel Miederhoff. To this second marriage were born three more children; Joseph, Bernard and Emma. When Henry died April 18, 1882 in

The Schuemer Family in New Hamburg, Mo, early 1900s. Seated: Joseph Schuemer and Christina Miederhoff Schuemer. Standing: Frank, Barney, Mary Schuemer Brockmeyer, Emma Schuemer Brockmeyer, and Louise Schuemer Steinnerd.

Biehle, MO, Christine was left with seven small children in her care. She kept the family together with determination and the help of relatives.

Christine moved to New Hamburg, MO with her children shortly after 1898 to join some of the Miederhoff relatives. They were Kaspar Miederhoff, a well-known photographer of the area, and his brothers, Frank and Henry. Christine and her family were farmers and members of the St. Lawrence Catholic Church in that community. Louise, the eldest, was employed as a housekeeper to the pastor there until she married Joseph Steinmann. After a time Frank went back to Perry County to marry Mary Zoellner; Mary married Theodore Brockmeyer; and Joseph remained single and continued to farm. Bernard, known as Barney, also remained single and established a ginseng farm and was involved in many other enterprises near New Hamburg and surrounding areas. Emma became the wife of Henry Brockmeyer, a brother of Theodore. Both remained for some years in the area where they were prominent farmers.

Christine Schuemer died June 10, 1930 at the age of 78 in New Hamburg, MO, leaving many descendants. She was buried in St. Lawrence Catholic Cemetery, New Hamburg, MO. Her father, Frank Miederhoff, and her son, Barney, were also buried in this cemetery. The remainder of the family moved to other areas, namely Perry, Cape Girardeau and Bollinger counties. The home in which she and her family lived can still be found in the village of New Hamburg. *Submitted by Mrs. George P. Jansen*

SEYER – F. Joseph Seyer was born August 1824 in Alsace, France or Austria, depending on the border disputes of those times. He came to America in 1852 at the age of 28 and settled near Dayton, OH where he married Richardia Wantz. Two children, Joseph and Lawrence, were born in that area. The year 1858 found them settled near New Hamburg, MO where the remaining 13 children were born. His occupation was farming.

On May 5, 1861, he enlisted in the Missouri Home Guard where he served honorably until Aug. 5, 1861, then with Company F, 79th Regt. E., M.M. Volunteers from September 1863 to March 1864. According to his military records, he had also seen duty in his homeland before coming to America.

The Joseph and Richardia Wantz Seyer family was listed in the first 31 families in St. Augustine Parish in Kelso, MO in 1878 when it was founded. In the spring of that year, those families met to build a church. The Seyers were an active family in the parish and Joseph was a member of the choir. Their home was located on a farm about two miles southeast of Kelso, MO.

The Lawrence Seyer family of Kelso, Mo., ca. 1898. Mary Elisabeth, Regina, Elisabeth, Joseph, Philip, and Lawrence.

Their surviving children included Joseph, Lawrence, Frank, Sister Augustine, John, Margaret, Jacob, Leo and Ferdinand.

Richardia died at the age of 49 years on Feb. 7, 1883. Joseph passed away at the age of 82 years in Kelso, MO.

Born Oct. 21, 1856 near Dayton, OH, Lawrence was the second son of Joseph and Richardia. He was about 2 years old when he came with his parents and his brother, Joseph, to New Hamburg in Scott County where they were engaged in farming. On April 14, 1885, at the age of 28, he took Mary Elisabeth Urhahn, also of the Kelso-New Hamburg area, as his bride. She came to the area with her parents, Peter and Elisabeth Kunz Urhahn, and her brothers and sisters from Indiana. Children born to them were Philip, who married Alvina Dohogne; Elizabeth, wife of William Blattel; Joseph, who married Pauline Dohogne, and Regina, the wife of Albert Frederick. Two daughters and one son died in infancy. Mary died in childbirth April 23, 1905, leaving Lawrence at the age of 47 with four children in his care.

A year later, July 12, 1906, Lawrence married Elisabeth Logel Felden, whose husband had been killed in a steam engine boiler explosion while threshing wheat. Lawrence and Elisabeth lived in a home in the Ancell, MO area after the marriage.

Six years later, on Aug. 8, 1912, Lawrence died at the age of 55 years, 10 months, leaving one minor child in the home. Lawrence was laid to rest in St. Augustine Catholic Cemetery in Kelso, MO, as were his parents and other members of the family.

Joseph Seyer and his family left many descendants still living in Scott County. They and other members of the family who were not included here left a heritage covering areas far and wide. *Submitted by Louise Sobba Jansen*

SEYER – Phillip Jacob Seyer was the first-born son of Lawrence and Mary Elisabeth Urhahn Seyer of Kelso, MO. After his birth, Feb. 28, 1886, he was baptized in St. Augustine Catholic Church, where his parents were among the first families in the parish.

Alvina Dohogne, daughter of Constantine and Rosina Heisserer Dohogne, was born July 25, 1887, the tenth child of 12, just a short distance west of Kelso. Her father's family had immigrated from Ster, Belgium and was one of the first families to settle in New Hamburg.

Both were educated in the Kelso Community, and were involved in the community and church through all their growing up years. Philip was 22 and Alvina 21 when they were married in the same church they had attended all their lives and set up housekeeping on the farm his father owned west of Kelso.

About November 1911, several families from the area moved to rural Advance, MO hoping to find better land to farm and raise livestock. They went through the depression with the financial difficulties that went with it. Heartbreak came as they lost their little son to pneumonia. Disaster came as they watched their home and outbuildings go up in flames on the night of Feb. 3, 1934. After losing nearly all their belongings, Philip once again made the decision to relocate his family to a farm west of Oran. He and his neighbors established a local party telephone line in this community called Caney. There were many birthdays celebrated with card parties and social gatherings.

Over the years many hours of worry and countless prayers were offered as five sons went to serve in the armed forces. Two daughters entered the convent, and six daughters-in-law and two sons-in-law were welcomed into the family. Philip and his sons continued to farm and raise cattle and hogs.

Children born to them and spouses were Zeno (Rachel VanderMierden); Alma (became Sr. M. Michaelette); Syvilla (Mr. Clem Sobba); Agnes (became Sr. M. Agnes); Henry died at age 2; Raymond (Rosemary Hoffmann); Albert (Charlene Maller); Paul (Bernadine Olsen); Lawrence (Ida Glasscock); Elmer (Susie Bucher) and Mary (Charles Woltering).

Philip and Alvina Seyer family, August 1958. Front row: Alma (Sister Michaelette), Philip, Alvina, Agnes (Sister M. Agnes). 2nd row: Zeno, Mary, Syvilla, Lawrence. Back row: Albert, Raymond, Elmer, Paul.

Alvina created many fond memories for her family. Even with endless gardening, canning and housework, she always had time to play games with grandchildren. Often the kitchen table was moved to the side and the youngsters were taught to dance while some of the popular tunes of the day were played on the phonograph. Many times she could be found at the old treadle sewing machine mending and singing. There always seemed to be a pot of soup simmering on the back of the stove.

Philip, after retiring to the town of Oran, became ill and passed away Feb. 25, 1961 at the age of 75. Alvina lived another 14 years before she died of the infirmities of old age March 11, 1975. They are both buried in the new Guardian Angels Cemetery, Oran, MO, leaving many descendants in the area. *Submitted by Louise Sobba Jansen*

SHUMATE – John Lewis Shumate, M. D., born in Manchester, MO in St. Louis County on Sept. 3, 1832, was one of the earliest physicians to settle in pioneer southeast Missouri. His parents were the Reverend Walker Daniel Shumate (1809-1872), a noted Methodist circuit rider, and Sarah Wheeler Williams (1811-1836), both natives of Fauquier County, VA, who had emigrated to St. Louis County about 1830. Sarah Williams' family was prominent in the Revolutionary War; her great-uncle, General Charles Williams was with Mad Anthony Wayne at the battle of Fallen Timbers in 1794. In addition to preaching the Gospel, the Reverend Shumate founded a school in St. Louis County called "Oakley Seminary," which featured both English and Classical curriculums. The ancestry of Dr. Shumate can be traced to Jean de la Chaumette, a French Huguenot, whose family fled Catholic France because of religious persecution and settled in England during the 1680s. The same Jean de la Chaumette emigrated to the Virginia Colony in the early 1700s, and there the name was changed to "Shumate." Dr. Shumate completed medical studies at St. Louis University, and in the fall of 1855 came to New Madrid County, settling along "The King's Highway," between Sikeston and New Madrid, not far from the present-day town of Matthews. As a bachelor, Dr. Shumate shared households with Captain Tom Jenkin Phillips, originally from Louisville, KY, who was the first commander of Co. I of the First Missouri

Dr. John L. Shumate 1832-1892

Confederate Infantry. At the close of the Civil War, Dr. Shumate wrote to his father seeking spiritual renewal and thought of returning to St. Louis, but instead he removed to the fledging town of Sikeston in 1867. There he married Lucinda Jane Magee (1847-1879), daughter of Adam Magee, a former overseer in New Madrid County. Lucinda Magee was the granddaughter of Dr. Alexander Magee, originally of Wheeling, WV; Dr. Magee was judge of the New Madrid County Court from 1838 to 1844. Their union produced five children: 1. Sarah "Sallie" Arminda Shumate (1868-1937), who married Henry Clay Watkins of Oran. He was the grandson of prominent Scott County attorney, Nathaniel W. Watkins, half-brother of renown Senator Henry Clay of Kentucky. Nathaniel W. Watkins served briefly as brigadier-general in the Confederate State Guards, the pro-Southern Missouri militia. 2. Mary "Mollie" Lucinda Shumate (1869-1956), who married William H. Stubblefield Jr. of St. Louis. 3. Henrietta "Etta" Shumate (1871-1944), who married twice; first to John Perry McMullin, substantial farmer of Scott County, and second, after the death of both her first husband and her sister, Grace Ann Shumate Moore, to Alfred Joseph Moore Sr., her brother-in-law, of Sikeston. 4. Walker Adam "Doc" Shumate (1873-1932), also a physician, who graduated in 1896 from Missouri Medical College in St. Louis; unmarried, he practiced briefly in St. Louis and later retired to Sikeston. 5. Grace Ann Shumate (1878-1915), who married Alfred Joseph Moore Sr. of Sikeston. Alfred Moore was, for many years, assistant cashier at the Bank of Sikeston. Over the years, Dr. Shumate developed a large practice in the Sikeston area. A devout Methodist, he died on Aug. 22, 1892 and is buried at the Sikeston City Cemetery. See McMullin and A. J. Moore family histories. *Submitted by Tom Moore Root*

SIKES – The Douglas Wilson Sikes family moved to Scott County on November 6, 1993 upon purchase of a house and 8 1/2 acres of land on the southern edge of Morley, Missouri. They came from their native home in Paducah, Kentucky, along with Doug's mother, Rebekah Ruth Sikes, to further expand westward his work in history publishing and even more to lend support to the relatively new Gospel Assembly Church in Sikeston.

This family was formed by the July 30, 1983 marriage of Doug (born June 15, 1963), son of Wilson Davis Sikes (born August 2, 1932) and Rebekah "Becky" Ruth (Crotchett) Sikes (born May 13, 1933), to Mary Kelly Mitchell (born April 17, 1966), daughter of Jesse Willard "Pete" Mitchell II (born Aug. 13, 1939) and Mary Ann (Pardon) Mitchell (born June 3, 1942) in Paducah, Kentucky. On May 11, 1984 their first child was born, a daughter, Emily Kay Sikes. Three more siblings were to follow: Elizabeth Bonnie on January 2, 1986; Wilson "Wil" Douglas on February 14, 1988; and Mary Ellen on January 16, 1990. Both Doug and Kelly were graduates of Reidland High School in 1981 and 1983 respectively, and were residents of Paducah, KY until the move.

Upon arrival, they immediately began to enjoy rural life raising gardens and various pets such as dogs, cats, rabbits, and chickens. The children's interest began to develop in several areas including Boy Scouts and Girl Scouts, basketball, baseball, softball, skateboarding, track, art and music, participating in many area teams and playing instruments in their church band. All four began and continued their education as home schoolers participating in several local support organizations, while their father, Doug, continued to expand his publishing business of history books including the one you're holding in your hands now. Soon this expansion afforded the opportunity for Emily, and later Elizabeth and Wil, to learn

computer graphic design, this young team producing books that are sold in bookstores nationwide, as well as this one. In May of 1999 Rebekah moved back to Paducah, KY. In September of 2002 Emily began attending Southeast Missouri State University in Cape Girardeau, MO as a freshman.

Emily Sikes, age 18

Elizabeth Sikes, age 17

Wil Sikes, age 15

Ellen Sikes, age 13

On October 31, 2001, they, along with several area families, helped found a new church in Morley known simply as The Church at Morley on 202 E. Harding St. in a converted truck garage. There, while lending their humble efforts, they have witnessed God's notable activity in Scott County through people's changed lives, healings and increased knowledge of the Bible.

Their family has and still enjoys life in Scott County and looks forward to being here and contributing to their community for many years to come. *Submitted by Doug Sikes*

SITZES – Jacob "Jake" Marion Sitzes was born on Nov. 4, 1868 in Bessville, MO (in Bollinger County). He was one of 10 children born to Edward Allen Sitzes (1837-1918) and Frances Ann Sanders (1838-1905). He came to Sikeston in 1894 when he was a young man of 26 and lived here with his family until he died on Aug. 10, 1941.

Jacob and Anna Sitzes

Anna Whitener Sitzes was born on Oct. 11, 1891 near Marquand, MO and died July 11, 1967 in Sikeston. She was the daughter of Joseph H. Whitener and Frances Effinar Tucker Whitener. She was a direct descendant of Captain Henry Whitener, a hero of the Revolutionary War after whom the Fredericktown chapter of the DAR is

named. In 1917, she was wed to Jacob Marion Sitzes and they subsequently became the parents of four children: Jake Jr.; Robert Joseph; Frances Anne and Grace Marie.

Mr. and Mrs. Sitzes built a family home on North Kingshighway and their children grew up there. Their oldest son, Jake Jr., enlisted in the Army at the beginning of WWII. After completing Officers' Candidate School at Fort Knox, KY, he was commissioned as a 2nd Lieutenant and was assigned to Patton's Third Army, 33rd Armored Division. He was later promoted to 1st Lieutenant. He was reported missing in action on Sept. 18, 1944 and on November 18, his mother was notified that he had been killed.

A second son, Bob, died of a heart attack on Sept. 5, 1960 at the age of 41. He was survived by his wife, Rachel Ruckel Sitzes, and their four children: Jacob Marion "Jay" III; Robert William "Buzz;" Edward Alan "Ned;" and Susan Claire. Another daughter, Rae Ann is deceased. She was born on Feb. 15, 1946 and died on April 9, 1947. Jay, who is retired, pursued his career in the field of engineering.

During the Vietnam war Buzz enlisted and served with the 101st Airborne Division in Vietnam. While in Vietnam he was diagnosed with Hodgkin's disease and he died on Dec. 5, 1986 from complications resulting from the disease. He was survived by his wife, Sandra Byrd Sitzes, and two daughters.

Edward Alan "Ned," RN, served in the Army and Air Force for 20 years, retiring with the rank of Captain. Susan Claire Sitzes McDonald, RN, currently serves in the Naval Reserves as a Lt. Commander.

Of the children of Jake and Anna Sitzes, Frances Ann and Gracie Marie survive. Grace was married for 54 years to Nathaniel C. Watkins Jr., who died on Oct. 15, 2000. They are the parents of two daughters, Jan Watkins Georgen and Frances Watkins Meador. Both daughters are pursuing their careers in the field of education. Jake and Anna Sitzes had 12 great grandchildren and three great-great grandchildren.

Jake Sitzes was a successful and prosperous farmer. Early in his career he bought and cleared a large farm at Brown Spur and he later lost that farm during the Great Depression. He was a devoted husband and father and a respected citizen who showed much interest in his community and church. He was a trusting man and a friend to all who knew him. He lived and believed in the words "let your word be as good as your bond." He and his wife, Anna, were living examples of that attitude and had the ability to carry on in spite of adversities as well as when they were experiencing so-called "smooth sailing." Both are buried in the mausoleum at the Sikeston Cemetery. *Information furnished by Grace Sitzes Watkins, Rachel Ruckel Sitzes, Frances A. Sitzes*

SMITH – The earliest history I have found of George B. Smith (1812-1867) was in the first book of Marriage Records on the first page in Canton, Stark County, OH, when George B. Smith and Mary Grisenger (1814-as 1858) were married March 9, 1837. They came to Scott County around 1846 near Kelso from Canton, OH. They are buried off Highway H, three miles south of Highway 77. To this union, were at least seven children:

1. John Henry Smith (1838-1883). He married Margaret Winchester on Oct. 15, 1867. He had three children; George W., who never married; James Alexander, who married Eva Snowden (a sister of Tom Snowden); and Newton Aaron Smith, who had no children.

2. Catherine Smith (1840-?). She married Asa Hawkins (1864-1879).

3. Marion Francis Smith (1842-1863) who

never married and died as a Union soldier in the Civil War at Vicksburg, MS.

4. Jacob A. Smith (1845-1891) married Allie Morrow and later Amanda Humpheries. He had two children, Jim and Delia, who married Roy Kneezle of Benton. He is buried in Pollard Cemetery in Scott County, MO.

5. Mary R. Smith, born in 1847 the first child born in Missouri.

George B. Smith descendants, ca. 1894. Left to right: Nora, Stella (Nuckles), Luther Nuckles (holding son Lawton), Jake B., Polly Ann, Phillip Newton, Delia (Kneezle), Laura, Anna (Darby), and Will Darby.

6. Phillip Newton Smith (Nov. 10, 1849-Sept. 20, 1898) born near Morley in the Hickory Grove Community. He married Polly Ann Collins (Sept. 1, 1848) in Scott County on Sept. 20, 1871. They were my grandparents. They had the following children:

A. Louella, who married Thomas George Snowden. They had 14 children: Ethel, who died when 9 days old; Charles Ray; Raymond Brook; Polly Annie; Estella Vyeve; Tommy Loyce; Mabel Lee Philys; Sibel Dorris; Ester Joy; twins Myra Reba and Thyra Ruby; Loula Faye; Melba Jane; and Paul Sidney Phillip who was Japanese prisoner of war in WWII and buried in Arlington Cemetery.

B. Harriet Estella married Luther L. Nuckles and had a son, Lawton.

C. Elizabeth Anna married William Alexander Darby and had Leslie Howard and Ila. She died young and is buried in Hickory Grove Cemetery.

D. Nora Louise married Charles David Powell and had Fred, Mazie, Stella, Ina, Freda, Gwandolyn, Jake and Birdie.

E. Jake B. married Pansy Lane and had 9 children: an unnamed; Wanda Mae; Jake Jr.; John Earl; Mary Ann; Ruth Jean; Henry Ulys; Lillian Louise; and Shirley Jo. Records show Jake was the ninth child.

F. Laura A. married Edgar Daniel Freeman and had Juanita and Estella.

G. Roy lived nine days.

Phillip Newton and Polly Ann Smith are buried in Hickory Grove Cemetery. *Submitted by Mary Ann Phillips*

SMITH – James Thomas and Philamina "Mina" C. Smith moved to the Klugg's Hill area of Scott County, MO during the early 1920s. They were from the Mokane-Tebbits communities near Jefferson City, MO.

They raised hogs, cattle, poultry, row-crops and also ran a dairy for many years.

They were the parents of four children:

Mary Susan (Smith) Wyman, Lorainne (Smith) Burgess, Harold G. Smith and Buddy F. Smith.

Mr. Smith was killed accidentally at an early age in front of the family home on Highway 61 while helping victims of an automobile accident.

Mrs. Smith, or "Mina" as she was called by her many friends and neighbors, was well known for her homemade bread and sugar cookies. She lived to be 92 years old.

SMITH – Burton J. Smith was born in Calloway County, KY in 1844. Burton was the son of William Smith of Virginia and Catharine Ann Duncan of Ohio. William and Catharine were married in Benton, Scott County, MO on Nov. 1, 1840.

In 1860 Catharine was living in the Twappity Township of Scott County with her sons Burton, William, Richard and John. On July 17, 1862 Catharine became the fifth wife of Ephraim Lemley, born April 11, 1801 in South Carolina. They resided on his farm near Benton, MO.

Burton Smith enlisted in the Union Army at Benton, MO on Oct. 18, 1862. He, along with brother William, were assigned to Company K 29th Missouri Infantry. Burton and William Smith saw their first action on Dec. 29, 1862 at the battle of Chickasaw Bluffs outside of Vicksburg, MS. Here Burton received a head wound that would keep him out of action for the next two months.

After this the 29th Missouri went to Chattanooga, TN where they participated in the battle on Lookout Mountain in November of 1863. The spring of 1864 they began the campaign for Atlanta, GA. While in Atlanta, the 29th Missouri became Mounted Infantry to lead the Army on the rest of their journey. Sherman used Mounted Infantry because of the failure of his Cavalry to perform any mission other than to fight the Southern Cavalry. This period included the March to the Sea and the March through the Carolinas. The 29th Missouri dismounted after the surrender of General Joe Johnston's Army on April 26, 1865. They marched in the Grand Review in Washington D. C. and then went to Louisville, KY to be mustered out.

Burton and William returned home to marry daughters of Ephraim Lemley, both born in Scott County, MO. Burton married Lucy Emeline Lemley on Aug. 17, 1865. Lucy, born about 1845, was the daughter of Ephraim and Margaret McDaniel. William married Margaret Malinda Lemley on Feb. 14, 1867. Margaret, born May 1850, was the daughter of Ephraim and Nancy Ann Pritchett.

Burton and Lucy lived out their lives in Scott County, farming and raising their family. Their children were: William W. Smith, September 1867 to November 1900; Elizabeth Smith, 1868 to 1870s; Richard "Orange" Smith, April 1872 to May 1945; Laura Viola Smith, February 1876 to unknown; Jasper Adustin Smith, August 1879 to January 1965; Clara Agnes Smith, March 1882 to unknown; and Burton Jasper Smith, March 1885 to 1898.

After suffering severe headaches for several days, Burton passed away on Nov. 30, 1884. Lucy received a pension for Burton's war service until her death. The under-aged children, starting with Laura Viola, were placed under the guardianship of Dr. Joseph S. Freeling of Scott County until they were old enough to go out on their own.

SMITH – Gladys Raines Smith was born Aug. 26, 1942 at St. Francis Hospital in Cape Girardeau, MO. Her parents, Leslie R. and Neta (Peetz) Raines, lived on a farm across from Harris Field, which is now Cape Municipal Airport. She was baptized and confirmed at Eisleben Lutheran Church, Illmo, MO. Her great-grandparents were Heinrich and Wilhelmina (Meier) Peetz; her grandparents were Henry and Mary (Roth) Peetz, who lived on a farm where Bob Kielhofner now lives. (See the Peetz family history). She has two brothers, Wilford (Sharon Steger) Raines and Marvin (Bonnie Hawn) Raines. Her sister, Alice Raines Getz (Austin) passed away in 1988 in Fairmont, WV where she had lived all of her married life.

Gladys started to school in 1948 at the old Ancell Grade School, Ancell, MO. When the school system consolidated, she attended the old

Junior High School on Fifth Street in Fornfelt, MO. In 1956 she graduated from the eighth grade and attended Illmo High School, Illmo, MO. In 1957 the students were moved to a new high school and elementary building, Illmo-Fornfelt-Ancell R-1 School, just west of town. 1960 was a big year for her: she graduated from high school and got her first job as a medical

John Z. and Gladys Smith Family, November 26, 1996. Clockwise from left: John Z., Leslie Kriete, John, Anita, and Gladys.

secretary for J. Marshall Jung, M. D., who set up a general practice in Illmo, MO. Her dad died on July 14, 1960.

John Z. Smith was born March 30, 1939 in Jackson, MO but lived most of his life in the Scott City area (Illmo-Doomstown area). When he was 10 years old, he worked at the old Red Brick store owned by Red and Gert Henson. They gave him his first job and helped him to buy his first bicycle. His parents were Henry and Mary (Lynn) Smith. His brothers are: Hubert (Jean Kent); Loyd; Frank; Tom and Jim. His sisters are: Addie Mae (Junior Russom) and Mary Lee (who was married to Lloyd Ford who died in 1986 and later married Joe Davis). He attended the Illmo Grade School, the old Junior High, and Illmo High School. At one time, he had seven jobs. Johnny and his family attended the Assembly of God Church as a young man.

Gladys met Johnny Smith when she started high school. They were in some of the same classes. His dad had a heart attack and he could not finish school, so after his junior year, he quit school and began driving a school bus to help earn money for his family. He also worked for the school as a janitor. He joined the National Guard in 1961 and served for six years. On April 7, 1963 they were married at the Eisleben Lutheran Church, Illmo, MO. From this marriage came three children:

Leslie, born July 13, 1965, who married Greg Kriete on Nov. 18, 1995. They have one son, Connor Robert Gregory Kriete.

Anita, born Feb. 5, 1968, who married Bryan Kinder on March 7, 1997.

John Franklin Smith, born June 22, 1973.

John received his high school diploma through a correspondence course. On Dec. 1, 1965 he hired out as a brakeman on the St. Louis Southwestern Railroad, also known as the Cotton Belt. Later, he was promoted to a conductor and maintained that position on the Union Pacific Railroad until he had a heart attack on March 3, 2000. He also served as an alderman for many years. Gladys was a housewife, mother, Girl Scout leader, taxi driver, church worker, cook, nurse, and everything that goes with being a parent.

Johnny was acting mayor when the overpass in Illmo was dedicated on Sept. 29, 1979. This was the only official function they participated in as "Mayor and the First Lady" of Illmo. They are members of Eisleben Lutheran Church, where she is presently employed and where the Peetz family has a long history of working in the church and attending worship there. One of the highlights for them was being a part of building a new Parish Hall in 1997. It was a dream come true.

Even though they were not born in the 1800s, they feel that they are still pioneers of today. They have seen many changes in their towns, including the consolidation of Ancell and Fornfelt into

Scott City; then Illmo and Scott City into now Scott City. They have seen many changes in their world – modern conveniences, modern technology, the building of Interstate I-55, etc.

Now, they are the parents helping their children to be the mainstay of tomorrow. The most recent joy is their first little grandson, Connor Kriete, who was born on April 18, 1999. He weighed in at 1 pound, and 12 ounces; and was 12 inches long. It has been a remarkable experience to witness his life thus far. *Submitted by Gladys Raines Smith*

SMITH – James Thomas Smith was born in 1885 in St. Aubert, MO. Jim acquired a love of music, hunting and baseball. He was elected to the local school board and joined the I.O.O.F. As a young man, he played semi-professional baseball in St. Louis. He also played the violin.

Wilhelmina Caroline "Mina C." Lohear was born in 1889 in Warren County. Mina attended what is now Central Methodist College in Fayette, where she was a member of the a cappella women's chorus. Later she clerked at Haffner's Store in Tebbetts and joined the Rebekah Lodge and the Order of the Eastern Star.

Jim and Mina married at the state fair in Sedalia in 1913. The birth of two daughters, Mary Susan and Margaret Lorraine, coincided with WWI and increasingly hard times. The family loaded their possessions into boxcars and headed to Scott County, buying Julius Kluge's small farm that included the northwest corner of the New Madrid fault. The Smiths joined the Farm Bureau and cooperated with neighbors in harvesting crops. Jim was elected to the school board for rural Scott County in 1920s and Mina to the Sand Prairie School Board in the 1930s.

In the 1920s three sons were born; James Martin, who died at birth; Harold Gene; and Buddy Frank. Each of the Smith children learned to play the piano and at least one band instrument.

Mary and Lorraine graduated from Vanduser High School. Mary earned a B. S. in Education from SEMO and taught in several area schools. She married E. T. Wyman in 1945, and they had a daughter, Jane, and a son, James. Lorraine briefly attended SEMO before entering Brown's Business College in St. Louis. From there she pursued a career as a bookkeeper and office manager for auto agencies in St. Louis and, after marriage to Gordon H. Burgess, in North Carolina. Lorraine died in May 2001 and her ashes were placed in a niche in the memory garden nestled beside Centenary Methodist Church in Winston-Salem.

In March 1947, Jim died in an accident near the McMullin Community. Harold graduated shortly from Sikeston High School where he was active in the band and FFA. He served briefly in the U. S. Army but returned to work on the farm. After Mina acquired farms in Cape County and Salem, IL, Harold bought a plane and learned to fly. He and Mina farmed until her death in December of 1976.

Mina C. (Lohear) Smith and James Thomas Smith of Kluge's Hill near Morley, Mo., 1930s.

Shortly after graduation from Morley High School, Buddy served in the Medical Corp in the Korean War. He drove auto transports out of Memphis, Tulsa and Phoenix, retiring with a safe driving record of 24 years. Buddy married Doris Lowe of Henderson, TX in 1960 and they had a son, Jeffrey Scott. A few years later they divorced. In 1970 Buddy married Mildred Matlock Yokum.

Their legacy passed down and their time on this earth ended, J. T. and Mina rest side by side in the Morley Cemetery…in Scott County. *Submitted by Jane Wyman Conner*

SMITH – Eugene Herbert Smith was born in Garrard County, KY March 25, 1865, the second child of the eight children of the Rev. Mr. Henry Ackerman Smith and Almira Clay Potts Smith. His father was a schoolteacher and a minister of the Methodist Episcopal Church South. Herbert was a precocious child. His father was his principal teacher, beginning his education at the age of 4 years. Many a night, he recalled, he cried because his father kept him studying Latin and Greek when he would have liked to do something else, or nothing at all. With English and German, he could read in four languages before he was out of knee pants! Despite a busy schedule, his father also found time to play with his children.

Herbert must have at one time considered a career in the ministry, as he once told this writer that he decided he would never be a minister when his father figured his net profit for a year of preaching and found that he had netted sixty-five dollars!

When Herbert was 10, his father bought him a small printing press and he was able to get a job as a "printer's devil" when his father moved to Cape Girardeau to organize what is now known as the Centenary United Methodist Episcopal Church.

With the family settled at Cape, Herbert's father tried to interest him in enrolling in the Normal School (now Southeast Missouri State University), but Herbert thought he had burdened his parents long enough and went to work – first at the *News*, then at a temperance paper in St. Louis. Later he accepted a job teaching a six-month term at Neely's Landing. After it closed for the season, he enrolled at the Normal expecting to complete the course and become a professional teacher. In response to a letter from J. F. Mitchim of Benton, MO who needed a printer, Herbert went to Benton, little thinking it was to be his home for over 20 years. After switching briefly to papers in Charleston and Sikeston, Herbert became the owner of the *Benton Record*.

During the time in Charleston, he met and married Miss Stella Rowe. After they moved back to Benton, two children were born to the marriage – Ernest Harold and Faye Dorothy. Circulation of the *Record* increased to 650 or 700, enabling Harold to build a new home for his family and better printing equipment. Unfortunately the equipment was lost in a fire that burned every business house in Benton. After nearly 21 years in Benton, the family moved back to Charleston where a son, Rowland Haw, and a daughter, Lois Rhea, were born. Herbert worked at the *Courier*. In about 1910 he changed professions for a couple of years trying to sell automobiles in Clinton, KY. Deciding he was a better newspaper man than auto salesman, he took over the *Charleston Courier* again while his wife and older son closed out the auto business.

Not long after his return to Charleston, Herbert bought out the *Enterprise* and consolidated it with the *Courier* forming the *Enterprise-Courier*, which is still published now. He also found time to serve as Postmaster of Charleston under the appointment of President Woodrow Wilson.

Then in 1922, his wife, Stella, died following an operation in St. Louis. Herbert's son, Harold, became co-owner of the paper but became dissatisfied and insisted on selling his interest. After considerable dickering, Herbert and his son sold the *Enterprise-Courier* to a friend, Mr. Simon Loebe. It was Herbert's understanding that Mr. Loebe would employ him at the paper, but it did not work out and soon he was out of work. Attempting to make a living as he best knew how, he spent seven years running a new newspaper – the *Charleston Democrat* – but he had made the mistake of agreeing in writing not to establish a new paper in Charleston when he sold the *Enterprise-Courier*; and Mr. Loebe was finally able to force him out of the *Democrat*. These were the most strenuous years of his life.

In 1925 Herbert married again. The second marriage was a disaster. In a few years the home, car and office had been lost and the new wife was in a mental institution. For a while Herbert ran the Brewer's Lake Club. He drew an "old age assistance" pension for a while. Then he was offered a job at Clarkton, MO, running the *Clarkton News*. Eventually he became owner of the paper. He ran this paper until 1940 when the infirmities of age persuaded him to sell it. He moved to Poplar Bluff where he had a sister. He died there in February of 1956.

SOBBA – Clemence P. Sobba was born in Willowdale, KS Aug. 23, 1910 to Frank and Christena Olendorff Sobba. His family had lived in Kansas and Oklahoma where his father followed the wheat planting and harvesting. In 1927 they located in southeast Missouri, living in several places including Risco, Advance and Malden.

It was in Advance, MO that Clem found employment as a farm hand for the Seyer family where he met their daughter, Syvilla. After the marriage Jan. 23, 1934 in St. Joseph Catholic Church, they moved to a farm near Gideon, MO. Daughters Louise, Marie and a son, Leon, were born but their only son died shortly after birth. Clem rented a farm west of Oran and they set up residence near Syvilla's parents in January 1939. Two more daughters, Phyllis and Alice, were welcomed into the family.

Clem worked hard at farming, and was always ready to help out a neighbor, friend or relative in need. He was known for his generosity to everyone, especially his children. He donated his labor to help build the new Guardian Angel Grade School, and served as usher for many years in the church. The stories he told of his early life, as his family moved from place to place, were a source of entertainment and history for his children, especially in Kansas and Indian Territory, OK.

His wife, Syvilla, was born in Advance, MO May 17, 1915, daughter of Philip and Alvina Dohogne Seyer. She remained there with her family until she and Clem married and set up housekeeping. Syvilla was always a dedicated homemaker tending her children, gardening and sewing for herself and four daughters.

Syvilla and Clem Sobba, 1956.

Many hobbies filled the little spare time she had, including crocheting, quilting, various types of needlework and keeping scrapbooks. One hobby provided many handmade flowers for weddings and special occasions in the area. Syvilla was a perfectionist in everything she did and was an inspiration to her family. She strived to instill in her children a sense of responsibility, integrity and compassion while teaching them homemaking skills. A great void was left in the family when she died suddenly Oct. 26, 1973.

Clem continued farming and living alone in the home west of Oran for the next 20 years. Even after he felt he could no longer farm by himself, he was always ready to work for someone else. He died July 23, 1993, one month before his 83rd birthday. Both he and Syvilla are buried in the new Guardian Angel Cemetery at Oran, MO. They passed on a lifetime legacy of love, work ethic and high standards to their daughters and sons-in-law and to the grandchildren who were always so special to them and benefited from their love and caring.

Their daughters, Louise, who married George Jansen; Marie, married to Omer Seiler; Phyllis, wife of Henry Trankler and Alice, who married Robert Urhahn all settled in the southeast Missouri area. *Submitted by the Sobba daughters*

SPALDING – The Spaldings migrated to Scott County, MO from Kentucky in the 1800s. Edmund Franklin Spalding (b. Dec. 18, 1817, d. Nov. 7, 1899) was married on Feb. 16, 1844 to Martha Ann Walker (b. 1828, d. Jan. 2, 1902). Their son, William Edward Spalding (b. Dec. 17, 1844, d. Jan. 5, 1915) was married April 17, 1965 to Sophia M. Scherer (b. June 15, 1843, d. Oct. 25, 1895). Their son, John Lucias Spalding (b. July 8, 1867) married Aug. 26, 1890 to Ida Josephine Profit (b. April 13, 1872, d. Nov. 30, 1938). To this union were born: Charles Doc Spalding; Lillian, who married Coot Cannon; Josephine, who died in her early 20s; Ada Belle, who married Calvin Dirickson; and Joseph Lucias. Mr. John Spalding was the Superintendent of the Scott County Poor Farm. This consisted of 352 acres of land which they cultivated. There were orchards and cattle to raise. Mr. Spalding, with his family, lived in the main house with additional housing for the residents (one for the males and one for the females). He paid the county $752 a year rent for the farm and received $2.50 per resident per week from the County for board and care. The family provided for all the residents' needs, including caring for them when they were ill, acting as undertaker when they passed away and burying them in a cemetery on the grounds. The son, Joseph Lucias Spalding (b. Nov. 18, 1901, d. Feb. 21, 1942) married Feb. 24, 1925 to Mary Johanna Enderle (b. Nov. 22, 1903). Due to the need of transportation to haul produce and cattle from the farm, Joe started the Spalding Trucking and School Bus Business. Mary helped Joe by driving a school bus for some 30 years. She lived in her own home until she was 97. She is now age 98 and a resident of a nursing home. Joe and Mary's children are: Martha Ann married Daniel Dempster; Joseph John "Amos" married Lois Dirnberger; Ida Louise "Susie" married James Roper; Mary Alice married Melvin "Bud" Schweer; and Blanche Marie "Sally" married Alfred Asmus. The only son, Joe "Amos," took over the trucking business upon the death of his father in 1952.

Joe "Amos" (b. July 9, 1930, d. Dec. 13, 1995) married Sept. 26, 1953 to Lois Rebecca Dirnberger (b.. Oct. 26, 1932). They had four children: Joe Wayne (b. 1954), his children Joseph and Justin Thomas; Rebecca Mary (b. 1956) married Charles Schwartz, their children Suzanne Rebecca, Stephen, Gregory; Melissa (b. 1959) married Jeffrey Lee, their children Jared and Jordan; John (b. 1961) married Lisa Ann Duke, their children Emily and Katie Johanna. Joe Amos operated the trucking business. He drove the school bus until he turned the bus business over to his brother-in-law Bud Schweer. Joe and Lois supervised the Commodity Food Program in Scott County prior to the issuing of Food Stamps. Lois

then worked for the Division of Family Services for 20 years. At the time of Joe Amos' death in December 1995, he was serving his fourth term as Associate Commissioner of Second District of Scott County. The family were members of St. Denis Church and the children attended the parochial school. All

Joe "Amos" and Lois (Dirnberger) Spalding

four children graduated from Southeast Missouri University in Cape Girardeau. The Joe Spalding Trucking Business is still in operation under the supervision of Joe Wayne, John and Becky. This has been a family-owned business from 1925 to the present time.

Lisa Ann (Duke) Spalding, John's wife, opened a Floral and Gift Shop in the same building of the trucking firm in 1996. This has been a full-service floral facility for six years, the first in town of Benton, county seat of Scott County. The Spaldings have been involved in county business for many years. *Submitted by Lois Spalding*

STOFFEL – Hazel Eunice Stoffel Luebbers (married Winefared Daniel Luebbers on Nov. 4, 1933 in Benton, MO) was born on Dec. 20, 1914 in Delta, MO, daughter of Patrick Jessie Stoffel (born May 25, 1880 and died on Jan. 1, 1952), and Iva Clubb Stoffel (born Oct. 20, 1886 in Oran, MO and died Dec. 21, 1976 in Cape Girardeau, MO). Patrick Jessie Stoffel was the child of Ernest D. Stoffel and Sara A. Stoffel. Patrick and Iva were married on Aug. 1, 1907 in Oran, MO.

Here begins the history of Iva Clubb and her ancestors. Iva Clubb was born on Oct. 20, 1886 in Oran, MO, the daughter of Mary Elizabeth West Clubb (born July 10, 1862 and died May 1, 1951) and Anthony L. Clubb (born Aug. 23, 1860 in Oran, MO and died Oct. 13, 1946).

Mary West Clubb's parents were James Buck West and Martha Phelps (1837 to 1893 in Scott County, MO). James Buck West's parents were Bayless West (1802-1862) born in Persia, Hawkins County, TN and died in Scott County, MO and Mrs West (only record found) married about 1830 in Tennessee. Bayless West married Nancy Jane Brown (born in 1830 in Scott County, MO) in 1851 in Scott County, MO.

Bayless West's parents were James West and Nancy Grigsby. James West was born Oct. 12, 1772 in Hawkins, TN and died Feb. 5, 1834 in Hawkins, TN. Nancy Grigsby was born in 1786 in Hawkins, TN and died in September 1838 in Hawkins County, TN. She and James West were married in 1807 in Rogersville, Hawkins County, TN.

Nancy Grigsby's parents were John Grigsby Jr. and Winifred Winney Ashby. John Grigsby Jr. was born Oct. 5, 1752 in Culpepper County, VA and died Sept. 28, 1826 in Hawkins, TN. He is buried in Grigsby-Arnott Cemetery, Hawkins, TN.

John Grigsby Jr.'s parents were John "Soldier John" Grigsby and Rosanna Etchinson. John Grigsby Jr. married Winifred Winney Ashby around 1772 in Hawkins County, TN.

Winifred Winney Ashby was born in 1757 in Virginia and died in 1830 in Hawkins County, TN. She is buried in Grigsby, Hawkins County, TN. Rosanna Etchinson was born in 1735 in Orange County, VA and died around 1761 in Rockbridge County, VA. She married "Soldier John" in 1753 in Prob, Culpepper County, VA. "Soldier John" Grigsby was born in 1720 in Stafford County, VA and died April 7, 1794 in Culpepper County, VA.

"Solder John's" parents were Charles Wilkerson Grigsby and Sarah Wilkerson. Charles Grigsby was born in 1682 in St. Pauls Parish, Stafford, VA and died Nov. 11, 1740 in St. Pauls Parish, Stafford, VA. Charles Wilkerson Grigsby's parents were John Grigsby and Sarah Jane Rosser. Charles Grigsby and Sarah Wilkerson were married around 1705 in St. Pauls Parish, Stafford, VA. Sarah Wilkerson was born in 1697 in Stafford, VA and died in 1756 in St. Pauls Parish, Stafford, VA. *Submitted by Jan Drury*

STOFFEL – Patrick Jessie Stoffel was born on May 5, 1880 in Kentucky. He later came to Scott County as a small child. His parents were Ernest D. and Sarah A. Stoffel. He married Ivah Clubb on Aug. 1, 1907 in Oran, MO. Ivah was born on Oct. 20, 1886 in Oran, MO. Patrick and Ivah had seven children.

Jessie Patrick Stoffel was born on April 6, 1909 in Oran, MO. He married Letha French on Aug. 7, 1939 in Delta, MO. He died on Aug. 31, 1975.

Gladys Elizabeth Stoffel was born on July 7, 1910. She died at the age of 10 from a ruptured appendix on Feb. 19, 1921.

Grace Vera Stoffel was born on March 19, 1912. She died at the age of 11 from typhoid fever on Nov. 14, 1923.

Luther Floyd Stoffel was born on March 10, 1913. He married Hallie. He died Feb. 19, 1976.

Hazel Eunice Stoffel was born on Dec. 20, 1914 in Delta, MO. She married Winefared Luebbers on Nov. 4, 1933 at the courthouse in Benton, MO. Winefared Daniel Luebbers was born on April 8, 1913. Their children are: Shirley Jean Luebbers, born on May 26, 1935. Shirley married Charles Louis Drury on June 11, 1955; Bobby Luebbers, born on Aug. 14, 1937. Bobby married Sylvia Dwanna Lufey on March 10, 1962; Jackie Wayne Luebbers, born on Sept. 18, 1945. He married Cynthia Gail Seabaugh on July 2, 1977.

Bertha Helen Stoffel was born on March 2, 1916 in Delta, MO. She married Roy Meyer. She died on June 11, 1986 in Cape Girardeau, MO.

William Clyde Stoffel was born on Sept. 20, 1917. He later moved to Effingham, IL.

The family was raised in a four-room house with an upstairs. The walls and floors were bare. The family was very poor. They did farming and raised chickens, pigs and cows. Pig sties are a very vivid memory for Hazel. Hazel, at the age of 15, lied about her age to go to work. She had to go back to school until the age of 16. The family was so poor the children would do anything to make money to help the family.

Patrick and Ivah moved from Oran in 1937 to Cape Girardeau, MO. Patrick Jessie Stoffel died when he was 71 years old. He was living on 513 South Pacific Street in Cape Girardeau, MO. He was a retired farmer. He died of a heart ailment while assisting Fred Hoffman, a contractor, pour concrete at a residence on Highway 61. The heart attack was the first attack he had ever had.

When Patrick Clubb died, Hazel hurriedly got her three children ready. She took a bath and on the way to the funeral chapel, she said, "Oh my, Winefared, I left without my panties on. I can't go to that windy hill at the cemetery (Oran, MO) without my panties on." They stopped at a local store and bought underwear for her. *Submitted by Jan Drury*

STOWE – James Stowe was born in what is now Germany in 1872 and in the 1890s he came to Hickory Grove, Scott County, MO. He later told his family he was escaping political and religious persecution from the Kaiser of Prussia and that he hid inside a pickle barrel on a ship across the Atlantic. He was referred to as "the stowaway" and to hide his identify he kept the name Stowe. In 1897 James Stowe, known as Jim, married Francis Beckman in Scott County. Francis was the daughter of Henry and Amelia Beckman. Jim and Francis had two children, Jesse Myron (born May 1, 1899, died 1975) and Howard Wayne (born Sept. 11, 1908 died Aug. 29, 1962). Jim died at the young age of 35 of pneumonia in 1907 before his second son was born, and Francis remarried Carter Foster. Jim is buried in the Hickory Grove Cemetery and the headstone reads "Jim Stowe."

Jesse Myron Stowe received a certificate for perfect attendance for 8 years to Hickory Grove School in 1913, which is still proudly displayed today by his son, Jim. Jesse was a handsome and very strong man who was very mechanically minded. He operated steam powered thrashing machines and managed cotton gins in and around Scott County. Jesse married Minnie Lucille Atherton in 1919 and they settled in Morley, MO. Minnie Lucille was born in Scott County in 1898 to Richard H. Atherton (born 1863 died 1903 and buried in the Morley Cemetery) and Mary Belle Butler Atherton (b. Aug. 5, 1869, d. 1928, buried in Morley Cemetery). Mary Belle and Richard were married in Scott County in 1885. Mary Belle's parents were Charles F. Butler (born May 15, 1839, died Sept. 23, 1908) and Sarah Smith Butler. Jesse and Minnie Lucille's first born arrived Dec. 7, 1923 and they named him James Richard Stowe after Jesse's father and Minnie Lucille's father. Their second child, Mary Francis, was born June 13, 1928, named after Lucille's mother and Jesse's mother. Jess and Lucille, as they were called, moved to Ottawa, OH in their later years to be near their son and his family. Jesse and Lucille are buried in Harman Cemetery near Ottawa, OH.

James Richard Stowe "Jim" graduated from Morley High School in 1941 and was drafted into the U. S. Army. Beginning in 1942 he was sent to Jefferson Barracks, MO and then on to General Patton's Desert Training Center at Indio, CA for six months, and from there to Fort Pierce, FL for amphibious training for the D-Day invasion. In England he continued his amphibious training and during Operation Tiger on April 28, 1944 he was on *LST 513* IN THE English Channel when their convoy of 8 LSTs were torpedoed at 2:00 a.m. by ten German PT boats. Two of the eight LSTs were sunk and one badly damaged and over 1000 lives were lost in this practice exercise for the D-Day invasion. This tragedy was not made public until 1992. Jim went on to participate in the D-Day invasion on Utah Beach on June 6, 1944 with the 3207th QM Service Company attached to the 1st Engineers Special Brigade. Jim was also involved in the Battle of the Bulge in Belgium, supplying equipment and supplies to the front lines. After WWII on Nov. 21, 1947 Jim married Betty Jean Clauser of Fredericktown, MO. Betty was the daughter of Samuel Clauser (born in Luckey, OH Oct. 29, 1880, family moved to Fredericktown, MO in 1888 where he died Dec. 16, 1969), and Eustacia Mouser (born Jan. 27, 1890, died March 14, 1973). From 1950-52 Jim and Betty lived at Fort Lewis in Washington, while Jim served in active duty during the Korean War. Jim graduated in 1953 from MSM-UMR at Rolla, MO with a B. S. degree in electrical engineering. Jim moved his new family to Ottawa, OH in 1953 after accepting a job with Sylvania Electric at the largest TV picture tube plant in the world. He was engineer in charge of processing and during his 35 years there he received three patent awards related to vacuum equipment, gettering, HV processing procedures. Jim retired in 1986 after Sylvania had passed to GTE and then to Phillips Electric. Jim and Betty raised four children. Samuel Myron (Aug. 20, 1949); Bruce James

(June 29, 1951); Robert Paul (Sept. 16, 1952, died Oct. 10, 1964) and Mary Jane (Nov. 21, 1955). Jim's wife, Betty Jean, graduated from the Jewish Hospital in St. Louis in 1947 with a degree in nursing and was a County Health Nurse for Putnam County in Ottawa, OH for over 20 years before retiring in 1986.

Jim's sister, Mary Francis Stowe, joined the Women's Air Force (WAF) in 1951 and obtained the rank of Master Sergeant before retiring in 1973. She served during the Korean and Vietnam Wars. Mary was very active in the WAF Sports and traveled the globe playing against the other women's teams in the armed forces. She excelled as pitcher for the women's soft ball team, pitching one no-hit game with a batting average of .360, played on the basketball team, and was also a star bowler leading the WAF bowling team to three world victories. After serving the Air Force in bases across the USA (Lackland AFB in San Antonio, TX; Keefler AFB in Biloxi, MS; George AFB in Victorville, CA; Shaw AFB in South Carolina; Donaldson AFB, North Caroline; March AFB in Riverside, CA; the New Orleans Recruitment Office; ENT AFB at Colorado Springs, CO; Otis AFB at Cape Cod, MA) Mary served 18 months at Kadena AFB on Okinawa during the Vietnam War and in 1970 finished her military career with three years at Edwards Air Force Base in California. Mary has worked 10 years with the Los Angeles County Library, has volunteered for over 20 years with blood drives for the American Red Cross, is active in her local American Legion, is a Disabled American Veteran, volunteers for many organizations and is active in her Lutheran Church were she resides in Palmdale, CA.

Minnie Lucille and Jesse Myron Stowe, 50th Anniversary, 1969.

James R. and Betty Stowe live in Ottawa, OH and are enjoying their retirement and celebrating their 55th wedding anniversary in 2002. They travel throughout the USA and have been to many parts of the globe (Kenya, Australia, England, France, Germany, Austria, Switzerland, Portugal, Spain, ,Scotland, Italy, Belgium, Mexico, Brazil, Argentina, New Zealand, Hawaiian Islands, Nova Scotia and P.E.I., Fiji, to name a few places). As well as being active in their local Methodist church, Betty has her beautiful plants and flowers, and Jim has been active on his bowling league for nearly 50 years. They keep in touch with their three children and their grandchildren. Samuel M. Stowe married Joyce Hooper in 1972 and they have two sons, Ryan Jamison (Aug. 20, 1981) and Andrew Paul (Sept. 7, 1985). Sam has a Master's Degree in Hydro-geology from Ohio State University (B. S. from Miami University) and has a company designing water systems and wells worldwide called International Wells, Inc. in Worthington, OH. Bruce is an artist (MFA from the University of Denver, B.F.A. from Miami University) with his own business, Stowe's Art and Antiques located in Ottawa. Mary Jane has a Bachelor of Science from Ohio State University, works at Oakland Nursery in Columbus, OH, is

married to Dr. Bobby G. Joyner (a doctor of plant pathology with True Green Chemlawn), and Mary is a step grandmother to four grandchildren.

STUBBLEFIELD – William Thomas "Tom" Stubblefield born in Commerce, MO (b. Sept. 15, 1873, died Dec. 22, 1939).

Thomas' father was M. G. B. Stubblefield (b. May 8, 1826, d. Oct. 31, 1898). His mother Roanna Terry Stubblefield (b. May 1842, d. Jan. 20, 1882) was born in Ireland. His father taught school in Morley and Pleasant Hill, MO. Roanna was M. G.'s student in school and later became his wife. They had six children: Thomas; Montie; Robert; Carrie; Daisy and Rose. Montie Stubblefield was clerk of Circuit Court at Benton, MO. Robert was Recorder of Deeds at Benton in the late 1800s and early 1900s.

Tom Stubblefield and Amanda Birdie Lennox, daughter of John Patrick and Elizabeth Hill Lenox, married Jan. 10, 1897. They lived in Commerce, Blodgett, and McMullin, MO areas. Seven children were born of their marriage: Robert Paul; John Harley; Anna Lucille; Kathleen; Bettie Roanna; Lorene and Edna Blanche. Amanda Birdie Stubblefield passed away Aug. 25, 1910. Tom later married her sister, Anna Alice Lenox, Feb., 15, 1915. They had one daughter, Amanda Birdie (1916).

In 1916 the family moved into their home north of Sikeston at McMullin, MO between the road to Cape (Highway 61) and the Frisco Railroad tracks. It is now County Road 450. Mr. Stubblefield farmed 80 acres and farmed 50 acres for other southeast Missouri farmers. They moved to Sikeston in the late 1930s.

Their daughter, Anna L., married N. G. "Nick" Kindred; Bettie Roanna married Lowell Greer; Kathleen married Jere Caverno; Amanda Birdie married C. Linn Smith; and Robert P. married Helen Rachel Hollister, one of three daughters of Clarence Ward and Eva Mae Cunningham Hollister. The Hollisters moved to Sikeston in 1913 from Avon and Onarga, IL.

There were seven grandchildren: Virginia, daughter of Bob; Jo Ann, daughter of Kathleen; Lowell Jr. and Billy Jo Greer, sons of Bettie; and Francoise, Bettie Lucille and W. T. "Bill" Kindred, children of Anna.

Tom and Amanda's oldest son, Robert, left to serve in WWI but the war ended before he could be sworn in. He and his first wife, Helen, were divorced and he was drafted in WWII. While in service, he married Malita Provort in Goldsboro, NC (Dec. 23, 1941).

W.T. Stubblefield Family Home, McMullin, MO., early 1920s.

Grandsons Lowell and Billy Joe Greer, and Bill Kindred, served in the Korean War. Great-grandsons, Gordon Deason Jr. and Earl Lewis Jr., served in the Vietnam War. Earl Lewis Jr., a Naval flier, was a prisoner of war in the Hanoi Hilton for five and one-half years, returning to the states in March 1973. Great-great-grandsons, Earl Lewis III and Eric Workman, served in the Desert Storm War.

Anna Alice Stubblefield died April 19, 1957 and all children, except for Edna Blanche, who lives in La Bonn Maison in Sikeston, are deceased. Three grandchildren are living: Bettie, Virginia and Bill. Tom and Anna have 11 great-grandchildren and 16 great-great-grandchildren living at the present time.

Tom Stubblefield is buried in Carpenter Cemetery beside his first wife, Amanda. Anna A. Stubblefield is buried in the Stubblefield plot in Garden of Memories Cemetery. *Submitted by Virginia Lewis, Bettie Deason and W. T. "Bill" Kindred*

STUBBS – Henry Freeman Stubbs, born Sept. 15, 1877 in Hickman, KY, came to Blodgett with brother Harry about 1903, married Tempie Moore of Mansfield, MO. They had four girls, one boy Clyde Moore Stubbs, born April 21, 1905.

Henry "Major" opened Stubbs Hardware, Furniture and Funeral Home in newly incorporated Chaffee late in 1905. His motto was "We Serve You From The Cradle To The Grave." Cradles and caskets were sold there.

Clyde married Ruth Adeline Wilson (born Jan. 6, 1905, Old Town, Stoddard County), March 7, 1925. Initially they lived in East St. Louis, IL. Clyde worked for Endicott Johnson Shoe Company in St. Louis. On July 14, 1927 James Milton was born. A few months later, race riots occurred with blacks thrown off the bridge Clyde crossed getting to work. They returned to Chaffee.

"Major" sent them to operate his funeral home in Benton. Oct 23, 1930 Jimmy became ill. Recovered, Ruth discovered he couldn't stand. He had contracted polio.

After President Franklin Roosevelt's inauguration, March 1933, Ruth wrote Mrs. Roosevelt asking how to get 6 year old Jimmy into Warm Springs, GA for treatment. Mrs. Roosevelt sent Ruth a name and address to contact. Jimmy was accepted. In August 1933, Clyde took him by train to Warm Springs, checked him into the facility and returned home. Depression years, with little money, Clyde had to return to work.

Jimmy was the only patient from Missouri, had no visitors, saw no family for one year. Nurses took pictures of Jimmy to send his mother. Halloween was a costume party for the children. Most children had families bring them costumes. Jimmy had none. Nurses found a set of red flannel underwear, used a red rubber tube from an enema can as a tail, fashioned a set of horns making a little Red Devil. Jimmy won the contest. The prize was sitting beside the President when he came for Thanksgiving dinner with the patients. This was the first Thanksgiving he spent there with the children. It became a yearly ritual for his entire presidency.

Annual President's Birthday Balls were held each January 30 (FDR's birthday), a means of raising money for polio patients' treatment. To publicize the event, three young boy patients held three puppies while pictures were taken. The pictures were sent nationwide to newspapers and magazines, including *Literary Digest* and *The Weekly Reader*, and were used each January from 1934 through 1937, making the cover of the *Literary Digest* in 1937. For the first time children were photographed to generate money for a specific disease – the original Poster Children. Jimmy is one of the boys. He returned home in August 1934.

Jim attended the Kansas City School of Watchmaking, owned his own jewelry business from 1947 through 1997, is married to Marlene Mirly, has three children and five grandchildren.

April 12-15, 2001 Warm Springs, GA held its first ever Former Patients Reunion. Unearthing the original picture, and with Jim's help, the three little boys were reunited – the first time in 67 years the three were together again. Jim said, "We were three little boys with three young puppies, now we're three old men with three old dogs." *Compiled by Marlene Mirly Stubbs*

STUCKER – Elisha Kimuel Stucker, born Jan. 29, 1863, died Aug. 23, 1941 and Della Florence Muir Stucker, born Nov. 4,1 875, died July 13, 1944, were married Oct. 20, 1895. Della had two brothers, James B. Muir, born March 22, 1874, who married Daisy D. Garrett. A sister, Mary Elizabeth Muir, was born March 26, 1878 and married Charles W. Spitler, Sept. 13, 1903.

Della's father, James W. Muir, was born March 16, 1832 and died June 1905. His first marriage was on Sept. 9, 1858 to Annie L. Payne, who was born June 15, 1838, and died June 13, 1871. His second marriage was to Mary E. Calloway on Feb. 22, 1872. She was born Feb. 1, 1851 and died March 30, 1878. This third marriage was to Elizabeth Calloway on March 23, 1879.

Elisha Kimuel Stucker's mother was a McCall. He had one brother, Halley Stucker, and one sister, Auntie McKinney. Grandfather Stucker owned a drug store in Mokane, MO. He was of Irish descent.

Elisha Kimuel and Della Florence Stucker had two children, Leland Stanford Stucker and Erma Mae, who married Charles John Engler, who was born Nov. 2, 1895 and worked for Barker Blis Service Inc. in St. Louis, MO. Erma Mae was born March 8, 1896 and worked in a milliner shop, Stix, Famous and Vandivers. They had no children.

Leland and Betty Stucker Family, 1954.

Grandfather on mother's side was James Eugene Drury. His mother, Elizabeth Debora Drury, never married. Grandfather Drury was born Oct. 6, 1871 at Owensboro, KY and died April 3, 1960. He married Anna Marie Cramer, who was born Oct. 20, 1875 at Evansville, IN and died Nov. 8, 1940. Her mother's name was Anna Marie. Dad was Charles Cramer. They were from Holland (Dutch) descent. James and Anna Marie Drury had three children: Lotus, Gene and Geneva Alma.

Leland Stanford Stucker Sr. was born June 13, 1899 at Mokane, MO and died Dec. 23, 1976 at Missouri Delta Community Hospital. He met and married Geneva Alma Drury at Pinetree, AR. They later moved to Scott County. Geneva was born Jan. 21, 1898 in Evansville, IN and died Oct. 15, 1968 at Missouri Delta Community Hospital.

Leland S. Stucker farmed and worked at New Madrid County Courthouse. He measured land, worked as a clerk for Beck and McCord Auction, owned and operated Shady Grove Service Station near East Prairie between 1960-1963 and worked a ticket agent at the Greyhound Bus Station for Don Kellet in his late years.

To this union was born seven children: Evelyn Mae Stucker (Huls), born Oct. 9, 1924 at Juanita Switch; Virginia Elizabeth Stocker (Parker), born Aug. 8, 1927 at Cape Girardeau, MO on the Crawford Place at Marquette Cement Plant; Leland Stanford Stucker Jr., born Sept. 8, 1929 at Cape Girardeau, MO; Mary Imogene Stucker (Mitchell), born April 3, 1932 at Cape Girardeau, MO; Linda Lee Stucker (Fisher) born Mary 31, 1934 at Cape Girardeau, MO; Rita Ruth Stucker (Miller), born Aug. 17, 1936 in St. Louis, MO; and Betty Jean Stucker (Strickland), born Nov. 18, 1938, Brown spur Road, Walker house, Scott County, MO. *Submitted by Rita Miller*

STULL – Bob J. Stull was born Jan. 4, 1942 in Advance, MO. He is the son of Elvis and Oma Stull. They later moved to Illmo, MO where Elvis worked at Southeast Missouri Lumber and later as a custodian of Illmo High School. Oma was a homemaker. Bob has six brothers and two sisters: John; James; Thermie; Donald; Bill and one half-brother, Paul; two sisters are Arletta Washburn and Betty Doria.

1988, left to right, Tina, Bob, Robin, and Margie

Bob attended Scott City High School. Bob worked at the International Shoe Factory at Chaffee, MO. He later worked for Ely Walker in Scott City, Atlas Plastic in Cape and in 1967 landed a job with Wetterau Foods in Scott City, MO, from which he retired in 1997 at age 55, after 30 years of service.

In 1961 he married Margie Meyer from Benton. Margie was born and raised in Benton. She is the daughter of Ben and Lorena Meyer. The Meyer family (family of 14 children) lived on a 120-acre farm north of Benton. Ben farmed, raised cattle, hogs and chickens. Lorena was a homemaker. Margie was born Sept. 17, 1943. She attended St. Denis Grade School and later Kelly High School in Benton. Margie worked at Cannon's café in Benton throughout her high school years. She later worked at Ely Walker factory in Illmo, MO, then in 1969 found employment with Drury Inns that would last for 31 years. Margie retired from Drury Inns in 2000 at age 56.

Bob and Margie have two daughters and five grandsons. Robin Stull-Haight, married to Tim Haight, has two sons and lives in Manassas, VA. Tina Stull-Schlosser, married to Randy Schlosser, has three sons and lives in Kelso, MO. Bob and Margie lived in Scott City, MO from 1961 – 1997. In 1997 they moved to Benton, MO. Robin and Tina graduated from Scott City High School. Robin graduated from Washington University in St. Louis, MO. She spent two years in Paris, France. Later she came back to the U. S. and joined the U. S. Army as an officer. During her six years in the Armed Services, she spent two years in Korea. She departed from the Army in 1995. In 1997 she returned to school and completed her Psy.D. in Clinical Psychology from George Washington University in Washington D. C. in 2002. Tina graduated from Metro Business College in Cape Girardeau, MO. Her employment includes Tanksley Trucking, Jerry Lipps Trucking and she currently works in the Safety Department at Delta Express.

During their retirement years, Bob volunteers many hours to the Knights of Columbus in Scott City and also works at MFA during the farming seasons. Margie works part-time at CSPrinting in Cape Girardeau and also part-time at the Cape Girardeau Convention and Visitors Bureau.

Bob and Margie are one of four partners who have developed Meyer Lake Estates in Benton,

MO. Meyer Lake Estates was developed in 1991, with the first lot being sold May 1991. Other partners are John Meyer, Tom Meyer, brothers, and Marie Rankin, sister.

SUVER – Alma Augusta Enderle was born Aug. 28, 1913 (the day of the dedication of St. Augustine Church and named for it) of Kelso, daughter of John Baptist Enderle and Mary Elizabeth (Dohogne) met Virgil Suver of Sikeston at a dance. They dated a while and then married June 2, 1938 at St. Mary's Catholic Church in Cape Girardeau, MO. He was born March 12, 1915, the son of Clyde Suver and Alice Rose (Story).

Alma Enderle and Virgil Suver, George Bartlett and Norma Enderle

They had many struggles through the years but the first one must have been the worst. He contracted tuberculosis (TB) shortly after the birth of their first child in 1940. He was sent to Mount Vernon, MO to be kept in confinement for one year and while he was there, their first child (Judith Ann) also contracted TB, as did his mother. Alma had to care for a sick child, make a living, help with a dying mother-in-law, and bury her only child during this time. He only was able to come home for the funerals and was sent back immediately. Alma and Virgil persevered and owned or operated several businesses together in Sikeston and had five more children: John Jeffrey, a son that was stillborn; Margaret Rose married Jerry Wayne Palmer, son of Charles Turner Palmer and Drucille (Brashier) on March 8, 1969 in Church of Christ at Lilbourn, MO. Jerry served in the United States Air Force three years in Madison, WI and 12 months in Seoul, South Korea, being discharged in 1968. Margaret and Jerry's children, Jerry Kirk, born June 11, 1970; John David, born Sept. 15, 1971; Jason Bradley, born Aug. 11, 1975 (died in infancy); and Justin Blair, born June 4, 1982.

Alma's daughter, Martha Jean, was born July 4, 1953, and the youngest child, Paul David, born Feb. 4, 1953.

Alma died Dec. 27, 1993 and Virgil died Nov. 1, 1986. Both are buried in Garden of Memories Cemetery in Sikeston, MO. *Submitted by Margaret Rose (Suver) Palmer*

TANNER – Harrison Tanner's grandfather, Samuel Tanner, was born Dec. 14, 1838, in New Hamburg, the son of Lewis and Elizabeth (Dobbins) Tanner. Samuel married his first wife, Amelia Evans on Oct. 8, 1858. She was born April 15, 1838 and died March 14, 1871. They had three sons and one daughter: John Lewis, Charles, William and Margaret.

Harrison was the son of Charles Samuel and Ella (Sayers) Tanner. Charles and Ella were married on Dec. 31, 1890. Charles was born on Jan. 13, 1867 and died Feb. 19, 1935. Ella was born Feb. 23, 1874 and died Feb. 26, 1950.

Henry Harrison Tanner was born Oct. 14, 1912 in Sikeston, MO. He attended Sikeston High School. There he met Ethyl Dunn and they graduated together in 1932. They were married on Oct.

23, 1932. She was born in New Madrid County on Nov. 18, 1914. Her parents were Fred and Edal (Jones) Dunn.

Harrison and Ethyl had two sons: Samuel Harrison, born July 19, 1935 and John Russell, born Aug. 30, 1938. The Tanner's built a new home at 617 Tanner Street in 1941.

Henry Harrison Tanner

Harrison was employed by the US Postal Service while maintaining ownership of the family farm. He retired after 30 years. After retirement, he enjoyed traveling during his leisure time.

Ethyl cared for her family and home. She was a member of a Sewing Club and a Garden Club. She and Harrison were active members of the Wesley United Methodist Church.

Their two sons graduated from Sikeston High School.

Sam graduated from Arizona State University with a B.S. degree in Agronomy. He married Retha Holloway. They had two sons: Richard Russell, born Feb. 8, 1960; and Robert Sean, born May 10, 1963. After retiring from Farmland Industries in Little Rock, AR, Sam moved back to Sikeston.

Russell graduated from Central Methodist College at Fayette, MO with a B.S. degree in Education, major in Biology. He served in the US Navy seven and a half years and retired with the rank of Lt. Commander. He married Angie (Vasquez). They had three children: Joseph Harrison was born July 20, 1967; Anna Kathryn was born July 26, 1969; and Felicia Renee was born Feb. 2, 1975. Russell worked with the Department of Corrections in Santa Claire, CA.

There were eight great-grandchildren in the Harrison Tanner family.

Harrison died Jan. 21, 1995 and is buried in the Sikeston City Cemetery.

TANNER – John Lewis Tanner was born March 6, 1860 in New Hamburg. He moved with his father, Samuel Tanner, who was born in 1838 in New Hamburg, Scott County, MO to Sikeston in 1871. His mother, Amelia Evans, also born in New Hamburg on April 15, 1838, died March 14, 1871 and this was probably the reason for their moving. John married Nannie Eliza Harris on May 4, 1893. She was born in Milan, TN, Feb. 10, 1860, the daughter of Dr. Christopher C. Harris, who was born May 10, 1835 in Stewart County, TN. He served as 1st Lt. In Gen. Nathaniel Bedford Forrest's Calvary, CSA. After graduating from Cincinnati Eclectic Medical Institute in 1871, he moved to Morley and established his medical practice. He died April 5, 1903 and is buried in the Old Morley Cemetery. Nannie's mother was Mary I. Townes from Virginia. John and Nannie Tanner had three children: Myra Irvin Tanner, 1894-1989; Bernice Harris Tanner 1895-1970; and Kathryn Handy Tanner, 1896-1939. John was a landowner and a businessperson. He helped to organize the Peoples Bank in Sikeston and served

John L. Tanner

on the Board of Directors. The Bank could not reopen after President Roosevelt declared the Bank Holiday in 1932. John purchased farmland from his father on June 10, 1887. The farms area located just west of the city of Sikeston on parts of Section 3, 10 and 22, T26N, R13E and is still being farmed by his grandson and great-grandson John L. Wilson Sr. and John L. Wilson Jr. This Tanner land became a 1987 Missouri Century Farm, Scott County, College of Agriculture, University of Missouri. The Tanner estate now reaches seven generations. John Lewis Tanner's wife, Nannie, was a schoolteacher. Their home, located at 412 North Kingshighway, is still in the family and now owned by John Lewis Wilson Jr. and his wife, Jan Ingram Wilson. *Submitted by John L. Wilson Sr.*

TANNER – Lewis Hatcher Tanner was born January 1810, near Smithland, KY. He married Elizabeth Dobbins Sept. 6, 1831 in Livingston County, KY. They moved from Livingston County, KY along the Pioneer Trail, crossing the Ohio River at Smithland, KY into Golconda, IL. They then traveled across Illinois to the Mississippi River. They crossed over to Commerce, Scott County, MO. Thence they traveled along the hill line west into central Scott County. In 1835, the settled in the Caney Creek area where they established a home and farm. They had at least two sons, Samuel and Henry Tanner.

In 1840, German settlers traveled west out of the low land of the Tywappity bottoms because of fever sickness to the higher land. The Germans stopped for the winter on the Lewis Hatcher Tanner farm. During one night, a hard winter storm blew the German's temporary shelters away and Lewis Tanner, by lantern light, brought all of the Germans into his home until the storm was over. The many families of this German group, along with the Tanner family, built a Catholic Church (although the Tanners were not Catholic) because all of the Germans were Catholic. The place was called Hamburg that was later called New Hamburg because there was already a Hamburg in Missouri. There is a Tanner name on the Tablet of the New Hamburg Catholic Church.

Samuel Tanner was born Dec. 14, 1838 at New Hamburg, the son of Lewis and Elizabeth (Dobbins) Tanner. He married his first wife, Amelia Evans, on Oct. 8, 1858. She was born April 15, 1838 and died March 14, 1871. They had six children. He then married Francis Annie Applegate on Aug. 27, 1875. They had four children together.

During the Civil War, Samuel Tanner served as a Captain in Company F of the 79th Regiment of the Northern Militia out of Cape Girardeau, MO. He fought as a scout against the Confederate forces and against the guerilla forces and bands of outlaws. There is also a record of "Tanner Infantry" but also original orders state he was to report with his Company mounted. Records show there were many skirmishes or "bushwhackers" activity in southern Missouri. A bullet wounded him in his head while scouting in the Ozark area. He rode horseback to his home in New Hamburg and family tradition tells blood was dripping from his horse blanket. He was then transported to a Cape Girardeau hospital in the family wagon. The bullet wound was plugged by a silver plate and left a hole in

Capt. Samuel Tanner

his head that you could put your thumb in. Samuel's brother, Henry Tanner, enlisted in the Confederate forces so they fought brother against brother in the conflict of the War Between the States.

With the death of his first wife, Amelia Evans, in 1871 Samuel Tanner moved with his six children to Sikeston in southern Scott County at the young age of 33. He was a businessman, farm owner and developer of farms and properties in the area. He was a partner at times with Dan McCoy and at times with Reece Applegate. They built some of the downtown buildings and you will find their activities in the old newspapers, city records and church records. Capt. Sam (as he was known) owned some farms just west of the Sikeston ridge on the Salcedo Road. On the property was a house on the farm that he rented to a widow lady and her children. Family folklore handed down tells that while Jesse James was visiting the lady and he hid while she was paying the rent to Capt. Sam and after he left, Jesse James robbed him of his money and returned it to the widow before leaving for the west.

He sold his Scott County farmlands to his sons and daughter of his first wife in 1887. He and his second family moved to Poplar Bluff, Butler County, MO to continue developing farms south of Poplar Bluff. The Iron Mountain terminal rail yard Poplar Bluff was his demise. He was killed while crossing railroad tracks with his mules and wagon. He was transported to St. Louis, MO by the train and died in St. Louis hospital of his injuries on Oct. 14, 1912. He is buried in the Sikeston City Cemetery on Kingshighway. *Submitted by John L. Wilson Sr.*

TANNER – This narrative adds to Tanner family information printed in the March 2001 Scott County Historical Society newsletter and then continues with one family branch.

In the 1850 census, Lewis H. Tanner and Elizabeth Dobbins Tanner had three children, Henry (17), Nancy (15) and Samuel (12).s During the Civil War, Sergeant Samuel and Private Henry served in Captain Daniel's Co. C, Scott County Battalion, Missouri Home Guards from May to August of 1861.

Private Henry was mustered into the 79th Reg't, E.M.M. (Enrolled Missouri Militia) August 20, 1863 with "Capt. Tanner" appearing on the record card. Private Henry served in Tanner's Six Months Reg't E.M.M. Co. F from August 29, 1864 to March 12, 1865. Capt. S. Tanner is shown as the commanding officer. As all the above archival information shows Union service, it appears to conflict with an old letter that says the brothers were on opposite sides. Official activity reports exist for some of Capt. Tanner's actions.

Samuel Tanner (1838-1912), a widower, married the widow Frances Annie Applegate Moore (1838-1925) in 1874. One of their chil-

Murray Quinn Sr.

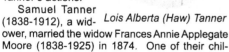
Lois Alberta (Haw) Tanner

dren, Murray Quinn Tanner (1881-1943), and a brother bought a steam thrasher engine and worked on harvests. The money earned paid for Murray's attendance at the Missouri Military Academy and he was an un-appointed alternate for West Point. At about 21, he was supervising installation and wiring of the town electrical system in Oran when he met his future wife, Lois Alberta Haw (1884-1959). She often told of him being up on a wire pole near her Uncle Dr. Wescoat's house when they first met and then he returned in the evening to sell electrical service to the Doctor. Lois was a daughter of Dr. Joseph Lindsay Haw, Sr. (1836-1910) and Mary Ann Vernon Haw (1838-1893). Murray and Lois were married in 1906. There were four children, Frances Phoebe (1907-1998), Murray Quinn Jr. (1908-2000), Mary Ellen (1912-1982) and Lois Haw (1914-2001). Murray Sr. was an executive with the Scott County Milling Company when the family moved to Webster Groves, Missouri in the 1920's.

Murray Jr. was a graduate of Washington University in St. Louis. In 1935 Murray Jr. married Marceline Holekamp (1912-1977). There were two sons, Murray III (1936-) and Robert H. (1941-). Murray III is an Engineering graduate of Northwestern University and Robert is a Forestry graduate from Oklahoma State University.

Murray III married Donna Sue Thornhill on September 12, 1958 in Gray Summit, Missouri. Children of Murray III and Donna are Russell M. (19S59-), Daniel Q. (1960-) and Cynthia K (1962-). *Submitted by Murray Q. Tanner III*

Some sources of reference: Missouri State Archives, Census Reports, "The HAW Family Ancestry" by Joseph L. Haw III, official records of the Union and Confederate Armies by the War Dept., original CW orders in possession of the writer, notes and letters from past research, and inquiries by family members, especially W. H. Tanner, verbal accounts from interviews and tape recordings.

TAYLOR – Emily Jane Taylor was the first of 12 children born to George Washington Taylor and Massa Parker Taylor. Emily Jane was born on Aug. 13, 1829 in Hardeman County, TN. She was about 5 years old when she moved with her parents and younger brother and sister, Miles and Martha Ann, to Scott County about 1834.

Emily was married at Commerce to Phillip James Miller on Nov. 24, 1850 when she was 21 years old. Phillip was born William Miller, son of Phillip Miller and Mary Smith, and Elizabeth R. Price/ Pryce, daughter of William Price and Sarah Williams. Emily Jane and Phillip James Miller were the parents of George W. Miller, Mary Matilda Miller, Andrew Christy Miller and Elizabeth Pauley. These children were living in Scott County in 1869 when their grandfather, George Washington Taylor, died as they were listed as his heirs. Phillip

Mary Ann (Vernon) Haw

Dr. Joseph Lindsey Haw Sr.

James Miller died May 10, 1862 at the age of 36, probably in the service of his country. Tragically, his young wife Emily died just six months later on Nov. 21, 1863 at the age of 34. Emily Jane Miller is buried in Old Commerce Cemetery. Their orphaned children were taken in by family members.

Mary Matilda "Molly" Miller was born Sept. 30, 1853. She married John Mack Sanders on the first of May 1870. John was born Feb. 8, 1849. Interesting to note: this couple was born, married, died and were buried at Commerce, MO. They died exactly two weeks apart. First, John Mack died on Nov. 16, 1932 when he was 83 years old and Molly joined him on Nov. 30 at age 79. Bohnhardt, Terry, Uelsmann, Sander and Held are family names.

Andrew Chrisy Miller was born Nov. 29, 1857 and on April 13, 1879 he married Mary Elizabeth Spradlin. Mary Elizabeth was born on March 29, 1860 at Piedmont, MO. Andrew passed away on Dec. 16, 1941 at the age of 84. Mary Elizabeth died on Feb. 5, 1943 when she was almost 83. Both are buried at Oakdale Cemetery.

Mary Elizabeth Spradlin was the daughter of David Spradlin and Myriah Adeline Sanders. Her grandparents were Obediah Spradlin and Mary Elizabeth Driver, as well as Richmond Sanders, who was the son of William and Mariah Sanders. Richmond's wife was Mary, daughter of William Rasberry and Sinah Hooper.

Andrew and Mary Elizabeth had a daughter, Fannie, who was born on Aug. 25, 1887 at Commerce. She married William Joshua Belk on March 6, 1907. William was born March 9, 1882 at Kelso to Thomas G. and Texanna Belk and died on Oct. 30, 1923 at only 41. His widow, Fannie, lived a long time and died on Aug. 26, 1981. She was 94 years and one day old. Both Fannie and William are buried at Oakdale Cemetery. *Submitted by Toni Martinazzi*

TAYLOR – George Washington Taylor was born in Virginia about 1800 and he married Massa Parker, who was born in Illinois Territory about 1810. They were married in Hardeman County, TN, on Sept. 12, 1828. Massa's father may have been Gamaliel Parker, as he entered a marriage bond with George and that document was usually contracted between the groom and the father or brother of the bride. The young couple had three children while they were in Tennessee: Emily, Miles and Martha Ann (McIntosh). Around 1834 they moved to Scott County, where they probably joined several relatives. There were several Taylor families who lived in the area. Over the next 20 years George and Massa had another nine children: Catherine, Mary, William Broom, Andrew, Mildred, Mariah, Isham, Sarah Ann and Joann. They were probably Baptists.

George farmed 140 acres but was also a Justice of the Peace. Activities included executing documents for a sheriff's sale on Nov. 29, 1840 and performing the marriage of Patrick Tobin and Arminta Rasberry on May 4, 1854, among other chores.

The war took a huge toll on ordinary people and although George and his family were diligent workers, and responsible citizens who contributed greatly to the development of Kelso township and the county, they, along with everyone else, suffered both financially and emotionally during that great conflict. George and Massa lost family and sources of income. Debts began to pile up.

George Taylor was 69 years old in early 1869 when he died, and surprisingly, he left no will, which was a grave loss to his family. By that time the eldest son Miles had died and left a widow and orphaned children. So on April 9, 1869, Wiley A. Hughes, Clerk of the County Court at Commerce, appointed George's second born son, William Broom Taylor, administrator of the estate. He had to hire appraisers, lawyers, auctioneers, accountants and clerks. He had to pay up back taxes. He had to pay court costs and place ads in the *Commerce Dispatch* newspaper. All of this ate away at the once large estate of his parents. If George had only left a will, all the land and property would have passed on to the heirs. As it was they got nothing, except what some of them could buy themselves. Massa could keep some land and a few household items and animals.

The G. W. Taylor tax bill, for example, for the year 1868 on 160 acres was only $15.88 and his personal property was valued at $389. The tax bill reflected a total value of $1,229.00 for which he owed the $15.88. But there were many unpaid tax bills.

Much paperwork filed with Scott County Probate Court demonstrates William's valiant struggle to make ends meet and provide for his mother. So there was an Administrator's Auction Sale on Nov. 14, 1872 and it must have weighed heavy on the hearts of the family to see beloved possessions sold.

However, both William and Andrew bought tools, animals, and farm implements at this sale. Finally, three months later, on Feb. 18, 1873 some of the real estate had to be auctioned off on the courthouse steps in Commerce in order to pay debts of the estate, which was not closed until 1877.

Massa Parker Taylor probably died between 1870 and 1880 and she rests with her husband in the Taylor Cemetery. The old part had been destroyed, but the newer part has been incorporated into Lightner Cemetery. *Submitted by Toni Martinazzi*

TAYLOR – Miles N. Taylor was the second child and the first-born son of George Washington Taylor and Massa Parker Taylor. He was probably born in Hardeman County, TN in 1831. He moved to Scott County, MO with his parents about 1834, along with his two sisters, Emily Jane, who was older, and Martha Ann, who was younger.

He married a Percilla or Drucilla ___ who was born about 1839 in Missouri and they became the parents of at least two children. Charles A. Taylor was born about 1858 and John A. Taylor followed about a year later around 1859. Miles probably served in the Civil War and may have lost his life then. This is based on the fact that when his own father died in early 1869, Miles was already dead but would have been at a prime age for military service during the war. These two sons of Miles were thought to be living in Butler County, MO when their grandfather, George Washington Taylor, died. *Submitted by Toni Martinazzi*

TAYLOR – William Broom Taylor was born Nov. 24, 1837 in Scott County, MO at what is now Illmo. He was the son of George Washington Taylor and Massa Parker Taylor who had moved to Missouri from Tennessee about three years before William was born. At the time of his birth, William had five elder siblings: Emily Jane (Miller), Miles, Martha Ann (McIntosh), Catherine and Mary.

When under 3 months old the lucky child was named in a will to inherit 40 acres of land from the old man for whom he was named, Mr. William Broom. It is uncertain what relationship existed between the Taylor family and the Brooms, but since other Taylor's also inherited from William Broom it suggests a blood relationship. A Mary Jane Taylor was to get a 3-year-old filly from his stock of horses and little William Broom Taylor's father, George Washington Taylor, witnessed the associated will on Feb. 20, 1838.

William and Martha had a daughter, Minerva Hutson, who married William Hutson and she was probably dead at the time of the writing of William Broom's will, as she is not named. After his wife, Martha is provided for, the next person in line was Louisa Hutson, daughter of William Hutson, and she was to get a Negro girl named Betty. Thus, if Louisa was his granddaughter, perhaps the Taylor children were related in some way also.

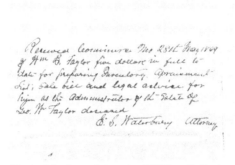

Reciept for the estate sale of William B. Taylor.

At any rate, over the years William Broom Taylor was joined by siblings Andrew, Mildred, Mariah (Marie Bena), Isham, Sarah Ann and Joann. He, and probably most of them, had attended the Old Lishman School. William married Adaline Pryce/Price and they were married by William Miller, M. G. at Wrays Landing on June 6, 1861 and it was not recorded until Sept. 21, 1863.

William B. Taylor was a well-respected member of the community. When his father passed away, William was appointed administers of the estate, as his elder brother, Miles, was deceased. The appointment was made on April 9, 1869. For the next eight years this occupied a great deal of the son's time. William Broom Taylor lived his entire life in Scott County, MO.

In later life William joined the Methodist Church, and he and his wife, Addie, lived at Morley. William Broom Taylor died Jan. 2, 1929 in Scott County at the age of 92. He was buried from the home of his son, Marvin, of Morley. Rev. D. M. Margraves, pastor of the local Methodist Church officiated at his funeral. Both William and Addie are buried in Oakdale Cemetery in Commerce. Their surviving children at the time of William's death were Robert Taylor who lived at Swindon in 1929 and Marvin Taylor born 1883-1950 who had married Bertie ___ and a daughter, Mrs. R. L. Buck of Benton. *Submitted by Toni Martinazzi*

THOMAS – George Joseph Thomas, born Jan. 25, 1876, New Hamburg, Scott County, MO, was the son of Mathias Thomas, who came to Scott County from Ohio in about 1849 and Marie Theresa Dumey, who was born in Scott County in 1850. George's dark hair, dark eyes, and slight stature reflected his Belgian heritage. His mother's Dumey ancestry can be found in Steven Dumey's *Genealogy of the John H. Dumey Family* and his father's ancestry in *John Thomas and Catherine Kettel: from Lexembourg, Belgium to Scott County, MO (1809-2001)* by Kay Thomas Brusati.

In 1900, George living on the family farm was a farm laborer. On April 7, 1905, he purchased Lots 9 and 10, Block 3, first addition to the town of Ancell, now Scott City. The house he built there was at 2500 James Street; it was sold June 10, 1925. George J. Thomas and Catherine Seifert were married at Quincy, IL, Sept. 25, 1907. Catherine, born Jan. 20, 1886, was the daughter of John Seifert and Katherine Herold. In 1910, George was a salesman for a lumber company. At the time of his registration for military draft at age 42 in 1918, he was employed as a car re-

pairer for the St. Louis and Southwestern Railroad Company in Illmo, now Scott City. He also worked in a merchandise store in Kelso, at the Cotton Belt Railroad Station in Fornfelt, now Scott City, and for a short time, at Ford Motors in Dearborn, MI. In 1913, the family moved to Quincy, IL, but soon returned to Scott County until permanently relocating to Quincy in 1925, where George worked as maintenance man for the Irwin Paper Company 16 years until retiring in 1941. In Quincy, the family lived at 318 South Tenth Street. George is remembered for his thoroughness in reading the newspaper and his love of the card game pinochle. George and Catherine Thomas died at Quincy, he on Feb. 19, 1955, and she Jan. 21, 1961. Both were active members of St. Boniface Catholic Church and are buried in St. Boniface Cemetery, Quincy. They had nine children: Marguerite Catherine Dorothy Thomas, born June 20, 1908, Ancell, died June 1, 1986, Dallas, TX. She married Alexander Sconder Haroz.

George Joseph Thomas

Gertrude Cecelia Thomas, born July 6, 1910, Ancell, died July 6, 1992, Quincy.

Helen Magdalene Thomas, born April 21, 1913, Ancell, died Dec. 8, 1981, Solon, OH. She married James John Sullivan.

Clara Mary Thomas, born May 9, 1915, Ancell, died Sept. 19, 1972, St. Louis, MO. She married Levi Peck.

Joseph George Thomas, born Oct. 25, 1917, Ancell, died Aug. 15, 1987, Rockville, MD. He married Ann Lourdes Burke.

Kenneth Charles Thomas, born Nov. 7, 1921, Ancell, married Margaret Mary Snyder.

Frederick Louis Thomas, born Nov. 28, 1924, Ancell.

Mary Ann Thomas, born Oct. 27, 1930, Quincy, married Wendell Prather.

James John Thomas, born Oct. 3, 1933, Quincy, married Charlotte Deane Burrows.

TODT – Carl, son of John and Bertha Todt, was born June 15, 1927, in Montgomery County, IL. The family moved to New Madrid County in 1929. In 1936 they moved to Scott County two and one-half miles south of Morley on Highway 61. Carl attended school at Landers Ridge 2-1/2 years, finishing the third grade in Guardian Angel School, Oran. Carl entered the fourth grade in Morley and graduated from Morley High School in 1945.

I had chores to do as do all farm children. I started at an early age to pump water, turn the cream separator; milk cows by hand (later with a milking machine), and worked a team of mules plowing corn and a lot of other chores. While in high school I mowed highway right-of-way from Morley to Grant City. I liked all sports playing basketball and softball in high school and played softball with the Catholic Youth Conference.

In 1948 I joined the National Guard 140th Infantry at Cape Girardeau. I served three years until a tractor accident in 1951. I crushed my left heel bone and was in and out of Barnes Hospital for a year.

In June 1952 Carl and Kathryn Dumey, daughter of John and Bertha Bles Dumey, were married. The Dumey family had three boys and seven girls. John Dumey was from Kelso; Bertha from New Hamburg. They farmed seven miles north of Sikeston, moving to Oran in 1946. Kathryn graduated from Oran High School and attended Steimle Business College in Cape Girardeau. She worked with Division of Family Services quitting work to raise her children. I continued to farm the home place after my father died in 1951, becoming the second generation to farm Todt Dairy Farm. In 1963, while in partnership with Sylvester and Robert, I took a part-time job with Missouri University Extension as supervisor of Semo Dairy Herd Improvement Association. I had as high as 24-dairy herds (1500 cows) in Scott, Cape, Stoddard, Perry and New Madrid Counties. I took a milk sample and weighed the milk from each cow. I calculated the value of each cow's feed to come up with a net cost per cow so herd owners knew which cows were profitable. At first the butterfat test was done with a Babcock tester. Later this information was processed in a laboratory in Springfield, MO. I retired from this position in 1993 after 30 years.

Our first daughter, Mary Beth, was born in 1954. She attended Guardian Angel School and graduated from Oran High School. She attended Murray State University in Kentucky and obtained a Masters in Early Childhood Education from Terry Haute University. She is now Director of The Children's Place in Columbia, SC.

Our son, Carl Jr., born in 1959, attended Guardian Angel Grade School, graduating from Scott County Central. He graduated from Southeast Missouri State University with a degree in Agriculture and continued to farm.

Carl and Kathryn Todt Family. Front: Mary Beth, Kathryn, and Susan. Back: Carl Jr. and Carl Sr.

In 1960 our second daughter, Susan, was born. She attended Guardian Angel Grade School, graduating from Scott County Central. She graduated from Southeast Missouri State University with a major in Agriculture and a minor in Social Work. In 1982, Susan and Mark Howard of Jackson were married. They live east of Fruitland on highway 177. They farm 400 acres of corn, soybeans and do some construction work. They have two children, Stephanie 10 and Tyler 5.

In 1995 I retired and Carl Todt Jr. "Eddie" became the third generation to farm Todt Dairy Farm. *Submitted by Carl Todt Sr.*

TODT – Cletus John Todt was born May 1, 1922 in Raymond, IL, the son of John and Bertha (Hoehn) Todt. The family (Harold, Herman, Regina, Cletus, Geraldine, Theresa and Carl) moved to Missouri in 1929, New Madrid County, three miles south of Morehouse. We started to school at Landers Ridge, a one-room school. A brother, Sylvester, was born Oct. 5, 1930; another brother, Robert, was born Jan. 23, 1934 at Morehouse, MO. We moved to Morley (Scott County) in 1936 and I went to school one half year at Oran, MO (seventh grade). The next year I started school at Morley the eighth grade then on to high school where I played some basketball in my free time, graduating in 1941. In 1942 I enlisted in the Navy. I went to Great Lakes, IL for basic then to machinist's school. After that I

went to New York for diving school and became a salvage diver. I went overseas for WWII in 1943. I was in Sherburg, France five or six days after D-day. Here my duty was to repair a dry dock gate then on to LaHarve, France. My job here was search and recovery of boat "ducks" which was unloading freight from transport ships. The next stop was Bremer Harven, Germany. We patched and raised a freight ship there. After two and a half years I came home or back to United States, traveling on troop ships. Returning to Morley I farmed together with family.

Cletus J. Todt family, Back row: James, Brenda, and Steven. Front: Cletus, Daniel, and Lorena.

In 1949 I married Lorena Dohogne, moved to Sikeston for six months then to Oran and farmed on the "Friend Family Farm."

Our first son, James, was born in 1950. We moved to Benton and farmed until 1955. Here our daughter, Brenda Sue, was born in 1951. A son, Steven, was born in 1953 and a son, Daniel, in 1954. In 1955 the family moved to Cape Girardeau (Cape County). I started working for my brother, Herman at "Todt Sheet Metal." After Herman's death (1975) I continued managing the shop for his wife, Louise. In 1983 my wife, Lorena, passed away. I kept working until 1985 retiring to part time.

In December 1985 I married Hannah Geringer, a retired school cashier and cook. We are still living in Cape and enjoying traveling.

We have a Navy Salvage Divers reunion each year. There is a plaque at "Pier 88" in New York with my name along with others for helping raise the ship *Normandy*. Along with my gardening and woodworking hobby I'm kept quite busy. We attend St. Vincent De Paul Church here in Cape.

TODT – John and Bertha with their seven children, Harold, Herman, Regina, Cletus, Geraldine, Theresa and Carl, left Harvel, IL (Montgomery County) in 1929 for southeast Missouri. They loaded mules, cows, sheep, and a tractor along with some equipment in a boxcar. They went by rail to Morehouse, MO. Household items were loaded on a Model T Ford Truck and a 1924 Dodge touring car. Crossing the Mississippi River on a ferry they came to a farm three miles south of Morehouse in New Madrid County. They farmed there for seven years raising corn, beans, and wheat. Cream from the dairy cows was shipped by rail from a junction near Canalou. They had sharecrop families that grew cotton on a crop-share basis.

Sylvester and Robert were born in New Madrid County. The older children attended a one-room school, Landers Ridge, with the oldest son, Harold, graduating from Morehouse High School in 1934.

In 1936 the Todts bought 160 acres in Scott County two and one-half miles south of Morley on Highway 61. There were nine children, six boys and three girls. Herman, the second son, graduated from Oran High School in 1936. The rest graduated from Morley High School. In 1938

an adjoining 120 acres were purchased and in 1950 another 80 acres. In all businesses there are always some natural disasters. In 1939 a tornado blew half of the barn away leaving the part we milked in. That fall a new barn was built, which still stands. With 360 acres the family continued to farm. With additional cows they started selling whole milk in ten-gallon cans to Reiss Dairy. Milking was done by hand until 1941 when a milk barn was built and milking machines were purchased.

On March 17, 1942, the farmhouse burned, a total loss. The recently completed shop building served as our house for a year. With generous neighbors and friends we had enough furniture to get by. We built a new house in 1943, the present house. Our dad, John, died in July of 1951 of a heart attack. Carl, Sylvester and Robert continued in partnership. In 1957 we built a new dairy barn equipped with a pipeline milking system allowing the milk from each cow to go directly into a bulk cooler. After Reiss Dairy in Sikeston closed, milk went to Paducah Greater Milk Association later known as Dairymen, Inc. of Louisville, KY.

John and Bertha Todt Family. Back row: Theresa, Herman, Cletus, Regina, Harold, and Geraldine. Front: Robert, John, Bertha, Sylvester, and Carl.

Our mother, Bertha, passed away in 1963. A year or so later Sylvester and Robert decided to pursue other interests and Carl became the owner of the 360 acres, the second generation to farm the home place. Dairying and grain farming continued with additional rental land. A new machine shed was built in 1994 next to the shop building, which was once, our house. In 1995 Carl retired and his son, Carl Jr., Eddie, became the third generation to farm the home place. In 1997 Carl and Eddie decided to quit the dairy operation. In April 2001 a fire destroyed the shop and machine shed. In December 2001 Eddie built a new shop and in February 2002 a new machine shed was completed. *Submitted by Carl Edward Todt Sr.*

TODT – Robert "Bob" Leo Todt was born Jan. 23, 1934 at Morehouse, MO, the son of John T. Todt and Bertha Hoehn Todt. They moved to Scott County and resided on a dairy farm located at the Blodgett Road and Highway 61. Bob graduated from Morley High School in 1952. Together, he and his brother, Carl operated the Todt Dairy Farm until Bob purchased the Oran Tavern in 1966 from John Houck.

He married Mary Frances Vetter, daughter of George and Alvina Compas Vetter of Benton, MO on July 7, 1962. They have four children: Thomas "Tom" Allen Todt, April 19, 1963, who resides in Yukon, OK; Donna Todt Ross, April 21, 1964, now living in Scopus, MO; Gail Todt Dame, Oct. 24, 1966, or Wolf Lake, IL; and Sandra "Sandy" Leigh Todt, March 23, 1970. Sandy died May 24, 1995.

After selling the Oran Tavern, Bob went to work for Todt Sheet Metal Company in Cape Girardeau, MO until 1983. He then became an Insurance Representative for the Knights of Columbus, retiring in 1996. He drove a school bus in the Oran R-III district for 25 years. He is a past president of the Oran Chamber of Commerce.

Bob is a charter member of the Oran Knights of Columbus Council 4311, a member of Thomas Langen Fourth Degree Assembly in Cape Girardeau, MO and a member of Guardian Angels Catholic Church.

TODT – Sylvester Todt, son of John T. and Bertha Hoehn, who originally was from Harvel, IL, came to Missouri in 1929 to New Madrid County in the Canalou Community where Sylvester was born Oct. 5, 1930. John and Bertha, with a family of nine children, later moved to Scott County to a farm on Highway 61, three miles south of Morley in 1936. They row cropped and later started dairying. Sylvester entered school in the old Morley school, completing and graduating from Morley High School in 1948.

Sylvester was engaged in farming when he met Della June Moore, born April 18, 1934. She is the daughter of Marvin Moore and Mae Back Moore, of Oran, MO. Sylvester and Della married and had seven children. Twin boys, Larry Allen and Gary Wayne, were born on May 9, 1952. Pamela June was born on March 29, 1953.

Sylvester and Della, along with their three children moved to Kansas City, MO, where Sylvester was a truck driver for Auto Transport Company for two years. They moved back to Cape Girardeau, MO where Sylvester worked with Todt Sheet Metal Company for one year. They moved to Pickins, MS where he was engaged in Farm Management with his Uncle Lawrence Todt for three years. They had a daughter Peggy Ann Todt. She was born on July 12, 1956. Later, she died Dec. 18, 1956.

Moving back to Oran in Scott County he was engaged in farming with his two brothers, Carl and Robert.

Son Gregory Raymond was born on Oct. 11, 1960; Vance Christopher was born March 29, 1962; Brian Sylvester was born Nov. 29, 1963.

Gary Wayne graduated from Oran High School in 1971 and attended Southeast Missouri State University. In June 1973 he married Sharon Ann Scheeter. They had four children: Jason Allen, born July 26, 1976; Jill Ann, born Dec. 23, 1978; Justin Michael, born Oct. 29, 1980; and Jared Raymond, born Aug. 8, 1982. Gary died Dec. 31, 2000, the result of an automobile accident.

Larry Allen graduated from Oran High School in 1971 and attended Southeast Missouri State University. In 1985 he married Barbara Fieldhein. They had a daughter, Rachel Davie, born Sept. 1, 1985.

Pamela June graduated from Oran High School in 1971. She graduated from Southeast Missouri State University with a B.S. in education, and received her Masters Degree from Northern Arizona University. On July 9, 1988 she married Donald Eugene Wilgus. Donald was born March 16, 1930. Donald is a retired teacher. His parents were Fred Wilgus and Elsie Rucker. Pamela is employed at Puxico High School as principal.

Gregory Raymond graduated from Oran High School in 1979, and attended Southeast Missouri State University. He married Lori Diebold, daughter of Jerome Diebold and Marilyn LeGrand, on Sept. 29, 1984. Lori was born on Aug. 6, 1962. They have two daughters: Angela Renee, born March 12, 1981; and Lexie Dawn was born Sept. 15, 1985. Greg is employed at Procter and Gamble. Lori is owner of Clippity Clip Beauty Salon.

Vance Christopher graduated from Oran High School in 1980, and attended Southeast Missouri State University. On June 18, 1983, he married Tammy Glastetter, daughter of Ralph Glastetter and Doris Dannenmueller. Tammy was born June 5, 1963. They have two children: Logan Christopher, born Jan. 15, 1991 and Morgan Sophia, born Dec. 29, 1995. Vance is employed at Industrial Systems. Tammy is employed at Dr. Fenton's office.

Brian Sylvester graduated from Oran High School in 1982, and attended Southeast Missouri State University. On June 14, 1986 he married Crystal Sallee, daughter of Charles Sallee and Claude Ann Phillips. Crystal was born March 2, 1964. They have two children: Austin Brian, born Sept. 12, 1992; and Courtney Lynn, born April 8, 1998. Brian is employed at Procter and Gamble. Crystal is secretary at Oran High School.

Sylvester farmed in the Morley and Oran communities until the mid 1980s. He then returned to truck driving with Allied Automotive, until his retirement.

TOTTY – The Totty family originally came to Tennessee from Virginia. They settled in Hickman County in what came to be known as Totty's Bend. William H. was the son of Asa and Polly Totty and Sarah S. was the daughter of Lewis Perkins and Athelia Baird Totty. They were distant  *Sarah S. Totty*
cousins. William and Sarah came to Scott County in the early 1870s from Hickman County where they were married in 1861. William had served in the 9th (Gantt's) Tennessee Cavalry Battalion. He was a prisoner of war, having been captured at Fort Donelson, TN and imprisoned at Camp Douglas, IL. They were paroled and released at Vicksburg in September 1862. The company was re-organized and fought at Port Hudson, LA; Kennesaw Mountain and Atlanta, GA; Nashville, TN; Kingston, NC and Bentonville, NC. They surrendered on March 19, 1865.

William and Sarah had ten children. In January 1883, they bought 80 acres outside of Commerce, MO for $1000.00 with 10 percent interest. In June 1884, William at the age of 48, died of TB and the land was sold at auction on the courthouse steps in Benton, MO. Sarah died at the age of 87 in April 1931 and is buried in the Commerce Cemetery. William's place of burial is unknown. The names and birth dates of the children of William and Sarah are as follows: Tennessee "Tennie" (b. 1862), Guse Leonidas "Lee" (b. 1865), William c. (b. 1868), Dora (b. 1870), Josephine Narcissey (b. 1872), Levicy "Lou" (b. 1874), Louis Perkins (b. 1877), Robert "Bud" (b. 1879), Edward (b. June 4, 1881) and Benjamin (b. 1884). Louis Perkins (b. 1877) was the last of the children to pass away. He died in 1969 at the age of 91.

URHAHN – James Monroe Urhahn was born Dec. 29, 1947. He was the son of Theon and Lorena Urhahn. He was raised in Benton, MO, the youngest of five boys, and two girls. He attended St. Denis Grade School and Thomas W. Kelly High School. He graduated from Kelly in 1965. He joined the Army and served in Vietnam from October 1967 to October 1968. He married Barbara Scherer on July 26, 1969 at St. Denis Church in Benton, MO. Barbara Scherer is the daughter of Cletus L. and the late Ivy Scherer. She was born June 25, 1946, the oldest of three children. Jim and Barbara purchased a house in Benton at 41 County Highway 250 and Barbara still resides there. On Nov. 14, 1969 they had a son, James Joseph Urhahn. He was born at Southeast Missouri Hospital.

Jim worked as a truck driver for a few years and then became a manager of Campus Auto and Tire for 11 years. Barbara had worked at Thorngate LTD for 38 years.

On June 24, 1997 Jim passed away. He is survived by his wife, son, daughter-in-law, Shelly Urhahn, and two grandchildren, Hunter and Kaelyn Urhahn.

UHRHAN – John Uhrhan and Rosa (Glasser) Uhrhan are my grandparents. My great-grandfather, Peter, and his brother, John, came to America from Germany about 1850. They were first located in Indiana, then in Ohio, coming to New Hamburg, MO in 1856. John subscribed to work on the new church in 1857, but Peter was back in Ohio by 1858 where a child was born.

Peter married Elizabeth Kunz and John married her sister, Katherine. This probably occurred in Ohio because Elizabeth was living with her parents, Jacob Kunz and Barbara (Zeichel) Kunz in Ohio in 1850. Peter and Elizabeth's first four children were born in Ohio. My grandfather, John, was born in Ohio on Jan. 21, 1856. He married Rosa Katherine Glasser in Scott County, MO on Nov. 21, 1882. They had seven children who lived to be adults. John married Stella Schlitt- four children Otto, Juanita (Jake), Ralph (Sweetie) and Wilford (Dusch). Alvina married Adam Felter- six children Lorena, John, Sylvester, Zeno (Sam), LeeAnn and Mildred. William "Bill" married Amelia Scherer- eight children Leon, Ervin, Vernita, Lucille, Raymond (Pat), Mildred (Tootie), Edvera and Clemens (Dusch). Rosa married Leo Essner- five children Vincent, Simon, John, Herman and Paul William. Emaline married Leo Menz- five children Cyrilla, Arbella, Marie, Ernita and Cletus.

The Uhrhan Family. Back row: John, Bill, Emaline, Rosa, and Alvina. Front: Stephen, John, Valentine, and Rosa (Glasser).

Stephen (my father) married Agnes Berghoff, daughter of John and Elizabeth (Droste) Berghoff, Valentine never married.

These couples all lived in Scott County all their lives and many of their children still live in Scott County. All of them were farmers most of their lives. My dad, Stephen bought the family farm after his mother died. He was a farmer all of his life. He fed his cattle the morning of the day he died. He died very suddenly at age 78. The farm is still owned by the Uhrhan family. It is three miles north of Benton just off of Highway 61. My dad hauled gravel to help build the first Highway 61.

Stephen and Agnes had five children: Irene married Cornelius Blattel; Vernon married Jerry Glueck; Cletus married Sue Koester; Rosemary married Ronnie Kern; and Helen married Fred Drew.

Since my great-grandfather and his brother

married sisters all the Uhrhans in the area are related even though some spell their name different. Our grandparents spelled it Uhrhan; my dad spelled it Uhrhan but his brothers spelled Urhahn. *Submitted by Irene (Uhrhan Blattel)*

UHRHAN – Stephen Lawrence Uhrhan was born Aug. 10, 1900 and died Dec. 13, 1978 on a farm three miles north of Benton, MO where he lived most of his life. He lived on a farm a few miles away for a few years. After his mother died, he bought the home place. His parents were John Uhrhan and Rosa (Glasser) Uhrhan. He had three brothers (John, Bill, and Valentine) and three sisters, Alvina, Rosa and Emaline.

The Steven Uhrhan family: Helen, Cletus, Rosemary, and Vernon; (front) Agnes, Irene, and Steven.

On April 16, 1929 he married Agnes Elizabeth Berghoff. At that time the Berghoff family lived across Highway 61 from where the Uhrhans' lived. My mother, Agnes Berghoff, was born in Prairie Du Rocher, IL, daughter of John Berghoff and Elizabeth Droste Berghoff. The Berghoff family moved to Arkansas about 1918. After living there two years, they moved to Fornfelt, which is now Scott City. John and Elizabeth had three children: Theodore (b. Nov. 9, 1905; d. Feb. 25, 1987); Agnes (b. April 16, 1908; d. Sept. 28, 1986); and Magdalen (b. March 29, 1910; d. Jan. 17, 1996).

Theodore married Lorena Georger. They had two children: Leo (b. July 28, 1935) and Betty (b. June 29, 1949). Magdalen married Matthew Urhahn. (This is the way he spelled his name. He was my dad's first cousin). They had two children: Gilbert (b. March 6, 1935) and Marilyn (b. March 12, 1937).

Agnes married Stephen Uhrhan. They had five children; Irene (b. Feb. 1, 1932); Vernon (b. July 20, 1934); Cletus (b. April 25, 1937); Rosemary (b. Nov. 14, 1941) and Helen (b. March 18, 1944).

Vernon worked at the shoe factory at Chaffee and at Todt Sheet Metal Shop. He served in the army from 1957-1959 and again from 1961-1962. After that he worked for B&J refrigeration and joined the Pipe Fitters Union No. 562. He worked for the pipe fitters until he retired. He married Jerry Glueck June 4, 1960. They lived in Cape Girardeau. They had three children: Sandra (b. March 23, 1961); Tamara (b. Dec. 3, 1968) and Michael (b. June 15, 1977).

Cletus lived in Scott County with his parents until he was 35 years old. He worked in construction as a laborer, truck driver and heavy equipment operator. He married Sue Carolyn Koester July 29, 1972. They lived in Jackson, MO. They had two daughters: Brenda (b. March 19, 1974) and Erin (b. Sept. 12, 1976).

Rosemary married Ronnie Kern Aug. 4, 1962. They live in Scott City. They had two children, Sherry (b. May 21, 1963) and Gary (b. Oct. 25, 1966). Rosemary worked at the shoe factory in Chaffee, Holiday Inn in Cape Girardeau, library in Scott City and is currently working at the Post Office in Benton, MO.

Helen worked at the Scott County Court House, first as a typist for Frobase Abstract Company and then for John J. Bollinger at the recorders office. She became a deputy recorder of Scott County on her 21st birthday. Helen married Fred Drew on April 23, 1966. She moved to St. Louis and now lives in Imperial, MO. They had five children: Timothy (b. Jan. 31, 1967); Jeffrey (b. April 27, 1968; d. July 8, 1968 from Infant Death Syndrome); Daniel (b. Feb. 10, 1970); Paula (b. Nov. 20, 1973) and Patty (b. Dec. 21, 1979).

I, Irene, started working at the International Shoe Factory in Cape Girardeau when I was 16 years old. I worked there for nine years, and then stayed home to raise my family and be a farmer's wife. I married Cornelius Blattel on May 8, 1954. Cornelius was a son of Herman and Blanche (Hamm) Blattel. When we married we moved into the house that Cornelius's grandfather, Joe Blattel, and built. Our farm is located two miles east of Kelso, MO. We lived all our married lives on this farm. Our son, Larry, now lives in the house that his great-grandfather built. His children are the fifth generation of Blattel's to live there. Since Cornelius died Feb. 29, 1996, Larry has taken over the farming operation. Cornelius and I had three children: Darlene Marie (b. June 11, 1958) and twins Larry Joe and Mary Jo (b. July 4, 1961). Larry married Tina Marie Beussink on April 16, 1983. They had three children: Emily Renee (b. Jan. 20, 1988); Elaine Marie (April 4, 1990) and Nicole Elizabeth (b. Feb. 26, 1993).

Mary married Jim Brinkmeyer on April 12, 1986 and had two children: Elizabeth Ann "Beth" (b. Feb. 23, 1987) and Stephen James (b. Sept. 3, 1989). Mary is a teacher. She works at St. Joseph School in Imperial, MO. They live in Barnhart, MO.

Darlene married John Beardslee on July 19, 1980 and lived near Hillsboro, MO for seven years and then moved to Bloomsdale. They recently bought a farm near Altenburg, MO where they plan to move soon. Darlene is a teacher in St. Genevieve, MO. They have two children, John Paul (b. Jan. 7, 1983) and Julie Marie (b. March 5, 1984).

My hobbies are quilting and family tree. I went to Germany in 1992 and visited the area where my ancestors came from. We stayed with and met many cousins on my mother's side of the family. Many of them are teachers. I also saw the church where my great-grandfather was baptized. It was beautiful. *Submitted by Irene Blattel*

URHAHN – Lawrence Urhahn was born in New Hamburg, MO, Nov. 10, 1876, the son of Peter Urhahn and Elizabeth Kunz Urhahn. Lawrence married Catherine Geisner (b. Dec. 3, 1882; d. May 3, 1938), at Guardian Angel Church in Oran, MO on Nov. 7, 1899. She was the daughter of Joseph Geisner and Mary Gosche Geisner. Lawrence and Catherine had ten children: Theon, Zeno, Matthew, Leo, Henry, Gregory (served in WWII in Navy), Clara, Harold (died in infancy), and Raymond (died at 5 or 6). They were a farming family. Lawrence died Dec. 1, 1958.

Theon was born Jan. 22, 1901 at New Hamburg, Mo. Theon married Lorena Wesley Hawkins (b. Nov. 14, 1907) at St. Lawrence Church in New Hamburg on Oct. 26, 1926. She was the daughter of Wesley Hawkins and Anna Bollinger Hawkins. Theon and Lorena had seven children: Wesley (Boodle, b. May 11, 1928; d. Aug. 14, 1981), Marvin (Curly, b. Dec. 5, 1931; d. July 16, 2001), Patricia (b. Feb. 23, 1936), Edwin "Butch," (b. Aug. 19, 1942), Joan (b. Nov. 17, 1944), and James M. (b. Dec. 29, 1947; d. June 24, 1997) and Harold, who died from jaundice and liver failure at two weeks old (b. Feb. 3, 1939; d. March 18, 1939). Theon was a carpenter for several

years. He worked winters for Maas-Steffen Fur Company in St. Louis, MO and worked at Urhahn Service Station in Benton for 40 plus years. Lorena was a homemaker and wonderful cook. Theon died April 30, 1977. Lorena died Aug. 1, 1985.

Left to right: James, Wesley, Theon, Joan, Lorena, Edwin, Pat, and Marvin, 1976.

Wesley married Edith Muriel Eastwood May 7, 1951. They had five children: Brenda Jenkins, Deborah, Thomas (died age 7), Darlene and Dennis. Wesley worked at the Sinclair Gas Terminal in New Madrid, MO and the family resided in Benton. Marvin married Ruth Ann LeGrand Oct. 13, 1951 at Guardian Angel Church in Oran, MO. They had six children: Gail Ann, Charlene, Richard, Kenneth, Sherry and Jackie. Marvin managed Urhahn Station in Benton for 40 plus years.

Patricia married William Schlosser Nov. 20, 1954 at St. Denis Church in Benton. They had four children: Denise, Ronald, Carla, and Alicia. Patricia "Pat" is bookkeeper for Schlosser Construction Company in Benton.

Edwin married Darlene Schwartz. He is president of First Tire and Wheel in Cape Girardeau, MO. They live in Cape Girardeau.

Joan married John A. Kerby Aug. 30, 1973 at Metropolis, IL. John is a retired towboat pilot. Joanie is a singer-musician and homemaker. They reside in Benton, MO. Joanie had one daughter, Mary Morrill, who was born and died Oct. 31, 1964.

James "Jim" entered the Army Oct. 26, 1966. He served in Vietnam from Nov. 19, 1967 until Oct. 18, 1968. Jim married Barbara Scherer July 26, 1969 at St. Denis church in Benton. They had one son, James Joseph. Jim worked in tire sales, most recently at Campus Auto in Cape Girardeau.

URHAHN – Marvin Zeno "Curly" Urhahn was born in Benton, MO on Dec. 5, 1931, the second son of Theon and Lorena Hawkins Urhahn. His older brother was Wesley, better known as Boodle, and his younger siblings were Pat, Edwin (Butch), Joanie, and Jim. Curly attended St. Denis Catholic School until eighth grade and then graduated from Benton High School. He started working with his dad at the service station in Benton in 1947. In the early years Curly and Boodle sometimes slept at the station so they could service trucks that came through the busy highway during the middle of the night. Later on, both Butch and Jim worked at the station as well. Curly operated Urhahn Service Station, at the corner of Highway 61 and Highway 77 in Benton, until November of 1990. He sold gas, fixed flat tires and serviced cars and trucks of all varieties.

On Oct. 13, 1951 Curly married Ruth Ann LeGrand (b. Jan. 25, 1932), the fourth child of Zeno Peter and Welden Stike LeGrand of Oran, MO.

Curly and Ruth Ann had six children. Gail (b. Sept. 14, 1952) teaches in the Psychology Department at Southeast Missouri State University.

She is married to Daniel Overby and has two sons, Jeffrey Leonard (b. July 4, 1982) and Douglas Marvin (b. Jan. 30, 1986). They live in Cape Girardeau.

Charlene (b. May 25, 1954) is bookkeeper for Scott County R-IV School District. Charlene is married to Mark Camren and has two children, Travis Glenn Green (b. Feb. 13, 1976) and Audrey Marie Camren (b. March 30, 1993). They live in Benton.

Richard (b. June 5, 1955) is a marketing associate with Hardin Sysco Food Company. He is married to the former Doris (Jeanie) Asher. Richard has three children and one grandchild. Neil Richard was born April 15, 1979 and is the father of Ava Nicole Urhahn, born April 7, 2000. Casie Nicole was born Aug. 16, 1981. Austin Andrew was born March 24, 1991. They live in Cape Girardeau.

The Marvin Urhahn Family. Back row: Charlene, Kenny, Richard, and Sherry. Front: Gail, Marvin, Ruth, and Jackie.

Kenneth (b. July 28, 1956) works for Schlumberger-Sema Services. He is married to the former Kelly Kremer and has three children, Blake Kenneth (b. Oct. 25, 1985), Haley Brooke (b. Nov. 28, 1989) and Chase Andrew (b. Aug. 9, 1996). They live in Cape Girardeau.

Sherry (b. Dec. 29, 1958) is a nurse at Scott County Health Department. She is married to Jamie Burger and has three daughters, Vanessa Marie (b. July 23, 1979), Allison Anne (b. July 30, 1982) and Paris Nicolette (b. Jan. 7, 1991).

Jacqueline (b. Aug. 15, 1961) is a homemaker. She is married to Frank Rodriguez and has three children, Frank Andrew (b. July 14, 1992), Danielle Elizabeth (b. Sept. 29, 1994), and Christina Marie (b. March 25, 1998). They live in St. Charles, MO.

Curly passed away on July 16, 2001. He is sorely missed by family and friends who love him dearly. He is buried in St. Denis Cemetery in Benton, MO.

VERNON – Josie Mae Watts Vernon was born Nov. 25, 1898 in Richwood, MO. Josie was the daughter of Robert Mitchell Watts and Cynthia Boutwell Watts.

While quite small, the Watts family moved to Dexter, MO where Josie and her sisters, Lennie and Bertia (twins, Roberta Morris Hutchinson and Robert D. Morris) grew to womanhood, and were educated in the public schools.

On Dec. 23, 1916 Josie and Harry Lehman Vernon drove to Bloomfield, MO in a horse and buggy to procure a marriage license. They were accompanied by her sister, Lennie Watts and his sister, Isabelle Vernon. They were married that same afternoon by the Methodist minister at his home.

They were given a "linen and granite" shower on their return to Dexter.

Harry worked at the Dexter Ice Plant before becoming the bookkeeper for Scott County Milling Company for 20 years. He later owned Vernon's Hardware and Lumber Company in Bloomfield until his death on July 27, 1959.

They had three daughters, all born in Dexter, MO: Virginia Mae Vernon Keaton, (one daughter, two grandchildren, five great-grandchildren); Doris Elayne Vernon Davidson (two children, four granddaughters and three great grandaughters); and Harryette Elizabeth Vernon Aslin (six sons, and nine grandchildren).

Harry and Josie were members of the Methodist Church and took an active part in church work. Harry was the Church Treasurer for 20 years before becoming a member of the Official Board. He was a member of the Masonic Lodge.

Josie was a member of the Methodist Church for over

Josie Mae Watts Vernon

65 years, working many of those years in the primary department. She also belonged to the Order of Eastern Star. Josie was chosen "Woman of the Year 1975, by the Dexter Business and Professional Women's Club and the Stoddard County Soroptimist Club. She received this honor for her outstanding contributionsof her time and work toward the betterment of the community. Josie was Chairperson of the Easter Seals work for 16 years, helping children who could not help themselves. She was a volunteer worker in cancer efforts and for many years a member of the Monday Club plus a member of WCTU.

Josie helped and touched many individuals for many, many years. She died of cancer May 5, 1977 at Sikeston, MO.

VETTER – Vernon Linus Vetter was born Feb. 2, 1935 at Commerce, MO. His parents were George William Vetter, born March 17, 1899 at Oran, MO and Alvina Compas Vetter, born Jan. 20, 1906 at New Hamburg, MO. They were married May 18, 1926, at St. Denis Church at Benton, MO. They were members of this church and were residents of the Benton, MO area all their married life. George Vetter was a farmer all his life. George died Nov. 14, 1983, and Alvina died Nov. 29, 1990.

George Vetter's father was John Vetter, born Feb. 22, 1860 at New Hamburg, MO. He died June 22, 1940. His mother was Rose Scherer, born July 22, 1861, at New Hamburg, MO. She died June 14, 1947. Alvina's father was Henry Compas, born Aug. 27, 1864 at New Hamburg, MO. He died Jan. 22, 1943. Her mother was Regina Scherer Compas, born May 17, 1871 at New Hamburg, MO. She died Jan. 16, 1957.

George and Alvina had six children. Loretta Clara Vetter, born June 17, 1927. Loretta is a nun with the Order of Sisters of St. Francis, in Joiliet, IL. Alfred George Vetter, born July 21, 1929. Rita Marie Vetter was born July 13, 1931. Rita married Thomas Drury from Kelso, MO. Thomas Drury died May 22, 1970. Vernon Linus Vetter was born Feb. 2, 1935. Georgia Ann Vetter was born June 17, 1937 and died May 8, 1939. Mary Frances Vetter was born June 12, 1942. Mary married Robert Todt of Oran, MO.

Vernon Vetter was married on Oct. 11, 1958 at St. Lawrence Church at New Hamburg, MO to Janet Sue Dirnberger, born Dec. 20, 1939. Vernon and Janet are members of St. Denis Catholic Church and residents of the Benton, MO area. Vernon has been a farmer all his life. His two sons, James and Jeffery, are in the farming business with him. Vernon and Janet had four children: Victoria Ann (b. July 13, 1959)'; Cynthia Marie Vetter (b. June 25, 1960); James Andrew Vetter (b. July 8, 1961) and Jeffrey Gerard Vetter (b. July 27, 1965). Victoria married Randol Thomas Hagar, at Benton, Mo. They live in Wake Village, TX. They have one daughter, Rachel Elizabeth Hagar, born in Jackson, MS on Dec. 23, 1984. Cynthia married Franklin Thomas Glueck at Benton, MO. They live in New Hamburg, MO. They have one son, Adam Francis Glueck, born in Cape Girardeau, MO in Dec. 19, 1985 and one daughter, Hannah Marie Glueck born in Cape Girardeau, MO on April 14, 1989. James married Christina Webb at Kelso, Mo. They live in Benton, MO. They have two sons, Brady James Vetter, born in Cape Girardeau, MO on March 10, 1994 and Caleb Christian Vetter, born in Cape Girardeau, MO on Jan. 18, 1999. Jeffrey married Jamie Spane at Benton, MO. They live in Benton, MO. They have one daughter, Ashley Renee Vetter, born in Cape Girardeau, MO on Sept. 24, 1988 and one son, Benjamin George Vetter, born in Cape Girardeau, MO on Feb. 9, 1994.

WADE – Montrose Pallen Wade, eldest son of Dr. R. Bay Wade and Ann Henderson Wade, was born Aug. 13, 1866. He attended the public schools of Benton, Bellevue Collegiate Institute of Caledonia, MO and the Rolla School of Mines and Metallurgy. He was a member of the Knights of Pythias and AOUW. At the age of 22 he was appointed Deputy Sheriff under Sheriff J. B. Greer. He also served as Sheriff of Scott County and at the time of his death, was a Deputy US Collector of Internal Revenue,

Montrose Pallen Wade

It was near midnight when Mont Wade, Judge O'Bryan, Charley Hawkins, Clark Russell, W. H. and Mike Heisserer, John Hutson and others visited Bonnefon's Saloon for a "nightcap." They were chatting and enjoying a pleasant evening, when after two attempts by Will Heisserer to have their order filled by Dave Matney (temporary barkeeper, who was being very indifferent and insolent), Heisserer joking remarked, "If you can't wait on this crowd I'll do it myself." This angered Matney and he swore and became more sullen. Heisserer apologized, saying all was in good humor. This apology seemed to cause Matney to feel his importance and he indicated by his actions all was not right. At this time Wade spoke and said no harm was intended and no one wanted to put him out. At this time Matney insulted Wade. Wade spoke up to chastise him for his attitude of indifference towards his patrons. Only a few words were uttered before Matney took a .44 revolver from the cash drawer and shot Mont Wade in the chest. Wade fell on the floor. The patrons all rushed out except James Humphrey, who was holding Wade. Matney held the gun on them, robbed the cash drawer, and ran. Drs. Freling, Butler and Wade (Mont's brother) were summoned, but Mont Wade died in about 15 minutes and never spoke a word. His funeral was reported as the biggest since his father died 20 years before. Charles Speck, US Collector of Internal Revenue, praised Wade highly. He said, Wade during his two years with his office; had not a blemish on his official conduct and it gave him pleasure to testify to his high character, earnestness and efficiency as an officer. From all reports Mont Wade was held in high esteem. He was only 29 years old at his death on Oct. 29, 1895. *Submitted by Lisa Wade Vetter*

WADE – Dr. Robert Bay Wade was born at West Liberty, KY on July 24, 1832. As a young man he immigrated to Scott County, MO and settled in Benton, MO. He married Ann Henderson, daughter of Dr. Alex S. Henderson and Mary Duncan, Nov. 17, 1858 in Benton, MO. She died Nov. 2, 1900.

They had nine children as follows: Mary Adeline and Gertie Delilah, twins, born Sept. 6, 1859, and they died in infancy. Gertie died Sept. 6, 1859 and Mary Adeline Sept. 4, 1862. An infant daughter was born Sept. 2, 1862, and died the same day. Other children were: Lelia M. Wade, born

Robert Bay Wade

Aug. 8, 1863; Montrose Pallen Wade, born Aug. 13, 1866; Chapman Walker Wade, born May 11, 1868; Julia Victoria Wade, born April 14, 1870; Sydney Johnson Wade, born Nov. 10, 1872 and Robert Bay Wade Jr., born Jan. 7, 1875.

Dr. Wade practiced medicine in Benton and the surrounding territory and from 1872-1876 he served in the Missouri House of Representatives.

During his tenure in Jefferson City some of the legislative topics were the same as we have today: schools, revenue and roads. However, one big difference was the Civil War had ended a few years back and there was a problem of rebuilding the state. In a letter to the editor, D. L. Hoffman, *The Morley Advocate*, he reviewed some ideas Bate County was using and thought they could be applied to Scott County.

Much of the time he was in Jefferson City he corresponded with his wife and children on a regular basis. Anne Wade was home in Benton with their small children. These were love letters of a different nature. From these letters, it is evident he was a concerned and caring husband and father. He continually saw to their welfare even when in Jefferson City. He sent remedies for the children's ailments, advised on discipline, and had household items delivered to them. Once on a trip through St. Louis on his way to Jefferson City, he sent a keg of molasses. He sent reading material and gifts to the children regularly. He always signed letters to his wife Ann, "Thine forever, R. B. Wade."

On the morning of his death, May 28, 1876, he had delivered a baby. Later in the day he suffered a heart attack and died.

Descendants of Dr. Robert B. Wade: Montrose Pallen Wade, oldest son, attended Benton schools. During 1883 he attended Bellevue Collegiate Institute of Caledonia, Mo and in 1885-1886 attended Schools of Mines and Metallurgy of Rolla. He was a Deputy Sheriff at age 22 under Sheriff of Scott County and, at the time of his death, was a deputy US Collector of Internal Revenue.

Dr. Sydney J. Wade married Lillian Proffit and practiced medicine in Benton as his father had. He also served in the Missouri House from 1906-1908. He was a Democrat and his father had been a Republican. This couple had one adopted son, Sydney J. Wade.

Lelia M. Wade, daughter of Dr. R. Bay Wade and Ann H. Wade, married Dr. J. S. Freling. They had one daughter, Cleopatra Freling Margiott; no grandchildren.

Robert Bay Wade Jr. and Julia V. Wade, son and daughter of R. Bay Wade and Ann H. Wade, after school in Caledonia, MO, spent most of their lives at the family home in Benton. Robert was the overseer of the farmland in the area. A family tree was compiled by Julia V. Wade of her mother's family going back to 1796. She was bedfast for a good part of her later years. She faithfully researched this genealogy and wrote several copies by hand.

Chapman Walker Wade, son of Dr. R. Bay and Ann Henderson Wade was born May 11, 1868 in Benton. On July 3, 1889, he was married to Lula Perry at Charleston and May 22, 1892, was united with the Benton Methodist Church. Seven children were born to this couple: Charles Byron Wade, Clara Wade Wood, Jessie Wade Wolsey, Marvin Wade, Robert Wade, Carrol Wade and Allen Wade. The family lived on various farms near Benton and in Benton. Mrs. Wade died April 20, 1906 and was buried in the Benton Cemetery. A couple of years after her death Chapman lost his sight. He moved to Oran and for the exception of portions of 1910 and 1911, which were spent in Montana, "Chap", as he was familiarly known, spent all his life in Scott County. He was sick for about six weeks with Bright's disease and died July 31, 1931. It is interesting to note all the living descendants of Dr. R. Bay Wade, are Chapman's extended family of great grandchildren and other great-greats down the line. Some of those descendants still living in the area are: Mary Jane Wade, Oran, daughter of Carrol and Mary Wade; Charles B. Wade Jr., son of C. Byron and Cora E. Wade and Wilma Wade Cox of Carlisle, AR, daughter of C. Byron and Cora E. Wade. *Submitted by Evangeline "Lynn" Wade*

WAGONER – Allerson Alexander Wagoner "A. A." was born on Oct. 21, 1864 in Illinois to David and Fannie Wagoner. He married Sarah Frances Hamblin on Sept. 18, 1887. She was born Aug. 19, 1869, the daughter of Henry Hamblin and Anna Breedlove, in Tennessee.

They farmed in Kentucky and Tennessee until 1900- 1907 when they moved from Austin Springs, TN by covered wagon to settle in the Diehlstadt/Blodgett area. They crossed the Mississippi River on a ferry and since the trip took several days they spent their night on quilts under the stars. In 1926 they moved between Morley and Oran. Sarah Wagoner died on Feb. 15, 1930, and A. A. Wagoner died on Feb. 10, 1937. They had six children, the youngest dying at birth and is buried by them in Blodgett Cemetery.

Zora Wagoner was born April 29, 1889 in Tennessee. She married Oda Felty (Feb. 5, 1883) on March 20, 1907. Oda Felty died on June 26, 1957 at Chaffee. Zora Felty died on Nov. 17, 1976 at Chaffee. Both are buried in Cape City Cemetery. They had nine children: Pearl Felty Sandusky (b. Feb. 5, 1909); Ruby Felty Sandusky (b. Oct. 11, 1910); Opal Felty Cook (b. May 6, 1912); Grace "Gloria" Felty Weinberger (b. April 26, 1914); Zella Felty Story (b. Sept. 21, 1918); Doris Felty Scott (b. Jan. 3, 1923); Odell Felty (b. May 15, 1925); Marvin Felty (b. July 11, 1927) and Melvin Felty (b. Jan. 19, 1930).

Anna Wagoner was born in Kentucky Dec. 7, 1891. She married George Brent in 1913. George Brent died in Chaffee. Anna died and is buried in Brownsville, TX on April 6, 1954. They had one daughter, Christine Brent Rydel, born November 1912.

Bertha Wagoner was born on July 27, 1895 in Austin Springs, TN. She married Otto Rettig on March 21, 1915 at Benton, MO. He was born Nov. 24, 1892 in Evansville, IN. Bertha Rettig died in Sikeston on Oct. 22, 1971. Otto Rettig died on Aug. 8, 1987 at Sikeston. They are both

buried in Memorial Park Cemetery. They had eight children: Sherman Rettig (b. Oct. 24, 1912; d. April 1, 1976 in Sikeston); Laverne Rettig (b. Oct. 24, 1918; Cleo Rettig Davis (b. Oct. 19, 1920); Willine Rettig Miller (b. Feb. 14, 1922); Sadie Rettig James (b. Sept. 9, 1924); Lola Rettig Adock (b. June 30, 19270;

Back row: Zora, Bertha, and Beatrice. Front: A.A. and Sarah Wagoner.

Dorothy Rettig Broderick (b. July 29, 1931; d. Dept. 2, 1997) and Harold Otto Allen Rettig (b. Jan. 10, 1937).

Allen Wagoner was born in Tennessee on Oct. 18, 1897. He married Agnes Patton. She died on May 25, 1954. Allen Wagoner died on Sept. 6, 1974. They are both buried in the Oran Cemetery. They had one son, Hershel Wagoner, born Aug. 3, 1920.

Beatrice Wagoner was born Oct. 11, 1907 in Diehlstadt, MO. She married Leslie Inman on Aug. 29, 1923. He died Sept. 26, 1978. Beatrice died Jan. 26, 1996. They are both buried in the Oran Cemetery. They had two children: Jean Inman Wolsey (b. Jan. 23, 1925) and J. L. Inman (b. Dec. 19, 1926; d. July 3, 1971 in Illinois). *Submitted by Willine Rettig Miller*

WALDSCHMIDT – During the advent and period of the 1930 Great Depression, Mary Waldschmidt was born on June 28, 1926 the daughter of Louis and Margaret McKamie Waldschmidt. Lester Miller Jr. was born July 30, 1926, the son of Lester Miller Sr. and Easter Farris Miller. A letter written by Louis Waldschmidt during those troubled times expresses the hopelessness of many citizens. Dec. 11, 1932 "We have all done without money so long that we are used to it. You would be astounded to know how little people have to manage with. As for myself, I can't for the life of me see how we have managed to live – I do always manage to raise a good garden and plan to put up everything in the way of food such as potatoes, dry beans and peas, turnips, onions and nuts, etc, - leaving only a few other essentials to buy, and when I say essentials, it is surprising how these can be limited through necessity. I want to be doing something, but cannot find a thing to make a dollar. My desire is to get a small farm and raise a little truck farm stuff, a couple cows, a few chickens, and sell enough to buy the essentials. This is only a dream now, for it takes a little money even for such a moderate desire, and I see nothing in the future to build any hopes on."

Louis Waldschmidt (b. March 1, 1883; d. Sept. 22, 1951) and Margaret McKamie Waldschmidt (b. March 21, 1901; d. June 10, 1988), both having grown up in Cairo, IL were newly married when they settled in Benton, MO in 1921, where he established a sawmill in Lambertville, taking advantage of the fine timber growing in the area, along with access to the Frisco Rail Line nearby. After the depression, in 1934, he was able to sawmill again, this time moving his mill to McMullin (near Sikeston, MO), then on site south of Benton and big Island near Commerce, MO and finally Wickliffe, KY.

Lester Miller Sr. was born April 4, 1906 in Bollinger County, MO moving to Morley, MO with his family in 1918. Easter Farris was born Feb. 23, 1907 on the Harbison farm south of Lambertville, later moving to Benton with her family. She and Lester were married in 1925 and spent all their life in Benton. Easter will be remembered as the first librarian of Benton Branch of Riverside Regional Library, which opened May 12, 1957 in the vacated Frobase Drug Store building. Lester served as deputy sheriff during the terms of Sheriff's John Hobbs and Early Malcolm. He worked for Texas Eastern Transmission Company in Oran, Mo from 1948 until his death April 30, 1967. Easter died Oct. 29, 1997. They were parents of three sons: Lester Jr. (b. July 30, 1926), Jean (b. July 15, 1928;d. Dec. 19, 1928) and Thomas (b. March 24, 1936).

Lester Jr. and Mary graduated from Benton High School in 1944. Lester enlisted in the US Air Force during WWII and reported for duty January 1945. He was discharged October 1946. Lester and Mary were married Oct. 20, 1947 in the Benton Methodist Church and lived in Cape Girardeau, MO three years after their marriage. In 1950 they moved back to Benton and Lester went to work for Waldschmidt Lumber Company in Wickliffe, KY where he remained until his retirement in 1995. In 2001 they moved to Cape Girardeau. They are the parents of three children: David Miller of Cape Girardeau, MO, Rebecca O'Neal of Denver, CO, Sarah Boeker of Arnold, MO and six grandchildren, Brian and Derek Miller, Margaret and Michael O'Neal, and Irina and Anton Boeker.

WALTER – Ludwig "Louis" Walter, born about 1806, married Anna Maria "Mary" Eidol, born about 1805. They had four children: Barbara, Jacob, Louisa and Louis. Jacob was born July 25, 1835, in Alsace, France. Alsace was then a part of Germany. Jacob came to America with his family about 1844 in 1845. The family settled in Pittsburgh, PA, before moving to Monroe County, OH in 1849. Jacob married Margaretha Hoffman on March 30, 1856. They had four children: Emile "Amelia", George Wilhelm "William", Mary Salome "Sally", and Elisabeth "Lizzy".

Jacob served the Union forces in the Civil War from Aug. 15, 1862 until May 30, 1865. In 1866, Jacob Walter moved his family to Little York, Washington County, IN, where Albert was born. In 1867, the family moved to Scott County, MO and lived on a farm near Kelso. Jacob was the overseer of a sawmill at New Hamburg.

Two children died in 1867, apparently of typhoid fever. Albert died May 11, 1867, and Amelia died Aug. 30, 1867. Both were buried in the old Eisleben Lutheran Church Cemetery. Six additional children were born to Jacob and Margaretha in Scott county: Ottillia Louisa "Tillie", Magdalena "Lena", Anna, Louis David "Louie", Emma Julia, and Louisa Barbara "Lou".

Left to right: Anna Marie, Otto Walter holding twin great granddaughters Karen and Sharon Roth, Richard Roth.

George Wilhelm "William" Walter (b. July 27, 1858; d. Feb. 14, 1949), second child of Jacob, married Augusta Sander (b. 1860; d. May 16, 1907) in 1879. They had eight children: Elizabeth, Heinrich, Anna, Wilhelm, Otto, Albert, Augusta, and Emma.

Otto Friedrich (b. May 17, 1889; d. Dec. 13, 1971) married Anna Agatha Sander (b. Jan. 4, 1889; d. Aug. 30, 1935) on June 2, 1912. They had 11 children: Anna Marie, Martin George "Tige", Aletha Emma, Otto William "Pete"; Orville Calvin "Butch", Dorothy Elizabeth, Kathleen, Alfred "Irish", Lenos "Alex", Henry, and Charles Eugene. Of these children, three and/ or their families still live in Scott County.

Marie Walter (b. March 2, 1913; d. July 28, 1995) married Ernest Theodore Roth on Sept. 5, 1936. They had six children: Richard Walter, Ralph Leon, Rose Marie, Franklin Dorris, Donald George, and Ernestine Ann.

Dorothy Walter (b. May 16, 1922) married William Avery Hamm on Oct. 27, 1941. They had six sons: William Douglas "Doug", Jackie Ray, Glen Dewayne, Roger Keith, Mark Eugene and Bruce Alan.

Henry Walter (b. Aug. 24, 1931) married Rose Edith Lindeman on March 28, 1964. *Submitted by Richard Roth*

WELCH – Lawrence E. Welch, born Feb. 11, 1906, was united in marriage to Lottie B. King, born Jan. 22, 1907, on Jan. 31, 1925 in Pangburn, AR.

They spent several years farming in the Hayti, Portageville area. They farmed their land walking behind a plow that was pulled by two stubborn ole mules named Jake and Kate. They moved to the Sikeston area in 1944.

Lawrence and Lottie had ten children born to them, six sons and four daughters. Two of the sons died as infants. The sons are: Leon, married to Lea Sajez; Thomas (now deceased) married to Marie Dorlaque; Billy, married to Min Kowalchuk; and Larry, married to Donette Rinehart.

Lawrence and Lottie Welch's wedding day, January 31, 1925.

The daughters are: Laverne (now deceased) married to Kenneth Daucett; Ruth, now married to Howard Lane; Lillian, was married to Carl Weston; and Loretta, married Leonard M. "Jack" Skelton (now deceased).

After moving to Sikeston, six of the children, Thomas, Billy, Ruth, Lillian, Loretta and Larry attended the little one room Hunter School taught by Susie Cline. Leon, the oldest son graduated Wardell High School at the age of 16. Laverne, Billy, Lillian, Loretta, and Larry were graduates of Sikeston High School.

Lawrence died Feb. 29, 1948. Lottie and son, Billy, built a house at 807 East Kathleen in Sikeston.

Lottie worked in numerous restaurants and at the Missouri Delta community Hospital in order to care for her children.

All four sons served in the military. The two oldest sons, Leon and Thomas, served during WWII. Leon went on to make a career in the Air Force and later worked for Hues Airport before retiring in Rocklin, CA. Thomas owned and operated an automobile dealership. Billy worked for Hills Brothers Coffee Company in Kansas City before transferring to Cupertino, CA where he is currently retired. Larry owned and operated an automobile dealership in California and in Indianapolis, IN, where he now resides.

The oldest daughter, Laverne, and Kenneth owned and operated a florist shop in California.

Ruth and Howard were in real estate land development before retiring. After moving from Chicago to California, Lillian was employed by Lockheed Airport and the Los Angeles Police Department. She is currenlty a licensed Real Estate Broker for Re-Max in Valnecia, CA. Loretta was eployed by the Federal Reserve Bank in Downey, CA and in alterations in a men's specialty store in Sikeston for many years before retiring.

In 1953, Lottie Welch leased and operated the Palace Café on North Kingshighway. Lottie was known in the Sikeston area for her home cooking and her cloverleaf yeast rolls. She also leased and operated the Dunn Café Shop and the El-Capri Restaurant before she retired. While she was the proprietor of the Dunn coffee Shop, she was hosting a dinner for the Rotary Club to raise donations for the Ridgeway Home for homeless boys. She made the first contribution by endorsing their dinner check back to them. She also made many contributions to the Shady Acres Children's Home.

Lottie Welch died Aug. 30, 1984, leaving eight surviving children. These were four sons: Leon, Thomas, Billy and Larry and four daughters: Laverne, Ruth, Lillian and Loretta. She was also survived by 15 grandchildren and six great-grandchildren. *Submitted by Loretta (Welch) Skelton*

WELLS – Owen Dudley Wells Sr. (1889-1960) one of eight children of William Wells and Caroline Wyatt of Ravenden Springs, Randolph County, AR married Lavinia Jane Eaves Wells (1891-1968) one of nine children of Benjamin L. Eaves and Jane Smith Eaves of Ravenden Springs, Randolph County, AR. There were six children born to this union, four born in Arkansas and two in Missouri; Sylvia Wells Hunnicutt Manis (1909-1973), Opal J. Wells Harris (1912), Rose Marie Wells Bryan (1915), Unnamed (192?), Unnamed (1923) buried in Old Benton Cemetery off Highway 61, and Owen Dudley Wells Jr. (1925) born in Scott County, MO.

Lavinia (Eaves) Wells and Owen Dudley Wells Sr. (seated) with their children: Owen Jr., Sylvia, Opal, and Rose Marie.

Owen Dudley Wells Sr. and a hired hand came to Missouri in 1923 in a covered wagon with all their belongings, including cows, horses and chickens. The family came later on a train because his wife was pregnant. They were one of the first families in Scott County to raise cotton for a living. They lived and worked the same farm until his death. A portion of the farm is still in the family. Both are buried in Forest Hills Cemetery on Highway 61-77, Scott County, near Morley.

WELLS – Owen Dudley Wells Jr. (1925) the sixth child of Owen Dudley Wells Sr. (1889-1960) and Lavinia Jane Eaves Wells (1891-1968), and Ruth Jean Smith Wells (1929) the sixth child of Jake B. Smith (1884-1977) and Pansy Louella Lane Smith (1901-1976) were married Jan. 29, 1947 at the Morley Baptist Church. Both were born at

Benton, Scott County, MO. Owen and Ruth Jean were both delivered by the same Dr. Hall of Benton, MO. Owen attended school in Benton, Scott County, and served in the Navy during WWII in the Pacific and helped bring troops home from France after the war, from 1943 to 1946. Ruth Jean graduated from Morley High School and worked for several companies in Cape Girardeau and Scott Counties.

Wells - Smith family gathering

To this union four children were born: Carolyn Kathleen Wells (b. June 14, 1950); Marilyn Jean Wells (b. March 19, 1954) married William Kluesner and Robert Tuey; Owen Dudley Wells III (b. June 1, 1958) married Maureen J. Stengel; and Sherilyn Diana Wells (b. Aug. 27, 1959) married David Burger and Robert Hasselback.

There are nine grandchildren: William James Kluesner (b. July 4, 1975); Jennifer Leah Burger (b. Nov. 4, 1977); Jeremy Jason Kluesner (b. Feb. 11, 1979); Charles Jacob Wells (b. Aug 8, 1979); Christopher Joseph Tuey (b. June 3, 1980); Kristina Dawn Tuey (b. Oct. 12, 1984); Owen Dudley Wells IV (b. Dec. 16, 1985); Ryan Justin Wells (b. Nov. 24, 1987); and Daniel Joseph Wells (b. Nov. 24, 1987; d. Nov. 26, 1987).

They have five great-grandchildren: William Robert Burger (b. Sept. 20, 1993); Stephen Douglas Burger (b. Nov. 19, 1999); Anna Marie Burger (b. March 15, 2001); Letycia Kluesner (b. Feb. 22, 1998) and Larissia Love Kluesner (b. Feb. 14, 2001).

WELTER – Edward Leo Welter, the son of Michael Welter and Magdalena (Diebold) Welter, was born on March 21, 1894. He was one of nine children born to Michael and "Lena", who were the third settlers in Kelso, MO. He was baptized in St. Augustine's Catholic Church, and attended St. Augustine's Elementary School. After completing the eighth grade, he went to work at 13 years of age for the Kelso Milling Corporation.

On Sept. 25, 1917 he married Eleanora "Ella" Pfefferkorn, the daughter of Mathias and Caroline "Georger" Pfefferkorn, also early farmers in the Kelso community.

Ed and Ella Welter 50th anniversary, 1967.

On Oct. 2, 1917 shortly after their marriage, he was inducted into the Army during WWI. He was sent to Camp Funston, KS and served as

Bugler for his company. ON May 10, 1918, he was sent to Brest, France. He served overseas with Company F, 110 Engineers, 35th Division.

He saw active duty in the Argons Forest and St. Mihiel Drive in France. During this time he kept a daily diary describing the progress of the War, his work in the Engineers, and other incidents as they traveled through France. They also dug trenches and strung barbed wire in preparation for the final battles. He remained in France until the end of the war and returned to the States on May 3, 1919.

He served from Oct. 2, 1917 until May 3, 1919 (579 days).

The diary is on microfilm in the archives in Rolla, MO.

On his return to Kelso, he returned to work for the Kelso Milling Company. He took a correspondence business course, and became manager of the Mill in 1919. Ed and Ella Welter became sole owners in 1937.

He retired in 1959 after 52 years of continuous service. Edward Leo Welter died of cancer of the palate on June 6, 1975.

Ella Pfefferkorn died of emphysema and chronic bronchitis on July 4, 1983. Three children were born to Edward L. Welter and Ella Pfefferkorn Welter: Doris Marie Welter, married John S. Smith; LaVerne Caroline Welter, married Robert C. Rosenquist; and Laura Jean "Lolly" Welter, married Paul L. Robert.

Eleven grandchildren were born to Edward L. Welter and Ella Pfefferkorn Welter: Jack E. Smith, Myra E. "Jill" Smith Glaus, Richard E. Smith (stillborn), Luann G. Smith Pfau, Geralyn M. Smith Beussink, Carl E. "Dusty" Rosenquist, Roger A. Rosenquist, Chris R. Rosenquist, Cheryl L. Robert Ziegler, Daryl G. Robert, and Lisa K. Robert Beussink.

Twenty-five great-grandchildren were born to Edward L. Welter and Ella Pfefferkorn Welter: Vivian Yvette Smith Bohannon, Michael Edward Smith, Heidi Nicole Glaus, Jodi Rae Glaus, Erin Elizabeth Pfau, Matthew James Pfau, Casey Marie Beussink (stillborn), Cory John Beussink, Brooke Allison Beussink; Robert Lee Rosenquist, Ryan Christopher Rosenquist, Kara Rosenquist Amos, Christopher Rosenquist, Nathan Alan Rosenquist, Megan Elizabeth Rosenquist, Matthew Oliver Rosenquist, Elizabeth Marie Rosenquist, Madline Jo Rosenquist, Michael Christopher Rosenquist, Toby Lee Holmes, Jason Paul Robert, Nicholas Kent Robert, Miranda Nicole Robert, Madison Elyse Robert and Courtney Nicole Beussink. *Submitted by Mrs. Paul L. Robert*

WELTER – This is the story of the Victor and Lillie Welter family. Victor "Vick" was born in 1911 to Henry J. and Juliana (Westrich) Welter of New Hamburg. He had five brothers and sisters: Joe, Tony, Zeno 'Sam", Rose (Dannenmueller) and Sylvia (Glastetter).

Lillie was born in 1915 to Nick and Nellie (Arnold) Ledure of Commerce. Her three brothers were Bill, Leo and Frank.

They were married in New Hamburg in 1933 and moved to Benton in 1947. They had 12 children, Dewayne, Patsy (Peters), Jerome, Geraldine (Lawson), Larry and Garry (twins), Linda (Hite), Charlie, Marion (a.k.a. Murphy), Paul (a.k.a. Dudley), Michael (a.k.a. Melon) and Vicky (Guth).

Vick served in WWII and was employed at Theon Robert Farm, Eli Walker Garment Factory at Scott City, Pat's Gas at Benton, and as a mail carrier.

Lillie also worked at Eli Walker, picked cotton for Ben Meyer, picked blackberries, cooked, sewed and ironed on many occasion, all while

raising 12 kids. She enjoyed dancing, quilting and bingo. She is a member of the American Legion Ladies Auxiliary.

Front row: Geraldin, Gary, Vickie, Paul, Larry, Charlie, and Michael. Back: Linda, Marion, Patsy, and Jerome. Not pictured: DeWayne.

Vick passed away in 1975. Lillie still lives in Benton. Half of her children still live in Scott County and all still live in Missouri. Dewayne passed away in 1987. Lillie has 33 grandchildren and 35 great-grandchildren.

WELTER – Nickolaus/ Nicholas Welter a farmer, born March 18, 1818 in Belgium, immigrated to America in 1832, married Katharine Gosche, the daughter of Henry Gosche and Barbara (Peters), on March 6, 1848 in Canton, OH. Two children were born in Ohio: Henry in 1845, served as a private in Company "B" 5th Regiment, Missouri Calvary during the Civil War. He died in the US Hospital at Mounds, IL on Sept. 6, 1862 and is buried in the National Cemetery in Mounds City, IL. Louisa Anna (1848-1940) married John B. Messmer on Aug. 10, 1865 in St. Vincent's Catholic Church in Cape Girardeau, MO. They were the parents of 10 children: John Valentine, Mary Katharine, John William, Catharine, Maria Rosalia, Frank Peter (died in infancy), Frank Joseph, John Frank, Albert Louis and Theresa Alvina. Mr. Messmer died on July 22, 1908 and Louisa Anna married Charles Heisserer on Feb. 20, 1912, as his third wife. Louisa died Dec. 28, 1940 and is buried in St. Augustine Cemetery at Kelso.

June 21, 1959. Back row: Andy LeGrand, Ed Welter, Emil Dohogne, Joe Welter, Gus Welter, Leo Welter. Front: Agnes Welter LeGrand, Eleanora (Pfefferkorn) Welter, Dora (Welter) Dohogne, Theresa (Heuring) Welter, Emma (Schlosser) Welter, and Pauline (Welter) Menz.

The family came to southeast Missouri about the mid 1850s, and they had eight more children: John Henry (1852-1925) married Sophia Dannenmueller on Feb. 9, 1875 at New Hamburg. They were the parents of three children: John Louis, Mary Catherine and Mary Sybilla. Sophia died in 1883. John Henry's second marriage was to Mary Louise LeGrand on Sept. 30, 1884 and six children were born to them: Otto John, Eleanora, Benjamin John, Bertha Josephine,

Corina and John Louis. She died in 1948 and is buried in Memorial Park Cemetery at Sikeston, MO.

Michael Welter (1854-1942) married Magdalena Diebold on Feb. 16, 1882, daughter of Dennis and Magdalena (Wantz/ Wanc) Diebold. They had nine children: Leo, Rosalie, Dora, Albert, August, Edward married Ella Pfefferkorn, Pauline, Agnes and Joseph.

Peter Welter (1857-1945) married Louisa Diebold (1860-1932) on May 3, 1881 in St. Augustine Catholic Church in Kelso. Louisa was a sister to Magdalena. Peter and Louisa were the parents of nine children: Frank (1882-1918), Charles J. (1884-1948) married Regina Essmer. Their children are: Paul A., Mildred, Herbert L., Elmer, Maurine and Mary Margaret.

Alvina (1886-1973) married Joseph Burger on Oct. 2, 1907. They were the parents of nine children: Bernadette (Monroe Drury), Harold, Mary Josephine (never married), James J., Adolph, Dorothy, Ralph, Thomas, and Alice Theresa died in infancy.

Rosalia (1888-1891), Bertha (1890-1977) never married, Lawrence I. (1893-1961) married Anita Rodamier/ Rodenmeyer (1894-1918 during flu epidemic). They were the parents of three children: Anna (1913-1918), Lena (1915-1916) and Fred (1917-????) married Mavis McCombs.

Adolph (1895-1971) married Bertha Schwach on Aug. 2, 1922 in St. Mary's Church in Cape Girardeau, MO. This union produced one child: Alene (Joseph Cullen).

Anna (1899-1977) married Owen Rogers on Feb. 6, 1928, their children were: William O., Owen Jr. (never married), Margaret, Charles, and Mary Ann (John Bles, son of Ed Bles and Clara Scherer). They live in Oklahoma.

Josephine (1901-1996) married Mason August on Aug. 20, 1919. Their children were: Mason Jr. (1920-1931 from acute pneumonia), Geraldine, Eddie, Florence and Douglas.

Joseph (1859-1946) married Susanna Compas on April 25, 1882. Seven children were born to this union: Henry Charles and Frederic Joseph both died in infancy, John Joseph, Emma Maria, Fredolin Peter died at age 6, William Joseph (married Coletta Enderle) and Lorena.

Nicholas (1862-1890) married Elizabeth Scheeter on Aug. 22, 1882 and she died Aug. 4, 1883. He then married Mary Kielhofner on Nov. 8, 1883. Children were: Josephina, Ida Katherina and Ida Rosalia. Henry Joseph (1863-1936) married Mary Julia Westrich on April 25, 1893. They were the parents of nine children: Hermina Ida, Zeno, Anton Clemens, Coena Magdalena, Ermina, Joseph, Victor Louis, Philomena and Rosalia. John, twin to Henry Jacob, died in infancy. Jacob born Jan. 13, 1866 at Vanduser married Josephine Pfefferkorn. They had ten children: William Peter, Maria Regina, Andrew John, Pauline Katherine, Nicholas, Albert, Martin, Theodore, Margariette, and Hermina Bertha. Jacob died in 1927 and is buried in Catholic Cemetery at Kelso.

WESTRICH – Jacob and his wife, Katherine Steinmetz, were both born in Schirrhein, Alsace France and came to the United States prior to 1854. Jacob was born March 7, 1822 and died March 16, 1885. Katherine was born Nov. 9, 1833 and died Sept. 21, 1917.

The Westriches were a farm family in the old country and also in the new one. They settled in the New Hamburg area and started to raise a family. Ten children were born to them in Missouri. They were: Phillip, born June 6, 1855. His wife was Louise Bisher and they had four children: Jacob Jr., David, Simon and Alvina. John was born in 1865 and was married to Caroline Glasser.

Nine children were born to them: Albert, Steve, Fridolin, Gregory, Anton, August, William, John Jr. and Linda. Catherine was born in 1857 and married Edwald Hamm and four children were born to them: William, Ed, Philomena and Lena. Frank Westrich was born in 1855 and married Mary Scherer. Three children were born to them: Monica, Paul and Adelia. Rosa was born in 1865 and was married to Casper Menz. Six children were born to them: Leo, Theon, Clemence, Ida, Clara and Christine. Leo was born in 1866 and never married. Louis was born in 1867 and was married to Martha Kilhafner. Ten children were born to them: Bertha, Ludwina, Benno, Frieda, Tillo, Martha, Ida, Jennie, Theckla and Frank. Joseph Westrich was born in 1869 and married Sophia Gosche and ten children were born to them: Mamie, Agnes, Cecilia, Rose, Anna, Antonette, Raymond, Cletus, Mike and Paul. Julia Westrich was married to Henry Welter and their children were: Joe, Anthony, Sam, Victor, Rosalia, Coena and Philomena. Clemence Westrich was born in 1877 and married Rosena Heisserer and their children were: Carolina, Coletta, Lawrence and Clara.

The Jacob Westrich family has lived in Scott County over 134 years and six generations. *Compiled by Martha Westrich Robert, Submitted by Glenda Kenkel*

WESTRICH – Phillip Westrich (b. April 15, 1796; d. July 16, 1862) and his wife, Anna Mary (Fohr) Westrich (b. Aug. 10, 1798; d. Oct. 25, 1868) came to America around 1852. Their children were: Johann, Katharina, Jacob and Phillip. Jacob Westrich (b. March 7, 1822; d. March 16, 1885) married Catherine J. Steinmetz (b. Nov. 9, 1833; d. Sept. 21, 1917) on Jan. 11, 1853. They had 11 children: Phillip, Katherine, Jacob, John, Mary, Rosa, Leo, Louis, Joseph, Maria and Lawrence.

John Jacob Westrich (b. Dec. 16, 1860; d. April 27, 1955) married Caroline Glasser (b. Feb. 3, 1867; d. May 15, 1952) on Oct. 25, 1887 at St. Lawrence Catholic Church in New Hamburg, MO. They had 11 children: Raymanda Katherina (b. July 30, 1888; d. May 11, 1890), Albert, Stephen, Fridolin, Otto Daniel (b. July 5, 1896; d. June 15, 1898), Gregory (b. July 6, 1898; d. April 4, 1917), Anton, August, William, John and Linda.

Seated: John, Linda, and Caroline. Middle row: William , August, and John. Back row: Anton, Albert, Stephen, Fridolin, and Gregory.

Albert (b. Aug. 26, 1890; d. April 4, 1966) married Estella Enderle on Oct. 23, 1917. They had seven children: Chester, Alfred, Roy, Leon, Marie, Vera and Alma.

Stephen Jacob (b. Aug. 14, 1892; d. March 30, 1963) married Coena LeGrand on Nov. 27, 1917. They had five children: Michael, Anna, Lucille, Herman and Edward.

Fridolin Phillip (b. July 23, 1894; d. March 8, 1978) married Agatha Glueck on Nov. 18, 1919. They had six children: Gilbert, Clyde, Rita, Quentin, Agatha and Herbert. Agatha died at birth. Herbert died as a baby of whooping cough.

Anton (b. Nov. 27, 1900; d. Jan. 30, 1976) married Anna Marie Felter on Oct. 24, 1922. They had three children: Agnes, George and Sylvester.

August (b. Dec. 15, 1902; d. Jan. 5, 1974) married Louise Blattel on April 18, 1925. They had seven children: Erwin, Virginia, Arnold, Theodore, Robert, Adolph and Rosa Marie. Robert died at 6 years of age.

William Sylvester (b. Dec. 29, 1904; d. Sept/ 22, 1950) married Blandina Blattel on April 24, 1928. They had five children: Charles, Viola, James, Joseph and Clarence.

John (b. Dec. 13, 1906; d. Jan. 30, 1988) married Frances Hess. They had two sons: Francis and Andrew.

Linda Bertha (b. March 6, 1909; d, Feb. 17, 1989) married Frank F. Kenkel on April 29, 1929. They had seven children: Bernard, Rose Marie, Paul, Caroline, Doris, Elmer and Larry. Bernard died at birth. *Submitted by Doris (Kenkel) Roth*

WILSON – Farrell Daniel Wilson, son of Woodrow and Virgie (Cates) Wilson was born in Bloomfield, MO on March 5, 1942. When Farrell was 1 year old, they moved to Morehouse where he attended school and graduated. While in high school he delivered groceries for Pal's Grocery and after graduating worked for Dacus Manufacturing Company in Morehouse.

Ferrell, Mildred and Danny Wilson, 1990.

Mildred Ann (Patterson) Wilson, daughter of Clarence and Emma (Lingle) Patterson was born March 26, 1939 near Charleston, MO. When about 3 years old, the family moved to California, living in various locations and working in the fruit harvest; finally settling near Marysville. In March of 1949, they returned to Missouri where they sharecropped for E. P. Coleman and attended the Matthews School, and later Grey Ridge and Morehouse. After graduation Mildred worked in the office at Lewis Furniture Company in Sikeston.

Farrell and Mildred were married May 3, 1963 and moved to Sikeston where they still reside. A year later, Farrell, too, went to work for Lewis Furniture, first as a collector, then as manager of the used furniture department, and is now a salesman at the store on West Malone.

In October 1966, Farrell was drafted into the Army. He was trained at Fort Leonard Wood, MO and then sent to Cam Rohn Bay, Viet Nam where he was a cook/ truck driver. After eight months he was eligible for R & R and he and Mildred met in Hawaii for seven days. Upon his return to the states, Farrell was stationed at Ft. Campbell, KY (where Mildred joined him), and later Ft. Riley, KS. While in Kansas, Farrell was sent to Germany for six weeks. Farrell was discharged in 1969 and they returned to their home in Sikeston.

On July 6, 1973 Farrell Daniel Wilson Jr. "Danny" was born. Danny was in the scouts, played t-ball, and soccer, and was a newspaper carrier for *the Daily Standard*. He also worked at Hardees. He graduated from Sikeston High School in 1991, earning a scholarship to Southeast Missouri State University. While at Southeast Missouri State University he worked in the bookstore on campus and later at Dana Manufacturing. He received a scholarship from T.G. (USA) and graduated in May 1994 with a degree in engineering. On June 3, 1994 Danny and Tanya McElrath were married in Cape Girardeau where they still live. Tanya is a remedial reading teacher at Franklin Grade School in Cape, while Danny is an engineer for Galaxy Cablevision in Sikeston. They attend Bethel Assembly where they are active working with youth.

In 1994, Mildred returned to the work force as an employee of Buck Food Services where she enjoys participating in the company sponsored corporate games.

Farrell and Mildred are charter members of Christian Tabernacle United Pentecostal Church of Sikeston. They are avid campers and enjoy traveling; the highlight being a ten-day trip to Israel in 1999. After retirement at the end of 2003, they plan more travel.

WILSON – John Lewis Wilson was born September 15, 1917 in Sikeston, Scott County, Missouri, at 731 North Ranney Avenue. He was the son of Randal H. Wilson [1897-1958] and Kathryn Tanner Wilson [1896-1939]. He felt that the best way for his children, grand-children and great grand-children to know him would be to write his history, because families today are growing up in a society that is moving so fast that their is no time left for real family closeness and to get to know each other personally.

He became a Boy Scout at age twelve and attained the rank of Eagle, served in the drum and bugle corps and was twice awarded honor camper. During this time he worked as a manager for a miniature golf course and as a carhop for the Galloway Drug Store, making the sum of $2.50 per day. He graduated from high school in 1935 and then attended the University of Missouri, Columbia, Missouri for two and one-half years in the school of engineering and agriculture, The Sigma Nu fraternity pledged him and he become a member.

His grandfather, John Lewis Tanner [1860-1947], made him a partner in his land holdings, which included three farms of 570 acres. This was done upon his graduation from high school and he was learning the management of farmland. He married Hazelle Young [1916-] at her home

John Lewis Wilson Sr.

on North Street on January 30, 1938 and honeymooned in Memphis, Tennessee with the sum of twenty-five dollars. He went to work for the Farm Security Administration [FSA] as a County Assistant in New Madrid, Missouri, during the roadside demonstration along Highways 60 and 61 just south of Sikeston, which began on January 10, 1939. The demonstration was because of the living and working conditions of the farm sharecroppers and tenants. The number was about 1500 families who camped along the highways in the snow and cold for almost two months. He walked the highways and gave government vouchers to the families at the rate of $15.00 per month per family and two dollars for each child. He then became County Supervisor for Mississippi County. The F.S.A. helped lower-income farmers acquire loans and technological knowledge as well as make more available loans and grants for feed, seed, and livestock.

He went to the Marine Corps in March 1944. After going through Boot Camp for two months and being assigned to a school for two months and earning a rank of PFC and 501 classification he was transferred to Camp Mirimar. He worked as 501 Clerk in the office of the Squadron Casual Group who sent the Marines over seas into the combat zones and after a term brought them back. He served in the same capacity also in Cherry Point, North Caroline, the Camp in Walnut Ridge, Arkansas, and Camp Pendleton, California. He received an Honorable Discharge from the Corps in March 1946.

All this time he remained a partner with his grandfather in the farming enterprise and returned to a more active part after his discharge. He took over the farmland and began actively farming. His grandfather told him he had held it altogether while he was gone and he did help him get started. He died in 1947 at the age of 88. It was a struggle to begin, with the lack of machinery due to the war and the expense. It was necessary to sell his home on North Ranney Ave., which he just bought as a Veteran with a four percent mortgage, in order to finance his fanning operation. During this period from his discharge in the Marine Corps and to get started back working and supporting his family of Hazelle and two children, their daughter Kathryn Penney Wilson [March 18, 1940] and John Lewis Wilson Jr., [February 25,1943], he worked as a teacher in the high school as a Veterans teacher for discharged veterans three times a week. The government paid for the schooling and for the time spent in schooling. All veterans received benefits of different kinds for their service. They could chose and were paid for the benefit they choose. He received payment for teaching. He also took up flying at the Robinson Flying School in Sikeston, Missouri and received a license. This also was paid by the Government. He served as Hail Adjuster on agriculture crops for insurance Companies mainly on corn, wheat and cotton. Due to his schooling as an Appraiser he did Appraisals on small farms and residential homes that were financed by the Veterans Administration and received $15.00 for each appraisal. He also did Appraisals for banks, real estate businesses and individuals for a time factor charge. All this time the farming was progressing and growing by renting more land and hiring more people. There were two main employees and four families working full time.

During this period he had joined the Lions Club and rose to be President for a year. He became a Mason in the Sikeston Masonic Lodge #310 and worked part time in the chairs in Sikeston. Then he became a 32nd Degree Mason of the Ancient and Accept Scottish Rite in the Temple in St. Louis, Missouri. Also in St. Louis, Missouri he advanced into the Shrine at the Moolah Temple. A branch of Moolah Temple was formed as the SEMO Shrine Club. He rode in the SEMO Shrine horse patrol. He served as Chairman of the Agriculture Committee in the Sikeston Chamber of Commerce and organized the 100-bushel Corn club in order to help the farmers do a better job of utilizing fertilizer on their farms for a higher yield.

From 1949 through 1956 he ran a fertilizer selling and applying business, mainly anhydrous ammonia, along with his farming. In 1956 he had a complete farm auction and sold all of his farm machinery and rented all of the farm land out for the regular crop rent, still retaining the management. In 1956 a group of large landowners in four counties organized a Corporation for the purpose of manufacturing liquid fertilizer and delivering to their companies for their use and to sell to their customers. John Wilson headed up this organization and was the manager and President of the company. In February 1961 he went to work for

Sagimon Grace Company a subsidiary of W. R. Grace and Company. The purpose of the company was to buy and organize retail outlets for the sale of anhydrous ammonia and other fertilizers. He and his family lived in Decatur, Illinois during this two years. After two years he realized he did not like large corporate work and resigned and returned to his home in Sikeston. For the next two years in Sikeston he studied and passed the Real Estate broker exam in Missouri and Arkansas and became a licensed Real Estate Broker and opened offices in Sikeston and Walnut Ridge, Arkansas. While in Walnut Ridge for the purpose of establishing a office to handle the agriculture businesses, mainly developing farm land and clearing land from the woods and making it ready for farming and selling it. He was also appraising land for banks and insurance companies. The residence and business in Sikeston still was operating and the management of the farms continued. In 1964 John L. Wilson Jr. wanted to leave school and start farming.

Penney Wilson had finished the University in Cape Girardeau, Missouri, and married Michael King [1943-] on January 15, 1966 and was living in New Madrid. They moved to Sikeston and Michael went to work in the Real Estate office. John Wilson Jr. had gone to school in Decatur, Illinois and graduated from high school and then attended the University of Illinois in Urabana, Illinois for one year and then attended the University in Cape Girardeau, Missouri for one year and then attended Clerical school in Memphis, Tennessee.

John L. Wilson Sr. and John L. Wilson Jr. in 1964 formed a farming partnership and rented the Tanner land for crop shares, paid as rent 1/3rd of the proceeds of the corn, wheat and soybean crops and lt4h of the proceeds of the cotton crop. With supervision John Jr. farmed the land and John Sr. continued the Real Estate business. In 1969 John Jr. having already married Mary Janet Engram [1945-] on December 28, 1966 and had started their family bought out the farming partnership and could continue on their own. John Jr. also took the Real Estate exam in Missouri and received his license.

As a part of the Real Estate business John Sr. became an Agent for the Mutual Life Insurance Company of New York [MONY]. The business of the Agent was to appraise land for farmers and to loan them money to develop or to buy farms and to also service the loans in Missouri, Illinois, Arkansas and Kentucky, a radius of 150 miles of Sikeston, Missouri. This position continued until 1980.

During the seventies and eighties along with the farming management business and the real estate business he joined with a group of partners for the purpose of buying, clearing and developing land for sale, mainly to foreigners from European countries. The agricultural depres-

John L. Wilson Sr.

sion of the Reagan Years, the cost of farming, the cost of developing, the cost of money at the rate of 20 - 22 per cent put a stop to this business. Two of the partners went bankrupt and left him with a large loss.

Semi-retiring in the late eighties, he dropped all of the businesses except the farm management, mainly the Tanner Estate Farms.

John Jr. and Jan continued the rental farming

and reared three children, Machelle Alivia Wilson [1968 -], Julie Leah Wilson [1970 -], and John Lewis Wilson III [Trey] [1976-].

Penney married Thomas Michael King and to this union was born one son Matthew David King [1966 -] and they adopted a girl, Linda Marie King [1979 -]. Penney and Michael were divorced and Penney remarried to Richard Albert Limbach on December 31, 1968. They live in Birmingham, Alabama at this time.

Myra Irvin Tanner died in 1989 and that left John L. Wilson the remaining heir of the Tanner Estate. He sold the Tanner home on 412 North Kingshighway to John and Jan Wilson and they did restore the home to the original design and developed a beautiful home.

The John L. Tanner Estate Trust was formed of Heirs and Bodily Heirs so on the death of John L. Wilson the Trust will be over. There have now been seven generations associated with this land trust.

Since 1974 John and Hazelle have had six motor homes and have traveled all over the United States and parts of Canada and Mexico. The early motor homes were also used in the real estate business. Hazelle is now 86 years young and John is 85 years young. They live at 1212 Sikes Ave, Sikeston, Missouri. *Submitted by John L. Wilson on May 28, 2002*

WOLPERS –

Wolpers Family. Front row: Joella Wolpers, Mary Frances Atkisson, Joy Wolpers, Sue Wolpers, Paul Evans, and Myra Wolpers. 2nd row: Lanu Propst, Myra Propst and Myra June, Lillie Minner, Elmira Goza Bynum, Luta Evans, Edythe Wolpers, Earlie Bynum, Mayme

Joy Wolpers Brown, 1925. First place in baby contest.

Wolpers Family

Eskridge, Byrdie Atkisson, Ella Evans, Basil Atkisson, and Amy Mayes. 3rd row: Sinus and Maybelle Evans, Dick and Marge Evans, Milford Minner, Minnie Bynum, Laura Bynum, Myra May Bynum, Maxine Eskridge, Jim and Ella Lee Evans, Grace and Murl Stanfill. 4th row: Tom Bynum, Hunter Bynum, unknown, Jeanne Wolpers, Murriel Wolpers, Cass Wolpers, Basil Atkisson Jr., Gayle Evans, Valree Minner, and Elinor Atkisson.

WOOD – Roy A. Wood was born Jan. 2, 1932 in Flint, MI. His mother was Laura R. Smithson, born in Fornfelt, MO and his father was Roy A. Wood Sr., born in Pargould, AR. His grandparents were Clarence Smithson (died November 1918) and Grace Smithson. Grace then married Robert "Bob" Murphy.

The family moved to Morley, MO in 1937. Roy

started school at Morley Grade School, but the family moved back to Michigan in 1939. When the family moved back to Morley in 1945, Roy attended Morley High School.

He worked on the river for Shell Oil Company after leaving high school (1946-1947); then went into the Army in 1947 and was stationed in Japan. Roy re-enlisted in 1949, serving in Korea. He was wounded twice before his discharge in 1953.

After his discharge, he lived in St. Louis and attended the David Rankin Trade School for air conditioning and refrigeration repair. Roy worked in this field in Missouri, Texas and Florida, becoming an A/C contractor in Naples, FL in 1982. He retired to Casslberry, FL

Roy A. Wood

WRIGHT – Arthur Newton Wright was born Aug. 3, 1887, in Golconda, IL to James G. Wright and Sarah Ann Jaco Wright. His maternal grandparents were Andrew Douglas Jaco and Nancy Saylors Jaco. The earliest records of the Jacos show they originally came from the Cornwall area of Southern England. They arrived in the United States in the early 1700s.

Arthur Wright came to Commerce, MO as a young man and lived most of his life there. He married Zelma O'Guin June 29, 1910 in Cairo, IL. Six children were born to this union: Viola Wright William Dec. 16, 1911; Ruby Wright Varnon Dec. 27, 1913; Cleo and Leo Wright, twins June 25, 1919; Evangeline Wright Wade Nov. 3, 1929 and Gary Jarrett Wright Jan. 24, 1938.

He worked at various jobs from the age of 9 to help support his family. One of his jobs as an adult was lamplighter on the Mississippi River under the US Coast Guard during WWII. He traveled by boat from Gray's Point to Price's Landing to maintain these lamps. Many times during bad weather and rough water it became impossible to stay on the water. He went ashore and stayed the night. Like everyone else during the war, he was subject to rationing of some necessities, but due to the nature of his work, gasoline and kerosene were always available. He lit these lights several years for Tillman Anderson, and after 20 years under the Coast Guard retired in 1957.

Arthur Newton Wright

He was a member of the Commerce Missionary Baptist Church. He died April 18, 1976, Easter Sunday, and was buried in Oakdale Cemetery near Commerce. At this time two daughters survive, many grandchildren, great-grandchildren and great-greats. *Submitted by Jim Wade*

WYMAN – Edwin Thomas Wyman was born in 1916 in Lowes, KY. He graduated from Sedalia High School and completed his BS degree in education at Murray (Kentucky) State Teacher's College, his MS in education at the University of Illinois, with postgraduate work at Southeast Missouri State College, Memphis State College,

George Peabody College, and the University of Cairo, Egypt.

Mr. and Mrs. E.T. Wyman, May 1970.

In 1939, Ed moved to Diehlstadt to teach business education, where he met and taught with a Scott County girl, Mary Susan Smith, the older daughter of J. T. and Mina C. Smith of Kluge's Hill. A graduate of Southeast Missouri State Teacher's College, Sue taught in schools in Crowder, Essex, Fisk, Lutesville, and Vanduser. Ed and Sue were married in Sikeston Methodist Church in June 1945.

During WWII, Ed spent three years in Communications in the Army Air Corps 12th Bomb Group, 15th Air Corps in Brazil and various sites in the Mediterranean Theater. Post war teaching took him to Illinois High Schools and LaGrange Junior College. In 1952 he settled in Sikeston as a teacher and/or administrator for schools in Matthews, Essex, Bell City and Sikeston. In 1965, Ed returned to Illinois to serve as a special administrator for schools with serious financial and administrative deficiencies.

Ed always said one of the greatest difficulties in educating the children was educating the parents. In later years as a school administrator, the "Professor" as he became known, earned the reputation for personally administering the "Board of Education" only once to any particular student. Healthy respect often grew into loving admiration between students and "The Professor." This love was returned to students with countless hours of firm but patient instruction in the classroom and with a mountain of after-hours time devoted to supervising ball games, chaperoning parties and dances, and coaching thespians. There were even some Saturday sessions at home for students who stopped by with needs unmet by Friday's last bus out.

The Wyman household never lacked momentum, and civic responsibility and community service were an important part of family life. Casting an informed vote in local and national elections was a privilege more than an obligation. Ed served as VFW Commander and as a member of the Sikeston Little Theater. He was a member of the Men's' Bible Class at First Methodist and regularly took his daughter, Jane, and son, James, to Sunday school and later to MFY. Sue was active in the Rebekah Lodge and the Order of Eastern Star and worked in support of the Cancer Society making bandages by the box full.

A life well lived has its rewards. A silver wedding anniversary for Ed and Sue, celebrated in Sikeston in 1970, was sweetened with the birth of the first of three granddaughters.

Ed suffered a fatal heart attack in his Illinois home in November 1982. He was buried in Sikeston City Cemetery. Sue continued on in Illinois into the new millennium, enjoying her crafts and industrial arts activities. *Submitted by Jane Wyman Conner*

YOUNG – Charley Herman Young Sr., born Nov. 7, 1899 in Cline's Island, MO, the eighth child of William Clayton and Nancy Tunel Young. William was born Sept. 26, 1856 and died Feb. 29, 1904. Nancy was born Feb. 4, 1861 and died Feb. 10, 1904. Both are buried in Ellis Cemetery in Idalia, MO. Charley did not remember his parents, as he was only 4 years old when they died. A married brother raised him.

Charley was a car inspector for the St. Louis Southwestern Railroad and worked in Illmo (now Scott City) and in Malden, MO.

Charley was an active Mason, served as Master and Chaplain of the Masonic Lodge in Illmo. He was Worthy Patron of Madonna Chapter 314 and Worthy Guard of Bethel White Shrine.

Charley was a strong man. His son, Lloyd, has signatures of six men who witnessed Charley lifting a set of RR Wheels off the ground with two men standing on them, in fact, one of his friends wrote that "Charlie was the strongest man he ever knew." His nickname was "Pappy" because he usually had the stem of a pipe in his mouth like the cartoon character in "lil Abner." Charley was a jolly person and loved to be around friends and family.

A favorite family story is when he decided to make his own wine. He heard the corks popping and went down to the cellar to see what was wrong. He decided to drink all he could to keep from being wasteful. I think he fell asleep there.

Charley and Norma Young

Charley and his wife Norma loved to hunt, fish, and play cards. Another favorite story was when he told his wife "Hold still Normie" and he shot her. He was trying to shoot a rabbit but some of the shot ricocheted off a rock and hit her in the shoulder.

Charley died Nov. 27, 1971 at Southeast Hospital, Cape Girardeau, MO and is buried in Lightner Cemetery, Scott City.

Charley married first Nellie Moore, one daughter Opal Mae Young (b. Jan. 29, 1921). Nellie and second daughter died at birth. Opal married first Jesse Trosper divorced and married second Claude Albert Riggs (b. July 1, 1919). Opal's four children born while living in Illmo: first one Jerry Lee Riggs (b. Jan. 27, 1946). Jerry had three children: 1) Belinda Popineau. Her children are Natalie and Vanessa. 2) Carolyn Derifield who had two children: Shelby and Brandon. 3) Joanne who had one child, Larissa. Claudi Kay Williams (b. Dec. 6, 1950) who has three children: Leslie Williams Jr., Curtis Williams and Lisa Williams.

Marjorie Ann Riggs (b. Feb. 2, 1951) has three children: Pamela who had three children, Preston, not married; Morgan, not married. Patricia Ruth Riggs (b. Oct. 12, 1954) who had three children: Dawn who is married with children, Troy not married and Claudia not married.

Charles Herman Young Jr. (b. Sept. 7, 1925) Fornfelt, MO and died March 10, 1971 of cancer. He was a Conductor for the Frisco Railroad 25-1/2 years. Married Jan. 21, 1945 Ruth Virginia Eaves (b. Feb. 9, 1929). Ruth is retired from Southwestern Bell Telephone Company. They have two children, six grandchildren and four great-great grandchildren.

Lloyd W. Young (b. April 29, 1933) is listed in separate article.

YOUNG – Devon Wesley Young was born May 28, 1963 at Southeast Missouri Hospital in Cape Girardeau, MO, second son of Lloyd Wesley and Shirley Ann Sample Young. (See Lloyd Young in separate article.)

Devon graduated from Scott City High School where he played fullback for the Rams and was a captain of the team. He played trombone in the band.

Devon graduated from Southeast Missouri

State University in 1986 B.S. business administration with minors in math and computer science. He is a member of Pi Kappa Alpha Fraternity. He passed the Certified Public Accountant Exam (CPA) on the first sitting and is currently employed as a Commercial Insurance Broker at A. J. Gallagher in St. Louis.

Devon W. Young family, 2001. Left to right: Cameron, Devon, Ann, and Anastasia.

Devon was married April 27, 1991 at St. Gerard Majella Catholic Church, St. Louis, MO to Ann Marie Barreca (b. June 20, 1964) daughter of Tony and Sallie Sterling Barreca.

Ann graduated from Sikeston, MO High School in 1982 and graduated from Southeast Missouri State University in 1986 with a B.S. in communications/pr. Ann was a member of Alpha Delta Pi Sorority and member of Student Government. Ann is employed part-time by State Farm Insurance as a claim specialist.

Devon and Ann have two children: Cameron Wesley Young (b. March 23, 1993) St. John's Hospital St. Louis, MO. Cameron is a student at St. Gerard Majella School and plays baseball, soccer and basketball. Cameron loves computer games. Anastasia Marie Young (b. Feb. 3, 1998) Gomel, Belarus (former Soviet Union) adopted by Devon and Ann on April 16, 1999 in Belarus. Anastasia enjoys ballet and tap dancing and loves to swim.

Devon and Ann enjoy spending time with family and bike riding. Devon works out at the YMCA and Ann loves walking and scrap booking.

YOUNG – James Bert Young was born in Liberty, KY, on Dec. 10, 1867. His parents were Sampson Young and Sally (Branson) Young. The Young family had moved from Tennessee into Kentucky shortly before the Civil War. During the war Sampson Young served in Company B of the 13th Kentucky Cavalry, US Army. The family remained in Casey County, KY until James Bert brought his family to southeast Missouri in December 1911.

James Bert Young married Lucy Elizabeth Grider on Dec. 30, 1886. Lucy Elizabeth was born Dec. 8, 1865, the daughter of John Grider and Emeline (Coffey) Grider. Emeline's great-grandparents were John and Martha (Pettigrew) Witherspoon. This Witherspoon family was of Scottish descent and produced many politicians and patriots including John Witherspoon, signer of the Declaration of Independence.

John Sampson Young was born to James Bert and Lucy Elizabeth Young in Liberty, KY on Aug. 1, 1893. He

John Sampson and Claudia (O'Guin) Young with children: James Edward, Francis Alene, and Johnny Wilbur.

married Claudia O'Guin in Charleston, MO on June 8, 1916. The couple lived in Commerce and Illmo in Scott County before moving to Cape Girardeau in 1942. John Young was a farmer and later worked for the United States Corps of Engineers until he retired in 1950. He was a charter member of the National Association of Retired Federal Employees. John Young died on July 29, 1974.

Claudia O'Guin Young was born Sept. 11, 1891, in Waverly, TN. She was the daughter of William O'Guin and Lillie Lee (Hedge) O'Guin. For many years Claudia was president of the Ladies Aid Society of the General Baptist church in Cape Girardeau. Through her work in the church, she taught many women the beautiful and creative art of quilting. Claudia Young died Nov. 21, 1974.

Claudia's grandparents were William O'Guin Sr. and Margaret (Alexander) O'Guin. The Alexander's were prominent in early North Carolina politics and six family members signed the Mecklenburg Declaration of Independence n 1775. The Alexander's were Scotch-Irish. The O'Guin's were Irish.

The four children of John and Claudia Young were James Edward, Francis Alene Young Rhodes, Johnny Wilbur, and Nine Marie Young Sommers. The Young children grew up in Commerce, MO and have many pleasant memories of growing up in a small Mississippi River town.

On Nov. 22, 1937 James Edward Young married Mary Elizabeth Caldwell, another Commerce native. The couple had four children: Evelyn Delores, Charlotte Elizabeth, Karen Ruth and Donald Ray. The Young's presently live at Chateau Girardeau in Cape Girardeau, MO. *Submitted by Karen Ruth Young Lang*

YOUNG – John Alfred Young, son of John William Blackford Young [1843 - 1913] and Sophronia Ann Orange, his wife [1851 - 1932], was born in Woodbury, Butler County, Kentucky, on June 1, 1872 and was the eldest son of 10 children. The family moved to Millersville, Missouri, when John Alfred was 14 and then in 1886 they moved to Blodgett, Missouri for one year and then to Bertrand, Mississippi County, Missouri. John W.B. Young carried on the trade of Blacksmith during these moves.

John Alfred Young married Lillian Elizabeth Bush [1874 - 1950] on May 18, 1893 in Bertrand, Missouri, and to this union one son was born, Harry Culen Young, March 15, 1894 in Bertrand, Missouri. He operated a Drug Store and then went into the Building Trade and also

John Alfred Young

served as a salesman for the McCormick Harvester Co. During this time as a salesman and repairman of farm machinery he worked from Southeast Missouri all the way to the Canadian line for a period of seven years. He was then given the opportunity to locate in Sikeston, Missouri, by Mr. Charles F. McMullin, then the president of the Sikeston Mercantile Co.

They moved to Sikeston, Scott County, Missouri on February 14, 1905.

He worked in the Sikeston Mercantile Co. as manager of the Farm Machinery Department and was given the responsibility of the retail Lumber and Coal Departments. He returned to the construction business and then organized the Sikeston Concrete Tile and Construction Co. in

1909. In 1915 he bought out his partners and continued the business. He built more than 500 homes, churches, and business buildings. In 1918 he with his son went into the lumber business [Sikeston Lumber Co.] and continued the construction business.

John Young, politically, favors those principles and policies of national affairs that are represented by the Democratic Party. He was deeply interested in public affairs and served seven years as Chairman of the Board of Aldermen for the City of Sikeston. During the seven years so serving, he may be given credit for putting in the municipal water-works systems, for promoting the paving of all the streets that are paved with brick, for building the city hall and fire station on Center Street, and for getting the city to take over a plot of ground from the Malone family and turning it into a park [Malone Park]. He served four years as President of the Chamber of Commerce, during which time he promoted and helped to build up the Sikeston branch of the International Shoe Company factory at the cost of $86,000. He served as president and as director for twenty-one years in the Sikeston Building and Loan Association. He also served fourteen years as Chief of the Fire Department in Sikeston.

John Young served as County Judge of the First District of Scott County in 1934, having been appointed by the Governor to fill an un-expired term for six months. The latter part of 1934 he served as County Chairman on the Missouri Relief and Reconstruction Commission. He was also local chairman of this work in the City of Sikeston.

Harry Culen Young, born on March 15, 1894, the only son of John and Lillie Young. A partner with his father during all of the early building and construction times and in running the Sikeston Lumber Company. He was also in the insurance business, the seed business with the McCoy Seed Company, and a short time in the Post Office. His life's ambition fulfilled was the opening of the first radio station KSIM in Sikeston, Missouri.

He married Hazel May Penney in Poplar Bluff, Missouri, on August 30, 1914 at the residence of Rev. R.L. Russell, Pastor of the Southern Methodist Church. They took up residence in Sikeston where he was in business with his father. The children of this union are Harry Culen Young Jr. [7/6/15 - 11/23/86], Hazelle Penney Young [12/10/16-] and John Richard Young [4/6/31 - 12/31/96]. *Submitted by John L. Wilson - May 28, 2002*

YOUNG – Lloyd Wesley Young, son of Charley Herman and Norma Ann Chaffin Young was born April 28, 1933, Fornfelt, MO; married Oct. 7, 1956 Centenary Methodist Church, Cape Girardeau, MO to Shirley Ann Sample, born May 2, 1936 Sedgewickville, MO, daughter of William Rudolph and Reva Genora Niswonger Sample. Their two sons are: Richard Lloyd Young (b. Sept. 26, 1959, Cape Girardeau, MO) and Devon Wesley Young (b. May 28, 1963, Cape Girardeau, MO). Lloyd graduated from Fornfelt High School and attended Southeast Missouri State University three years then received his degree from Columbia College, Columbia, MO. Lloyd and Shirley are members of Eisleben Lutheran Church where Lloyd serves as Elder and Shirley sings in the choir and was chairman of the 150th Anniversary Committee in 2001. Lloyd retired from the US Army as a LTC on April 30, 1988 having served in the Missouri Army National Guard for 36 years. During that time, he served in Europe, Asia, and Central America. He graduated from the Basic Infantry Officer Course at Fort Benning, GA April 19, 1958. Lloyd is an Army Aviator. He completed Primary Flight Training at Camp Gary, TX Oct. 21, 1958 and completed Army Aviation Tactics course and received his wings on Jan. 31, 1959 at Fort

LTC. Lloyd W. Young and wife, Shirley.

Rucker, AL. He became rated in Helicopters at Fort Wolters, TX March 23, 1964 and completed Helicopter Instructors Course Oct. 7, 1966. He graduated Engineer Officers Basic Course Dec. 4, 1963, Fort Belvior, VA, Engineer Officers Career Course Fort Belvior, VA, June 12, 1968, Construction Planning and Operations Course, Fort Belvior, VA, Chemical, Biological and Radiological course at Fort Riley, KS June 13, 1969, Civil Disturbance Course at Fort Gordon, GA Nov. 20, 1970, Graduated from Command and General Staff College July 24, 1971, Senior Officers Preventative Logistics Course at Fort Knox, KY April 13, 1978, and Senior Commander's Orientation Course at Fort Knox, KY Sept. 29, 1978.

Lloyd always wanted to be a pilot and started very young by jumping off a shed with an umbrella. When the umbrella did not work, he thought it was because he was not high enough so the next time, he made a parachute out of sheets and jumped off the house. He decided when he got up off the ground limping that he would have to wait until he was old enough to fly in a real airplane. Lloyd was in grade school during WWII and saved ten cents per week and bought a stamp for his saving bond book, which was traded for a $25.00 bond. He saved enough for three savings bonds and was able to buy a 1937 Ford with two of the bonds when he was 16 years old. Later, when he was in college, he charged people who rode to Cape with him to help pay for the gasoline.

After Lloyd retired, he graduated from the Police Academy at Southeast Missouri State University Nov. 19, 1989 and the Hostage Negotiations Workshop at Southeast Missouri University Feb. 16, 1990. He served as Chief of the Police Reserve in Scott City for several years. Lloyd worked for a while as a Private Investigator. Before he went into the military full time, Lloyd worked on the Frisco and Cottonbelt Railroads and operated a real estate office in Scott City.

Shirley has been an active volunteer in Scott City. She was a member of the (now Scott City) Women's Club for 25 years serving as president twice, vice president, secretary, etc. She served as an officer in the PTO and was a band and sports booster. She was elected president of the MOARNG ASSN AUX., organized the first city wide celebration in 1976 called the "Bicentennial Celebration" and had the honor of naming future celebrations by submitting the winning name "Mid-Summer Festival." She was first elected to the City Council in 1982 and then was elected mayor in 1989. She did not run for another term but was elected president of the Chamber of Commerce in 1993, a position she held for 5 years. Shirley is currently serving as Missouri State Organizing Secretary of the Daughters of the American Revolution, and stands for election to State Corresponding Secretary in 2002. She is a member of the John Guild Chapter, National Society of the Daughters of the American Revolution where she has served as Regent, Vice Regent, Chaplain and Treasurer. She is a member of the State Officers Club, Chapter Regent's Club, State and National Speakers Staff and sings in the MSSDAR choir. She served as Southeast District director 1998-2000. Shirley is Secretary of the Historical Conrad Reunion and helped her sister write the Conrad

Genealogy book in 1986. She is currently working on the Sample Genealogy book.

Richard Lloyd Young (b. Sept. 26, 1959 Cape Girardeau, MO) is listed in a separate article in this book.

Devon Wesley Young (b. May 28, 1963 Cape Girardeau, MO) is listed in a separate article in this book.

YOUNG – Richard Lloyd Young was born Sept. 26, 1959 in Cape Girardeau, MO, the first child of Lloyd Wesley and Shirley Ann Young. Richard "Rick" graduated from Illmo-Fornfelt High School in 1978 and graduated Cum Laude from Southeast Missouri State University in 1982 with a BS in historical preservation. (Additional hours for major in history and minors in art history, astronomy and economics.) He received four Gramling semester scholarships. He was a member of Pi Kappa Alpha Fraternity where he held offices and received two"best active" awards and Pi Kappa Alpha Scholarship Award. He served a three-month internship with the Missouri Historical Society in St. Louis. (Attended the 1982 World Series seventh game in St. Louis and slid into second base after Cardinal victory.)

He graduated with honors from Texas Tech University, Lubbock, TX 1985 MA Museum Science. He served as chair and vice-chair of Museum Science Student Association. He performed a six-month internship at Missouri Historical Society January to June 1985 and began work in June 1985 as Curator of Collections at Fort Casper Museum and Historic Site in Casper, WY. He was promoted May 1987 to Director of Fort Casper Museum and Historic Site.

Rick is an avid reader, loves hunting, camping, golf and bowling. (Bowling league president last three years.)

Professional involvement: Colorado-Wyoming Association of Museums: Board of Director, 1987- 1991 and 1998-2000, 2002-2005: Vice-Chair 1990, Wyoming State Representative 1998-2000; Program Chair 1988, Local Arrangement Chair 1990 and 2002; (tentative) Chair 2002, assorted committee positions, Mountain-Plains Museum Association: Board of Directors, 1998-2003-; Wyoming State Representative 1998-2000, Councilor-at Large 2000-2003; Wyoming Membership Chair 1988-1992, Nominating Chair 2000, Local Arrangement Chair 2004; assorted committee positions.

Richard Lloyd and Tami Young with son David, 1995.

Other memberships: American Association for State and Local History; Wyoming Awards Chair 1990-1992; Smithsonian Associates Program: Wyoming Coordinator 1990; Casper Area Convention and Visitors Bureau: Executive Board 1989-1994; City of Casper Historic Preservation Commission: commission member 1989-1991 and 1997-present. Staff Liaison 1989-present. National Historic Trails Center Foundation: Board member 1990-present. Casper Museum Consortium: Member 1999-present; Chair 2000-2001. Friend of Education Award Recipient, Natrona County School District 1993; Master of Ceremonies for Wyoming, Phillip-Morris Bill of Rights Tour, 1995; and Arthur H. Mattingly Award for Outstanding Achievement in historic Preservation, 1995.

He married April 1, 1995 Tamara "Tami" Marie

Meade (b. Dec. 18, 1959 in Hollywood, CA). She moved to Fortine, MT in 1972 and to Casper, WY in 1974. She was a graduate of Natrona County High School in 1978. After high school she spent some time traveling for a survey company. She moved back to Wyoming as manager for Pizza Hut and then acquired her Real Estate License in 1990. She received her Broker License in 1995. She is employed at Broker One Real Estate.

Tami has five brothers in Wyoming and Colorado. Tami is an avid reader and gourmet cook and does needlework.

David Andrew Young, born Aug. 22, 1984 in Beeville, TX, son of Tami by previous marriage, was adopted by Richard after his marriage to Tami. David is a senior at Natrona County High School 2002. He has won many awards in weight lifting to include state champion and Regional Champion in his weight class.

ZIEGLER – Gary Ziegler was born May 23, 1945 in Benton, MO. He is the oldest son of Joseph J. Ziegler (b. Aug. 27, 1915; d. Feb. 2, 1980) and Linda Marie (Burger) Ziegler (b. March 1, 1916). Gary's parents were married in Los Angles, CA on Nov. 6, 1943. Gary's father served in the US Army during WWII and was taken prisoner by the Germans during the Battle of the Bulge.

Joseph and Linda had five children: Gary, Norbert (b. Nov. 26, 1946), Geroid "Roy" (b. June 24, 1949), Ralph (b. Nov. 12, 1950) and Therese (b. Dec. 22, 1952). Gary and his three brothers and one sister were all raised by their parents on a farm five miles east of Benton. They all attended St. Denis Grade School and Kelly High School in Benton. Gary joined the US Marines and saw active duty in the Viet Nam War. After his military service, Gary attended and graduated from Southeast Missouri State University in Cape Girardeau, MO. Roy served in the US Army and Ralph served in the US Navy.

The Gary Ziegler family. Front: Anne, Brian, Kimberly, and Addison. Back: Alan, Roxie, and Gary.

On Aug. 12, 1967 Gary married Roxanna "Roxie" Reinagel of Kelso, MO. They were married at St. Augustine Catholic Church in Kelso. Roxanna was born Sept. 14, 1947. She is the oldest of five children (and only daughter) born to Leroy Reinagel (b. Aug. 17, 1926) and Bernice Glastetter (b. Aug. 8, 1926). Roxie's brothers are: Tom (b. Dec. 12, 1949), Allan (b. Nov. 4, 1953), Ray (b. Oct. 10, 1957) and Kenneth (b. Aug. 30, 1962). Roxie and her four brothers attended St. Augustine Grade School in Kelso and Notre Dame High School in Cape Girardeau, MO.

Gary and Roxie have two children. Brian Scott Ziegler was born July 18, 1969 in Cape Girardeau, MO and Alan Lee Ziegler was born April 11, 1971 in Mexico, MO. Brian and Alan attended St. Augustine Grade School in Kelso and Notre Dame High School in Cape Girardeau. Brian served in the US Army with the 101st Airborne based at Fort Campbell, KY. Brian is a registered nurse at St. Francis Hospital in Cape. Alan graduated from

St. Louis University in St. Louis and is a physical therapist in San Jose, CA. Brian married Kimberly "Kim" Essner of New Hamburg, MO on July 22, 1995 at St. Lawrence Catholic Church in New Hamburg. Kim attended Kelly High School in Benton and is a registered nurse at Southeast Missouri Hospital in Cape Girardeau. Brian and Kim have two children: Anne McKenzie Ziegler, born Nov. 17, 1997 and Addison Marc Ziegler, born March 11, 2000. Brian, Kim, Anne and Addison live in Kelso.

Gary and Roxie live in Kelso. Gary has worked for Shelter Insurance Company as a claims adjuster for 23 years. Roxie had worked for Missouri Dry Dock in Cape Girardeau for 25 years as a secretary. Gary and Roxie are both active members at St. Augustine Catholic Church in Kelso and enjoy spending time with their two granddaughters Anne and Addison. *Submitted by Gary J. Ziegler*

ZIMMERMAN – Billy Charles was born Sept. 25, 1933 in Illmo, MO Scott County, to Charles Edward Zimmerman and Edna Hulda Brenneisen (daughter of Frederick and Elizabeth Heiling Brenneisen, married in Kelso, MO, Dec. 28, 1894; Elizabeth died Nov. 25, 1918 in Illmo, MO; buried in the Eisleben Lutheran Cemetery). "Bill" has lived in the Scott County area most of his life, living in East Scott City, MO (Old Illmo) at the present time. He married Geraldine (Kohl) Jan. 29, 1960 and they have two sons, Mark Colin of Bettendorf, IA and Randy Wayne, who lives in Scott City, MO.

Charles Edward Zimmerman was born May 9, 1897 in Dongola, MO, son of William Lee Zimmerman and Sophronia Jane Pierce. When Charles was 16 years old, he moved to Scott County from Dongola because his father had a job with the Johnson Land Company near Commerce, MO, clearing the swampland. Charles married Edna Dec. 21, 1926 in Lutheran Parsonage in Illmo. She was born Dec. 14, 1897 in Cape Girardeau, MO, died April 11, 1974 and is buried in Eisleben Lutheran Cemetery Scott City, MO. Charles died June 1, 1971 and is buried in the Lightner Memorial Cemetery, Scott City, MO.

William Lee Zimmerman, born Dec. 25, 1869 in Franklin County, MO and Sophronia Pierce (the daughter of Zachary Taylor Pierce and Hannah Niesewanner), born July 20, 1872 in Bollinger County, MO were married March 16, 1890 in Marble Hill, MO. William and Sophronia had seven children, six of whom grew to adulthood: Charles Edward, William Henry, Theodore Roosevelt, Mamie Gertrude, Lilly Mae and Opal Marie. William Lee served 12 years as town marshal in Fornfelt, MO; being elected April of 1931. A newspaper account stated he had 37 relatives voting for him. He was also a foreman at the Messmer Box Factory in Fornfelt, MO. Sophronia died Jan. 7, 1951. William died May 26, 1953; both are buried in the Lightner Memorial Cemetery in Scott City, MO in Scott County.

William Lee Zimmerman was the son of Samuel Zimmerman (b. September 1838) and Sarah Catherine (Fisher), born in April 1838. Samuel was a Civil War Veteran, enlisting in the Union Army in August of 1862 at St. Clair, MO. He was discharged in August 1865 at St. Louis, MO. Samuel and Sarah were married

Lee Zimmerman and his mule team

April 22, 1866 at Richwoods Township, Washington County, MO. They lived in Dongola, Bollinger County, MO. Their children were: William Lee, Parker Lonzo, Effie Henrietta (all who came to Scott County in the early 1900s, moving from the Dongola area) and Frederick, who moved to Oklahoma, where he died in 1937. Samuel and Sarah lived in Dongola, MO at the time of their deaths. Samuel died April 10, 1905; Sarah died in December 1908. They are both buried in the Collins-Schlatitz Cemetery in Dongola, MO.

ZIMMERMAN – Frank O. Zimmerman was born in Commerce, MO on May 28, 1913, the son of Parker and Margaret "Dolly" Storey Zimmerman.

Parker, born in Bollinger County, MO, was the son of Samuel and Sarah Fisher Zimmerman. Sometime after the death of Samuel (1905) and Sarah (1908), three of their children, Parker, William Lee and Effie Henrietta, moved to Scott County. A third son, Frederick (Ferdinand), moved to Oklahoma.

Settling first in the Commerce area, they later moved to Fornfelt. At one time, all three siblings lived on what is now Mary Street in Scott City. Frank always said, in a joking manner, the Zimmerman boys (both those of Parker and William) earned that area the name of "Rascal Flats."

Frank's father, Parker, had children

Parker Zimmerman holding son, Harry, and wife Dolly holding Frank. Commerce, MO., 1913.

by two wives. Five children were born to his marriage to Mellie Bollinger: Ida May, twins Lonzo and Reuben, and twins Oliver and Dollie Marie. Mellie died at the age of 29 after a tragic accident (her skirt caught fire from the flames under a kettle). After her death, Parker married Margaret "Dolly" Storey.

Parker and Dolly had six children: Robert Harry Lee, who died at the age of 30 when he fell into the Mississippi River from the construction steamer *Penniman* in July of 1936, Harry was married to Geraldine Crader of Oran, MO; Frank Otis (b. May 28, 1913); Norman Harlan (b. March 2, 1915; d. April 1986 in Indianapolis, IN) married Hazel Marie Poe; Charles Francis b. Feb. 28, 1918 at Commerce, MO, d. April 1981 in Beech Grove, IN, married Pauline Swinney; Mamie Juanita b. Feb. 27, 1920, at Oran, MO, d. September 1987 in Hanover, Il, married Elmer Joseph Yount; James Elvis b. Feb. 2, 1924, d. September 1998 at Cape Girardeau, married Evelyn Pettengill of Benton, MO.

Frank married Eloise Deweese Swindell, the daughter of Charles and Neva Edna Preyer Deweese, in Cape Girardeau. Their daughter, Soundra Joy, married Robert Eugene Eifert at Illmo, MO; they have two daughters, Debra Ann and Kay Francis. Their first son, Kenneth Wayne, first married Patricia Ellis; they had three children, Kenneth Wayne Jr., Sheri Renee, and Rebecca Marie. Kenneth's second wife was Theresa O'Brien Higgason, who had two daughters by a previous marriage, Theresa Ann and Victoria Lynn. Kenneth died July 7, 1999, at Cape Girardeau. The second son of Frank and Eloise, James Ray, died in an automobile accident July 17, 1967. Their third son, John Franklin married Deborah Sue Kinder; they had one daughter, Jennifer Leigh. Dana Mark, the youngest child, married Laura Buccheit Carpenter with whom he had two children, Lucas Matthew and Barry Ian. Frank also raised his stepdaughter, Willa Lee Swindell, who married Lloyd Zimmerman, the son of T. R. and Anna Lee Zimmerman. She and Lloyd had two sons, Michael Keith and Daniel Scott.

Frank worked many years for the US Corps of Engineers. He and Eloise lived in Cape Girardeau until 1949 when their neighborhood was destroyed by the tornado that killed his father and seriously injured his mother. They then moved to Illmo, MO. Frank died of cancer at the age of 57 at Chaffee General Hospital. Eloise passed away at her home in Scott City (old Illmo) on March 27, 1998. They are both buried at Lightner Cemetery. *Submitted by Soundra Zimmerman Eifert.*

LATE ENTRIES

CHASTEEN – Hartle Harvey Chasteen was born at Long Lane, MO Nov. 14, 1901 (died April 28, 1989). Ava Henderson Chasteen was born at Parthenon, AR Nov. 4, 1912 (died Dec. 12, 1990).

Hartle and Ava were married Dec. 25, 1935 at Deere, AR. They came to Vanduser on April 12, 1948 from Parthenon, AR to sharecrop for a year or two. They had always planned to go back home to their place in Arkansas, but this became their home. They stayed in Scott County until their deaths. The Chasteen's were members of the Church of God in Vanduser.

Hartle worked for the Vanduser and Scott Central School systems as a janitor and bus driver from 1950 until he retired in 1972.

Their children (all born in Parthenon, AR) are Wayne Eldon of Arnold, MO; Leeman Allen, deceased (drowned in Lake Wappapello in a boating accident Sept. 3, 1966); Jane Hanback of Vanduser, Bonnie and Lyda also of Vanduser.

The Chasteen's have five grandchildren: Larry Hanback of Chaffee, MO; April Westrich of New Hamburg; Timothy Chasteen of New Madrid; Allen Chasteen of Florida; and Sheila Casali of California. *Submitted by Jane Hanback.*

FREY – Carolyn (Graham) Frey, Vice-president of the Scott County Historical and Genealogical Society was born in Sikeston, Missouri on June 6, 1949 to Levena (Johnson) and Theodore Graham. She married Steven Frey in Cape Girardeau on May 17, 1974. They have no children.

Carolyn Frey

Much of my childhood was spent in rural Scott County where my brothers and sisters and I enjoyed climbing trees, riding bicycles and playing in the sand – like most kids before the Computer Era. Our family moved to Illinois in 1967. After graduating from high school, I worked three or four jobs, finally staying in retail for 23 years. After I left my job with Wal-Mart, my husband and I moved to Morley, MO. It was familiar territory to me.

I am pleased to have played a small (very small) part in getting this book compiled. I wish to extend a very special thanks to all those who contributed family histories and pictures. And "Thanks" to Peggy for her help. I hope all who read this book enjoy learning about the people who have made Scott County what it is today.

LUBER – John B. Luber, Sr. came from southern Germany in 1857. He had been born in Auerbach,

Bavaria, Germany in 1816. The family arrived at the port of New Orleans in 1857. They came up the Mississippi River to the town of Columbia, IL. The family consisted of John Sr., his wife Catherina, and three children.

The Luber family, Cape Girardeau 1896. Front row, left to right: Catherine Reminger holding Jacob Adam, Joseph, Frank, and John B. Jr. holding Mary. Back, left to right: Louisa, Henry, John J., and unknown.

John B. Luber, Jr. moved with his family to Scott County in the early 1880s. The family eventually grew to 14 children. He farmed in north Scott County. He moved to Arkansas about 1901. He was a postal rider. He established the town of Luber, Arkansas. The post office for Luber closed in 1976. Mrs. Luber, who died in 1906, is buried on the farm they owned. John B. Luber, Jr. is buried in Kelso.

John B. Luber, Jr.'s son Henry A. Luber moved back to Scott County with his family in 1921. He farmed in the Vanduser area until his death in 1947 and was buried in Kelso. He and Bertha Luber had six children: William, Henry, Ann, Powell, Lawrence, and Catherine. Bertha Luber died in Sikeston at the age of 93 in 1973. Bertha is buried in Sikeston.

Lawrence B. Luber married Beulah Faye Boatner in 1941. The family lived in Sikeston. Lawrence and his wife operated several businesses in Sikeston for 40 years. Lawrence died in 1978 and is buried in Sikeston. Beulah died in 1991 and is buried in Sikeston as well. They were the parents of six boys.

Larry B. Luber is an attorney in St. Louis. Byron D. Luber is an Associate Circuit Judge in Caruthersville. Charles B. Luber is retired and living at Kentucky Lake. Paul C. Luber lives in Sikeston and works for the Missouri Department of Corrections. Greggory A. Luber is an attorney living in St. Louis. Thomas J. Luber lives in St. Louis.

NORRID – Henry Harold "Hal" Norrid was born October 10, 1917, in Benton, MO. At the age of four he moved to Detroit, Michigan, with his parents, James Henry Norrid and Alma Blocker Norrid, where he graduated from Wayne State University in 1940. He served five years in the Army during World War II.

Hal Norrid

He married his high school and college sweetheart, Charlotte Martha Carey (born Feb. 25, 1918 in Detroit, MI), on December 20, 1941. With his wife and seven children he moved from St. Clair Shoes, Michigan to Arizona in 1959. While in Ari-

zona he was co-owner of the Rex Precast Concrete Company and later worked for the City of Tempe Public Works Department.

His interests in photography, bird watching and oceanography inspired many interesting trips with his wife and family in the United States, Mexico, Galapagos, South America, Central America, and Africa. The family also enjoyed his tradition of baking whole wheat bread.

After being hospitalized with pneumonia on December 27, 2000, Hal Norrid passed away on January 8, 2001 at the age of 83 in Tempe, Arizona. He was survived by his wife Charlotte; daughters Martha Carr, Virginia "Gena" Hall, Nancy Gwilliam, Barbara Lacey; sons Lawrence and William; 19 grandchildren; and a sister, Nancy Bosaen. He was preceded in death by his daughter Carolyn Ruth Norrid in 1985 and by his brother James Maurice Norrid in 1998.

Hal's family is one of the pioneers of this section of Missouri and many ancestors are buried in the Benton Cemetery. *Submitted by Charlotte Norrid.*

WATKINS – Sterling Peal Watkins was born February 11, 1910 in Sikeston, Missouri. He was the son of Louis Watson Watkins (1873) born in Scott County, MO and Pearl Mack Peal, a native of Humboldt, Tennessee (1879). He married Lexie Helms, daughter of Lorenzo Bow Helms, a native of Greene County, Indiana and Flora Brendel, a native of Bollinger County, MO, on January 9, 1932 in McMullen, MO. Lexie Helms was born December 20, 1914 in Vanduser, MO. They had two children. One son, Louis Sterling Watkins, born February 16, 1937, married Carol Gay Sewald of Festus, MO. One daughter, Margaret Watkins, born November 6, 1938 in Vanduser, MO, married first James Pobst of Scott County, who died May 10, 1978 in Sikeston, and then married Jerry Ford of Cape Girardeau, MO. Sterling P. Watkins was a farmer in Scott County all his life.

In the Sikeston Standard, July 25, 1961, Page 1, one headline read, "S.P. Watkins of Vanduser gets FHA Post." The article read, "Appointment of Sterling P. Watkins as a member of the Farmers Home Administration County Committee has been announced by A. Allan Brock, the agency's County supervisor serving Scott and Mississippi Counties.

"Mr. Watkins operates approximately 400 acres of land one and one-half miles north of Vanduser. He and Mrs. Watkins live on the farm. They have two children, Mrs. James Pobst of rural route, Bell City, and Louis Watkins of Vanduser, Missouri.

"Mr. Watkins was selected for this position because of his good knowledge of agriculture, both as to land and people, in Scott County.

"Two other members make up the three-member committee which works with the county supervisor to see that the best possible use is made of the agency's farm credit service program consistent with local farmers' needs. The other two members are Colie B. Taylor, Route 1, Benton, and K.M. Streeter, Route 1, Painton. Mr. Taylor will serve as committee Chairman during the 1962 fiscal year. Each member is appointed for a three-year term. Mr. Watkins succeeds Vernon Shelton whose three year term expired this year."

Sterling and Lexie were of the Methodist faith. Sterling Watkins died February 3, 1964 in Sikeston and Lexie survives. Sterling is buried in the Watkins Cemetery, on the old Beechland Plantation, near Morley, MO along with other descendents of General N.W. Watkins. *Submitted by Margaret Watkins Ford*

VANDUSER – John Sylvester Vanduser was born March 23, 1855 of Dutch ancestry. The original spelling of the family name was Van Duser. He married Florence Viola Tull who was born December 31, 1864 and they first lived in the area of Morley, Missouri. After moving their household goods and farm implements over trails, about twelve miles west of Morley, through marsh land by horse and wagon the Vanduser's homesteaded their land and then bought addition acres for $1.00 per acre. At the time they moved to the area it was without the benefit of elevated road beds or railroads for transportation. Oran was the nearest large town for supplies.

John cleared the land, improved it by 1895, and had a saw mill and farmed. The Vanduser house was large with a porch on three sides and it had a cellar. The Vanduser's donated land for the Vanduser Baptist Church as well as some land for the town to be laid out. For this reason the people living in the area named the town Vanduser.

John and Florence Vanduser had seven daughters and one son. The oldest daughter, Bertie married Charles Chaney; Gertrude married

John Gibbs; Lula Ethel, born February 14, 1888, married Andrew Houston Phillips and remained in Scott County. She died on April 3, 1981 and was buried in the Old Morley Cemetery; Inez married and moved to Tucumcari, NM where she died; Clovis died in infancy; Iva moved away and

John Sylvester and Viola (Tull) Vanduser, August 1898.

little is known of her; Thelma married a Mr. Miller and was living in Tulsa, OK at the time of her death. Their son, Guy, married but had no children and died in Wichita, KS.

John worked all day for his family on farm and saw mill, then worked until midnight building the Vanduser Baptist Church. The town was supposed to have an association that fall and they were trying to get the church ready for the associational meeting. They did get the church ready enough for the meeting. The first thing John Vanduser did was to hold a prayer meeting right there in the church. He took a chill walking home from church, went in, went to bed, and never was up another time. He took pneumonia and died on Christmas morning, 1898. His widow, Viola, was considered wealthy at the time of his death. After raising her children she died with little of material value. However, she was a happy Christian woman who attended the Vanduser Baptist Church until her death on November 18, 1943. Both John and Viola Tull Vanduser are buried in the Old Morley Cemetery. *Submitted by their granddaughter, Hester Doyle of O*

Index

193

195

196

197

198

Printed in the USA
CPSIA information can be obtained
at www.ICGtesting.com
JSHW060053150824
68134JS00032B/2723

9 781681 624501